Kill the Prisoners!

By Don Wall

By the same author

Singapore and Beyond	1985
Sandakan – The Last March	1988
Revised Second Edition	1989
Revised Third Edition	1992
Revised Fourth Edition	1995
Abandoned?	1990
Heroes at Sea	1991
Heroes of F Force	1993

ISBN 0646 278 347

Published by D. Wall

98 Darley Street West, Mona Vale, NSW 2103

Typeset and assembled by PS Graphics, 139 Regent Street Chippendale, NSW 2008

Printed in Australia by Alken Press Pty. Ltd. – Smithfield

Introduction

Preface

There are many relatives of prisoners of war who were not given a satisfactory explanation of how and where and under what circumstances their loved ones died as prisoners of the Japanese in the Far East during 1942-1945 – fifty years on they still want to know.

In 1949, one of the commanding officers of a Royal Artillery Unit sacrificed in Java, wrote and suggested that the date and cause of death of men lost in Borneo should be withheld from relatives and next-of-kin as "the true cause of death would give undue distress to the next-of-kin". Consequently, the reports received from the International Red Cross [and supplied presumably by the Japanese] were adopted.

It is well established that the Japanese falsified their death certificates of prisoners of war to cover up the real cause of death. It is outrageous that Authorities should accept the Japanese version of death.

The real reason of death is to be found in the records of the War Crimes Courts: ill-treatment, cruelty, starvation, murder and massacre.

After researching and identifying the Australians lost in Borneo hundreds of letters were received from relatives seeking more information on their loved ones, and the phrase which stood out in all the letters was: "It's the not knowing which has caused us so much grief".

It is the right of the relative to choose to know the tragic facts of the loss of their husband, son or brother, and it is the obligation of the Authorities to provide this information free and without delay when requested.

There were no survivors from any of the massacres carried out by the Japanese, and only through the Trials of the War Court did some of the truth emerge. Many of these records were restricted for years, and it is sad that so many of the files have not been accessed for public scrutiny.

This account endeavours to relate the sequence of events in North Borneo, the loss of the Gunners' 600 party from Singapore sent to the Solomons and their final massacre; the exposure of the loss of Royal Air Force and Royal Artillery personnel parties on board the SUEZ MARU and the massacre of those who survived the sinking.

Many questions seemed unanswered: Why were the British party of 300, who died at Labuan and in the Brunei area, not honoured on the nearby Labuan War Cemetery and Memorial. Answers are required for the Gunners' party – the remains of 438 lie in Bomana Cemetery, Port Moresby, but they are honoured on Singapore Memorial.

Many Australians feel it is regrettable that their British comrades, who died in an Australian territory under such tragic circumstances, are not suitably honoured.

Acknowledgements

I acknowledge the contributions of the Diaries of Peter E.I. Lee, CBE, MID*, who has spent several months copying by hand diaries he had so meticulously recorded in pencil over 50 years ago. Because of their age, these diary entries represent an important contribution to the History of British Prisoners of the Japanese in Borneo during 1942- 1945. It is rare to discover records so important to the relatives of those men who died there.

The Director and Staff of the Australian War Memorial, particularly Mr. Bill Fogarty, Manager Research Centre; Pam Reay, Ian Affleck and Staff of the Photographic Archives; Darren Watson of the Australian Archives.

In Britain: Brian Denson of Cambridge (we shared a tent in Thailand on the Railway in 1943) who set in motion the responses I have received from former Officers of the Jesselton Party; Geoff Threadgold and Donald Yates who were fortunate to be moved from Sandakan to Kuching in 1943; John Chambers of 35 LAA Regiment, who survived Kuching; John Bessant whose father, W.O.1 John Bessant, died at Sandakan; Neville Watterson, Author of Prisoners of Borneo Prison Camps; Christopher Elliott for various pictures and to his daughter, Anne Elliott, for her verse.

Captain Jack Burnett, MM, who commanded the War Graves Unit which completed the Sandakan War Cemetery; Ray Battram, Len Evans and Graham Robertson; Peter Gorrick; Alex Dandie and Tom Connolly for his maps.

Pru Row-Cusack, Danielle Jones, Janet Border, Annette Cassidy, Molly Garland, Pat Meilleur (Canada), Elizabeth Kessler (Illinois) and Wong Yu En of Ranau.

Dedication

Dedicated to the memory of British Prisoners of War
who died in the Far East during 1942-1945.

*"...Not the great or well- bespoke
But the mere uncounted folk ..."*

Rudyard Kipling

THE BIG TREE: Towering over the parade ground, the drab huts and the bare soil within the imprisoning wire, "The Big Tree" was a symbol that gave hope and strength to the inmates of Camp 1; its dominance, its seeming impregnability, its resistance to the powerful storms and lightning of the rainy season and its resilience were the very characteristics that the prisoners intuitively knew would be those needed for their own survival. Yet the hopes were in vain; finally, neither the living tree nor the living humans could overcome the enemy's persistent onslaught.

Caption: Russ Ewan Pic: AWM.120461.

Chapter One

1942

Emperor Hirohito decreed the establishment of the Prisoner of War Information Bureau: its task seemed to be to record the deaths of Allied Prisoners of War and to adopt a policy to ensure that by the end of hostilities all Allied prisoners of war and internees would be eliminated.

Throughout Asia prisoners were told by their guards that in the event of an Allied assault they would all be killed. Imperial Headquarters advised all Commands that under no circumstances would prisoners of war be allowed to fall into friendly hands.

In 1942 aircraft from the carrier, USS HORNET, in a flight led by Cdr. James Doolittle, made an audacious attack on Tokyo. Several pilots were shot down and captured: the Emperor ordered the execution of these men as a warning of what would happen to other prisoners.

In 1943 the tide was turning against Japan with the loss of Buna, the Battle of the Bismarck Sea and Guadalcanal – the killing of combat troops in the water certainly produced the climate to kill the prisoners at Ballale Island.

The early impression in this Chapter indicates the Japanese were observing the Hague Convention: officers were not forced to work, they were paid and provided with Japanese newspapers to translate the progress of the war.

By now the Allied leaders had met at Casablanca and announced the elimination of German, Japanese and Italian war power, this statement demanded unconditional surrender.

Up to this time the Japanese committed many atrocities on American Prisoners of War, these were unknown to the Allies until POWs were rescued by U.S. submarines following the sinking of the RAKUYU MARU in 1944.

The evidence of the Ballale Island and SUEZ MARU massacres exposed the Japanese planned to kill all the prisoners, and the prohibition of purchasing food from the local people represented the first phase of the starvation policy as part of this program.

Peter Lee's diary records the beginning of the events in the Officers' PW Camp and at this stage there is no indication of what was happening elsewhere or what lay ahead. I asked Peter Lee how he was able to conceal his diaries over all that time and he replied:

> *My diaries were concealed at various times in a variety of places – under the huts, in the attap (dried leaves) roofs etc. The main reason for diary writing, in my case, was to keep my mind active and enquiring – all my life I have believed in the need to keep both physically and mentally fit – so I aimed to "fill every minute with full sixty seconds of distance run" as Kipling said. My secondary aim was to be a good reporter not only of events but of my feelings – there was no question of either offending or not offending the Japanese – the facts – the malnutrition, starvation diets, sickness, beatings and deaths spoke for themselves. Written abuse of the Japanese would have served no useful purpose and so I did not indulge. I was not too worried about the Japanese reading them – why? Because the number of those who could speak or presumably read English with any fluency was clearly very limited. I think, given the hundreds of papers they would need to read, the capacity wasn't there. They were probably most interested in sketch plans about possible escapes etc.!*

The War-time Diaries
of Peter E. I. Lee

1942 – Jesselton,
British North Borneo

Changi, Singapore, Friday 9th October 1942: Haversack rations and Red Cross gifts distributed after Roll-Call this morning. At a special parade which I called at 10.15 a.m., Colonel Hingston said a few words of farewell to the troops and complimented them on their behaviour and sportsmanship. I replied on behalf of all ranks, and dismissed the parade. The Colonel told me how much he had enjoyed our stay, and that Divisional H.Q. had been much more impressed with my party than with the Java "B" crowd. On the Gun Park just before 1200, Capt. Wilkinson, "Richard" and Padre Cordingley and others of the 9th Royal Northumberland Fusiliers, R.A.S.C., R.A.O.C., and the 4th Norfolks came to see us off. We were counted at Changi Gaol, embarked at 1330 hrs. and sailed at 1700 hrs., anchoring in the Singapore roads for the night. Slept on top of a crate on deck.

Saturday, 10th October: Sailed 8.30 a.m. Our ship is very old, some say British, ship of about 6000 tons. Conditions are a little less crowded than on the KALGAN (which took us to Singapore from Java (Batavia)), but facilities are fewer. There is very little drinking water and no space at all for bathing. The R.A.F. and some of the Army are in two of the holds forward, on two decks. Spent most of the day on deck watching the eternal sea, and some of the less eternal creatures on board! Some excitement was caused when we sighted what appeared to be a lifeboat with several waving people in it. A closer view showed it up as a matted section of undergrowth with several seagulls on board. Started a violent zigzag course at about 1800 hrs. Slept below.

Sunday 11th October: In spite of obvious difficulties, shaved and washed in salt water! Many didn't bother. Ploughed a very slow course all day, much the same as any other sea voyage, but without, of course, the usual amenities. Food is not very good, but one does occasionally get some meat in it. About 1400 sighted a number of fairly large islands which we thought might be the Anambas or Natunas. About 1800 the coast of Sarawak, mountainous in places and obviously swampy on the coastal plain, was sighted. A very beautiful sunset coloured the sky in many hues for about half hour, but did not

3

Some of the 20 survivors of the 410 R.A.F. personnel who landed in Borneo in 1942. Taken at 9 A.I.F. Division Camp, Labuan. Front Row L.to R.: Canadian Pilot, W.O. Beckett, B.E.M., Flt. Lt. Peter E.I. Lee, Flt. Lt. MacIntosh, Flt. Lt. Elliott   *Pic and Caption: Peter Lee.*

impress one as much as those at Malang. Anchored for the night off a headland with a lighthouse.

Monday 12th October: Spent most of the day at anchor off a point with a white temple-like building and an attap hut high above the headland. There seem to be a number of sand bars in the bay, and quite a number of small sailing craft including catamarans. At about 1400 weighed anchor and moved up the Kuching River, after taking a pilot on board. Passed several native waterside villages built on poles over the water. Anchored off a small jetty at 6 p.m., a few miles up the river. During the evening, which was made memorable by the most remarkable and almost continuous display of tropical lightning I have ever seen, Hardie made several of his usual dramatic statements that all were getting off etc. Quite a cool night down below.

Tuesday 13th October: Disembarkation of 1st Party of about 1000 started at 0830 and finished about 11.30, 2 very fine lighters (diesel-engined) being used for the purpose. The Japs chose the moment when one of the lighters was alongside to clean out our deck bogs with the result that a load of shit just missed about 10 soldiers who had just boarded the vessel. Loading and unloading of M.T. and dry goods during the remainder of the day. Food now so poor that we are obliged to dip into our Red Cross supplies of bully etc.

Wednesday 14th October: Everybody is getting heartily sick of the steamy swamps of Kuching. Today, loading of what looks like tapioca and demerara sugar went on apace. Some airmen and soldiers managed to get some of the sugar from burst bags. This afternoon a Major Suga who is Commandant of POW Camps in Borneo came on board and read us out a long statement in English, promising to look after our health, but reminding us that our quarters at Jesselton were going to be very crowded. He introduced Lt. Nagata who is to be our C.C. at Jesselton, as a refined Japanese gentleman [PL: I recall a sotto voce comment of one of the men at the time "Looks more like a bloody thug to me!"] a graduate of the Imperial University of Japan. [Now Tokyo University, still the most prestigious in Japan.]

Thursday 15th October: Sailed at high tide this morning, which was about 0730. The ship was in sight of the coast until about midday. Sat on top of water-tank with Grey-Jones most of the morning and afternoon and got badly blistered for my trouble. Grey takes a poor view of Doc Daniels and his pessimism. The Doc's most amusing (? cynical) statement was that he would be the happiest man alive if he thought our imprisonment would only last 15 years! I think he rather prides himself on his sardonic witticisms – he was much the same at Seletar (main air-base in Singapore, bordering the Straits of Johore) two years ago. In circumstances like this, however, some people are apt to become depressed on hearing statements such as from an Officer.

5

Friday 16th October: Arrived Miri at 1000 hrs. and anchored off. Seems to be the last place God made. Disembarked some troops and started off-loading cargo, including M.T., large crates and about 500 tyres – the off-loading of the latter proceeding until almost 11 p.m. The consensus of opinion which, of course, usually errs on the optimistic side, is now about 6 months, based on the Changi canards, and what we know of Am prod and the geography of the islands. [This was a veiled reference to speculation that American industrial and production and technology would enable them to retake the "islands" in a very short time. At Changi, there was quite a cottage industry in producing such speculative guesses!]

Saturday 17th October: Another blazing day. The usual comings and goings of lighters, small tugs and motor launches. Spent most of morning with Grey-Jones, wedged between the water tanks and rail, watching the off-loading of a miscellaneous cargo of paints, M.T. springs, general engineering equipment, batteries (Vesta). F/Lt. Jones (Hardie's Adjutant) decided today to "permit" the opening by each man of 1 tin of Red Cross veg., on doctors wishes!! This created quite a lot of amusement amongst the men, most of whom have already eaten the greater bulk of their Red Cross supplies! Another case of not knowing the men and refusing to face facts.

Early in the afternoon the Japs took off the two large crates, containing oil machinery I imagine, on which quite a number of officers and men have been sleeping. Later in the evening two 40 ft. invasion barges were brought on board with a number of Annamese and 2 European Frenchmen! Another memorable sunset. Talk with Vernon Smith on world affairs and in particular, Empire affairs, was interesting. He has had quite a lot of bad luck in his career. In 1928 he bought a 600 acre farm in Western Australia, and was swamped by the slump in 1930. He has tried colliery and lumber work, and the trip to Malaya was his first outside Australia. He lost his Masonic regalia on Alor Star* (an R.A.F. Station in North-West Malaya, near the Thai border).

Sunday 18 October: Awoke in morning to find we were under way and out of sight of land. Rained most of the day in alternate drizzles and downpours. Was therefore obliged to spend a lot of time in a smelly, overheated and sweat-producing hold. Many people had rain baths on deck, but some were caught by gusty winds and showered with soot from the smoke-stack. The dysentery cases on deck had a very thin time, and one is now so weak that he has to be bathed and helped into the lavatory. Brown and Hardie still have slight squitters.

The stew today was particularly bad, being in the main just coloured water. Saw the 2 Frenchmen today – they looked furtive – gave the men cigarettes, and one $10. They had been sent to Sarawak on the orders of the Vichy

Government, and had been there since January – (oil) wells at Miri had been effectively destroyed by depth charges. They were quartered in the hold with the Japs, Annamese and our own troops. (PL: NB: These rather cryptic sentences indicate that the Frenchmen had been sent to Miri to repair the oil wells destroyed by the British prior to the Capitulation.)

Sighted Jesselton at 1820 hrs. at the base of a long range of mountains, thickly forested, and the surrounding sea studded with small, thickly wooded and apparently uninhabited islands. The highest peak (Mt. Kinabalu – 4101 metres – so the guess was accurate!) in the range we estimated to be 12, 000 ft. high. Started H.C. Armstrong's biography of General Smuts, "Grey Steel" just before going to bed. I think it will be interesting.

Monday 19th October: A body of Jap M.O.s came out to the ship in the trim-looking M.V. KITTIWAKE – registered Singapore. They seemed worried about the dysentery cases on board, and went through the vessel very thoroughly. Eventually, we started to disembark about 3 p.m. down rope ladders fore, aft and midships. After another farcical disinfection and kit inspection, seeing a glimpse of Kobashe, we marched through Jesselton to our new Camp about 3 miles out, in the old Gaol next to the North Borneo Volunteer Force Barracks now occupied by the Japs. The men are quartered in attap huts, each man having about 2½ sq.ft.! We are in cells (2 to a cell) in a concrete "jug" which is, however, well-lighted at night. I share with Grey-Jones. There has, I notice, been a general post amongst officers' room mates, which I think is a very good thing in the circumstances.

Tuesday 20th October: On leaving Malang, S/Ldr. Hardie was given an Imprest in Dutch Guilders by W/Cdr. Welch. I was given a share of this when the 1st Java Party left Koan School en-route to Singapore.

Spent most of day 'settling-in'. The Camp nestles in on the seaward side of a small hillock covered with bracken and fern with a few small trees. It has a one-storied gatehouse and two permanent concrete blocks of cells, in the most modern of which officers and W/Os are quartered, and in the smaller, the Senior NCOs. Each cell measures 6' x 8' and holds 2 officers. The remaining buildings are of wood, attap and kajang, and of different sizes – each man has about 15 sq.ft. (2½' x 6') to himself. A protest about the very cramped conditions has been made to the Japs. The Camp, which has night-soil sanitation, holds about 800-900 people and would be overcrowded with 400. Climate is milder than Singapore, and heavy rain falls each night about 1800 hrs.

Wednesday 21 October: Main event today was the issue of cocoa and sugar, which I made to my party. The cocoa, which Grey-Jones and I tried tonight was good! This morning went for a walk round the Camp perimeter which takes

Jesselton

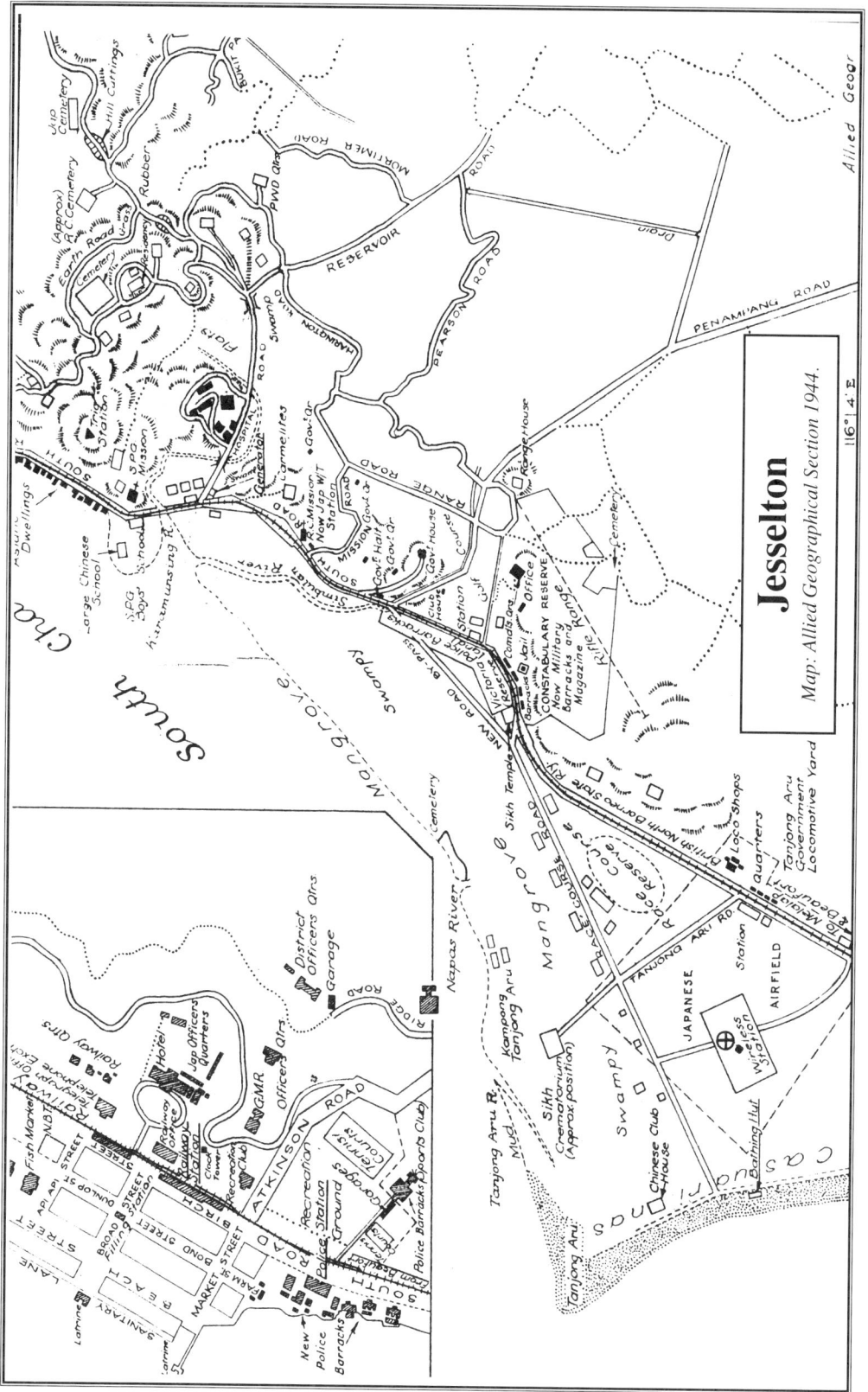

Map: Allied Geographical Section 1944.

116° 4' E

South China Sea

Mangrove Swamp

Reservoir

MORTIMER ROAD
BEARSON ROAD
PENAMPANG ROAD
RANGE ROAD
HARINGTON ROAD
SOUTH ROAD
NEW ROAD
PWD Qtrs
Golf Course
Rifle Range

CONSTABULARY RESERVE
Now Military Barracks and Magazine
Comd Store
Jail
Police Office
Victoria
Club House
Gov. House
Station
Mission
Now Jap WT Station
Gov. Qr.
Court Hall
Carmelites
Hospital

Cemetery
Jap Cemetery
(Approx) R.C. Cemetery
Earth Road
Rubber
Hill Cuttings

Large Chinese School
S.P.G. Boys School
SPG Mission
S.P.G. Station

Fishing Dwellings
Sinsuman R.
Sembulan River

British North Borneo State Ry.
Sikh Temple
Race Course Reserve
Loco Shops
Quarters
Tanjong Aru Government Locomotive Yard
Tanjong Aru Rd.
Beaufort
Station
AIRFIELD
JAPANESE
Wireless Station
Bathing Hut
Chinese Club House
Sikh Crematorium (Approx position)
Kampong Tanjong Aru
Tanjong Aru R.
Mud

Napas River
Mangrove
RIDGE ROAD
District Officers Qtrs
Garage
Cemetery

Railway Qtrs
Jap Officers Quarters
Hotel
Railway Offices, Telephone Exch.
Railway Office
Officers Qtrs
GMR
Recreation Club
Police Station
Recreation Ground
Country Club
Garages
Police Barracks Sports Club
New Police Barracks
NBT
Fish Market
ATKINSON ROAD
BOTTOM ROAD
SOUTH ROAD
MARKET STREET
BOND STREET
BIRCH
DUNLOP STREET
API API STREET
BEACH STREET
SANITARY LANE

about 5 minutes. On one side, bounded by the Gate House, on 2 sides by a high red-corrugated iron fence, and on the other by a crumbling stone wall, worn away to holes in places.

Thursday 22 October: Finished "Grey Steel" this morning, and got some very useful points from it. Jones today dissolved our two parties and has organised the Unit into flights of 30-40. I command No. 4 in Hut 3, of 32 men. Spent the afternoon in restarting Beatrice Webb's autobiography "My Apprenticeship", the first chapter dealing with Charles Booth's great inquest into the condition of life and labour in the London of the '80s and '90s of the last century.

The Japs have asked us to fill in another form with the usual rank, name and nationality, where and when captured, father's and mother's names, place of origin, next of kin. Visited my men in Hut 3 at 1930 hrs. and found them all pretty cheerful. They were much amused by Jones' order that 1 tin of Bully could be opened by every four men!

Friday 23 October: Reveille this morning 0615, Roll Call 0630, breakfast for Working Party 0640 and Working Party (the first at Jesselton) marched off at 0730. Jones, Caruth, Mac(Intosh), Jackson, and W/O Sanders went with R.A.F. and 230 men. The Army sent 10 officers and 220 men owing to their larger number of sick.

In a conference yesterday, Nagata promised "wider" quarters, better food pay for aerodrome parties, "salary" for officers, more cooking utensils and a reconsideration of the long working hours which break the promise given to us by the Commandant of POW Camps in Borneo (i.e. Suga) in Kuching. Rained heavily and continuously during the day. The Working Party returned early, having worked only about 4 hours, the remainder being spent in attap sheds. Jones apparently again distinguished himself at lunchtime by addressing the men as a "lot of oafs"!!

Saturday 24 October: In charge of our 230 RAF Working Party today. Marched off at 0730, and after the inevitable countings and gesticulations by the Japs, we moved off at 0800; after an easy and pleasant 20 mins. march, arrived at the Landing Ground. This is separated from the sea by a thin belt of trees, and it seems to be the intention of the Japs to construct two grass runways running roughly NE-SW and N-S. The aerodrome has a W/T Station which was left intact by the BNB authorities, and is backed on the landward side by a low line of hills. Not much work was done during the morning and, realising this, the Jap Boy Scouts became very energetic during the afternoon, resulting in much futile grousing by our men! We got back at 1730 feeling quite tired. The rest of our Officers' party included Burgess, Pethybridge, Price, Smith and W/O Whiteside. Concert at 1930 tonight fell rather flat owing to the absence of lights and sufficient time for rehearsals. There were, however, two very good bass saxophone and piano accordion players there.

Sunday 25th October: Owing to the extremely heavy rain which fell during the night and until about 0900, today's working party was cancelled, much to everyone's joy, especially Jackson and MacIntosh!! Rain fell intermittently during the morning, but the weather cleared after lunch. Made passable progress with Beatrice Webb this morning, and slept very soundly during the afternoon. At night, Padre Wanless held our first service in Jesselton at 1930, just as dusk was falling; he delivered a very good and appropriate sermon on how to live together, the basis being respect for oneself and for others. Holy Communion afterwards behind the officers cells! With a row of earth closets facing us, a standard lamp giving illumination and the Cross mounted on a biscuit box, this was the most primitive Communion we have had to date!

Monday 26 October: Jackson and Mac had unfortunately to go to the aerodrome today! Weather fine all day. B. Webb becomes more interesting with every page – I am becoming infected with her enthusiasm. She must have been an exceptional woman in the England of the 1880s and 1890s. The description she gives of life in the dockland slums of that period is both vivid and frank – overcrowding, filth, squalor, moral degradation, sexual perversion, immorality and drunkeness. On such, perhaps unavoidably in the amazing progression of the 19th Century, was the greatness of our country founded.

Lt. Geoff Threadgold: "I was the first British Officer at Jesselton to attend to a cremation – in this instance Gnr. John Needham of my "A" Troop 242 Bty. 48 LAA Regt. who died shortly after we got to Jesselton.

"The Japanese called for an Officer and six men – marched us to some waste ground where there was a pile of logs; they indicated the coffin bearers to place it on the logs. The Japanese NCO sprinkled petrol over the lot, handed matches to me and told me to light the pyre. I was at a loss as this was so alien to us but managed to call the men to attention. I led them with the 'Lord's Prayer' and then set the fire alight.

"The Japanese marched the men back to camp but kept me there all night with two guards who had me stoking the fire.

"When morning came they had me raking through the ashes for bones from each part of the body which were put into a small wooden casket. I was then marched back to camp carrying this and reported to Sqdn. Ldr. Hardie, the senior British Officer.

"After this our dead at Jesselton were just slung on to an open fire with a wood party in attendance … "

Tuesday 27th October: Aerodrome today. Except for some rather threatening clouds around midday, the weather behaved itself quite well. Started the levelling job, but as the Jap guards were quiescent, not much work was done. One small incident – when a "boy scout" (Guard) picked up a couple of baskets filled with earth, and ran with them, and was promptly jeered by our men, he became very obstreperous with a stick and very voluble in Japanese, but cooled down after a few minutes. Spent most of the day trying to cheer up our "doubting Toms" with their predictions of 2 years etc. – particularly Capt. Bazell of the R.A. – I think I succeeded – somewhat. He, incidentally, is a cousin of

Lieut. G. Threadgold, 242 Bty. 48 LAA Royal Artillery. ''Thready'' of the Diaries.

F/O. Mansell-Lewis, a Battle of Britain fighter pilot, who came out to Singapore to fly the first Buffaloes to arrive, and who was killed as a passenger in one of 27 Squadrons' Blenheims.

Wednesday 28th October: Another quiet day with my book. In the morning, read the 27th Sept. '42 copy of the "Syonan Times", the Jap Singapore propaganda paper in English. No war news but glorification of past Japanese victories. Apparently the "Tatura Maru", which left S'pore as we entered on the 18th, arrived in Japan on 26th. The Japs seem to be Nipponising Malaya pretty thoroughly, starting, of course, with the youth of the country.

Heard from Padre that Hardie never goes to conferences with Jap Commandant, but always sends Young – I think this is all to the good! Apparently Elliot is not to be allowed in town again, but a native will be allowed to come to the Camp to sell anything that is available. Nagata has promised to look out for English books, to supply communion wine (port), and to fix transport twice a day to take tea to the aerodrome parties. The breeding of maggots in the lavatories, caused by overflows etc. on to the earth, is also to get attention.

Thursday 29 October: Very quiet but very hot day on the 'drome. Tea arrived for the first time both during the morning and the afternoon. Jap reconnaissance

11

aircraft on 'drome this morning. Took off at 0900, circled, landed, and took off again in southerly direction. Feeling runs high today on the autocratic manner in which Hardie and Jones have handled the proposed levy of 20% from the airmen's pay. They declined to listen to the just enquiries and views of the men (I explained the Scheme to them last night – viz. 20% daily rates SSQ – 2 cigs (?cigarettes) per sick (?patient) a day, bananas etc., payment of bootless, sick, sanitary party, cobbler, tailor.) Men had objected to (i) 20% (ii) Payt. of Bootless etc. (iii) the Committee of Hardie, Jones and Mills. The latter had adopted a "take it or leave it" attitude; I advised the men to leave it, which they did. All other RAF also turned down the scheme unanimously. Most men would have welcomed an extra diet scheme and supplementary SSQ. Mentioned this to Jones who said it was "not in the terms of reference"!! Sgt. Allsop discussed the scheme with me on the 'drome and said that the men did not trust officers, with one or two exceptions including myself. He said the could not stand Hardie at any price. Tonight Wag Price's flight said that they would subscribe the 20% if the fund was administered by F/Lt. Lee, 2 Senior NCOs and 2 Airmen.

MacIntosh* was told tonight by Jones that his conduct since he became a POW had been unbecoming as an officer, that it was all recorded against him, and that he would hear more about it. Mac retorted that he would also put in a report on Jones ! Mac also reported by Johnstone for criticising the lunchtime fish stew, and was ordered to apologise, which he refused to do. Poor lad!! [*PL: Mac was a very tough young Scot, who joined the regular RAF before the War – I think as a boy entrant at Halton. He was commissioned before arrival in Singapore. He had a great sense of humour, did not take himself too seriously he was the complete antithesis of Jones!]

Friday 30 October: Today's W.P. sent back from the 'drome at 11.30 a.m. on account of rain. Made good progress with B. Webb's chapter on "Why I became a Socialist", which discusses the origins, personalities, aims and methods of the Co-operative Movement. She deals, with particular clarity, with the differences in theory and practice between producers and consumers co-operation and why the early attempts at running self-governing workshops failed.

Dealt with A.C. Kitchingham's claim that he handed Fl. 5 (Five Netherlands East Indies guilders) to W/O Whiteside for exchange at Changi. I think he is telling the truth – Whiteside being no organiser, and having lost or destroyed his records. Read out the points elucidated in past conferences with the Japs to my flight, tonight.

Saturday 31st October: Turned out fine again for our day on the 'drome. In the morning a very pleasant breeze in evidence, but became very hot in the afternoon, with our warmest march-back so far. Was appointed by representatives of Room 3 to take over the organisation of subs. for sick RAF. Explained to them the basis of the Flight Scheme which thought was better.

A/C again took off to the south. Padre enquired of Hardie today the possibility of using the shed near the baths for meetings etc.; he was told that it was required for a detention room!! A hushhush policy is being pursued about the new quarters which are being prepared for us. Needless to day, everyone knows about it! Felt very irritable and bored today, mainly due, I think, to the uninspiring environment and company. *Sic transit mea horae*!

Sunday 1st November: Finished Vol. 2 of "My Apprenticeship", from which I have taken notes and references for, I hope (!), future use. Am about to start, as a slight relaxation from the concentrated effort required by B. Webb, a small Penguin Special "Science in War".

The meals today were rice, boiled cucumber and water – without salt. Somebody is not up to his promises, but things are probably scarce.

Wallis appointed P.M.C., at the meeting tonight. Elliot was elected Mess Secretary, Bickerton, Army Representative, Burgess for the RAF, and W/O Sanders – Warrant Officers. Proposals re the new quarters and subs. from officers who work, discussed.

Monday 2nd November: Today on the 'drome we had one major incident a Jap Boy Scout became rather incensed at the jeers and general attitude of our men, and struck 2 RAF airmen on the head with the butt of his rifle, having completely lost his head. Lt. Bagnall who was near at the time, at once took the two men to the Jap NCOs in the attap hut they refused to do anything, and on return both Bickerton and Bagnall had their faces slapped by Boy Scouts, who also tried to make them do press-ups. They refused and Bicky had a loaded rifle shoved into his stomach. He took it very well indeed. The matter was resolved by the arrival of some english-speaking Jap 'drome engineer.

The chain-gang principle was put into operation this morning and will produce more work, but will tire the men more. I mentioned this to Nagata when he arrived at the 'drome about 4 p.m. I also registered a protest about food – which he said was the same as the Japanese Army's. I would willingly swop my grub for that supplied to the Nip guards.

Tuesday 3rd November: A slight experiment in dieting (!) as a result of a slight attack of squitters, just before morning rollcall. Ate plenty of rice and stew, but kept off cocoa and tea. Result – successful! Again spent quite a time on "Science in War". The opening chapters deal mainly with the problem in a general sense, stating that the resources of British science are only being half-used (this was in Nov. 1940), and that no coordinated effort was being made – they instance camouflage, which is being handled by 4 Departments.

Rain fell today about 1600 and continued at intervals until after sundown. Nagata apparently gave out some news on the aerodrome yesterday, that since April 770 Allied aircraft, 5 Cruisers and about 26 destroyers, and 5 aircraft carriers had been destroyed by Japs, with the loss to themselves of 70 aircraft etc. He said that the Yanks and Australians were still on the Solomon Islands.

Wednesday 4th November: A holiday (?) today for me, I am told! Spent most of it reading "Science in War" and ruminating on things in general. Old Stan Cressey is looking rather under the weather these days. He has got a rather bad dose of Changi Balls – his look as though they were raw beef. I am now hardly amazed, but always constantly reminded of the complete uselessness and ineffectiveness of Hardie as C.O. He spends a little time during the morning thinking out a letter to send to the Japs, and having sent it, sits around the front of the cells in a sarong, or merely reclining on his back in his cell; announced very proudly that he had had a tin of curried chicken for his lunch. As an example to men he makes a good latrine wall.

Thursday 5th November: Perfectly uneventful day on 'drome. Wallis's system of half the men working and half resting has worked very well. Most interesting event today was a Mess meeting in the evening. The Committee brought forward these suggestions: that 50% of officers' 'drome pay be paid into a Mess Fund, out of which extra messing payments would be made. Batmen would be paid $1 a month. C.O., Padre, Adjutant and Linge would receive extra messing free, and in addition $1 a month. Was proposed by Pethybridge that these officers should go on the 'drome. Hardie said that the Adjt. could not, two were non-executive (!) and – himself. General sympathy with Pethybridge's views, which Hardie squashed by refusing to allow these officers on 'drome. I proposed that they should not be paid (except Adjt.), but was defeated. Only 7 of the officers out of the 20 odd who were against it so vehemently beforehand, having voted. Still, a valuable lesson! We are always learning!!

Friday 6th November: During my day "at home" started Norman Angells "The Great Illusion – Now", a book published originally in 1908 and proving remarkably prophetic as regards both war and peace. It has been brought up to date by chapters written after the fall of Czechoslovakia in 1938. His theme, as far as I have got, is that of collective security with Russia, and the impossible position in which France has been placed by the military hegemony of Germany and Italy. He also emphasises that continued retreat before aggression does not prevent, but encourages war, instancing the examples of Manchuria, Abyssinia, Spain and Czecho-Slovakia. I had a word with the

Padre about last night's meeting. He feels a kind of self-righteous grievance which I find hard to support. I find the number of people willing to retreat before facts in order to avoid unpleasantness really amazing. My Malayan experience all over again!!

Saturday 7th November: Sky overcast most of the day on the 'drome Result, very pleasant coolness, men quite happy and worked cheerfully, and Japs quite quiet. One incident – 2/Lt. Nicholas, R.A., was hit with a rattan (stick/cane) on the head and across the rump by a Jap guard for attempting to remove the cane after the striking of a soldier. The Chief Boy Scout also handed out an open-hander – Nicholas, after being stood at attention for about quarter of an hour, was taken to a hut near the runway and given cigarettes and cake and "shake-hands"!! The marsh is now almost completely filled in. One 2E Bomber Reconnaissance flew over from the sea, circled, and flew off about 10 a.m.

A good concert in the evening after dinner. There is a definite dearth of talent here, but they make the best of things.

Sunday 8th November: Made considerable progress with Angell's "Great Illusion"; the illusion being that a mere exchange of territories between the "haves" and the "have nots" would not prevent war. His analysis of self-sufficiency is very revealing and one which I should like to verify with figures when opportunity offers, He argues that, *per se*, Germany is not self-sufficient, but neither is Britain – and self-interest prevents G.B. from handing over the territories it now controls. Possession of our territories by Germany would not prevent the economic phenomena of boom-depression etc. which is a potential cause of war.

Slept fitfully during p.m. o/a heat, which was more oppressive today than for some time past. Usual church services at 1930 and 2015 hrs.

Jones told us tonight that Nagata had ruled (i) that officers were not in any circumstances to be struck, (ii) men were not to be struck with canes or rifle-butts (iii) men could be struck with the flat of the hand as a disciplinary measure, such as used in their own Army. Issue of soap today.

Monday 9th November: Only the RAF on the 'drome today – the Army having been given the day off for dhoby-work – our turn tomorrow. Cool most of the day, which we spent filling in drains and ferrying Hudson trucks levelling-off the ground. Had talk with Jap. C.C. Nagata who said that owing to a shortage of cement in Jesselton the only runway was to be "stoned, soiled and turfed". Remainder was to be unturfed presumably, and rolled. I again pressed the question of food, which, he said, was difficult owing to increased population of prisoners and native labourers.

15

He said he was a pioneer who built roads, bridges etc. and that his Boy Scouts were the POW Guards. He had fought in Shanghai, Nanking and Borneo and had come from Hanoi.

Elliot gave a very Interesting talk on tea tonight to TOC H. [Tom Elliot had been employed in Java pre-war by a British Merchant house – Swire MacLane, I think, which dealt in tea amongst many other tropical products.]

Tuesday 10th November: Our turn off today. Spent half hour doing my dhoby which, owing to lack of soap, I am cutting down. Generally, the smell test is applied before anything is washed nowadays!! Finished Sir Norman Angells' introductory Chapters on the "Great Illusion – Now" "Now as then". He argues that to prevent an internal collapse of the German industrial machine it was necessary for the City of London to finance Germany, i.e. to secure her external loans. On her defaulting on these in 1931, it was feared that England would not be able to meet her own external obligations, and there was a run on money on demand and short-term call; we were thus forced off the Gold Standard.

Boxing tournament this evening, tho' much of it was brute force and b——ignorance! Ended up with a very amusing comic round.

Wednesday 11 November: Spent early part of morning doing my small amount of dhoby, consisting of stockings and handkerchiefs. Remainder of day with "The Great Illusion", in which the author develops his theme by illustrations of the effect of conquest on foreign markets and the effect of modern interdependence on the latter.

In the evening a short Armistice Day Service was held on the "square" at 1930, including the 2-minutes silence at 1945. The Padre Wanless read the lesson beginning "Let us now praise famous men and our fathers that begat them etc.", and read Laurence Binyon's lines "To the fallen"; the service ended with the National Anthem. A community sing-song followed, which included last war favourites, and the tunes of the moment (or up to March 1942!) ending with "Land of Hope and Glory" and God Save the King.

Tuesday 12th November: A perfect scorcher of a day on the 'drome with hardly a cloud overhead – a long line of clouds hung around the Kinabalu Range as usual, but did not move in our direction. 5 lines of skips 60 men to 4, and 70 to 1, and 140 on baskets – filling drains. 8 men sent back to Camp, some with fever, and others with stomach troubles. Japs seemed to feel the heat probably more than our own men! Was again disgusted by the rush by our men for the food left-overs of the Japanese guards. The acceptance by some officers of food from those quarters is also deprecated. Wag Price told me something of his insurance valuation business in Tientsin today.

Friday 13th November: Finished "The Great Illusion" today. Whilst it is obvious that certain of the author's assumptions are still true, some of his conclusions, tho' borne out by the 1914-1918 war, have been falsified by the methods adopted by the Dictator states in post Great War history. Got several new angles and valuable guidance on future reading material. Started a book by Maxim Gorki – "Fragments from my Diary". I found I was under a misapprehension regarding his period – he is quite a modern Russian author. As with novels by most of his countrymen, there is a strong undercurrent of melancholy and mysticism in his writings. His descriptive powers are, however, magnificent. His contrasts and similies are vivid and in some cases inspiring.

Monday 16th November: Doc came in with a cheery (piece of page missing) this morning … clouds very low and thick … marched out this morning. As we reached the 'drome rain fell heavily and continued steadily until 1030, when we were marched back to Camp, most of the 'drome being under water. During the rain had a chat with Capt. Bird and 2/Lt. Hammond on their war experiences in England. Talking with various people on the same subject convinces me that I have gained much more from a personal point of view from my experiences and life in the Far East than I would had I remained at home. There seems to have been the same chaos, incompetence and selfishness there as in Malaya. As I hear more about the campaigns in France, Greece, Crete, and Egypt, the more I am absolutely convinced that the Malayan shambles was not unique but typical, of something basically wrong in our body politic.

Tuesday 17th November: Rain again stopped work on the 'drome, much to (missing) delight. A heavy and continuous fall most of the morning. Finished first of my report notes on Far East Command, Singapore, Prestige, and thought over rough draft for second and third, Discipline and Morale.

One feels the need of a table and chair or bench when working sitting on a camp bed is not an ideal position! Usual milling crowd in our mess-cells; some playing bridge, one or two couples bending over chess-boards, and the remainder either sleeping, reading, or talking over other days in small groups. Made one or two attempts to cheer up Stan Cressey, Price and others by suggesting a possible threefold attack from Burma, China and Australia. This evening a boxing tournament in three 1½ minute round contests. Highlights were A.C. Grange and Cpl. Thompson (R.A.) and F/Sgt. Potter and Cpl. Griffiths. The final round between the "Jesselton Terror" and the "Batavia Basher" created some amusement. The sound of the choir practising Christmas carols brought back a strange nostalgia of things past that I have now decided to leave resolutely out of my mind.

Wednesday 18th November: Almost finished rough draft on Discipline this morning. Padre managed to get "The Good Soldier Schweik" for me today, which I began to read in the afternoon.

After three days in this dump, I am very anxious to get onto the 'drome again; the working party today managed to do their full spell and get back to Camp before the rain started at 1730, and continued more or less all night. Concert arranged was cancelled. Talk with Stan Cressey tonight was mainly on house plans. When he returns to England to retire he aims to build a house in Kent or Sussex, around the 1000 pounds mark. Several other people seem to have got this house plan craze. Several talks with Paterson, Davies (R.C.S.) and Yates (who has just come out of the dysentery ward) on the possible position of things in this area.

Thursday 19th November: Quite warm on the drone today, though not so warm as our record about 4 days ago. Our tall young boy scout who was in charge got rather mixed up in his initial organisation, and was in his usual changeable mood all day. However, he gave 70 of their 'prizes' as a magnanimous gesture before we returned to Camp.

In the evening we had our long postponed concert including a topical sketch in old time melodrama style: "Sir Jasper Jesselton", an interlude by A.C.s Gordon and Shackleton, songs by Garner and Community singing led by our (?) Army accordionist. Afterwards we had our daily dose of liquid yeast which the M.O. hopes will keep down the vitamin deficiency cases.

Friday 20th November: A very quiet day in camp. Finished "The Good Soldier Schweik", a very amusing story of the adventures of a rather dumb Czech soldier in the Austro-Hungarian Army in the War of 1914-18, ending in his transfer to the Galician front. Stressed throughout was the underlying rottenness of the Dual Monarchy.

Did a spot of dhoby in the afternoon, and then started "The Story of Mankind" by Hendrik Van Loon, whose "Story of the Pacific" I had read whilst at Malang. Int. conf. of details heard the other day by convs. on working party [PL: This is clearly shorthand for some "confirmation of details heard through working party conversations" – it may have referred to a rumoured visit by Major Suga, see notes for 21, 22 and 23 November.]

Jackson returned from 'drome this afternoon with dysentery, and with 30 others was sent to the outside dysentery hospital. This type of sickness seems unfortunately to be on the increase. Shared a tin of M&V with Padre as the stew was so poor this evening. Hope to do a deal with Jacko re shoes today.

Saturday 21st November: A very hot day on the 'drome which seemed to make

18

the Japanese very lethargic. Our genial machine gunner spent most of the day sleeping in his 'crows nest'! The Japanese Major Suga was expected by air today, but was told he is coming by ship. A patrol recce machine circled the 'drome today at 1 pm but did not land. The "Gen" merchants were again busy today, making mountains out of molehills! Chief sources were the Japanese soldiers whose remarks in pidgin English are usually interpreted very many ways. Today Jones and I were on the 'drome together for the first time.

At the evening's sing-song, Hardie addressed the men for the first time, asking them to back up their Officers and NCOs and promising to keep them informed of everything. It went down very well, but to have been fully effective it should have been made when we first arrived here. The concert compere Shackleton, tried hard, but made a hash of it, I'm afraid.

Whiteside and MacIntosh went sick today.

Sunday 22nd November: Very heavy rains this morning, which caused the working party to return before lunch. More fell during the afternoon and evening.

The Japanese Major Suga did not arrive today, but is promised for tomorrow morning, at 0900; the morning's work party being cancelled, one to take place in the afternoon. Church at 1930 hrs. followed by Holy Communion.

Had slight dust-up with Jonah this evening re my supposed refusal to give commands in Japanese, which was cleared up when I heard that Lt. Nagata had given the order. Was ordered to parade for lunch with the Japanese tomorrow at 11.30 hrs., but felt obliged to refuse for reasons I explained to Jones and the Padre. A peculiar position to be placed in, but one on which I think I have taken the right decision.

Greatly absorbed today in "The Story of Mankind".

Monday 23rd November: The event today was the visit of Major Suga – the long expected!! I was in charge of Room 3, and after he had asked A.C. Burroughs if he was well, and had received the answer that he had a bad heart, * he didn't ask any more questions!!! [*PL: The Japanese frequently used "bad heart" as a form of abuse, meaning insincere, untrustworthy, unreliable etc.]

After inspecting the Camp he made another of his "look at me" speeches in which his English got rather tied up. He announced that today would be a holiday for "harvest-thanksgiving", which was very popular.

I refused Hardie's order to attend a lunch party with the Japanese, and was placed under open arrest!! The whole affair grows more phantastic each day. 12 officers, including the Padre, attended this beanfast with our enemies. They were given soup, rice and pork, coffee and saki. None of the complaints

19

about which so much has been said, were apparently mentioned. A lot seems to have been said about officers' conditions, but little or nothing about Airmen's and/or Soldiers'. Considering our leadership, this is hardly surprising. Officers returned from lunch like a lot of excited schoolboys.

A very good concert this evening which, being in "open arrest" I did not attend. I am hoping that they will make this a Court Martial case after the War.

Tuesday 24th November: A very heavy shower delayed our departure for the 'drome for about 3/4 hour. Much to most peoples chagrin, however, off we went, and in spite of a very heavy shower of rain, we had to start work. Quite an uneventful day.

A very good boxing display again tonight, which a slight drizzle failed to mar. A minor sound-off over another case of the officers getting a little more meat than the men, or so it was alleged. All due to rather tactless handling on the part of Captain Wallis and RQMS Salter, one of the Messing Officers.

Wednesday 25th November: A fairly quiet day which I used to do a spot of dhobying and read Van Loon. About 1800 hrs. we were told that we were to move out of the Gaol into new quarters at 0800 hrs. tomorrow morning. The only 2 officers being "left-in", being the M.O. and the Padre. No contact will be allowed between officers and men except, of course, on the 'drome. W/O. Whiteside becomes "Camp Master" of the Gaol, with ASM. Laing as his Assistant. Hardie and Young fill these roles in our (new) place. They are all provided with special armbands. Managed to change Fl.*20 (N.E.I. Guilders) for $ with S/Sgt. Rooker, and also lent Padre $5. Later took $10 to Jacko in part payment for his shoes. Said a few words of farewell to my flight after rollcall, and they seemed to appreciate it.

In the new quarters there will be 42 officers (including four W/ Os.) 3 cooks and 7 batmen.

Thursday 26th November: Moved out of the Gaol at 0800 hrs. to new quarters opposite the railway level-crossing and the Guruduwara (Sikh Temple). Made 3 trips before all kit, food and cookhouse utensils were moved.

There are 14 rooms in the new building, which is built of wood, with a very high roof of shingles, the whole being raised about 6ft. from the ground on piles. Two of the rooms are being used as Mess Quarters the others having 4 or 5 officers in each. I am sharing the end room nearest the Gaol with Stan Cressey, Dicky Caruth and Grey-Jones. We have 5 windows and a very pleasant end-verandah which possesses distinct possibilities. After bedding down, we bathed in a corrugated-screened "double Dutch" [PL: Not sure why it was so called – it was simply a screened, open-air bathing place with 2 cold showers, and a small space for changing] bath, and enjoyed a grand meal – the best since Changi. Fish – fresh fish – at 2100 hrs. Ye Gods!

Friday 27th November: Only 151 R.A.F. and 142 Army on the 'drome today. Everything peaceful but very hot.

According to all accounts our removal has made no difference to the accommodation problem in the Gaol. The dysentery figures are rising rapidly, and as a result the one-storied building by the gate has been converted to a hospital, the previous hospital now being used purely and simply as an isolation ward.

One gunner died today (dysentery). The Japanese are now taking stool tests on banana leaves. Out of 15 tests taken 2 days ago, 15 were positive, and 15 of 30 taken yesterday were also positive, the results of the remainder not having been received.

Had a long talk with Sgt. Vickerman on Tjilitjap, in the Far East, and Asian War events in general. Another cracking meal tonight a-la Foley, and all done out of rice.

"Won" a broken-down wicker chair from the Japanese today the only one in the Mess!

Saturday 28th November: Spent part of this morning as one of "Linge's Labourers"; Eric Foulkes and I were detailed to clear a path to some of the latrines at Hardie's end of the building. This was completed in about 3/4 hour, during which we had an interval for coffee!

The Japanese demanded 400 men for the 'drome this morning and W/O. Whiteside was therefore obliged to send 100 sick men (B and C) about 60-70 of whom came back during the a.m. and p.m. The presence of W/O. Bessant for the first time caused much amusement amongst the 'drome parties.

Jones gave his summary of evidence on the "case"* (i.e. My Case* of refusing to obey? a lawful order!) during the p.m., followed by Whitworth. I asked Jones several questions.

We have now constructed a small table, which has been put on the verandah, covered with a small sarong of Grey-Jones's. Stan and I sat around it and chatted most of the evening, being joined by Mac(Intosh) and Thready.

Sunday 29th November: Finished "The Story of Mankind" by Van Loon, last night.

Our morning fatigue took the form of moving some bricks and cutting up some corrugated iron sheeting. Afterwards I got a rather tiresome head cold which kept me blowing hard all day! Only 320 on the 'drome today – apparently Nagata had seen about 15 people frolicking round the Camp and had thus ordered 400 out.

W/O. Whiteside seems to be doing very well in the Camp much more successful in getting things than our incompetent gang has been. Up-to-date, he has obtained (i) 300 grass mats (ii) bathing parades for skin disease cases. Doc Daniels is very pleased as he can now get things done without going "through the usual channels."

The *Syonan Times* (Singapore Times) from Sept. 10th – Oct. 19th arrived today and provided quite interesting – and encouraging reading. Reading between the lines, I am more than pleased.

Monday 30th November: The aspirins and hot water last night seemed to have done my cold some good; spent a very quiet day in an attempt to dislodge it. In the p.m. the barber called for the first time, from 3-5 p.m. but was too late in learning of it, to have my hair cut.

Foley put on his first menu in French tonight – 3 courses (rice of course), followed by coffee.

Holiday for the 'drome parties. 2 parties of skin diseases sea-bathed this morning, and about 150 fit men this afternoon, but no officers. A spot of bother in the Jap guard-room tonight, when one of the Nips turned up tight. Coming on to our verandah at rollcall, Stan Cressey, Orderly Officer, he started to embrace Wag (Price), but on the Jap Guard Commander attempting to calm him, he drew his bayonet and started to flourish it – he was knocked down the steps (a fall of 6 ft. on to concrete, it sounded as though his skull (where he landed) had cracked) – where he lay concussed. After anxious consultations, visits by officers etc., he was dragged away with bandages round his head.

Tuesday 1st December: Hardly a cloud in the sky today, which made things hot at the 'drome. Rain clouds came over from the S.W. mountains about 4.30 p.m., and produced a very cooling shower for our march home. The men appreciate the sea-bathing very much indeed, so they told me; the beach is of fine white sand, about 5 miles long, the sea is quite shallow and clear for some distance out, and there appear to be no sting rays, jellyfish or sharks. They found a number of seats and a changing hut which had clearly been used by the British population.

Today, my thoughts went back to a year ago, when I was on leave in Penang, just prior to my recall on the mobilisation of the Federated Malay States. Conversation tonight hinged on memories and their value.

Wednesday 2nd December: Cpl. Kerslake, who died in the Civil Hospital from a perforated appendix yesterday, was buried today with military honours. Saw Doc in Camp who said that Kerslake was taken to hospital in an open truck in pouring rain, resulting in partial collapse on arrival. English Doc at Hospital thought him fit for operation after 3 days and sent for Daniels, who got the message 3 days later. On operating, he found the case hopeless.

Although Padre was out, had a long chat with W/O. Whiteside, who seems to be making very good progress without interference from Hardie and Co. Doc told me that he can now get things done without going through "usual channels" and that there is now no crime in the Camp at all. He looks tired and it appears that all this sickness is worrying him considerably.

Thursday 3rd December: A completely blank day. Managed to do a little to the Far East Command notes, but very little else. Very oppressive afternoon, which I used for sleeping, and woke up with a mouth like the bottom of a birdcage. Before dinner had a quite interesting conversation with Dicky Caruth on life in the East, Java and Malaya particularly, in peace time. Life during the sugar boom about 1926 must have been extremely hectic for the Dutch. Apparently the Simpang Club in Surabaya used to run a ball on Queen Wilhelmina's birthday, with 5 dance-bands – one each in the Palm Court, Ballroom, Billiard Room, Bar and Entrance! Also instanced case of a Sugar Mill Managing-Director, whose bonus for boom years was Fl.1, 000, 000. Not bad squeeze!

Friday 4th December: 'drome today, passably cool. Airmen still very cheerful, although numbers today were the lowest ever 136 R.A.F. and 144 Army. Dysentery is still claiming one or two people a day, the latest to go down being F/S. Warner. Bathing parades are still popular with the scrotum cases (tinea), especially as transport is now often provided. Its practical value does seem doubtful to me, however; I think the object should be to keep the private parts dry and avoid friction, although I admit that under present conditions this is almost impossible. F/S. Stammers and I went over old times at Alor Star, Tengah and Seletar, and the history of 205 Squadron.

An "extraordinary" Mess Meeting was held tonight to discuss the Canteen. Grey-Jones, Cressey and I did not attend. The usual, windy, "much-ado-about-nothing". Hardie and Co. had a "Canteen Board" rigged, but were forestalled by one of the Army, who proposed the present Mess Committee.

Saturday 5th December: After the rain which fell last night, today was quite cool. Spent an hour or so cleaning camp drains with Dicky Bird and W/O. Sanders, showered and took notes from the Syonan Times which may prove useful later. Finished the synopsis to G.B. Shaw's "The Intelligent Woman's Guide to Socialism, Capitalism, Communism and Fascism", which is going to be very interesting. The news events of yesterday were a prominent subject of conversation here today* [*An example of obscure writing to conceal some rumour with political or military implications]. Another very important event was the arrival of Canteen supplies – ours consisting of 25 oranges, 12 bananas, 3 papayas, 3 packets of tea dust – a great luxury this – and about 1½ katies of unshelled peanuts. As a reserve ration I bought one large tin sardines for a possible future boat journey – one never knows!

Sunday 6th December: Drains again this morning with Jones and Cressey. Did 15 chapters of "The I.W.G. " this morning, dealing with Distribution of Wealth in theory and practice. He (GBS) argues that socialistic theory is that every-one should receive an equal share, irrespective of character, ability and class. This obviously does not take human nature into account. His case looks good on paper, e.g. it is difficult to determine the respective monetary values of a padre and a blacksmith, as one gives an intangible service and the other a material benefit.

My day off tomorrow, but as Bickerton has gone sick, and his relief, Hobbs, has also – yours truly parades again!

Monday 7th December: Quite a pleasant day on the 'drome mostly overcast all day. 7 R.A.F. Officers were out – Jones, Burgess, Smith, Sanders, Brown, Grey-Jones and myself, and three Army – Paterson, Bird and Mason. 151 Air Force ORs and 144 Army. On talking with some of the men today, was struck by the number who had come direct to Java from U.K. or the Middle East; no wonder most of them feel pretty grieved and depressed about the whole busi-ness. One young lad I spoke to had been in the RAF 2 years, before which he had been a grocer's assistant 6 years – he was 23. He did not like regular RAF service, but thought that grocery would be too dull to go back to!! I imagine that quite a number of them feel like him!

Tuesday 8th December: Holiday for all today. Drains this morning with Burgess, Cressey and Grey-Jones – we finished in record time. Afterwards spent time with Shaw's I.W.G.A whitebait tiffin of which I ate both my own and Cressey's portion.

Mac(Intosh) at last finished the Summary of Evidence which I signed today.

We developed quite an argument on Socialism just before dinner tonight, Stan Cressey taking the right wing and trotting out all the stock arguments, whilst I took the left wing. A much more profound discussion on the same subject developed after dinner with Paterson and Yates, on equality of pay and incentives.

24

The date cast my mind back a year to Tengah – 1.30 a.m. bombing of Kota Bahru (Kelanton, Malaya) and 4.15 a.m. bombing of Tengah. [PL: I was quartered at the RAF Station, Tengah, Singapore, when the war started on 8/12/42 – my first experience of bombing and of a (collapsed) air raid trench.]

Wednesday 9th December: At 0730 we learnt officially that officers were no longer required to work on the 'drome, marking another stage in the Jap administration of POW Camps. We also heard last night that all senior NCOs were to work, with the exception of one per railway. On being notified that they were not required this morning, a cheer went up from the Army Officers in front of the men who had just arrived in front of our quarters. A very sorry show from a few British officers, indicative of the complete lack of interest they have in their men. Capt. Larder, R.A. (!!) said that he didn't give a damn about his men, as they didn't seem to care about him, and would not do anything he told them! An illuminating confession. This cannot be the type of officer they have at home.

We all wonder when they will be creating a second front in Europe, as our armies must be pretty well trained by now.

Thursday 10th December: Visited the Camp this morning on reporting sick, and saw Doc Daniels and the Padre, who both seemed well, although the Padre had had a touch of Changi balls! The Doc showed me his report on Cpl. Kerslake's death, which is certainly a revelation. Things in the Camp are going on very well. They held a competitive "Song Bee" between the Army and R.A.F. last night, which was a great success.

Doc reports that he now gets things done without obstruction; Padre likewise. The sickness incidence is now more or less static, but another hut is being taken over today, making 3 in all. Number of patients in Camp – 150 and in the Civil Hospital – 78. Doc received long expected medical supplies the other day – one half envelope of rice polishings, 1 day treatment for his stomach ulcer case etc.

Friday 11th December: Rose at 0625, roll call at 0630, shave, wash and note-taking all before 0730. I find the early morning hours amongst the freshest of the day, so am resolved to make good use of them! One or two grumbles from Grey-Jones about "people not going back to bed after roll-call, making a noise etc. ", but he is always half asleep at this hour, and very much worried at the moment about his cough which seems to come more frequently in the past few days.

Padre did not pay his usual Friday 3-5 p.m. visit, either on account of the very heavy rain which fell most of the afternoon (first for weeks) or because of a bout of squitters. Had a chat with 2/Lt. Hammond tonight about leadership in the campaigns of the present war. We agreed that an element we missed was the definite aim or fervent belief in the ultimate objective, which the Axis countries seem to possess.

Saturday 12th December: Drain fatigues this morning, followed by a very refreshing cold bath. One appreciates these simple pleasures to a remarkable extent nowadays. The relativity of pleasure to circumstances is impressed on one every day.

Hardie's talk with Cressey amused me a lot this morning, being mainly concerned, as usual, with Hardie. His statement that he was always bored with those people at home who had never been East, was very revealing. He must be bored with about 48, 000, 000 people!!

Today – big event – we ate our pomelo, which proved exceptionally good. Conversation after dinner hinged on plans for the post-war years. For Dicky (Caruth) and Stan (Cressey) things should be more or less comfortable, but I am prepared for very hard times personally, – if, of course, we all stay the course!

Sunday 13th December: Today, one of rumour and counter-rumour. Started badly for some of us when the expected sea-bathing was cancelled this morning. Spent most of it in speculations with (Vernon) Smith, (Dicky) Bird, Johnnie (Johnstone) and Co. on possible present moves.

Our batman then produced a rumour, just before tiffin, that we were to move on the 15th, and that work on the 'drome was to be finished by 22nd. By post-tiffin this had been further elaborated – our destination being Singapore, where we would arrive before Christmas, the troops apparently leaving on 4/2/ 43 for an unknown destination!!

Bell again conducted a very simple yet sincere service tonight at 1900 hrs. in the Mess Room. In preparation for any eventuality did some dhobying tonight.

Monday 14th December: Two Gunners, Lawrence and Hill, died in the Camp Hospital today from dysentery. Hill we all remembered for his outstanding performances at our Camp Concerts and particularly in "I'm an Old Cow Hand". The Doctor has had no sleep for 3 nights, as the sickness incidence is rising. There are now 278 in the Camp and outside hospitals.

W/O. Hynes returned to the Mess today and reported that food is plentiful but always stew, that Mac has gone into the outside hospital, and that W/O. Whiteside is receiving very little support from the NCOs. The men on the

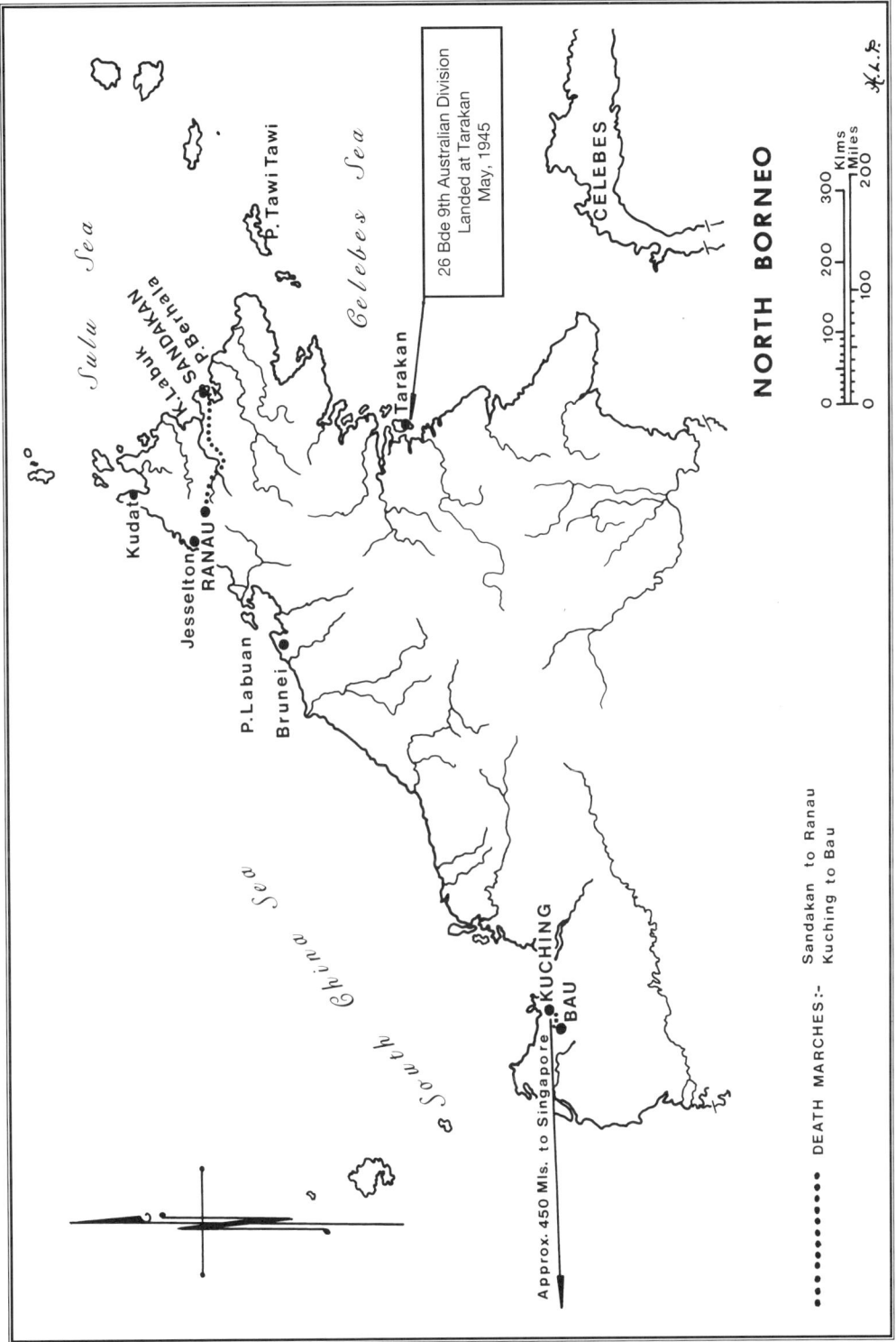

NORTH BORNEO

26 Bde 9th Australian Division
Landed at Tarakan
May, 1945

CELEBES

Klms
Miles
0   100   200   300
0   100   200

Sulu Sea

P.Tawi Tawi

Celebes Sea

Tarakan

K. Labuk
SANDAKAN
P. Berhala

Kudat

Jesselton
RANAU

P.Labuan
Brunei

South China Sea

KUCHING
BAU

Approx. 450 Mls. to Singapore

•••••••••• DEATH MARCHES :-   Sandakan to Ranau
                              Kuching to Bau

27

'drome are being made to work harder by the Japs, and there have been several instances of men being struck with rifle butts etc., proving, I think, that our presence had a restraining influence on the Japanese.

After dinner W/O's Hynes and Bessant had a chat about Changi.

Tuesday 15th December: Went into Camp on "Sick Parade" this morning, and saw Doc, Padre and Whiteside. Padre had just returned from Hill's cremation. The poor lad had to be folded up to get him into the box, and as only 2 Boy Scouts were detailed, Padre had to start the fire himself.

Whiteside told me that Hardie had been into the Camp on two occasions to see the M.O., but had not been to ask him how things were going. Hynes also remarked the other day that Hardie, known to the men as "Big Chief Sitting Bull", had had his finger dressed outside S.Q. without once going inside to see the men. All this has naturally produced unfavourable reactions in the Camp.

After hearing Doc's 'gen' (news), went to see the men in the various wards, and found most of them remarkably cheerful. Was surprised to see Cpl. Holdsworth in the Dysentery Isolation Ward, as he has been one of the most regular attenders at the 'drome.

Wednesday 16th December: Two more gunners died today, making four within 36 hours. On protest to the Japanese Camp Commandant, Doc Daniels was told that the men were eating too much. Capt. Mills told me that he was worried about the situation, and that after much pressing Hardie had reluctantly agreed to ask the Camp Commandant to give him an interview. Hardie and Mills went to see Nagata about 4 p.m. The latter expressed regret but said that 10 soldiers had died from dysentery in Kuching. He was indignant when it was suggested that the Japanese Government was responsible, and said he had done his best. The pair also came back with a lot of information about officers' pay, and the fact that saki would be allowed on Christmas Day. Selfish motives seem to have crept in again. Most of the talk in the Mess was about the latter; the fact that their men are dying daily does not seem to worry some officers.

Thursday 17th December: Heavy rain fell most of the day, and the clouds were unusually low and heavy. Took notes from Vol. 1 of Shaw's I.W.G. in the afternoon, dealing with Chapters 1-8 up to the seven means of distributing wealth.

Hardie made an announcement after dinner this evening dealing with the interview which Mills and himself had yesterday with Nagata. He seem anxious to impress on everybody that he had impressed on Nagata that Japan was responsible for the deaths of the seven airmen. It seems to me that he has started his protests rather late in the day.

Stan Cressey again preoccupied with plans for after the War. After 9 p.m. parade we went over to the Maos train incident with 'Dean' Linge (who was on the first train), Rollinson, Cressey and self, of course. Shanghai news was well to the fore, and very interesting it proved.

Friday 18th December: As the men passed our quarters this morning we noticed that there were only about 216 on parade, which is very low for the 'drome party. Very sultry afternoon during which I tried taking notes from the I.W.G. but, finding myself dropping off to sleep, went to bed. Was awakened by the arrival of Padre on his weekly visit.

Cpl. Albert Tyrrell. 11900 A.I.F. Joined Capt. Daniels in Java and went to Labuan with Flt. Lt. Blackledge as one of the nursing Orderlies. Died Labuan 24 June 1945. Nedlands, W.A. *Pic: Vic Tyrrell.*

He brought back "Science in War" and took back Beatrice Webb Part II. He told me that the events of the past week had profoundly affected him, and he felt particularly bitter against Hardie for his obvious lack of interest in the welfare and concerns of the men. After all this was over, he was prepared to be most vindictive. In this case, it is entirely warranted and I shall, D.V., back him up to the hilt.

Saturday 19th December: Visited Camp this morning and found Doc Daniels in bed with a fever which, however, he hopes to dispose of by having a day in bed. He and his Nursing Orderlies are doing a marvellous job of work for the men. Cpl. Tyrrell, especially, is putting up a very fine show, although the strain is beginning to tell on him; he has red rims round his eyes through lack of sleep – up to date, 60 hours at a stretch. Visited W/O. Whiteside and found him looking over photographs of Singapore and Tengah Yacht Club in particular, with F/S Stammers. Visited as many of the men as I could in the time, and found them all very cheerful, especially Cpl. Holdsworth who is in the Isolation Ward.

One more Gunner died yesterday in the outside hospital and was brought into Camp without having been plugged and in a state of decomposition, necessitating the destruction of some of the underbearers' clothing.

Visit from the new Japanese Commandant at 1600 hrs.

Sunday 20th December: Had to suffer an hour or more of drums, pipes and chanting from the Guruduwara across the road this morning.

Nagata left with some of his soldiers by the 0800 hrs. train.

Started Susan Stebbings "Thinking to Some Purpose" which should prove of great use to me. The opening chapter is headed "Are the English Illogical?" and she quotes Austin Chamberlain "We are prone to eschew the general, we are fearful of these logical conclusions pushed to the extreme, because in fact, human nature being what it is, logic plays but a small part in our everyday life. We are actuated by tradition, by affection, by prejudice, by moments of emotion and sentiment. In the face of any great problem, we are seldom really guided by the stern logic of the philosopher or the historian, who, removed from all turmoil of daily life, works in the studious calm of his surroundings."

Monday 21st December: At our usual Sunday evening service last night, conducted by 2/Lt. Bell, we had our first carol "Once in Royal David's City".

Today, made good progress with Stebbings book, and took notes on 12 Chapters of Shaw's I.W.G., which brought me to Chapter 20.

This afternoon received the last of the 'drome pays: in my case 73 cents, of which I took 35¢ in cash. Had my hair sheared off again by LAC Spencer on his weekly visit; he told me that, apart from sickness, everything goes well in the Camp, Mr. Whiteside apparently getting no trouble from any quarter. The men have bought a rice grinder at a cost of $28, which will do 1½ 100 kilo sacks of rice a day, with 2 men working it. At present the ground rice is being used solely for hospital use, especially for the dysentery patients.

Tuesday 22 December: Today at lunch time Hardie addressed one or two remarks to the Mess. He said he had been to see the new Japanese Camp Commandant, Lt. Nagai and had found him a very charming fellow indeed, with a perfect command of English. He had asked him about salaries and was told that he had the papers with him but that it would be a week or so before final arrangements were made. Hardie said, however, that Nagai had made the extremely generous gesture of lending us $700 personally. He had enquired about saki and was told that that would be arranged. Hardie said that he had invited the Japanese Camp Commandant for drinks on Christmas morning, but he had merely smiled. If Hardie could have read my thoughts at that moment he would not have looked so pleased with himself. As an after-thought he said that when he mentioned dysentery to Nagai he said that the position was just as bad at Sandakan and Kuching and that Jap soldiers had it too.

Wednesday 23rd December: Went into Camp this morning. W/O. Whiteside had just forwarded 2 letters to Hardie, which he showed me. One dealt with Hardie's order that as only 8 lbs. instead of 13 lbs. of sugar had been sent round, the balance should be sent round at once. Whiteside replied that the officers had received their proper share and that, as sugar from the airmens rations was being given to dysentery patients at the hospital, the other ranks were actually getting less than the officers. The other was a complaint about a Pilot Officer and the rations. Apparently the officer and his ration party had arrived at No. 1 Camp before W/O. Salter and his men were allowed out. In the interim the officer had picked up a piece of beef from the ration lorry and had given orders for it to be hidden under some vegetables; when Salter came out the officer was given his usual supply of meat. This was all witnessed from No. 2 Block by 2 Gunners whose 2 signed statements formed the basis of the complaint. The Padre and Doc were rightly very bitter about it all, especially as most of the disease in the Camp is caused by malnutrition.

Thursday 24th December: Spent most of the day re-reading "Grey Wolf" by H.C. Armstrong, a biography of Kemal Ataturk. It makes extremely vivid reading as it traces Kemal's career from his boyhood in Salonika, through the military schools, campaigns against the Druses in Syria and the Italians in Tripoli, and the Bulgars, Greeks and Serbs in the Balkans.

Friday 25th December: In spite of hanging up two stockings (really to dry), got nothing in them! Most people were wishing each other a Merry Christmas 1943! Went, with 9 others, to 0700 Communion in the Camp, and found the cold rather intense. Saw Doc and Padre who, for obvious reasons, are not dining with us tonight.

1100 hrs. Carol Service in Camp also was well attended by the men and by 24 officers. Afterwards we had time to go round to see the men, who seemed remarkably cheerful. There is no doubt that this experience is bringing out the best in the men. Many thoughts of home today, wondering if there will be the usual gathering at Broadmeadows (My sister and brother-in-law's home in Country Durham, where we all spent Xmas Day in previous years); and whether the usual toast will be drunk at 1 o'clock? But for the misfortunes of war, I might have been there myself! At 1800 hrs. dinner was served in the Mess Room, which had been transformed by the efforts of our decoration committee into something resembling a pukka Mess; sheets on the tables for cloths, menu cards very artistically drawn by Whitworth and Bagnall were stuck in clay holders, paper streamers made from newspapers, a Xmas Tree complete with fairy lamps (torch bulbs), beautifully arranged sarongs on the walls, together with imitation berry holly stuck in our pictures. And the menu – hors d'oeuvres, soup, beefsteak, chicken, a very cunning Xmas pudding made of rice, and black coffee – a triumph for Cpl. Foley. Dicky Caruth proposed "The King" and Hardie "Absent Friends". Then "us four" having drunk our private toast to our relatives and wives, the fun and games started. A broadcasting programme, charades, telepathy, "Up Jenkins", Community singing (Ilkley Moor, Pack Up Your Troubles etc.) Auld Lang Syne, "The King" and so to bed, after a grand evening. Strangely enough, most of us could have eaten another dinner after our feast tonight!! Grey-Jones and Dicky (Caruth) waxed well on the saki and samsu, whilst Stan and I stuck to ginger beer.

Saturday 26th December: Finished "Hags Hook", a mystery yarn. A very quiet day, the morning being spent woodchopping, and at a TOC H Meeting called by "Thready" Threadgold. Was surprised to see the men marching to the 'drome today, as we understood that a holiday had been granted. Stan Cressey at last achieved a reasonable plan of a house today!

Sunday 27th December: Continued Susan Stebbings "Thinking to Some Purpose" today, but whether on account of the muggy weather, or the reaction from Christmas, I made very heavy weather of it. Stan has almost finished his house plans and hopes that these will not be confiscated this time. Rain fell at the usual time, about 1630 hrs. for about an hour. Football match cancelled this afternoon – "match prolonged owing to wet and grass has not been cutted." Did not attend evening service tonight – watched sunset instead.

Monday 28th December: Finished "Thinking to Some Purpose" today must get this on our return to civilisation. After yesterday's holiday, slightly more men turned out for 'drome today – about 240.

One more gunner (Hicks) died today (dysentery) and four more are dangerously ill. Diptheria, too, seems to be becoming a menace now. Doc Daniels has been abed again with his temperature – if anything happens to him, the picture will be very serious. I think his work here alone deserves a decoration, when one realises the difficulties he has had to contend with depressing living conditions, lack of hospital space and supplies, malnutrition, and obstruction from Nips.

Threadgold had that bloody gramophone on most of the evening.

Tuesday 29th December: 2 more deaths from dysentery today A.C. Mendy – our first R.A.F. dysentery casualty, and Gunner Hall. Ken Whitworth attended the cremation of Mendy, and was much disgusted at the method of carrying it out. Blood was oozing out of the coffin, running down the bearers' shirts and splashing into a trail down the path. The smell was also fairly high.

Went into Camp and found Doc drawing airmen's teeth; he has been in bed again for 3 days, and thinks he has some form of malaria. Padre has now got beri-beri in his feet and so gets little sleep at night; what little they get is frequently interrupted by the spasms of the dysentery patients in the adjoining ward, or calls for the M.O. They are both doing a fine job.

Whiteside told me that Hardie did not mention anything of the meat or sugar incident, but that he was not letting the matter rest there. Good for him!

Started 2nd Volume of I.W.G. – 1st Chapter dealing with nationalisation of the banks. Took notes.

Wednesday 30th December: In process of doing drains this morning when 27 officers were called for to move the Jap Guard House opposite our room, to a site on the road leading to the Jail. Work began at 0930, and after a break of 1 hour for lunch, continued from 1330 to 1930. Demolition and erection within 1 day: that's the stuff to give 'em! Some very tired, but quite happy bodies tumbled into bed just after 2100 hrs. roll call!

After finishing drains with Cressey, a party of six of us collected firewood and rations from the Camp. After tiffin did rice cleaning with Johnstone, Young and Hammond; collected hundreds of rice maggots, which we bottled!!

Started R.S.M. Jacobi's copy of "Winged Words" – a collection of broadcast talks by R.A.F. personnel. Had a fierce argument tonight with old Stan Cressey, our staunch supporter of the "upper classes"! Jock, our batman, told us some interesting stores of the first air raid on Glasgow – raid commenced at 2100 and lasted till 0600.

Thursday 31st December: Quiet day. Prepared for inspection by Japanese Camp Commandant which did not come off. Read "Winged Words" and Country Life Book of Air Force photos.

Good riddance to 1942

1943 – Jesselton

Friday 1st January 1943: Today we start a New Year which we are all hoping will prove to be Liberation Year, if not the year of final victory for our cause. We remember the Prime Minister's prediction in 1940 that 1943 will be the year of offensives that will bring us to our goal, and remembering, take courage!

A holiday for the Camp today, during which a bathing parade was authorised for both men and officers. With 24 other officers I marched down to the beach which is one of the best I have seen in the tropics; it is bordered by a wide fringe of fir trees, consists of a gently sloping gradient of fine white sand, and overlooks a sea which includes one or two large tree-covered islands to break the monotony. The day was perfect. A cloudless sky, and a suspicion of a breeze, which induces the slightest of swells on an otherwise glassy sea. Most of the time I spent in obtaining "water-confidence" and attempting, rather unsuccessfully, to float! Afterwards wished all the senior NCOs and a number of the men, a happier year than the last. Back for tiffin and a very heavy sleep in the afternoon.

Celebrated the New Year by putting on fried eggs for breakfast and an extra special dinner at night.

Saturday 2nd January: Another bathing party today, which was again very popular; they do help one to forget the circumstances of the moment. Had chat with several airmen who seem to be keeping remarkably cheerful despite the upsurge of dysentery and beri-beri cases. L/Bdr. Fields, our very popular camp accordionist, and A.C. Myers, one of my 1st Java Party at Changi, died this morning (dysentery). The death of Fields had a very depressing effect on the sick in the Camp, as he had been the mainstay of the very popular concerts and sing-songs which had been arranged from time to time. To enable me to go swimming, Stan Cressey had taken over my duties as Orderly Officer, and was detailed for the cremation party which, I think, depressed him. The Padre had also been rather short with him, when he made an enquiry about his health. I think that conditions in the Camp are getting on the Padre's nerves to the extent of a somewhat unreasonable bitterness against all officers. Whilst there are quite a number of the latter who are entirely selfish, there are some who would have preferred to stay in Camp to do whatever was possible for their men. [All the officers had been moved from the Jesselton Prison, some time before, to what had been the Warders' Quarters a few hundred yards away, on the main road to the beach.] Among the latter I naturally include myself.

Sunday 3rd January: Today was our last bathing parade for the time being, as the airmen tell me that working parades are recommencing tomorrow. With the aid of "Wag" Price actually managed to float on my back for 5 minutes and swim for about the same time; as ! "Wag" had a firm grip of my legs, in 5 feet of water, I hadn't much option! Was told today by one of my ex 152 M.U. crowd that young LAC Matthews had been taken ill with cerebral spinal meningitis, and had been taken to the Civil Hospital. Hope to get some news of him in a few days time from the Doc.

Monday 4th January: As the working party went by this morning, noticed that the numbers had increased to about 300, as (W/O) Whiteside told me the other day. All the men looked much more lively and cheerful after their holiday in spite of the fact that A.C. MacLeod and Gunner Hall had died during the night. Rain fell very heavily during the morning, but in spite of this visited the Camp, and arrived just as the coffins of Hall and MacLeod were being taken out for cremation. Had a long chat with the Doc on the way things were shaping. His diptheria cases had had swabs taken, but no results were to hand. He was still concerned over the eye-sight of three of his Army beri-beri cases; the buying party had managed to get a bottle of concentrated Vitamin B in Jesselton, with which the sight of one man had been saved – unfortunately no more supplies of this essence were available. Owing, too, to the entire absence of incoming supplies, prices of quinine had risen to 8¢ per tablet: as the normal dosage in cases of dengue or malaria is 6 tablets per day (4 or 5 grams apiece). The Doc himself looked better than he has been for some weeks. On my way out, Doc took me to see Gunner Keaney who was isolated in the old lepers' lavatory near the old Guardroom. He was dying and uncon-scious, and looked a horrible sight, poor chap, with only the whites of his eyes showing, and his mouth open. As he had thrown up some blood over another patient's food, he had had to be isolated.

Tuesday 5th January: Gunner Keaney died yesterday and was cremated. There are now five lots of ashes awaiting burial: was detailed for the funeral with 2/Lt. Coleman, R.A.

Wednesday 6th January: Stood by all the morning for the funeral party which did not, however, mature until 13.30 hrs. Went round to the Camp and found everything prepared for a memorial service; five boxes were lined up on the stage, with flowers beside each, and the altar covered with our R.A.F. altar cloth. Had to wait about half an hour for the Japanese Camp Commandant, which was rather trying for the sick men who had been detailed for the ser-vice. He arrived and put some flowers on the remains. After service, I then slow marched the funeral party to the waiting mosquito-bus, which took us to the Christian cemetery. The route took us up a winding road to the rear of the Civil Hospital, through a plantation of young rubber, to the landward side of

35

Revd, J.T. Wanless. 77336. Chaplain to the Forces 3rd Class, Royal Army Chaplains' Dept. att. R.A.F. Died Sandakan 30 June 1945.
Pic. The Revd. John Hyde.

Captain J.F.D. Mills. 73787. 77 HAA Royal Artillery. Died Sandakan 3 July 1945. Age 30.
Pic: Donald Yates

the hill dominating Jesselton. From the entrance to the cemetery we had a magnificent view over rubber estates, an extensive salt-water marsh to our left, and the long Kinabalu range. Our patch of ground was on the lower slope, and we just managed to make a row of 15 graves Gnr. Needham, the 16th, being buried elsewhere. The Japanese Camp Commandant allocated another patch of ground for the next batch of burials. Having dug the graves, we held our service, filled in the earth, saluted, and came back via Jesselton by the European residential quarter, from which we had a magnificent view of the bay.

Thursday 7th January: Started Konrad Herden's "One Man against Europe", a detailed account of the rise of Hitler and the NDSAP in Germany, their acquisition of power, methods, and successes in Europe since 1933.

Friday 8th January: Paid another visit to Camp this morning to see Doc. Found both Padre and he quite cheerful, and heard about tomorrow's dysentery test, by which the Japanese Camp Commandant hopes to increase the number of those on the 'drome. Doc not in favour of this, and anticipates the worst. Padre also very sceptical; incidentally he gave me this dreary book. Went into 4 and 5 and found some very bad skin cases; speaking generally, the men did not seem quite so cheerful as before. I do think that the holding of memorial services in the Camp should be discontinued: it is bound to have a bad psychological effect on the men, all of whom are sick. Saw Groundon and one of my men from Bukit Panjang who had been operated on the day before, for stricture, at the Civil Hospital. Matthews will live, but will be permanently paralyzed in both legs (from the hips down) so the Doc told me but he is keeping remarkably cheerful. Sent him a message. Did quite a lot of dhoby work today.

Saturday 9th January: Held meeting of TOC H this morning in the Centre Stable – it was a covered open-sided shed – at which I read the minutes of the last two meetings. RSM Jacobi elected Jobmaster. Finished off "One Man against Europe" and began to take notes from it, also got this diary up-to-date. Another TOC H meeting at 4.30 p.m. at which Thready read a chapter from the TOC H book, entitled "The first friend of TOC H – a hymn of praise for Archbishop Davidson"! After dinner, 'Wag' Price gave a talk on life in peacetime China, particularly in Shanghai and Tientsin. In the case of Shanghai, he based his remarks on an imaginary tour of the city, starting at the Whangpo, passing the Waterworks and Power Station, and eventually arriving at the Bund. Our route was then down the Nanking Road, past Wing On and Sinceres (Department Stores) to Bubbling Well Road and the Racecourse, with its variety of sporting facilities, all of which were reserved for Europeans. All racing in Shanghai is done by amateurs, on ponies, which most Europeans can afford to own and run; there is a considerable volume of betting, particularly amongst the Chinese, with the result that the Turf Club is one of the richest institutions in the city, and can afford a large amount of philanthropy – they run, amongst other things, a Union Jack Club for our troops. Cost of living etc. was briefly outlined. A two-room apartment, will cost from two pounds ten shillings to four pounds ten shillings a week, and servants, exceptionally good there, another $150/- per month. Sketching the history of Hi-Li (or Pelota) in China, Wag went on to discuss life in Tientsin, which has more foreign concessions than Shanghai, all adjoining each other, and each with its own police. His varied experiences during the civil wars, students demonstrations, and finally, the Japanese War, closed the talk.

Sunday 10th January: 'Drome party worked only 1/2 day today, returning at 1330. Doc came in to see Davies this morning: there are now seven more on the dangerously-ill list, mostly suffering from starvation. Read some of the Japan Times Weekly supplements (dated 22nd and 29th Oct 1942 and 5th November 1942) this morning and was interested in their comments on the Battle of the Solomons, and on Burma, Australia and North Africa. Evening service conducted by Lt. Hammond, R.A. Afterwards took notes from Konrad Heiden's book, watched Jacko (F/O Jackson) and CO. play poker for a while, and so to bed.

Monday 11th January: The Japs turned out 30 sick men for the 'drome working party this morning. These men had previously been working on a slight levelling job just outside the Jap Guard Room and opposite their double-storied quarters (i.e. Jap guards' quarters); this morning they were therefore turned out for the 'drome. They made a pitiful sight as they lagged behind the main body. They consisted mainly of beri-beri cases, but as they struggled along, they looked like a crowd of crippled decrepits. One man only got 10 yds. beyond the railway line when he was "all-in" and had to be sent back by a passing mosquito-bus: most of the others also came back during the course of the day, by buses and lorries. At 1100 10 of us were turned out to erect posts and barbed wire around the building and area which is being turned over to the ORs camp and which will afford them some relief to their overcrowding, and a little more ground to exercise in. At 1400, 30 of us were turned out; 15 to finish off the erection of the posts etc., and the remainder to commence the clearance of the derelict garden in front of the Boy Scouts (Jap guards) quarters. We knocked-off at 1715, and obviously afforded the troops a great deal of amusement as they returned to the Camp. Noticed that the Army particularly are feeling and showing the strain of the continuing work on an inadequate diet. After a cold shower and change into clean clothes, felt fit, hungry and pleasantly tired! Most of my brother officers, however, agreed that it was "disgraceful" that British officers should be made to work, and resolved to make a strong protest. I did not participate, feeling (i) that our work had probably relieved some of the men in the Camp from doing it, and (ii) it had done us good to get out and take some exercise. Spent evening in Mess taking notes. Gunner Scullion died today in the Civil Hospital (dysentery) and Cpl. Harrison (RAF) is now on the D.I. list from the same complaint.

Tuesday 12th January: More grouses when another officers' working party of 30 was ordered out at 0900 this morning; same numbers on the same jobs as yesterday. As I had sunburned my back yesterday through working without a shirt, took the precaution of wearing one today. Again on our market garden job, which a well-timed rain shower terminated at 4 p.m. Rain fell heavily between 5 and 6, but cleared up by 6.30 pm; the weather remained cold all night, however, making it necessary for me to wear my pullover. I hear that a letter of protest about Officers working parties was sent to the Japanese Camp Commandant by 'Sitting Bull' today; he obviously intends to keep his "hand-in" at letter-writing!

Wednesday 13th January: Our job this morning was the levelling and filling of the padang (open space) outside the ORs Camp Guard Room, and in the afternoon, our garden 'allotment'. Hardie went to see Camp Commandant this morning re officers working parties, having rightly refused to see the Japanese Sergeant, who had apparently "hung up" Hardie's letter of yesterday. Nagai was asked whether, in view of the Japanese Government's intention (as reported in the 'Japan Times') to try and adhere to the Geneva Convention on POWS, it was his order which had resulted in officers doing what amounted to coolie work. Nagai said that he had visited POW Camps in Manila, Singapore and Bangkok, but that he did not work from the book, but from the heart! He said that the turning out of officers was due to a misunderstanding on the part of one of his NCOs. What he really intended was for 30 volunteers to do the work which, he said, was for the good of the whole camp. Asked why he had sent 30 sick men to the 'drome, he replied that he was aware that they would not do any work, but he did it to get them out of the camp and into the fresh air. He said his one wish was to look after the happiness and welfare of the men. He hoped that when the padang was finished, they would be able to play games, as he was very keen on these, and when the weather cleared, soccer would be possible on the other pitch (the poor devils in the Camp hardly have the strength to walk, never mind playing games). Hardie next asked him about Red Cross supplies, to which he replied that base areas always got the supplies in preference to the front line. I gather from Hardie's remarks that they both laughed over this, and nothing more was said. Hardie winded up by saying that, as a result of this interview, his opinion, formed at his last meeting, that Nagai was utterly sincere in all that he said, had been reinforced, and that he was "full-out" for our troops. Signalman Druce, R.C.S., died 0715 today – another dysentery starvation case.

In the evening 'Dean' Linge and I had a chat about old times in Malaya. He reminded me of old Fogden's evidence in the Loveday Cases [USA notorious Civil case before the Singapore Courts in 1940 or 1941 involving corruption by British Officers and Civil Contractors employed on military work]: explaining why he had been struck off the Admiralty and War Office Contractors' lists for refusing to tender, he gave reasons as follows: (1) bank charges on loan of money for periods up to one year, as they were invariably kept waiting for their money; (2) any possible increases in materials costs; (3) ditto as regards labour costs (4) to cover penalty clause, they were never allowed a bonus clause (5) to cover costs of delays, and modifications etc. by Government Inspectors etc. Also gave some of his experiences during Group Captain Macauley's (RAAF) period as C.O. (he afterwards went on to Palembang) – S.H.Q. officers "beating it" on receipt of an [here page of diary torn but continues]

There were pilots who showed up extraordinarily well in 21 RAAF (F) Squadron – were F/O Kininmont (6) and a Sgt. Pilot (9). I can substantiate this as we had to send 2 bomber pilots (Lancaster was one) from Taiping to ferry down to Ipoh, Central Malaya, 2 Buffaloes that had been left by 21 Squadron when they went away from Sungei Patani in Kedah, Malaya. (N.B.

Mandore (a Ganger in charge of Coolie labour) and his remarks to Linge when taxed with coolies running away from Sembawang (an Air Force Station on Singapore Island): "But, Tuan, the white man goes away in lorries, we have to walk.")

F/O White of 21 Squadron was shot down at Ipoh.

Thursday 14th January: Gunner Bareham, G.A., died at the outside hospital (dysentery).

Spent most of the day on the garden scheme, 25 officers turning out for the duty.

A great deal of satisfaction was caused by the apparent absence of results of Hardie's interview yesterday with Nagai, and the rather obstreperous attitude of the Jap guarding us. This all came to a head at a Special Mess Meeting at 1930 tonight, at which Hardie explained (reluctantly) the way in which he was tackling the job, i.e. of sending 19 out on the Work Party tomorrow, and retaining the 6 extra for camp fatigues, and seeing what happened. He said, quite rightly, that as the Japanese had the big stick at the moment, he could make it compulsory or voluntary at will, and there was nothing we could do about it. This all seemed quite a sensible way of doing things, and met with general approval. Bill Wallis, however, expressed doubt whether the matter would be pressed.

Spent the evening on note taking from "One Man Against Europe". 'drome party did not return until 1800 hrs. today, but some sick were given a lift back in the mosquito bus.

Friday 15th January: My 27th birthday! Greetings all round, and a present of 3 razor blades from Stan (Cressey)* [PL: Before the outbreak of the Far Eastern War on 8/12/41. he had been employed by the Government Printer in Hong Kong]; poured with rain all day! In celebration opened my only tin of sardines at tiffin and shared them with my room-mates, Stan Cressey, Dicky Caruth and Grey-Jones. Rain fell so heavily during the afternoon that we had to close all doors and windows for the first time since our arrival here. During morning went along to see Doc and Padre, and found them both looking fitter than for some time. Still no medical supplies or improvements in rations by the Japs; but the Messing Committee found it possible to buy 30 katies of soya beans at a cost of $3 which apparently produced the best stew they have had in Jesselton. Gave them both the gist of Hardie's interview with Japanese Camp Commandant the other day. Had our hair clipped short again, and spent remainder of my time visiting our sick men whom I found generally more cheerful than on my previous visit. Cpl. Pearson, who is in the Dysentery Ward after his relapse is looking very thin, but keeping his spirits up. Padre has started a book club on Tuesdays, which is proving popular. Spent evening with my notes in the "Mess". B.Q.M.S. Draper died today (dysentery).

Saturday 16th January: Heavy rain fell during the night and continued most of the day. Finished off my notes on Heiden's book during the morning, slept until 1630 during p.m. and attended TOC H 1630 – 1730 – only 6 present today. Humphrey Burgess gave a talk on the brick and tile industry in the Mess tonight, most of which I had heard at Malang and on the 'drome! This morning Hardie was laying down the law again on our verandah to Stan and Dicky.

Sunday 17th January: Morning dull and cloudy, in spite of which there was a bathing parade at 0830. Water cold, mainly, I suppose, on account of the almost continuous rainfall for 3 days, so only stayed in for about 20 minutes. Saw Hodkinson, my batman at Malang, who is now looking very much better – he had dysentery shortly after we arrived in Jesselton. F/Sgt. Stammers, cheery as usual, had seen a Syonon (Jap name for Singapore) Times dated Nov. 24th, '42 which contained news of Darlan's transfer to our cause, the capture of Algiers, Tunis and Benghazi (for 3rd time 1942) and the bombing of those places by the Italian and German Air Forces. There was also something about a 3rd Battle of the Solomons. Back to camp for tiffin and a sleep. Read lesson (Luke viii, v.36-end) at this evening's service, which was taken by 2nd Lt. Bell, R.A. Afterwards started my notes on "Equipment in the Far East Command". Weather cleared at 1500 hrs. for first time for 3 days, altho' this evening's moon (¾ full) still looked watery.

Monday 18th January: L.A.C. Speed, our Camp tailor since Tusik Malaja, and entertainer on the guitar, died this morning (dysentery and beri-beri of the mouth – being fed by rubber tube). Gnr. Nash also died at the Civil Hospital today (Septicaemia from skin sores caused by starvation diet). One airman, (L.A.C. Enoch Beardsley) was carried to the Civil Hospital last night, on a stretcher, with appendicitis. Today was warm and sunny, and consequently most of the Mess stocks of bedding and clothing were put out on the lines. 2/Lt. Canty gave the second of his talks on "Furnishing" at 11.15, which dealt mainly with equipping a dining-living room: he did not produce any startling information. No Work Party today, a party of ORs being employed on the garden. Dicky Caruth feeling very sorry for himself today with a dose of colic: apparently he kept Stan and Grey (Jones) awake most of last night!!

Tuesday 19th January: Nothing of interest today whatsoever. In the evening took down various A/C particulars from the "Country Life" R.A.F. book belonging to G-J. Thready brought in his album of photographs to show me tonight. Most of them are war-time snaps of home, taken during training and at O.C.T.U's etc. Notwithstanding all these reminders of home, I don't regret one minute of my time spent in the Far East: it has taught me more in 3 years than I should have learnt in 10 at home. I could well have done without this present experience, however, which palls badly, particularly at the moment!!

Wednesday 20th January: Gunner Brennan died, and was cremated this morning (dysentery). Finished my A/C notes, and began those on loading tables, supply, and A/C Bombs and Pyrotechnics. Very clear and beautiful moonlit night, with the singing cicadas and the note of the TocToc bird being very distinct. Reminded me very much of happy evenings spent at the Gap in Singapore.

Thursday 21st January: Finished off my drawings of A/C bombs in pencil colours borrowed from Young. Gunners Watson and Harvey died this morning (dysentery) – the latter was a very good man, one of the older types who possessed a very fine waxed ginger moustache(!) and was generally a very willing worker on the 'drome – too willing, I thought, and very popular with his fellow-men. The disturbing element in these deaths is that the men are not fighting back at disease as they used to, but are just throwing-in the sponge. A.C. Phillips is also on the danger list, so I hear today. About 50 men from the Camp (all with dysentery and/or beri-beri) were working on the garden today, and like yesterday, a further batch of skin disease cases went down to the sea for bathing this afternoon. This evening, at 19.30, gave the batmen a talk on the history of the Malayan Campaign, which we followed up with questions and a discussion.

Friday 22nd January: To the Camp this morning. (W/O) Whiteside showed me his letter to Hardie in which he asked for a reduction in the officers' sugar ration for the benefit of the sick. He seems very pale and worried nowadays, and small wonder! Gunner Griffiths, a young chap of 21, had just died as I arrived, and was being carried away to the mortuary. Doc and Padre were looking better and were much more cheerful then for some time. The Doc told me that his visit to Nagai is bearing fruit, 25 pints of Soya Bean milk are now supplied to the Camp daily, and 50 sacks of rice polishings have been promised. The Japanese Camp Commandant has also promised to try and substitute brown beans for cucumbers etc.

So far so good! A party of 150-200 is shortly to be moved to a spot inland in the near future. It is 1000 ft. up, and 20 miles from the railhead; this distance will have to be marched in 2 days, i.e. 10 miles a day. Nothing has been prepared at the destination, but there will be plenty of bamboo etc. with which to build huts and other accommodation. The district is in the centre of the food-growing area of Borneo, and better food is promised. The work will be the construction of an aerodrome without the assistance of native labour, and a greater measure of freedom is promised them. A job after my own heart, for which I would gladly volunteer, only Doc tells me that no officers are to be sent.

Saturday 23rd January: Doc came to the Mess this morning to see Lt. Davies's foot, and took the opportunity of informing Hardie on the results of his interview with Japanese Camp Commandant. Hardie naturally claimed credit for much of what the Doc had achieved "Doubtless the result of my many letters etc." What he did actually achieve was to ensure that the Doc saw Nagai, by requesting it in his letter re officers working. In the late afternoon, TOC H at 4.30 p.m., Threadgold gave a talk on his experiences in the R.A. before the War which was rather long-winded and slow, mainly on account of his detailing of the most ordinary of everyday events. Gunner Helliwell died today (dysentery).

Sunday 24th January: Drains this morning. No bathing parade today, although the troops did not go to the 'drome. I gather that the day is being used for a general "cleaning-up" and dhobying in No. 1 Camp. Padre visited us at 6 p.m. and conducted our first communion service in these quarters. Thready had fixed up a very attractive altar in the centre stable out of our TOC H box and a couple of sarongs: about 20 officers attended. Afterwards Padre had dinner with us for the first time and appeared to enjoy it. Owing to the late arrival of his escort he did not leave until 8.15 p.m., and would thus be late for his Camp service. Rain fell at about 5 p.m., for the first time for several days.

Monday 25th January: Spent most of day reading from a collection of the best short stories of 1935 (English and American authors) (Jonathon Cape). Some very excellent descriptive pieces with, *mirabile dictu*, quite a large, though discreet smattering of sex! Pay arrived at last this afternoon, and we were paid out at 1715 hrs. from the 16th August last! I received $101. 25; the basis for captains is $122.50 per month, $60 of which is deducted for accommodation and rations (!!), $40 is credited to our accounts in the Yokohama Special Bank at Kuching, and $22.50 is received monthly in cash. The W/Os, as they are not commissioned, are not included in the scheme: the biggest surprise was that the Padre also is not paid. At Kuching, Lt. Col. Russell has evidently classed his W/Os as 'commissioned' to the Japs, resulting in them being paid the same as 2/Lts. Our receipt for the cash, by the way, was the tip of our thumbprint. Grey-Jones, Stan Cressey, and Dicky Caruth, like many more "indigent" officers, were rather excited at the sudden acquisition of 'wealth', after so many months without. Gave my views on distribution of cash to our Mess Rep, F/O Burgess, tonight.

Tuesday 26th January: Morning produced a peculiar "false dawn" to the left of Kinabalu which was impressive though hardly beautiful. Read over one or two of the "Short Stories of 1935" during the morning, chief amongst which was "Michael's Wife" by Frank O'Connor, a tale of an Irish-American girl's first visit to her husband's parents in Southern Ireland. After tiffin, was 'collared' for a fatigue party in Jesselton, which proved to be the loading of rice at a godown on the seafront near the jetty at which we landed, and its unloading at the Jap Barracks. On our first trip we went back to Camp via the Cemetery Hill Road: there had been a funeral of 5 Gunners attended by (Capt.) George Larder and one other Army officer, and we picked them up just past the Civil Hospital. The next loads were unloaded at the Camp end by an other-ranks fatigue party, and whilst waiting for the return of the 15 cwt. van, we were allowed to wander around the harbour area. Sat awhile, watching the whitebait swimming around in shoals of millions underneath an Asiatic sea latrine and the lazy graceful dhows and catamarans moving between the islands and the shore. "Home" again for bath and dinner at 6 p.m. In the interim the Mess Committee had sat from 9.30 a.m. – 3.30 p.m., and had produced 2 schemes for the disposal of our salaries. Hardie had squashed these immediately, saying that they were against K.R's and all the other usual Hardie nonsense. He was countered by being reminded that one of the schemes was based on that approved by the G.O.C. Malaya Command at Changi and put into operation there.

Wednesday 27th January: Did the Camp drains this morning with George Larder and Ian Rolfe, and had a slight disagreement with a small Jap on saluting as we were leaving the Camp !-!?-* (Indicates a face-slapping, kick, punch or whatever!) After a very refreshing bath, a meeting of RAF officers re our salaries and the method of their allotment. Result: 13 officers in favour, Hardie, Jones and Whitworth against. Afterwards went in to Camp at 1 o'clock – rather late and without tiffin! Explained scheme to Doc and Padre who agreed with it, and wished to come in. Doc said that he would prefer all accounts to be kept by an Accountant Officer, who could supply him with cash as he needed it. Both Padre and he are to come in to our Quarters tomorrow, to discuss the scheme with Hardie. Saw W/O. Whiteside who is content to keep his 25 cts. a day, which he gets from the Japs. Mac is also agreeable to enter the scheme. A great deal of discussion amongst Officers during the afternoon.

Padre and the sick got soaked on their return from bathing parade – some of our chaps being supported back to Camp by others they looked more like wounded soldiers coming back from the front line than prisoners of a "civilised" nation.

Thursday 28 January: Today Jones appointed himself and Pethybridge (an RAF Accounting Officer) as RAF representatives on the Other Ranks Aid Fund. As he (Jones) is not a 100% contributor, there is a strong feeling that he is not eligible for the post. Decided to call a meeting of officers to elect representatives, in our room after tiffin tomorrow. Very large canteen supplies came in today, as a result of payment of our salaries, out of which we got 14 eggs, 2 papayas, 21 bananas and 5 biscuits each. Mess meeting was held at 1915 hrs to discuss various matters arising out of the establishment of the Mess Fund. Mess subscriptions fixed at $4., batmens' wages increased from $1 to $2, and Lt. Mason appointed "Nursing Orderly" after it had been decided to collect a medical chest to avoid the over-buying of medical supplies by individuals, to the detriment of the hospital in the ORs Camp. In addition to the latter I also raised the question of the overbuying of eggs by individual officers. The P.M.C. promised that the Mess Committee would look into this. Tom Elliott resigned from the Mess Secretaryship (after his bust-up with Hardie), and, after some close voting between Yates, Smith and Price, Yates was elected.

Friday 29th January: This morning a large party of officers visited the (ORs) Camp, taking with them a contribution of 100 eggs from the Mess. As I went in, stopped to have a few words with W/O Whiteside, Padre and Mac(Intosh), and was glad I did so, being considerably cheered after my conversation with them. Men also much brighter; although dysentery and skin diseases figures are about constant, beriberi cases are increasing, especially the opthalmic species. Saw A.C. Hodkinson, whose eyes were covered by dark glasses; Cpl. Tyrrell showed me the white spot in the pupil of his right eye, which is the beginning of the ulcer which eventually covers the whole eye. The cause is lack of Vitamin A which only the Japanese can remedy. On our return we found that 2/Lt. Bell (Author of Undercover University) had been diagnosed as a diptheria suspect, and that Hardie had ordered everyone to gargle 3 times a day: after each roll-call and at 1400 hrs. A meeting of RAF officers was held in our room after tiffin to elect representatives on the Other Ranks Aid Fund – Pethybridge, an Accountant Officer, and myself were duly and unanimously elected. Did my weekly dhoby in the afternoon, and as the Padre did not turn up for the TOC H meeting, slept for an hour, after which Capt. Mills and I discussed various topics ranging from post-war economics and events at Tjilatjap (Southern Javanese port), to various incidents he had experienced during the Battle of Britain. Bell was taken to the Civil Hospital, Jesselton this afternoon by lorry.

Saturday 30th January: Main events of the day were the TOC H meeting, and the weekly post-dinner talk in Mess. Threadgold continued his experiences of R.A. life in war-time England up to the time of his embarkation for the Far East.

Mills gave a most enlightening talk on English Law, or more properly, the "Laws of England", from the time of Edward the Confessor to the present day. I learnt a lot about the procedure of the Law Courts, and law etiquette, that was new to me.

After the debacle in the Far East I am afraid that officers who have been in the Far East Command won't be very popular or in demand at home. Another case of give a dog a bad name and it sticks!

Sunday 31st January: Our hopes of a bathing party were disappointed this morning. Instead, the Japanese had organised a series of basket-ball games to which 12 officers were invited (as I was on "drains" I couldn't manage it.)The Army was beaten by an Officers team, the RAF beat the Army, and Officers beat the RAF. The victors received 12 bottles of orange crush as a prize! In the absence of Bell, our weekly service was taken by Ken Hammond, with "Wag" Price leading the 'cantors'. Spent the rest of the evening in a series of RAF reminiscences with W/O's Hynes and Sanders, mainly about Seletar (RAF Station, Singapore) and its characters such as F/Lts. Bralby, O'Toole and Shrapnell-Smith – a very enjoyable evening!

Monday 1st February: Went over to No. 1 Camp this morning, and handed over the balance of the Malang Canteen A/C ($215/60) to Mac, for disposal as the airmen think fit; this was done on behalf of 'Jonah" (F/Lt. Jones); the fund was converted from Dutch guilders to Jap dollars by officers – I took $10 worth, but main amounts were taken up by Hardie, Jones and Whitworth. Told Doc, Padre and Mac that I thought that, if the airmen put all this cash into the Doc's Fund, through Imprest, we could reclaim it from the Air Ministry after the War for the benefit of the RAF Benevolent Fund. Went through the skin ward this morning and found most of the fellows pretty cheerful, although some are in a hell of a mess, with sores on the backsides and legs particularly. After tiffin we were hauled out, 28 of us, to move 270 lOOK sacks of rice which had been brought in by a Jap coastal steamer the day before. They had been dumped by the side of the railroad and had to be moved 30 yds. to some stores behind the NCO's new quarters. Jonah, Ken Whitworth, Young and myself got cracking with a wooden sack carrier. The heaviest work we have been asked to do so far! I think the airmen – they were all RAF – were rather grateful for our help, as they stopped carrying 1 sack per man, and emulated us at 4 men per sack! The rice they sent in to Camp was of particularly bad quality, and certain sacks had actually begun to ferment. The Doc and Whiteside went to see Nagai immediately about it, as the latter had promised only the best quality native rice for the men. We did not, of course, get the result this afternoon. We finished at about 1600 hrs, when a slight drizzle began; shower, dinner and coffee and did I feel good! I could do with more of this work. RSM Jacobi and 2/Lt. Bagnall took a board from our front verandah this evening and managed to collect from the inside wood quite a number of bees eggs and honey; Baggy is starting off his new, patent, glass-fronted hive!! A chat with Grey-Jones about his college days at Cambridge post the last War (like Hardie he was a RAF/RFC pilot in WW.I.), the removal of Jesus College souvenir gun by Cains etc., – and so to bed, very pleasantly tired.

Tuesday 2nd February: A thoroughly lazy day which I spent finishing off "Short Stories of 1935", which were good descriptively, thought-provoking as far as characterisation is concerned, but they fell far short of my ideal short story which would have an ending more satisfactory to the reader. Borrowed a spy thriller from Whitworth – "Stealthy Terror" by John Ferguson, on which I spent most of afternoon and evening. It is easy reading, and deals with a 1914 "Invasion Plan".

Wednesday 3rd February: Most of morning spent on 'fly-swatting' fatigue outside the cookhouse, a duty which has now been made a daily routine for all officers. It seems that the flies are being kept in check by this method. Slept very soundly during the afternoon, and started "China Struggles for Unity" for 2nd time. Today we all began to take the "muscle and bodybuilding" pills which the Japs have asked us to take after each meal (3 per day). They have a taste suspiciously like carbolic soap! Perhaps they are meant to disinfect our stomachs in some way? Cpl. Bond (RAF) was cremated today (dysentery) – he was 37.

Thursday 4th February: Did wood-chopping fatigue this morning, with Vernon Smith, who did most of the chopping! Thereafter to Mess to do a spot of work on China, using "China Struggles for Unity" as a guide, but seeing my map, a crowd collected and the inevitable discussion began. Dicky Caruth laid down the law by saying that the only possible basis of future peace in the Far East was a pact between the U.S., Japan and ourselves, but then, he always does ignore facts! Dai Davies, George Larder and Eric Foulkes also joined in, and the conversation switched to A/C Davies' brother was in the R.N.R. at home, and was with the "Cossack" when she took the "Altmark". He was also in another destroyer in the attack on Narvik (Norway), when they dropped a battalion of South Wales Borderers, who were to attack up a slight slope. 500 Jerries appeared over the crest of the hill, and the SWB's, led by their Colonel, were mowed down in dozens. They (the survivors) were returned to England. After this episode, the destroyer turned its multiple pompoms on the Jerries, and cleaned up all but 1O of them. The French Foreign Legion were put in the firing line, and marched into Narvik the next day. In the evening was again drawn into an argument on the campaign in France and Flanders 1940, and on Dunkirk. Bill Wallis maintained that Dunkirk was a blessing in disguise as, if the fighting had continued, our reserves of A/C, arms and personnel would have been thrown into a fight we could not then hope to win, with the result that when the German air offensive came on Britain, we should had had no fighter force to beat them off. This sounds very plausible, but as George Larder remarked, were the fighting tools there to fight with? Tonight had my first cup of cocoa for 2 months!.

Friday 5th February: Finished off, for 2nd time, "China Struggles for Unity".

Hardie today put the Camp out of bounds for officers on account of Bell's diptheria – this is going to make it rather awkward for me to see the men, Doc and Padre, as apparently personal permission has now to be obtained from H. before we can go into Camp. Very beautiful rainbow and sunset this evening – when NCOs moved into their new quarters facing the road. Big noise arrived today by air. (We speculated it was the Borneo C. in C. Had it been Suga we should have been so informed.)

Saturday 6 February: Gunner Cousins died today (dysentery). A thorough spring cleaning of our room this morning by Jock, our batman, which certainly improved things. At 11.30 our second beginners class lecture (not stated on what!) and at 4.30 p.m. TOC H. when RSM Jacobi gave us a talk on "Highbury", the Arsenal Football Club ground. A four-course dinner tonight, one of Foley's masterpieces, consisting of a shrimp hors d'oeuvres, soup, beef rice and yams, and 2 small coconut cakes. Chopping gave the talk tonight on "Life as a Magistrates Clerk" which was very rambling and not very interesting.

Sunday 7 February: Morning started by "Sexy", a young Jap guard, cracking the convict latrine coolie over the head and back with the butt end of his rifle, because he did not bow low enough. The native warder gave the Jap a look that should have killed, and a significant look at us! The evening service tonight was taken by 'Wag' Price, the lesson being read by Pethybridge. Slight dose of squitters today.

Monday 8 February: Spent most of morning note-taking on the IWG Part 2, mainly dealing with National Debt Redemption Levies and "How the (last) War was paid for". In the evening started A.P. Herbert "Uncommon Law", a series of imaginary cases taken before the C. of A., Assizes, etc., but I found I was not really in the mood to appreciate them fully. Orderly Officer today.

Tuesday 9 February: More I.W.G. note-taking in the morning, sleep in afternoon and diary at night!! Young was called to Jap H.Q. this morning, and closely questioned about the right procedure to be adopted at funerals, which would henceforth be conducted in batches of two or three! He was also notified of some Jap celebrations to take place on the 11th, which we were ordered to attend. Included in it would be a 'prize-giving' to young Jap soldiers and also to POW – best Camp Master, best workers on 'drome, best Medical Orderlies etc. – we are expected to clap the recipients! All most distasteful, and about which I had quite an argument with 'Wag' Price, who always emphasises Jap courtesy etc. etc. !

Cressey has been ill for a couple of days, and has been rather irritable, so we have left him alone in his little corner.

Wednesday 10 February: The practice of buying eggs from the latrine cleaning convicts is growing, and will, if detected, inevitably result in the stoppage of privileges, and possibly of purchases, if my knowledge of Japanese tactics provide any guide. Again, the action of the selfish and thoughtless few.

Had a very amusing yarn with Jackson about common experiences with NORGROUP during the campaign, including F/Lt. Loftus Paton, the Intelligence Officer (afterwards at Tengah RAF Station on Singapore Island) who had a F.M.S. Volunteer shot as a spy (on the authority of General Sir Lewis Heath, Commander of 3rd Indian Division and one of the few outstanding leaders of the campaign) for searching his papers. Also P/O. Dick at Port Swettenham.

Young collected 7 clouts on the jaw from the Jap guards for being offhand when notified of a change in tomorrow's parade times.

Thursday 11 February: Reveille 0630, Roll-call and breakfast 0700, Stand-by 0730, move-off 0815. Paraded in front of a stage erected in one corner of the basket-ball pitch, decorated with palm-fronds and a large Jap flag in the centre. The men were drawn up behind, and in front of the whole parade the detachment of Jap "Boy Scouts". The Japanese Camp Commandant came out, the usual commands were given and a certain amount of mumbo-jumbo, and the Jap National Anthem was sung by the Japs. We were then, under Hardies' "inspiring" lead, ordered, with the Japs, to bow to their National flag which I did with a feeling of impotent rage and silent imprecations. After the "Boy Scouts" (Jap guards) had been given badges of rank by Nagai, prizes were given to our men for 'best work on 'drome etc.', a sight which also revolted me.

The prizes were cartons of Javanese (B.A.T.) cigarettes. The basketball game which followed was won by the men 5-4 against the officers. Again more prizes. The men then put on quite a good variety show, with a certain amount of community singing (not very good); after a series of boxing contests (3x2 or 12 minute rounds), the proceedings closed with a group photo of officers and a certain number of ORs! Saw Padre, Doc and F/Sgt. Bowden – the latter told me that the "Up Country" party might mature towards the 14th or 15th, but others said that the No. 2 Jap had vetoed it, after a visit, on account of the malaria. The star-turn of the morning was, of course, the speech by the Japanese Camp Commandant! Spent the afternoon "head down". Note-taking I.W.G. at night.

Friday 12 February: Gunners Butterfield and Bentley and A.C.J.B. Booth died today (dysentery). Spent most of morning, after digging drains, in playing my first games of chess with W/O. Bessant. Afternoon ditto. Stan Cressey and I again discussed the war situation and a possible major offensive on the Continent this year, dealing mainly with morale. He made the very important point that in the training of a first class fighting force, hate must play an important part. We agreed that, from our own knowledge of the equipment the troops in Malaya had, and from what we heard subsequently from people who had come direct from U.K., that the first few weeks of any continental invasion would be very worrying from our point of view. I have come to the conclusion that, for the aims I have in mind personally, a hard and uncompromising mode of life will be essential, with the pleasures and distractions inseparable from the average man's life put resolutely aside. Everything in the nature of the personal must be sacrificed to the attainment of the aims. As this has crystallized, must think out possible ways of putting it into effect *Deus Vult*!! (God Wills It)

Warrant Officer John William Bessant. 355412. R.A.F. Died Sandakan 4 April 1945. Age 45. Liverpool, U.K.   *Pic: John Bessant.*

Saturday 13 February: TOC H at 4.30 p.m. – rather uninteresting this week, with Thready reading from the Book. In the evening, in place of the usual talk, we held a general knowledge and spelling bee. I was Captain of the RAF team, which included Jacko, Burgess, Pethybridge and "Wag" Price. Army team – Yates (Captain), Bazell, Rolfe, Wallis and Chopping. We won the Spelling Bee, but fell down on general knowledge; net result being a win for the Army 29-24. One of the best 'turns' was the drawing competition which followed the lines of the one held at Christmas. Bickerton, Johnstone and RSM Jacobi wound up the evening with a very amusing sketch, answering 'letters' from Dicky Caruth, Brown, Elliott and Capt. Mills!

Gunner Eastwood died at the outside hospital this evening (dysentery).

Sunday 14 February: I. /Bdr. Wood died in camp today (dysentery). Grey-Jones attended the cremation. Other ranks worked today. Did a spot of work moving Jap rations (salted!) 1/2 hours work this afternoon for which we received one cake of Java soap each! Chess-League arranged self, being a beginner, in the 3rd Division as "Sunderland". Service tonight, taken by Hammond, 2/Lt. Nicholas removed to hospital again tonight, with fever and squitters, after about 4 days with us. Mac hopes to return when his feet heal up.

Monday 15 February: 1st Anniversary of the fall of Singapore. What memories it conjures up! After the morning fatigues spent ½ hour doing notes, and then, at 11 a.m., we attended the funeral service for the 4 Gunners and 1 Aircraftman; this time held on the basketball pitch instead of in the Camp. Some duff (rumours) came in at tiffin time – oh for 1944* Still no canteen supplies – we wonder why? Very cool throughout the day with rain at night. (*Such rumours were sometimes brought into our quarters by a young Chinese bringing occasional canteen supplies. He spoke good English, and after a time put out 'feelers' about anyone wanting to escape, offering to lead them! But after the Malang executions, and the knowledge that the Japs offered large rewards to anyone turning-in escapees, there were no takers!)

Tuesday 16 February: A new batch of "Japan Times Advertisers" Oct. 30th, Nov. 30th and 'Japan Times Weekly' ending Dec. 3rd, '42, arrived today, with the news of 3rd Battle of the Solomons and the Battle of the South Pacific, also of British and U.S. landings in Algeria and Tunisia. The Russians appear to be holding the Jerries on all fronts.

Wednesday 17 February: Spent most of day reading the Jap papers. Got some quite useful 'lines' from them. From pictures of 'dromes they have established in New Britain and New Ireland, they seem to have the right idea on how to get a patch of virgin jungle shaped into a 'drome by 24 hours forced labour etc. Canteen purchases arrived today – no peanuts or cocoa-abis !!

Thursday 18 February: Drains this morning. 10 Officers went to Jesselton to collect some cooking oil; and R.C. priest apparently got into some trouble with the Japs for looking at them, or something like it! (a local civilian). Chess today with Stan Cressey. Thoughts very occupied with 'wild-cat' perambulations!!

Friday 19 February: Working party of 400 this morning. Went into Camp this a.m. and found Doc and Padre very much more cheerful about the health of the Camp, although the supply of beans has now run out. They attribute this to the extra food bought with the officers contributions. A bathing party of 20 officers went down to the beach with the skin cases from No. 1 Camp, at 1400 hrs. A perfect day, cloudless sky, warm sea, 1/2 hours bathe and 2 hours sunbathing and talking to the men, some of whom seem to be benefiting from the sea bathing. Had chat with airman who got 1 letter and a postcard from home the other day; his letter was numbered 130 by his wife and was addressed to his last known address at Kluang. After collecting some wood from the patch from which they are clearing firs from the beach, we marched off at 1730 hrs. and arrived back at 1830. The pleasantest afternoon I have spent for many a long day! F/Lt. Blackledge (MO) closed down hospital today.

Saturday 20 February: Another bathing party this afternoon. The usual Saturday evening entertainment took the form of an "In (Jesselton) Town Tonight". The first introduction was W/O Bessant by Capt. Wallis. Old Bessant gave his experiences as a POW in Germany from May-November 1918. He was captured near Arras whilst a L/Cpl. in the East Yorks Regt., and taken to a camp whose prisoners worked in salt mines. Apparently treatment was bad, and likewise the food. They escaped on Nov. 12th 1918, not knowing that the Armistice had been signed! A "Puzzle Corner" by Capt. Paterson followed, and the entertainment ended with "Do You Know?" by Professor Jackstein (RSM Jacobi). An early 'Lights Out' at 10.30 p.m. for those going on the route march tomorrow.

Sunday 21st February: The "March of Joy" (so named by the Japs) route march to Lekas Beach, 5 miles distant, began at 0800, and returned at 1300. It took 2 hours each way, and went via the Civil Hospital, where our patients and the doctors wives waved to them. The beach was disappointing, with the shallow water extending some miles out. I did not go, as my sunburnt feet were somewhat swollen! In the evening, I conducted the evening service at 7.30 p.m. 'Pat' reading the lesson.

Monday 22nd February: Sgt. Potter, R.A. died today (dysentery). A spot of bother at tiffin time over a 'black market' in bananas and eggs which was suddenly opened by a Malay woman and small boy by our back fence, under the aegis of a Jap guard. Hardie made another emotional speech, threatening dire penalties for this 'open disobedience of orders' by a small selfish minority (incidentally it was a large majority who bought from it!) etc. etc. Jacko thought it was 'sour grapes' as H. hadn't got any! I was much amused as the PMC had participated, Hardie, as usual, did not know the facts. This afternoon finished "Doomsday" by Warwick Deeping, a sombre tale of grey post-war disillusionment and emotional struggles. As a result of the tiffin-time outburst, Ken Whitworth has started a SHITZ Club for all bounders, cads and rotters and the S.S.M. (small selfish minority). Rumours today of a move to Changi and the repatriation of some "other ranks" on an exchange basis. We have heard these stories before! Weather miserable, wet and damp today, with very low cloud. The North Borneo No. 1 Jap arrived today by air.

Tuesday 23rd February: Another 'gem' from Jones; "The C.O.(H) passed unfavourable comment on the fact that you continued to eat food whilst he was making his speech yesterday." Comment was completely superfluous!

Wednesday 24th February: A very restless day – feeling very irritable and moody. Eventually got down to the first chapter of Keith Horsfield's? "The Real Cost of the War", dealing with the war as it effects the consumer. As far as I can see it is going to deal mainly with the National Income and National Output, as effected by wartime economic changes.

Thursday 25th February: A fatigue party was called for today by the Japs, to construct a pathway round the perimeter of the Camp, presumably so that the Guard can walk round it. From 10.00 – 12.00 and 1500-1700. Umanada told Linge that in 3 months India and Australia would be in the possession of Japan. Another guard is supposed to have told 'someone' that the war will be over in 9 months time when Japan will have Australia! We should all very much like some genuine news about Russia/ Burma, and the Solomons!

Friday 26th February: Finished off Price's copy of A.P. Herbert's "Common Law", which I found both entertaining and instructive. Some of his situations, although framed in a very light-veined manner, are, nevertheless, ones that can, and have, arisen in everyday life. His chapter on the Divorce Laws was particularly scathing. In the afternoon, the fatigue party duty was to cut down 5 trees from the hillside estate of some Englishman, which overlooks the 'drome and the sea. Whilst we were in the elevated grandstand, a Douglas came in and, after a number of circuits, landed. We carried, rolled, and kicked these logs along the railway line, having been caught in a rain storm (during which we sheltered under a bungalow and ate coconuts), arriving at the Mess about 6 p.m. I was unfortunate in having Tom Hobbs as my carrying partner – he wasn't feeling very strong! During a rest, 7 of us went along to the 'drome, where I had a chat to Shaw and one or two of our men.

Saturday 27 February: No fatigues today. Very sultry until about 5 p.m. when it started to rain. Japs altered the time of roll call to 8 p.m. and lights out to 9 p.m. Hardie has written a letter of protest to the Japanese Camp Commandant. At today's meeting of TOC H "Wag" Price gave a talk on his experiences as an observer in the R.N.A.S. during the last war. He was trained on a kite balloon, and saw overseas service at Dunkerque, St. Pol and Bergues(?)

Sunday 28th February: Padre arrived this morning and conducted a combined service and communion, and afterwards stayed to tiffin. He brought us some of the Camp news; both Docs (Daniels and Blackledge) are O.K.A.C. Fox and 1 Gunner are seriously ill with dysentery; all patients in the outside (Civil) Hospital are getting on well, including Bell, Cpl. Jefferson and F/Sgt. Stammers. Nicholas is now off the D.I. list, but the Doc thinks he will be a chronic dysentery case most of his life.

Monday 1st March: Nothing doing in a.m., but fatigue party of 15 at 14.30. We took a small hand-cart to the beach, filled it with sand – 10 minutes – 1 hours bathe, and back to ORs camp where it was needed for "fire precautions". Met several airmen down on the beach who seem very cheerful. Some of them are learning the geography of these parts P.I. (Philippine Islands), Celebes, New Guinea, Ambon etc. I think it is a good thing that they should take an intelligent interest in their surroundings.

Tuesday 2nd March: Game of chess with W/O Bessant this morning, and was beaten by a narrow margin. As 30 were required for fatigues in the afternoon, was roped in, and spent the time until 1730 weeding in the Jap barracks area. How are the mighty fallen! Patience, my friend, patience! Mills approached me this morning and informed me of Hardie's action in sending round money to RAF 'needy' personnel. He had remonstrated with Hardie about the inequality of it, and reminded him of his responsibility as O.C. of both Army and Air Force. His reply was "It has nothing whatever to do with you, and I certainly have no intention of assisting the Army." Mills naturally felt rather strongly about this, as the Army are producing the bulk of the hospital contributions, and would have been quite justified in cutting off the R.A.F. from benefiting from their funds. Instead, he has written a letter to the Doc suggesting (1) that the RAF men who receive Hardie's money be approached, informed of the position, and a suggestion made to them that they share with the Army (I'm not very sanguine about this) and (2) that he allocates an equivalent amount of money from their funds to an equal number of Army 'needy'. To increase our RAF contributions to $35 per month, and to show our appreciation of the Army contributions to our men, I proposed to the RAF that we decreased our monthly salary to $9 a month each. This met with general approval, although Johnstone and Linge thought that the RAF men should be shown on which side their bread was buttered! Jones was a listener as I expounded my views on the irresponsibility of Hardie as a C.O. I have no doubt that he was a faithful reporter!

Interesting chat with (W/O) Hynes about various service reminiscences he tells me that almost all 242 Squadron with the exception of the C.O. and 5 pilots were taken prisoner in Java.

Wednesday 3rd March: Another morning off, during which I again played a couple of chess games with W/O Bessant. Mills told me that he had had another up and downer with Hardie, who told him (1) that he was causing disaffection among the officers and (2) that he had 'misunderstood' his statement of yesterday, and that he would now ask the Padre to send in a list of needy cases, Army and RAF, and he would send in cash to them. A climb down my talk of last night seems to have borne fruit!! Fatigue party putting up barbed wire in front of our favourite latrine, in the afternoon!

Thursday 4th March: Managed another 'swimming' fatigue this afternoon, and found the sea quite warm, with few jelly-fish about. Had a chat with F/Lt. Blackledge for first time in about four months. Found him quite cheerful and well except for usual spots! Managed to get some coconuts on way back. Officers cleaned out No. 1 Camp Urine Drain this afternoon (including Jones) but no protest made.

Friday 5th March: *Mirabile dictu*, a whole day off today, during which I started Warwick Deepings "Ropers Row", a tale of a lame medical student's struggle, against poverty, ignorance, prejudice and snobbery. His characterization of Chris Hazzard, and his mother Mary, are very fine, whilst he pokes not so gentle sarcasm at the sow-like Mrs. Prosser's of the world – prolific, gossiping and jealous.

Saturday 6th March: Drain fatigues today outside No. 1 Camp very easy work, most distasteful part of it being the smell! A very fine dinner was put on tonight, followed by our usual Saturday night "In Town Tonight". Cpl. Foley and Bdr. Bayer gave us their experiences as hotel and restaurant chef and waiter respectively. Some of their reminiscences, being highly coloured and amusing. Impersonations of film stars and brother officers also proved popular.

Sunday 7th March: No fatigues today – camp working party did not go out. Inspection by Jap NCO of our quarters at 5 p.m. today, in preparation for the visit of some "No. 1" on the 9th. Hardie, the petulant schoolboy as always, said that ours was the only room commented on – mentioned mugs and fruit, and otherwise, he said that this was the cleanest camp he had been into. Hardie was as pleased with this 'tribute' from a Jap NCO as though he had received a mention in despatches! Did not feel in the mood to attend evening service tonight.

Monday 8th March: We have now one year behind us as POWs. One year of disappointments, observation of my fellow men such as I have been unable to do for years, a year of reflection and general mental stocktaking. The experience has greatly widened my knowledge of human nature in its reactions to various situations, mainly adverse! I feel, however, that we have all had enough of this experience!!

Tuesday 9th March: A day of "excitement and bustle" as Stanley Holloway (Yorkshire comedian pre-WW.II) would have put it. Reveille and Roll-call at 0630, breakfast 0700, and parade to Jap Guard Room at 0800, where we were drawn up for the arrival of Major Suga, the No. 1 of POW Camps in Borneo. At 0830 we were again paraded, together with the senior NCOs and other ranks on the basketball pitch. Here Major Suga made one of his usual speeches in which he reiterated the same points – that he would try to get us food and clothes, notwithstanding the fact that these were difficult to get. He urged the growing of our own vegetables and fruit, and the keeping of pigs! In spite of the fact that Great Britain and the U.S.A. had ill-treated Japanese internees, he would allow no thoughts of revenge to affect his treatment of us – afterwards he inspected our quarters, and the men were sent to the aerodrome at 1000 hrs. At about 11.30 a Jap General and his staff inspected us – he was very small, but very dignified, as are most of their higher ranks, and is presumed to be the No. 1 in Borneo. He was accompanied by an Army press photographer who took 3 snaps. And that was all for the day! Apparently their Boy Scouts (troops) got a ration of brandy (probably sake or samsu) and ice-cream!

Wednesday 10th March: Finished "The White Cockatoo" – a Penguin thriller by an American author, W.G. Eberhart; the plot of which is laid in A —, which betrays itself as Avignon (France), of which I have a brief, but happy, pre-war memory. A hair cut today by our amateur barber, 'Dean' Linge, (a 'take-off' from Dean Inge, pre-war St. Paul's Cathedral, London) who does remarkably well.

Thursday 11th March: No purchases. No fatigues. Started "The Real Cost of the War" by Keith Horsfield, for 3rd time.

Friday 12th March: No fatigues. Jap General and staff left today in rail cars. Gunner Hitchings was cremated this morning, having died of dysentery and vitaminosis – this making the 38th death since our arrival in Jesselton about 4 months ago. Defeated Rollinson at chess this morning, my first victory, although not a particularly creditable one, as we both played badly. This afternoon, got down to Horsfield's analysis of the National Output – in its essential convertible and inconvertible aspects.

Saturday 13th March: Orderly Officer today w.e.f. 7.30 p.m. Our usual Saturday night concert was held at 8 p.m. Ken Whitworth was 'interviewed' by Bill Wallis, and gave us some quite interesting details of newspaper production. A quizz between the under and over 30's. followed, and finally a charade by Room 6.

Sunday 14th March: Usual Sunday service at 1930 hrs., taken by Ken Hammond, with an attendance of 20.

Monday 15th March: A rice carrying fatigue for 1 hour this morning, for which we received an extra cake of soap – very acceptable. In the afternoon, a wood-chopping fatigue on the hill overlooking the 'drome. Cutting 4' posts for the cemetery which we are apparently going to construct for our casualties. We also managed to buy some eggs and bananas individually, and also 100 ducks eggs for the Mess – only to find on our return that the purchases had arrived! A large dinner tonight which, after this afternoon's bananas, left one feeling very full – a strange feeling! LAC Robertson and a Gunner died today – the first from septic sores and the latter from beri-beri, making a total of 40 deaths in all.

Tuesday 16th March: Wood-chopping fatigue this afternoon. Very pleasantly overcast, and the "fritter" woman in attendance. The Padre visited us in the morning to discuss plans for the formal cemetery which we are to construct on

Sunday. Both he and Doc Blackledge are suffering from septic sores.

Wednesday 17th March: Played chess with Elliott this morning and beat him. Spent rest of the morning studying the Atlas and reading some of the articles in the Japan Times. I found further confirmation of the Jap policy of deliberately weakening the morale and unity of British OR PWs by creating bad feeling between the latter and their officers. Wood-cutting fatigue after tiffin – when we reached the drome, found that the three twins (2-engined 'planes) had gone, but one ? 'plane arrived just before our departure.

Cpl. D.V. Elliott. 574596. R.A.F. Died 17 March 1945. Age 23. Beccles, Suffolk
Pic: Christopher Elliott

Thursday 18th March: Beat Elliott again in our last game of chess, making the 1st complete series of three I have won. Padre called for Les Coleman this morning, prior to viewing the cemetery for layout plans. Burgess and Mason brought back news that Nagai intended to move the S.Q. to our present quarters, we were to move to the Sgts. Qtrs., and the NCOs back to the main Camp. Burgess heard that this had been suggested to the Japanese Camp Commandant by Doc Daniels and the Padre! Our quarters would certainly make a very fine hospital. Nagai, it appears, told Hardie about it yesterday, saying he was thinking it over. A short fatigue in the afternoon, carrying fuel wood to the cremation pyre for LAC Morgan, who died today. Almost everybody, I'm glad to say, takes a reasonable view to the projected move. Total deaths to date 41.

Friday 19 March: A fatigue into Jesselton this morning with two 40-gallon drums of gasoline. The town looks very 'dead', with all the shops practically empty of goods; got back at 1 p.m. Incidentally, noticed a large photo of the King and Queen in an upstairs room of a Chinese shop. The Nip War map also needs a spot of revision in respect of the Solomons and New Guinea. No fatigues in the afternoon.

Saturday 20 March: No fatigue today. In place of "In Town Tonight" (a pre-war radio show), Les Coleman gave a talk on his experiences as an anti-aircraft

(LAA) Gunner with the B.E.F. in France. Very little seems to have been done with the months from September 1939 to May 1940, except for perfunctory training, and a number of pleasure jaunts to WW. I battlefields. His impressions of the actual fighting were of continual retreat, never knowing the why and wherefore of what they were doing and where they were going. His description of Dunkirk was a vivid one – their Colonel, Greville-Smith, a regular, getting the D.S.O.

Sunday 21 March: Reveille at 0630 hrs., breakfast at 0700, march off at 0800, arriving at the Christian Cemetery about 0900, with 300 other ranks. Going past the English Doctors' Quarters, we gave the Docs and their wives "There'll always be an England", at which they waved enthusiastically.

On arrival at the Cemetery the officers were told to clear the raised bit of ground on which the Cross is to be placed, on a plinth. Lt. Nagai, the Camp Commandant, took off his shirt and gave us a hand with the chunkeling (spading), which we thought was a good effort, and which provoked Hardie to a half-hearted attempt at work.

Tiffin was sent up from the Camp and we had it on the side of the shady road above the Camp. The Japs provided pomelos, papayas, wax fruit, guavas and coconuts, which were enjoyed by everybody. The whole job, raised gravel paths, cross plinth, two strand fence, and reinterment of caskets, was finished by 4 p.m., the coffins being left where they were. During the day had chats with most of the Senior NCOs and quite a number of airmen from my old Singapore unit, including Curtis, Maitland, Patchesa and others. We marched back about 4 p.m., gave the Britishers at the Hospital the "Roemah Sakit", "Smile, Boys, Smile", and arrived at Camp about 5 p.m., after an enjoyable day. In the evening, managed to get an anthology from Bill Wallis, "Multum in Parvo", containing some of my favourites. Hardie again put his foot in it by telling the Padre he could not join us for a meal as it would "throw our numbers out"! Our usual service at night with the choir excelling in their Nunc Dimittis, but things went sadly wrong with the works in the last hymn!!

Monday 22nd March: Today, there were 2 fatigue parties – one of 5 officers to Jesselton in the morning, and one of 8 officers wood-chopping in the afternoon. Out of the latter an incident arose! F/Lt. Jones complained to Hardie that Bickerton, being a junior Captain to him, had taken charge of the party of 8, i.e. he had marched it off! Hardie, through Mills, explained to Bickerton that the seniority in this Camp was (1) himself (2) Jones and (3) Mills. Bickerton came to me to enquire about Jones's seniority, on which I could not help him. He was very annoyed with both Jones for childishness, and Hardie for his officiousness. He said that when he returned to the U.K., he was going to see that Hardie was reported on through Sir Robert Fanshawe(?), his uncle, who was at the War Office.

Tuesday 23rd March: An exceptionally 'heavy' sort of day, similar to the ones which in Singapore always indicated thunder and rain. No fatigues. Stan Cressey's 46th birthday – gave him ¼ of a ripe pomelo – the only thing in the gift line available!

Wednesday 24th March: Went to see the Doc and Padre this morning. Found an overdose of flies in the Camp. Beri-beri and skin diseases are on the increase, mainly, the Doc thinks, on account of the 250 sacks of bad rice (much of which was fermented) which they have had for the last month or so, and which are now nearing the end. Blackledge is sceptical as to the practicability of using our (officers) quarters as S.S.Q., as they have 250 patients and 50 staff to get in, and very few cooking utensils! Saw W/0 Whiteside and F/Sgt. Warner, both of whom seemed pretty cheerful. F/Sgt. Merchant was also his usual cheery self. Most of the billets have now had the wooden sleeping boards removed, which has got rid of the bugs, but I noticed there were dozens of flies on each man's blanket. LAC Fox and Gunner Henderson died yesterday (dysentery) – the former after a brave fight lasting about 6 weeks. Started Samuel Butler's saga of country vicarage life in the 19th Century – "The Way of All Flesh". The long threatened rain arrived today and cooled things off very effectively.

Thursday 25th March: Moved some planks this morning from No. 1 Camp to our own for the construction of a floor in the stables for proposed new S.S.Q. Rumour that our new abode is to be in quarters previously occupied by Jap regular soldiers. Paterson and I had an interesting chat today over the news contained in the "Japan Times" papers; a talk continued later in the day with Bill Wallis. Most of day with "The Way of All Flesh". a talk with Larder, Bird and Thready on regimental histories and marches proved quite informative.

Friday 26th March: Funeral of 5 today at 10 a.m. Cogitated some time today on the cost of a 2 or 3 year course in Economics at the London School of Economics – London University, on the basis of figures which Dai Davies, who took an Arts Degree at King's College (Ldn. U.), gave me I reckon I could do it comfortably on 175 pounds per annum – fees, digs, clothes, and a little pocket money for extras. If things have gone financially as I hope, I should be able to manage this with about 200 pounds to spare. This is, of course, dependent on a number of contingencies about which it is impossible to speculate not least amongst them is safely getting out of this mess!

Saturday 27th March: "Tinker" Bell returned to the fold today from the Civil Hospital, looking not much worse for his diptheria experience. Cressey remarked that his appetite has not been affected – the Jesselton Cat Club!! The "In Town Tonight" consisted of an Inspector Hornblower murder case, with excellent sound effects, and a Puzzle Corner conducted by P/O Pethybridge, W/O Sanders and myself representing the RAF and Dicky Bird and Lt. Nicholas the Army. We won 35-32½, after giving as our 'tableaux' the Death of Nelson, Hardy (no relation to Ted Hardie!) saying: "You can kiss my arse, I'm next on the list for Admiral", and Mark Anthony's speech: "Thank God the old b…'s dead, he's left me a million!"

Sunday 28 March: Padre came over this morning at 11 a.m. and took a short service and communion. Most of the men are spending their day off cleaning up the Camp, whilst quite a number of them are working on new decorations for the Church. This morning the bluebottles started to swarm from our borehole latrines, so an intensive smoke drive was made against them. Again very sweaty during the afternoon. Usual service tonight taken by Bick(erton). Sent Matthews and Cpl. Harrison $1 each today via the Padre and Doc.

Monday 29th March: Gunner Blackburn died today (dysentery). Finished "Those were the Days", a collection of articles written for "Punch" by A.A. Milne some 20-30 years ago. Old Rollinson in a very pessimistic mood today – thinks it will be 2 years before our release and by then Singapore will have lost its entrepot trade. He is inclined to gloom!

Tuesday 30th March: A rumour that in a few days time we are all to move to Sandakan. The sick have already been examined to see whether they are fit enough to march. Met Jimmy Mills in the chess league and was beaten 4-2. Mills was at Rossall, but as he was in the 2nd XV, did not get up to Durham. [Rossall and Durham are 2 Northern English Schools, rivals for many years on the rugby field. I was at Durham School. PL.]

Wednesday 31st March: Five of us – Grey-Jones, Johnnie (Charles Johnstone), Threadgold, Yates and myself – went into Jesselton with the hand-cart loaded with 70 rice sacks, 1 44-gallon empty petrol drum and 5 5-gallon petrol tins! We dumped these at the docks, where there were a couple of junks anchored. Back in town, we collected our canteen purchases and were given coffee (with sugar!) and cakes by the Chinese shopkeeper. Returned to Camp feeling very fit and pleased with our cup of coffee! One Eurasian woman also gave us iced water and boiled peanuts whilst we were en-route to Jesselton.

Thursday 1st April: A quiet day waiting for news of our impending move. This came about 6 p.m., we were to be ready to move as from midday tomorrow. Started to pack at once. We also had an additional supper after roll call, to use up our remaining eggs and canteen supplies.

Friday 2nd April: Finished packing by 1100 and stood by. F/Sgt. Merchant came around to collect our gift of yams for the Camp, and gave out the 'gen' (RAF slang = news). A ship is in the harbour with 600 POWs from Java, who came via Changi. The sick were to go on (board) at 12, men in the afternoon, and officers and NCOs to move into No. 1 Camp for 1 night. None of this came off!! Spent p.m. reading Sinclair Lewis' "Mantrap" and chatting to Pethy on post-war prospects. He is 34, an A.C.A., and no job to go back to, with a taste to remain in the R.A.F. or come East on some post-war Settlement Commission. A concert this evening Don Yates on "Patents" – he is a technical assistant to a firm of patent agents: – followed by Puzzle Corner – run by Bazell and Yates. Examinees – Davies, Pethy, Rolfe and RSM Jacobi – good impersonations Bell and his "Bruce" scared a Nip guard! A coterie gathered in the Mess afterwards telling smutty stories over tea! One would think from such hilarity that our release was imminent! Still, variety is the spice of this sort of life too, I think.

Saturday 3rd April: Still awaiting the long-anticipated move; most people spending the day sitting on their kits. At 5 p.m. the NCOs and ORs in the hut opposite the Jap Guard Room were whisked away – presumably to a ship. Speculation rife. Were we going to another place, Singapore, for example?

Sunday 4th April: Party of NCOs etc. returned from the ship this morning. She is a small coastal vessel (British built) of about 500 tons but, as her diesel engines had broken down, they had been sent back. To my mind there is no doubt that we are going to the place stated, i.e. Sandakan. Our last evening service in Jesselton was held tonight, conducted by Ken Hammond. Visited Camp in the morning and saw Docs Daniels and Blackledge and the Padre. Doc Daniels (Capt. RAMC) was very amused at Jonah's pedantically-expressed thanks to him for what he had done for the R.A.F.

Monday 5th April: At last, we were told this afternoon that we should be moving at 3 p.m. tomorrow, with 147 NCOs and ORs. We now know where we stand!

Tuesday 6th April: Packed up early in the morning and afterwards stood by. Bath immediately after tiffin, and moved off from Quarters at 3.30 p.m. When we arrived at No. 1 Camp we found that some men had been brought from the 'drome, and that the party now totalled 200 all ranks. Soon after 5 p.m., we began our march to the docks, which proved to be fairly cool as the sky was overcast. Two small coastal vessels were lying alongside (ex-Straits Steamship Co.) and we embarked on the 2nd and larger one, the men being on the 1st, which towed ours. A beautiful sunset was our send-off from Jesselton – the Camp Commandant also saw us off. We passed several attractive-looking islands as the sun went down – small hillocks, native huts of attap, and stretches of golden sand. Spent the night in the rice stores

Wednesday 7th April: Woke fairly early and found that we were steaming near the coast with Kinabalu in the background. Passed a number of large and small islands and sandy-spits before we passed into the small bay of Kudat. Here there is a small jetty, a W/T Station, a very nice bungalow overlooking the harbour, possibly the former residence of the British Resident or Harbourmaster. Here we were trans-shipped to the other ship with the NCOs and men – conditions were over-crowded and cramped; a few Jap civilians were in evidence, one of whom took a photo of POW with evident relish. Various English-speaking and obviously sympathetic natives brought us bananas and tobacco – very cheap, too, before we cast off about 1.30 p.m., leaving the coaster with the cracked cylinder head behind. We passed through what must have been the Balabac Straits just before dusk, when I found a bed space at the top of a companionway leading to a tiny gangway aft of the wheelhouse. During the afternoon I had a long chat with an airman who had been a driver on the staff of my Port Depot in Batavia, Moore by name, and also with Sgt. Allsop, a young NCO, who I think would make a good man under proper guidance, and with Cpl. Clarke, who was with 211 Sqdn. in Egypt and the Sudan before coming to Java. So to an uneasy bed!

DIED JESSELTON - GRAVES LATER TRANSFERRED TO LABUAN

ROYAL ARTILLERY AND R.A.F. PERSONNEL

Number	Name	Rank	Regiment	Place of Origin	D.O.D.	Age	Place Died
1787581	Auerbach, H.A.	Gnr.	48 Bty. 21 LAA	Sth. Tottenham, Middlesex	16.04.43	36	J
6001252	Bareham, G.A.	Gnr.	95 Bty. 48 LAA	Great Clacton, Essex	14.01.43	39	J
1481414	Bentley, D.H.	Sgt.	48 Bty. 21 LAA	Enfield, Middlesex	12.02.43	31	J
1734012	Blackburn, James	Gnr.	95 Bty. 48 LAA		28.03.43	36	J
1216038	Bond, A.G.	Cpl.	R.A.F. (VR)	Victoria, London	02.02.43	37	J
987409	Booth, J.B.	AC.1	RAF(VR) 84 Sqdn.	Bolton, Lancashire	12.02.43	28	J
11052485	Brennan, D.G.	Gnr.	242 Bty. 48 LAA	Sunderland, Co. Durham	20.01.43	21	J
6461200	Butterfield, A.W.	Gnr.	48 Bty. 21 LAA	St. Marylebone, London	11.02.43	31	J
1222372	Chadburn, E.F.	AC.1	RAF(VR) 242 Sqdn.	Bulwell, Nottinghamshire	23.04.45	24	J
2368539	Cousins, Tom	Sgmn.	21 LAA Sig. Sec.	Wetwang, Yorkshire	06.02.43	26	J
13056649	Crossley, Selwyn	Pte.	Pioneer Corps.	Sowerby Bridge, Yorkshire	15.12.44	24	J
1828094	Daynes, E.W.C.	Gnr.	242 Bty. 48 LAA		10.04.43	33	J
1478306	Draper, R.C.	BQMS	48 Bty. 21 LAA	Enfield, Middlesex	15.01.43	31	J
5191726	Druce, E.V.	Sgmn.	21 LAA Sig. Sec.	Cheltenham, Gloucestershire	13.01.43	33	J
1117656	Durnford, R.G.G.	L/Bdr.	48 Bty. 21 LAA	Bishopsworth, Somerset	18.12.42	33	J
11052569	Eastwood, W.L.	Gnr.	242 Bty. 48 LAA	Shotton Colliery, Co. Durham	13.02.43	21	J
1489185	Field, R.J.	L/Bdr.	48 Bty. 21 LAA	Barnsbury, London	02.01.43	33	J

Number	Rank	Name	Regiment	Place of Origin	D.O.D.	Age	Place Died
1260307	LAC	Fox, I.E.	RAF(VR) 211 Sqdn.	Ely, Cardiff	21.03.43	20	J
1549382	Gnr.	Green, Harry	48 Bty. 21 LAA		05.04.43	33	J
1796103	Gnr.	Griffiths, Clifford	242 Bty. 48 LAA		22.01.43		J
1833263	Gnr.	Harvey, T.H.	242 Bty. 48 LAA	Totnes, Devon	21.01.43	36	J
1772160	Gnr.	Hellewell, G.W.	48 Bty. 21 LAA	Camberwell, London	23.01.43	31	J
1820156	Gnr.	Henderson, E.C.	242 Bty. 48 LAA	Dundee	21.02.43	33	J
1794649	Gnr.	Hick, Harold	242 Bty. 48 LAA	Bradford, Yorkshire	28.12.42	26	J
1486338	Gnr.	Hill, F.L.G.	48 Bty. 21 LAA		14.12.42	32	J
11052513	Gnr.	Hitchings, A.L.	242 Bty. 48 LAA		12.03.43	31	J
11052198	Gnr.	Hood, George	242 Bty. 48 LAA	St. Helens, Lancashire	29.12.42	21	J
1807855	Gnr.	Howard, J.R.	95 Bty. 48 LAA	Southport, Lancashire	27.11.42	33	J
1801624	Gnr.	Jones, Robert	242 Bty. 48 LAA		04.01.43	27	J
13056385	Pte.	Keaney, J.R.	Pioneer Corps.	Oldham, Lancashire	04.01.43	26	J
610608	Sgt.	Kerslake, W.P.	R.A.F.	Cadnam, Southampton	01.12.42	24	J
832284	L/Bdr.	Lawrence, A.E.J.	95 Bty. 48 LAA	Linford, Essex	14.12.42	29	J
1366156	LAC	McLeod, J.B.	R.A.F. (VR)		02.01.43	35	J
1309567	AC.1	Mendy, H.J.	RAF(VR) 211 Sqdn.	High Wycombe, Bucks.	28.12.42	29	J
646961	LAC	Morgan, R.H.	R.A.F. 211 Sqdn.	Rhyl, Flintshire	18.03.43	23	J
1171890	AC.1	Myers, J.G.	RAF(VR) 211 Sqdn.	Goring, Sussex	02.01.43	27	J
1621264	Gnr.	Nash, Edward	242 Bty. 48 LAA	Basingstoke, Hampshire	17.01.43	29	J

Number	Rank	Name	Regiment	Place of Origin	D.O.D.	Age	Place Died
11051911	Gnr.	Needham, J.B.	242 Bty. 48 LAA	Goole, Yorkshire	25.10.42	21	J
1655520	Gnr.	O'Brien, F.W.	95 Bty. 48 LAA	Bedminster, Bristol	15.12.42	22	J
1563222	Sgt.	Potter, C.A.	242 Bty. 48 LAA	Clacton-on-Sea, Essex	21.02.43	28	J
987515	AC.1	Robertson, J.D.	R.A.F. (VR)	Corpach, Inverness-shire	14.03.43	40	J
1808864	Gnr.	Scullion, Joseph	242 Bty. 48 LAA	Collyhurst, Manchester	11.01.43	22	J
1159728	AC.1	Smith, Sidney	R.A.F. (VR)		14.04.43		J
1104482	AC.1	Speed, A.D.	R.A.F. (VR)	Edinburgh	17.01.43	36	J
11052258	Gnr.	Stirzaker, John	242 Bty. 48 LAA	Preston, Lancashire	14.02.43	32	J
11052243	Gnr.	Thomasson, J.H.	242 Bty. 48 LAA	Salford, Lancashire	10.04.43	34	J
1827456	Gnr.	Venables, S.L.	95 Bty. 48 LAA	Streatham, London	07.02.43	21	J
1548471	Gnr.	Watson, W.A.	95 Bty. 48 LAA	Clacton-on-Sea, Essex	21.01.43	26	J
1523229	L/Bdr.	Wood, Harold	49 Bty. 48 LAA	Southend-on-Sea, Essex	13.02.43	35	J
1782806	Gnr.	Wright, J.W.	95 Bty. 48 LAA	Oldham, Lancashire	28.01.43	22	J
1592539	Gnr.	Young, R.G.T.	48 Bty. 21 LAA	Mill Hill, Middlesex	17.04.43	31	J

Plan of 8m Camp – Late 1943-45

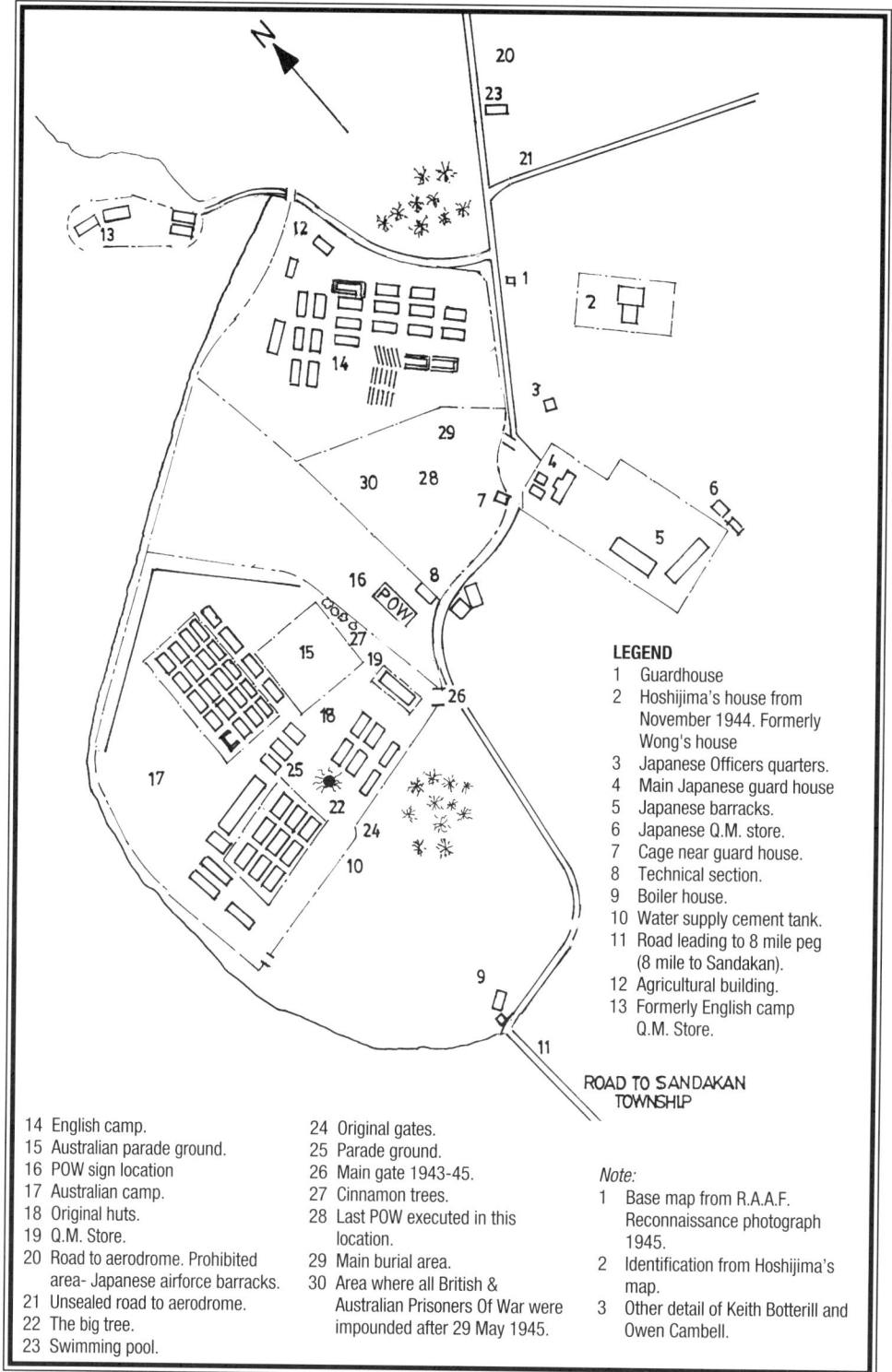

LEGEND

1 Guardhouse
2 Hoshijima's house from November 1944. Formerly Wong's house
3 Japanese Officers quarters.
4 Main Japanese guard house
5 Japanese barracks.
6 Japanese Q.M. store.
7 Cage near guard house.
8 Technical section.
9 Boiler house.
10 Water supply cement tank.
11 Road leading to 8 mile peg (8 mile to Sandakan).
12 Agricultural building.
13 Formerly English camp Q.M. Store.

14 English camp.
15 Australian parade ground.
16 POW sign location
17 Australian camp.
18 Original huts.
19 Q.M. Store.
20 Road to aerodrome. Prohibited area- Japanese airforce barracks.
21 Unsealed road to aerodrome.
22 The big tree.
23 Swimming pool.

24 Original gates.
25 Parade ground.
26 Main gate 1943-45.
27 Cinnamon trees.
28 Last POW executed in this location.
29 Main burial area.
30 Area where all British & Australian Prisoners Of War were impounded after 29 May 1945.

Note:
1 Base map from R.A.A.F. Reconnaissance photograph 1945.
2 Identification from Hoshijima's map.
3 Other detail of Keith Botterill and Owen Cambell.

Chapter Two

SANDAKAN

Off Sandakan, Thursday 8 April 1943: Woke at 5 a.m. and got up – pronto! Watched sunrise and had usual tasty breakfast of rice and tea that tasted like swill. About 8.30 a.m. we sighted the Gibraltar-like crags of sandstone (Berhala Island) that marked the entrance to Sandakan Bay, one of the largest natural land-locked harbours of the world. Docked at 9.30 a.m. and hung about on the otherwise deserted quay until the new Japanese Camp Commandant inspected us. We were then rested at an old godown behind the quay until the afternoon when we were marched, with our kit, about 1/2 mile to the local C. of E. Church which is situated on a hill commanding a fine view of Sandakan. The Church is stone built, wooden-vaulted, and has a raised organ-loft and concealed lighting. Above the entrance to the chancel is a large crucifix suspended from the ceiling. After a bath at the bottom of a small valley, on the opposite side of which is the Civil Hospital surrounded by cedars, we had dinner and a roll-call conducted by armed Japanese, inside the church, after which the Camp Commandant came in and looked around, accompanied by his dog. And so, in one of the transepts, to bed.

Friday 9 April: Reveille at 4.30 a.m., breakfast, and marched off at 6.30 a.m. March took us through the town, up a hill on the opposite side to the church, and from there on a fairly good road, into the open country. We sang all the old marching songs with gusto, everybody feeling like the morning – fine. Water was organized along the road, and rests were allowed about every 3 miles. After the 7th mile the strain began to tell on some – Ken Whitworth had to be supported by Bird and Coleman, and I relieved Stan Cressey of his haversack. "They" put on a lorry further down the road. We arrived at the site of our new camp about 11 a.m. and two parties of very fit-looking Aussies were formed up as a Guard-of-Honour."

The Australians first arrived in Sandakan on 18 July 1942; they were now well acclimatised and generally in good condition, their losses were only about 20 from a total of 1494 men.

Lieut. Tony White remembers the English arriving, led by R.A.F. officers, and marching to their camp which was located on the north eastern side of the road leading to the aerodrome. The Australians were working near the gravel pit and were generally shocked at the poor condition the men were in, later they learned these were Royal Artillery Anti Aircraft and R.A.F. Units, many of whom had spent nearly two months at sea before reaching the Far East and had already suffered losses at Jesselton. Contact was not permitted between the English and the Australians and later when an additional Australian force of 500 A.I.F. arrived, they were kept separately.

Friday 9 April: When we reached our own camp we found it to be a collection of coolie-lines with no water, sanitation or light. Before entering the compound our kit was searched very thoroughly for the umteenth time, all pencils, pens, knives and blank paper being removed. These latter were put in a box, locked and the box deposited with Hardie. We were then marched into the Camp, around which local natives were still busy putting up a double line of barbed wire. Our first job was to build latrines as those provided were not considered adequate or flyproof. All water, we discovered, was drawn from wells outside the camp, and very dirty looking water it was! At night the Japanese officer, Hoshijima, gave us a talk, through an interpreter, on keeping the camp "nice and clean and tidy". He also said that our work would be the construction of the aerodrome – we should be getting quite expert at it by now! And so, feeling very tired, to bed.

Saturday 10 April: Hardie gave us, and later the senior NCOs, a talk on discipline. This was certainly well-timed.

From 10-17 April: Our days seldom varied – 0700 Roll Call, a quick shave and breakfast; 0810 Working Parade – water carrying for cookhouse and washing purposes; men doing well-digging (also 2 parties of officers); digging new latrines and cleaning up the camp generally. 12.10 Knock-off parade.

12-15-1330 Tiffin and possibly a spot of reading; 1330 Working parade again – water carrying or wood collecting for cookhouse. 1720 Finish and a quick bath at the well or under our hut (all huts were on 'stilts'), with about 3" of water in a tin can. 1800 Dinner. 1900 Roll-call. As it is dark here about 1945 and no lights supplied one usually sits around the 'smoke-holes' and talks until either 2200 "Lights Out" or before, as the body dictates. Fortunately, it is very cool here at nights and there is a waxing moon, so things are not so bad."

When 'E' Force left Changi it comprised 500 British and 500 Australians under the command of Lt.Col. Whimster; on arrival at Kuching the British were disembarked and the senior Australian officers, Major John Fairley with his second in command and several Other Ranks were also off-loaded to remain. The Japanese decided that no officer above the rank of Captain would be permitted to remain with the main body of men. The Australians, now under the command of Captain R.J.D. Richardson, were taken on to Sandakan. When they arrived at Berhala Island at the entrance to Sandakan Harbour on 15 April 1943, they were placed in the Quarantine Station, now vacated by the Internees who had been moved on to Kuching.

As 'E' Force left Changi, the wireless components were given to the 20 officers on the Force. At this time most PWs had been away from Changi and were accustomed to searches – those not accustomed to regular searches often panicked and dumped vital parts – the responsibility was left to the technicians and Sigs. men who were allocated the task of assembling the wireless at their destination.

All components reached Borneo, despite nerve-straining moments during three searches. After some time it became known the Japanese acted on a directive that they must search for a certain item; in Borneo they were primarily concerned with writing material and were likely to overlook other incriminating items. In other searches in other countries they would search for salt – arms and other stolen goods they would be likely to overlook. On 'E' Force, one man was able to get a pair of Rolls-Royce headlights he intended to take home as far as Sandakan. Lieut. Rex Blow managed to conceal his .38 calibre pistol through three searches.

The second search at Berhala Island was witnessed by fellow officer, Lieut. M. Brennan, who saw Blow nonchalantly place his pistol under a groundsheet and hold it up – then in the final search Blow felt he was caught when the Japanese guards ordered the officers in the front rank to place all their belongings on the ground, he placed his groundsheet on the ground while another officer gave him a commentary on the position and movement of the Japanese guard conducting the search. Blow, with his hand under the groundsheet, frantically digging a hole in the hard ground to bury his pistol – the commentary was coolly maintained until the pistol was safely buried without the guard being aware of anything untoward going on.

The Japanese concentrated attention on writing material; the 'E' Force men were not to know the dramas taking place at the 8 Mile Camp where officers were sending out signed notes of world news, fresh from their wireless, to loyal civilians in Sandakan and to the English camp – nothing could have been more incriminating.

Lieut. Blow not only had his pistol to conceal but the complete power transformer, a bulky unit for the wireless set, which he concealed under the flap of his pack.

After the search carried out on their arrival at the Berhala camp, Lieut. Hoshijima, paraded the men then stood on a make-shift platform and told those present that he was the Commander of the POW Camp at Sandakan and said he knew all about Australians – they were a bunch of thieves, sons of convicts, and knew all about their tricks – there was nothing he did not know and he advised the parade what would happen if they attempted to escape. While this oration was continuing Blow murmured to his mate Lieut. Gillon: "We won't be staying around with this bastard!"

Lieut. Hoshijima returned to Sandakan by barge, he was beginning to have problems – he knew something was rumbling under the surface – the existence of an Underground organisation perhaps but nothing he could be positive about. The security of the camp perimeter was reinforced with wire and higher fences. Still, he was feeling uneasy, Southern Command in Saigon had ordered all officers above the rank of Captain to be removed to Kuching – all other prisoners were kept in separate camps and not permitted to make contact.

Saturday 17 April: Cpl. Foley (Cook) thinks that the greens are more plentiful here than at Jesselton, but the rice has been reduced. There is also a very pleasant tasting fish (fresh and salted) ration which is an improvement on that supplied at Jesselton. Our 'sick' officers during this period have been employed on cleaning yams and grating tapioca root for our evening doughnuts. During this period I developed a swollen right foot which went down in a couple of days, and a scratch from a rusty nail which required a little more treatment than I normally give. The animal life here is active. We have numbers of rats and small snakes in our attap roof beside the usual Cheechaks, and between them they manage to create quite a noise at times. Our largest snake to date was a 4'6" cobra caught in the latrines by F/S Stammers and subsequently skinned. The Aussie officers are, according to rumour, not paid, but receive extra rations in lieu, for which they sign. Their health record is very good – 26 deaths out of 1500 in nine months. The Aussie M.O. visited us one day but was closely followed by Hoshijima who would allow no one to speak to him. He sent over some mag. sulph. for the skin cases.

Sunday 18 April: We were told this morning that the remainder of the Jesselton party would arrive today. They did – about 1730 hrs., being assisted by 120 of our men who had marched out about one hour previously. Padre Wanless and the two Docs arrived in the first party, all looking very hot and jaded. They had been brought from Jesselton in a 1000 tonner – about 570 of them packed on to the decks and in the holds, including 240 very sick men, several of whom were dying. At night there was insufficient room to lie down, dysentery patients had pots and tubs to rear into, some of which were kicked over during the night as there were no lights. The loading of the sick at Jesselton had to be done up a sloping ladder, and then down a vertical ladder into the hold. At Sandakan they were all transferred into deep barges at 0430 hrs. in the morning, and taken up river to a landing stage near a drome in the jungle. Here they were landed and kept waiting during the heat of the day. The Aussies sent down two rissoles per man each for tiffin. About 1630 hrs. everybody was moved off, all the sick being made to march. During the transfer to the barges at Sandakan, one of the men carrying a dying man, Gunner Knutton, fell into the sea. Knutton was pulled back at the last moment but suffered from shock. Late afternoon they were then marched up a jungle track through which a narrow gauge railway had been cut, and eventually reached the drome and the camp. Some of them were in a pitifully weak physical condition on arrival – men whom I had known as strong healthy specimens of British manhood had shrunk away to gaunt hollow-eyed ghosts.

My job was to shepherd the men into their billets on arrival – 74 to a hut. In spite of their experiences they were all very cheerful – and very hungry. Owing to lack of water we could not satisfy their most pressing need – for a wash. Most of them went around contacting their friends from the first party, swapping yarns until about midnight. L/Cpl. Green and two other Gunners died at Jesselton before the rest of the party embarked.

Monday 19 April: Contacted some of the men today. Some seem to have lost weight rapidly and are mere skeletons of their former selves. LACs Parker, Thompson and Ramsay look like ghosts of what they were a mere 5 months ago. Thompson, particularly, seems to have lost about 6 stone. Cpl. Kleiser also looks an absolute wreck.

71

Most of them seem to appreciate the comparative "openness" of this camp after their surroundings of corrugated iron walls at Jesselton.

Tuesday 20 April: Today, the rather tedious business of water-carrying which up till now has been done daily by the officers, was taken over by the men.

Gunner Knutton died late this afternoon and was taken out of camp for burial after parade, about 19.30. Dusk was falling as we paraded to honour the cortege. The coffin was taken to a wood about 3 miles from the Aussie Camp, the Padre tells me, and the party did not return until 2330. The Aussies have apparently got their own electric light plant and water pump, which the funeral party could hear in the distance.

Thursday 22 April: First 'drome party of 270 men and 7 officers went out today. From reports received at tiffin time, when everyone returned to the Camp for food, the work is similar to that at Jesselton; working with bogies for 'drome levelling. Supervision is by the 'boy scouts', with a leavening of regular soldiers and seems fairly easy. The work party was allowed to buy fried fritters, native fish cakes and a few bananas and eggs.

Friday 23 April: Grey-Jones out today and reported a slightly larger supply of fritters. Finished Sinclair Lewis' "Work of Art" today, a life history of an imaginary American restaurateur – Myron Weagle. It give a very good insight into U.S. hotel life, its workers and habitues. Running through it all is the theme of the small town boy of Black Thread Centre, determined to make good in his chosen vocation and to learn from the bottom.

A Good Friday Service was held after parade tonight.

Saturday 24 April: In charge of No. 3 Party on 'drome today T.Q.M.S. and W.0.2 (BQMS) Salter who told me quite a lot about his Army experiences in France and Java and also about camp administration at Jesselton. Apparently there were a lot of adverse comments by Army ORs at Koan School just after the capitulation on the retention by Army Officers of imprest monies which they put to their own personal use instead of pooling them all for the benefit of all ranks. The sight of cooked chickens, whiskey, gin and sherry going in to the officers' quarters excited a lot of adverse comment. I questioned him on whether similar occurrences were noticeable after Dunkirk, and he concurred. To his knowledge, several Gunners, whilst at Bordon Camp (to which they were taken after Dunkirk) changed from 1000 to 5000 French or Belgian franc notes into English money! The element of personal opportunity seems very much to the fore in this War.

Sunday 25 April: Easter Day: Yet another Easter "in durance vile". Remember last year when our road convoy arrived at Malang about 5 p.m.

A parade service was held at 9.30 a.m. and was taken by Mills, as Hardie is sick in bed with a couple of small ulcers on his leg (the Doc tells me he is keeping him in bed to give the men a break!) Padre preached an excellent sermon on the relation of Easter to our present, and world conditions. We also had a voluntary evening service after parade which was well attended. The private cooking area has now been moved to a corner of the camp area which slopes down to the stream just outside the wire. It provides a pleasant sight at night, with groups of ORs bending over their pots and billy cans on twig fires.

Monday 26 April: To fill in the day with something useful Paterson, Foulkes and I started work on an attap sun-shelter over the officers "smoke-hole". By 5 p.m. we had put in the 4 main bamboo supports and the frame-roof. Also did a couple of journeys to the drinking water well with Jimmy Mills. TOC H met in the unfinished hut after parade, when Gunner Hart spoke on "Experiences as a Waiter in Lyons" (Lyons Corner Houses in London – pre-war equivalent of MacDonalds today). He is a Cockney, with all the racy fluency which characterizes them. After about 1 hour he seemed to be just getting into his stride, so I left! The association of food ideas was too much. I believe he eventually finished about 9.30 p.m.!

Tuesday 27 April: In the morning finished off the 'attaping' of our shelter roof. The finished product looks quite impressive and we were complimented by several of our fellow officers. Others made various suggestions for its further improvement, and got some brusque replies for their trouble! In the evening another talk with Doc Daniels and Padre Wanless about events in Malaya – it is amazing how we can still find additional facets of that campaign to discuss, so often. Book Society met tonight, discussed American drama, about which none of the speakers seemed to know very much. Discussion got onto general lines: I intervened when they touched on the attitudes of British – U.S. Forces when fighting in the Far East – why should we fight for Malaya and the vested interests? I asked whether the same spirit existed in the Middle East?

Wednesday 28 April: Again 1/C of No. 3 Party at the 'drome, with Sgts. Thomas and Burke (R.A.) as NCOs. Had long chat with them about their wartime experiences in London. Sgt. Thomas comes from Treorchy (South Wales), as does David Mason. Accompanied the water party to the Aussie Camp, and managed to get about $5 of food for the men, including $1 tapioca root, peanut toffee @ 2¢ small slab, bananas (1,1½ & 2½¢). In the afternoon had a spot of bother with a Jap 2-Star soldier, 2 of my men were struck with a thick stick across the back and behind, and I collected one across my left thigh which left a weal. My thoughts can be imagined. In the evening had a long conversation with Doc Daniels (Capt., RAMC), on our respective views of possible post-war events, national and personal. We both seem to have hit on the idea of a move to get us out of the "everyday rut" and he is keen to prospect Australia or the Colonies for openings. The Civil Medical Officer at Jesselton had told him that his salary was 1200 pounds a year free of income tax, with free quarters, light etc. Considering the not inconsiderable recreational facilities of the place, with generous leaves etc., it seems a very attractive proposition to the Doc. He seems determined not to continue his pre-war practice in Portsmouth, even though it was financially successful. He is about the only one of the "old stagers" here who had any sympathy with my own plan to study at the London School of Economics for an Economics degree in Finance and International Trade – and then possibly return to the East, China or one of the Colonies.

Held a meeting of the Northumberland and Durham Society after roll-call tonight. Padre presided. We went over the objects of the Society for the benefit of Army members and elected Sgt. Hall (ex 2nd Durham Light Infantry, India, etc.) as Secretary, Doc Daniels another Vice-President, and a Bombadier as Army representative on the Committee. We decided to meet every fortnight. Foley is to give a talk at the next meeting on his experiences in the Turks Head, Newcastle-on-Tyne (a very popular Hotel and Pub).

Thursday 29 April: The Emperor of Japan's birthday, for which we were given a holiday, 2 packets of Jap fags each, and permission to buy, at 15¢ a time, 12 tins (small) of pineapple chunks. Had a 10 minute ceremony in which we saluted towards the North-East; during rest of day I got down to Frida Utley's book "Japan's Gamble in China" published in 1938.

Friday 30 April: Another short ceremony at 1030 hrs, which we were told was for the "War Dead of this and other Wars". For most of us just another rather stupid parade! The 'drome party were sent back at 11.30 a.m. and Hoshijima made a speech telling us that (1) he had heard reports that our conduct at Jesselton was "satisfactory" and hoped it would continue to be so here, (2) as Borneo was not yet a "producing" country, food was not plentiful and that there were no clothes etc. obtainable, so he exhorted us to be economical in all things (many of the B.Ors in front of him were dressed only in loin cloths) (3) he had noticed that we had a lot of sick – unfortunately, medical supplies were scarce, but we were urged to "take great care of our health" (4) in the present state of things "even officers" could not be kept here without work, but would have to do manual labour (5) a copy of Camp Regs. had been passed to our C.O. – these were drawn up for the Australian Camp and would not necessarily *all* apply to us.

Hoshijima then took his salute, the 2/Lt. jumped on the table and took his, and so the parade ended.

Saturday 1 May: Working party suddenly returned to Camp about 10 a.m., having suddenly been dismissed from the 'drome. No Aussies were seen out. Later in the morning armed parties of Japs, led by natives, were seen beating the bush around the camp. It seemed obvious to me that some Aussies must have made a break, but all sorts of wild rumours circulated, amongst which was one which supposed that a tiger had been seen in the area! Hardie made an announcement on parade tonight re various Camp Funds viz: (i) Hospital (ii) Canteen (iii) Extra Messing. Rolfe is to be in charge of the monies with Paterson and Pethybridge as auditors. Burgess and F/Sgt. Merchant are to run the Canteen which hopes to serve coffee or tea and doughnuts at night. He was rather vague about the officers' contributions to the Hospital and Extra Messing funds, as he was not a contributor himself. I must look into the position.

Sunday 2 May: A Working Party today, of which I was in charge of No. 3 Party. Spent most of the day moving our rail bridge over the gully. Hoshijima visited the 'drome. Barnes, our batman, made some very good doughnuts, after roll call tonight, from the tapioca root I was able to buy on the 'drome. A very pleasant service was held tonight at 1930 hrs against a background of the very beautiful sunset; the altar was framed between 2 rubber trees and a very tall, straight palm tree. Communion service was held afterwards in the dark, with fires from the private cooking area throwing flickering shadows over us all. Heard from a Jap that 3 Aussies had escaped.

Monday 3 May: Enjoyed my day of rest today by looking thru' the Japan Times which had just been given to us: the latest is dated February 16th. There is much "between the lines" that is very encouraging, e.g. Pres. Roosevelt has made a statement to Congress that 1943 wd. be a year of v. large scale counter offensives against the Axis forces. The Casablanca meeting between Roosevelt and Churchill is also reported but none of the statements made were recorded except "unanimity of views etc.. TOC H held a debate after roll-call – our new "canteen Coffee Parade" "Should capital punishment be abolished?" proposed by Sgt.. Holder, R.A. and Staff Sgt. Ackland opposing. Some of the speeches were quite convincing but all lacked knowledge of the subject.

Tuesday 4 May: Another day spent in reading Japan Times and "Japs Gamble in China". Today is the anniversary of the shooting by firing squad at Malang ' Drome, Java, of Flt/Lieut. Gordon, P/O Cheesewright, W/O Kenason and F/Sgt. Poland in 1942, for attempted escape [NB: After about 2 days on the run they were turned in to the Japanese by Javanese natives for the large reward offered after their escaped.

Wednesday 5 May: An attack of squitters started during the night, so laid off from the 'drome today. Spent a.m. and p.m. reading Japan Times: noticed that at beginning of February Churchill stated that "Germany would be defeated within 9 months, after which Japan would be attacked." He also advised

Germany to capitulate. Some interesting interviews with Lt. Gen. Percival, ex G.O.C. Malaya, at Taiwan POW Camp. He ascribed the fall of S'pore to lack of equipment and personnel, and said he was confident that Britain would win this war. The Japs, in a very illuminating article also admit their withdrawal from New Guinea and Guadalcanal Island. Apparently the Aussie and U.S. troops operating in that area have learnt their lesson from the Battle of Malaya and are now adopting both Jap and Russian tactics of (i) firing from tops of trees and from holes in the ground, (ii) not retiring during nocturnal attacks but counter-attacking (iii) scattered groups operating individually in the jungle (iv) protecting 'dromes by pill-boxes etc. (v) constructing 'dromes at high speed with mechanical devices (obviously bulldozers) ! They also pay tribute to the new fighting spirit of the Aussies as compared with those captured in the past. Finished "Japs Gamble in China".

Thursday 6th May & Friday 7th May: Lazy days spent reading "Chez Les Francais" a book of French colloquialisms borrowed from Frank Bell. Most of the mornings taken up by filling in postcards for the men. These P.Cs which the Japs have promised to send by the "next ship" are headed I.J.A. and contain the following print:
(1) I am interned in …
(2) My health is excellent/usual/poor
(3) I am working for pay
(4) I am not working
(5) Please see that … is taken care
(6) My love to … Signature …

On the address side, top L.H. corner there is a square with spaces for name, nationality, rank and camp. Many of the men, mere skeletons of their former selves, covered with septic sores, scabies and wet beriberi put down that their health was excellent so as not to worry their people. I thought that my folks would understand when I wrote "usual" – as a family we are not given to over-statement in many things.

Saturday 8 May: On 'drome today 1/C No. 4 Party, which I found a very "dreamy" lackadaisical bunch. The 2 senior NCOs, both R.A.O.C., one of whom Sgt. Henschel told me they were conscripts and supplementary reserves respectively. Both were untidy in habit and address and appeared to have no control over their men … A quiet day during which I had long chats with LAC Gordon, who was in my old Unit, 152 M.V. (Bukit Panjong, Singapore). He told me he had been a student at the Royal College of Arts (Ldn.) whose principal was Sir William Rothenstein. An Arts Master (he himself was teaching at a Technical Institute in Dewsbury, Yorkshire) apparently organised a 4-year course in classical visual arts, sculpture, pottery, weaving, heraldry etc. Had the good fortune to borrow "Babbitt" by Sinclair Lewis from LAC Wallace today.

Sunday 9 May: Parade service at 0900 this morning. Sermon by Padre Wanless … As a "Parade" managed by F/Sgt. Potter it was a shambles! Our evening service was held as usual by the bottom smokehole, after which Doc, Padre and I sat and smoked, talked and admired the heavens – tonight being a new moon.

Monday 10 May: Working Parade cancelled this morning and all paraded for speech by Jap. Major Suga who arrived at 10.45 with Hoshijima, Nagai and Moritaki, Hoshijima's jacket was very small and showed a large expanse of backside which, with his unusually long legs, made him look like an overgrown schoolboy. Major Suga began with his usual "Look at me!" which caused a loud titter from the troops. His speech followed the usual lines; apologies for short rations, lack of boots and clothing, bad accommodation and shortage of water. In spite of these "due to shortage of food and materials in Borneo", he urged everybody to look after their health and take care not to get dysentery or beri-beri! He concluded by saying he thought the end of the war was in sight and reminding us of the righteousness of their war to liberate the peoples of East Asia from Anglo-Saxon oppression! The working party went out in the afternoon. At TOC H after Roll Call, Lt. Les Coleman, M.M., gave a talk on his experiences with the British Expeditionary Force at Dunkirk, to quite a large audience.

Tuesday 11 May: Another ½ day working party. The Book Club met tonight in the unfinished hut and discussed "Which of the forms of Art is the best interpretive medium?" LAC Gordon spoke for Art and Music, A.C. Pierce for Poetry, and Gnr. Russell for Drama. The last mentioned is a professional actor who told me last week that he was just making headway in the profession when the war started. He has acted in Repertory and spent the winter of 1938-39 at the Playhouse, Jesmond, Newcastle-on-Tyne. This was of interest, as I come from Durham in the North of England and Newcastle was our nearest large town. Russell had a minor part in Dame Marie Tempest's play, "Dear Octopus", when the war broke out – I had seen the play in London. As was expected from a debate on such a subject, it developed into a discussion of the function of the various forms of art. (Gunner Russell was the son of John Peter Russell, a famous Australian artist, and his second wife Caroline de Witt Merrill of Florida. John Peter Russell was a contemporary of Van Gogh and Tom Roberts and his paintings were exhibited throughout Europe.)

Wednesday 12 May: No guard turned up at 0830 for the working party, but we were suddenly called for at 11.30 a.m., marched outside to the guard-room and after hanging around for about 10 minutes, sent inside again. We went out again at the usual afternoon 'follow' time 1.30 p.m. and marched off. I was in charge of No. 2 Party which was amalgamated with No.1 on the 2nd line from the Aussie end. At about 4.30 p.m. a Douglas (DC3) aircraft landed,

77

making a very beautiful touchdown. Just prior to this we heard machine-gun fire and at 5 p.m. two parties of Aussies carried 2 coffins from the 'drome to their quarters. Two of the three men who escaped a week or so ago had been recaptured in a kampong about 40 km. from Sandakan, were tried by Jap Court Martial, and shot. The third member of the party is still at large.

Sgt. Wallace, the third member of the party, reached Heng Joo's house wearing only his bathing trunks; he had lost all his gear swimming a river. He was hidden here for some days until the women folk in the house insisted he be taken away. It was at this time that Wallace, through the Underground, sounded out Captain Matthews to see if he could return to the Camp but the Camp had already suffered enough having been on half rations for four days because of the escape and he was told he was on his own. Then, with the knowledge that the escape party on Berhala Island were waiting for a kumpit from Tawi Tawi Chin Peng Syn (known to the Australians as 'Little Synnie') conducted Wallace to Berhala Island where he escaped with the officers' party.

The machine-gun fire heard by the working party on 12 May was the shooting of Wallace's two companions, Sig. Harvey and Sig. Mackay (served as Mackenzie) by the Kempe Tai.

Friday 14 May: The dry spell broke today with a downpour in the afternoon which lasted about ½ hour. Everyone in camp rushed out with pails, cups, etc. to collect some decent drinking water – the first since we arrived here. It was a treat to drink clear cold water again. Others took advantage of the rain to have a natural shower bath. Tonight indulged myself in an argument with George Larder about the morale of our forces, drawing comparisons with Russia and China. He is difficult to argue with reasonably, as he only half listens to what his opponent has to say, with the result that he reiterates things one has never said! We both agreed, however, that the disasters of our first 2-3 years of war can be attributed to lack of both training and leadership, as well as the inadequacy of material resources. Capt. Foulkes chipped in to say that Jimmy Mills had been most impressed with the War Office when he was there in October-November 1941, and that arrangements for K Forces landing in North Africa were very complete, down to lists of contacts, telephone lines to be tapped, pictures of road junctions and the like.

Saturday 15 May: 'Drome today. Small canteen of attap has been built between lines 2 & 3. "Handlebars" (a Jap guard with handlebar moustache) spent most of his time supervising the purchase of supplies from the Malay vendor; there was tapioca root, 102 turtle eggs, bananas and fish for sale. Beautiful moonlit night and starry sky brought out a talk by Sgt. Littlewood of 205 Squadron on "The Heavens". He pointed out to us Orion, Cirius, Poseidon, Castor and Pollux, the Plough and the Pole Star. L/Bdr. Hammond (11/5/43) and Gunner Morton (13/5/43) died this week and were cremated in a small hollow just outside the Camp, within sight of the hospital. Incidentally, Stan Cressey (P/O) has been given the job of Adjutant of the Hospital. His main problem is to arrange feeding, extra-messing (when available) as directed by the M.Os; roster of hospital duties etc. Owing to heavy rain and wind, there was no concert tonight.

Sunday 15th May: Very clear and cool morning. Philip Young upset the Padre by failing to announce the Church Services, as a result of which I missed Communion after parade. In a very frank address at voluntary morning service attended by about 30, the Padre appealed for attendees to do some proselytizing among the backslides and complained of lack of support. He explained this afterwards to me that in an interview he had with Hardie, the latter had ordered 2 parade services a month (against the Padre's wishes) and thought that voluntary services could be dispensed with, – also the very successful meetings which the Padre runs on week-nights !! Usual service this evening.

Monday, 17 May: Tonight A.C. Rennie gave a talk on the Scottish Woollen Industry. His home was in Galashiels but after the small mill in which he served his apprenticeship closed down, he got a job in Paton & Baldwins. He seemed a typical Scot; stolid, conscientious, loyal.

Tuesday 18 May: On 'drome today I had No. 2 Party which is operated in conjunction with No.1. As Jones was busy haggling with the natives on makan, I had the job of supervising both. The Japs got rather excited, as usual, over line maintenance, which I quietened by putting 2 men, including Sgt. Hall on the job. Sgt. Hall was in the 2nd Bn. Durham Light Infantry, [PL: My father's old regiment in 1st WW] in India and spent a lot of time this morning telling me some of his experiences abroad and after he had finished his time. Coming out of the Service with 300 pounds, he devoted the first nine months of his freedom to enjoying himself and 'blueing' his cash! He then got married and "I got myself a job at the pits (coal-mines) and settled down". As his health cracked, he eventually got a job as a ganger with the Clacton-on-Sea (Essex) Gasworks.

L/Bdr. Prentice spoke to the Book Club tonight on "Famous Detectives in Fiction". In spite of his rather stilted style he covered his subject very ably, and had obviously read widely in that particular field. A particularly glorious sunset distracted my attention from the talk a little. Gnr. Pattison, who came from Sunderland, died from wet beri-beri just before parade this evening, having been ill since the forced march up here from the ship. I went to see him last night and found him lying back in a crudely-constructed armchair; his legs and private parts were swollen with fluid to grotesque proportions, and his breath came in short spasms. I did what I could to cheer him up, but one feels so helpless in these circumstances. The only people who could do anything are the Japanese. LAC Williams, who was in the Fabric Shop at Aircraft Depot, Far East Seletar, Singapore – one of my old units, who came out to Singapore on the same troopship (SS DUNERA) as myself, knew Pattison in Sunderland and tells me that he previously worked in Silkeworth Colliery, and had a wife and two pretty kiddies. Rotten luck on them, but war is like that.

Wednesday 19 May: This evening LAC Gordon gave a talk on "Heraldry", in which he dwelt more on the artistic side of his subject, rather than on the historical. I learnt a lot about heraldic metals and colours, quarterings, per bends, per fesse and artistic origins from this very absorbing talk.

Thursday 20 May: Borrowed "In Dubious Battle" from Tommy Hobbs today. The author is John Steinbeck, the American Dickens, all of whose novels deal with U.S. social and political problems from the socialist or communist standpoint; his greatest work "The Grapes of Wrath" published in 1939, was made into a movie picture which created a sensation and won the Academy Prize,

Saturday 22 May: Funeral (Cremation Party) this morning of Signalman Bird, who died yesterday of wet beri-beri. All men on the 'drome stood to attention whilst the Last Post was sounded, I heard later from Grey-Jones, thus following our example on Tuesday. Some Jap guards also fell into line. Concert tonight round smoke-hole; band played various selections from Show Boat, Maid of the Mountains, and modern waltz tunes, incl. "Who's taking you home tonight?" Our camp crooners also did their stuff. Concert ended with "There'll always be an England" and "God Save the King".

Sunday 23 May: Some doubt as to whether 'drome party was required today, so prepared for it – unnecessarily as it happened. Holy Communion 07.20 and Parade Service 0900; Padre preached a "Pulling Together" sermon. Evensong as usual. Arranged with "Tinker" Bell (Frank E. Bell, author 'Undercover University' and post-war founder of Bell School of Languages (UK.)) this evening to buy, jointly, a set of Hugos Spanish Lessons with which he will teach me Spanish.

Monday 24 May: 'Drome today No. 3 line. NCO's F/S. Boutcher and Sgt. Thomas, R.A. Moved line for about 4th time! Quiet day and pleasantly overcast afternoon. Jap guards mainly occupied with natives over purchases! Coffee with sugar, very acceptable, also arrived during afternoon. Downpour of rain started about 6 p.m. and lasted about 2 hours. Rapidly filled up latrines and thus caused a hell of a smell to waft thru' the whole camp. TOC H cancelled. Rain continued intermittently whole night.

Wednesday 26 May: Gunner Potter died today (beri-beri and dysentery) and was cremated on 27th.

Saturday 29 May: No concert tonight in spite of our holiday (in lieu of Sunday). The office was informed today that an "Amusing Hour" would be permitted each Saturday from 7.30 – 8.30 p.m., but that no war or marching songs must be sung or played – the weekly program to be submitted before Tuesday morning each week. Heavy rain today which satisfactorily topped up our wells. L/Bdr. Waite died today (dysentery and beri-beri).

Sunday 30 May: Usual Sunday Services – but evening service marred by flying-ants.

Monday 31 May: At TOC H tonight we had a debate "Should conscription be continued in Great Britain after the War", proposed by Sgt. Holder, R.A., and opposed by S/Sgt. Ackland Both made poor work of their respective cases. To keep the subsequent and rather desultory debate going afterwards, I intervened and spoke for about ¼ hour "in favour".

Tuesday June 1st: On 'dromc today on No. 3 Line, with F/S. Boutcher and Sgt. Thomas, R. A. as senior NCOs. Boutcher and 10 men got into a spot of trouble with 'Bill the Basher' for non-compliance with his orders. I am afraid that Boutcher, like many present-day technical NCOs, has very little control over the men. Sgt. Thomas provided two very acceptable cups of coffee during the day, and also told me some of his very interesting experiences as* gun-layer of an A.A. Unit. He was closely connected with the (deleted) [PL: Self-censorship at the time] side of the R.A.F. at home, and seemed pretty well versed in the ins and outs. At the Book Club tonight, held in the C.O.'s office, Doc Daniels gave me an exceptionally good summary of "The Citadel" by A.J. Cronin, and a commentary on it afterwards. His opinion was that as Cronin himself had a very poor medical qualification (L.R.C.P., L.R.C.S. Edinburgh) and had failed to stand up to the rigors of general practice, he should hardly have presumed to write about the G.Ps. The characters, he thought, were all overdrawn and representative of a very small minority of the medical profession.

Wednesday June 2nd: My second Spanish lesson today, which I found very interesting. The pronunciation I find fairly easy, but the stress on syllables is still rather tricky. Round the smoke-hole tonight LAC Gordon continued his art talks by telling us something of lithography and printing. He knows his subject and puts it over in a very attractive form. Before the talk he brought along some photographs which he took at Bukit Panjang* (*No.152 M.U. Bukit Panjang, Singapore – his and my last Unit in S'pore]. As photos they were not very good, but most of the people and places on them were recognizable.

Thursday June 3rd: Detailed for the funeral party which was scheduled for 1.30 p.m. today. Seven boxes of ashes were to be buried – an accumulation of the last 3 or 4 weeks. We also took crosses for the graves of A.C. Smith and Gnr. Starmer who were buried shortly after our arrival here. No transport was provided, and the party of 15, including the Padre, Lt. Threadgold and myself (in charge) moved off just before 2 o'clock. The march of 3-4 miles, which took us 1-1/2 hours, was down the Sandakan road up to the crossroads, where we forked right. Altho' there wasn't a cloud in the sky, a very pleasant breeze was blowing which somewhat tempered the heat of the sun. To get to the burial place we left the road and climbed a small hill which was used as a grazing ground for several cows and their calfs. On top were a number of byres and the hut of an Indian family who apparently looked after the animals, most of which were sheltering under their house in company with hens and chickens and a solitary, mangy-looking mongrel. On another small eminence some 50 yards away, we found the place, an irregular-shaped, very uneven bit of ground about 60 yards by 15 yards, forming the crest of this small undulation. We found that our two graves had been badly trampled on by the cows, as had also the graves of 2 Australians who were shot for attempted escape and which were about 15 yards away. We began the grave-digging, which we found somewhat difficult as the ground was a clayey shale. 8 men were taken away for about ½ hour, to bring up baskets of fruit from the road to the cemetery. Most of the men naturally thought that it was for them! Natural exclamations were … "I wonder how we are going to get thru' all that!" This done we proceeded with the Service which was attended by Nagai and 2/Lt. Morotaki, whom we have christened "Moriarty". After the committal, which was done by Thready and myself, we placed bunches of wildflowers (collected by the men) on the graves, saluted, and stood back whilst the Japs paid their respects. Then came the surprise of the afternoon. Nagai solemnly placed one basket of fruit on each grave and saluted! Afterwards he told us that the fruit was to be taken back to camp for the hospital. As we seemed to have reached the place by walking in a semi-circle, the "boy-scouts" decided to try a short cut back to Camp. They were not very sure of the way, which took us cross-country and through the small holdings (coffee, banana etc.) of various Chinese, at one of whose huts we managed to get some water. I also distributed some of the fruit. We eventually reached the main road after a rough passage during which we saw the Jap barracks for the first time – a long hut similar to those in our own coolie lines, but with plank walls instead of attap. Thready and I carried one of the large baskets of fruit

Picture taken from 8 Mile Road of No. 2 Cemetery looking East.   *Pic: AWM.42553.*

Picture of No. 2 Cemetery taken from eastern side of hill. Note ''Big Tree ' on right. The English Compound would have been further north of the ''Big Tree''.   *Pic: AWM.*

between us back to Camp as most of the Army party seemed a bit lacking in guts. We made one last stop on the crest of the hill near the Aussie camp, where a native quite voluntarily brought us some water, and we reached camp just after 6 p.m. I got Doc Blackledge to deputise for me in the reading of my news summary (from the latest "Japan Times") to the 1st Hut at 6.15 p.m. I was annoyed to hear later that he said, after the reading, " … and if any of you think you'll be out of here by Xmas, you've got another think coming." In these circumstances, depressing statements like that to the men are not only unnecessary but dangerous (to morale). Padre held his "Question-Hour" after rollcall, when Doc Daniels and I started a provocative argument on the Church and sex. Doc maintained that every man before marriage should have some experience of the sex act, as he knew of many marriages which had been wrecked by bad techniques! Padre did not agree. I spoke in favour of licensed and inspected brothels for troops in garrison towns like Singapore, to prove a clean outlet for a natural appetite, and to avoid infected troops going home to U.K. to infect English women. With certain reservations, the Padre agreed, after he had tried to sidetrack me!

Friday June 4: In consideration of the strenuous (! … actually was glad to get out of camp) day at the funeral yesterday, I was exempted from the 'drome today by Jimmy Mills! Read over again certain parts of the "Handbook to British Malaya" which I bought from A.C. Clarke the other day for 75 cts. Before roll-call read over news summary to No. 3 Hut; the interest shown is amazing, and does show how much the men appreciate any attempt to give the real 'gen'. (Although the news came from the Japan Times, I attempted to analyse, what the real situation behind the propaganda might be.) After roll-call, a chat with Bazell and Davies about the simple things of life, previously taken for granted, which this experience had made us appreciate: good beds, clean sheets, showers, clean table cloths, chairs to sit on etc. etc.!!

Meanwhile, on Berhala Island the escape group decided they would leave the camp together prior to the force being transferred by barge to Sandakan. Contact had been established with Cpl. Koram, who had arranged with Filipino traders and members of the U.S./Filipino Guerrilla Movement at Tawi Tawi to collect the Officers' party which comprised Capt. Ray Steele, Lieuts. Rex Blow, Gillon and Wagner; they were obliged to take W.O. Wallace who had been transferred to the Island by Chin Chee Kong (Little Synni). Pte. Jock McLaren, Pte. Kennedy and Dvr. Butler decided they would paddle their own canoe to Tawi Tawi. They left first after stealing two canoes from the local Leper Colony – one canoe was to travel and the other was to be sunk as a ruse to indicate to the

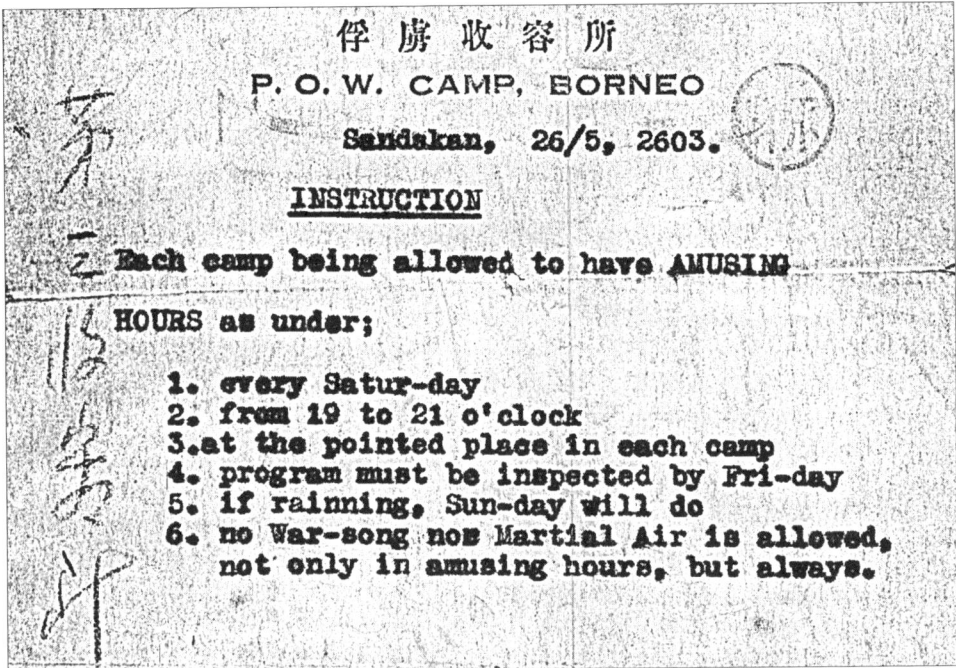

俘虜收容所

P. O. W. CAMP, BORNEO

Sandakan, 26/5, 2603.

INSTRUCTION

Each camp being allowed to have AMUSING

HOURS as under;

1. every Satur-day
2. from 19 to 21 o'clock
3. at the pointed place in each camp
4. program must be inspected by Fri-day
5. if rainning, Sun-day will do
6. no War-song nor Martial Air is allowed, not only in amusing hours, but always.

Amusing Hour

Japanese the rest of the party had also left the Island – they were to 'sweat it out' until the kumpit arrived from Tawi Tawi.

McLaren's party paddled at night, hiding their canoe during daylight hours and avoiding local people; they arrived safely at Tawi Tawi where contact was made with Colonel Suarez, Commander of the U.S. Filipino Forces. He was informed of the party hiding out on Berhala Island and immediately despatched a kumpit to collect them.

Saturday June 5: Spent most of the day reading out my news-sheet to the men, as a whole day's holiday had been given. During course of the day finished the last four Huts. Ostensible cause of the holiday was the arrival of 500 Aussies from Berhala Island at No.1 Camp, our guards being required for escort duties. They arrived by the same river route as our No. 2 Party. Our 'Amusing Hour' was held tonight from 7.30-8.30 p.m. Consisted mainly of items by our two-piece band – bass saxophone – piano accordion, and one or two solos by Sgt. McComisky, Les "Somebody or other" – a gunner, and A.C. Lucas, whom the men know as 'Sunshine'.

When the men lined up to be counted at Sandakan and the guards established there were seven men missing, they were counted, re-counted and counted again – four Officers and three Other Ranks.

In the short time 'E' Force were on Berhala Island, the POWs had christened one of the guards "Pants" and when it was known the seven men were missing he said: "Ah so! I know the men swimming up and down the beach!" He had seen these officers swimming, exercising and cutting wood, getting themselves fit for the task ahead. Rex Blow was a powerful swimmer and had represented Queensland in the National Titles.

The guards informed the NCO who informed the Officer-in-Charge. Face-slapping commenced, the Sergeant got his share and then he gave to all the ranks below. Hoshijima was informed – it then became a matter for the Kempe Tai Patrol boats were sent out, these were observed by the officers hiding out, while McLaren, Butler and Kennedy were well on the way to freedom.

Sunday June 6: As usual, holiday, church services etc. Attended service in skin diseases hut this morning. We sat on one of the raised platforms which serve as a bed space for the men, and which are separated by the earth gangway down the centre. The morning was hot and moist, so most of the patients were naked, and had all their running sores, ulcers, scabies, and Changi Balls exposed. One poor lad was so tormented by flies that during the whole service he remained entirely covered by his blanket, industriously scratching under it the whole time. Young Plummer still looks like a shrivelled up ghost, his skin looks like cracked mud, and one could get one's fingers round his arms, but he is tremendously plucky and keeps very cheerful. Still, he is, after all, a North-Countryman from Tyneside, and one expects it from them!

Monday June 7: Work party recommenced today – several incidents – perhaps most amusing concerns poor old "Wag" Price [PL: His initials were W.A.G.] he fell off a small bridge and dropped 5 feet into the gully, cutting his head and right leg. He now looks very sorry for himself, with a green handkerchief draped bandana-like round his head and a convincing looking bandage round his leg.

Tuesday June 8: A series of reported incidents on 'drome today. The Basher had a busy day, and 3 men were sent back to camp after being beaten up with his stick. L/Bdr. Prentice gave a talk on J.B. Priestley's place in English Literature and dwelt on most of his work as an author and playwright.

After roll call tonight Hardie made a farewell speech to the troops. He said how sorry he was to leave, how he admired the way in which they had taken everything on the chin – dysentery, beri-beri, skin disease, bad food, accommodation and treatment; this all showed remarkable spirit, and he hoped that his message might be conveyed to the relatives of those who had died. As he was being sent to a senior officers camp, he would not be with them on release as he had hoped – however, if any of them met him afterwards he hoped they would stop him and have a word. He already had appointments with the old No. 4 Malang Squadron and with the North-Country Society at the "Torks Heed" ("Geordie" or Northumbrian dialect) in Newcastle-on-Tyne. This was not something in Japanese, but the name of a Pub in Newcastle – the "Turks Head" (laughter). He wished them all Good Luck and an early release, and was greeted with loud applause. During his talk to the men S/Ldr. Hardie used all his old mannerisms – the catch and pathos in his voice, and his deep sympathy with the plight of the men. Unfortunately, I have heard him describe these same men, so many times, as "an undisciplined rabble", "useless lot of bastards" etc. etc., that the effectiveness of his speech was rather lost on me. The men, however, who have very short memories, and in the main are, I have found, pretty good chaps, liked it, so everything in the garden was lovely. I found afterwards that the 2 Docs and the Padre had also derived a considerable amount of amusement from it. Tea at tiffin today smelt very strongly of latrine excreta, so I ditched it. It was found out later that the new latrine disposal pits in the NW corner of the camp have seeped through to our drinking water well about 25 yds. away. I am told that the responsible officers were warned of this by P.O. Smith. This now puts our best well out of action.

Wednesday 9 June: Spent morning doing this diary from my rough notes. Was inoculated against T.A.B. at 1.30 p.m. The vaccine was supplied by the Japs in a bottle covered with Japanese characters; the Doc *thinks it is* T.A.B., but is not quite certain! The hut this afternoon presented its usual appearance – most officers stretched out on their beds either asleep, or reading tattered books; Coleman, Bazell, Hobbs and Wallis playing bridge; Burgess eating a banana and looking vacant; Paterson reading, with his pipe and his usual paternal expression! Mac (Intosh) in the next bed to mine, is interrupting my diarising efforts by tales of his previous service in the ranks. Gordon gave another talk tonight on "Book production and book-binding", and as usual, seemed very well-versed in his subject. Talk on this, of course, set me wondering about how my old folks were getting on at home. (My father was also in the printing and bookbinding business.)

Thursday, June 10th: On 'drome today for the first time for over a week. Sky overcast all day, fortunately, but as the breeze dropped after tiffin, the afternoon was very sultry. Had as my Senior NCO "Q" Willis (a W/O.2 in the RAOC). He is an engineer, only about 5'4" tall, and has no control whatever over the men. Sgt. Hall was also on my No. 1 Line – for an Ex-Cpl. of the

2/D.L.I's he is also very dis appointing from the disciplinary point of view. In the evening our North Country society met and I gave them a talk on Malaya and Singapore about ½ on the country and its people, and ½ on the Malayan campaign. Quite a crowd collected and they all seemed interested, especially in the Campaign part of the talk, about which quite a number of questions were asked. The talk lasted 1½ hours – questions 20 minutes. Afterwards the Doc said a few words about Hardie's departure, including how well he had looked after our interests, the pertinacity with which he had tackled the Japs, and would not take no for an answer, and he was quite sure we owed the present condition we were in to S/Ldr. Hardie! I found it difficult to keep my face straight but, with the men, I applauded politely!! Doc, Padre and myself walked up and down the parade ground until 10.45 p.m. in the strong light of a half-moon, talking over experiences and reminiscing. There were also quite a number of the sleepless from the hospital walking around, talking and most of them scratching themselves, poor devils.

Friday, June 11th: Made further progress with my Spanish lesson today, and am still finding it a most absorbing study. We met round the log circle again tonight for the Padre's question hour. I arrived early and got mixed up in a choir practice, much to my amusement. The discussion followed closely the lines of last week, i.e. on sex, inaugurated by Doc Daniels, and proved quite as provocative. The Padre held his own very well, and drew on his own marital experiences to support his points. Afterwards, Padre and I compared notes on English periodicals. He maintained that the "Listener" is one of the best informed, and has taken it since its introduction; binding cases are available from the publishers every 6 months. Batch of letters and cards for Mac, Bazell.

Saturday, June 12th: Our weekly concert was held on a specially constructed stage in the workshop tonight. P/O. Linge had made 4 'shields' at each corner, each of which cont'd a small oil lamp. I did not attend, but heard most of it as Stan (Cressey) and I had our moonlit constitutional on the path between the main gates and the cookhouse. Tonight, Hardie not being present, the concert closed with "God Save the King".

Sunday, June 13th: Holy Communion after Roll Call, and a Spanish lesson from Bell at 1300 hrs; apparently my progress is satisfactory. Evening Service at 19.30 hrs. when Padre preached a very good sermon.

Monday, June 14th: 'Drome today – extremely hot after the very heavy rain which we had during the night; this latter, incidentally, drenched Larder and Mason who now sleep in hammocks slung under the hut. They were unfortunately on the windward side last night. In spite of this the enthusiasm of both has not abated a bit for their hammocks. Old Grey-Jones favourite remark re one of his colleagues is "To think that stupid bastard was a Battery Captain – Jesus!" Sgt. Littlewood supplied me with tea in both the a.m. and p.m. sessions, which was v. acceptable, even tho' it seemed to ooze out almost immediately. Paterson and I talked for some time about prospects of compensation for kit lost in the campaign, and plans for re-kitting. He is in a better position than myself, as most of his civilian clothes are intact at home, whilst I have now absolutely nothing, either service or civilian. He tells me he is now preparing a list of stuff he will need on release; this seems rather premature to me. I do feel, however, that when the opportunity does eventually arrive, I shall be much more discriminating in my buying them had this experience not come my way. A lot, of course, will depend on the value of money after the war. I doubt whether cost of living will ever go back to pre-1939 levels. S/Sgt. Ackland, R.A., spoke to TOC H tonight on Big Game Fishing in the West Indies, where he was stationed for 4-5 years (at Port Royal). Most of his fishing was for sharks, which they did with home-made equipment consisting of a hook made from a broken ramrod and a reel, on the shore. They were also very fortunate in catching a barracuda, a quick-moving fish about the size of a 13 lb. salmon. Afterwards discussed Far Eastern and Empire politics with Doc Blackledge, with Vernon Smith as an interested listener. Told them something of the antiquated systems of government in operation in the Malay States and Straits Settlements, and as an outcome of the conversation we decided to start a weekly discussion group on "The Br. Empire and the Post-War World" by which we hope to stimulate interest in imperial problems.

Tuesday June 15th: Yesterday Nagai lent a portable HMV gramaphone and about 30 records for use in the hospital wards, for 3 days. Inside the portable was an inscription: "Presented to Captain Nagai by Dr. MacArthur, Jesselton, Jany 10th 2603". Most of the records were classical or light operatic: "Lilac Time", "Oransay, Awake, Beloved", "Hunters Chorus from Der Freischutz" and "Die Fledermaus", "Jerusalem" and a selection of Oxford Group songs (e.g. Drums of Peace). Visited No. 1 Ward and sat with the men for about an hour whilst they (the records) were being played. It was good to see the obvious enjoyment which the men got out of them. This evening the Book Club met on the stage at the end of the Workshop, and the Padre read a paper on "The Child in Literature and Actual Life". He thought that the period of realism in the portrayal of children in fiction began with Wordsworth's "Recollections of Early Childhood", selected extracts from which he read. He then traced the development of children in literature through Lewis Carroll, A.A. Milne, Ethel Manning and others, including the biography of Sir Edmund Goss (the literary critic) who was brought up by a Plymouth Brethren father. Extracts from "Gone with the Wind" by Margaret Mitchell, were also read.

Wednesday, June 16th: Padre today fixed Doc Blackledge and self up for a serious of either weekly or fortnightly talks entitled: "The Br. Empire and Post-War problems". LAC Gordon started a new series of art talks tonight on the "History of Art", which he is taking from earliest times. He began with the prehistoric cave paintings of Spain (Burgoa) and S. France, thence to Egyptian, Sumerian, Babylonian, Assyrian and Chaldean art, during which he spoke of the excavations of Sir Leonard Woolley at Ur of the Chaldeans. After going very thoroughly into the art of the Greeks and its devotion to the human form, he concluded by describing Roman art as a copy of that of the Greeks. The 3 phases of Greek art were Doric, Ionian and Corinthian.

Thursday, June 17th: 'Drome today with No. 2 Party. Day very hot and little cloud in sky, spent most of my time walking up and down the lines – Larder, as usual, occupied himself in helping Paterson with the fritters in the Canteen, and generally being genial with the Jap guards. We were to have had Hardie's farewell talk to the North-Country Society tonight, but as he was ill, Padre deputised and spoke on his visit to the Island of Skye, home of the MacLeods (Dunvegan Castle) and I acted as Chairman. Afterwards had 2 hour chat with Private Metcalfe of the A & S Highlanders; he comes from Gilesgate, Durham City, and as he was a keen supporter of the City Rugger Club, we found that we both knew many of the same people – Vern Ferons, Pitt, Blagdon etc. He told me he joined the A.S.& H. in 1937 and went out to India with them in the same year. About April or May 1939 they were transferred to Singapore. During the Campaign, they first went into action at Baling then Telok Ansor, but about general details he is rather hazy. I must investigate exactly how he got out of Singapore when the Battalion was taken prisoner in that town. He knew, of course, both Moss and Pace when they were with the battn.

Friday June 18th: Was booked for a talk in the top hospital tomorrow night (Sat.) by Cpl. Tyrrell, one of our Australian Nursing Orderlies, who told me that the patients, not being able to go to the concert, liked to have something to listen to. This evening Padre held his usual "Question Hour". Instead of speaking himself, he had asked A.C. Pearce and LAC Wallace**, two young professed agnostics, to give a statement of their beliefs and answer any questions. Whilst subscribing to Christian ethics, they said they could not accept the Church's doctrines. Wallace got rather tied up in what he did or did not believe, but Pearce was more honest in professing himself as communist. On the practical side of their beliefs they were rather hazy. [** Wallace was a personable and intelligent man, whose father, Lt.Col., won the D.S.O. and M.C. in WW.I. After the War, I went to see his parents in Berkshire and I saw Mrs. Wallace who told me her husband was still too upset about his son's death, to see me or talk about it.]

90

Air Photo of Sandakan Prisoner of War Camp May 1945.　　　　　*Pic: RAAF Air Photo.*

Saturday June 19th: Had a smoke-hole talk with Doc Daniels on last night's meeting. He maintained that, to a Christian, one need not subscribe to *all* the creeds and doctrines of the Church. He instanced the Virgin Birth and the Resurrection – I agreed with the former, but I do think that acceptance of the latter is necessary for a Christian "else, wherefore born?" Gave a talk to the top hospital on Malaya and the Malayan Campaign, which seemed to interest them.

Sunday June 20th: Short parade service this morning, which lasted 10 minutes. The Padre hits back! Usual Sunday today; service at 7.30 p.m. Hardie gave his delayed talk on Ceylon tonight, after Church, to the Geordie Society, and was most interesting.

Monday June 21st: Today we were told that, as from now, we would not work on the 'drome again. 3 'Crows Nests' were brought over from the 'drome and resited on the cleared area behind our camp. We were then marched round to this area and given our new job – cutting down rubber trees and removing tree stumps. "A change being as good as a rest", the men seemed to enjoy the new work today, but I don't think it will last long. Sgt. Littlewood gave a talk to TOC H tonight on "Observing with the R.A.F." He was posted to 202 Squadron at Gibraltar after finishing his training in 1941. On his first trip they had to pick up a convoy of 36 ships which were approaching Gib. at 6 knots. When they reached them, only 23 were left, and eventually only 3 arrived! They usually patrolled on the increasing square system; they were armed with Catalinas, having relieved a Squadron of Londons. When they were posted to Singapore in the middle of Dec. 1941, to reinforce 205 Squadron, their place was taken by a Squadron of Australian Sunderlands. They flew out via Cairo, Aboukir (where 230 Squadron were still stationed), Basra, Karachi, Colombo – Singapore, where they arrived on New Year's Eve. He was taken ill shortly afterwards and did no operational flying in S'pore. He did some, however, from Gosthaven, sighting a couple of convoys off the Anambas (or Natunas) in the S. China Sea: they proved to be Japs – they proved this by flying down to mast height and were promptly fired at. They dropped the A.S. bombs they were carrying, on them, and cleared off as they anticipated the arrival of fighter aircraft, as no naval escort was in sight. Littlewood also told us about the sinking of the "Ark Royal". The pilot of a Blenheim passing thru' Gib. from Malta en route for Britain casually passed a remark whilst having lunch that he had seen 2 subs in the vicinity of the Rock. Flying boats were immediately sent out but by that time the 'Ark' had been torpedoed. They were sent out from Gib. and succeeded in finding her within sight of the Rock when, however, the Captain decided that he would like to make the Gib under its own steam. He ordered the engines started and the ship promptly sank.

Tuesday 22 June: Hardie asked me into his room tonight in a very friendly manner, and on my arrival explained that it was in connection with the Summary of

Evidence (NB: Taken at Jesselton by P/O MacIntosh in connection with the Court Martial charge laid against me of "refusing to obey a lawful order to have lunch with Major Suga and officers of the Imperial Japanese Army"!) that he wished to see me. He was at pains to explain that it was a very bad summary, and that under normal circumstances MacIntosh would have been told to make out a new one, but as paper was short at Jesselton at that time etc. etc. He went on that "I had not confined myself to a mere statement of events, as one should in a summary, i.e. in my case, that I had received an order, but on grounds of principle I could not obey it, but I had stated things which should have been reserved for my defence. Accordingly, instead of himself only writing a brief 1/2 foolscap page report on the case, he had been obliged to write 3 full pages of explanation (? exact word). In the circumstances he had talked the matter over with Jones (F/Lt., his "Adjutant"), "although naturally he had nothing to do with it", and had decided that, if I was agreeable he would order the old summary scrapped and the taking of a new one on the lines he had suggested. He explained that if I wished the old summary to stand, he thought that it would prejudice my case, not that it will come to anything in any case. I said I would consider the matter and let him know later. Talked over the position with Doc Daniels and the Padre, and they both thought, like myself, that it was a confession of weakness.

Wednesday 23 June: Told Hardie tonight that I wished the Summary to stand in its original state. I added that I should like a copy of it as soon as possible, as he was due to leave us at any moment for the Senior Officers Camp at Kuching; he promised to get a copy made for me at once. In view of the fact of his imminent departure and possible separation on release, I asked him whether he intended to give F/Lt. Jones a copy of his remarks on the Summary which could be handed to the Air Officer Commanding of the first Group to which we would be posted. The reply was: "No, I shall forward them to the first A.O.C. or A.O.A. I come into contact with". Relations throughout the exchange were perfectly cordial!!

Thursday June 24th: Held our first and introductory Post-War Discussion Group tonight, about 80 turning up, which we consider very satisfactory. Doc Blackledge made a 10-minute introductory speech in which he explained how the idea of the series had arisen, through a discussion between our two selves on the future of the British Colonial Empire. I followed with an outline lasting about ¾ hour on some of the problems which we hoped to discuss in future: demobilisation, absorption of discharged men into industry, possible continuance of high taxation and rationing as a means of combating an orgy of inflationary spending, continuance of conscription, and new parliamentary methods or systems to replace the present cumbersome procedures. Our national ability to support a colossal burden of war debt, especially after the sale of overseas investments and the consequential virtual disappearance of invisible exports as a stabilising budgetary factor, the probable necessity of a lower standard of living and a harder standard of work. I also touched briefly on the concentration of gold in the United States, the possible establishment of an International Bank and currency, leading up to European Federation, or federation with the United States. From this rather sweeping survey a hot argument was started which was only ended by the 'Last Post'. In view of the interest aroused I was billed to give another talk next fortnight.

Sunday 27 June: Today, a group of about 25 excited British officers put on their best khaki drill, polished their boots and Sam Brownes' and looked anxiously at their puttees. "Do I look all right, old man?" "Do you think there'll be much to eat?" "I hear that old Nagai is producing some cherry brandy. Anyhow there's sure to be sake". The occasion – the Japanese Camp Commandant had invited the officers from this Camp to his "Canteen" known as Hakko Yen – adding, of course, that they would have to pay for the eats themselves!

They duly turned out at 8.45 a.m., 25 in all, headed by S/Ldr. Hardie and Capt. Mills, and including the Padre and the 2 Doctors, and were marched off down the road like a crowd of school-kids going off on a Sunday School out-ing. They returned about 1 p.m. They had been taken to a 2-storied wooden building near the main Jap Guard Room, and shown upstairs to a room which had been decorated with paper streamers – more Sunday School stuff – and with a long trestle table on which were bananas, pineapples, doughnuts, and toffee, coffee etc. No Jap turned up so they all moved in, being served by a native. When they had had enough, they were told that the charge was 75 cts. each, and marched back. Prior to going in they had had to do a mass salute for a Jap 2/Lieut. who came out specially for the purpose. I naturally did not attend. I wonder if these people ever had any pride of race: if they are typical of the 20th Century Britisher, then God help us.

Thursday 1 July: Again a new month – I wonder what this one will bring forth!

Friday 2 July: Gave my talk on "Malaya and the Malayan Campaign", for the 7th or 8th time, to the skin ward of the hospital tonight! Again, they all seemed very interested.

Saturday 3 July: Main event today was the concert in the evening, which for the first time was entirely produced and acted by the officers. The new stage which had been put up at the open end of the workshop by 'Dean' Linge and his men has been christened 'Dean's Theatre'. It is well lit with about 15 coconut oil lamps, some of which form the footlights, others being suspended on a board just above the front of the stage, and four being in the wing. Mac and Ken Hammond appeared in the first scene, gorgeous in blue and khaki service dress, with Thready, well made up as a rather buxom wench, to supply the female interest: 'she' was loudly applauded by the men! The "In Town Tonight" of our Jesselton days was repeated in the programme as "Inspector Hornblower Investigates", and went down very well. The only snag, it seemed to me, was that Alan Bazell's puzzle corner lasted too long, 40 mins. instead of 20, and this rather spoilt the balance of the show. But I think that on the whole everybody enjoyed the change.

Sunday 4 July: Parade service this morning which lasted about ten minutes, ending with the National Anthem. To me, these services seem rather a mockery, consisting as they do of a few perfunctory prayers and The King. Better that they should be cut out altogether.

Monday 5 July: 'Drome today, but in spite of this, managed to finish the News Summary which I read over first to the senior NCOs after dinner, and then to the officers at the smoke-hole – as it started to rain I finished it off in the hut. The rain having sent all the men into their huts, I took the opportunity of getting the Japanese news across and finished these before Last Post. I had to read by the flickering lights of improvised oil lamps (standing on tin mugs!) with a very attentive audience grouped around, sitting and lying on the bed boards, and standing in the gangway, an average of about 70 in each hut.

Skips used on aerodrome constructions   *Pic: R. Battram*

95

Tuesday 6 July: Missed the poetry reading which Padre had arranged for tonight, (with Blackledge, LAC Gordon, Gnr. Russell, A.C. Pearce and Lt. Bell), as I had to continue the reading of news summaries extracted from "Nippon Times", to the remaining huts. Started to rain about 8.30 p.m. and rapidly became a downpour. Again, the "gen" seemed to interest the men, and I had to spend some time in each hut in discussions.

Wednesday 7 July: Today, we moved house; as our hut, the hospital hut opposite, and the Admin. Bldg. are required for re-erection at new location, thought to be near the Jap Main Office which is fairly close to the Aussie Camp. We moved after tiffin, those without beds and the sick, going upstairs into a por-tioned quarter of the Sergeants Mess, those *with* beds, including myself, going below. Main drawbacks are the earth floor, the wide spacing of the floor-boards above, which results in our being showered in dust every time someone starts sweeping upstairs. Still, we are used to these somewhat primi-tive conditions by now! I now have Yates on one side of me, and Jacko (Jackson) on the other, Grey-Jones being upstairs. Between us we managed to put up a shelf and rig up some floor-boards – little things which make life liveable nowadays! A really terrific storm blew up about 8 p.m. which, by 9 p.m., seemed to be almost directly overhead. I have seen some vivid electrical storms during my short 4 years in the Far East, but never has one been so vivid or seemingly so close. By 10 p.m. a semi-gale had arisen which threat-ened to blow away our mosquito nets – so much so that I had to anchor mine at the four corners of my bed for the first time. The officers on the other side of the hut had by this time about three inches of standing water under their beds. So much for the first night in our new slums! Finished reading of news to Hut 6 tonight.

Thursday July 8th: The 2nd meeting of our Post-War Discussion Group was held tonight. 70 men attended, about 10% of the Camp, proving that this meeting is by far the most popular of those held on week-nights, concerts excluded, of course, which is very gratifying. Bill Wallis gave a 'continuation' talk on "The Conduct and Finance of International Trade", which obviously the audi-ence found of absorbing interest. Unfortunately, he was unable to finish on account of the time, and questions were cut short by rain. Most of the 3 build-ings (huts) were taken down today.

Friday July 9th: Tonight F/S Warner gave a talk to us at the officers' smoke-hole, on his experiences with the F.A.A. (Fleet Air Arm) with which he spent a total of about 7 years. He was lucky enough to be on the "Courageous"(?) when that ship accompanied the Prince of Wales on his South-American trip. From his accounts, they were given exceptionally warm welcomes at Buenos Aires, Montevideo, Bahia Blanca, Rio de Janeiro etc., and did some good work propagating the efficiency of British aircraft – notably the Osprey which was our latest at that time. 'Drome today.

Saturday July 10th: The Concert tonight was given by the ORs Concert Party who named themselves for tonight "The Tapioca Coons" – a nigger minstrel troop. The show was compered by Sgt. Walker in the role of an officer of the "Old South". Although it was a good attempt at a new and "continuous" programme, it somehow lacked punch. Still, quite enjoyable.

Sunday July 11th: Today our Camp Basketball League was inaugurated. There are 10 teams ranging from the "Teetotalers" (Officers), "The Rebels" (Nursing Orderlies) and "The Craps" (Admin. Staff). Matches started at 1.30 p.m. and continued until about 4.30 p.m. The idea is sound, but I feel that the men should conserve their remaining strength as much as possible. Our present food, although certainly better than that at Jesselton, is hardly sufficient to support 'drome work, easy as it is, and *violent* exercise as well. Doc Daniels tells me that he himself is not sure of what the effects might be, but is going to give it a trial. Many men complained of the hardness of the ground (parade ground clay) – no sand being available. Usual Sunday evening service after rollcall parade and coffee.

Monday July 12: A.C. Sands knocked unconscious on Working Party by a blow to the head from a Jap guard armed with a stick. Gordon gave the last of his talks on the history of Painting tonight. As usual, it was lucid and interesting, and covered the period from Constable, at the turn of the 18th/19th Centuries, through the pre-Raphaelites to the Impressionists and Surrealists. His next series will deal with hand crafts, pottery, weaving etc.

Tuesday July 13: 'Drome today. Very hot but otherwise uneventful. Men seem to take a delight nowadays in building huge pyres of tree trunks and brushwood which, when lit, send up flames some 30'-40' high. Work is still very easy and progress very very slow. After watching some of the men I don't think I would care to employ many of them after the war, as quite a number seem to have lost all powers of concentration! Eric Foulkes gave a talk to the Book Club tonight on "Beyond the Blue Sierras", a tale of the Spanish colonization of California and San Francisco in the late 18th Century. Foulkes has a very stilted delivery and either the book itself must have been very dull or else his interpretation of it was at fault. Anyhow, I almost went to sleep over it!

Wednesday July 14: Waxed irate this morning over some water which the NCO above us threw out of his window and splashed my bed! This, on top of the razor blade and dust-sweeping incidents was rather too much. So I asked Jones to speak to W/O Hynes and either (1) have an order issued re general consideration for others or (2) tell Hynes to give the NCOs a very straight talk. Spent morning writing up this diary, a spot of Spanish revision, and a sleep in the afternoon.

97

Saturday July 17th: Spent some time with Ken Whitworth's atlas this evening, tracing the probable course of the War from the "Japan Times". If we have now got the whole of North Africa, then Sicily or Italy would seem to be the next natural objectives. There also would appear to be something blowing up on the Burma Front. 'Drome today with a new Jap guard Commander who seems a poor type. He speaks neither English nor Malay, and as usual with this type, has an inferiority complex and is rather truculent. Most of the difficulties are, however, caused by language problems, as for example this morning when 5 NCOs were told to clear a certain area of ground, they didn't understand but gave the usual OK! Consequently, when the G.C. found that his instructions were not being carried out, he lined them up and struck them in the face with his clenched fist, knocking 2 down. An airman was also caught smoking at work and consequently our rest periods were delayed for ½ hour. The afternoon was quiet. About 10 parties were engaged on digging out rubber trees due south of the cleared area – all in an area about 25 yards long and 10 yds. wide! I forecast quite a number of accidents in the near future. In the evening the officers gave their second show. The scene was laid in a supposed night club, "The Pineapple Slice", which an ex-officer POW had established in London. RSM Jacobi was 'Joe' the bartender, Jackson was 'Flash', the waiter – and incidentally the success of the evening. A new female in the form of "Susie West" (Lt. Chopping) was introduced, in addition to "Pat" (Lt. Threadgold) and went down very well. Capt. Bickerton and Doc Blackledge did a very popular duet about work on the 'drome. Bill Wallis acted as compere and Pethybridge sang Sterndale Bennet's "Leanin" and the Drinking Song – unfortunately they were under-rehearsed and the accompaniment was very bad. But that did not effect the high standard of the show which was very well received.

Sunday July 18th: Usual Sunday. Another group of 25 hungry officers went off to a Sunday morning treat or Hakko Yen, I am told that the translation is "Friendship Garden"!!

Monday July 19th: No work on 'drome today as the Jap guards are having a day out in Sandakan. A talk was to have been given tonight to TOC H on "The Dartmoor Mutiny" by one who was in it, actually a Gunner, but as an electrical storm blew up about 8 p.m., it was postponed to next week. The storm continued until about 10.30 p.m., when rain began to fall, altho' not very hard.

Tuesday July 20th: LAC Gordon gave a talk on "Industry and Art" tonight. He traced the utilitarian side of art, and stressed that in its archaic forms, art is always ahead of the life of the times. He gave examples of the conservatism of industrial organisations forwards designing art – Wills Ltd. would only allow their "Gold Flake" packets to be re-designed over a period of years, so as not to upset their sales. He held strong views on the modern tendency to copy period designs in house building, furniture etc. and considered that we should aim at making the most of the materials with which modern science has provided us. He instanced as a good example of modern designing a firm of Swedish metal smiths who produce an entirely new conception of table silverware, i.e. table knives with a short cutting blade and a long handle, properly balanced soup spoons etc. The new profession of art designing for industry is, he stated, producing an entirely new class of artist, more a business or professional man than a cultural type.

Wednesday July 21st: Spent most of the day writing up this diary. Padre has promised me "Oliver Wiswill" which I have been looking forward to for some time. Our tiffin-time extras nowadays consist of fried Bindjaws (? brindjalls), cucumbers, spring onions and very occasionally hen eggs!! Tonight Padre arranged a "Brains Trust" with Capt. Bickerton as Chairman and Sgt. Holder as Compere. Five questions were submitted: (1) On emigration, answered by LAC Sheriff very fully in respect of New Zealand (2) On the detection of hereditary traits in children before adoption, answered by Doc Blackledge. (3) On a man being posted "Missing, believed Killed" and whether his wife would be able to marry again immediately? Lt. Chopping answered this in his usual disjointed way, but still quite a satisfactory answer. (4) Define a gentleman, answered in a very amusing way by the Padre, with a footnote by Chops. (5) Define Art, which LAC Gordon did, very effectively, in about 10 minutes. The whole show lasted about an hour, and seemed to both interest and amuse the men, who voted for it to be a monthly function.

Thursday July 22nd: Officer in charge 'drome again today. In the morning it was very cool, and a slight drizzle fell until about 10 o'clock. We were delayed until 2.30 p.m. for the afternoon "Fall-in" as the Japanese guards had had no tiffin! When we did eventually get out, the main event was the moving of a "crows-nest" to the top of the hill, which caused quite a lot of expletives amongst the men! Our third meeting for the Post-War Discussion Group tonight, when our speaker was LAC Sherriff on the politics-economic aspects of agriculture after the war. His main thesis was that agriculture had in the past suffered through the vested industrial interests and exporters, who wished to maintain the policy of cheap food in order to maintain their markets. He hoped there would be a wholesale migration of the industrial populate ion to the Dominions in order to bolster up their new industries, and leave the U.K. in the position of more or less self-sufficient agricultural country. We had a very interesting discussion amongst the 70-odd people attending – and managed to draw attention to the strategic aspects of the questions. Doc Blackledge was Chairman tonight. LAC Wallace made a nuisance of himself by persistent questioning and refusing to be convinced – I think he is passing through the young man's phase of believing that cynicism is modern and "clever"!

Friday 23 July: Tonight, attended the Padre's discussion group and found that he is now dealing with Old Testament history, which he presented in quite an interesting fashion.

Saturday 24 July: The ORs produced "Snowdrift and the Seven?" an exceptionally good burlesque. [PL Note: ? normally indicates I can't decipher the word in my diary – all written in now faded pencil in a very small mode – to get the most out of the precious paper. ? can also indicate that I was unaware of a fellow POW's name, and didn't follow-up the omission.]

Sunday 25 July: First of all notified that a Church Parade would be held at 8.30 a.m. but when the Japanese asked for the "Hakko Yin" officers to parade at 8.15 a.m., then the Church Parade was cancelled. 19 officers went to the Japanese party and returned at 12.45 p.m. The usual Sunday evening service was held after roll-call. I find the services very pleasant; the evenings are cool, we usually have as our back-cloth the flaming splendour of a tropical sunset, for our roof the rustling green of 3 solitary rubber-trees and the star-spangled expanse of the sky. Here then, in this prison camp, one can find half an hour of peace and reflection.

Monday 26 July: On 'drome today with Jones as Officer in charge. Some excitement in the morning. The guards suddenly loaded their rifles and ran into the wood, some of them asking me if I had seen a Chinese. They then went on, and seeing Cpl. Guerin and another airman working on a tree slapped their faces for speaking to this mythical Chinese! They seemed not a bit surprised when both of them explained that they hadn't even seen a Chinaman on the workings. After the tiffin interval they did, however, catch a Chinese and presumably his small son, a lad of about 6, in the wood. The man had a British Army-pattern haversack with him, which contained a K.D. shirt. He was then seized by one of the guards, who threw him over his shoulder a couple of times; at this the small boy ran screaming through the wood in the direction of the small kampong behind it. The Chinese was marched to the cleared ground and given a terrific beating-up. Again, he was flung over a guard's shoulder several times, had his hands tied behind his back, was flung to the ground again, and was kicked in the back, stomach and face with the hobnailed boots of the guards. Afterwards he was marched off to the Guard Room, presumably for another exhibition of sadism and followed by the "Basher" carrying an axe – a typical bit of exhibitionist "terrorism" which impressed neither ourselves nor the poker-faced Chinese. Previously one of the new guards had distributed over 120 cigarettes to our men, and yet he gave one of the worst exhibitions of brutality on the unfortunate Chinese.

The wood is beginning to show the effects of our mens' work, and in a week or so's time, we should be through to the clearing on the other side.

Tuesday 27 July: On going out of the gate this morning, Lieut. Threadgold was stopped by the guard known to us as "Sexy", for not saluting. The guard ordered a British soldier to strike his officer in the face for this. 'Thready' gave the man permission to do so, but as the weakness of the slap did not please the Japanese, he struck Threadgold himself. If this is allowed to continue, it is difficult to see how the Japanese can expect us to maintain discipline in the Camp. Our own people (Hardie!) are so supine, however, that I doubt whether any protest will be made.

About 10 a.m. those remaining in the Camp were fallen in on the Parade ground. A body of guards with Lt. Hoshijima and the small interpreter (Osawa) arrived shortly afterwards, and it was explained to us that a search was about to begin of our kits. The search took two and a half hours and was very thorough. Some pens, ink and paper were taken. Some were left. I lost "China struggles for Unity" which I had lent to 'Wag' Price, but the interpreter explained apologetically that it would be returned in a week's time.

The ground around the Camp, the Cook-house, and even our new garden were prodded and gone over. The Working Party was searched before they were allowed into the Camp. The Japanese Camp Commandant classed the search as satisfactory and retired with his guards. It is understood that the Aussie Camps have already been done. LAC Gordon continued his "Art in Modern Industry" talks tonight. Managed to go over the "Nippon Times Weekly', 3 copies of which have arrived – without the newspapers, however. There is no news whatever in them about Russia, Middle East, India, Burma and very little about China or the S.W. Pacific. The numbers end at May 13th. There is one special "Co-Prosperity Sphere Special Number"; all of them go over

Sketch: Captain Hoshijima Susumu.
Clem Seale.

101

the fall of Malaya, the N.E.I. and Corregidor again, and are mainly filled with the history and current process of rehabilitation work in the "Southern Regions".

There was chaos in the Australian camp at this time – a Japanese spy had fallen out with local people friendly to the Australians and reported the fact the Australians possessed a wireless in the Camp.

Names were mentioned and Hoshijima decided to search the camp and during this search he found Lieut. Wells' diary. Hoshijima confronted Wells, who was in charge of the Wood Party; he told him he had found his diary during the search and claimed Wells had written in the diary that there was a radio set in the camp. Later, when Hoshijima was interrogated he said: "In the beginning of the Sandakan incident I found Lieut. Wells' diary. In it it said there was a radio set in the Compound so after the wood cutting party had finished their work I lined them up and took Lieut. Wells to a spot about 30 metres from the wood cutting party and I accused him through an interpreter of having a wireless set in the Compound. He denied this, so I repeated the question and asked whether he was absolutely sure of this and he said there definitely was not a wireless set; then I told him that if he was lying I would hit him and he answered: "That will be alright". At the time I had Wells' diary in my pocket, I took it out with my left hand and showed it to Wells and with my right hand I hit him. I only hit him once. I did not hit him repeatedly or tried to strangle him."

What happened after that Hoshijima was asked, and he answered: "I told him to take me to the spot where the radio was. He took me into the Carpentering Room and we looked for the set in this room and could not find it. After this he took me into the office. This was the Technical Section of the office of the POWs and Wells opened a hidden compartment under the desk and even then there was not a radio set.

"After further investigation two Captains told me the following: On the previous night they saw Captain Matthews coming back from the latrines with a shovel. This was about 11 o'clock at night."

Next morning the officers were ordered to the latrine area and told to start digging and prodding for the radio; eventually it was located and, according to former officers, the senior Captains went into a conference and decided it would be best to tell Hoshijima the wireless was found. In the interests of the whole camp it was probably the best course to take.

The wireless was the principal exhibit at the trial of Captain Matthews at Kuching in March 1944.

Wednesday July 28th: Working Party cancelled today. Permission refused for entertainment (Spelling Bee) tonight.

Thursday July 29th: No Working Party again today. Plenty of speculation! Started "Seven Red Sundays" by Ramon Sender today.

A difficult but enlightening book. Doc Daniels gave our North-Country Society a talk on "Shooting, Fishing and Poaching in Northumberland", which carried me back to days spent at Weldon Bridge (Northumberland) with Dora and Bill. [PL: My sister and brother-in-law, both very keen on river fishing (trout and salmon)]. His tales of duck and goose shooting on Holy Island and the Fames took our minds off present circumstances very success-fully for over an hour.

Friday July 30th: Very large fires were started just over the hill to the west of our camp about 1 p.m. today. They were obviously burning trees as quite a lot of burnt leaves etc. drifted over. The pall of smoke particles obscured the sun for about 12 hours. This, with again no Work Party, caused our rumour-mongers to get active again. Gave my talk on Malaya to No. 2 Hut tonight to approxi-mately 100 – as usual, it seemed to cause a lot of interest.

Saturday July 31st: No Work Party. Managed to obtain "Dodsworth" by Sinclair Lewis at long last! Officers' Concert Party gave "Borneo Assignment" tonight, with Doc Blackledge and Bick(erton) as "Banyak and Bagoes", Grock(?) and Bazell as Chaprewoman (Charwoman) and Son, and a song quartet consisting of Price, Pethy(bridge), Burgess and Bell. The show was well received and enjoyed. As usual, helped Tom Elliott back to the hospital with his stool. He seems to be getting a little thinner in the body, and rather haggard-looking, poor chap – he has had a bad time of it, and his voice shows no sign of returning to normal. Dicky Caruth is much as usual; Tom tells me he is getting rather childish nowadays and is trying to remember the nursery rhymes of his childhood. He woke Tom up at 3 a.m. the other morning and said that had he made the Army his career as was originally intended, and had he had the luck he had had in planting**, he would have been a General in this war!! Tom's comments can be imagined! Dicky is still very keen on a political career when he gets back, as he considers he has the necessary quali-fications, i.e. he knows nothing whatsoever about politics, but has quite a number of relatives and others who can "pull the strings." [** He was, in peace time, an "Estate Agent" in Malaya, i.e. he supervised a number of rub-ber estates in his particular Malang State. He eventually died in Kuching

Camp Hospital only about 2-3 months before liberation. He was a man of great charm and traditional manners, but a bit 'vague'. In modern parlance, he was showing signs of the onset of Alzheimers Disease.]

Sunday August 1st: Church parade at 8.45 a.m. – usual farce. All sorts of conjectures being voiced on the present "holiday" from working parties. Some of the are (1) the Japanese have been warned against employing Allied POWs on military objectives on pain of reprisals against Japanese internees (2) Peace negotiations are proceeding (3) Some of the Japanese guards have been moved and there are not now sufficient to go round! (4) Some priority work is in progress which necessitates extra guards. One takes one's pick! Incidentally, the Aussies have not been working on the 'drome during the past few days, but do seem to have been engaged in their garden or a road. Service tonight, Bird reading the lesson.

Monday August 2nd: No Working Party – more rumours. Finished "Dodsworth" today, and found it, up-to-date, the most engrossing of Sinclair Lewis' works.

All our tools were removed from the guard room today. A very vivid sunset followed by an electrical storm and rain drove our talk from the smoke-hole to our rabbit warren tonight. Gunner Maguire gave us his experiences as a convict in Dartmoor Prison during the mutiny of November 1931. He was sentenced to 3 years penal servitude at Liverpool for a crime of which he gave us no details, but which I believe was robbery and car theft – the length of the sentence for a first offender suggests with violence. He gave us details of 16 ozs. bread per day, porridge and plum duff etc. Very similar to British F(ield) S(ervice) Rations. He did 18 months in the quarries, where each man had to obtain 6 marks for good work, otherwise 1 days remission was stopped. Hours were 0630 Reveille, 0730 Breakfast, 0800 Working Parade. Work ceased at 4 p.m. in the Winter and 4.30 p.m. in the Summer. Lights Out at 9.30 p.m. The cells were about 10 x 5' and contained bed, mattress (coir), blankets etc. and washing implements. All this seems strangely familiar after our experiences of the last 18 months!

Tuesday 3rd August: No work party and another rather lazy but not entirely wasted day, as I started Spanish revision once more. Thinking over the things that Paterson told me the other day about events immediately before and after the capitulation in Java, my belief in the necessity for complete remodelling of our armed forces after the War, have been reinforced. Apparently he (Paterson) was in possession of a large amount of public funds in guilders when the capitulation was signed – these were used in past to re-kit Army officers with blankets, clothes, toilet necessities and suitcases etc. which were bought in Garoet, a town in Java, and also to lay in large stocks of tinned chicken, sausage for personal use; the remainder he kept. Each officer was also given 200-300 guilders by the Army paymaster at Headquarters. There was no mention whatsoever of any payout to the men or of any supplies being bought for their benefit. This confirms B.Q.M.S. Salter's story of the officers at Koan School P.O.W. Camp having fried chicken and sausage dinners and plenty of gin, whiskey etc., whilst many of the men were without toothbrushes and other necessities. Paterson also mentioned an R.A.F. officer at Glodok, Batavia, P.O.W. Camp who had had a large sum of public money when he was captured and who did quite a brisk business with the troops by changing their one pound notes at Fl.4 apiece, i.e. 50% discount. The spirit of comradeship, responsibility and esprit-de-corps seems to have been sadly lacking throughout.

LAC Gordon held a Question-Hour tonight instead of his usual talk. As usual, the questions got right off the track, but I did manage to get in one or two questions on Art, Propaganda and Design generally, in industry.

Wednesday 4th August: Again, no work party, but a general cleanup of camp drains, grass verges etc. was decreed by the Japs, who notified Rolfe that in a few days time the Camp would be inspected by Major Suga and another Major from Singapore. Permission for our Question Bee was refused again today. In its place the Padre arranged a scratch talk by LAC Keaney on "Pawnbroking". He worked for a high class pawnbroker's shop in Holborn (London), and they took in pawn anything from Old Masters to Diamond Tiaras and fountain pens, and even, on one occasion, a skeleton from a medical student!! The values of paintings, furs, foreign stamps are estimated by expert advisers from London firms, and a price offered on their valuations. He gave us some very amusing stores of the various types of customers they get, from prostitutes to night-club proprietors, and of the various shady deals which some of them try to put over. His talk was generally voted one of the most interesting we have heard.

Thursday 5th August: Camp working party only. Complaint from Hardie and Linge this morning about the uncooked state of the breakfast rice. Chopping explained this by stating that the Japanese had ordered the fire to be put out last night on account of the high wind and danger of sparks setting fire to the wood. This seemingly satisfied "Sitting Bull"!

Tonight we held our fortnightly Post-War Discussion Group, when Doc Daniels gave a talk on "Medicine and the Post-War State." He favours the complete socialisation of medicine, involving the widening of opportunities to promising youths to take up medical careers (all this was remarkably prescient of the future Welfare State!); the absorption of the medical profession into the Civil Service, the establishment of a regional hospital system with one central and modern hospital for each region, fed by subsidiary hospitals and dispensaries in the towns and cities. Each doctor would be responsible for about 1000 people who would be examined at least once a year. Sterilization of the mentally, and in some cases physically, unfit, euthanasia, abolition of nursing homes and voluntary hospitals were other points which he favoured. This discussion which followed was not quite so brisk as in previous weeks, as the subject had been so well-covered by the Doc and, in any case, most peoples' opinions of post-war medicine seemed to be quite hazy. We had one good contribution from Gnr. Fayles who told us about the postgraduate course at Hammersmith Hospital (London). Friday 6 August: LAC Keaney gave his talk on "Pawnbroking" to the Officers tonight, at their 'smokehole'. Again listened and was again very interested!

Saturday 7th August: The Senior NCOs gave a presentation of "The Ghost Train" tonight, and were, I thought, extremely successful. As they had no script, it was compiled from memory by A.C. Pearce. The costumes, made out of old sarongs etc. by Sgt. Walker, and the sound effects (F/S. Stammers) were up to the usual standard. Capt. Tregarth was played by Sgt. Holder; Mrs. Masky by QMS Rooker (very true to Yorkshire type); Sgt. Bradley, RAF, by S/S. Ackland and F/S Warner, the woman mental patient by Sgt. Cunningham, and "Mabel" and her husband by Sgt. Tugwell and Sgt. Waidson.

Sunday 8th August: Started "Main Street" by Sinclair Lewis. A very beautiful sunset again coloured our evening service with scarlet and gold. If every church could have such a setting!

Monday 9th August: LAC Simpson talked to a good crowd of officers tonight on "Trawling". He served an apprenticeship in the hull trawler fleet before going into the Merchant Service. Amongst his experiences was a trip to the Cape on board the "Herzogin Cecilie", a windjammer, which had a mixed crew of Finnish men and women on board, a trip with Skipper Osborne of "Girl Pat" fame, a voyage to Tierra del Fuego for guano, and the comments of his mother when he and his father returned, "What a bloody smell!" His descriptions of some of the characters he met with in trawling were very amusing, particularly "Shitey" Brown – so called because he was so lucky! Book Club also held tonight under threatening clouds. Bell spoke on Blaize Paschal, the French scientist, mathematician, and theologist:- greatest work his "Pensees", died at 39.

Tuesday 10th August: Decided, at suggestion of Bill Wallis, to have a bi-weekly musical appreciation talk by Sgt. LeClerq, to alternate with LAC Gordon's art talks.

Thursday 12th August: Our North Country Society Question Bee was again rained off.

Friday 13th August: Gave talk on Malaya to Hut 5 and again had an attentive audience.

Saturday 14th August: ORs gave a concert party tonight. "The English Family Juggins", featuring Mabel Constantsorearse! (A play on the name of Mabel Constantoluros, a popular entertainer in pre-war and war years) LAC Gordon took the name part and played it exceptionally well. Gnr. Olding played "Father", and Sgt. Walker "Grandma". An amusing show with good effects made, as usual, by 'Dean' Linge out of wood and attap. The Welsh Choir under Sgt. Thomas also got a warm reception.

Sunday 15th August: Communion after roll-call parade and evening service as usual at 7.30 p.m.

Return to Kuching

Monday 16th August: Informed at 10 a.m. that all officers with the exception of 9 Admin. Staff were to be moved to Kuching immediately. We were to be ready with our kit at 3 p.m. Spent most of morning packing, and most of afternoon saying my goodbyes to the officers remaining, the Senior NCOs and Other Ranks. A number of Sgts. I had missed came and rooted me out to say good-bye – F/S. Bowden and Stammers, Sgts. Freeman, Tugwell, Allsop and Tennant. Also went round the hospitals. Paraded at 3 p.m. for another kit inspection; most of ORs paraded to see us off. Very minute search of kit, ended abruptly by a torrential downpour of rain. Helped with kit by 2 of my Bukit Panjang (No.152 M.U., S'pore) airmen – Elder and Knapper – had said "Cheerio" to others before. Taken down to docks in 2 lorries. As rain still continued, troops waved goodbye to us from the doors of their huts. Stan Cressey was given permission to stay as Hospital Adjutant at the last minute. Officers staying are Mills, Young, Rolfe, Daniels and Blackledge (M.Os Chopping, Padre Wanless, Burgess and Linge.

As Jacko, Mac, Paterson, Foulkes and myself were without overcoats, we were soaked to the skin on arrival at the docks, so changed from my wrecked suitcase. After a meal, we dumped our kit in a rat-infested godown and then watched a baseball match between 2 Japanese teams. Embarked on a small steamer of about 400 tons, formerly belonging to the Sandakan S.S.Co., at about 3 a.m. and sailed at about 3.30 a.m.

Tuesday August 17th: Very choppy sea which had Bird and Hobbs "over the rail". Felt rather unsettled myself! Arrived at Lanai Island just as dusk was falling. Beautiful entrance in the De Vere Stacpoole tradition. I imagine that the main exports are fish and copra – quite a well-made wooden quay and a small typically North Borneo Company village (they ran the territory pre-war) behind. Stayed there the night. I slept on deck next door to the latrines. Notwithstanding – from the rats and the hardness of the deck, slept fairly well.

Wednesday August 18th: Left Banggi at dawn – 6.30 a.m. and crossed the bay to Kudat, where we docked about 10 a.m. Left again at 12 after loading some stores. As soon as we left the shelter of the bay, the sea again had a fairly severe swell! The coastline here is undulating and rises in stages to the foothills of Kinabalu: there seems to be a considerable amount of rubber and coconut cultivation for some miles inland. Slept on table between engine-room hatches and rail and found it hot and cold in draughts.

Thursday August 19th: Arrived at Jesselton at 6 a.m. The wooden godowns seem to have been completed since we left about 4 months ago, otherwise nothing

Lintang Barracks   *Pic: RAAF*

changed. I should have liked to have seen our 8 men whom we left in the Hospital, but there was apparently no chance of that. Managed to buy a quantity of eggs to supplement the meagre quantity of rice, Brindjaws, sweet potatoes, cucumbers, fish and bananas which the Japanese had provided for the journey, which was estimated to last 7 days. Our meals are cooked by Vernon Smith and Threadgold, who are not allowed to use the galley until the Japanese food had been cooked. We thus get our meals about 10.00., 1500 and 1930. Owing to the totally inadequate size of the rice boiler, our rice was usually only half-cooked, which did not add to the pleasure of the trip. Spent most of the day on the small after-promenade deck where most of the other officers were bedded down: usual serum for better places at Sandakan. Left Jesselton at 3 p.m. in glorious sunshine, Kinabalu being capped by a large bit of drifting cloud.

Friday August 20th: Reached Labuan at about 10 p.m. and tied up for the night. Lovely sky and cloud formation as we came in.

Saturday August 21st: Left for Brunei about 9 a.m. There was very little to see at Labuan with the exception of a large scrap-iron heap which had been accumulated on the docks, and which included a couple of old British cannon. About the 1830's it was intended to make Labuan a British Naval Base in

109

preference to Singapore, largely owing to the presence of coal in mineable quantities. It was here that Admiral Keppell brought his ships when he came to suppress the native uprisings at the request of the Sultan of Brunei. As a result of this assistance, the Sultan ceded the island of Labuan to the British Crown, and it is now included in the Straits Settlements. The trip to Brunei took us into the vast expanse of Brunei Bay and up a fairly wide river, navigation on which seemed to be fairly tricky. At about 1 mile distant we saw the low-roofed godowns of the town. The Sultan's palace, a strange mixture of Victorian and Mohammedan architectural styles, showed its four towers over the trees about 2 miles further up the river. Opposite the town, the main feature of which seemed to be a long wide street running at right angles to the docks, there was a squalid and closely-grouped collection of native houses built on stilts over the river. There appeared to be little doing. At 3 p.m. we left, passing what seemed to be a European Club and quarters on our left, out into the bay again back to Labuan, which we reached just after dusk. Slept in the small saloon for'ard of the funnel, and found it rather too warm.

Sunday August 22nd: Coaling all morning. This was done by coolie labour working with small hand baskets, and was a slow business. Left at 3 p.m. towing a large, power-less wooden vessel, built on the lines of a yacht and with a small superstructure. We had seen several under construction at Sandakan. Christened her the "Ark Royal".

Monday August 23rd: Arrived Miri about 4 p.m. and found quite a few ships, mostly small, in the harbour. Power-driven barges came alongside and we off-loaded our 44-gallon drums into here. 'Wag' Price got a crack over the back for laughing at the aquatic antics of a Japanese. Jacko was also taken to task when looking at some of Ken Whitworth's snaps. He had previously told the Japanese that he had no snaps himself, and as he was seen looking at some, there was some jumping to conclusions. A most amazing dialogue follows: "You bad man, have no good heart" – "Soria no photos, my heart number one!"

Tuesday August 24th: Left Miri about 8 a.m., after having bought some meat via the cook. This we had in the form of steaks for supper, and very good they tasted, too. Our first meat for about 3 weeks.

Wednesday August 25th: After sighting the South Natunas we saw land again on our port bow, and anchored in the mouth of the Kuching River, about 6.30 p.m., where we spent the night.

Thursday August 26th: This was the day of our landing in Kuching and effectively ends our Sandakan experiences.

Chapter Three

Ballale Island

The Jesselton party, now at Sandakan, were not to know a relatively unknown event was taking place on a tiny island, Ballale, in the Shortland Group, south of Bougainville; the "Gunners 600", who left Singapore about the same time on 18 October 1942, and were now in the process of being totally eliminated.

The first evidence which emerged regarding POWs on Ballale Island came from Mr. Seaton – formerly Captain Seaton, a Coast Watcher on Choiseul Island – when, in late December 1942 the natives reported to him that there were European POWs working on the island who had come from Singapore, and that they were working on the airstrip. The natives did not offer to work with the Japanese; he heard nothing further until late June 1943 when about 30 survivors of the captured natives returned to Choiseul Island; one was Peter Topoto, he said while he was working on the airstrip he frequently saw several hundred Europeans working there, he often attempted to contact them but he was not permitted to get close enough to hold a conversation. When the American air-raids occurred and all took cover, these Europeans refused to leave the target area and he saw more killed by the bombing.

When the airstrip was finished and the Choiseul natives were waiting to return, certain Japanese told him that they had killed all the white men as they had no further use for them.

In October 1945 statements were made by seventy Chinese witnesses and two

Korean witnesses that a shipment of European prisoners of war arrived at Ballale Island in early December 1942. This was confirmed when Lt. Comdr. Ozaki, Commander of 18 Construction Unit and the Army Commanders on the Island were interrogated. Ozaki confirmed a shipment of 517 English POWs from Singapore arrived on the Island early December 1942.

Karehara Kanseyo stated: "In November or December 1942, a party of white men came to the Island. I heard from the Japanese there were five or six hundred. I first saw them after they had landed from a big vessel and barges brought them from the ship to the jetty. The day after the prisoners landed Ozaki himself beheaded a white man, the Japanese said the white man had not obeyed orders.

"The white prisoners were quartered on the western end of the Island which was out of bounds to us Koreans. I was working in a different part of the Island and did not see them at work but I used to see them going to and coming from their work. I never had any opportunity to speak to them. I heard from the Japanese that they were English prisoners from Singapore, I do not know if they were Army or Navy troops. They wore khaki coloured clothing and some had caps or hats.

"I overheard the Japanese troops discussing that a lot of PWs were killed by Allied bombing and many wounded and they had buried the dead; they also said that the PWs who had died of illness before the air raids had been put in rice sacks and dumped at sea.

"After the air raid I saw about 100 PWs who were gathering rock at the northern end of the Island for the airstrip but I could not get near them.

"When the air raids came the Japanese took shelter in their own air raid shelters but they made the PWs remain in their huts. I heard that three bombs fell in the PW compound and afterwards I only saw about 100 PWs. I do not know what happened to the wounded and I did not see any other PWs after the end of May. In June 1943 an American warship bombarded the Island but no landing was made.

"I heard from the Japanese that the remaining PWs, about 70 or 80, were all killed; a big hole was dug and the PWs were shot and put into it."

Kateshiro Fukukan, another Korean and a guard on the Island, stated: "I was returning from work when I saw the PWs marching from the jetty to their compound, I heard the ship had come from Singapore. I saw the PWs at various times, I think they were Englishmen; they were dressed in light khaki coloured clothes with slouch type hats, some wore forage caps and some officers type caps. They wore boots of different sorts; some of the men had tattoo marks on them showing anchors and some English words. We overheard the Japanese say they were English prisoners from Singapore – I overheard a group of Japanese soldiers talking about Ozaki and how he had beheaded an English prisoner and that he was buried in a grave beside the road.

"The Japanese used to beat the prisoners with a pole if they did not work quickly enough. Where the prisoners lived was out of bounds to us and we would have been punished if we went near them.

"After the air raids I only saw about 70 to 100 white PWs. The airstrip was

Ballale Island

(Enlarged Detail)

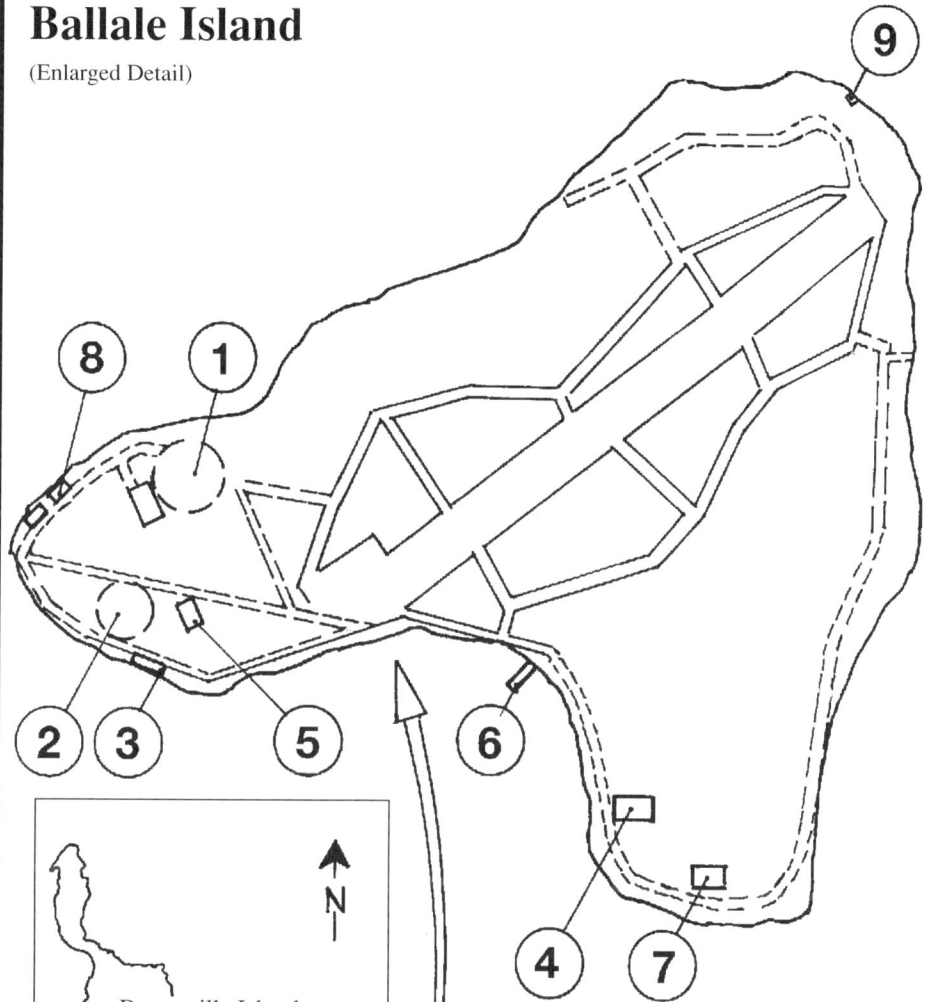

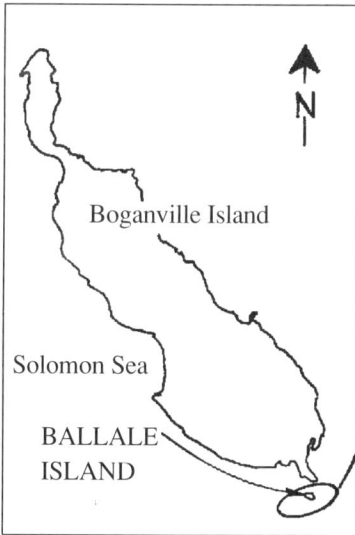

9

8 **1**

2 **3** **5** **6**

N

Boganville Island

Solomon Sea

BALLALE
ISLAND

4 **7**

Legend
1 British Compound
2 Chinese Compound
3 Japanese Hospital
4 Ozaki H.Q.
5 Tower
6 Jetty
7 Japanese Hospital
8 Generating Plant
9 Landing Place

never finished, there was always some work to be done repairing the bomb damage.

"On the night of 30 June 1943, the place was shelled from the sea, the Japanese were afraid of a landing and killed all the PWs next day by bayonets or swords."

Following Captain Seaton's statement in 1945 many Chinese were interviewed and they all told of the atrocities committed against the white prisoners. They confirmed that many were killed by aerial attack and the 40/50 who were wounded later died, they were not allowed to use slit trenches; the Japanese were seen to beat the prisoners until they became unconscious and were revived and beaten again. They all appeared to be weak and thin.

At this time most of the Chinese thought the prisoners were Australians from Singapore until they were questioned regarding dress. In November 1945 when the War Graves Unit moved into the area, items found belonging to the British Royal Artillery personnel soon established their identity.

Hong Luen said: "One night Allied planes came over about midnight and bombed the Island heavily, a number of bombs fell in the prisoner area. Next morning prisoners were marched past and there were only about a hundred of them left, the Japanese did not allow them to dig trenches for themselves for protection against air raids. I saw the prisoners carrying the bodies of their dead and I know that they were buried in one grave. The Japanese permitted the Chinese to dig small trenches for themselves, there were about 30 Chinese on the Island at the time.

"Within the next fortnight I saw about 40 bodies of the POWs put into rice sacks, which contained big stones; I saw them loaded on to a motor boat which went a short distance out to sea and they were thrown overboard. When I left the Island there were 80 prisoners alive."

The Japanese were also committing atrocities against the Chinese, natives and Allied pilots who were shot down. Cheo Chee said, " … in May 1943 I saw a white man dressed in overalls like a pilot would wear, he was a young man and the Japanese tied his hands behind his back and made him sit on the ground; they put a drum of boiling water beside him and nine of them filed past, each one pouring a tin of boiling water over him, the man screamed in pain, I saw him fall flat on the ground, lie still and stop screaming, he appeared to be dead. The Japanese were soldiers, not officers, the white man was tall, of medium build, clean shaven and fair, the overalls were khaki, I was the only Chinese who witnessed this." Unbeknown to Cheo Chee there were other witnesses.

Lim Leow claimed he witnessed the incident described by Cheo Chee, and also Lee Chew Lim, he said that he was 30/40 yards away, that he was there for about an hour carrying rice at the time when he first saw the white man who was standing and the Japanese were pouring hot water over him, the Japanese were also hitting him in the face and he did not see him except standing up. "The prisoner was still there when I moved on to another job, I heard the prisoner screaming as if in pain while I was there."

Another Chinese said that he also witnessed the Japanese pouring tins of boiling water over a prisoner and as they poured the water the man was screaming in pain and the Japanese were laughing and clapping their hands, some of the Japanese slapped the prisoner with their hands and some with sticks. "The Japanese were speaking to him in a language which was not Japanese and which I think was English."

Lin Chin Fook said on one occasion a bomb dropped on a Japanese kitchen during a raid: " … that was before the bombs had killed the white prisoners. The following afternoon I saw the Japanese beating the white prisoners, the Japanese used to beat them almost every day and mainly with sticks, but the day after the Japanese kitchen was bombed was the most serious beating, the Japanese appeared to come from a Naval Unit, it was the Osaki Unit."

Major Milliken was appointed to investigate the alleged war crimes on Ballale Island during the period November 1942 – September 1943.

He soon established that about 600 Royal Artillery personnel from Singapore arrived at Rabaul on 6 November 1942, one man died on the voyage. The party remained at Kopoko for about a week; the main party embarked on a ship, leaving behind 82 men who were too weak to continue on the journey. This group came under the control of Higaki who could speak English. These men, apart from three reasonably fit men left as cooks and orderlies,** were suffering from beri-beri, malaria and other sicknesses. By March 18 the number had been reduced to 48; on the Japanese surrender there were 18 survivors who were evacuated to 2/7 Australian General Hospital at Lae.

Of the 517 men who were put on a ship and departed for an unknown destination Major Milliken was unable, despite repeated enquiries, to establish anything about their fate at the time.

By this time the Australian War Graves Unit began to exhume the graves and the evidence emerged that items found belonged to British troops from Singapore.

On 29 November 1945, War Graves Unit reported the exhumation of 438 Europeans and 14 Asiatics, believed to be Japanese, together with a number of items which indicated the Europeans were British and belonged to the Gunners' party which left Singapore for Rabaul. The senior British Officer was Lt.Col. Bassett of the 35 L.A.A., Royal Artillery. The Japanese claimed a complete record of the prisoners was kept and forwarded to the proper authorities.

Those suspected of being implicated with the atrocities were Vice Admiral Kusaka Jimichi, Commander of the South Eastern Fleet; Lt. Commander Ozaki Noriko, formerly Commander of the 18 Construction Unit, Ballale; Lt.Commander Miyake Isamu, formerly Commander A.G. Gun Unit, Ballale, and Captain Senda, former Commander, Army Battalion.

Both Ozaki and Miyake were held in custody at this time and both made long statements about their respective roles – both admitted they signed a defence plan

---

** This period is described by one of the survivors: Alf "Blackie" Baker, in his book, "What Price Bushido?"

for the Island which stated that in the event of an Allied attack the plan w000ould be implemented which meant all the prisoners would be killed.

Ozaki claimed that while virtually local Commander, he was not responsible for the guarding of the prisoners; however, he admitted receiving the 517 prisoners to be used on the construction of the airfield and denied having beheaded a British officer soon after the prisoners disembarked.

About this time, news of the discovery of remains of British POWs on Ballale Island leaked to the British newspapers. The War Office sent a Signal to LAND-FORCE (Australian Army Headquarters):

> *"Use your efforts to obtain further news Ballale much appreciated. Should mention however that no information had previously reached this office regarding 517 British P/W Ballale December '42, with subsequent deaths of 300 by bombing.*
>
> *"Last sight June 1943 and execution same month, we would point out if this party had connection with party 512 P/W from lost Japanese transport reported sailed from New Britain early March 1943 date of arrival in Ballale stated by you is suspect. Request therefore this date be confirmed."*

Up to this time the War Office were well informed on all matters relating to Ballale and for some unknown reason were adopting a rumour that the ship carrying the POWs from Rabaul was sunk by American aircraft and all those killed were buried by the Japanese on Ballale Island. This position was published in War Graves Register Bomana Cemetery 1957: "The 438 unidentified soldiers of the United Kingdom forces were all Royal Artillery personnel. They lost their lives as prisoners of war while being transported from Singapore to the Solomon Islands, when their ship was bombed by the American Air Force. These men were first buried on the Ballale Islands, and later reburied in a temporary war cemetery at Torokina, before being transferred to their permanent resting place at Port Moresby.", and seemed to remain the official War Office version of what occurred.

Meanwhile the English press. "Daily Telegraph" of 4 February 1946; "Daily Express" of 5 February 1946 and "News Chronicle", published an account on remains being found on Ballale. Anxious relatives began enquiries, however, it seems the War Office attitude remained the same. In May 1946, ALFSEA decided Ozaki and Kusaka would be tried by an Australian Court in Rabaul with a United Kingdom member. On June 6, 1946, Major Wait was appointed and stated he was unable to add any thing to what was already known, except Kusaka accepted responsibility as Commander but denied knowledge of events.

By September 1946, reports of interrogations were forwarded to ALFSEA. From that time on the investigation was exclusively in the hands of British War

Crimes Section. In December 1946, Vice Admiral Kusaka was repatriated to Japan and released without being interrogated. Lt. Comdr. Ozaki was released in April 1947 but subsequently arrested by the British Minor War Crimes in Tokyo.

After the British had apparently lost interest, they formally transferred the suspects in this matter to Australian War Crimes Section tion in November 1947: two years after the first report was sent to TROOPERS (War Office London).

One would have expected the most important question would have been investigated: who ordered the prisoners of war to be dispatched to a war zone and confined without protection? The Americans were quick to try the Japanese who placed B29 pilots in a prison located in a target area.

In the early part of the war, orders went out from Japanese G.H.Q. on how to treat prisoners of war, and as late as March 1945, it was repeated:

> *"Prisoners of War must be prevented by all means available from falling into enemy hands. They should either be relocated away from the Front or collected at suitable points and times with an eye to enemy air raids, shore bombardments etc. They should be kept alive to the last wherever their labour is needed. In desperate circumstances, where there is no time to move them, they may, as a last resort, be set free. Then emergency measures should be carried out against those with an antagonistic attitude and utmost precautions should be taken so that no harm is done to the public. In executing emergency measures care should be taken so that no harm is done to the public.*
>
> *In executing emergency measures care should be had not to provoke enemy propaganda or retaliation. The prisoners should be fed at the end."*

The action of the Japanese at Ballale was a "blue-print" laid down by Tokyo. No action was taken by Investigators to identify the source of the original order to move the prisoners from Singapore to the Solomon Islands; the Investigators then interrogated the Navy Commander Kusaki and so it went down to the Commander who was in charge, Ozaki. He was now interrogated again and stated: "In fact I was absolved of war crimes' responsibility through an investigation by British Authorities in Singapore two years ago and was released. This was the only course of action."

At this stage Ozaki was very confident: "I earnestly request that the truth be ascertained from an impartial stand-point so that the false charges against me be retracted as soon as possible."

So now it appeared the Japanese were confident of charges having been dismissed by the British – the Australian investigation could not succeed.

117

In July 1949, FARELF advised the U.K. Liaison Mission in Tokyo in the following 'Confidential' cable:

"CONFIDENTIAL

FROM: FARELF

TO: UK LIAISON MISSION TOKYO

Subject: Ballale Island case. Our 22008 WCS of 21 June 1949 to British Minor War Crimes Tokyo Info yourselves refers.

TROOPERS decision now received. Evidence insufficient to warrant prosecution. First. Ozaki Toshihito. Second. Miyake Isamu. Third. Kusaka.
Request you inform Australian War Crimes this decision and arrange with SCAP for release Ozaki and Miyake. Understand Kusaka not in custody. If otherwise arrange similar release. Inform Australian War Crimes case file being held this GHQ unless otherwise requested."

These victims of the "Gunners 600 Party" are honoured on the Singapore Memorial as having died 5 March 1943. Remains found on Ballale are buried in Bomana Cemetery, Port Moresby.

Chapter Four

SUEZ MARU

Sunk 29 November 1943

Unknown to those in Borneo, by the end of 1943 thousands of POWs had been dispersed from Singapore and Java to construct the Burma-Thailand Railway, shipped to Japan to work in industry and to work in the old, abandoned, and now re-opened, coal mines.

The lucky ones remained in Changi, complaining about their lot and not having any idea of what had happened in Thailand until the ghost-like survivors of the men of 'F' Force began returning to Changi late 1943.

In Java, "Black Force", comprising mostly Australians and some British – 6000 in all – went off to Burma. A large group of 4000, including some Dutch, were shipped to Ceram to construct airfields at Ambon, Ceram and Haroekoe: these parties were similar in composition to the "Java" parties of R.A.F. and Royal Artillery men now in Borneo.

The Commander of the POWs in Java at the time was Major General Saito, later to be sent to Singapore to command POWs and Internees, and remembered by many who often saw him in his baggy britches when he visited Changi Gaol.

Nothing was known of some 548 Allied POWs until 1949 when the conscience of a Japanese Lieutenant began to worry him. The Lieutenant was in charge of a shipment of POWs whom he had convinced the Japanese High Command at Amboina should be returned to Java because (1) the task of constructing the airfield had been completed and (2) the POWs were in a weak condition and in Java they would be able to recover from their illnesses – the only vessel available on which these men could be shipped was the SUEZ MARU.

In 1949, the Lieutenant, Koshio Masaji, wrote to Far East Command disclosing the details of the sinking of the SUEZ MARU and requesting a full investigation into the massacre of British prisoners of war at sea.

He wrote: "The Japanese should know for themselves what atrocities. inhuman brutality existed in the shadow of the Pacific War. They should be awakened to know, no matter how secretly an act was committed, one day that act shall be known to the public. We should build up Japanese with strongness for Justice and who love peace."

Who was Koshio? He was Lieutenant Iketani Masaji – he had changed his name and was now known as Koshio Masaji; he was, in fact. the Officer who was appointed to command the Japanese sick and POWs on board the ship. He asked his superior officer: What happens if the ship is attacked and sunk? How shall we care for the POWs? and the officer replied: The prisoners will be shot!

In July 1949 he made a comprehensive statement which triggered off an Enquiry involving the Captain of the SUEZ MARU and the escort Minesweeper No. 12.

Koshio stated: "The unit commander, Lt.Col. Anami, was in command during the time the POW boarded the ship. As the No. 1 and No. 2 hatches were already occupied by Japanese patients, the sick POW were accommodated in the No. 3 and No. 4 hatches. There were ten to twenty persons brought aboard on stretchers. Since I was the last one to board the ship, I witnessed the leading of prisoners aboard the ship. As the sea in the vicinity of that place was very dangerous at that time, I said to the Unit Commander, "If this ship is attacked by torpedoes from enemy submarines and sinks, what measures should be taken? And what should be done if the escort ship is a small minesweeper which hasn't the capacity to accommodate everybody?" The Unit Commander replied promptly: "You may shoot them. Shoot them!" Unit Commander Amani harbored a great deal of animosity toward the POW. This can be seen by the fact that he did not quickly agree to our advice previously given to send the sick POW back to Java immediately.

"Then both our small transport, the SUEZ MARU, and the minesweeper, left the port of Ambon. I believe it was past noon on the following day, the 25th. The 26th and 27th passed without incident, but on the night of the 28th our ship reported that the minesweeper had disappeared, apparently having sighted a submarine on the same night, so we felt quite helpless. Prior to this, I ordered the posting of one sentry over No. 4 hatch on three-hour shifts, but on the night of 28th I issued an alert order to all the passengers of the transport to be prepared for any emergency, and also increased the number of sentry posts to two so that the POW would be able to receive appropriate instructions in case of an emergency. I saw that the rafts above the No. 3 and No. 4 hatches were generally sufficient and the number of life jackets was also, generally speaking, sufficient.

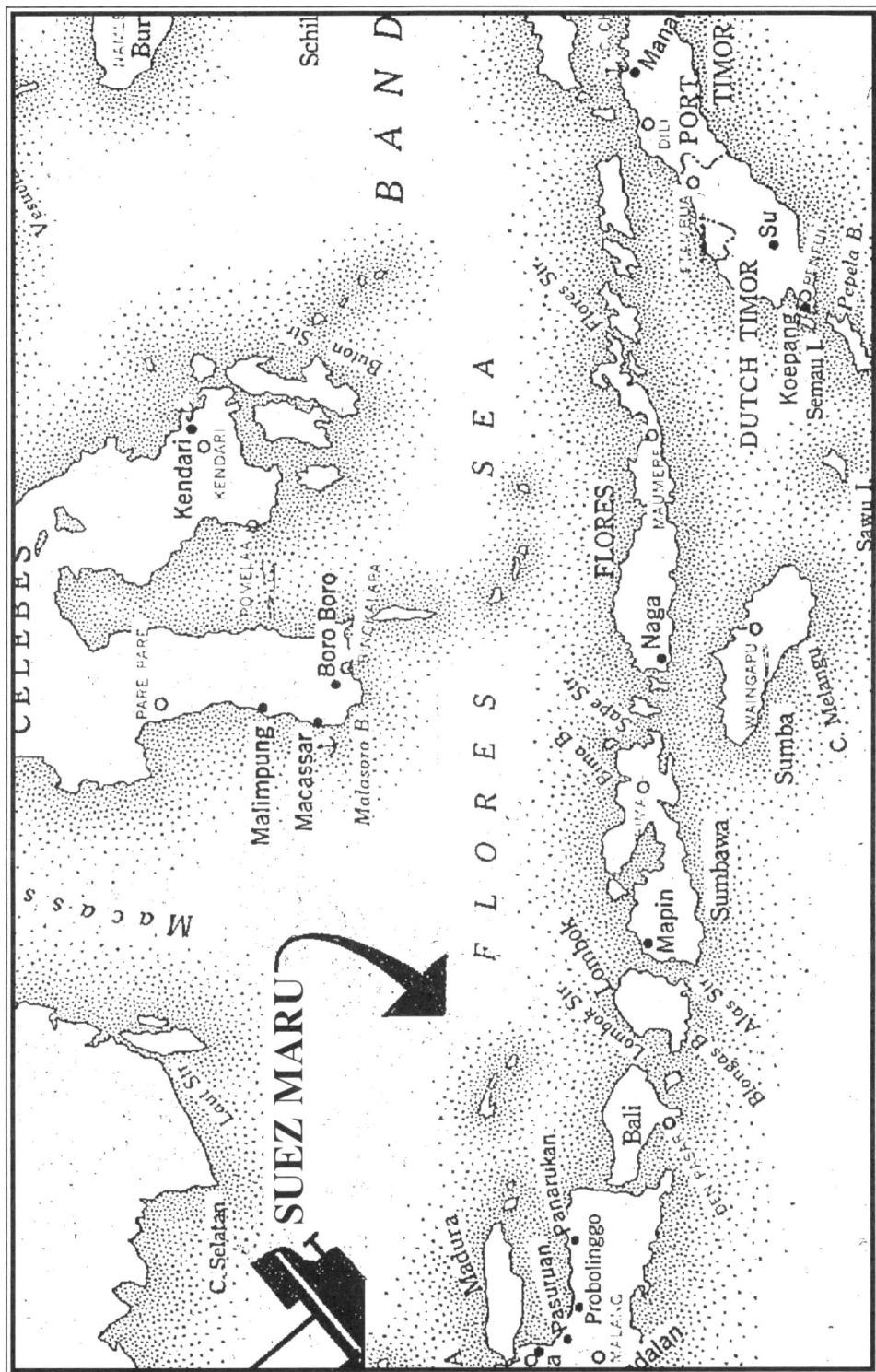

"When on the morning of 29th, we saw the minesweeper far to the rear and saw it steaming towards our transport at full speed, we felt relieved, assuming that we were out of the danger area. However, the alert order remained in effect and a strict watch was maintained. By the time we finished our breakfast and were on the ship's bridge, the minesweeper was seen emitting black smoke leisurely and sailing in front of the transport at a speed corresponding to that of the transport. Then suddenly a shout, "Torpedo!" was heard from the lookout. It was probably at about 0920 hours. Looking in the direction of the stern of the transport, I clearly saw two white traces of a torpedo. The transport was apparently trying to dodge the torpedo by making a big turn at full speed. Would the transport be able to succeed completing or not? For that moment, we prayed to God. Simultaneously with the sound of an explosion at the stern of the transport, our bodies were thrown around by the concussion. We suffered two direct hits.

"I immediately sent the Sanitation non-commissioned officer and a Korean civilian employee of the Army, Hoshino Fumio, on message duty to get information concerning the situation at the stern of the transport. The purpose of sending the messengers was to get information on the damage caused by the torpedo attack and, also, to transmit my order with instructions to take appropriate measures. The messengers returned with the following information:

    a. The two sentries are missing; they apparently fell into the ship's hatches due to the concussions.

    b. The majority of the POW in the No. 3 hatch are coming out of the hatch with their life jackets on. In view of the fact that very few prisoners were moving in the No. 4 hatch, it seemed that the No. 4 hatch had had a considerable number of victims because it had received a direct torpedo hit.

    c. Without delay, those in the No. 3 hatch were instructed to rescue those in the No. 4 hatch.

"Since the ship was in the condition mentioned in the above, I asked the Captain of the ship whether or not the ship would be able to continue. Then the Captain said, "Since the shaft of the ship is broken and the engines have ceased to function because the engine rooms are flooded, it will be utterly impossible for the ship to continue."

"In view of the confusion at the stern of the ship and also in consideration of the fact that almost all of the POW were ill, I presumed that it would be quite impossible for them to throw the heavy rafts into the sea. Therefore, without delay I gave the following order: "The remaining Koreans shall throw all the rafts into the sea. When this is done, all the passengers shall abandon ship." The Koreans seemed to have obeyed my order. The POW apparently jumped into the sea for prisoners were no longer seen aboard the ship. Since all of the Japanese passengers seemed to have left the ship and the list of the sinking ship gradually became steep, I jumped into the sea with the senior crew of the ship who had remained on board to the end.

"During the time we were swimming desperately to be clear of the sinking ship, it sank stern first. I remember that approximately ten to twenty minutes elapsed from the time the ship was torpedoed to the time it sank. Apparently preparing for the subsequent situation, the minesweeper came cruising around us in a large circle. Meanwhile, those who had jumped into the sea simultaneously with us were clinging to the floating rafts or the floating pieces of wood while drifting in the currents. They were floating in a long row. Between approximately two hundred and two hundred and fifty POW seemed to be floating. It seemed to me I was floating for three hours or less. However, I was probably floating longer. At any rate, I was picked up by the minesweeper near dusk.

"I had an interview with Kawano, the Captain of the minesweeper. We, as well as the crew of the minesweeper, felt hostile toward the unseen submarine which had torpedoed the transport.

"The rescue work was continued until shortly after I was taken out of the sea, at which time the boat was already full. At that time the Captain of the boat confronted me with a problem on which I was to render a decision. It was as follows: "Having accommodated the Japanese the boat is already full. In order to prevent the boat from capsizing, we cannot accommodate any more persons." I had no alternative but to nod in acquiescence. He also said, "It is dangerous to leave the POW drifting in the sea. There is a fear that they will be rescued by a submarine. [Presumably an Allied Forces submarine.] I would like to kill them with machine guns, but what do you think should be done?" I stared at the surface of the sea. Since there were approximately 200 to 250 POW floating on the sea, I then learned that there was an unexpectedly large number of them who had been killed simultaneously with the terrifying explosion of the enemy torpedo in Hold No. 4. Together with the terse remark of, "Well, what you say is true", I quoted the orders issued by Lt.Col. Anami at the time of departure from Port Amboina. Whereupon it seemed that the Captain was planning some sort of order to the executive officer standing nearby. Soon thereafter the whistle blew and there was much commotion aboard the boat.

"It seems that a machine gun was readied at the bow of the boat. It also seems that about twenty sailors appeared with rifles. As I could no longer bear the atmosphere, I crouched down on the bridge of the ship where I pressed my eyes shut and avoided looking at the surface of the sea. It must have been about twenty minutes after I had the foregoing conversation with the Captain of the boat that the machine guns started making piercing sounds across the surface of the sea, which was strangely silent due to the deceleration of the boat.

"The noise of rifle fire was intermingled with that of machine gun fire. The boat carefully made four or five rounds of the surrounding sea. I also heard the voice of a person who seemed to be an officer of the boat, and who seemed to be pointing out the positions of floating POW while he scanned the surface of the sea with a pair of glasses. It soon became dark. As had been decided, it seemed that the minesweeper had killed the remaining prisoners. Finally we began to sail west at full speed, after destroying the empty boats with the bow of our boat. I was taken over by a completely gloomy feeling and I dejectedly ate the food given to me as I crouched in a corner of the officers' cabin. It seems that I was in a completely abstract state of mind.

"As soon as we arrived at Batavia, I immediately made a detailed report to the commander of the Main Camp, Maj. Gen. Saito Shosi, of the incidents which took place from the time of departure to the time of arrival, and relayed the orders issued by Lt.Col. Anami, in regard to which the Main Camp commander said nothing. He merely said, "That was probably the only method available at that time", and avoided making any express statements as to whether the method was just or unjust. I do not know what his opinions may have been concerning the issue, but he did not seem to want to become deeply involved in the matter. Furthermore, he added that I should discuss the disposition of this matter with the officer in charge of POW, Army Captain Suzuki Hiroshi, and make sure there were no oversights. Therefore, I once more related to Capt. Suzuki the things I had told the main camp commander. He thought the matter over for a while and told me to wait a day or two.

"Later, he brought me a draft which he told me to print and affix my signature thereto. This is the report I submitted after writing it in Japanese. Upon examining the draft I found the text was contrary to the facts. Therefore, I asked him if it was all right to leave the draft as it was even if the text was contrary to facts, whereupon he said it was all right to leave the text. As I was a supply officer, I did not know the details of writing reports. Therefore, I printed and affixed my seal to the report as I thought it was supposed to be written. Kawano told me where the SUEZ MARU sank.

"I took the report to the Captain of the boat anchored at Tanjanpriok and asked if it were all right with him, after telling how I was told to write the report on the incident. He then replied, "I approve of the report and you may handle the matter as it suits your position." I, therefore, offered one copy of the report to him. He accepted it."

The Koshio statement continues reporting a conversation between the Captain of the Minesweeper vessel and 2/Lt. Iketani:

"Captain, Minesweeper: "Now are we going to dispose of the POW? Have you received any order from higher authorities?"

2nd Lt. Iketani: "We have orders instructing us to shoot them if the ship were sunk. I request that proper disposal be made by the escort ship."

Captain, Minesweeper: "Is that so? Then we shall shoot them."

2nd Lt. Iketani: "I will leave it to you, Captain."

Senior Officer (myself): "Captain, it is not right to kill POW by shooting. I think it would be all right to leave them alone since the boats are afloat. Let us start immediately."

Captain, Minesweeper: "It is the expressed wish of the Army. Also the enemy submarine is bound to emerge after we leave and rescue the survivors. Then information about the Japanese forces will be come known to the enemy and will affect operations adversely. We must not let the POW fall into enemy hands. If we cannot accommodate all of them, death is the only answer. Shooting them is unavoidable."

Koshio continues: "Making up his mind thus, he ordered me to shoot them. I thought it was futile murder, but that was the situation; furthermore, we were facing the enemy submarine.

"Complying with the aforementioned order, I recognised the need for killing the POW speedily, and immediately called Warrant Officer Niyauchi Toshimori, materiel assistant to the mine officer, to the Bridge. (I think it was he, but it may have been Ensign Noromaga Tomakishi). I ordered him to take charge of the rifle unit and deploy approximately 12 men of this group (there were approximately 12 rifles on the minesweeper) on both sides of the foredeck and shoot the POW. Also, I ordered the commanding officer of the rifle unit and the lookouts to be sure they made no mistakes as to the target, because about 20 of our men were still missing. The Captain assumed command from the Bridge and I stayed either on the Bridge or on the foredeck and assisted him. I also supervised the shooting. In addition, I gave advice as to the disposition of the wounded we had aboard.

"After preparations for firing were completed, the Captain had the ship cruise at a slow speed within 50 metres of the POW, the left side of the ship facing the POW. He had the firing begin around 1715 hrs. At first the POWs were lying down since they were tired and hardly paid any attention. However, when they heard the sound of firing, saw their comrades fall to the left and right, they tried to protect themselves by hiding behind anything that would shelter them.

"The water in the vicinity was coloured by the blood and the scene was so distressing it made one cover one's eyes. The lookout, probably it was Superior Petty Officer Yoshino, who was posted at the 12-centimetre binoculars on the Bridge, said that he could see a Japanese, so I took his place and saw a completely naked man with closely-cropped black hair lying on a board. When the SUEZ MARU Captain was called and he looked at the scene, he said it was a crew-member of the SUEZ MARU and asked us to save him. We ceased firing and taking the ship close to the man, pulled him aboard. We saw at this time that the torpedo explosion had taken the flesh off his back and that he seemed to be nearly dead."

Fujimoto, Takeshi: "I moved to a spot over the boiler room on the upper deck, and looking down to where a POW was clinging to a life preserver, I saw blood spurt from the back of the man's head as though he had been shot from somewhere close to the minesweeper. Profoundly shocked, I hurried at once to my cabin to regain my poise. I had never before seen a man killed, even in combat.

"Around 1600 hours, I could still hear sporadic firing. Making my way gingerly to the top deck, I heard the rescued Japanese, who were apparently rather excited, saying, "Shoot every POW in sight!" At approximately 1600 hours, I saw about 200 dead men on the surface of the sea. I returned once more to my cabin.

The sound of firing was still audible.

"About 1630 hours, the firing stopped. I went to the top deck three times, and looking out at the water I was surprised to see that about 200 to 250 bodies seemed to be floating around. I did not see any survivors. The minesweeper was gradually moving away from the scene."

"We headed for Soerabaja, but later the engineer officer told me that we had changed course and were going to Jokjakarta because magnetic mines had been dropped by planes at the entrance to Soerabaja Harbour."

Koshio continued: "After returning to our former positions, we approached the scene of our last firing and again started shooting at the POW in the water on the port side of our ship, while simultaneously keeping watch for the submarine. There were some brave POW who, knowing they were going to be shot, stood up on the boards and presented themselves as targets for our bullets. There was nothing to hide behind as it was an open sea, and the number of POW floating gradually decreased as they were hit one by one and sank.

"What an inhuman thing to do – to kill unresisting men – although it was war and we had to do it. I could not help saying to the Engineer Officer, Lt. J.G. Tanaka, whose first name is unknown, standing beside me: "Even if it is war, this is a distasteful thing, isn't it?" The Engineer Officer also said in low voice: "It is pitiful, isn't it? However, if this was one of the means of winning the war, it had to be carried through at any cost." "

No further action was taken to indict Kawano Osumu, the Commander of the Mine-sweeper No. 12, for the killing of Allied prisoners of war after the sinking of the SUEZ MARU.

This followed a message to Army H.Q. Melbourne from 2 Aust. War Crimes Sec. SEAC:

> *U.K. Mission Tokyo has been advised by FARELF that War office decision terminate Japanese War Crime Trials 30 September. Must be maintained. FARELF instruction Mission release any suspects unless required by Australian and U.S. Authorities end mission.*

The account of the SUEZ MARU: the vessel was sunk by the USS BONE-FISH, commanded by Cdr. Tom Hogan. The BONEFISH was the Flagship of Admiral Christie of Task Force 71, based at Fremantle and the location of the sinking was about 300 miles N.E. of Kaengan.

Diaries of Flt. Lieut. Peter E.I. Lee

1943 Kuching, Sarawak.

Thursday August 26th: Weighed anchor 6 a.m. and moved up the Kuching River with the "Ark Royal" lashed on to our port side. Passed the spot where we had anchored off last October en route to Jesselton (from Changi, Singapore). Entering the upper reaches we noticed an increasing number of clearings on the right bank. Brickworks, Sawmills and Godowns, mostly in very dilapidated condition straggled one after the other like a crowd of ragged unkempt children. Then the biggest surprise of the trip. A large expanse of riverside vegetation, a 400 ft. hill was in process of excavation at the rear, and in the space left vacant slipways had been constructed with the accompanying paraphernalia of attap huts and small-gauge railways. About 14 wooden vessels, similar to the "Ark Royal" were in varying stages of completion, although nowhere could I see any signs of any engines to power them. Turning a bend in the river we came suddenly on – Kuching! Standing alone on the left bank stands the old Fort which seems at some time to have been gutted by fire. Surrounding it was an almost English-like park scene of trees, flowering shrubs, winding pathways, small summerhouses and little wooden bridges. The Istana, home of the Rajah Brookes, stood to the left of a small creek, and had on the river bank an imposing white colonnaded entrance. The house itself was, in the main, obscured by trees, but from what one could see of it, it seemed fairly small and modern in design. The most incongruous part seemed to me to be the native kampong which nestled almost up to the Istana itself: again a most extraordinary contrast of wealth and poverty. The Japanese seem to have occupied most of the Istana area with officials who use small motor boats to reach the town proper. The Jap, Lt. Nagata, whom we had as Camp Commandant for a couple of months in Jesselton, met us at the quayside. Before we were driven off in lorries I noticed that the Chinese and Malay women passengers, and also the Jap soldiers, had their kit searched before being allowed to land; whether this was a military or purely customs measure I could not make out. The town, as we passed through it, appeared typical of any medium-sized town in the East: many open-fronted shops, mainly Chinese, with a small covered pathway or arcade in front of them, formed by the rooms above. The most elegant-looking building in the town was the Post office, built in Grecian-style and capped by the coat of arms of Sarawak.

The residential area outside the town seemed well laid-out with good roads and thick creeper covered green hedges which were reminiscent of English country roads. When we arrived at the Camp, about 4 miles outside the town, we found that it was a miniature Changi, containing separate wired off compounds for British Officers, British ORs, British Internees (Men and Women separately), Dutch Officers, Ambonese, Dutch Catholic priests, and Nuns, mainly Dutch. On arrival before the main office we saw 3 Englishwomen waiting for rations, a sight that sickened me considerably. They all looked neat and their clothes appeared clean and fairly new, but they all looked pale and worn-out. I found out later that there are also about 20 children who are apparently given extra milk. Apart from this, one gathers that the Nuns do cooking and also sewing for the Japanese.

After a speech by Major Suga welcoming us to Kuching, and giving us general details about camp life – rations being short, no intercourse between areas, necessity for maintaining our health and avoiding typhoid, cholera, dysentery, beriberi etc., we had our kits searched and disinfected again – all my papers, nominal rolls, were taken away, and we were at last admitted to the Officers Camp. Capt. 'Jerry' Skey and several other officers came out to welcome us, and to help us in with our kit. Most of the area has been cleared of rubber trees, and the ground turned into vegetable gardens, which however, does not seem to have been cultivated for very long. There are 3 huts, two of which previously accommodated the 66-odd officers who were here before our arrival, the third being used as a Mess Canteen and batman's quarters. With our advent, the Mess was scrapped perforce and all huts turned into sleeping quarters. Besides the original officers and men who came with us from Java, we found that another contingent of 500 men and 20 or so officers had arrived from Changi in May this year. From them I learnt that Changi is gradually being cleared of troops, but that the 18th Division is still there. About a month after we left, about 1000 R.A.F. from Java passed through Changi en-route to Bangkok for railway building work. Very many Dutch troops were also being sent to Bangkok from Java for similar work.

Eventually I found a bed-space between Lts. Banton and Metcalfe, both R.A.S.C. I mess with 4 other officers who are fortunate enough to have a table – Lt. Phillip Lovely, R.A.; Capt. Hare-Scott – regular R.A.; Dicky Bird and Ewart Metcalfe. Roll-calls are held twice a day, usually – at 7.15 a.m. and 6.45 p.m., and in contrast to our Sandakan show, are short and sweet! Breakfast is at 9 a.m. and almost invariably consists of burnt rice porridge and a teaspoonful of sugar and one sweet potato cake. For lunch there is vegetable soup, and either a kedgeree or plain rice and a prawn curry. Dinner is the main meal of the day, at 7 p.m., at which we have vegetable soup, nasi goreng with prawns and peanuts, a potato and veg. (and sometimes meat) casserole and katjang ejan (a small bean supposedly rich in Vitamin B) and on high days and holidays – a banana rissole, joy of man's desiring! The Canteen is open daily between 11 and 12.30 and is run by an F.M.S.V.F. Lt.

Allan Dant, very successfully. The main 'buys' are blachang, the so-called caviar of the East, which is really a type of fish paste, peanut toffee, small sweet biscuits, a sweet crisp optimistically called brandy snaps. Also of course, for the smokers, tobacco, cigarettes and native cigars. The only thing we ex-Sandakanites miss is fruit; the small amount which does come in is very rightly taken by the Mess.

There is a small Mess Committee presided over by Lieut. Perry, R.A. – a monthly mess sub. of not more than $4.50 is levied; the average is, I understand, in the region of $3-$3.50. Contributions to the Men's Camp are made at the following monthly rates: Lt.Col. $15; Majors $10; Capts. $5; Lts. $3 and 2/Lts. $2. Arrangements have been made with the Japanese to have contributions from our Sandakan officers sent to the men there. Learning that there are 34 R.A.F. other ranks in the men's camp here including the 8 whom we left in hospital at Changi, we had a 'whip around' amongst RAF Officers and realised $19., F/Lts. paying $3, F/Os $2, and P/Os $1 – Hardie giving $4.

There is a well-run library here, the librarian being Lt. Metcalfe and membership is achieved by donating one book. Camp fatigues are done by detailed officers permanently – gardening, camp hygiene, Camp 'Doc' (Victor Anderson), Canteen – Lt. Dant, Admin. (Col. Whimster, Jerry Skey), John Bailey, about 3 or 4 others and Ken Whitworth – most of the latter do such things as water and ration-carrying etc. I, and 39 others, am detailed for wood-chopping and carrying. For this, we go outside the wire, usually on Tuesday and Fridays, cut down 5-7 rubber trees and carry them inside to the cookhouse.

There are about 3 electric lights in each hut, but as the wattage of each is low, and the current weak, there is normally insufficient light by which to read. Most people play cards: bridge, poker, piquet, etc. until lights out, which is at 10 p.m. We can hear the bugle calls from the Other Rank's Camp, and also from the Japanese barracks on top of the small hill above us. Spare time during the day is generally spent reading library books or in the study of languages etc. At the moment (9th September) there are classes in French, German, Spanish (these 3 I am taking myself), Dutch, Italian and Malay, Accountancy and Philosophy.

Every other Sunday we have a visit from the Bishop of Labuan and Sarawak, who is interned here. His first visit was on Sept. 6th, when he arrived to take early morning communion at 8 o'clock. He is a tall man of about 50, but looks considerably older, with a long, narrow, aesthetic-looking face the colour of old parchment, strangely enough he reminded me very strongly of the Assize Court Judges I used to see on "Judges Sunday" at Durham Cathedral, before the opening of the Assizes. As he came striding down our garden path in his white cassock, red sash and scarlet-trimmed white cape, I wondered whether many bishops of modern times had had his experiences. His name is, I believe, Hollis, although no one seems quite sure – he is always referred to as the "Bish". From the form of service he took, I gather he is a High Church man, which, with Roman Catholicism is perhaps the type of Christianity most amenable to Asians. Apropos of this, he is apt to complain bitterly, I gather, of the competition he receives in normal times, from the Catholics, who have more money to spend on what seems more like Christian bribery than Christian charity! Free rice is a potent proselytizing weapon in these 'ere parts!

Tuesday September 28th: Since writing the above life has, on the whole been uneventful. Our wood-cutting area has been changed, and we are now slowly clearing an area of mangrove swamp just outside the Camp to the right of the main guardroom. It is not so pleasant as working on rubber trees, one of the main drawbacks being the swarms of red ants which are everywhere and which have a most vicious bite.

On Sunday 17th September, Padre Staunton, one of the Padres from the Civilian Internees Camp, came over at 4 p.m. and conducted a short service which included a very fine address on Christian living, in which he very sensibly stressed that, although God can help a lot in an individual's efforts at right-living, it is, in the end his own endeavours which must pull him through.

The Canteen has been disappointing recently as regards food supplies, and, apart from meagre rations of sago biscuits and peanut toffee, there has been little of interest. Fruit is still absent.

We now introduce some variety in our diet by making blanc-mange from coffee, sago biscuits, peanut toffee and a portion of our sugar ration! All the ingredients are broken up and dissolved in hot water; the mixture is then boiled and decanted into mess tins, dixies etc. It sets very quickly and passes quite creditably for a blanc-mange – although, of course, not quite the same as Mother makes!

A ripple on the surface of our placid life today, when Alan Dant received a letter dated March '43 from his mother in Durban, South Africa. She stated that she had heard of him from England, so one hopes that by now news has reached home of our whereabouts.

Camp amusements have gone back to children's party days for inspiration. On Sunday nights we play "Silly B's", a variation of charades, in which one has to act a given book-title or famous name, which the rest of the side must guess. An initial try-out between a team of Ex-Sandakanites and the "Old Hands" ended in a defeat for the former, which was, however, revenged by a victory of over 10 minutes two weeks later on 26th September. "Consequences" and a drawing game which a small group of us played a couple of days ago, also gave us a great deal of amusements. In the party were Tony Hare-Scott, Phil Lovely, Dicky Bird, John Gardiner, Alan Dant, "Tink" Bell and myself. I laughed so much that I gave myself stomach-ache, which was probably a pretty good thing.

The gardens are doing quite well now, in spite of a mysterious blight which occasionally attacks marrow plants. With the opening up of the ground immediately inside the gate, all available land is now under cultivation. I feel we shall be very grateful for this some day.

I was elected a member of the Camp Committee for this hut on the 21st September. Owing to my relatively recent arrival at Kuching, I was reluctant to stand, but was persuaded to do so by Phil Lovely, who proposed me, and Dicky Bird who seconded. I was one of 4 candidates, 2 of whom were required as representatives of the No. 1 Hut on the Mess Committee; the others were Capt. Taylor, RASC, Capt. MacArthur 2/15 Punabs, and Lt. Nordeman, RASC. Against this competition I did not feel particularly confident of my own chances, but much to my surprise the voting went as follows; Nordeman 26, Lee 22, MacArthur 17 and Taylor 12. Our election takes effect from October 1st. At a subsequent election Capt. Kettlewell (Ordinance) was elected to the post of Messing Officer in place of Lt. "Shot" Spurway, 2/15th Punjabs, who has held it for 9 months. (A former Sarawak Government Civil Servant who, when asked how he got his nickname, would reply – "Because I was always half-shot – old boy!")

The unsuccessful candidates were Whitworth and Hodges (16 votes each) and Lt. Harris, who was 'Kettle's' closest competitor in the 2nd Ballot. 'Kettle', a rather tall and ungainly chap with a pair of horn-rimmed glasses which always seem to be balanced on the end of his nose, has a most inventive brain, and has done some very useful work for this Camp, including the construction of a rice-grinding machine and, originally, the installation of the electric light wiring – this latter done mainly with strands of barbed wire and broken bottle tops as insulators. In his present job, I am afraid that his imagination is about the only thing he will have to work on!

Friday 1st October: Although I am always up, dressed and shaved before the rest of the hut, I almost managed to miss roll-call yesterday, and just made it after a hurried call from Dunderdale. The "stay-in-beds" eagerly seized the opportunity to do a lot of leg-pulling on the virtues of REST! The other morning I discovered that John Gardiner had been to Ashridge College, and that Alan Bazell knew it well although he had not actually attended a course there. During the War it has been turned into a hospital, so I was told. Canteen supplies were a little more generous last night, and we received quite a useful supply of sweet potatoes, a sack of maize and some bananas, the latter, although not so numerous as to support an issue to individuals, will at least mean a resumption of the banana rissoles as a "dessert"!

On looking back through these notes, I notice that no mention has been made of the increase in pay which we received about a month ago. Captains received an extra $10 a month, making a total of $32.50, Lieuts. $25 instead of $15, and 2/Lieuts. and P/Os $20.83 instead of $8.83. Lt. Colonels were reduced from $70 to $60 in the same revision, and Majors pay remains unaltered. This has achieved, with the messing rate and contributions to the men, a much-needed levelling-up in officers' pay.

At our Mess meeting yesterday, it was decided to increase the compulsory minimum Canteen deposit to $6 on account of the "more prawn" policy, to make up for a deficiency of proteins, notably greens. A vote of thanks was proposed to retiring camp 'officials' by Lt. Col. Whimster and the new ones, including myself, welcomed.

Sunday 3rd October: The Bishop came over this morning and took Communion Service, which was attended by 26 Officers. The rest of the day, which was hot and sultry, I devoted to finishing the reading of General Lee's letters.

The weather is now changing perceptibly. Afternoons are generally hot and oppressive, the rain arriving fairly punctually every day between 5.30 and 6.30 p.m., during and after which things are very pleasantly cool. When the North-East Monsoon arrives in December, I expect very heavy rains here.

Dinner tonight was a "Kettle" special – Vegetable soup, which had a small piece of pork boiled in it, a prawn and peanut rissole with beans and maize, and sliced papaya and a biscuit. A noble effort! Conversation after dinner started on the subject of jobs after the War. Jerry (Skey) would, I think, like to settle down in England* with his wife and son, now aged 6 years old. [NB: He emigrated to the USA not so long after the War!] Out of those (his son's) 6 years he has been with him for approximately 1½, and feels it rather badly, not unnaturally. From that we got on to the old topic*, which occupied us until 'Lights out'. {*This would be the current war situation, as far as we could summarise it, and its possible effect on our own situation. One had to write in these vague and obscure terms, because of the ever-present possibility of searches by Jap guards and subsequent scrutiny of seized diaries.] Phil Lovely put forward his point of view very well, but I think it is a subject on which each must formulate his own opinion on the basis of his own observations and knowledge. The evidence on the other side of the picture is so very conflicting.

We were informed on Saturday by the Japanese authorities that they were unable to send officers' contributions to the POW Camp at Sandakan, and that no further such donations could be sent to the men's camp here.

Our C.O. here, Lt.Col. Whimster, belongs to the Ordinance Corps, and was in Malaya from about the middle of 1940 until the Capitulation. He knew Colonel and Freda McLare, Colonel Eveleigh and a number of others whom I knew either socially or from duty contact. I found that he knows the North Country (in England) very well too, and has stayed several times in Durham. He also seemed to know the history of the Finchale Abbey Road house (a small hotel built near the ruins of a mediaeval Benedictine Priory, near Durham City, just before the 2nd War) very well. What a small world we live in! There are two other North Countrymen here amongst the staff – Sgt. Hinckley, who lives in Jesmond, Newcastle-on-Tyne, and Private Morley of the Argyles, a native of Gateshead.

Friday October 15th: Almost the end of a very depressing week. On Sunday I caught a touch of the sun, and on Monday, had all the symptoms of a chill – high temperature – 101.5°, slight shivering bouts and a general feeling of "being out of sorts". Our amateur Doc – Victor Anderson who, incidentally, managed extraordinarily well, advised bed, keeping warm, and gave me 4 quinine tablets to take. So, after missing my Spanish and French lessons this week, I am now more or less fit again with, however, a reminder in the form of herpes on my nose and upper lip!

Sunday October 17th: A morning remarkable for its freshness after the chills and damp heat of the last few days. A clear sky, and a crispness in the air that was both welcome and invigorating.

The Bishop conducted a short afternoon service at 4 p.m., and preached on the "looks" of Christ and of mankind in general. Urged us to look upwards and forwards, which is very good advice for our and every circumstance.

A new batch of internees arrived the other day, which included the 2 doctors from Jesselton, who were seen by one of our party who had been in hospital there.

Today finished "The Master of Ballantrae" by R.L. Stevenson; a tale of Scotland in the middle 18th Century which, I feel, must have been written for schoolboys but which I enjoyed very much. I think the last of R.L.S. I read were "Treasure Island" and "Catriona" many years ago.

Tuesday October 19th: Another book with a Scots flavour which I finished last week was "J.M.B.", a biography of Sir James Barrie, O.M., by Dennis Mackail. Starting with his birth in the Tenements, Kirriemuir (the "Thrums" of his later novels) it traces his boyhood through Glasgow Academy and the School at Dumfries to his undergraduate days at Edinburgh University, of which he became Chancellor some 40 years later.

Don Westwood, who was taken to hospital on Sunday, is still unconscious and having strychnine injections. His chances, according to Lt.Col. King (RAMC, I/C the Camp Hospital), are 50:50. He is an Australian, previously in the RAAF, but now a Captain in the R.A.S.C. He had a bad attack of dysentery about November last year, which almost finished him, and left him with a weak heart. He is, like so many, groping for a creed which will provide him with some guiding force in life, and is a member of Ron Green's psychology class.

Wednesday October 20th: Major Suga came into Camp this morning and told the Colonel that the Australian officers from Sandakan were expected down here shortly. He did not know whether the rest of the British officers would be coming with them.

Finished "The Spirit of London" by a naturalised foreigner Paul Cohen-Portheim, who apparently spent part of the last war (WW.I) in an internment camp. It is a well-written and beautifully illustrated book in the Batsford series. He covers London remarkably thoroughly and there are chapters on traditional London, amusements (from Hampstead Heath to the Royal Opera) and eating places varying from the Savoy Grill to Lyons Corner House. An entertaining book.

Thursday October 28th: Last Sunday listened to a very delightful concert given by a male-voice choir, which sang quite a lot of old favourites including excerpts from "The Desert Song", "White Horse Inn", "Student Prince", etc. A song which appealed to me very much was "Yesterday", which I had not heard before, and which seemed to have a rather haunting nostalgic quality. In spite of the intermittent rain showers, about a dozen of us sat outside under the rubber trees until the concert finished.

A feature of this past week was the arrival of the party of Australian officers from Sandakan. To accommodate them, the Dutch officers were moved to the old Rice Store, and their hut was taken over by the new arrivals. The barbed wire fence was adjusted by Indian details the next day. I notice that the Dutch have been allowed to keep most of their gardens. Our daily wind and rain storms are now generally later than for the past few weeks, and now start about 7 or 8 o'clock at night.

Thursday October 28th: Our first all-day wood party. Turned out 20 in morning and 40 in the afternoon, and as a result, managed to get in one week's supply of wood. We understand that in future, the Japanese are going to organise wood-cutting on a schedule basis each week, and that our days are Tuesday and Wednesday. The new area is outside the perimeter wire, about 100 yards to the left of the Main Guard Room, and is well wooded with rubber trees. The Australian officers, Dutch Fathers and internees were also out on the same job. We were also notified today that permission for a joint Concert with the other Camps on November 3rd, was now cancelled, but that we would be allowed to have one in our own area on that date.

Friday October 29th: F/Lt. Jones today received a letter from his god-mother, who lives in Zurich, Switzerland. It was addressed "British P.O.W., Borneo Camps," which address she had received from his mother. 2 theories account for this – (1) that the Jap Govt. have notified our Authorities that we are held in Borneo and (2) that our Changi postcards, before despatch, were overprinted "Borneo".

Saturday October 30th: Pay parade held this a.m. at 11.30. Gnr. Ralf Eaton, one of Tony Hare-Scott's battery, died this morning at 6 a.m. from suspected cerebral malaria and was buried at 11 a.m. Tony, John Bailey and Douglas Dewar and the Colonel being present. Eaton was on the usual working party yesterday, woke this morning with a high fever and died on the way to hospital. The officers who attended the funeral report that the cemetery looks very unkempt, but Maj. Suga has promised to have it cleaned up.

Finished a short, light and readable biography of the amorous 18th Century adventurer Giacomo Casanova de Seignalt by Bonamy Dobree today. It is rather superficial and I think that Casanova's actual "Memoires" should be more entertaining.

Sunday October 31st: The other O.R. who was taken to Kuching Hospital yesterday with suspected Q spotted (?) fever died, and was buried today.

Tuesday November 2nd: All day wood party. Quite pleasant – spent most of the day "carrying" with Alan Bazell.

Today, LAC Wilson and A.C. Mockeridge arrived very unexpectedly from Sandakan. They were both at Sandakan Hospital – Mockeridge an appendicitis case and Wilson his Nursing Orderly. As they had come into contact with some Australian officers who had been sent to prison, they were sent down here. From them I gather that our people moved to the new camp at Sandakan 2 days after our departure, that there are 14 huts, most of which have 40 men in them, 2 being used as a hospital and one as an Officers Mess and Medical Inspection Hut combined. The sick have declined to 80 and there are now, again, 'drome working parties working at the old spot. They leave the Camp at 8 a.m. and return at 6 p.m. as the march takes an hour each way. "Q" Willis is permanently in charge – this seems rather strange. Tiffin is cooked on the spot. In the Camp itself, the huts are similar to the ones here – clapboard and attap – but there is still no running water or electric light. There is, however, a swimming pool, but neither airman seems to know if there are any means of changing the water. Linge and his assistants, we hear, are engaged in the laying of bamboo water pipes into the Camp from a stream some distance away.

Wednesday November 3rd: A parade for all camps in the area. Facing the stage in the main square, there were, from left to right (1) the women and children internees (2) the Mother Superior and Nuns (3) the small Punjabi Contingent (4) ourselves (5) Australian officers (6) Dutch Officers and Dutch Fathers, 24 in number (7) British ORs. The parade was addressed by Major Suga of the Japanese Army who said that today was the anniversary of the death of the Emperor Moiji, the founder of modern Japan. In Japan, the day was called Moiji-Setsu, and as the climate in the country is at its best about now, is generally devoted to sports. He concluded that he had always been magnanimous in his dealings with us, and he hoped we would be as happy today as the circumstances of our confinement would allow. I was particularly impressed with the cheerfulness and neatness of the women and children whom I saw today for the first time en masse. Most of them are from British North Borneo, I understand, and have been interned well over a year. But in spite of this most of them looked very attractive this morning, some even having obviously some make-up left!! Our anticipated concert was rained off tonight.

Thursday November 4th: The concert took place tonight in the Square. A stage had been rigged up with branches of rubber trees and blankets, and an electric light extension from one of the huts. Victor Anderson was compere, and introduced the 3 sketches (including one by Paterson) and individual turns, mainly songs by a quintet lead by 'Wag' Price and a trio with Monty (Montgomery)-Campbell as leader. Compared with concerts we have had at Malang, Changi and Sandakan, the standard was poor, but it did provide a welcome change.

Sunday November 7th: The Bishop (Hollis – an Anglican) came over this morning and took Holy Communion. He rambled rather badly during the service and does, I believe, freely confess that his memory is not now so good.

The weather of late has been treacherous. Rain lasting several hours during the day sends the temperature down to the 80°s F (today was 82°F) and the sun then comes out with its usual strength. These rapid changes of temperature have sent a large number of people down with head and chest colds recently.

The only book I read during the past week proved most interesting. It was "Renown" by Alan Hough, a biography of Benedict Arnold.

Monday November 8th: Am writing this in the shade of our hut – Bulford is repairing the roof of No. 3 Hut with attap and he looks far from safe – first fine morning for days reflected in the amount of bedding out to air. "Digger" Marchmont [PL: A remarkable, older Australian who claimed to have invented a tubeless tyre – unknown in those days] sits and reads under his tree, Miles the batman polishes a Rolls razor from Jones' case, Bick(erton) and Pat(erson) scrape away at the drains and John Bailey and Taylor work away at their shorthand. The gardens come on apace. Tony Hare-Scott produced some potato tops for our soup for the first time yesterday. The Indian corn, beans and brinjals are also doing well, but there seems to be far too little chikor manis to me: from all accounts this latter seems to be most prolific in Vitamin B.

Sunday November 14th: Am writing this to the strains of Monty Campbell's* [PL: Lt. Montgomery-Campbell, Argyle & Sutherland Highlanders – with Geoff Threadgold, one of the youngest officers in the Camp] during his weekly practice ½ hour 6-6.30 p.m. The past week has been uneventful. Canteen supplies were a little more plentiful than usual: each officer got 7 packets of Sago biscuits and 4 of peanut toffee, whilst the Mess got papayas, bananas and limes. For the first time since our arrival here, we have been given rice polishings in bulk, of quite good quality, and not too badly riddled with maggots. I generally put 3 dessertspoonfulls on my rice porridge in the morning. Our 2-day weekly wood-party is still very successful despite our depleted numbers. Still more people seem to be going sick with scabies, ringworm, tropical ulcers and the like. There has also been a mild epidemic of sore throats, colds and diarrhoea recently, due no doubt to a change in the weather. Yesterday, Grey-Jones lost his ruler!

December 27th: Big event of today was the Camp Concert which was suddenly announced at 2.30 p.m. We all trooped up to the main square, where a high stage had been rigged up. The arrival of the various camps provided continuous interest, particularly, of course, the women internees. The way in which they managed to turn themselves out under these conditions simply amazes me: some seem even to have "make-up", and their morale seems very high. The weather, which was overcast at the beginning, with threatening black clouds in the background, eventually cleared up into a very fine afternoon, with the sun breaking through intermittently.

PROGRAMME – CAMP CONCERT, 27/12/43.

1. Camp No. 4 (Children)	Dance: Pop goes the Weasel. Songs: Santa Claus has come to town. Recit: Footsteps in the Snow (Julie Tuxford) Song: A Christmas Wish	
2. Camp No. 2 (Internees)	Entertainment, Songs, Etc. Mr. H. Bishop	
3. Camp No. 4 (Ladies)	Songs we used to sing – 1943 Version Carol: Silent Night	) Ladies) Choir
4. Camp No. 6 Dutch Fathers)	Carol: Stille Nacht Ewe sig God Koo de Radice Jesse	)) Choir)
5. Hospital	Songs & Entertainment by Compton & his Iodoform Boys	) Sgt. Burnley (?)) Trigg, Compton
6. Camp No. 5 (Indonesians)	Lagoe: Lagoe di Padang Terang Bulan	))
7. Camp No. 1A (Australian Officers)	Songs: Waltzing Matilda Volga Boatmen Marie When Day is done Dinah I'm going to lock up my heart Brahms Lullaby Carol: O Come, All ye faithful	)) Choir) and) Sextet)))
8. Camp 1B (British Officers)	Clerkots (?) Apache Dance	) Lieut.) Allan
9. Camp No. 4	Songs: Toscelli's Serenade One Fine Day (Butterfly) Loch Lomond My Hero (Chocolate Soldier Un pen d 'amour	)) Mrs. Wands) (with piano) and violin))
10. Camp No. 3	Variety and Pantomime with Lou Levy and his Band. Tarleton, Pasquill, Ditchfield, Hardy and Company.	

****

138

The rest of the old year I devoted to taking over the cookhouse from "Kettle" (Capt. Kettlewell). He works very hard, but I get the impression that his constant presence in the cookhouse is a source of embarrassment to the cooks, especially as his temper is rather short, due to his poor health. The two cooks, Sgt. Roberts and Cpl. Martin, run the Cookhouse with the assistance of 2 other ranks – Morley and Moxon – and the part-time assistance of any batmen available. They work extremely hard, and are kept going from 5.30 a.m. until almost 8 p.m., which is a very long day on these rations. Roberts belongs to the Royal Army Catering Corps and a pastry cook in civil life in Newport, Monmouthshire.

Brunei Bay and
Labuan Island

NORTH BORNEO

BORNEO

JESSELTON

Jesselton

Papar

KENINGAU

Beaufort

Weston

Sipitang

Sapong

Brunei Bay

Labuan I.

LABUAN

Muara I.

BRUNEI

Brooketon

Brunei

SARAWAK

BRUNEI

Seria

Lutong

MIRI

80 MILES

60

40

20

0

MILES 20 10

LABUAN

LABUAN ISLAND

TIMBALAI

BROWN BEACH

Labuan

Victoria Hbr.

KIAM ROAD

Hamilton Pt.

MILES

0 1 2 3 4 5

Chapter Five

1944

A number of events occurred in 1943 which were instrumental in influencing the Japanese Imperial H.Q. ordering the re-organisation of the Borneo Garrison into the 37 Army structure to counter the threats which were developing from within the area.

They were concerned about the large number of Chinese who were preparing a guerrilla organisation and endeavouring to obtain supplies of arms from the U.S.-Filipino Forces which, at this time, were beginning to receive arms from Australia via U.S. submarines. The Chinese realised Jesselton was lightly defended and on the 10th October 1943 they led an attack on the Japanese Garrison at Jesselton which was brutally put down by the Japanese forces. The Chinese had endeavoured to get the POWs involved at this time and were told any action such as an uprising was premature and nothing should be done until instructions were received from the Allies.

In the meantime, General MacArthur had structured the loosely organised bands of guerrillas in the Philippines into separate Military Commands and supplied them with radio transmitters by submarine, he requested and was granted the huge cargo submarine, USS NARWHAL, to be placed in his command for that purpose. The NARWHAL had the carrying capacity of about 100 tons, as against the Fleet submarines of about 3 tons. Every small group was provided with a transmitter and were able to maintain contact with the Command Stations who were in touch with Australia.

In June 1943, eight Australians escaped from Berhala Island – they had arrived there with 'E' Force. When they arrived at Tawi Tawi after their escape they were put on strength with Colonel Suarez and later ordered to Mindanao; in the meantime, they clashed with a force of pro-Japanese Moros and lost Driver Butler. Later, they captured a group of Japanese seamen; unable to keep them as prisoners or feed them, they took them out to sea and put them to death with the parang. The Japanese Command would have received the news of this massacre of their seamen by the Australians.

About this time, Captain Hamner, U.S.N., arrived at Tawi Tawi with radio equipment. Australian L.H.Q. was fully aware of the escape of the eight POWs -

Also at this time G.H.Q. approved a Special Operation landing an Intelligence group at Labian Point, just 100 miles south of Sandakan, in October 1943 and codenamed PYTHON I. The area overlooked the important Sibutu Channel where much of the tanker traffic to and from the oil ports could be observed.

This mission, under Major Chester, a former resident of British North Borneo, operated for three months successfully reporting the movement of shipping to Australia, who, in turn, advised the submarines in the locality details of the positions. Often the operators would witness the sinking of Japanese tankers. This group was reinforced in January 1944; during this operation one of the party, Brandis, became lost and after wandering from some days was found by the local people and handed over to the Japanese.

The Japanese reacted swiftly to this capture – Colonel Otsuka, Commander of the Sandakan Garrison, dispatched Captain Takakuwa with a Company of men to the Labian area to round up the rest of the party. Here they found a well-worked track from the lookout tree back to the camp site and they set a trap. They caught Sgt. McKenzie and Lieut. Rudwick and took them back to Sandakan where the Kempe Tai commenced their torture.

The Japanese later claimed the Australians endeavoured to teach the Japanese how to use the equipment – it is most likely the Australians would have made some attempt to contact their Base.

Early 1944 Major Nishihara, the Judicial Officer at 37 Army H.Q., was recalled to Tokyo. It seems the Japanese were growing more concerned about the security of the region; disturbed at the wide-spread guerrilla activity in the Philippines, they were unable to garrison the hundreds of islands and villages; then there was the Jesselton uprising; the serious charge against Captain Matthews was insurrection, endeavouring to obtain arms, and possessing arms to assist an invading force – the PYTHON activities – the massacre of Japanese seamen by escaped prisoners – and they believed an Allied air-borne invasion of Sandakan was imminent to use the airfield the POWs were building for advanced operations. They were convinced of the threat, and ordered the Yamamoto Battalion from Manchuria to be stationed at the 9 Mile to protect the airfield. The POWs' rations were reduced even further to render them ineffective to assist an invading force.

In March 1944, the gallant Captain Matthews was shot by a firing squad of three at Kuching. Several Australians in 'F' Troop Kuching Other Ranks' camp were taken away from a work party to dig a grave. Roy Kent said it was about midday, the sun was directly overhead, when the truck arrived with a blood-soaked coffin. They learnt it was Captain Matthews. The order to prepare the grave was given while the Court proceedings were in progress. Major Nishihara, with instructions from Tokyo, had appointed the Judges and given them instructions of what was expected of them. The eight local people, mostly from the North Borneo Constabulary, were found guilty and killed by Nishihara's firing squad.

The remaining officers and men at Sandakan were now on a starvation program, their rice issue was about 7 ozs. per man per day; deaths were mounting, hospital huts increasing in number. The dead were placed in a mortuary by the main gates for the allocated burial parties to collect and carry down the road to the Cemetery. Here the Japanese removed any form of identification.

At all times the Japanese held the fate of the prisoners in their hands; heavily armed machine-gun posts were constructed just outside the English and Australian Camps.

Peter Lee's diary continues
1944

New Year's Eve was ushered in in the traditional manner on the Square (i.e. our Camp Square) where we formed a circle, sang "Auld Lang Syne" under the direction of Mac(Arthur) and Monty Campbell (Montgomery-Campbell), and the New Year with 3 very hearty cheers. Handshakes all round followed. Not many of us thought that we would still be POWs now at this time last year! Still, we are again confident and optimistic about our chances for 1944!

Victory for the Allied Nations! It is perhaps strange that our optimism should be based on the scraps of news which we have been able to pick out from the "Nippon Times"!! [PL: In fact, we were getting BBC News from the clandestine radio in the Mens' Camp, built and operated by W/O. Beckett, (at that time substantively a Corporal I recall). It was brought in to us, at first, by word of mouth from an R.C. Padre in the Civil Internees Camp, on Sundays, and thus, inevitably always thereafter referred to as "The Papal Bull!"]

Am taking over the job of Messing Officer, my main task will be the variation of the Menu as much as possible: no easy job in these circumstances. Breakfast provided the starting point, and as an experiment I put on the usual quantity of porridge plus boiled fish and rice – it was received very well indeed. Other innovations tried during the first 10-day period were – duff (ginger and peanut flavour), banana sauce and rice for breakfast, a new type of angel-on-horseback, biscuit, and nasi goreng fried in pork fat.

Sunday 9th January: Little of interest during the past week. The work-party was cancelled yesterday, but a load of wood was delivered at the gate in lieu, so all is well! Our hens, bought at Christmas, are now producing an average of 8 eggs a day, on a diet of prawn ends and rice; these are being issued, fried, each morning on a roster basis. We also have 4 ducks or rather, 3 drakes and 1 duck – their sex has proved the No. 1 mystery of the past week. In spite of a physical examination by our poultry experts, nobody seemed quite certain as to their gender. However, it was decided yesterday to kill and raffle the 3 drakes on account of their depredations in the garden, 'Shot' Spurway having, in the meantime, done his best to maim them by well-directed clods of earth. The draw took place this morning, and the 3 prizewinners were the Punjabi Officers, Sgt. Hinckley and L.A.C. Stridgeon.

I was fortunate enough, during the past week, to borrow from Don Westwood, the first of the Pelman series of Grey Books, to which I intend to devote at least one hour a day. He told me that he bought them from an O.R. in the Men's Camp for $10.

Saturday 15th January: My 28th Birthday today A lot of good-natured chaffing and "Happy Returns" (but not as a POW!) and a birthday greeting in the form of a Union Jack, with a centre-piece inscribed "Happy Birthday – Many Lagis! This day we all extend our greetings to the Officer I/C Messing." Up to date everyone seems satisfied with the changes I have been able to introduce into our messing arrangements; so much so that the slogan "Lee's Larger Lagis" has been coined! I always remind my brother officers, however, that as yet only 15 days of my 3 month period have elapsed! The affair of the 32 extra rissoles a "one-days wonder". I do find, however, that intelligent supervision rather than constant interference with Cooks and their staff – Sgt. Roberts, Cpl. Martin (Royal Army Catering Corps) and Privates Morley, Moxon and Shropshire, produces much greater interest and co-operation. I visit the Canteen at 8.30 pm each night and discuss the following day's menu with the cooks. Every morning I receive the previous day's issues from Sgt. Hinckley and bill the menu for the day on our slate notice-board – as is natural, the interest displayed in the day's food is very keen! Rations are collected from the Japanese ration store every other day by Philip Lovely and myself. For the first time, today (16th Jan.) we received some yams in our rations; these make a very good potato substitute and if anything are better for fritters etc. than the sweet potatoes we have used so far.

Thursday January 20th: High jinks in the Batmens' Quarters! [PL: Cannot remember details!]

Another batch of "Nippon Times" arrived the other day dated 1-30 September 1943. They contain some very interesting accounts of the Capitulation of the Italians on Sept. 3rd '43, which was not announced until 8th September. Mussolini was apparently arrested on July 25 by the Badoglio regime, after an interview with King Victor Emmanuel, and was later rescued from Ponza, an island in the Gulf of Gaeta, by German paratroops! During the negotiations General Carton de Wiart V.C. was released from his imprisonment which had lasted 3 years. The 4th or 5th meeting between Churchill and Roosevelt is reported as having taken place at Quebec in August last years, as a result of which Vice-Admiral Mountbatten was appointed C.in.C. Allied Forces in S.E. Asia.

Wood parties are now announced as being suspended indefinitely and wood is supplied as required – about once every 3 days. A very large area of ground to the rear of our camp has recently been cleared, dug over, and wired-off by other ranks, and is being converted into a kitchen garden. Canteen supplies during the past 2 weeks have been plentiful especially fruit: bananas, plantains, langsats, mangosteens, small oranges and even a few soursaps (durian blanda). We received rather a shock however, the P.M.C. and I, when we costed them on the 20th – $792!! As we saved $340 by the absence of prawns, I was reckoning on cutting down the Messing Sub. to about $4-5 per head. The best laid plans oft go astray!

Sunday 30th January: Messing for the period under review totalled $9.50. per officer which, with batmans' salaries, worked out at $10.25. High, but everyone has seemed satisfied with the messing during the month. Last Sunday we were fortunate enough to get a sack of tapioca root which provided us with some grated tapioca doughnuts, which proved extremely popular.

The Colonel was taken into hospital on the 15th, suffering from a slight attack of dysentery, and was followed afterwards by Tom Huggins with the same complaint. Charles Farmer of the Royal Army Pay Corps was taken to hospital with a large ulcer on his thigh, and Don Westwood (RASC) with nervous trouble. Digger (Marchmont) returned to the fold with some very amusing accounts of his hospital experiences. During the Colonel's absence, Major 'Nobby' Clarke, R.A., took over command.

Major Suga also returned to Kuching during the period from his long journey. He came down to our Camp one morning and conveyed belated Christmas and New Year greetings to us. Major Clarke had an interview with him shortly after his return and brought up various subjects – amongst which was the question of payments of the ORs Canteen by this Camp, letters and Red Cross parcels, clothing, and library books. Apropos the latter, he was told that the removal of library books was a reprisal for similar treatment alleged to have been meted out to Japanese internees in the U.S.A. and Canada. However, they were promised back shortly. A change of Japanese command has also taken place. Lt. Nagata has been placed in charge of the Civilian Internees, and all POWs have been "taken-over" by Lt. Watanabe.

Various letters arrived recently. Jerry Skey got 3 – his first – one of which announced the birth of a son to his wife 18 months ago. They have called him Simon, and Jerry, tho' very proud of having another son, is not particularly pleased with the name! Bill Saunders too was notified that he became the father of a daughter – Jennifer – about the same time ago. He is absolutely appalled at the name! Evening roll-calls are now held at the gate, and the Japs insist on all officers wearing at *least* shirts, shorts and a hat. This is a good thing.

One more gunner died – of quinsy, and also an elderly Nun – this latter is the first death amongst the women.

The Bishop still continues his visits on alternate Sundays, and is as cheerful as ever. His cassock, however, could do with some soap and water! Messing became more difficult at the beginning of February, as canteen supplies showed a great decrease in quantity. Innovations include a Mark II rissole, made from grated tapioca root and sweet potato, and two varieties of jam –

papaya and lime, and marrow and ginger, all popular. The Sandakan banana doughnut still proves popular. The garden is now proving its worth by supplying us with a fair number of sweet potatoes, brinjals, chillies, beans, chikor manis, onion leaves and potato tops. I also tried boiling (twice) leaves from the tapioca plant, but in spite of their 3-hour cooking they were still tough and rubbery – not a success. A few hundred rambutans came in during the first week of February, 10 for 16¢. In spite of their expense, it was good to taste them again.

Sunday 13th February: Sports, rather suddenly announced a few days ago, were held on the Square at 10 a.m. Consisted only of volley-ball – a type of basket ball played with a centre net and a team of 9. We were beaten by the Dutch Fathers, the Aussie Officers beat the Dutch Officers, Indian ORs beat the Indonesians, and the Male Internees beat the British ORs! Two Japanese photographers were in evidence and took photos of the proceedings, including the prize presentation by Major Suga, during which everyone was asked to clap. The day was dull and overcast. I was busy in the Cookhouse and did not attend.

Spent some time chatting to Digger (Marchmont), about some of his experiences in Tanjong Priok and elsewhere, also, later to Tuppy Hancock, whose father had been Commissioner of Prisons in Singapore, on the same theme. Thoughts:-wonder how Mother's garden is getting on at home – the privet hedge must now be quite high. Dora's (my sister) fir trees also must be over 8' high now – wonder if she and husband Bill are still living at Broadmeadows, or whether petrol restrictions have driven them into Durham again.

Friday 18th February: Two "major" events today. I received a German Red Cross Reply Letter from family friend Michael McCarton in Jersey; and a Concert was held on the Main Square in the afternoon. Mac's letter – 24 words on a single sheet of paper – was dated 24th July 1943 and gave his address as still "Kathmaur", Top of St. John's Road, St. Helier, Jersey. The message was: "Glad to hear news of you via Tokyo and German Red Cross. Have informed your sister. All well here. Kind regards." It bore no signature but was over-stamped "Bailiff of Jersey's Enquiry and News Service". The printed text was in French and German, and bore the Red Cross sign and the address of the Deutsches Rotes Krenz in the Bluchestrasse, Berlin. It had passed through the International Red Cross at Geneva on Oct. 16th, 1943. I replied on the back as follows: "Greetings to all! Delighted hear both well. Many thanks informing Dora. Am fit and cheerful. Happy memories Jersey, am looking forward our next meeting. Warmest regards." Jerry Skey took the reply to the office, and the Japanese promised to send it off. On the assumption it should take 6 months to get to Jersey, they should get it about Sept. or October this year.

The Concert, the mainstay of which was a local violin and mandolin band from Kuching – there were 7 performers, and the music played was almost wholly Japanese. The first 3 numbers were very pleasing, and with a certain rhythm, but most of the other tunes seemed alike. Still, they put up a good show and were well received. The Australian Officers put on a very good South American sketch, with their "Swing Sextet", and managed to bring in most of the more popular S.A. tango songs such as "Lady in Red", "Lady of Spain", "Down Argentine Way". The women internees were represented by a very game old Scotswoman, about 50 I should think, who sang, in an atrocious voice "Loch Lomond" and "I belong to Glasga!" She was old enough to be most people's Mother, had grey hair and a very homely face and manner, and got a rousing reception. The ORs were represented by Levy and his accordion and trumpet band, and the usual crooner, but in the middle of their act, the weather, which had been overcast most of the day, finally broke in heavy rain, and the rest of the concert was abandoned. And so back to Camp.

Our largest consignment of bananas had arrived the day before – in all about 6000, all of which were handed over to me for Messing use. Besides their obvious use for fritters and fruit salads, they will provide a very welcome filling for the evening kedgeree which now consists almost entirely of kong stalks, dried cucumber and baked potato. The gardens are now providing a useful and continuous supply of potatoes, potato tops and greens generally, which are tiding us over this rather lean period quite well.

Friday 25th February: Pte. Farr of the R.A.O.C. died yesterday of galloping TB and was buried today – Capts. Skey, Paterson, Saunders and Lt. North attending the funeral.

Some cameos: (1) Our pet cat dragged in a rat trap, complete with dead rat, about 12.30 a.m. this morning, woke up almost the whole hut. (2) Our 2 families in the poultry world – one of 12 and the other 8, going out on their daily expeditions in search of worms – quite a number of helpers ready to dig over the ground for them! (3) The daily burial of excreta – Jonah finding a foot-long tapeworm therein! (4) Major Swaine cutting the toes from his stockings, and inserting a 2-inch long extension in each. (5) The skin cases – particularly Jimmy Grieve and Alan Bazell, having their hot-water baths – young Macintosh is doing a good job in the No. 2 Hut as a volunteer nursing orderly. (6) The afternoon race in the Canteen, "Kidda", W.A.G. Price etc. and their systems.

The Bishop no longer conducts our services, as each Camp has now been allocated a Padre without possibility of interchange. The Bishop now does the Men's Camp exclusively, and our Church of England Services are taken by Padre Sponton, who paid us his first visit under the new arrangement last Sunday.

Sunday 27 February: Pte. Farr of the R.A.O.C. died and was buried yesterday, from nephritis. Don Westwood, who came out of hospital yesterday, told us that this particular man had given a talk to the men in the hospital on Friday night, and was found dead by orderlies on reveille. There are apparently several more cases of nephritis, 2 [or 7] of TB and about 700 of general skin diseases in the Camp. One man's foot was so badly ulcerated that his tendons were showing. Don himself looks well, and says he is sleeping very much better now.

The weather for the past 3 or 4 days has been persistently wet and cheerless, and has had marked effect on the rations. Had a long chat with Thready last night on post-war personal problems; he still hopes to stay in the Army afterwards. Talk then developed into a discussion of various types of M.T. and the large numbers which were left in Java. John Harris and Alan Bazell still looking rather thin.

Monday 28 February: A torrential downpour last night about midnight woke me up, with rain driving into my mosquito net. In the ensuing melee to close our window, heavily encumbered, as usual, with towels, sarongs etc., I managed to knock over 2 of Banton's bottles and general paraphernalia, but by that time most of the hut was awake. Had some difficulty in getting off to sleep again, and had barely succeeded when reveille sounded. Another grey damp morning – the rain last night had cleared away the mud from paths etc., but had left everything feeling rather moist.

Had a chat with Col. Whimster this morning.

Tuesday 7 March: The weather, which during the past week continued wet, damp and overcast, has showed definite signs of change during the past 2 days. Rain during the night is slight, and falls only in short intermittent showers during the day.

Skin disease such as scabies and ulcers still continue to increase in the Camp. Young MacIntosh is doing some very valuable work as the "Medical Orderly" for No. 2 Hut, which seems to have the greatest number skin cases. He had scabies very badly himself when at Jesselton, and has evidently now acquired quite a professional touch. Jimmy Grieves has shown the most marked improvement of late, but Alan Bazell is still very much scarred, and very thin. Bickerton was taken to hospital last week, for observation, after one of his fainting attacks, but was back again after 2 days. John Harris took his place: for no accountable reason John began to lose weight very rapidly about 2 weeks ago, and with it, his appetite. He is only 21 or 22, and naturally became worried, which did not improve matters.

Colonel King took to his bed at the beginning of last week, and has been replaced with Col. Shepherd of the R.A.A.M.C. All officers who have been treated by him speak very highly of his work. Digger (Marchmont) still pursuing snails, and has now constructed a special trap to house them. His pursuit of these things has created some amusement recently in the Camp.

The Colonel (Whimster) has now resumed command of the Camp after his convalescence: there are now no "Red Ticket" officers (excused from duty) left in the Camp. Last night spent most of the late evening walking up and down the garden path with Gerry Skey; there was a full moon and practically no cloud about, and the result was a fine study in strong moonlight and shadow. The cicadas, we have noticed recently, are becoming more noisy, and are especially active on cool, dark, nights.

Tonight, another perfect evening, cool and clear, I listened to some of Thready's view on life: he is now toying with the idea of the Colonial Police after the War.

The chicks continue to flourish, and we now have another brood of 10, making 28 in all. Was amused to notice the fuss one of the old hens made when she successfully attacked a small flying lizard; she was very determined that none of her brood should go near it. The lizard was a pretty little thing with a speckled grey-brown body and triangular wings, pale brown underneath, which folded neatly into his sides. Rations continue poor – today's consisted of 6 cucumbers, 13 small pumpkins and 1 bundle (?) cabbage. I am hoping that better weather will mean better rations.

Monday 20 March: *The Social System*

> The British, with their tidy minds,
> Divide themselves up into kinds.
> The common kind, they call the masses,
> The better kind, the upper classes.
>
> In either case it's really not
> A specially inspiring lot.
> The common ones play darts in pubs
> The others slowly die in Clubs.
>
> (From: The British Character by Pont?)

Friday 24 March: Two disturbances on the millpond of our existence during the past week. On Monday, the area was visited by Lt. General Yamawaki, the Japanese Chief Army Commander in Borneo. He arrived in the centre of a cortege of 3 cars, his flying 2 flags – one red and white and the lower one yellow. He inspected various Camps, including the Australian Officers and the British ORs, but did not enter our own. The other event was the arrival of about 300 packages of American Red Cross on Wednesday, quite a number of which, we are pleased to hear, are medical stores.

John Harris, who was diagnosed as suffering from "general weakness", still continues to lose weight, in spite of the extra diet in the shape of eggs, extra fruit and vegetables which we are giving him. A couple of days ago, dysentery again broke out in the Camp and today there are 66 cases – all the ORs are being inoculated today.

The Colonel and Jerry Skey had an interview with Major Suga about a week or 10 days ago, in which they brought up the usual subjects – Red Cross supplies, clothing, rations, health, canteen etc. One very satisfactory result of the interview was that permission was given to us to send money to our men at Sandakan, much to the surprise of S/Ldr. Hardie with whom, incidentally, I had a long talk on Tuesday evening.

Weather has been wet and unsettled during the past week, but fortunately during our surprise search of our belongings – which happened without warning – last Saturday, the afternoon was fine and we were thus able to sun ourselves near the gate whilst it was proceeding. Jerry Skey and I have had several interesting yarns of late, after dinner, in the cool of the evening. I find these late evening walks and talks rather stimulating. Of course, one of the chief defects of this note writing is one's inability to express all the thoughts which pass and re-pass through the mind during this period of forced inactivity.

Monday 27 March: Owing to the recent outbreak of dysentery in the ORs camp, figures of which reached 86 yesterday, we were today inoculated with the first of 2 anti-dysentery vaccines at the Camp Hospital. Colonel King and Capt. Bailey did the inoculation, watched by Lt. Yamamoto, the Jap Doctor.

Was yesterday re-elected Messing Officer for the next 3 months, unopposed. Dant and Green were also re-elected, the latter finishing first in a 20-18 fight with Jeff North. John Perry was reappointed as P.M.C. for the ensuing 3 months by the Colonel. Little dust-up re our Camp Nursing Orderly just now. Hardie making himself rather unpopular.

Friday 31 March: Second dysentery inoculation was "done" by Colonel King, assisted by Docs. Bailey and Dutch Doc. Beeking.

Wednesday 5 April: Weather for the past few days has been extremely changeable, alternating between hot, sticky, blinding and cloudless days and cold, squally, overcast periods, sometimes lasting the whole day. As a result there have been a large number of very heavy head colds – Jerry, Dicky Bird, Phil Lovely and Tony Hare-Scott. Today wrote "Federal Union" (for some debate or group discussion).

Tom Elliott's flower-garden now progressing well – 3 beds each with red border of cannas.

25th May: After so long an interval, I think now is an opportune moment to recommence my epistle. The past few months have been tranquil ones on the whole, with only the small upsets which have now become part of one's daily existence, to disturb slightly the placid waters of Kuching life. But I still think the word "existence" is more apt than "life".

New regulations were announced about the beginning of April, which banned all classes, discussions, talks and the like; the library which now runs quite smoothly, helps to make up for the deficiency. A good deal of card-playing and the like is now done in the Camp, and helps to pass the time of those who are unable to study or amuse themselves otherwise.

Undoubtedly, the main event of the period was the arrival of the first really large consignment of mail since our captivity began 2¼ years ago. As all of it was for the 2 Java Parties, we were all very pleased indeed. I was fortunate enough to get ten – 2 from Mother, 1 from Dad, 1 from Mother and Dad, 3 from my sister Dora, 1 from Canon Wallis, 1 from Mrs. McLare, and one from the Air Ministry about my short-service commission gratuity. The letters were all written between March 2nd 1943, when apparently notification was first received that I was a POW, and July 12th 1943. Although the news they contained was extremely scanty, due no doubt to censorship regulations, it was a terrific thrill to receive them – my last letters from home being received at Tengah (RAF Station, Singapore) in December 1941. From them, I gather that Mother, Dad and Dora aren't too fit, although they say they are. Dad has retired (in September '42?) but does not state when and why, although it was obviously on grounds of health. I hope they are managing alright, but with prices rising, one is rather doubtful. If only one could help. Must devote my next postcard to Cox-King's, my branch of Lloyds Bank in London, two pounds a week should help, I think.

We now have a number of "new" fathers in the Camp; Ken Hammond, whose wife had twins 2 years ago; Ken Allen, father of a daughter; George Nordeman, now the possessor of a son and heir, David. Something must have gone wrong with the baby Bickerton's wife was expecting when he left England in December 1941, as his sister makes only cryptic references to it. The new fathers held a "happy dodger" dinner to celebrate their new offspring, all of whom are now 2 years old!! We managed to put on quite a good menu for the occasion. Our next big occasion was Empire Day, for which we killed our goat. It yielded 28 lbs. of meat and etceteras, and about 2 pints of blood: everything was used and "Big Lix" was the order of the day. Our 14 Infantry Officers held a dinner that night and finished with the Royal Toast.

On 28th May 1944, Paddy Girvan gave another of his monthly "Girvan's Gaieties" programmes. The Batmens' Choir sang the usual swing number, Smith and Glasgow as Reg Rissole and Dickie Duff did their "barbed" dialogue, the 6 Lead Swingers sung and Pip Parsons did a monologue "John Thomas". They all tried hard, but the mediocrity was very apparent compared to some of the shows we have seen in POW Camps.

2nd June: Had an interesting couple of hours with John Harris the other night at the water tongs, (collection points for garden water) in bright moonlight. The subject – wines. His father is solicitor to the London County Council, and is also a member of the "Court" and of the Wine Committee of the Ironmongers Company (one of the so-called 'Livery' Companies of the City of London).

3rd June: H.M. King's Birthday. We have been fortunate in the past few days, to get 200 katies of Pusu and Rusup (two varieties of whitebait, the latter rather like anchovies) through the Canteen, and we are also promised 50 ducks for killing, and eggs, if and when hospital needs are satisfied. With the rice polishings (256 lbs. obtained for 200 lbs. rice), the greens, and now the whitebait, I think that the health of the Camp, which has been extremely poor recently (skin diseases mainly – scabies, ulcers, ringworm) should show some material improvement.

The weather recently has been most unseasonable, heavy and sultry in the afternoon, with heavy, massive cumulus storm clouds coming up from the South and S.W. about 5 or 6 p.m. Sometimes the storm passes us by, but we usually get some rain either about 7 or 8 p.m. or during the night. The storm is usually preceded by a fresh breeze which sets the rubber trees rustling, and has a marvelously invigorating effect on one, both mentally and physically. Collected the following notes from Ken Allen on dress (he is in the Trade) which should be useful when re-stocking one's wardrobe – especially the bits about cloths etc. [NB: A description on every aspect of menswear, from worsteds, wools, tweeds and flannels, to dressware, single and double-breasted suits, evening ware, country and sports wear and the like.)

Writing the above has made me positively homesick! Roll on the boat!

Sunday 4 June: On the first anniversary of Colonel Russell's death, a party of 25 officers, 5 ORS, the RSM (Sunderland) and Liaison W/O. (Southern) from the ORs Camp, and Colonel King, were allowed to walk down to Kuching Cemetery and hold a memorial service for him. I represented the R.A.F., with Johnnie (Johnstone) and Pethybridge. Going down, we walked together, but split up on the return journey; on the latter my companions were MacArthur and Monty-Campbell, the former pointing out to me places of interest en route. The day was fine, and as we marched off at 08.30, there was a very pleasant coolness in the air which was an added bonus.

153

On arrival at the Museum, we were joined by Lt. Ojima, our new Camp Commandant, formerly in charge of Dahan, and Miss Takada, the new office interpreter vice Lt. Fujita Major, now Lt.Col. Suga, joined the party in the Cemetery. The ceremony, which was brief, was taken by the Bishop. Wreaths were laid by Col. Suga, who also made a eulogistic speech ending with God's blessings which passes all understanding, and by Major Whiting representing us. After which the "Last Post" and "Reveille" were sounded, all officers saluting on the "Reveille". The quiet was only broken by the noise of a car starting, and the lazy hum of insects. Chinese Christian graves, some in characters, some in English, looked forlorn.

The past few weeks have seen a rapid increase in sickness in the Camp. Colds in the head and chest became so general that we had to put on a course of 3 nightly drinks at 9 p.m. for the whole Camp. Skin diseases, too, showed a tendency to increase, a particularly bad case being young John Farwell. But perhaps most disturbing of all was a minor epidemic of dysentery which started with Don Westwood (who has chronic bacillary) and LAC Wilson, and ended in 10 hospital cases by the 16th. People affected were Paterson, Larder, Coleman, MacIntosh, Harris, A.C. Smith, Maddox, Campbell. Fortunately none were serious. As, during the period, we had received extra-large canteen supplies, including 200 Katies of Whitebait (@ 68 cts. a Katie) – 3 jars, many hundreds of pineapples, bananas and pisang tandok, besides rice polishings and larger quantities of greens from the garden than usual, I was inclined to put it down to the cumulative effect of all these.

Chutney, Potato and Onion Soup, and Ersatz Sausages were Messing innovations. Vinegar was made from pineapple juice. Peter Huish and Bick(erton) interested in this.

Monday, June 19th: A gardening exhibition was held today on our Camp Square, which was opened by Major Clarke, who is deputising for Col. Whimster, now in hospital. The main exhibit was arranged by "Baggy" (Bagnell) and showed of produce which the garden grows. Quite a number of sideshows were run by various officers, including a "biscuit-biting" contest, horse racing (Chasing the Aces) run by "Gypsy" Smith and "Bookie" Foulkes, "Hidden Treasure" by Alan Dant, weight-guessing run by Ron Green, "Coin-in-bucket" by John Harris, and "Lifting Peppercorns" with a pair of chopsticks. We produced special menus for the occasion. A most successful exhibition which did impress on quite a number of people the very sterling work which the gardeners are doing for the Camp.

Author's Note: Here I was forced to curtail the entries because of the printing schedule

1944

After the departure of the officers in August 1943 and a short time later LAC Mockridge and A.C. Wilson arrived at Kuching, there was no further flow of information from the English Compound at Sandakan. Those remaining moved into the area described as No. 2 Compound.

The strength at this time would have been by the beginning of 1944 about 600. The officers were Captain Mills, R.A., Camp leader Captain Daniels, R.A.M.C., Flt. Lt. Blackledge, Medical Officer with the R.A.F., Sqdn. Ldr. Chaplain Wanless; F/O. Burgess; P.O. Linge; F/O. Cressey; Lt. G.H. Chopping, R.A.; Lt. P.H. Young, R.A. and Lt. I.D. Rolfe. The senior Warrant Officers were RSM Jacobi, J.W. Bessant, G.A. Hynes (who would go to Labuan): W.O. Sanders and R.M. Whiteside. The R.A. W.O. BSM. G.E. Wilson; AQMS F.A.J. Willis (Labuan).

Captain Nagai acted as second in command to Captain Hoshijima but seemed to take more interest in the English Compound which remained completely isolated from the Australians; occasionally they would endeavour to make contact when close by at the aerodrome. The death rate during the first half of the year was steady, however, it was known the number of those unable to work was increasing.

In June when the Labuan party was ordered to assemble, no one would have known its destination, it is not known how they were allocated. It is interesting to note the Australian nursing orderlies who joined Capt. Daniels in Java were placed on the draft with Flt. Lt. Blackledge. They may have felt, as did the Australians at Kuching, any other place would have to be better than Sandakan or Kuching.

In March 1944, Capt. Ray Steele arrived in Australia on board the USS NAHWAHL with one hundred other evacuees from the Philippines. He was the senior officer who escaped from Berhala Island back in June 1943 to the Philippines where he joined the U.S./Filipino Guerrilla Forces; he was able to give Allied Intelligence Bureau a report on the dispersement of Allied prisoners from Singapore from the fall of Singapore to the departure of 'E' Force in April 1943. With him was W.O. Wallace who filled in on the state of conditions in the Sandakan Compound and the fact it was lightly defended.

Army H.Q. in Melbourne commenced planning a possible rescue operation and used the idea as a training exercise for the 1 Battalion Australian Paratroop Regiment which was formed in 1942 after the return of the A.I.F. from the Middle East.

The plan was based on this now out-dated intelligence – Allied Intelligence did not know of the collapse of the Camp Underground and the wide-spread cruelty inflicted on the local people who had relatives connected with the Australians – nor did they know in March 1944 those involved in the movement were executed at Kuching or of the capture of Australians at Tambisan Point and that as a result of these incidents the Imperial General H.Q. substantially reinforced the garrison at Sandakan.

The proposal was studied by planning officers at S.W.G.H.Q. and found impracticable. The operation would have drawn off substantial forces from the proposed Leyte operation and caused postponement for a further two months. There were numerous other issues involved; there was no military advantage to such an operation; Sandakan was not rated highly – it had 23 miles of roads and depended on sea transport for survival; the airfield, like Tarakan, was likely to be water-logged and finally, politically, it would have created considerable pressure on General MacArthur on the rescue of American prisoners of war held in several camps in the Philippines. Prisoners of War were expendable, any such rescue operation would have caused a spate of massacres throughout POW Camps in Asia. The plan as submitted was severely flawed. The only rescue operation of prisoners of war was carried out by the Americans when they had overwhelming military forces nearby.

1944 was to be disastrous for Allied prisoners of war. On the completion of the Burma-Thailand Railway the Japanese decided to dispatch 10,000 of the fittest prisoners to Japan to work in industry and reopen mines. Most of these prisoners were embarked from Singapore to join convoys.

As MacArthur's return to the Philippines approached, U.S. Task Forces set about sweeping the South China Sea and the various sea routes to Japan of shipping likely to assist the Japanese in the Philippines. It was during September in 1944 when huge numbers of Allied prisoners of war were lost at sea. If the POWs in Borneo had known of these events they would have been convinced Borneo was comparatively safe.

The survivors stated that conditions were quite bearable until June 1944 when the rice ration was cut to 7 ozs. This was followed by the bombing raids which commenced in October 1944. Earlier in September reconnaissance aircraft were seen overhead which gave the PWs a great boost of confidence – "We'll be out of here by Christmas!" was always the slogan since 1942.

The reduction in rations was ordered by Tokyo as one of the Staff Officers stated at the Yamawaki trial: "Amendments in regard to food were made to the Hague Convention." The Imperial policy towards prisoners of war was put into effect as the great American armada sailed towards Leyte.

1944 was a disastrous year for about 10,000 Allied prisoners of war being transported to Japan; battened down in foul smelling holds with no ventilation, little or no food, subjected to Allied air attacks on the unmarked ships. Many of these ships were sunk and some PWs managed to reach China ; they were quickly flown out to the U.S. where they joined "MIS-X", an organisation to search for missing personnel and prisoners of war. One of those officers who escaped from the jungle camp north of Davaò on Mindanao was Colonel Mellnik; now with "MIS-X" and an advisor to the President on Prisoner of War matters.

Soon, a "MIS-X" advisor was dispatched to Colonel Fertig, the leader of U.S./Filipino Forces on Mindanao, to ascertain the possibility of rescuing prisoners. The contact came away convinced of all the problems involved – the principal concern was the repercussions which were occurring when PWs left the Camp – the Japanese would take 50 to 100 PWs out and massacre them in retaliation and to act as a deterrent to escape. "MIS-X" concluded rescue plans could not be achieved without overwhelming forces nearby or because of the risk of repercussion in other Camps.

Tokyo ordered another squeeze on the prisoners – under no circumstances would prisoners be permitted to purchase food from natives – to do so was a punishable offence. The starvation program was under way; by the end of 1944 the rice ration was cut again – by January 1945 there was no rice issue at all.

Hoshijima, on his own initiative, created about 40 acres of garden – tapioca and potatoes which kept the prisoners living a few months longer. All these measures by the Japanese were probably the results of all the events which went against the Japanese during 1943.

The most devastating was the huge loss of shipping in the Sibutu Channel as a result of the reporting of shipping movements by the PYTHON party in September 1943 – January 1944.

In October 1944 the Yamamoto Battalion arrived from Manchuria and established camp at the 9 Mile near the airfield – precisely where the rescue drop-zone was planned. Sandakan now had been considerably reinforced by the Japanese, and in April 1945 they carried out a practice parachute drop at the aerodrome – it was believed this was carried out to test the reaction of the prisoners. There was none -

Captain Mills and Captain Cooke had convinced Lieut. Hoshijima it was International practice to display a POW sign in the camp earlier – this was placed between the English and Australian Camps and remained there until ordered to be removed by Southern Headquarters at Saigon following a visit by Colonel Takayama to Sandakan in April 1945.

The submarine traffic to the U.S./Filipino Guerrilla movement was constant; most Fleet boats travelling north dropped off supplies at various localities.

By 1944 there were about 47 transmitting stations throughout the Islands with major networks in constant contact with Australia. General Headquarters South West Pacific were anxious to extend arming guerrillas to Borneo, however the British feared they may have to fight the Borneo movement after the end of hostilities. G.H.Q. approved the various intelligence gathering parties under the code-name AGAS; in addition organised SEMUT parties inland to support the Dyaks in harassing the Japanese.

Sandakan Airfield, 1945

Pic: AWM.044659

Labuan

In June 1944, Captain Nagai was ordered to take a party of approximately 100 British POWs from Sandakan to Labuan, where they were to be put to work on constructing an airfield. Flt./Lt. Blackledge, R.A.F., Medical Officer, was the senior POW Officer with this group. They arrived at Labuan on 16 June 1944 and were later joined by Captain Campbell, R.A.M.C., and his party of approximately 200 POWs who had come from Kuching.

Captain Nagai became known to the prisoners of war at Jesselton in October 1942 when the "Java 1 Party" first arrived there before he took a party on to Sandakan. He was known to be reasonably fluent in English and Mandarin, and was reported to have relatives in California. Those who had met him said that he was a smooth-talking officer who, in the early days of Sandakan, did not give any indication to those around him he could understand or speak English.

He was now responsible for some 300 prisoners of war – of whom there were to be no survivors.

About September 1944, in preparation for MacArthur's return to the Philippines, the Allied air forces were attacking every airfield in the region, particularly staging airfields in Borneo to prevent reinforcements from Singapore reaching the Philippines. American B29 bombers operating from India had annihilated Singapore Naval Base. The submarines were active, the last regular ship went into Sandakan in July and the last ship seen there was in October, however, limited shipping continued to visit the oil ports of Brunei and Miri for bunker oil.

It was too late for the Japanese to construct an airfield, they were quickly running out of aircraft, and when MacArthur's forces landed at Leyte in October 1944 very few aircraft were reaching the Philippines. Food became short, deaths occurred and Nagai blamed the deaths on to malaria.

Up until October 1944 there were very few sick, bombing commenced, rations were reduced and from then on malaria took a heavy toll. Nagai states that the POWs were issued with quinine which did not halt the incidence of malaria and which caused the POWs to be "very sick on the stomach". No doubt due to lack of food. Nagai states that food was very short both for the POWs and for Japanese. From the time the bombing commenced, the Japanese began reducing rations in accordance with a Directive to Yamawaki's H.Q. where "Amendments" were made to the Hague Convention in regard to food.

During the latter part of 1944, many deaths occurred: the bodies were cremated and buried in No. 1 Cemetery. As a result of bombing, the POW Camp was moved to the 3 Mile. The dead at this Camp were buried at what was called "No.2 Compound", in an area at the foot of a hill about 300 yards north of the Compound.

It is possible that some of the deceased POW were buried in other areas such as in a Chinese Cemetery near No.2 Compound.

Sgt Major Sugino, who took over from the fortunate Captain Nagai, stated: "I left Labuan on 7 March with 112 POWs and 15 Formosan civilian guards. We reached Brunei on 8 March 1945 and remained there until 2nd or 3rd May 1945, during that time 30 POWs died of malaria and beri beri. I issued medicine for malaria and beri-beri to the medical orderlies, who in turn issued it to the sick POWs.

"One of the POWs tried to escape here and I know that the Kempe Tai took him and I did not see him again.

"On about 2nd or 3rd May with 82 POWs I left Brunei for Kuala Belait and arrived the next day. On arriving at Kuala Belait I reported to 1st Lt. Kamimura and a W.O. in command of Kempe Tai. While I was in Kuala Belait the POWs camped in the old picture theatre, where we remained until 26 or 27 May 1945. While in Kuala Belait, 37 POWs died of malaria and beri-beri. During this time I received 7 Indian POWs from Lt. Kamimura of whom one was an Officer.

"We left Kuala Belait on 27 May 1945 and arrived in Miri on the following day. On arriving in Miri I reported to Lt. Nishimura, who was 0. C. of 20 Aerial Supply Coy. He ordered me to go to Cape Lobang and the POWs were camped in a house inside a barbed wire compound. The POWs house was made of bush timber and roofed with coconut leaves and was built ready for us when we arrived there. The POWs remained here until 8 June 1945. During this time they were employed growing vegetables in the vicinity of the POW Compound, except that for two days they worked in Miri township unloading rice from boats and loading trucks.

"On arrival at Cape Lobang I reported to Capt. Hasegawa but after that I had nothing whatever to do with him. While the POWs were at Cape Lobang, four of them died of malaria and beri-beri. There were two English doctors amongst the POWs and they examined the dead men and signed the death certificates stating the cause of death to be malaria and beriberi. Copies of these certificates were forwarded to Kuching.

"The POW were buried in four graves near the Compound. Most of the POWs were sick with malaria, beri-beri sores and ulcers. While at Cape Lobang the POW diet consisted of meat, rice, sugar, tea, vegetables and tobacco. Those POW who were not sick were fat and well.

"At 1500 hrs. 8 June 1945, the Sgt. Maj. of Hasegawa Tai told me that an English Fleet was approaching Borneo. I became anxious for the safety of the POWs and decided to move to a safer place. I then ordered the POWs to make small bundles of their personal gear to take with them. We left the Compound at 2000 hrs. and went via jungle track over the hill to Riam Road and reached the 3½ Mile Riam Road at midnight. The whole party remained here until 0400 hrs. 9 June 1945, when a party of 15 fit POWs and 5 Guards returned to Cape Lobang to pick up stores consisting of rice, salt, office stores and medicine. There were at this time 20 fit men but only 15 went back, and of the remaining 28 sick ones, 5 were unable to walk and had to be carried by the fit men. The carrying party of fit men returned about 1000 hrs. At about this time one of the POWs died of malaria and beri-beri. In this move down the Riam Road I was responsible to no-one and in complete charge of the POWs.

"At 0400 hrs. 9 June when the 15 fit POW returned to Cape Lobang I sent a written message by one of the guards of Nishimura telling him that I was going down the Riam Road. At 1800 hrs. that night I received a written message from Nishimura telling me to take plenty of food and go to the mountains.

"At 1300 hrs. 9 June, 15 POWs left 3½ Mile and again returned to Cape Lobang with 5 guards. They returned at 1800 hrs. carrying similar stores to the last trip. All the POWs had a meal at 1800 hrs. and then at 2000 hrs. the whole party left and went to the 5½ Mile Riam Road, arriving at 2200 hrs. The whole party made camp in a deserted house and went to sleep.

"At 0600 hrs. 10 June 1945, the POWs arose, breakfasted and then were allowed to rest throughout the morning. The POWs had a midday meal and at 1500 hrs. the same healthy POWs and four guards returned to 3½ Mile Riam Road to bring back stores. At midday I burnt some old POW documents and letters. The only documents I kept were those relating to the living POWs and pay matters. Documents concerning POWs who died at Brunei and Kuala Belait had already been forwarded to Kuching.

"While I was burning the documents about 100 metres from the house I saw Captain Campbell going into the house acting in what I thought was a suspicious manner, as he was looking to all sides as he walked. Capt. Campbell was amongst the party who went back and I told Nago, the civilian guard in charge, that he would probably try to escape, in which case he was to be killed.

"At 1900 hrs., five or six men, led by Sgt. Ackland, jumped up from where they were sitting outside the house and started to run away. I called out the guard to open fire on the escaping POWs. In the confusion some of the bullets went in the house and caused the POW to come out. As they came out of the house they were shot and bayonetted by the guards. The sick POWs tried to crawl away and they were shot or bayonetted coming out of the house or outside the house. I did not give any orders to cease fire in order to save the sick because I was so excited that I did not know what was happening. Those POWS who were not killed outright were put out of their agony by shooting or bayonetting. When this was over there were 32 bodies. I then ordered three or four of the guards to bury the POWs. I then heard a burst of firing coming from about 100 metres back along the Riam Road. I called out about 6 guards and ran in the direction of the firing. When I arrived there I found that the POWs were then dead and were being carried to one place for burial by the guards. In addition to the guards I saw eight men belonging to the Nishimura Tai. Several men were digging the two graves that were about one foot deep when I arrived. When the graves were dug, the POW were buried and the whole work was completed by about 2030 hours. I asked Nago what had happened and he told me that the POWs had been shot trying to escape and that eight men of Nishimura Tai had helped to kill them. I did not ask any further questions because I understood that the POW had not been trying to escape when they were killed. Although I gave orders before they left to kill the POWs if they attempted to escape, I knew myself that they would be killed in any case. After the POW were buried at the road I

Pte. H.J. Murray. 582690. 4th Bn. The Suffolk Regiment. Sent from Kuching to Labuan. Died 19 November 1944. Age 26.
Pic: W. Murray.

Cpl. George Barclay. 996234. R.A.F. (VR). Sent from Sandakan 1944 to Labuan. Died Brunei 10 June 1945. Age 29. Glasgow, Scotland
Pic: James Barclay

returned to the house to supervise the burial of the others, which finished at midnight. Some personal belongings were buried with the POWs and the remainder were burnt. After saluting the dead all the guards went to sleep.

"We arose at 0400 hrs. 11 June 1945 and departed for the mountains. I sent a civilian guard back to Nishimura at the 1 Mile to tell him that the POWs had been killed trying to escape. I reached the 7 Mile on 11 June, the 10 Mile on 12 June, and on 13 June I returned to Cape Lobang to pick up stores and burn down the Compound. Lieut. Nishimura was with me and it was he who gave orders for the compound to be burnt down. We threw oil all over the building and set it on fire.

"The following men were guards with the party of POWs killed on the road: Nago Kiroshi, Kamamura Toryuhoshi, Nakayama Konishi, Makayama Koji. The following men were guarding the POWs killed at the house: Umemura Susumo, Hirota Seiichi, Kamashige Masayoshi, Matsumoto Hideo, Yamada Yoshimasa, Fujikana Tolsuo, Kumada Morihoi, Yokoyama Nobuo, Hirayama Hideo."

Sugino refers to Captain Campbell as "Captain Chambers" in his statement.

But Sugino had second thoughts after his first statement, and says "he will now tell the truth":

"I now admit that the statement I made on 11 October 1945 was not completely true. I will now tell the complete truth.

"The information I gave concerning the killing of the 21 POWs at the house

162

at the 5½ Mile Riam Road is all true.

"After the killing of the 32 POWs, I, together with six or seven Formosan guards, immediately went to the 5 Mile and waited until the arrival of Nago and three other Formosan guards escorting 15 POWs, who rested on a small track leading off the road and opposite us. Shortly afterwards, L/Cpl. Kaneko and eight members of the Nishimura Tai also arrived from the 5½ Mile.

"I thought at the time that as food was getting short, some of the POWs might try to escape and I decided that it would be better that we kill them. After the POW had been rested about ten minutes one of the European POW tried to escape by running into the grass. I then gave the order to shoot the whole 15 POWs. All the Nishimura Tai and five or six Formosan guards took part in the shooting.

"After the shooting, some of the POW were not dead, so I ordered that they be shot and bayonetted as they lay on the ground. The man who had previously run into the grass was also shot. We then buried the bodies in two graves and I sent the members of the Nishimura Tai straight back to 7 Mile and together with my own men, I returned to 5½ Mile to complete the burial of the POWs killed there. I later went to 7 Mile, where I spent the night."

There were no British POWs left, they were all murdered by superior orders issued by Tokyo. The Emperor would have been pleased. The Japanese then started to torture and kill the Indian POWs.

Major Ikegami Tomoyuki, 110 Air Field Maintenance and Supply Battalion, stated:

"I came to Miri on 6 March 1945 from Kudat and took over 110 Air Field Maintenance Supply Battalion … When it appeared an Allied landing was imminent all Units in Lutong area were re-formed and placed under my Command.

"I left Lutong on 20 June 1945 preceded by advance parties who left some days earlier. Roma Tai was one of the units preceded me. On about 26 June 1945 at 1600 hrs. I arrived at Pangaran Piniku and found the Roma Tai already there. When I arrived there I issued orders for the deployment of units under my command. After I had had a wash and a meal, Lt. Takahashi Yoichi reported to me, in the absence of Lieut. Shimizawa, OC of Roma Tai. He told me the Indian POWs were getting troublesome and out of hand and that about 20 of them had escaped. As there were not many guards, Takahashi asked for more men. As I was busy at the time I did not give him any more guards, Takahashi then told me some more POWs were preparing to escape and asked me what he would do. I then ordered Takahashi to kill those intending to escape. At this time I heard the sounds of Indian POWs being beaten about 50 to 60 metres away. Takahashi gave the orders for these Indians to be beaten.

"At 1000 hrs. on 27 June 1945 Takahashi came to me and said, "Let's execute the POWS". We then took the POWS, numbering about eleven, to a gully about 300 metres away from H.Q. and there we executed them. The execution party consisted of myself, 1st Lt. Takahashi Yoichi, 1st Lt. Takahashi Tatsuo, 2nd Lt. Hisano, 2nd Lt. Hiyoshi Ken and Cpl. Takahashi.

"I shot one of the POWs with my pistol and beheaded one with my sword.

163

The remainder were beheaded or bayonetted. Everyone else beheaded one or two of the POWs but I do not know about Takahashi Yoichi. I do not know the names of the POWs but Takahashi Yoichi does. As there was no doctor in the area he was not present at the execution. The POWs were buried in three graves dug by themselves and soldiers. I sent a written report to Aikyo Butai stating the POWs were killed because they were preparing to escape."

On 6 June 1945 Bui Chan was carrying water to his house at the 5½ Mile Riam Road, when he saw a truck pulled up in front of his house. There were 10 European POWs and some Jap soldiers, they all got out of the truck and were met by 10 more Jap soldiers. One of the Japs ordered Bui Chan to go away and not come back for two hours. Bui Chan went a short way, then hid in the jungle and waited and watched. The Japs closed the area to all civilians and during the next hour he heard shooting and moans of the POWs but could not see what was happening. After 2 hours he went back to his house and found the area covered in blood, there were two freshly dug graves with trails of blood leading to them, one grave was about 10 ft. diameter, the other about 4 ft., and they had been roughly covered with grass and pineapple plants. Two days later Bui Chan went to the graves and covered them with more earth and grass. Bui Chan's wife was further along the road when the shooting was taking place and she asked the Japs if they were killing Chinese and they replied that they were twelve white men.

At 1600 hrs. on 6 June 1945, Yong Chan was in his house on 5½ Mile Riam Road when he heard the sound of firing coming from further up the road. He did not see any POWs but his neighbours told him that the Japs had shot 30 European POWs. Yong Chan went to the scene of the shooting next morning and he saw there were two fresh graves covered with earth and scrub. He did not see any clothing or personal belongings.

On 9 June 1945 Yong Ngiak said four white men came to his house to borrow a hoe and some water buckets so that they could prepare a meal. They were in very poor health. Later on Yong Ngiak went to the place where the POWs were to collect his buckets and hoe and he said there were about 30 POWs guarded by about 20 Japanese, most POWs were too weak to walk. There were about 20 Japanese guards. Later in the afternoon he heard noises and looked out to see some POWs trying to run away but they were caught and dragged back where he could see the Japanese using rifles and bayonets on the other POWs. He could hear the Japanese wielding rifles and swords on the POWs on the ground but could not see them for the long grass. At the same time he heard sounds of gunfire coming from another point a little way up the road. Next morning he found two fresh graves and some personal belongings, but in the afternoon about 10 Japanese came back and burnt everything in the area.

Two to three days before the shelling of Miri, Yong Fam saw over 30 white and Indian POWs resting by the roadside at the 3 Mile Riam Road, the Japanese took the sick POWs into Yong's house and sent the rest back to fetch more food. When the POWs returned with the food, the Japanese blocked the road about a quarter mile each way from where Yong was hiding in the scrub about 300 yards from his house and he had a clear view of where the men were. He saw the Japanese bring the sick from his old house and kill them slowly, bayonetting and cutting them with swords and native parangs. Yong saw there were about ten men killed this way. At the same time as the Japanese were killing the sick men Yong heard gunfire from the area where the rest of POWs were but he did not see any actually shot. The next day he went to the scene of the killing and there were two graves, the area was covered with blood and personal equipment was lying about, photos, papers and things. Yong did not touch anything. Where the shooting took place was near Yong's neighbour, Bui Chan, and there were two graves there.

On 6 June 1945 Yong Thian saw about 30 white POWs carrying rice arrive at the 5½ Mile Riam Road. Curious to see them he started to go closer but a Japanese told him that if he went into the area where they were he would be shot. Yong Thian saw that there were a lot of POWs stark naked and also that the road had been blocked at both ends to stop any civilians going into the area. During the day the Japanese borrowed hoes from the farmers in the area and in the evening Yong Thian heard shooting. Next day he went to the area and saw two freshly dug graves.

On 4 June 1945 Chin Mai counted 34 Europeans, 3 Eurasians and 5 Sikh POWs, guarded by 40 Japanese. One of the Europeans he recognised as a man who was second in charge of the water at Kuching and he had worked under him 21 years ago. Chin Mai could not remember his name but he understood he later became head of the Public Works Department in Kuching. Chin Mai said that 12 of the Europeans were young men and Hong Su Kian told him that three of the Europeans died at the 3 Mile Riam Road and were buried there, near the shop-houses. None of the POWs were wearing any uniforms, only shorts. Chin Mai could not identify them, and he heard that the POWs stayed at the 3 Mile from 7 a.m. to 2 p.m.

During the afternoon Chin Mai went hunting for wild pigs near the 5½ Mile Riam Road. He climbed a tree and was able to get a clear view of the road. About 3.30 p.m. a party of 12 POWs guarded by one Japanese officer and 18 soldiers arrived in a truck; the POWs were told to sit by the road side and 6 Japanese went a short distance away and dug two graves while the other soldiers stayed guarding the POWs. Among the POWs was the man Chin Mai had recognised earlier as being from the Public Works Department. The Japanese officer then gave an order, the POWs stood up and walked in file to a position about 20 ft. off the road, here the two leading POWs were ordered to move over near the graves and the two Japanese soldiers shot them, the soldiers who had dug the graves in the morning then dragged the bodies over and threw them in the grave. This went on until all the prisoners were shot. Two of the POWS were shot 3 times, some of them were still alive when they were thrown into the graves which were then filled in, it was not done properly for when the Japanese had finished there were still heads showing above the grave. This killing took about two hours.

Chin Mai came down out of the tree and was going home through the jungle close to the road and when he got to the 5 Mile mark he saw a further party of

European and Sikh POWs coming along the road guarded by about 40 Japanese. The time was now getting dark and Chin Mai could not recognise any in the party or the exact number.

Next morning he went back to the scene of the shooting and saw the graves, the area was covered in blood and the two heads were still showing out of the grave.

Chin Mai identified the Japanese guarding the POWs at the 3 Mile as belonging to Kabotai, and he would recognise the killers again.

At midnight on 7 June 1945 Ng Lim Oun was in his house on Riam Road when a party of about 40 European POWs guarded by 4 Japanese arrived and stayed the rest of the night around his shop.

Next morning when he got out of bed he saw two Europeans who had died during the night lying under his verandah. At 9 a.m. the Japanese buried the dead men behind the Police Station which is opposite his shop. Ng Lim Oun saw three of the POWs wore naval type caps but he could not remember the badge. During the day he saw the Japanese beat three of the POWs with a piece of 3 inch thick wood. At 10 p.m. on 9 June 1945, the party left the 5 Mile and went up the road, next morning about 12 POWs returned and carried away food-stuff and personal belongings. He could identify the guards as all four Japanese guards spoke Chinese Khek dialect and one could speak the Hookien dialect as well.

Two days before the Australians arrived in Lutong on 18 June, Lam Yin was moving along the Miri river in his sampan when he was taken by the Japanese near the Fujut-Lintong Bridge, it was nearly dark, the bridge was on fire throwing the light across the river. There were five Japanese in the party, three armed with swords, the other two with rifles, they had two Javanese, eight Chinese and one Sikh as prisoners, Lam Yin thought the Sikh was of a Punjab Regiment. Lam Yin saw the Japanese take the prisoners to an area on the bank of the river, it was then about 10 p.m., he saw the Japanese make the Sikh take off all his clothes then they beheaded him, four of the Chinese were killed, three were beheaded and the fourth bayonetted. Just after this killing an Allied plane came over, the Japanese ran away and Lam Yin escaped in the confusion. He did not know what happened to the other Javanese and Chinese. He thought the Japanese were members of the Kempe Tai and he would recognise them.

A marked pack was found on the track along the ridge to Riam Road and a large quantity of personal gear etc. has been found at Tg Lobang, giving credence to the policy of the Japanese to carry out the elimination of POWs should an Allied invasion occur.

Tg. Lobang is a completely isolated compound, not located until 17 June 1945; out of bounds to the local people during the Japanese Occupation.

Items found here were: personal effects, badges, charred letters, maps, equipment, razors, cigarette and spectacle cases. Badges found were: A.I.F. (AUSTRALIA, and hat badges); R.A.A.F., R.A.F., Royal Artillery, Royal Engineers, Royal Corps of Signals, R.A.S.C., Gordon Highlanders, Cameronians, Royals, Royals (North Lancs. Regiment); plus some unidentified Officer's pip (British); part of an M.O.'s outfit: scissors, scalpel, glass syringe tube, plaster, alabaster pots.

A number of Mess Kits recovered indicates a possible 20 to 25 POWs left in the Compound.

The Japanese took every precaution to remove identifications from all POW effects, of nearly 100 items found, only three had markings on them which could be identified.

A local man, Lo Hing Koo, living at Tutong, stated he knows of 5 English POWs at Miri and that sometimes there are 10 at Seria. The POWs are moved between Miri-Seria-Lutong, all are in very bad health and are able to do little work – this statement was made on 15 June 1945.

At 1600 hrs. on 6 June 1945 10 POWs were killed by Japanese at 5½ Mile on Riam Road, a Chinese witness saw a mass grave partly covered and next day he threw more soil over it.

The investigation of the Labuan – Brunei area was carried out by Captain A.F. Boyland, A.I.F. He reported:

"No. 1 Compound – the original compound was built close to the harbour in the grounds of Victoria Golf Club. The compound has since been razed and the B.B.C.A.U. Bulk Store has been erected on its site. NO personal effects or traces to indicate POW occupation could be found.

"No. 1 Cemetery was established near the compound, close to the beach. Many of the deceased buried in this cemetery were cremated. The graves were NOT marked. To date, 23 Australian War Graves Unit has exhumed 40 unidentified bodies.

"No. 1 Compound was situated on a spur at the 3 Mile Post on MacArthur Road. This area was the scene of fighting during the Australian action on Labuan, and the buildings of the compound were completely destroyed. A search of the area produced NO personal belongings as it had been covered in detail already by PWLO 9 Aust. Div. and B. Aust. Field Security Section."

Part Diary of Unknown British Soldier – Volunteers (F.M.S.V.F.)
Period November 1944 – June 1945: Men's Camp, Kuching

Nov. 25th 44: Decided to carry on a few notes again and try and cover past ground. 150 of our Dahan party left for Labuan on Aug. 8. since when they have been hit by M.T. malaria and it is now believed there have been 35 deaths. Spare and Read both went away leaving Tayler, Proctor and Price behind. Price has since died. About the same period the rice ration was cut to nearly ½ and more ubi kayu issued, since when the meals have improved in flavour although less in quantity. A typical days meal is now "Glue bu", i.e. buboh rice and about 25% sago flour for breakfast stew and ½ or light ¾ rice tiffin, stew and good ¾ kedgeree for dinner with occasional pork stews and fishy stew from pickled ikan belis – supplies of salt fish have stopped for over 2 months and fresh fish is available only on very rare occasions. Ikan belis is our own purchase. There have been 3 issues of … coconuts at 15 cts. each which are greatly appreciated and we can generally purchase odd ones from some chaps at 50 or 75 cts. All Coy. gardeners are now on camp work outside the wire and we only get one day in four on Coy. gardens which is not nearly enough, one can only just keep pace with digging for mashes and replanting. There's an air of expectancy about Camp since Major Suga told Camp Commandants the War would be over soon and gave news of our retaking Mariannas and Carolines and also landing on Leyte and Samar. Rumours are rife as usual and all of an optimistic strain, out by Xmas, Out by Feb. or Mar. etc. The veg. ration is very poor and we are being told by Nips to provide as much as we can from our own gardens. This week I tried snails both roasted and boiled and they are good and I propose to have more. I've been a long time making up my mind to eat them although they have been eaten by other chaps for over 9 months. I could not fancy the idea at first, but now once having overcome prejudice etc. they are definitely good and under present conditions will provide some much needed animal protein.

I am amusing myself polishing coconut shells, fitting lids and handles and making dixies of them and also making pipes. It all helps to pass the time away and keep one occupied in spare time. They are useful as food containers and also for storing "pig meal", the dried coconut meal we are eating.

Nov. 27 Mon.: Am selling a Penguin "Pride & Prejudice" at 3 sheets for 10 cents to raise funds and expect it to bring in about $5. Original cost 6d.! Paper is extremely scarce these days and smokers are at their wits' end for "rolls". I wish I had a few more books to spare. Pig meal sells at 50 cts/pint in Canteen, rice is over $1000 per sack in S'pore. Plantains are 20-25 cts. each in Canteen – when available and bananas about 5-6 cts. each. Am having a bit of trouble with my legs these days, numbness and aches and a "cotton woolly" feeling in the mornings. Am afraid shall have to report sick with them.

Nov. 30th: Reported my leg condition to Dr. as my feet had started to swell and show decided B.B. symptoms. Told to carry on at work and drink less fluid. ½pt. tea breakfast, none tiffin, ½ pt. dinner, so will have to cut down a bit. I don't want to go sick but would certainly like a few days off. Owing to the working party on the aerodrome being increased from 150 to 300 and now to 400 I'm doing makan orderly nearly every day this week. The weather is very showery and the gardens are growing weeds faster than I can deal with them as we only get in once in every 4, now we are working on Camp gardens outside the wire. We've been on this since Aug. and put in 7 bags of kang kong to cook house yesterday from gardens outside Camp. This has only been planted about 5 weeks but the beds were well filled with night soil. Had another snail stew tonight with a good bowl full of thick veg. and it was jolly good. Running short of snails now, found none for 2 days and had 7 in the stew.

Dec. 10th Sun.: Cinema show tonight on the Square outside Camp. All people there from all Camps. Had a gardeners 'stodge' for tiffin, 3 bowls full! and a grand snail and veg. stew for dinner, about 20 odd snails of all sizes (cost 5 of us 50 cts. apiece all round over 100 snails for $2.50). weighed again last week, still.3 kilos, unchanged for 3 months. There have been about 5 deaths again this month so far, 10 last month. The Labuan party figures now believed to be 79. Canteen sales last week, peanuts $1 per pint (bought 2), bananas 3 small and 1 large 20 cts. (got 2 lots), gula toffee $1.20 packed (got 1) Yesterday the Nips issued us with a set of eating utensils: 1 large bowl, 1 medium bowl, 1 small bowl (rubber cup size) and 1 spoon, all made of earthenware and incidentally totally inadequate for the quantities of food we get even though we are on ¾ rations. The rice issue by the way is improved and an issue of sago flour has been issued but tapioca root supplies have decreased and green veg. is also down quite a lot. Fortunately we can supply plenty of spud tops from Yamamoto's gardens and kong from our patch (29 sacks so far). There has been quite a lot of s/mail in during last 2 weeks but very little for our hut and none for me. There's a story rumoured round Camp that there's a lot more bags arrived on a ship last week, also stores of cigarettes and chocolate! the usual Red X bilge that goes around every time a boat comes in, a very rare occurrence these days, since … Nips themselves admit Borneo to be cut off and American forces on the Philippines. I'm making a fellow a pipe in exchange for a packet of pipe tobacco, value $1.20. Next time I'll ask 2 issues of cigarette tobacco at 50 cts., its better value now I'm smoking papaya leaf. Am trying to read Vol. 1 of Gibbon but its rather slow and heavy going but very interesting. Hoping to raise funds a little by sale of old watch and a shirt shortly, market prices are good just now.

Sun. 17th: Made $25. on watch and $20 on shirt so am set up for a while, at least over Xmas. Co. mash today and another snail stew tomorrow. Sold another pipe for $1.50. and 7 rations buboh in morning! very acceptable. Now have orders for 3 or 4 others as soon as I can get a saw to cut up my wood. Had 2 bad days with my legs this week. The weather is getting very wet again, rain nearly every midday and evening, stopped work on our gardens 2 afternoons and its been very cold as well.

Wed. 20th: Snail stew tonight again. Had python's eggs for tiffin and although they had a young snake inside we ate them all (3 each – 2 people). There was plenty of yolk left and no smell or bad taste, in fact they were quite good, snake and all. Cost us 50 cts. for 6 and we consider them good value at the price. Chicken's eggs are about $1.20 or more and are very little larger than python's. There's still some doubt as to what we are getting for Xmas although plenty of rumours. All we know is it will be plenty but plain. Had a carol practice tonight which I conducted, had about 24 people turn up and it went quite well. The Camp has ordered close on $10,000 worth of stuff for Xmas – I hope we get it. 800 katies of pork at $8.20/k! plantains, banana, peanuts, 1500 coconuts, oil, extra rice. We shall see what we get. 4 pts. gardeners 'stodge' Sunday again.

Mon. 25 Dec.: Had a snail stew Fri. and again Sun., – a bumper lot on Sat., $1 worth each just stewed and seasoned – no veg. We made a savoury sago kuch?? with some of them and had it after carols last night. Rice issue yesterday was a full issue for tiffin and dinner plus a little extra. Xmas presento from Camp so far 3 bananas, 4 biscuits, 1½ twists and 3 cheroots. I also drew an extra biscuit from 6 over for the hut. Each man was also given $1 from Internees with which I bought 10 spring onions. There was to have been a concert last night but rain stopped it, although it cleared later for the carols. Lights Out was 11. Breakfast this morning – full issue of proper buboh rice with coconut mixed in, 2 rice squares, chips and fried egg and a small piece of fried pork, coffee. 3 issues sugar and 1 issue pepper. Church service (Communion) this morning 7.15 after 7.00 reveille, carols 8-8.15. breakfast 8.15 approx. Managed to buy ½ pt. whitebait for $3. Also got a bowl full of pumpkin seeds from cookhouse for drying and roasting. Tiffin, pork stew (medium) rice, full issue, curried pumpkin and shrimp sauce, tea. Also had tea at 11 and 4. Dinner, rice square with banana and papaya 'jam', 2 rice rolls with a little chicken meat in them. Chicken and duck stew (very good) made with plenty of kong … ducks and 22 chickens. Present of 1 pkt. 3 Gold Cash? cigarettes per man. kedgeree (official 1½ issue nearly ?) tea and coffee at 10.30 after the pantomime. The pantomime was a jolly fine effort. Altogether the day was very successful. There should have been another rice square for 10.30 p.m. but as they were not ready in time they were issued next morning. 6 extra presento bananas.

Thurs. 28th: Had some more snails last night and also a good stiff 'stodge' made around a small chicken we caught (Gardening). Got another ½ pt. bait $3. also 9 onions 40 cts. These onions are being bought on the 'drome for about 12 to 2½ cts. each and sold at these higher prices when brought into Camp. My feet were swollen up again on Tuesday but are down again now. My leg is still troubling me and last night on makan fatigue I stumbled and spilled pork stew, got some on my arm and burnt it a bit so I hope it won't turn busoh.

Sun. 31st Dec. 1944: My arm so far is O.K. but I took a nasty tumble today off the slimy tap platform into the drain, hurt my leg and back and also got a nasty knock over the left breast which is very painful and stops deep breathing. Cut 10 sacks of kong this morning for stews tomorrow that's 74 bags since Oct. 19, just over 2 tons! Had a hot bath this afternoon to try and ease the stiffness after my fall. Since just before Xmas there's been a cut in sugar and salt so we get no salt in midday stews and only 4 sugar issues per week instead of 7. After tomorrow we have a rice cut again – 3¼ bags instead of 4½. Bought 25 decent size onions and about 6 small for $1 and 15 large chillies for 90 cts. Prices are getting fantastic $250 for a laying hen. $1.75 for an egg when procurable. Durians 1 medium and 1 small $5. Today is ½ day for Camp but 400 men on 'drome. Holiday tomorrow. Pantomime was repeated last night, there's a play tonight 'Crazy Gang' concert tomorrow. Puffed rice toffee came into Canteen during the week at $1.70. Had small … snail …

Mon. Jan 1st. 1945: Holiday fine in morning and noon, rain about 4 and through night. Breakfast – rather thin buboh and coconut, quite good.. 2 rice balls containing a very small portion of buffalo beef, tea. Tiffin – plain rice and beef stew, quite good, tea, curried pumpkin sauce, excellent, very hot with red chillies. Dinner which was very late, nearly 8.35, kedgeree, double issue, fair but quite nice, pork and beef stew, rice square and banana 'Jam'. Keladi chips, middling, poorly fried, tea. Lights Out 11, same as last night! I laid up nearly all day resting, feeling very shaken and stiff. Procter and Taylor each brought me in 10 cts. of onions from 'drome (5 each) so that's a help. I'm making a hot pickle, chopped onions, chillies and ginger papaya seeds in a brine solution and its pretty hot already. As … some pumpkin etc. from stews as well to thicken the … The R.S.M. came round the huts to give us New Year … 'Crazy Gang' show again washed out by rain. Got some more pump-kin seeds from cookhouse for drying and eating. 5 men died in hospital between Xmas Day and New Year's Eve, bringing the month's total to, I think, 11.

Sun. 7th: There have been 4 more deaths this week. "Crazy Gang', put on their show on Wed. and it was quite good. Have bought more onions this week at varying prices: 3½, 4 or 5 cts., also bought a 'sample' of ripe durian for 20 cts. and it's delicious, a grand fruit. Sold another pipe to the Dr., Capt. Bailey, for

$2.50. I've got over my fall fairly well with no ill effects other than a slight stiffness still over the left breast. Had a few more snails on Wed. and some more for tonight. We have some seal meat (pickled) for dinner and wonder what it will be like. The rations have been cut again, 3¼ bags of rice instead of 4½ and meals are pretty thin. I manage to augment my tiffin usually with some green salad and save the rice for the evening meal and make that fairly substantial. Bananas and papayas are being issued by Nips in lieu of rice. Bananas are also on sale today, 3 per man at 20, 15 and 6 cts. each. I'm taking up 2 issues although the price is pretty steep. Toffee is also on sale at $1.40/pkt. 10, used to be 20 cts.! Dinner was a really good pork stew and I got 2 lagi issues. The seal meat, what little there was in the kedgeree, was very tough, a fishy flavour. There was a little fried banana as well as... seal meat in the rice, rather a poor kedge but was accompanied by an excellent mash of pumpkin and keladi which all mixed in with my tiffin rice, ½ doz. snails and some onions made an excellent meal.

Mond. 8th Jan.: New ration scale: 3¼ bags rice/day. Breakfast usual pint "glubu" (3/4 bag rice) Tiffin stew, ½ issue rice, dinner ½ issue rice, stew, tea.

Tues. 9th: Changed over from Coy. Gardener to Camp gardening … mate. Had a spud mash tonight also some more snails and it was an excellent mixture. Had some leftovers for Thurs.

Wed.: Was pay day and I drew $5 after deductions. Pay has been raised to 20 cts.

Sat. 13th: Another funeral today. Had snails Thurs. and Friday, some more for today but am afraid rain will stop cooking. Yesterday was very wet in afternoon and evening and today it has rained all afternoon. Have a sore on my right forearm which is turning bad so had an iodoform plug put in by Dr.

Sun. 10th: ½ day's work on gardens this morning – no snails yesterday owing to rain so had them today, a good double … size ones and that with lagi stew kedgeree and ½ tsp. … me a really good blow out for dinner … another funeral today

Fri.: Another death this morning. Got a present of 5 wormy cheroots on the gardens yesterday and 5 more from another chap. No good themselves but quite O.K. in pipe.

Sun. 21: Another snail boil up tonight with a green papaya and it was jolly good. Had a bit of a blackout this morning and got this morning off. Glad of a full days rest. My foot is still pretty sore and further sores spreading on my legs and hands. Have 3 brews going, one banana skin only, one onion chill) and papaya seed and one mixture of cucumber, papaya, mango, banana skin,

172

chill), potato, brinjal etc. in sugar and salt. Am still buying onions and chillies when I can, there's nothing else to spend money on except other fruit brought in by aerodrome parties and sold at over twice the purchase price. Coconuts $1.20, $1.40, sold at $3 or $4, Jackfruit $1.50-$2 sold up to $5. Durians same. Seeds of Jack 3/5 cts. each, durian 25 cts. each. "Queenie" mangoes 20-50 cts. sold at 50 – $1.20. Cucumber 20 cts. sold at 50/60 cts. and so on. Had an excellent dinner tonight, chupatti, ½ tiffin rice, 3/4 issue rice for dinner. 12 issues Coy. potato mash double stew (a really thick one, plenty of veg.) 1 boiled banana and one ripe (saved for later) and our snails and stew.

Mond. 22nd: Another death today. Went to Dr. for another plug in my foot and he ordered me to rest off from work, attend C., so I'm going to get my long desired rest after all.

Tues. 23rd: Another death today. Bought $4 onions and about $2 worth small chili pedas at 1 ct. each, much better value than large ones at 4 & 5 cts. each. 2 crushed in a bowl of rice are quite sufficient. Bought 3 seeds complete with flesh of a roasted jackfruit for 20 cts. and they were delicious.

Sat. 27th: Had another snail boil up last night and also a 1/3 share in a jackfruit ($1). Thurs. I got ½ a small roasted jack for $1.10. I'm also in another share up between 4 tonight. These fruit are very expensive in camp and unless one is prepared to pay a high price, difficult to come by.

Sun. 28th: Bought 2 more jacks, one $5 and one $3.75 for sharing between 4. Had ½ share in 2 others for tiffin cost $1.50 but they were both ripe and excellent nicely roasted. Had an excellent kedgeree for dinner tonight flavoured with blachang and a full issue. I use chop sticks now for evening meals and find I get on quite well with them.

Wed. 31: Another death. Holiday on 'drome. Gave a continuation of my talk on Sussex tonight to about 6 people … a rice from last Tuesday and then more jack for last night and tonight. I must stop buying as money will not last for ever and at this rate I'm spending … week, and as I'm still attend C shall only draw about …

Sat.: 2 more deaths today. Had another jack and snail stew bought ½ coconut and 25 jack seeds for 50 cts.

Sun. 4th: Bought 10 jack seeds … for 50 cts. Very poor meals today, practically no veg in at all, plain rice and very watery stew for tiffin, plain rice and boiled bananas and thin stew for dinner. Mail in this week, had 4 cards 45 letters so far.

Wed.: Tonight another … 100 chili pedas $1 4 onions about 50 for $1. they are getting dearer now. Got a nice lime 10 cts.

Had more mail today. 1/4 jack 35 cts. Made 65 cts. on jacks trading with $5 capital.

Sat. 10th: 2 deaths again … Morgan from D.B. the camp breaker. Had a go at Jack … Birthday. Kongsi got about $4.50 snails. Pay day $3 … letters 1943 vintage.

Thurs. 15th: Anniversary of fall of S'pore … Had Coy. "Stodge" for dinner, spuds and tops. 1 pint extra for … issue. Jolly good stodge. Also had a good boil up of snails …. One death last night and 2 today

Frid.: Another death this …

Another death last night. I understand there are about 10 more …

Another snail stew tonight. Made about another $15 selling "Safety Instructions and Use of Lifts", 15 cts/sheet. Am now selling Race Course Tickets at 4 for 15 cts. There was a breakdown of the power early in the week and we have had no lights for breakfast these last 3 mornings and its pretty deadly serving out and feeding in the dark.

Sun. 18 Feb.: Managed to get a little oil from 'drome for hut lamps in mornings. No power morning or evening today, believed due to shortage of fuel oil at Power Station. Managed to bring my cash in hand up to over $56 again and am now stopping paper sales. Got enough cash in hand for a time.

Wed. 21: 2 more deaths today. Lights on at night again but not in mornings.

Thurs. 22: Snail boil tonight about 10 assorted.

Frid. 23: Snail boil. again tonight. Total buried in new Cemetery 47 from our Camp, 3 Dutch and 3 Internees. Total in Kuching 66. Grand total 113 in 2½ years.

Sat. 24th: Another snail brew. Another death in hospital.

Sun. 25: A further snail boil. There seems to be plenty onions. for a few days, no doubt they will

[next two lines illegible]

with election results. Got a ¼ share in a jack for 15 cts. and bought 14 onions 40 cts.; the season for both items appears to be at an end and prices are rapidly rising. One jack bought on 'drome for 90 cts. sold in Camp for $8.! There seems to be a fresh dysentery scare of a mild form again and more rules for Camp and personal hygiene have been issued.

Mond. 26: Snail again.

Tues. 27: Started work again. Afternoon only owing to the heavy rains in morning.

Wed 28: Another death. Snail for dinner. Prices are going up a little owing to a good supply at the moment and a more general interest on the part of the Camp.

Thurs. Mar. 1st: There is a strong story of Joe taking over the center of the sausage industry and of that industry having ceased.

Frid. 2nd: Rather a tragedy occurred today, an internee was made to stand in usual "arms up" position on Square and was subsequently put in guard room where he cut his throat and despite frantic efforts by the medical staff he died. Had $1 worth of snail tonight.

Sat. 3rd: Had to part with an old friend today and have my beard off owing to a camp order. The end must be near if they are trying to smarten things up! $1 worth of snail again tonight, also 75 cts. worth peppercorns (1/4 pint) and $1.50 onions. Canteen had for sale today: puffed rice $1.75; toffee $2; biscuits 70cts. (all previously obtained in Dahan for 10 cts.)

Sun. 12th: Another death Tuesday. Had 3 more snail boils this week $2 and also bought a pint of rice sweepings for $2 and made 2 lots of rice mash boiled in snail "zippo". Also had a small snake again with P.B. Tayler. There's been no sago flour in this month so we have a mixture of rice and grated tapioca "porrige" for breakfast and it's quite an improvement. Rice is cut again to 3 bags a day although there's quite a lot of ubi kayu in. Pork has also been reduced a lot more this month so far. Got a "presento" pair of shorts from Nips this week made from pink striped ticking. Everybody is being issued with them and later on shirts are to be issued as well. There are rumours of Red X stores again. Every time Major Suga goes away this rumour crops up and he has just returned (yesterday) from a long absence of some weeks.

Thurs. 15: 3 deaths today including David Wilson of Penang Volunteers … 4 blackouts last week.

Frid. 16th: Had another blackout … been another 2 deaths.

Sat. 17: Another death today. I was given 6 snails. Got about 1/3 pints each … food, also got a gardeners stodge. Every man was today issued with one coconut and I managed to acquire another "cheesy" one. A fund of 10,000 has been received from Officers for here, Labuan and Sandakan and its about $4 per man which is being spent on food, so far we have had … and 1 coconut each and about ½ egg in our kedgeree. There's further local purchases to come.

Frid. 30th Good Friday: Good in many respects! About midday the 'drome was
visited by 21 American planes, 4 engined bombers and 2 engined twin body
fighters who all proceeded to shoot up the place with machine gun fire. No
bombs were dropped so it looks as though the 'drome is wanted – possibly
for paratroop landings next time. All the various buildings were shot up and a
petrol dump set on fire. The planes just appeared out of low cloud did their
stuff in a very few minutes and were … was over. Speculation is rife now as
to when we shall be free?? Many people seem to think any day now while
others still think middle of the year. Personally I think within the next 3
months. The sight of these planes has had a tremendous effect on morale of
the Camp. These last 2 days I have developed a nasty abscess on my left wrist
and its giving me some little trouble.

Sat. 31: 3 more deaths today, that's 22 this month, the highest on record.

Mon. 2nd: Another funeral today.

Wed. 4 April: Another funeral today. Had another raid today – 24 4-engined
bombers passed over Kuching and 3 dropped some more pamphlets and also
a few bombs were dropped somewhere – not in the town – probably Pending
or the river mouth. Obviously Kuching is only a secondary target; also there's
no opposition at all – no fighters off the 'drome or even A.A. fire. Bought a
slab of toffee $1.50! also 2 pineapples at $1.50. Sold 1 spoon and 1 fork for
$3 and a knife for $1.30. Gardeners 'stodge' today and a snail boil. Coy.
stodge on Mon.

Thurs. 5th: 2 funerals today.

Sat.: Gardeners stodge, roasted some small pineapples (poor). Another funeral
today. Snails yesterday. The bombs on Wed. destroyed a saw mill and docks
at Lahas Corner and also stopped Pending and river mouth. No authentic
word of the content of the pamphlets.

Mon. 9: Another death.

Tues. 10: 3 deaths today, that's 11 in 10 days this month. The Nips have now decided to cut the 'drome party down by 100 and all "Stinga Mati" are to work on
Battn. gardens and have no guards.

Sun. 15th: 2 more deaths this week so far.

Mon. 16: Air raid warning but no planes. Sold my ring for $100. 10% to seller.
Now I have money there's nothing much to buy. However rumours are strong
and I don't think we have much longer to wait.

Wed.: Another plane over today, obviously on recoy. flight. There's tons of ubi kayu, keladis and plantains in again this week after a shortage. Changed over to Battn. gardens today.

Fri. 20: Another death today and also an "Alert" but no planes.

Sun. 22: 2 deaths yesterday and also an "Alert" again. Today we had another of Uncle Sam's Cabaret shows, 9 "Lightnings" came over and for over ½ hr. gave great attention to the 'drome, shooting up with machine gun and cannon fire. We had just started tiffin and had to leave everything and go to the trenches.

[indistinct illegible]

a day off by Dr. Bought a lot more chillies $1.50 and a good bunch of snails enough for 2 days. Having 60 cts. worth tonight

[illegible for two lines]

Sun. & Mon: Had snails again each evening. Started work again on Yamamoto's gardens Mon. Had a Coy. 'stodge' tonight which was very good and acceptable. Another death today, McLeod of Volunteers. The Nips have warned us again that air raids are probable any day now and we are not to wave or cheer the bombing planes as when this happened in S'pore prisoners were shot out of hand; thus confirming the rumour that S'pore had been bombed. There are stories of Sandakan being bombed and its only about 180 miles away from here so at long last things are really moving and coming our way. Got some more rice sweepings for $2.

Wed. 21: Another death today. Yamo's gardeners 'stodge' tonight and also some snails and a boil up of the rice sweepings. This week there's been literally tons of ubi-kayu and yams and some bananas came in after quite a shortage for 2 or 3 days. Let's hope it will continue! Whenever we get short in one direction something else always seems to turn up.

Sat. 24: 3 deaths today including "Musso" McKenzie of Malacca Vols. Had another rice boil up tonight together with one grated potato about 3/4 pint and also 80 cts. of snails approx. 30 each, small ones. The kongsi is now just about broke and will have to stop buying until funds increase by paper sales etc. Rain stopped work this morning.

Sun. 25: A red letter day. Without any warning and from a lovely clear sky came 2 American 4-engined bombers and dropped pamphlets followed by a recce plane that after having a good look round proceeded to strafe the 'drome, dropped bombs and shot up the place with machine guns. One large bomb was dropped plum in the centre of the old runway, another cut the railway, leaving the train on the wrong side of the breach. The crater in the runway was big enough to take a double-decker bus, over 40 ft. across. Another death today. Bought a huge piece of ubi kayu for $5, about 2'6" long and 3" in dia.

Mon: Another death. All the camp very cheerful after yesterday's raid.

Wed: 28: Another death this evening. Made a stodge

> Got another abscess coming on my right wrist these last 2 days and there also been an acute tobacco shortage for some 4-5 days. There's been a big increase in ulcers and sores lately, so much so that 2 more sick bays have been opened up. This has meant a general reshuffle of huts. 6 of our people went to sick bay and 6 men from "D" Coy. have come in to replace them. I have a filthy cold since Thurs. and am trying to shift it with ginger and sugar and creosote tablets.

Wed. 25th: Another death today. Reported sick with my wrist and had afternoon off for hot water treatment.

Thurs. 26th: Had another of Uncle Sam's shows. Reports state up to 15 planes bombers and Lightnings attacked the 'drome again shooting up buildings planes, 6 Nips were killed and one plane at least brought down as it was taking off. A few bombs were dropped on new works but the original runways are not being touched. They also gunned the river again and rumour says another plane was shot down. Had day off bathing my wrist.

Frid. 27th: 2 deaths again and 1 attempted suicide. Burst my abscess with hot water treatment. Attend 'C' again.

Sat. 28th: 3 deaths today. 16 planes 4-engined bombers visited the drome today and dropped a nice one on the junction of the road and the runway blocking the road to the dispersal points and so bottling up all the planes in the 'ulu' ground.

Sun. 29th: 22 4-engined bombers again visited the drome today and did the job properly – all bombs on the main runway. Estimates vary from 50 to 80 cratering. Anyhow the main thing is the runways are well and truly ruined and nothing can get up or down now for some time.

> Today was the Emperor's birthday and he got the "presentos" instead of us this time. We got nothing. Had the thickest Coy. 'stodge' we have ever had today also bought 2 pkts. biscuits at Canteen at 80 cts.! to celebrate. We also opened up a beautifully ripened pineapple between the 4 of us so with stodge pork stew, fried kedgeree, 2 pieces of fried yam, pines and biscuits we had quite a good feed.

Mon. 30th: Had 9 Lightnings over again today, obviously just to inspect yesterday's damage as there was no bombing or gunning this time.

Tues. May 1st: 5 funerals today and one other death over Tues/Wed. night. Total last month 26, the highest yet. Had an issue of ginger again today and as there's a tobacco shortage again I obtained 1 issue of sugar and one of ginger for 40 cts. issue of tobacco. Also changed a further issue of 6 of sugar. Sugar is selling at 20-25 cts. issue now. Also bought one decent issue of roasted tapioca for $1.20 and another small piece for 20 cts. and 1/4 pint of castor oil for frying at $6. Its terribly expensive but is the only oil available for cooking purposes.

Wed. 2nd: Had a visit from 4 Lightnings again today – just had a quick look at the drome and away again. Part of the drome has been made fit for a fighter take off and 2 have been up today. I came off hot water for my wrist yesterday and had plugs in and last night it gave me a lot of trouble and its plugged again today and it's breaking down a little.

Thurs. 3rd: Another visit from 8 Lightnings who looked at the drome and left it, followed up about 2 hr. later by a bunch of 2-engined bombers who proceeded to 'strafe' the docks and river.

Frid. 4th: I was moved into Sick Bay 19 hut where one is supposed to get extra food so will note the differences. Dinner today rice and stew and 2 tapioca 'cakes' done on a hot plate and boiled plantain that serve as camp issue. Extra good stodge 1 pt. per man and an extra cake.

Sat. 5th: 2 more deaths these last 2 days. B'fast usual 1 pt. of 'ubu' Tiffin usual 1 pt. rice and ubi. Dinner: fish kedgeree and stew camp issue, extra handful of fish heads and bones (very good) and a small banana. Also got a … 'stodge' 1 pt. per man and watery. Bought 1 pkt. rice toffee $1.10 to help things along. Dinner: boiled up in rice and stew and a curry sauce, all same as Camp issue. nothing extra all day.

Mon. 7th: 6 deaths again today, including A.R. Jones of Vols. Breakfast 1 pt. ubu, tiffin 1 pint ubi v. nice. Dinner 2 extra small ripe bananas and stew and fried kedgeree. I got lagi stew myself and also had another fellow so that gave me an extra pint and it was quite a good stew. Had an alarm today but no raid.

Tues. 8th: Breakfast: 1 pt. ubu and lagi, 1 pint, Tiffin 1 pt. ubi and rice as usual. Dinner 1 pint stew and ½ issue fish kedgeree. I got lagi stew from another chap and also bought a $1 stodge from the fires (not a very good value). Had a visit from Uncle Sam again, 8 Lightnings and some 2-engined bombers bombed and shot up the drome and other places.

Wed. 9th: Usual breakfast and tiffin. Dinner 1 pint of curried green buboh and a rissole. Extra 1 small banana, ½ pint Nut stodge and also swapped my rissole for a lagi stodge which was good value. Another funeral today. My wrist is healing well, nice and clean and healthy …

Thurs. 10th: Usual breakfast … Tiffin green buboh with greens and yellow brinjals of which … issue as lagi (1 pint). Jack (Jock?) Innis (Innes?) died today. Dinner green buboh again, there's no yam or tapioca in at all and no tobacco either.

Fri. 11th: Still no root crops. green buboh for breakfast and a very thin one at that. Same for tiffin a bit thicker. Got Coy. stodge last night 3/4 pint. 7 deaths again today. One 'reccy' plane over this morning having a look around. Dinner: Sick bay stodge, stew, 3/4 issue of slightly fishy rice. Extra 1 dessertspoon full of fish bones.

Sat. 12th: Breakfast 'soup' of thin rice and a little veg. Tiffin green buboh 1 pt. plus a lagi 3/4 from cook house after meals. Dinner: thin watery pork stew and green buboh plus some lagi pork stew from cook house at about 8 p.m. This lagi was thick with veg. and far more pork than previously. Got 3/4 pt. and it was good. Still no veg. or roots from Nips, only spud tops from Battn. gardens form greens these days. Had an alarm again again this morning but saw no planes. 3 deaths today including 1 internee.

Sun. 13: Breakfast fairly thick plain rice buboh. 4 more deaths. Tiffin 1 pint green buboh. Dinner a rissole and 1 pt. green buboh – also got 3/4 pt. stodge as 'perks' for lending my cooking tin. Bought 4 roasted spuds for $14 – a terrible price but that's how things are now with this food shortage. Got ½ issue/man of tobacco for 25 cts. which has eased the situation for some people a little, though I don't suppose it will last most people more than 2 days. Still no roots or veg. from Nips. Got paid. today $3.

Mon. 14: Bought 2 pieces of tapioca for $2 … it proved to be a bit woody. Breakfast very watery rice gruel with a few veg. leaves in it. Tiffin green buboh thinner than usual. I got lagi … issue. Dinner stew 1 pt. and light 3/4 kedgeree (fried) as a little ubi came in. Three deaths again.

Tues. 15: 3 deaths again today. Breakfast very watery rice gruel and a little veg. Tiffin green buboh. Dinner thin stew and rice and boiled ubi. 2 chaps were caught trying to pinch tapioca outside wire at night and also trying to get into Nip stores. As a result our supply of ubi has been cut by 50% for 5 or 6 days we get 27 sacks instead of 54.

Wed. 16: Alarm again today, one recce plane over. Breakfast thin buboh and coffee. Tiffin a more normal rice and ubi; Dinner Hut stodge. 1 pint nice and thick,

½ rice and 1 pt. stew and boiled ripe plantain (good) I got lagi ½ rice and ½ pt. stew, also 1 pt. stew from another chap so I had a jolly good feed for a change. It was very cold again after dinner and all night.

Thurs. 17: Breakfast very thin rice and gruel and a little pumpkin cut up in it, about the thinnest yet. Tiffin green buboh. Dinner stew and kedgeree and a boiled plantain for which we had to pay 50 cts. but it was a good ripe one. 3 more deaths.

Fri. 18: Breakfast thin buboh and keladi (grated) and some tree brinjals cut up in it. Tiffin green buboh. Dinner 1 pt. stew, 3/4 kedgeree and a plantain also bought for 50 cts. Only a few of us bought these. Two more deaths.

Sat. 19: *Sent Post Cards again.* Breakfast very thin buboh. Tiffin ubi and rice into which I put an egg ($2) which was very nice. Dinner Hut stodge containing 1 brinjal per man, 1 pint Coy. stodge 1 pint and more. Full issue rice and I got lagi ½ hut stodge

[line missing]

[line missing]

which the Nips very generously gave us. Even took the meat off the head first! Had a recce flying boat over today which shot up the river a bit and also parts of 'drome works. Managed to buy 2 eggs at $2 each. 1½ portions of excellent blachang at $1.20/portion brought in by working parties specially for this sick bay. Salt was also on sale at 50 cts./spoon full (soup spoon) but I did not buy. Ordered another plantain at 50 cts. An extra special addition to evening was 2 dessert spoonfuls of cooked blood per man and it was excellent.

Sun. 20th: A big change round in camp. 3 new sick bays opened and all old Coys. reconstituted and moved to cliff. huts J & K now become G & move to 13 hut. 3 more deaths. Started to organised talks in the hut today and hope for some measure of success. There's absolutely nothing done by the camp for amusement of sick people and most chaps in this hut are pretty badly "out" and need a leader, Brekker a very thin gruel with practically no rice whatever and a little tree brinjal in it. I had a 2nd lot from a chap who could not face it and also some stodge left over from last night which was perfectly sweet and sound. Tiffin rice and ubi (medium) into which I put my 2nd egg and a little blachang. Dinner stew and boiled kedgeree and tapioca 'cake' and ½ a boiled plantain. (Note on side of Diary: 8th weighed 57 kilos lost 6 kilos).

Mon. 21st: Usual sort of meals. Got 3/4 bin of rice and ubi at tiffin for hut which gave ½ issue to every man in the hut extra. Managed to buy a duck's egg $2 for tiffin today. 3 more deaths and one officer (Aussie). Had a 4-engined bomber over again today and a flying boat yesterday.

Tues. 22nd: Bought a hen's egg $2 and a portion of potato mash 50 cts. 3 more depths.

Wed. 23rd: Usual breakfast and tiffin, got lagi rice and ubi for tiffin. Dinner: Rice and stew and potato mash, got lagi stew and had another egg ($2) fried through my rice. Got another ginger issue. No deaths today. Had the usual morning warning and one plane over but did nothing. Sold a pair of shorts for $40 which will all help to buy eggs etc.

Thurs. 24th: Usual brekker and tiffin. Dinner: stew, boiled ubi and rice, kedgeree with a boiled egg ($2). One death today. Had an abscess on my right shoulder opened up a little and its darned sore. Bought blachang $1.50, salt 50 cts. and a stodge $1.25. Also got an extra ½ pt. stodge from loan of cooking pot.

Fri. 25th: 2 alarms today, an odd plane or so over in the morning, did nothing another in afternoon dropped pamphlets. Lagi buboh rice (1 pt.) for breakfast. usual tiffin, dinner hut stodge containing beans, tree brinjals, spuds and tops as well as cook house rubbish, very tasty, got extra ½ issue. Fried kledi and rice kedg and stew … had a boiled ducks egg $2. and bought $2 blachang. Bought 2 issues tobacco $1.20. First in camp for about 10 days.

Sat. 26th: 2 deaths today. Meals as usual, got extra ½ issue dinner from sick neighbor. Had another hen egg $2. ½ issue blachang 50 cts. My shoulder is giving me a lot of trouble and it is very painful when orderly is busy with scissors and forceps.

Sun. 27: Perfectly *foul* watery buboh for breakfast only about 3 spoonfuls of solid … in all. Tiffin: green buboh and a raw hens egg ($2). Dinner: rice and boiled ubi stew.

Mon. 28: Meals about as usual. 5 more deaths including Sgt. Curtis of Vols. I've developed squitters and sickness. Brought up all my dinner including a hens egg $2, had a bad night.

Tues. 29: Gave away most of my brekker, tiffin and dinner. Got another egg $2 but saving it until I'm better. Feeling very weak today, the ulcer on my shoulder is very painful. Another flying boat over today.

Wed. 30: 4 deaths today and 6 yesterday including Sgt. Bob Grey of Vols. Feeling a little better today and ate most of my breakfast and all tiffin and lagi. Dinner: Hut stodge, stew and mixed kedgeree.

Thurs. 31: Usual grub, another plane over, eating a lot better and feeling better. Had a ducks egg whipped up with sugar raw and it was excellent. 1 death.

Fri. June 1st: Usual food. Got a lagi breakfast from exchange while sick, lagi stew and kedgeree for dinner.

Sat. June 2nd: Good buboh rice for breakfast and had ½ lagi from exchange while sick. Tiffin rice and keladi. Dinner stew and kedg. fish and seal meat.

Sun. 3: Usual meals. Off my dinner a little with chronic indigestion. Had a beaten ducks egg and sugar ½ usual meals, getting an extra breakfast each morning in exchange made of mashed potatoes, beans, kong, blachang salt and pepper and it was a jolly good effort. My shoulder is getting better slowly but still channelling downwards and is about 3'' long and 1½ broad. The indigestion is still troublesome.

Tues. 5: Usual breakfast and tiffin – had a lovely raid on the drome again today – 3 flights of 6 4-engined bombers each dropped a load and then came back and gave it another 'do'. Dinner stew and dugong meat kedg. 3 deaths today. Total death roll last month 67. Extra breakfast again but stopping it I think, too much indigestion.

Wed. 6: Usual brekker and tiffin, Dinner had a fried egg with stew and fish kedg. and also put in $1 worth of fish. Indigestion all day. Legs very muscle bound and cramped and feet swollen so am stopping fluids for a bit. Had curried brinjal sauce for dinner these last two nights but they have been very bitter as the fruit is unripe and I gave all my stew including 2 'lagi' and ½ sauce away. 4 deaths again today including Robbie Boyd of Vols.

Thurs. 7: Stopped the extra brekker and got large tiffin. Had lightly boiled egg with tiffin and 3 very nice fat fried fish. I soaked the fish in water and am using that brine as salt flavouring and its good.

Fri. 8: Tummy out of order again, bowels very loose, usual meals but not eating them all, getting indigestion badly, stopped almost all fluids.

Sat. & Sun. 9 & 10: Bowels still very loose, feeling pretty crabbed all round, swapping my food forward until I feel better. Made measly $20 selling newspaper these last few days. All grist to the mill while going is good. There has been a 4-engined bomber over each day for 3 days straffing the river and it looks as though a little more attention is being paid here this time. Well it can't come too soon now.

Mon. 11: Green buboh brekker and tiffin which I ate. Bowels still loose legs still sore. Ulcer improving a lot. Tobacco issue 80 cts. No eggs for 3 days. Dinner stew and boiled kedg. 5 deaths today.

Tues. 12: Had a piece of papaya given from orderlies. Off rest of my food, giving ½ away. Planes over again today. 2 deaths. Cinema show on Square but nobody from sick bays allowed to go.

Wed. 13: 5 deaths again. Got 2 beautiful eggs from Sid Williams. Had my belt and cash stolen while I was asleep. Recovered belt but lost about $30 cash

Here the diary finishes abruptly.

Below is a sample of the author's handwriting; he is believed to have been a Malayan Volunteer.

Chapter Six

DEATH MARCHES

29 January 1945 - Sandakan

The most powerful Japanese figure in Borneo was Major Nishihara Shuiji better known officially as the Judicial Officer 37 Army H.Q. It was Nishihara who frequently went off to Tokyo Imperial General H.Q. to secure guidance on policy matters particularly relating to POWs.

Nishihara appointed the Judges for the Matthews' trial, and told them what was expected of them. It would have been Nishihara who would have informed the Generals that ultimately the surviving prisoners and internees would be killed; his orders would have been verbally relayed.

Wherever there were POW camps located there were Kempe Tai 'stooges' who were feared by the local commanding officers, in Sandakan camp there was Hinato Genzo.

The High Command were careful how they relayed messages of policy; when they decided to put the PYTHON party on trial the whole process was planned by experts from Tokyo – the prisoners were found to be 'spies' and, accordingly, were not treated as prisoners of war and were hanged at Jesselton in December 1944 in the very gaol the English were housed in. It was Lieut. Geoff Threadgold who inspected the gallows when his party first arrived there in October 1942 – wondering what the two-storey building was used for.

185

The Commanding Officer of the 37 Army was General Yamawaki who, as a former Vice-Minister for War, had come out of retirement to command the Borneo Garrison – at the time believed to be a comfortable job in a country insulated by captured territories from attack until General MacArthur advanced almost 2000 miles in 1943/1944 in striking distance of Borneo and the Philippines. Yamawaki got out while he could – he was replaced by General Baba in January 1945 who was then left to make the decisions he was obliged to regarding the movement of the POWs.

Baba was ordered by Southern Command to move eight of his ten Battalions from the East Coast to the Brunei Bay area to protect the oil fields. At the same time he decided to evacuate the Sandakan prison camp to Tuaran where he was expected to put up his final battle for Borneo.

Hoshijima was ordered to provide 500 POWs in what was the first movement of the fittest men; he could not find 500 fit men – he claims to have provided 470 however the individual officers in charge of the Groups claimed there were more like 450 men.

The Commander of the Sandakan Garrison, Colonel Otsuka, ordered the unfortunate Capt. Yamamoto Shoichi to collect the prisoners at the 9 Mile and march west in nine Groups with about fifty POWs in each Group. General Baba described Yamamoto's Battalion as one of his finest Units in Borneo. They first arrived in October 1944 to protect the airfield the prisoners were building against a feared Allied airborne attack to capture the airfield – with the assistance of fit POWs; that danger had now passed as the aerodrome had been destroyed by bombing since October 1944.

The Allies were now stepping up their progress. The Japanese realised Luzon was about to be invaded and that there was a large Task Force prowling west of the Philippines and they feared an imminent attack on Sandakan.

In late January 1945 Captain Yamamoto planned the march and logistics for the movement of the POWs. Structures were set up at intervals along the route, at these 'Rest Houses' the escorting Japanese and their prisoners were supposed to rest, receive medical treatment and food. Yamamoto planned the march of 165 miles from Sandakan to Ranau to take 15 days.

Hoshijima ordered the camp administrators to provide groups of 50 fit men to assemble at the 9 Mile, not far from the camp, on the Labuk Road. The first group was led by POW Officer Captain Rod Jeffery, Medical Officer of 'B' Force, and the Japanese officer in command was Yamamoto's Adjutant, Captain Iino Shigero who later stated: "The condition of the PWs attached to my group seemed to be fit to march as a whole. All of them brought with them four days' rations, clothing and other equipments.

"On the first day we reached the spot 23 miles apart from Sandakan. All the PWs were in good condition. We delayed the start for one day as it began to rain during the first night. From the point 33 miles apart from Sandakan the road grew very muddy, but we could reach Kolapis without any stragglers.

"On the fifth day a PW and a Japanese became gravely ill and died after arriving at Muanad This event made us stay there for one day. The group was given four days' ration each and 100 kilograms of cassava at that place.

"On the sixth day, though the weather recovered a little, the bad condition of the road made us suffer greatly. Causing some patients of malaria and beri beri amongst both POWs and Japanese. Those who could not walk alone were carried by Japanese and PWs by stretchers to the next rest house. The diseased PWs were looked after by a Medical Officer and two medical soldiers of PWs.

"After passing Mandrin and Sapiro, we arrived at Boto where we were given four day's ration and some amount of vegetables which were distributed equally to PWs and the Japanese.

"Leaving Boto on the next morning we reached Milulu where each was given 200 grammes of cassava and some vegetables and then started for Paginatan on the next day.

"At 6 p.m. of that day we reached Paginatan where three days' ration and some amount of potatoes and salt was distributed to each of us by a supply depot. I purchased two pigs from the natives for the group. At 9 p.m. of the night a PW died of illness.

"By the time we reached Paginatan, 11 PWs died at the rest houses. Four Japanese died.

"After leaving Paginatan two PWs got ill on the way and were carried by stretchers both by Japanese and PWs as far as the rest house of Nobutan. There they both died in the night.

"It was about 4 p.m. 12th February that we reached Ranau via Naraba. Then I was ordered to transfer 42 PWs to Major Watanabe.

"The Japanese of my group started for Tuaran on the following morning. Just when I was about to start I was told by Major Watanabe that two PWs died during the previous night.

"While on the march the Japanese co-operated with the PWs in looking after the patients and carrying them by stretchers, but fifteen PWs died out of 55.

"I admit that the difficulties and pains met by us during the march were far beyond our imagination. We tried every means to carry the group forward, because to leave off the stragglers meant their death and because we had to reach the destination as quickly as possible according to the order of the Headquarters."

Each group of the march found the track becoming more impassable; the continuous rain, swollen rivers and swampy ground; the prisoners began to die from exhaustion, illness, lack of food and shelter at the 'Rest Houses'. The Japanese officers in command of each group all stated their men were suffering as well as the POWs from the terrible condition of the track and lack of food.

W/Offr. Gotanda Koroku who was with the 3rd Group of 50 POWs and 47 Japanese was ordered by the group commander to arrange for the supply of food and lodging for the group. He stated: "I was to march more than one hour every day in advance, together with an orderly, to reach the point where the food would be supplied and arrange for its allocation. On one occasion the PWs came short of food

187

and I had to march Muanad and Beluran to obtain rice. At Paginatan we purchased a pig from the natives and distributed it equally to the Japanese and the PWs as we always did.

"Thus I seldom marched with my group, as my duty always made me march ahead of it. It was after we had reached the destination that I heard from my commander that 5 Japanese and 10 PWs had died on the way owing to malaria, dysentery and beriberi."

The commander of 4th Group, Capt. Mizuta Ryuichi, had arrived in Borneo from Japan just three months before he was ordered to take 55 POWs with 39 Japanese guards on the march; day one of the march quickly showed to him that the PWs were in no fit state to embark on such a journey. He stated that as the march progressed the PWs began to die, as did some of his own men, and he complained in his statement that there was a great lack of medical attention, medical supplies and food at each Rest House stop.

Lieut. Sato Tetsuo, No. 5 Group, reached Ranau with only 35 of his 50 POWs alive and he stated: "I consider that I did everything possible for the PWs. I was on friendly terms with the S/M. in charge of them owing to my ability to speak English. The march was carried out under very difficult conditions. The S/M. name was A.E. Johns."

Lieut. Tanaka Shojiro, commander of No. 6 Group, was in charge of 20 Englishmen and 20 Australians and accompanied by 42 Japanese soldiers. He too found the track conditions extremely difficult and stated: "I tried to make use of carts which had been made for an unexpected removal, but we had to discard them on the evening of the first day because the path was unexpectedly hard." (These carts were later found by the Australian War Graves Unit.) He continued: "When we reached Mandolin one PW was absent. I made a Japanese and 2 PW medical soldiers go back and look him out, but they could not find him. The next day the advance party of No. 7 Group came up and told me that a PW was seen dead at a spot 3 miles east of Mandolin. I dispatched my soldiers to look out and bury this man, the PW's name was Sarginson."[1]

Note 1:

Number	Name	Date	Number	Name	Date
543013	Sarginson, J.	09 Feb.	1478296	Tasker, E.L.	
1827527	Black, L.W.	13 Feb.	11052607	Thompson, A.	
1354117	Whitehead, R.M.	14 Feb.	842317	Roberts, B.	
749641	Moore, F.W.	15 Feb.	1548153	Bareham, J.J.	19 Feb.
548711	Deacon, W.J.		643141	Beardshaw, H.	20 Feb.
11051585	Jardine, R.		1274285	Price, D.J.	21 Feb.
972854	Street, A.	16 Feb.	1109837	Larter, G.	
1684076	Slade, A.E.	17 Feb.	1195700	Kearney, F.W.	
1278350	Austin, T.H.				
544332	Marriott, F.	18 Feb.			

The Japanese advised that these groups died on the march.

No. 7 Group was commanded by Lieut. Sugimura Shinichi and was composed of 50 English POWs and forty Japanese soldiers; six POWs died on the way and only 44 finally reached Paginatan where they were handed over to Major Watanabe. Lieut. Horikawa Keichi was also in charge of 50 English POWs and 46 Japanese soldiers, this was No. 8 Group. Sixteen POWs died on the track and the remainder were taken over by Major Watanabe; Horikawa stated later that only 13 POWs died – all from natural causes and weakness.

Capt. Abe Kazuo was commander of No. 9 Group and the last group on the march from Sandakan to Ranau. He stated: "I detailed a party of three to follow along behind the main party of 50 POWs. I had been told by Capt. Yamamoto that in case if both the Japanese and POWs had to die after trying every means to keep them on the march, we could dispose of POWs. Private Endo and Private Sato were the only ones behind as far as Boto. I then detailed Sgt. Sato to move with them as well.

"On 10 February 1945 when I arrived at Muanad with my group I received orders from Captain Yamamoto that if there was no other course available PWs too ill to travel were to be killed.

"This order was given to me personally by Capt. Yamamoto and there were no other officers present. They were given to me because I was in charge of the last party. Sgt. Sato reported to me at Paginatan that all PWs had died of illness."

Private Endo Hiraki stated: "When we reached Muanad, Pte. Sato and myself were detailed by Capt. Abe to follow at the rear of the main group to help the sick PWs that dropped behind. Those of them that were too ill to travel we were instructed by Capt. Abe to kill. This order was given directly to Sato and myself by Capt. Abe.

"Between Muanad and Boto eighteen men died; one of these was shot in accordance with orders, the remainder died of natural causes. Pte. Sato shot the PW. When we reached Boto, Sgt. Maj. Sato Shinichi of my unit was waiting for us; he had apparently received the same orders from Capt Abe.

"Shortly after leaving Boto another one of the PWs became too ill to continue the march. Pte. Sato and myself under the orders of S/M. Sato, then took the PW into the jungle at the side of the track and shot him. Again Pte. Sato did the shooting.

"Between Boto and Pugnitan a further 9 PWs died. The first four were left with Pte. Sato and then, later, I was left with a party of five. These five men were very sick and suffering a great deal. Although my orders from Capt. Abe were to kill them I did not have the heart to do such a thing and so left them behind, without food or water, to die. I believe that Pte. Sato did the same thing. On these occasions there were no officers or NCOs present to see that we carried out the orders.

"Looking back now and remembering how ill the PWs were I feel it might have been more humane to have killed them and buried them before going on."

Private Sato was later killed in action and Sgt. Maj. Sato Shinichi denied giving orders to kill the POWs.

Captain Takakuwa Takuo's second in command, Captain Watanabe Genzo, was ordered to ensure that Sergeant Tsuji would compile the names of all those PWs killed when they could not carry on on the march.

He stated: "I went along on the march. There were 99 members from the Suzuki Unit in the Okuyama Battalion who came to assist us in guarding the prisoners on the march. There were 48 men from our Unit that went along; these were divided into three groups, one being attached to the Suzuki Unit, another under Sgt. Maj. Tsuji and a third under my command. Every day the PW were split into three groups. The first group leaving at 0630 in the morning and the other two at half hour intervals after the first group. Then at about 9 a.m. I started out with my group of guards and Sgt. Major Tsuji started out at 10 a.m.

"My group would get the names and particulars of any prisoners that had fallen by the wayside and try to take them on with them; however, if the prisoner simply could not go on my group went ahead leaving one man to guard him. They would be picked up by Sgt. Maj. Tsuji's group. Every morning the guards in the three groups would be changed around and I would give Sgt. Maj. Tsuji orders as to what time to start and what to do. Then my group would leave an hour and a half after the prisoners and one hour before his group. My group would usually reach the resting place for the night at about 4 p.m. and Sgt. Maj. Tsuji's group would arrive about 5 p.m.

"After his group arrived, Sgt. Maj. Tsuji would come to me and make a report on the number of prisoners who had been shot, died of sickness or escaped. Then I would take this figure to my superior. In this manner we proceeded to Ranau.

"We did all we could to see that as many PW as possible made the march. Sometimes the Japanese guards would carry what luggage the PW had for them or give them a little extra food or do little things to make things a bit more pleasant. On one occasion I saw a prisoner being chased by Japanese guards while making an attempt to escape. I remember that I made a report to the effect that five prisoners had attempted to escape and while one had succeeded, the other four had been shot.

"When we arrived at Ranau the prisoners were quite weary. There was a shortage of food and although we did our best to try and obtain more it was not possible. We did receive tapioca from the Watanabe Unit which was camped at Ranau. Now and then we would go out at night and steal cattle which we would kill and share the meat with the PW. Although we did all this, it was still far from enough and the death rate increased all the time. The deaths increased until there were only 33 prisoners left. My C.O. told me that practically all of them were very sick and would die sooner or later and that they should be shot. It was 1 August 1945 when he gave me these orders.

"The prisoners and the Japanese guards had been together for three years and had become friendly with each other. The Japanese soldiers had had no wish to kill all the prisoners both on the march and later at Ranau, but they were given orders by their superior officers and they had to carry them out. Some of the NCOs and men refused to do this, but I told them it was an order and had to be carried out."

That was the Japanese version of what occurred on the march. Some of the guards wrote on the death certificates: "Total exhaustion"; "When body unable move"; others "Missed by Medical Unit"; "Died" – then signed by the executioner Lieut. Ino – the killer at the rear.

This knowledge soon was passed forward to those struggling to stay on their feet – "If you drop out you'll be shot". Eventually some 300 reached Ranau.

None of the prisoners found what the Japanese promised – plentiful food and better living conditions. The local people were warned not to give food to the prisoners, despite this warning they gave their children food to pass on to the prisoners or place it where the PWs would find it.

While the prisoners continued to struggle through the mud somewhere near Boto, they were not to know a major assault was taking place at Labuan, a small island in a commanding position at the entrance to Brunei Bay.

G.H.Q. S.W.P. were urging the British to establish a major Naval base there in preparation for its advance to Japan, planned for later in the year. The British replied it would not be required because they would have re-captured Singapore by September.

There were two airfields on the Island, one of which the British prisoners from Kuching and Sandakan were constructing with disastrous results to the prisoners.

The first assault was made at Victoria Harbour by two A.I.F. Battalions to secure a beach-head; other attacks followed and by June 13 two Brigades were established on the Mainland and the Japanese were heading inland where the Dyak headhunters were waiting.

The Japanese were now obeying Imperial Directives – under no circumstances were prisoners to be permitted to fall into Allied hands.

Bdr. W.D. Moxham: "All the PWs in my party were in a very weak condition; the Japanese guards all seemed very fit. We were given some rations and told when we left the camp that our ration had to last four days but later when we got on the road Lt. Sugimura told us it would have to last eight days.

"At Boto we traded our clothing with the natives for rice and tapioca but this was taken off us by the Kempe Tai. There were food dumps along the way but we did not get much although the Japanese always seemed to eat well. We were issued with rubber boots but they were not good for once we put our feet in the mud the boots would slip off and stop us. We were lucky in a way we did not have to carry any Japanese gear, but just a little rice and salt.

"It was the rainy season, the track was mud up to our knees and fording rivers – from Boto on there was very steep climbing all the way to Ranau.

"We lost seven men out of our party; the first man took ill at the 23 Mile Camp and he was sent back to Sandakan. The next man was Gnr. Coughlan, he took ill as we were coming into our camp, we could not see him and we left him. That night, W.O. Kinder, who was in charge of our party, asked permission from Lt. Sugimura to take a party back and bring him into the camp. We made up a stretcher and went back and brought him back but he died that night and we buried him before leaving next morning. We lost another man that way too, but the Japs would not let us go back for him. The Japanese soldiers went back and we heard no more about him. Then we left three men at Boto. We never saw them again. We lost another man when he became ill and we had to leave him, just near the foot of a big range. I think it was Milulu. Two of the guards stayed with him. At Camp that night W. O. Kinder met me and said we would go back and get the sick man and bring him in. When we got back to where we had left him the two Japanese guards, one a Corporal and one a Private, said they had shot the POW and thrown him over the side of an embankment. It was a very steep embankment and next morning we heard moaning and groaning from one side of the road about a mile up from the camp; two of us went over and had a look to see if we could find who it was and it was a soldier who had been in the forward party. He was not dead but was in great agony and he was paralysed and could not move. The guards would not let us remain, they hunted us straight off on our journey.[2]

" ... Out of my party of 50, about 44 reached Paginatan, but at Paginatan we lost a lot. We stayed there for about a month. The six who died there included a chap from the 2/10 Aust. Field Regiment. He just died from exhaustion and exposure; he could not go on any further. He stopped about 2 miles from where we camped. Four of us went back that night, after getting permission from the Japs, and brought him to camp but he was dead next morning. We buried him there. The next chap who dropped out was from the 2/15 Field Regiment. The Japs would not permit us to return for him however the Japanese themselves went back for him. It was a good way back, I supposed they shot him – they wouldn't let us go back for him.

"The guards kept us going at full pace all the time and along the track we smelt and saw bodies. They were Australian soldiers' bodies, from the previous parties, we could recognise them, some we knew personally. One was in the middle of the track with a shovel in his hands; we were not allowed to stop and investigate. A chap from the 2/10 Field Regiment was on a log beside the road – dead. I saw his colour patch, which was the same as mine. Just as I got over to the body and saw by his hat who it was that was lying there the guards were on to me. I could not see whether he had been shot or not.[3]

Note 2:

1753256	Baulcombe, H.J.	20 Feb.	1120396	Seal, C.A.	
951267	Watkins, K.C.	24 Feb.	1498100	Pearce, C.	05 Mar.
1758991	Bagwell, A.	27 Feb.	1550073	Payne, B.M.	06 Mar.
645710	Moore, T.		2329580	Said, A.	
912890	Toye,		3660151	Jones, J.H.	
1481305	Rookwood, L.J.		2317202	Roberts, R.J.	
1330266	Clarke, H.B.	28 Feb.	7630609	Henshall, N.H.	
1274978	Cryer,	01 Mar.	1294019	Newman, K.F.	07 Mar.
2346404	Tomkinson, C.N.	02 Mar.	1498158	Davies, J.	08 Mar.
11051563	Luscott, T.				

"On the way I suppose I saw or smelt between 20 and 30 bodies, there could have been a lot more …

"Men from my own party could not go on. Boto was the first place where we had to actually leave anyone; we had to leave four there as they could not proceed. At the next place at the bottom of a big hill, we left two more men and later heard shots. In all of my dealings with the Japanese I have never seen any of our chaps after they have left with the Japs. Once you stopped – you stopped for good. The Japs had no time for the sick, they would not even feed them.

"I was at Paginatan for a month; No. 6 party of Australians and all of the rest of the Englishmen – 6 to 10 – were there. They remained there. The previous parties 1 to 5 had gone on to Ranau. We were told the reason for our being retained there was that the Ranau barracks were not finished; but that was a joke because they were never built. Of those parties, 6 to 9, there were originally 200 men – less than that, there were three parties of 50 and one small party of 20, a total of 170. Of this 170 about 38 men marched out, fit to march, from Paginatan to Ranau. There were still 20 to 30 who could not march, they were very sick. The rest had died. We have been burying four to five a day every day for the month we remained at Paginatan. The men died from malnutrition, reaction, dysentery, malaria. On the march the men used to get some ferns and even snails and frogs to eat, and one party caught some pythons. They got anything at all to make up for the food they should have got from the Japs. We marched up and down big hills, up to our knees in water and mud and over and through rivers. Acting Padre Garland died soon after we arrived at Paginatan. There was a doctor who went with the first party in February, Capt. Jeffrey, he had gone to Ranau. We had no medical officer at Paginatan. There were some Jap medical officers there but they did nothing at all for us. The Japs had plenty of medical supplies but we got none from them. We set off with a party from Sandakan numbering 50 and after a month at Paginatan only about 6 or 8 of us were able to march on to Ranau.

"There were a lot of beatings there, sick and all. We had to carry and get our own wood, and clean up the barracks. Warrant Officer Kinder took charge of us, eventually taking charge of the whole of the parties at Paginatan. He went up to

Note 3:

1808998	Hardacre, G.	10 Mar.	11052237	Hodgkinson, R.D.	
1826671	Robinson, A.W.	11 Mar.	621324	Tugwell, W.P.	
1201580	Bluck, H.G.M.	13 Mar.	2313139	Beck, J.T.	
851182	Rogers, J.W.	13 Mar.	1729649	Baker, J.G.A.	
116351	Small, J.N.	14 Mar.	937033	Campling, F.	
1483130	Shipley, G.	17 Mar.	959838	Durham, J.A.	22 Mar.
935211	Littlewood, E.L.		2571826	Edwards, S.E.	24 Mar.
56591	Brett, P.J.	19 Mar.	1522707	Butt, H.J.	
6550836	Burke, G.H.				

some of the Japs and was able to get some food from some of them. Some of the Japs however would come down and beat the men and Kinder himself was beaten when he took somebody else's part. He was belted with sticks. The guards at Paginatan were new men. I believe they had come from Kuching.

"Under Kinder 36 men started out on the march to Ranau from Paginatan. I was one of these 36. We did the march in four to five days; we could have done it more easily but we were only able to do 6 or 7 miles a day. One day we only did 5 miles. We would start off at 7 o'clock in the morning and we would be beaten along to get to our destination – a set mileage. We might arrive at 10 o'clock and we would be knocked up completely. You could not then have a rest because we were split into small parties to go out looking for food for the Japanese. We were not given any rest. We went to the native places and the Japs would get stuff from them.

"The Japs would take our blankets and any clothing or anything else we had and trade with the natives. The Japs thus obtained some sweet potatoes and pigs. We got only a few sweet potatoes. On the march from Paginatan to Ranau, I think 24 of our 36 died. One was puffed up with beriberi in the legs and face and was getting along all right on his own and could have made it but the Japs would not leave him alone; they tried to force him along and eventually he collapsed. They kicked him on the ground, Kinder and I in front saw it. The Jap turned and saw the man had gone down and he struck him over the head with his rifle butt. The soldier was left there and the party marched on.[4]

"When this happened, Kinder told me that in several instances when he was at the rear of our party on this section to Ranau from Paginatan, wicked things happened. The Japs used to make him stay behind while a man was shot to death or kicked to death. They made Kinder watch it.

"On the scrounging parties on which we were forced to go, the Japs scrounged, in exchange for our own clothes, food and some pigs and boots. I was on one of these parties and we got very little of whatever food was obtained. All we were given were a few small sweet potatoes. Once we got the skin of a pig. Out of our party of 38 that left Paginatan about 12 died on the trip to Ranau."

"I travelled with the 3rd Group with W. Offr. Gotanda Kiroku." said Keith Botterill.

"At the start of the journey we were given three pounds of rice, 1/4 pound of dried fish and an ounce of salt and about one pound of sugar was given to the officer in charge of the party. We moved out the gate and down to the road and we were given 120 pounds of rice packed in Army packs. We carried that rice, each POW

Note 4:

816056	Thompson, S.	26 Mar.	644334	Bell, A.
1530389	Beardsley, J.	29 Mar.	1539977	Bayer, J.H.
1035626	Fletcher, J.		10541432	Sweeting, A.J.

A.C.2 K.F. Cosham. 1293357. R.A.F. (VR)
211 Sqdn. Died Ranau 8 March 1945. Age 24.
Ridgewood, East Sussex.   Pic: John Bessant.

A.C.2 J.L. Williams. 1077842. R.A.F. (VR)
Died Ranau 17 March 1945. Age 26.
Ammanford, Wales   Pic: John Bessant

A.C.1 H.B. Clarke. 1330266. R.A.F. (VR)
Died 28 February 1945
                    Pic: Christopher Elliott

Gnr. Bois Roberts. 842317. 48 Bty. 21 LAA
Royal Artillery.. Escaped from first march
with L.A.C. Beardshaw and two Australian
POWs. Died near Telupid 18 February 1945.
Age 28.   Pic: Mrs. Josephine Share

carried 40 to 60 pounds. Our loads consisted of ammunition, rice and Japanese officer's gear ; the rice was sewn up in a hessian bag and the ammunition was in a bag which was made into a pack and worn on the chest. There were about ten bags of ammunition. Before we left we were issued with a pair of secondhand shorts, a shirt or a jacket and rubber shoes which were no good as they slipped straight off our feet. Only about six or seven men had the boots they had been able to keep all along.

"It was the rainy season, the track was very boggy and above our knees a lot of the way; we had difficult crossings over creeks and our feet were cut going along the track. The country was swampy, hills, and no flat country at all.

"We passed through Boto, Paginatan, I can't remember the other villages, I had no idea of the direction we were travelling. The Japanese officer in charge of our party used to find camps along the road about every ten mile and we used to try to make them each day so we could sleep in them. We slept in about 5 camps during the march and the rest we couldn't make by dark so we couldn't sleep in them. Most of us only had a groundsheet because we couldn't carry the blanket. We came across 5 ration points and once we got six cucumbers between 40 men for three days, and a bundle of tapioca leaves. At some supply depots we got rice issued to us for three days until we reached the next supply place, that would work out at about 150 grams of rice per day. At some outposts we got no rice, we got tapioca and corn instead. The last three days of our march we got about one pound of rice per day and our officer let us trade two blankets for a small pig at Paginatan. We gave the Japanese half and we had half of that pig the second day out of Ranau.[5]

"The Japanese had at least three times the amount of rations we had, bar the first five days when we had as much as them. During the period when we had the 6 cucumbers, they did not have very much at that period but although I do not know how much they got, they got sufficient. Their ration was of rice.

"At the commencement, the condition of the POW was very bad. There were men, about one or two, left behind every second or third day. Of a morning, those who were too sick to move would tell our Australian officer in charge that they could not move with the party and the Japanese Sgt. or officer would count us and move us off and we would get along the road about 1/4 mile and we would hear shots. The Japanese officer would tell our officers that they had to shoot the men who were left behind. At times when we were marching along the road and the men were too weak to keep up and they dropped behind, the Japanese would shoot them.

Note 5:

651872	Parfitt, A.W.D.	07 Mar.	1077842	Williams, J.L.	17 Mar.
1293357	Cosham, K.F.	08 Mar.	1434295	Palmer, J.H.	
1484235	Eaden, R.S.H.	10 Mar.	574596	Elliott, D.	
1632166	Shippen, J.W.	15 Mar.	6343400	Laing, R.	20 Mar.
11052588	Gregson, A.	16 Mar.	1376881	Newman, F.R.	21 Mar.

The way I know the Japanese shot those men was the Japanese officer told us at night. I do not know the name of the Japanese officer in charge of us; I can remember going up a big mountain at Boto where we lost five men. They were shot and I myself saw a Japanese Cpl. shoot two of them. That day, Sgt. Gotanda went ahead of the party to Paginatan. That night we crossed the mountain and camped at the bottom and the next day we moved off towards Paginatan and there was one Australian soldier, whose name I forget, was crawling up this mountain on his hands and knees and we went past him and got into Paginatan. As we were going in we met Sgt. Gotanda coming out and he said: "Why have you got those mosquito nets?" and we said: "The Corporal made us carry them" and he told us to leave them behind at Boto. The Sgt. told us to leave them at Boto as we could never get over the hill with them and he told us to just carry what we had. When we told him the Corporal had made us carry the nets he said: "Why" and he asked us if we were all there; we said that there were two men about three miles back, one was very sick and the other was helping him along, so the Sgt. went back to them and came in with the Australian soldier who was helping the sick man. He came into Paginatan and after he arrived we asked this Australian soldier what happened to his mate and he said: "The Sgt. had to shoot him, he could not come any further."

"The journey took us 17 days altogether. The total distance was about 150 miles. From Paginatan to Ranau was 26 miles. I have been that distance five times and I know where the mile stones were and I counted them. When I got to Ranau, there were between 150 and 200 POWs.

"When I first got to Ranau about 75 had arrived before us. I discussed with other men of other groups the conditions of their trip; we worked out No. 6 party was the worst party of the lot. The Japanese officer in command of that party had about eight Australians carrying his gear besides the ammunition and rice; his gear consisted of large boxes and two Australians used to carry a box with a pole tied to the box and the pole on each shoulder. I have never seen the Japanese in charge of No. 6 Party.. I never heard him described to me. The Japanese guards of No. 6 Party used to take the Australians' rice issue after it was cooked, they used to steal it; there was a soldier in No. 6 Party who was wearing a gold ring and the Japanese soldier killed him and took his ring.

"On the fifth day out in the march this Australian Sergeant started to drag behind and said he could not carry on; the Japanese officer told him he had only about 4 miles to go to reach camp and he sort of went off his head and went insane and kept grunting at the Japanese Sgt. and asking him to shoot him. The Japanese officer came up and the Australian Sgt. kept asking to be shot and the Jap officer agreed to shoot him if the Australian officer would give him an O.K. to do it and then Sgt. Gotanda prepared to shoot him with a revolver; then he said he would not do it and gave it to the Australian officer and told him to do it and he agreed to do it. There was myself and two other Australians beside the officer there and the Japanese Sgt. and the Japanese officer and we moved along the road and caught up with the rest of the party. The Australian officer said that: "He had to be shot, he was struggling against us when we were trying to help him and then I shot him." That was the first case of anyone being shot."[6]

Those known to have been on this march are shown on the Honour Roll.

On 13 February 1945 when they were in the Boto area near the kampong of Telupid, Pte. Molde and Gnr. Fuller fell out to await their fate with two British PWs named Gnr. Roberts and LAC Beardshaw who were also in a similar position. Roberts was a member of the Royal Artillery and Beardshaw of the Royal Air Force. The four men knew it would not be long before the Japanese completed the job of their disposal and finally decided that they would split into two groups and make a break for it. The two Australians decided to move to the east and the British decided they would make for the river and hide for a day or two. Some guards saw the PWs when they made their break and opened fire on the Australians, a bullet tore through Molde's left elbow but he kept going and they managed to shake off their pursuers.

Hussin was grey-headed, moustached, tall for a Dyak and he lived at Telupid near the rentis. He was well aware of the fact that the Japs had warned all village people to stay away from the rentis and that they would severely punish anybody found there. Although Hussin was not now living in a Dyak kampong he still retained a Dyak's curiosity and often went on a personal reconnaissance of the rentis area.

On the morning of 17 February while moving through the jungle about half a mile from the Telupid kampong he saw two white men; they were hiding near the river and beckoned to Hussin when they saw him. When he came close to them he noticed their poor physical condition and knew they were prisoners who had escaped from the Japanese. They indicated to Hussin they wanted him to let them know when the Japs had gone and they would then go into the jungle proper. About 4 p.m. Hussin returned and took the PWs to his house. Molde spoke a little Malay which made things easier for the whole party. Each of the men in a signed statement offered Hussin $400 if they could get to the Allied lines with his help. (This note was later handed in to the S.R.D. patrol.) Hussin was apprehensive about the PWs remaining at his house so he decided he would take them to the kampong of Kemansi, about a mile away as he considered their chances of remaining undetected from the Japanese would be better there than in the larger kampong of Telupid.

Note 6:

1490050	Wilson, G.E.		750336	Jones, W.	01 Apr.
1478314	Jacobi, S.C.	26 Mar.	623055	Chapples, I.	08 Apr.
1028262	Morris, L.	28 Mar,	927421	Garrad, E.	
1734002	Aplin, C.E.	29 Mar.	1556169	Moore, J.E.	
994444	Grice, R.W.	30 Mar.			

Route of the Death Marches

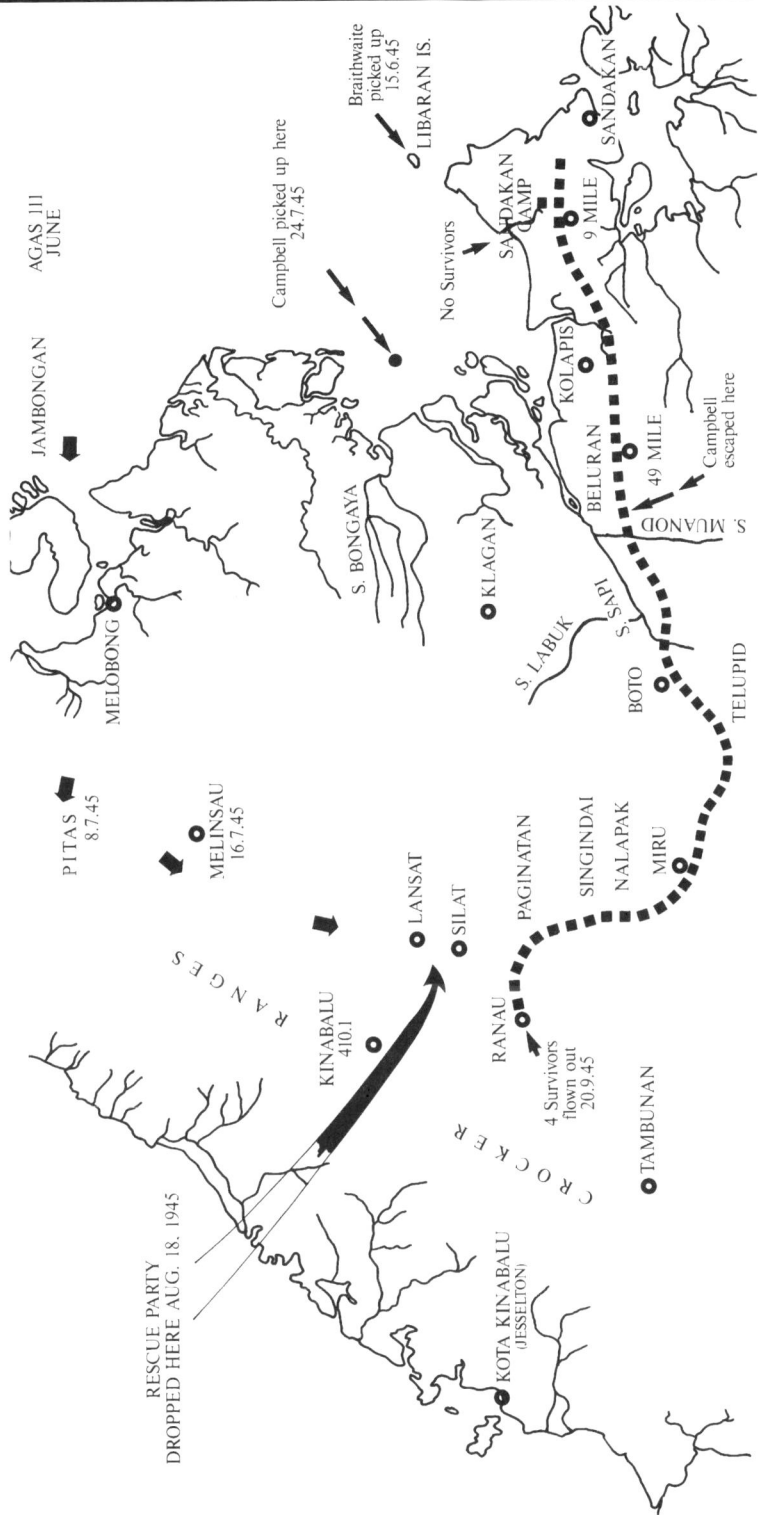

AGAS III
JUNE

Braithwaite
picked up
15.6.45

LIBARAN IS.

SANDAKAN

Campbell picked up here
24.7.45

SANDAKAN
CAMP

9 MILE

No Survivors

JAMBONGAN

KOLAPIS

KOLAPIS

S. MUANOD

49 MILE

BELURAN

Campbell
escaped here

MELOBONG

S. BONGAYA

KLAGAN

S. SAPI

TELUPID

S. LABUK

BOTO

PITAS
8.7.45

MELINSAU
16.7.45

RANGES

LANSAT

SILAT

PAGINATAN

SINGINDAI

NALAPAK

MIRU

KINABALU
410.1

RANAU

4 Survivors
flown out
20.9.45

CROCKER

TAMBUNAN

RESCUE PARTY
DROPPED HERE AUG. 18. 1945

KOTA KINABALU
(JESSELTON)

199

After the PWs had eaten a meal cooked by Hussin's wife and had washed themselves with hot water they felt better. Molde's elbow was attended as best they could and a parcel of food was given to each man for the journey to Kemansi. It was about 10 p.m. when they set out for the house of Orang Tuan (Headman) Onsi. The people of Kemansi went out of their way to do all they could to look after the white men. Orang Tuan Onsi told them to build a 'sulap' or lean-to for them and each of the twenty-one houses in the kampong shared in keeping the PWs alive with food and comforts. All the PWs had dysentery and beri beri and were in a weak state when they arrived at Kemansi. Three of the men had to be carried to the sulap. The village did not have any medicines apart from local herbs etc. and the PWs did not face a very bright future.

Early in March the first PW died, Gunner B. Roberts, 842317, R.A., Pte. Molde died towards the end of March and the other Australian, Gnr. Fuller, died five days later, LAC Beardshaw, R.A.F., was the last man to die in May 1945. The loyal people of Kemansi who had risked so much in harboring and trying to help the four men laid them to rest close to their jungle village and there they remained until their bodies were recovered by 31 Aust. War Graves Unit. They were re-interred in the War Cemetery in 1946.

Note: Pte. K.C. Molde served as Pte. Dawson, L.K.

Kulang described his part in the construction of the rentis: "I built the PW rest hut at the Japanese staging camp at Mile 48, the Muanad River (Tangkual) Crossing, with people from my kampong, Muanad.

"When the first march prisoners came through I was working on finishing the roof of the hut. It was in early February, the wet season, and the track is worse than it is in June (when the second march came through). Swamps start about the Mile 30 and continue to near Kolapsis (42 Mile), the mud would be knee depth in February – over the ankles in June.

"The prisoners I saw on the first march as they passed through were pretty fit. They used to sing at night. They had serviceable clothes and boots, except that some had beri beri and, with swollen feet, they could not wear. They had some blankets, soap and shaving gear – for the first time I saw a white man shave.

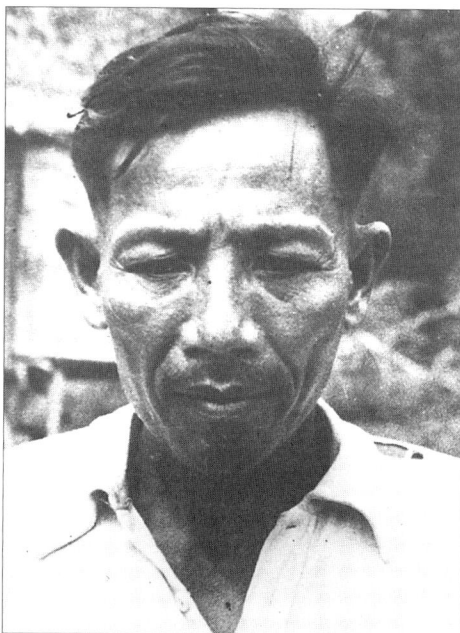

Orang Tuan Kulang. Worked for S.R.D. and assisted in rescue of Owen Campbell. Later played an important role in the recovery operations with War Graves Unit.

Pic: AWM.042512.

"I met Sgt. Major Johnny Land – he told me his name – he was down at the river washing when I met him, I did not know then whether he was Australian or English; he wore a broad-brimmed hat; he spoke differently to the way of speaking of Australians I have met since then and I think now he was English. [Author's note: "Land" or "Johnny Land" does not appear in the Australian or British Register of Sandakan Prisoners of War.] "He told me he was from No. 3 Compound at Mile 8 (the Australian Compound). He was a cheerful type, he liked to talk, he could speak Japanese. He would be about 28 years old I think. He was PW in charge of his group of 50 men.

"He told me that 421 men were on the march and including 15 who had died before Muanad was reached. He knew this because he had to call the roll. I have seen him doing this. I heard him say to the Japanese how many prisoners there were after the roll call and the Japanese asked was that number correct and he said it was.

"I asked him to give me a list of the names of the men, which I thought I could get to someone on the Allied side but he said no, it would be too incriminating if such a list were found on me by the Japanese. He told me to quit the Japanese and not to worry about the outcome of the war; he said the Japs would be beaten soon.

"Across the river from the main rest hut was a smaller hut. Eleven PWs were in this hut; I heard him call out across the river to come across for a meal; he joked and called out a list to them of things they did not get to eat: bread and butter and meat and jam and milk! They came over and got their meal, which was rice and tapioca."

"The number of Japanese I killed during the war I reckon was 96. I killed about 50 by shooting and the rest I killed with my parang, in many cases cutting off their heads. I killed many on the old British rentis which the Japs used to use between Sandakan and Beluran. Once a Jap officer from Beluran came to my kampong and complained to me as Orang Tuan that the Japs were being killed on the rentis and asked me could I throw any light on who was doing it. This was before I joined the SRD. I was having a little war on my own, in revenge for Jap depredations among my people. I killed some on the Sandakan-Ranau rentis near Boto in April 1945.

"My method was to wait in hiding beside the track until a Jap came along and then let him have it with my rifle or parang. I never took anything from the Japs I killed in case my house or I was searched and they found something on me. Yes, I did take a fountain pen I still use with the name NIRO carved into the barrel.

"When I was cutting a rentis for SRD word came that the war was over. I was disappointed that I had to go home and could not keep on killing Japs. I did not go direct to my kampong, but by a roundabout route and I killed a few more Japs on the way. I had joined Capt. Harlem's SRD party in May 1945. "

The account of conditions at Ranau is best told by the witnesses. Bdr. Moxham and Keith Botterill were responsible for bringing the killers to justice for the deaths of Gunner Crease and Gunner Cleary. Gnr. Crease was shot in the back as he tried to escape further into the jungle.

The deceased, along with another Australian PW, Gnr. Crease, escaped from custody during March 1945. Four days later Gnr. Cleary had been recaptured and was in the Guard House; this was a portion of a hut used by all PWs. It was a long hut, one end of it was used as a hospital, the centre occupied by PWs and the other end was used as a guard house. There were no partitions in the hut.

After his recapture Gnr. Cleary was made to kneel on the gravel floor, with a round rough bush log about 6 ft. by 3 inches tied to behind his knees. He wore only a 'G' string, his arms were tied high up behind his back and there was fresh and dried blood on his face and body – Kitamura and Suzuki were both present plus two other Japanese guards. Botterill saw Kitamura kick Cleary violently on the body, face and mouth; at times they held his head up and hit him on the throat with their knuckles, then charged him with fixed bayonets, stopping about an inch from his face. Both Kitamura and Suzuki jumped on the log at the back of Cleary's knees, causing him to scream in pain. Sometimes they stamped on the log with one foot and at times with both feet. Every half hour they would make Cleary stand up on his feet, causing him further pain. During this time Kitamura, Suzuki and the other guards struck Cleary with fists, sticks, rifle butts and anything else which came to hand; this ill-treatment lasted from 1400 hrs. to 1930 hrs. At 1930 the PWs were ordered to go to their bunks, but Botterill could hear Cleary moaning and crying out all night. During the night the log was not fixed to Cleary's legs but next morning at 0650 the Japanese again fixed the log to his legs and the ill-treatment continued until the guard was changed at 0845 hrs. The ill-treatment continued as Botterill went out on his work party and when he returned at midday the ill-treatment was continuing but this time Kawakami and four other Japanese were continuing the ill-treatment. Kawakami was thought to be the Guard Comd.

Shortly after midday a Japanese MP brought Gnr. Crease into the guard house; Cleary was then kicked under a bunk by Kawakami. At 1800 hrs. Cleary was ordered to come out from under the bunk and the log, which had by then been fixed to Crease's legs was also fixed on Cleary. The ill-treatment of jumping on the logs, striking with fists and rifle butts, and kicking continued. Cleary and Crease begged Kitamura and the other Japanese to stop, but the more they begged the more brutal the ill-treatment became. and kept on for one and a half hours.

The ill-treatment of the two PWs was punching on the throat, grinding the knuckles into the eyes of the men, bumping their heads together by catching hold of the hair of their heads, jabbing the muzzle of rifles into their chests and backs and hitting them on the head and side of the face with rifle butts. Botterill heard this ill-treatment continuing throughout the night, particularly when the guard was being changed.

Next morning at 0700 hrs. both the Australians were attached to the log again, Kawakami was the only guard present at this time. The ill-treatment meted out was particularly brutal. Kawakami stopped torturing the two men and was checking out the fatigue parties, an opportunity arose and Gnr. Crease managed to escape into the jungle.

Immediately after this Botterill was taken out on fatigue and did not return for four days; on his return he saw Cleary tied with a rope by the neck to a tree and he was still dressed only in a 'G' string; there were multiple bruises and blood blisters on his face and all over his body and his face and body were covered with dried blood. He was in a very filthy state – there was excreta on the ground and he was obviously suffering from a type of dysentery. The place where he was tied to the tree was exposed to the hot sun during the day and at night the weather was extremely cold and he remained there for four days. During that period the Japanese repeatedly struck Cleary with rifles and kicked him; this would occur on an average of 30 times a day. Kitamura, Kawakami and Suzuki all indulged in kicking Cleary and striking him with their rifles.

After four days, Cleary was moved to a place near a gutter on the road side; he was then in a very weakened condition and semi-conscious. Eventually he was released and brought back into the PW quarters in a dying condition and he died very shortly after. Repeatedly Kawakami said to the Australians: "If you escape, the same thing will happen to you!".

Top left: Gnr. J.C. Pratt. 11052555. 242 Bty. 48 LAA Royal Artillery. Died Sandakan 6 February 1945. Age 24. Ashington, Northumberland.

Pic: Adam Pratt.

Top right: L. to R.: Unknown; Gnr. N.J. Hannant. 11052590. 242 Bty. 48 LAA. Royal Artillery. Died Sandakan 13 February 1945. Age 24. Consett, Co. Durham; Gnr. Alfred Gregson 1105288. 242 Bty. 48 LAA Royal Artillery. Died Sandakan 16 March 1945. Age 23. Dean Bank, Co. Durham.

Pic: Bernadette Daly.

Left: A.C.1. Charles Waterhouse. 1073941. R.A.F. (VR). 84 Sqdn. Died Sandakan 8 February 1945. Age 36. Swinton, Lancashire.   Pic: G.G. Worrall.

Above left to right: LAC. J.B. Glover. 643685. R.A.F. Died Sandakan 3 April 1945. Age 28. Broughton, Lincolnshire. Pic: John Bessant; Sgt. P.R.C. Freeman. 565537. R.A.F. Died Sandakan 3 April 1945. Age 29. Felixstowe, Suffolk. Pic: D.H. Freeman; Gnr. F.G.H. Cole. 1801573. 242 Bty. 48 LAA Royal Artillery. Died Sandakan 10 April 1945. Age 29. Edmonton, Middlesex Pic: Patricia Meilleur

Sandakan Camp
February to 29 May

The condition of the men who remained at the 8 Mile Camp after the departure of the first march must have been critical for Hoshijima approving a lesser number than the 500 required to be escorted to Ranau by the Yammamoto Battalion.

The rice was denied from mid-January, the 25 acres of garden Hoshijima had established, on his own authority, was the only source of food to sustain the prisoners.

In the "Hospitals" or "Death Huts", no one recovered from any illness – there were no drugs nor any other medical supplies issued to the prisoners despite the fact Red Cross supplies were held in the stores. The Japanese denied the prisoners the opportunity to purchase food from the local farmers.

The appearance of Allied aircraft over the Camp, almost daily, gave many hope. Sandakan airfield was on the strike list since the bombing commenced last October; now, as planning for the occupation of Luzon was under way, more attention was given to the airfield to prevent air reinforcements from Singapore reaching the Philippines. In addition, as the OBOE planners were preparing to launch an assault on Tarakan, Sandakan became an alternate target in case Tarakan was clouded in. It was these attacks which caused casualties amongst the prisoners working in groups outside the camp. Many of the prisoners waved to the aircraft – in reported cases crew members could be seen standing in the doorway of the aircraft.

There was mixed feeling among the prisoners remaining in the two Compounds at the 8 Mile Camp. The POW sign was placed between the British and Australian Camp and it seemed Allied Intelligence had notified Allied air forces of its importance. The area was receiving constant attention from a squadron of "Lightning" long-range fighter aircraft.

At this time General MacArthur was moving in on Manila with his armoured columns while the VICTOR Task Force was occupying the western islands of the Philippines: Mindoro, Palawan and Tawi Tawi – just 100 miles south of Sandakan. It would have been an easy task for this force to have taken Sandakan, however Allied assessment was Sandakan had little military importance – just 23 miles of roads going nowhere and the airfield was already non-operational and peppered with unexploded bombs. Sandakan would be taken after the establishment of a major base at Labuan as part of the OBOE operations.

Many of the prisoners were optimistic that any day now an airborne force would take the Camp. The Japanese had constructed machine gun posts in such a way as to give a field of fire covering the two Compounds. They were adhering to the earlier order that no prisoner would survive to be handed over at the cessation of hostilities.

In March, Allied H.Q. approved the insertion of a British led party of Special Forces to the north of Labuk Bay. Their task was to gather intelligence to assist in the forthcoming OBOE operation and to discreetly investigate the condition of the prisoners.

In the Camp there were 400 plus stretcher cases. Hoshijima was having difficulty in finding sufficient fit men to take out to the airfield and remove the unexploded bombs. Most of those able to move around freely were working in the garden and on the wood collecting parties. It was these men who were often mistaken for Japanese and attacked by Allied fighter aircraft. Many of the casualties suffered during this period were killed as a result of these air attacks.

There was no contact between the British and Australians, occasionally they would sight one another, In April, Colonel Takayama, senior Staff Officer from 37 Army H.Q., visited the Camp and as a result of his visit Hoshijima was ordered to remove the POW sign between the two Camps.

Gnr. Peter Gorrick, A.I.F., requested the Japanese officers he was guarding at Labaun in November 1945 to write their autographs in his notebook. This is the message of Captain Yamamoto, Commander of the first death march, who was later hanged at Rabaul. Was the prawn meant to be a pawn?

Few men had any footwear, most were wearing only loin cloths. The food ration was now only tapioca and greens from the garden and very small in quantity.

In Europe, the war was coming to an end. The Allies announced the setting up of an International War Crimes Tribunal; this announcement brought immediate changes in command at Sandakan: Hoshijima was replaced by Takakuwa, Captain Nagai, the smooth-talking English-speaking officer whom Sqdn. Ldr. Hardie described as "a cultured gentleman", was removed from Ranau where he was in charge of the rice carrying parties and elsewhere in other POW Camps prominent Japanese officers were removed from sensitive positions.

Late April to early May the Japanese went through the huts and confiscated all forms of identification – identity discs and paybooks – and destroyed them. Soon after a rumour swept through the Camp that "All men move".

It was known, according to Hoshijima, that Captain Mills and Captain Cook, the respective Camp leaders, requested the Camps be evacuated to a safer area where food would be more plentiful but this request was denied. The Japanese seemed convinced the best way to dispose of the prisoners was to send them all on a forced march.

Second March

Colonel Takayama, senior Staff Officer responsible for POW matters, visited the 8 Mile POW Compound in April 1945 to inspect the condition of the prisoners and to talk to Captain Hoshijima. During the Camp inspection he observed the POW sign between the English and Australian Camps and asked Hoshijima who authorised the sign to be placed there, he replied he did, as it gave the Japanese some protection from the bombing raids. Later, Hoshijima was ordered to remove the sign on the grounds that it may give some advantage to the Allies.

About this time the Allies announced the setting up of an International War Crimes Tribunal; the Japanese took note of this announcement and immediately transferred Japanese officers in sensitive positions away to other Commands. Takahashi at Changi, who was not a criminal, just disappeared; Captain Nagai was recalled from Ranau and Hoshijima was soon replaced by Captain Takakuwa.

The Japanese believed at about this time an Allied attack would be made on the East Coast where two Divisions would be landed at Kudat and one Division at Sandakan. The 26 Brigade of the 9 Division (Australian) was already fighting on Tarakan and the Japanese were not sure where the next assault would take place.

On 26 May, the 37 Army instructed Colonel Otsuka, the Commander of the Sandakan Garrison, to prepare to move all the POWs and close the camp. This message would have been intercepted by U.S. code-breakers; at G.H.Q. it appears they decided they would endeavour to disrupt the Japanese and frighten them out of Sandakan.

No.2 Cemetery, Sandakan. Cross in the foreground: Gnr. Thomas Jones. 11051560. 242 Bty. 48 LAA. Died 7 February 1945.   Pic: G. Robertson.

On the morning of 27 May, P.T. Boats from Tawi Tawi, where the supply ship USS OYSTER BAY was stationed, attacked. Initially, two boats entered the harbour just after 0617 hrs., drew the fire of the 75 mm gun believed located in Sandakan, and commenced a run along the city front at 500 yards off-shore firing at shore installations. They remained on attack until 0930 hrs. then cleared the harbour at full speed with three 75 mm shells landing within 50 yards of their bow.

Altogether ten boats attacked targets around the harbour supported by twelve P40s of the R.A.A.F.; at the end of the day all boats returned to Tawi Tawi. The PT boats used torpedoes to explode under the docks to render them unusable. The Japanese were anticipating an assault, however, with no aircraft available they were preparing to evacuate the area.

It was on this occasion when aircraft were attacking the camp area an Australian produced an Australian flag he had hidden for such an event. About 40 A.I.F. were killed as they were working on the Wood Party, and a large number of British were reported to have been killed when they defied the Japanese and waved to the aircraft.

At this time, Captain Takakuwa called Captain Cook and Captain Mills (the Australian and British Commanding Officers) and informed them that the fittest men – which was about 500 – should prepare to move out. Later he confirmed the number at 536, which included 120 English, however the sick men remained.

Dick Braithwaite was the first survivor to be rescued, he described to the American Interrogating Officer at Sanga Sanga:

"On 24 October 1944 the night bombers came, then on 30th October the fighter planes came in and bombed the airfield, two men were killed in the Camp and a couple were wounded. Major Suga called all the POW Camp leaders together, he was very angry and told us that the American aircraft had attacked Formosa but that didn't mean we would be getting out of here. They were also attacking the Philippines but the Japanese were counter-attacking and driving them back. We didn't know whether to start to hope again for we had had so very little news of out-side events.

"But then on 1st June they began to fire Sandakan town and 11 a.m. that day we were given orders to shift out of our Camp. The British Camp Commandant, Captain Mills, and Captain Cook, the Australian Camp Commandant, were told to get their men together and every available walking man had to be prepared to march by 7 p.m. Everyone was sick, there only about 100 reasonably fit men and they were detailed to the essential jobs like cooking etc.

"The men of the British and Australian Camps all formed up and those who could walk were formed into groups of fifty men, each with Japanese guards in front and behind. Anyone too ill to walk was left behind. There were eleven groups all told, and they told us that we would have to march four miles a day. Then as we moved on they began to march us six miles, then seven miles a day and men began to drop out each night, next morning as we marched off we would hear gunfire and we never saw those men again.

"I began to get bad attacks of malaria and have blackouts each morning, the Japs would hit the men on the head with their rifle butts or gouge an eye out of the sick men if they could not go fast enough.

"At the 42 Mile peg there was a food dump but we only got half a pint of rice per day per man. Each man had to carry an issue of rice for his party and when any one dropped out and they were killed the Japs would go through their pack for rice or anything else. We were all being kicked and beaten every day to move us along and I decided that the only way out was to take to the jungle, stay out of sight of the Japs and try to get to the Coast.

"The track was very hard going, through the swamps and mud; by the time we had reached the 62 Mile peg I thought I just can't go on any further, sick and starving, I even thought about committing suicide, then I thought I will make a break for it now. When our party moved off next day, two men were left behind, Jacob Mildenhall and Rex Hodges. I was able to move away through the thick growth at the edge of the track, I don't know how I did it but somehow I managed to get back far enough off the track and down into the the jungle. I lay there for a time, and I heard sound of shooting. I stayed still where I was all day until I felt all the Japs had gone. Late in the afternoon and all was quiet I started to move and try and get down to the end of the river where I knew the PT boats were.

"I started back along the track and came to the camp site, I saw two Japs on the other side of the river lying under a shelter but I could see no sign of the men who had been shot the day before. I spent that night on the river-bank and next day I could only got about a quarter mile then I would have to rest for half an hour, it was very hard working along the bank, I came to two unoccupied Jap outposts but there was no food there. I managed to get some shellfish which I ate raw.

"After five days I was exhausted and near collapse and I had only come about five miles along the river. One night I heard two boats going up-river (probably the Lubak River); there was a swell on the river and it was running fast. I could not walk much further so I decided I would try and make a raft to float me down river, the track had come to an end and the river was deep, I was in a bad way. As I was struggling to make a raft I looked up and saw a local man coming across the river. He rescued me and took me back to his village, Sapi Village.

"I just collapsed unconscious and the next thing I knew the village people had me in their home, they were feeding me, I was warm, they were absolutely wonderful those people, they were so kind to me. They offered to keep me and shelter me from the Japs who they told me were still in Sandakan, but they said they would try and keep me safe until the Americans came.

"That night Armit, son of Abing, came and told me there was a man who had come back and that the Americans were near Sandakan. I was very happy then for I thought the men we had left behind in the camp now would be safe.

"Next morning, Abdul Rasid, who could speak very good English, told me he was prepared to take me down the river out to where the PT boats might be able to pick me up. I slept all that day and at 10 p.m. they carried me down to the river where eight men and two boats were waiting; these wonderful men paddled from 11 p.m. that night until 7 p.m. next night where we stayed in a camp just off Libaran Island. We could not across to the Island that night because of the naval restrictions but next morning we went across to the PT boats and safety.

"While we waited for morning I heard from one of the local people that several British prisoners were being held by 15 Jap guards in a camp near the wireless station near the 2 Mile peg on the Sandakan Road, but I do not know what happened to them."

Richard Braithwaite stated when being interrogated on June 15 that Armit came and told me "there was a man who had come back". Good news travelled quickly, right up through the kampongs, that a man had come back and the Americans were in Sandakan.

The man who had come back to assess the possibility of any rescue was Major Rex Blow, DSO. Blow, with seven others, had escaped from Berhala Island in 1943 and reached Tawi Tawi; after checking the credentials of the Australians by the U.S./Filipino Guerrilla Force, they were ordered to proceed to the H.Q. of the 10th Military District Mindanao.

Two of the escaped Australians were killed in action; one was Lieut. Wagner, and the other, Dvr. Butler who was the first killed on Tawi Tawi by the Moros.

The Australian Army H.Q. was informed of the escape and of conditions in the POW camps and it was decided that the senior officer of the escape group, Captain Ray Steele, be evacuated by submarine to Australia; with him went Sgt. Wallace and Dvr. Kennedy who was ill. Blow, Gillon and McLaren remained on Mindanao and later Blow was promoted and became Chief of Staff of the 10th Military District.

During 1944 Australian Army H.Q. wrote to General MacArthur and requested the Australians with the Americans in Mindanao be released for other operations. MacArthur declined the request and said they were too important to be released at this stage. In April 1945, Blow had led his Guerrilla forces and taken the important port of Malabang; he was invited on to the flagship of General Eichelberger where they took their next objective at Parang.

Blow and McLaren were later flown out and met General Blamey at Morotai. It was on this occasion Blow put the question: "What about our mates back in Sandakan?" Blamey replied that "If it could be fitted into on-going operations that they would be involved." But first of all the two men would be sent to Australia on leave for a few weeks and then join "Z" Special Unit for other duties.

It was early June 1945. Blow had come by American PT boats to Libaran island, just north of Sandakan; here he interrogated local people and was brought up to date on Intelligence regarding the positions of the prisoners of war. Despite having been told they had been moved from Sandakan, Blow insisted on having a look himself at the road leading to Ranau.

Taking two local men he was dropped off by PT boat further up Lubuk Bay, where they made their way up the Sandakan-Ranau track. Here he could see there had been considerable foot traffic over the road – many of the prisoners had left their bare footprints in the mud.

Blow was bitterly disappointed – it was too late to even risk one mission.

Soon after Braithwaite's rescue, news of the rescue of the POW was flashed from L.H.Q. Melbourne:

> "At Sandakan 1 June 500 Australian and British PWs moved west-wards from PW camp which was destroyed by Japs. 150 PWs too sick to walk remained fate not known. Prisoners dropping out of march reported believed shot. These PW believed now in vicinity Beluran or Labuk Bay. Effort being made to contact."

Meanwhile, Owen Campbell, who escaped from the march from somewhere near the 48 Mile peg had been rescued and was now being interrogated by Major Noone, S.R.D., on board the USS POKOMOKE. He gave his story.

On 29 May 1945, Campbell left the Sandakan PW Camp in Party No. 5. Each party consisted of 50 men and there were 11 parties numbered 1 to 11. The Japanese said the total number of British and Australian PWs was 536. They were not told where they were going; they marched all night and up to just before midday next day, 30 May. Allied aircraft came overhead and, as they usually did, the Japanese stopped and hid in the bush. They rested for the rest of the day.

On the following day, 31 May, they continued along the Beluran track and covered only four miles, after which they rested again.

The next day, 1st June, was a rest day. On 2 June they started off again at 0630 and covered seven miles.

By this time, men were beginning to fall out and die by the road side. Some were knocked on the head and killed by the Japanese. About 10 had died so far. PW were made to carry rice etc. and Japanese equipment.

On 6 June they had reached the 48 Mile, where there was a ration and staging point. It was situated in a clearing and consisted of shacks and three large sheds used to rest in. They were both sides of a river which was possibly the Muanad River (it was after the turning north to Beluran). There were many Japanese camped along either side of the road leading from Sandakan. At the 48 Mile they were told that there was another ten days march ahead of them, which would bring them to the 113 Mile. When they reached this point, they were told that they would reach an area where there was plenty of food.

The rations they had received on the march consisted of about a cigarette tin full of cooked rice per day and one tin of M&V for three days per person. They were given half a tin of sugar and half a tin of salt to last the whole trip.

Campbell decided he could not do the ten days trek which lay ahead, and he and four others decided they would escape. They had a compass with them and some odds and ends of equipment. So, when an Allied aircraft came overhead and the Japanese took to the bush, they raided their packs took some rice and tinned salmon and shot off into the jungle.

They travelled for 4 days in a direction inland, away from both the track they had been following, and the coast. They were afraid of meeting Japanese if they approached the coast. One of the party, Ted Skinner, developed dysentery, so they decided to camp for a few days. After three or four days, Skinner became worse and tried to persuade them to leave him, as he could not go any further. It was eventually arranged that the other three should continue on and try and get help, while Campbell was to remain behind with Skinner. He remained there a further four days, until the food had been finished. On the fourth day, Campbell went down to get water and returned to find Skinner with his throat cut. Campbell therefore pushed on in an attempt to catch up with the others. During that night he caught an animal (unidentified) which he ate raw.

Later he was near the river when he heard boats moving up and down. He followed the river down stream; it was very fast flowing. He came to a point where it was very wide and decided to attempt a crossing. He got hold of a log of wood and, half swimming, half floating on the log, set out to cross the stream. A Japanese suddenly appeared on the further bank, and whilst he was in midstream, fired at him. His wrist was badly damaged; he dived under water and swam to the other bank. Here he lay up for some time until the Jap had gone off. He crawled up on to the bank and dressed the wound with a field dressing.

Next morning, he pushed on down-stream and came to a lean-to where he found one of his mates, whom he described as Jack Austen but this man is believed to have been Hoston; there were two other men who were away fishing. The lean-to was about 60 yards from the river on which there were some Malays fishing. They decided to attract their attention and so Sgt. Ted Emmett and Pte. Sid Webber went to the river bank and hailed one of the prahaus. The prahau made in to the bank, and a Japanese popped up from the floor of the boat and shot both Webber and Emmett. Campbell was behind a rise in the ground and was protected. He ran back into the bush to rejoin Hoston who had dysentery very badly and could not walk.

They remained here for a further four days, living on soya bean powder, which was finished by the third day. That night, Hoston died in his sleep, with never a word. Campbell buried him as best he could and went on by himself. He was too weak to carry his gear, so he discarded it, and lived on fungus, crabs and fish, all of which he ate raw.

For eleven days he pushed on down-stream in this manner, camping overnight in hollow trees and under bushes to get out of the teeming rain. He had beri-beri now, and in the morning when he woke it took him some time to get his eyes to see properly. His mind began to wander and he suffered from delusions; many times he imagined he had his mates around him.

On the eleventh day he decided he could go no further, so he crawled down to the river's edge and came upon a track. There were natives on the further bank, to whom he called. They came across in a prahau and took him over to the other side of the river. He was taken into a Malay house back from the river, and fed on soup, rice and prawns. They washed his clothes and gave him others to wear. In the afternoon they took him still further in about one mile to a small village where he stayed for four or five days. During this period a policeman twice came to the village and Campbell was hidden away in a back room of one of the houses.

Finally, the Orang Tuan Kulang of Sungei Bongaya arrived and took charge. He looked after Campbell very well, clothed him, cut his hair and shaved him (with a very old cut-throat razor). He was given daily exercise and more food. After a further five to seven days, the Orang Tuan Kulang decided that he was fit enough to move him on again.

They progressed in easy stages, over a hill range through a swamp until they reached another village by a river. Here a boat was procured and they proceeded down river for three days, until Campbell was handed over to an SRD party under Lieut. Hollingsworth. From here on he was evacuated by Mariner flying-boat to Tawi Tawi on 24 July 1945.

* * *

"They started to muster us about 7 p.m. and orders were given to Captain Cook and Captain Mills that the Japanese wanted 500 from the Australian Camp and 100 from the English Camp, no reason was given, but it was for a very short journey,", recalled W.O. Sticpewich.

"Christmas 1944 I had been told on several occasions by several Japanese guards (one of whom was nicknamed "Masturbation") that we would all be killed; "Marti marti! All Australian English soldiers marti marti bagous", which meant that all the Australian and English soldiers were to be killed and that this was a good thing.

"I took charge of the second party with eight reasonably fit men from my technical staff. The balance of the party was made up of hospital patients and totalling 50 in all. The first party under Captain Heaslop were all hospital patients with the exception of himself.

"By this time I had got a hint that we were on the march to Ranau, 160 miles away; I was told by a Japanese guard that where we were going there was more and better food. We were assembled along the road in batches of 50, there were ten batches of 50 out of the Australian Camp. Just as the third party had got through the gate there arrived a company of Japanese old soldiers; Captain Takakuwa addressed them and told them that their duties would be to keep on us and nobody must escape; they were told they must keep four guards in front of each batch of 50 and four on each flank and that the remainder would stay behind and look after the rest of the camp.

"There were eleven parties in all – ten parties of about 50 and one party of 66.

"No. 10 party was composed of Englishmen and Australians and the last party of 66 were all Englishmen.

"While we were assembled on the road the Japanese burned down the

213

remaining barracks buildings including their own; there were no buildings left in the camp for the personnel who were to be left behind which would number about 288 to the best of my knowledge.

"At 8 o'clock we moved off along the road under guard and went out along towards Ranau, Captain Takakuwa was the Commanding Officer in charge of the march, his 2 I/C was Lieut. Watanabe.

"We marched all that night and all the next day. We had a rest of twenty to thirty minutes every hour and a half approximately. Our first stop was about 11 p.m. the same night when we got to the end of the bitumen road. We were given two 100 lb. bags of rice to carry, also pencil and paper and told to make a nominal roll of our parties. By this time I found six of my party had already dropped out and I was six short after the three hour march. Those who were struggling or lagging behind were belted along the road by the Japanese guards who used their rifle butts on the men. The rice was split up among the men and we were told that it represented ten days' rations which meant four pounds of rice per man for ten days. We kept marching along the road for the rest of the night and also the next day after until about 1300 hrs. At 1700 hrs. we were told we would stay there the night alongside the road. Then the Japanese took back 32 pounds out of the rice ration to each party. They then gave us our marching routine: the parties were divided up into groups, Nos. 1, 2, 3 and 4 parties were in No. 1 Group; Nos. 5, 6, 7 and 8 parties were in the second group and Nos. 9, 10 and 11 were in the last group. The groups were to move off at 6.30, 7 and 7.30 a.m. and were to follow in that sequence right throughout the march, leap-frogging through one another so that there was a different party leading each day.

"On the roll-call at 4.30 next day my party was then about 38 or 40 strong; when this was reported through Captain Cook to the Japanese they did not appear to be concerned at all about it, but Captain Cook was ordered that no officer was to drop out, that they all must complete the march.

"We cooked rice once a day in the evening after the march then we had to keep enough over for our morning meal the next day. We were having two meals a day, our ration was supposed to be 100 grams of rice per man per day; it worked out that 26 meals would be contained in one M&V tin.

"On the fourth day men dropped off along the track, no one was allowed to stop and help them, they were beaten by the Japanese guards and we would never see them after they had dropped out; I never saw anyone again after they dropped out of my party.

"We had our morning meal at 10 a.m. every morning; on the 10 a.m. stop on the fourth morning we were called back to Lieut. Goode, Q.M., to collect sugar and salt issue. We got about one and half pounds of salt and two pounds of sugar for the 50 men which I immediately took back to my party and hid among the men. I did not keep it in bulk as other parties who did so had it taken from them by the guards. When a guard asked me to produce my store I told him that the men had already eaten it. On each stop I found that there were men short in my party.

"We averaged about six and half miles a day; the track was deplorable, knee deep mud for most of the way for the first part of the journey and the track led over hills that you had to crawl up and slide down. When we were not going through mud and marsh lands you were marching up very steep pinches and down very steep pinches. The first party would stop marching about 3 p.m., the others would come in anything up to 4.30 p.m. or 5 p.m. Thirteen miles was our biggest march one day. When we moved out in the morning there would be some men who simply could not move, crippled by exposure and who were in bad shape before they started. I never ever saw any of these men again after we left them when we marched out in the morning. When we had marched about a mile or so from our overnight staging camp we would hear rifle and machine-gun fire [Author's note: The Japanese did not have machine-guns at this time ...] from the direction of the camp. Different guards told me that it was bad to stop because if you stopped you would be "marti" meaning dead. I never ever actually saw any of the stragglers shot although I saw a W.O. Dixon bashed to insensibility by a guard whose nick-name was "Top Hat" (also known to the Englishmen as "Gentleman Jim"). This happened because the guard wanted Dixon's gold ring which he refused to give him: Dixon at this time was right ahead of his party having leap-frogged into another party and this was the excuse for his bashing. He was left lying at the side of the road with another Australian soldier, Jimmy Barlow, who had dropped out; "Top Hat" was standing over them with his rifle. Dixon regained consciousness, so did Barlow, and they wanted to rejoin their party but the Japanese guard would not let them. I never saw either of them again but later in the march I saw "Top Hat" wearing Dixon's ring. During the rest of the march the beating of stragglers continued and the rifle fire from the stopping places was heard after we left each day.

"Before we continued our march each morning in the later stages certain men would be picked out and told they were not to continue. They were the ones who were fairly well done up and in poor shape. Padre Thompson was marching under difficulties because he had a big ulcer under his foot and as we were approaching a river he was stopped and told he was not to go on. I never saw him again.

"On one occasion when we were crossing a river on a single log one of the men from the front party fell down on the log, lost his nerve and could not move. There was a camp of Japanese civilians and soldiers on the bank of the river and they wanted to shoot this chap because he was blocking the crossing; I told them not to shoot that I would get the man off the log, I took off my gear went back and carried the man and his gear over. When we got to the other side the civilian who wanted to shoot him came up, took his gear and blankets and left him with nothing but what he stood up in. The man eventually reached Ranau where he died. I don't know the name of the civilian. When we reached Ranau we went to a camp 5½ miles out from the Administrative buildings on the Tambulan Road. There were 142 Australians on the night roll-call of 26 June; one man who was carried in died that day."

Captain Takakuwa was in charge of the second march and he would not have believed that his country would surrender within a few months.

When he was arraigned before the War Crimes Tribunal, he gave his account of the march:

"I was in charge of the Sandakan PW Camp and took command as ordered on 26 April 1945. I was not told what my duties would be, so I wrote down to Kuching, asking them for advice so during that time I really was not responsible for the PW Camp until 17 May 1945.

"On that day I received an order from Army H.Q. stating that as Sandakan was being subjected to Allied bombardment which also included the PW Camp, it would be best to evacuate the prisoners to Kemansi. I found that these orders had been received after I had taken over from Hoshijima. Hoshijima was not quite sure if there were enough rations for the prisoners at Kemansi so for this reason he sent 1/Lieut. Moritake to reconnoitre the place. Then on 20th May as they found it was no use sending the prisoners to Kemansi, Army H.Q. ordered them to be evacuated to Ranau. In the orders it stated that all the PWs were to go to Ranau and to be put into the compound with the other PWs already at Ranau and that I was to take command of the Ranau Camp and also to close down the Sandakan Camp.

"At this time in Sandakan there were many sick prisoners and I thought if they were to be moved to Ranau at least 400 would have to be carried on stretchers. There were very few who (could) bear the trip to Ranau, the rest would probably break down after two or three days marching.

"After thinking all this out, I thought that if I carried out these orders from H.Q. and marched the lot to Ranau, many of them would die, so I sent a message to Army H.Q. giving them the facts and asked for further advice. In the meantime as I had already received orders I had to act on it and made preparations. In the meanwhile I waited for an answer to my last message, but up to the day I was supposed to leave, none came. Aerial bombardment had become fierce and even the PW Camp was being bombed and strafed.

Some of the British PW became casualties in these air attacks and the head of the British PWs requested that they evacuate from the Camp. Also in the Australian Camp, over ten were killed from the result of these air attacks, and then the officer in charge of the Australians also requested that they be evacuated.

"Also at that time American boats were bombarding the shore and on the 27th a heavy naval bombardment started following by an aerial attack by hundreds of planes.

"The Garrison Unit (Otsuka Unit) had taken up the defence positions and then on 29th the Otsuka Unit received an intelligence report from Army H.Q. saying that one division intended landing on Sandakan and two divisions at Kudat. Following this, the Otsuka Unit took up their positions on the 11 Mile point. This left the PW Camp as the closest unit to the coast so I thought that it was best to withdraw back for the safety of the PWs. Then we received an order from the Otsuka Unit telling us to escort the Japanese sick patients and to evacuate them.

These orders were sent to 2/Lieut. Suzuki at the hospital and he came to show it to me, so I sent Capt. Watanabe to liaise with the Otsuka Unit. He arrived back that evening at 6 o'clock and we left at 8 o'clock that night. The reason for leaving at night was so that we would not be seen by aircraft.

"As the enemy were supposed to land on the morning of the 30th, we had very little time for preparations. I decided to carry out my original orders and called the officer in charge of the British and Australian PWs for a conference. As I said before, no reply was received to my signal to Army H.Q. so I decided to leave the sick PWs behind and send 500 of the best conditioned prisoners forward. Even then I did not think that many of these 500 would survive the trip to Ranau. So after telling the English and Australian officers in charge to send 500, they got together 540 for the trip. The road from Sandakan to Ranau was in a very bad condition and thousands of Japanese soldiers had died on the way.

"I gave each prisoner ten days rations of rice which provided for 550 grams per day. I also gave them pots and pans for cooking on the journey and advised them to take blankets and any clothes they wanted to. Army H.Q. had ordered that the PWs were only to receive 100 grams of rice a day but I knew this was not enough and gave them 550 grams. I also wished to give the medical supplies but as this was very scarce I could not do so. I requested some from the Sandakan hospital but was refused. Up to the time medical supplies for PW and Japanese soldiers were arriving from Kuching, in separate lots. The Japanese soldiers were receiving more medical supplies than the PW and so they were able to bring some on the march, but as they had plenty of gear to carry they could not bring too much. I then called my officers and NCOs together and issued out orders.

"The orders I issued were that as the march would be difficult and PW would probably die of illness on the way, and fall out because of weariness, the soldiers were to do everything they could to help them along, but as the enemy would be landing and advancing quickly, those PWs who could not go on any more and were likely to die would hamper the Japanese Army and could be put out of their misery by being shot. It was said that the Japanese soldiers had more rations than the PW, this is because all Japanese soldiers carried reserve rations with them and which were not issued to the prisoners. It was for this reason that I gave the PW 550 grams per day, but prisoners who fell down on the march used to throw their rice away so I ordered all the rice to be taken off the PWs and put together for safe keeping.

"Then, as there were eleven groups of PWs, I divided this rice into eleven parts.

"With regard to the PW compound at Sandakan, this camp could accommodate 2500 PWs and as I thought the enemy would utilise the buildings when they landed, I ordered the whole buildings to be burnt. I left one building standing to house the 288 sick PWs that were left behind. I also left them a stock of rice. I also left 20 or 30 thousand pieces of tapioca and spinach to enable the PWs to regain their health.

"I left orders with Sgt. Major Morozumi that when the sick PWs regained their health they could be marched to Ranau also and that Lieut. Moritake would take charge of them when he returned from Kemansi.

"As I had completed preparations for food and the march, I also left Sandakan. PWs who died on the way could not be buried as we did not have any shovels so I ordered them to be taken into the jungle where they could not be seen by people from the road. After I left Sandakan the death rate of sick PW increased greatly.

"It was the same with the Australians as we had been together for the last three years and had become affectionate towards each other. So the Japanese soldiers had never thrown away the dead bodies of PW and the soldiers took the dead bodies of PW and treated them reverently. I have also seen during the trip, Japanese soldiers treating the PW well and giving them food and tobacco.

"At Muanad I gave each PW three days rations of 100 grammes each. This was repeated at Boto and at Pagnitan. I gave them each three days rations of 200 grams per day. At Naraba I gave them two days rations of 300 grams per day. This was the way I supplied them with rice but besides this I let them gather the rice that was left by the dead PW. I also let them gather bamboo shoots, bananas and other roots on the way to cook at night. Therefore I do not think there was such a great difference between the PW ration and the Japanese rations. As I said before the journey was very difficult and many sick fell out on the trip. Also, every day there were quite a few attempts to escape, so I ordered that those attempting to escape could be shot, as they would not stop running even when told to stop, so there were some cases when the Japanese soldiers killed prisoners attempting to get away. Therefore, when I said before in my statement that about 90 were killed, this number included those who attempted to run away. The number that succeeded in escaping was 54. Of the 540 that left Sandakan, 183 arrived in Ranau.

"As the Ranau PW Camp was also being bombed by Allied planes, the camp shifted to the 110 Mile point and I took the PW up there.

When we reached Ranau I found that there was a shortage of food, so when the remaining PW arrived in Ranau I could only give them 100 grams per day; although they could get vegetables before, the position got worse at Ranau and no vegetables were procurable.

"On 2nd July I was wounded in the leg and confined to bed and I took every step possible to procure foodstuffs by ordering soldiers to do so. They managed to get some tapioca from the field warehouse and also kill a few cattle of which the intestines and other meat were given to the PW, but this became impossible later on and the death rate from those PW from Sandakan grew higher every day. Also there were other attempts to escape as the position became worse and many sick were dying and others were attempting to escape we did not have any more fit PW to carry rice and arms belonging to the Kanno Unit, I decided it was best to dispose of them as they became very encumbersome.

"So on the 1st of August I issued orders that all the PW were to be killed. This order of killing the PW was entirely based on the necessity of war operations and another reason was that the circumstances at that time had obliged me to take such a desperate action towards the PW.

"One further thing, it has been stated that the PW were killed with machine-gun fire also, this is not true. The machine-gun we had in the compound was only mounted for anti-aircraft measures. This can be proved by the MG ammunition which was left at Ranau and brought from Sandakan. Capt. Watanabe has a record of the number of rounds he brought to Ranau and not one round is missing. As I had issued the orders to the NCOs and soldiers to kill the PW and being a military order it had to be carried out. The entire responsibility is on my shoulders. I in turn had to carry out the original orders from Army H.Q. to march these PW from Sandakan to Ranau which I could not refuse to carry out the order."

Ranau

26 June – August 1945

W.O. Sticpewich continued: "No provision was made for our Quarters at all. The Japs had three huts built for themselves in the creek bed under cover of the jungle in hiding in preparation of an invasion by Allied Forces. We were camped in a valley in an area about 50 yards square and above the Jap quarters. The prisoners were all kept in this square, no building or tents were available to us and there was no provision for cooking. The only protection we had was to crawl under the scrub, we had no sanitary arrangements. We were here for three days, sickness increased and 19 died; we had no medical supplies or treatment. We had half a mile walk to get water from the creek and we were only allowed to bring a limited number of buckets of water as the Japs would not allow us to get around too much. We were made to get our water from below the Jap camp, and they would bathe, wash their clothes and urinate in the creek before the water reached our collection point. We had about 70-75 grms. rice per man per day, after this was cooked it would be about a cup full of very sloppy rice for each man for the day. No man in our camp was fit, they were all in bad shape and the Japanese called for working parties to cut bamboo to build huts for themselves and one for us. Men were often beaten during these three days. The weather was very bad, it rained at night and during the day which made ground conditions very bad. We also had to supply men for wood and vegetable carrying parties, this last party had to do a trip of 18-20 miles per day and carry 40 to 50 lbs. packs of vegetables which were never issued to us, the only vegetables we got were those which we could steal.

"After three days we were allowed to spread out a little more and were allowed to go up the side of the hill instead of remaining in the gully. The area was still restricted but we were allowed to set up shelters as best we could and everything had to be under cover and camouflaged. We also had to supply work parties for a rice carrying trip, about three miles and carrying 50 lbs. packs of rice; they had to do this trip twice a day which meant 12-13 miles a day.

"We were now located about 5½ miles out on the Tambunan Road; we were told that our strength would be increased by five Australians and one Englishman. When we went down to the river to cook that night we saw the Jap quarters and the six men mentioned. Two of them were very sick, we were not allowed to talk to any of them. I recognised the five Australians as members of the first party that left from Sandakan. I never ever saw any other members of the 370 Australians from that first party that left Sandakan except those five men.

"Within a couple of days I had an opportunity to talk with two of the men, Spr. Bird and Sgt. Stacey. They told me that all the others had died from malnutrition and exhaustion brought on by rice carrying from Ranau to Paginatan, 26 miles. They said the rice carrying was very arduous over this 26 miles of mountain track and the parties that left on the carry would come back considerably depleted and

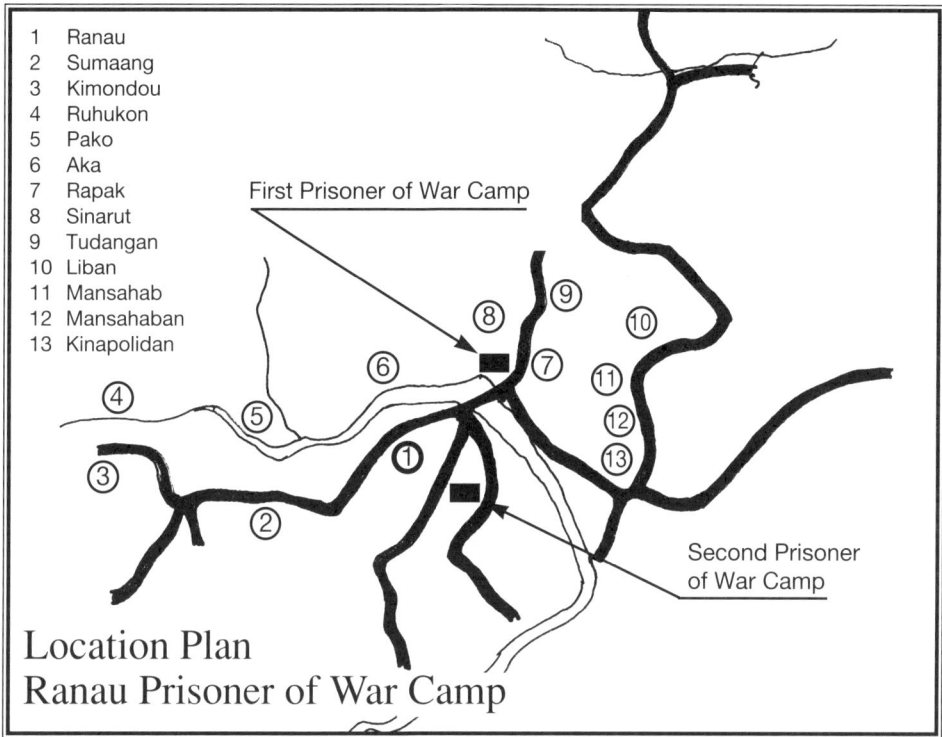

1 Ranau
2 Sumaang
3 Kimondou
4 Ruhukon
5 Pako
6 Aka
7 Rapak
8 Sinarut
9 Tudangan
10 Liban
11 Mansahab
12 Mansahaban
13 Kinapolidan

First Prisoner of War Camp

Second Prisoner
of War Camp

Location Plan
Ranau Prisoner of War Camp

that they never saw any of those who did not come back with the party again. Both these men have since died of dysentery, malnutrition and the effects of their bad treatment. They also told me that over 300 men survived the first march from Sandakan to Ranau. They did the march in a shorter period than we did but their men were much fitter than those of our party of whom 90% were hospital patients before we started on the march."[7]

On about 5 July, Bill Moxham remembers: "I was detailed to a work party for cutting cane. The parties formed up about 50 yards outside the perimeter of the camp, there were quite a number of men light on for the party and Sgt. Maskey, our Australian interpreter, told Fukushima Masao; he then went down to the lines and

NOTE 7:

British Died Ranau 1945 – from Jap PW Records

971437	Pearson, C.B.	02 Jun.
2562597	Stevenson, A.B.	07 Jun.
751161	Allsop, K.H.	24 Jul.
1472376	Charles, J.	25 Jul.
1687169	Davis, E.	25 Jul.
358213	McDermott, T.H.	27 Jul.
1592526	Stockwell, W.J.	29 Jul.
1684046	Picot, E.J.	30 Jul.
1025329	Smith, S.J.	01 Aug.
2369914	Hodgson, R.	02 Aug.
1374118	Sands, A.R.	02 Aug.
818029	Rooker, H.	04 Aug.
1592247	Edwards, J.	05 Aug.
539798	McCandless, J.R.	11 Aug.

Jul.-Aug. dates believed killed August 1st.

brought up several POWs including one man I knew well. Fukushima assigned them to our party and then ordered the guard to take us away. My friend was suffering from malaria and he had a fairly large ulcer on the side of his face, Fukushima was aware of this man's sick condition and also that he had been marked 'off duty' by our doctor.

"Our party moved off and we had not gone very far when my friend dropped back to the rear and told Fukushima, through Sgt. Maskey, that he could not go on as he was too ill; Fukushima then started swearing and shouting at him telling him to take his place in the party. When he did not move Fukushima came up and struck him 15 to 20 times very heavily across the face with his open hand. My friend collapsed to the ground and immediately Fukushima kicked him repeatedly around the face and head. Sgt. Maskey tried to help the sick man and pleaded with Fukushima to let him return to the lines, but Fukushima turned suddenly and smacked Sgt. Maskey right across the face with his open hand and ordered him to go back to the lines. Fukushima kept swearing and cursing my friend trying to make him rise to his feet; he could not do this then Fukushima gave him a very unmerciful, brutal, kicking about the head, face, body and testicles – this went on for quite a while. Then Fukushima ordered our party to move on, and ordered the guard to move us on.[8]

"The last I saw of my friend at this time he was lying on the ground, there was blood over his face and he seemed to me to be unconscious. At the time of this kicking Fukushima was wearing Japanese Army boots. It is very hard to say just how long he kicked my friend but it seemed to be at least ten minutes; what I relate I actually saw happen – we were about 15 to 20 yards away from Fukushima when he attacked my friend.

"On our return in the afternoon from the work party, my friend was still practically in the same position as when we left. We picked him up, carried him back to the lines and placed him on his groundsheet. We then called the Medical Officer, Captain Picone, over. When we picked my friend up to bring him down he was moaning and groaning of his stomach while we carrying him, and when we placed him down he was trying to cough and there was blood coming away from his mouth. Captain Picone shook his head and then I went on up to my tent-lines.

"Next morning my friend was dead at the same place on his ground-sheet."

NOTE 8:

1563215	Tritton, V.J.	28 Jun.	1782423	Forster, J.J.	08 Jul.
935920	Mahon, E.	03 Jun.	956498	Smith, J.T.	
3649933	Lomas, G.T.	01 Jul.	625094	Watson, A.J.	09 Jul.
1211353	Feltham, R.	02 Jul.	126045	Hughes, B.F.	11 Jul.
362816	Bowden, J.A.	04 Jul.	304115	Walmsley, M.W.	12 Jul.

On the afternoon of July 7 1945 the last remaining six survivors of the first march were placed with the survivors of the second march who had arrived a week before, in the open on the side of a hill. This group included Botterill, Moxham, Short and Anderson who decided they would leave that night. Botterill had located a rice dump. They asked Fitzgerald if he wanted to join them. He declined because of his condition. They asked others also, some wanted to escape but realised they would only be a hindrance, because of ulcers, to the stronger members. It was important the party was strong enough to fight off any unfriendly natives who might be seeking rewards from the Japs for jumping them.

About 10 p.m. that night they left and it was very dark. Moxham walked into the Englishman Frost's camp which was a ground sheet supported by sticks. Frost was startled and he asked them what they were up to? Botterill said "Shut up, we'll be back". He regretted he did not invite him to go with them because he was fit enough. There was only one way out. The camp was surrounded by jungle on three sides and on the cleared side there was no barbed wire. They moved out past the guards who were just sitting around, then continued on their way along a track for what seemed to be miles – each man was hanging on to the other in the dark. The track was faintly visible. Botterill could still recognise where the rice dump was located. They moved in quietly and felt around for the bamboo door and found it was locked. Their eyes by this time were fairly well adjusted to the dark and each member fumbled with the door until it opened. Apart from the rice the store contained baskets of native tobacco which they helped themselves to and also gathered what rice they could carry. They froze for awhile when one of the Jap guards went to the latrine at the back of the hut. When he settled down again the men went on, heading through what was Ranau – it had been previously bombed out by Allied aircraft – turned left and headed towards Jesselton.

Sticpewich continued: "I commenced building the hut on 30 June. The work parties carried on the same – attap carrying and rice carrying parties continued working up till about 13 July. During this period, 30 June to 13 July, about 40 of our men died and a greater percentage of the Englishmen died during this period. All these men I consider died from sheer exhaustion from the conditions of the working parties, malnutrition, exposure, starvation and the filthy conditions under which we were forced to live. The altitude of our camp was 3,300 feet above sea level so I was told by the Japs. During the day it was warm in the sun and cold in the jungle, at night it was very cold. We were not allowed out in the sun on account of air raids. Our clothing was only what we had left Sandakan with; some of us had blankets but a lot of others who were unable to carry anything arrived with nothing and shared with others. Men were still being beaten, I saw men receive severe beatings for leaving the area to defaecate or get water from the nearby creek; they were also beaten for not removing our dead quick enough when they had been ordered to bury them. Our men were in such poor condition by this time it was impossible for them to lift the corpses. A piece of rattan would be tied around the arms of the man and it would take about five men to drag the man along to the hole that had been dug. It would take four men 3½ to 4 hours to dig a hole two feet deep by six feet by four feet for the corpses. I have seen eight corpses put in a hole this size. The Jap guards would stand over the grave digging party and persistently harass and beat them. I could identify the guards who stood over the grave digging parties.

"On 18 July we had completed our hut and we moved into it. It was only a roof and a floor but a total of 72 men – English and Australians – moved down into the hut. This constituted the survivors, all the others having died. The hut was 30 ft. long by 18 ft. wide with a raised floor built on the side of a creek bed. 38 of us approx. occupied the floor but the rest of them were so sick from dysentery etc. they could only crawl under the floor, we had to keep those who already had dysentery away from those who had not yet contracted it. The men below had no control over their bowels and we were endeavouring to keep some of us alive. We had no medical treatment whatsoever. About 10 yards from the hut there was a pit latrine but after a few days it was a seething mass of flies and maggots.

"At this time it had become a great problem to bury the dead because of the weakness of the men. The Japs opened up a new Cemetery 20 to 30 yards above our new hut.

"Up to 20 July there was a working party working down in the Jap kitchen, carrying water, cleaning vegetables and chopping wood. There were six on this work party and every one of them died between 2nd and 20th July. They had to carry water from the creek, a distance of about a quarter mile, up a steep incline on which you could scarcely stand. The average was about 130 buckets of water a day for the Jap officers; one man did this, besides peeling vegetables and other kitchen duties. The other five men were on the Jap guards' kitchen, chopping wood, peeling vegetables, carrying water, all had to do washing of the Japs clothes too. As the man carrying water to the Jap officers got too sick to work he would be fallen out and another man would take his place. Every man who was on the job of carrying water to the officers' mess, with the exception of one, died within three to four days after knocking off the job. About 18 or 19 passed through that job and all but one died; he was still alive when I left, Dvr. Evans [Note: Dvr. Evans was the nephew of Maj. General Wootton now at Labuan and he is aware his nephew is being held by the Japanese in Borneo.] was his name, I saw Dvr. Evans receive a very severe beating one day from the Jap guards for failing to stop one of our men thieving some vegetables. He was beaten badly until he could not use his arms and was limping on one leg and he could not work for three days after the beating. Dr. Picone told me he was very badly injured internally and was in a very bad shape. He only worked for two days after that then he was too sick to move and was laid up in the hut, he was there when I left on the night of 28 July, and he was very ill.

"During the whole period at Ranau Jap guards were in the habit of going through our gear and thieving anything they wanted. On 15 July S/Sgt. Horder caught Pte. Suzuki and another guard going through his gear, they took a piece of jewellery out of Horder's gear, a watch and a ring, and Horder called them thieves and mongrels. He was immediately belted down by the two of them and kicked into insensibility while he was on the ground and finished up unconscious. They kicked him in the back of the head, the neck, stomach and in the testicles. They belted and kicked him around solidly for about ten minutes. Up till then S/Sgt. Horder had been in fair condition and had been the QM in the hospital. He was beaten so badly he never regained consciousness and died during the night.[9]

"During this period on three occasions work parties were sent out – eight men in each party – with two guards, to shoot a head of cattle. The cattle had to be dressed and the whole carcass carried back along the road, it was distributed to different Jap units on the way. All the hide, head and guts had to be carried as nothing was to be left at the scene of the shooting. On two occasions two head of cattle were shot; on these occasions they would average about 400 lbs. live weight each. On the single occasion it would be a big beast and would weight about 700 lbs. dressed. On each occasion all we got out of it was the stomach and intestines, we never got the heart or liver or any other part, apart from the two occasions when we got a portion of the lung.

"On the third day at Ranau one of the Jap guards, Takahara, who had been in charge of our technical party at Sandakan, took a message to me by one of my technical party, Spr. Moore, informing me that he could not speak to me in future and for me not to try and contact him as it was dangerous as he had been shifted from Sandakan in June the year before under suspicion of being too easy with us. This Jap guard, while at Sandakan, had been friendly towards us and treated us very decently. He supplied us with medical stores which he had stolen for us, also food, and he carried notes and communications for us to the native contacts we had. He was a Christian.

"At Ranau he sent this message and said he would give me a bottle of quinine that night and would point out where he would leave some bananas for me. As I passed him, a small bottle of quinine and atebrin mixed was slipped to me by him when I was on my way to do the cooking and he pointed to where the bananas were. This happened regularly throughout our stay at Ranau camp.

"On the night of 27 July I had just extinguished the fire, it was pitch dark, I had walked four or five yards down the creek bed when somebody grabbed me, it turned out to be Takahara, and the words he said to me were "You go now. Go Jungle. If you stay you will be 'marti'. All men very short time marti marti". I had

NOTE 9:

1563436	Collins, D.G.	14 Jul.	1108527	Foley, M.J.	21 Jul.
1482073	Frost, N.	15 Jul.	539095	Mellar, P.R.	
1387375	Stapeley, W.O.	16 Jul.	2358051	Sadler, F.E.	22 Jul.
505712	Merchant, A.H.	18 Jul.	1449675	Griffiths, D.	
928333	Roberts, W.L.		2351753	Waidson, F.	24 Jul.

225

previously been warned that we would all be killed, once by a Jap guard who later shot Captain Takakuwa and Lieut. Suzuki (he shot him dead), S/Sgt. Fujita and their batman, and also shot himself. This shooting took place about 15 July when a rumour went around amongst the Japs that an Allied invasion had taken place and they were advancing inland. This Jap guard – I do not know his name – shot at his officers, wounding those I have mentioned and killing Suzuki, then committed suicide. He told me the day before he did it on a cattle killing party that his officers would be 'marti' and he told me about the Allied invasion and also said in a short time we would all be 'marti'. The day before he had been beaten by Takakuwa and Suzuki for having a dirty rifle. I sympathised with him and told him that the Jap prisoners in Australia were treated well and he told me he knew the Jap prisoners in Australia were living better than they ever had in Japan. I was also warned that we would be killed by a medical orderly. I asked this man how he knew we would be killed and he said "I saw Takakuwa's papers which say you all be 'marti'". He immediately added, "You no speak other soldiers". He thought that was a great joke. Then when Takahara gave me the warning on the night of 27th I thought it was time I got out and got anybody else out who was willing to come and take the risk. I had a consultation with Captain Cook, Captain Picone and Captain Oakeshott, the two doctors, and told them the situation, the same way as I had kept them posted with all the information I got in the past. I had convinced Captain Picone that he could attempt to escape, Captain Oakeshott said he could not do it owing to his having no boots[11] and that he also had a big ulcer on his foot and said he would be too much of an encumbrance. Captain Cook was too sick to make the attempt. Pte. Reither was sick but was willing to have a shot[12]. The other men were all too sick or incompetent to make the attempt. The next day it was impossible to bury the dead because there was no one fit enough to do it. I laid up for the day with the pretence of being too sick, this was in preparation for my escape.

"On all occasions the dead were stripped of their clothing which was washed and rinsed in the creek, hung up to dry and the Japs then took possession, that is if others of us did not get to it before them.

"On the night of 28 July I cooked the meal and served it as usual; about 9.30 p.m. Reither and I sneaked out of the camp. The guard on the camp had been doubled from the time we moved down to the new hut. The guards' beat would be less than a quarter mile distance around where we were camped. The guard house was just above us and there were no sides to our hut so that they had a good view of us.

Note 10: A member of a previous escape party had stolen his boots.

Note 11: For ethical reasons none of the Medical Officers, Captains Daniels, Oakeshott or Picone, would have left their men. Maskey, the interpreter, the only channel on communication with the Japanese, would not have walked out on his mates, and it is doubtful if anyone else would have gone with Sticpewich because they regarded him as too close to the Japanese. It was not known how Sticpewich became in charge of rations.

226

We got up to the road and laid low the next day. We were still in the camp area and could see the general confusion in the camp at our escape. There was plenty of slapping of Jap guards' faces by the Jap officers. We saw the search party go out looking for us and return about 5 p.m. that evening. At dusk we made our way out along the road towards Ranau. When I left the hut there were 32 men still alive and I knew that at least 8 would die for certain that night because of their low condition. Six of the eight were already unconscious."

Bariga being interviewed. It was Bariga who befriended the escape party of Botterill, Moxham and SHort and led them to safety.
Pic: AWM. 042561

227

On August 1, 1945, Captain Takakuwa called his senior NCOs together and gave them the order to kill the prisoners – the last thirty two who were alive when W.O. Sticpewich escaped from Ranau on July 28.

Sgt. Beppu, an experienced killer who had come from Labuan early in the year, was given the order to kill the five officers: Captain Cook, A.I.F.; Captain Daniels, R.A.M.C.; two Australian medical officers, Captain Oakeshott and Captain Picone; F/O. Burgess, R.A.F.; and Lieut. Chopping, R.A. Heavily guarded, they were walked down the Tambunan Road to a site selected by Takakuwa where they were killed.

Takakuwa then ordered Sgt. Okada to take ten NCOs to a previously selected place. There has been evidence that some of this group put up resistance. They were all killed by rifle fire;

F/O. H.G. Burgess. 63906. R.A.F. (VR). Died Ranau 3 August 1945. Age 41. Stamford, Lincolnshire   Pic: Christopher Elliott

among them were S/Sgt. Jack Edwards, R.O.A.C. and Sgt. Rooker, R.A. There was some discussion whether the Australian interpreter, Cpl. Maskey, be killed with the officers, he was included with this group.

Sgt. Tsuji, who killed all those who were unable to continue on the march, was ordered to kill all those seventeen who were still alive. Sticpewich gave evidence that when he left on July 28 there were eight unconscious and no one was fit enough to bury the dead. Tsuji stated one or two crawled up to the cemetery where two holes had been prepared – one for those who died naturally and one for those who were murdered. The War Crimes Court found that this mass murder took place on or about 1 August 1945.

Takakuwa would have been carrying out superior orders and would have been aware for some time it was the intention of High Command to kill the prisoners and not hand them over at the end of hostilities.

In early 1944, it was Takakuwa who was responsible for the capture of three Australian commandos who infiltrated into the high ground at Tambisan Point, 100 miles south of Sandakan, where a British-led party, code-named PYTHON, was successfully reporting on shipping direct to G.H.Q. When the group was being reinforced, one man was lost; he was later captured and handed over to the Kempe Tai. Takakuwa was ordered to take a Company into the area to flush the party out; he was successful: two additional men were caught and handed over to Major Nishihara, the Judicial Officer, who would have been the officer who conveyed the sensitive messages to the Commander of 37 Army such as policy on prisoner of war matters. Takakuwa would have been briefed by Nishihara.

Now, Takakuwa, having disposed of the last prisoners at Ranau and possessing the knowledge the Australians had landed at Brunei and were in the process of chasing the Japanese out of the developed portion of Borneo, in accordance with verbal orders to ensure no prisoners were left alive carried out the orders then set out himself with his men to join 37 Army Headquarters at Tuaran.

The War Crimes' Investigators were never satisfied they extracted the whole truth and nothing but the truth as the guards had given conflicting statements as to the elimination of the prisoners, however, after strong pressure was applied to the killer guards confessions were made which amounted to confirmation that on or about August 1st, the last of those alive were killed.

Evidence suggested that the party of 10 put up some resistance, only seven remains were ever found which suggests the killing of this group would not have gone as planned. Personal knowledge of some of those men is that they would have made a break for it.

The grave site of the officers was confirmed: a shirt with a thermometer in the pocket, an English Sam Brown belt, Officers' pips and an R.A.F. officers' cap were found.[13]

The people of Ranau were having a hard time. The Japanese threatened to kill any of the local people who were caught assisting the prisoners; these people were very sympathetic and whenever possible would leave food knowing the prisoners would receive it and often, in many cases, they used their children to leave the food.

The Japanese confiscated livestock from the people, they took their pigs, their fowls, leaving many of them destitute.

During the Australian Pilgrimage of 1995, the Australians met many of these people who were children during the war years and who remembered "the white men".

Jahan of Kampong Matang near Ranau: "About 8 May 1945, many POWs were putting stones on the road near the 111 Mile peg, I was also working with them. An air raid started and the Japanese hid in a hole.

"I ran with five white men and hid in the long grass. Whilst we were in the grass I gave them cooked rice. One of the men gave me a wallet." (The wallet was

Note.

		Lieut. Chopping, R.A.S.C.	03.08.45.
Captain Daniels, R.A.M.C.	06.08.45.	S/Sgt. Edwards, R.A.O.C.	05.08.45.
Captain Cook, A.I.F.	12.08.45.	S/Sgt. Rooker, R.A.	04.08.45.
Captain Oakeshott, 10 A.G.H.	01.08.45.	These dates demonstrate how the Japanese cov-	
Flt. Lieut. Burgess, R.A.F.	03.08.45	ered up the massacres.	

embossed NX. 52402 with initials W.G.R. thought to belong to NX. 52402 Pte. W.G. Read, 2/10 Fld. Amb. Inside the wallet was a photograph of five children with the following writing on the back: NX. 68861 Dvr. L.E. Hardy, 2/3 M.A.C. 2nd A.I.F. Borneo Prison Camp, from Beryl Hardy, 4 Wynter Street, Taree, NSW).

On-being shown the Army photograph album Jahan recognised the photo of Pte. W.G. Read as the man who gave him the wallet, he wasn't sure about the photograph of Dvr. Hardy but thought that he was one of the five men who hid with him in the long grass.

Also in the wallet was a slip of paper with the following writing on it: Mr. C.P. Thane, Sungei Sekah Estate, Negri Sembilan, FMS.

Jahan: "The man who gave me the wallet said, "Hold these things for me until I collect them. If I don't collect them you will know that the Japanese have killed me." This man spoke a little Malay.

"When the raid finished the Japs called us and the PWs were marched away. I did not see them again."

Mrs. Palabiew of Ranau: "During the Japanese occupation, my family moved to Muruk, about 15 km from the POW Camp. I was 8 years old at that time.

"Earlier in 1945, my mother and I saw white men (POW) walking in very sick and weak condition. My mother asked me to give them tapioca and bananas;

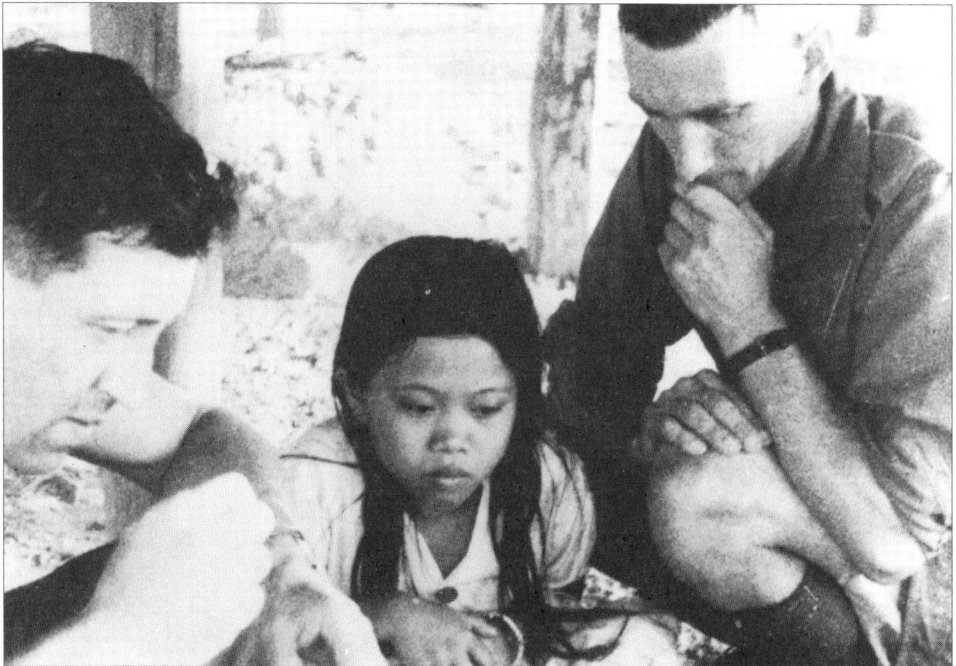

Mrs. Palabiew as child, centre. During Japanese occupation of Ranau she smuggled food to POWs.   Pic: AWM.042565.

sometimes I gave packets or rice, sweet potatoes, whenever POW passed by. I purposely put along the road so that they could take and eat for the journey.

"By that time our bamboo house was surrounded by jungle. Soon after the Japanese surrender, we moved to Ranau Town where I was asked to meet Australian Army in Government Office. They gave cloths, money, certificate and also took my picture."

Mr. Sing Kee of Ranau: "During Japanese time I was 8 years old and stayed in Ranau town. Early 1945 the POWs carried rice in very weak and sick condition. The older people were afraid to give food to POW because of the cruelty of the Japanese; so they asked me to give bananas and some food to the POW whenever they passed the shop.

"My family moved to the village because the town area was destroyed by aeroplanes. Somewhere in July 1945 I heard the news that Australia soldiers parachuted in Kampong Langsat, about 5 km. from my house in Kampong Boongkud, so I followed the local people to meet Australian soldiers where I was offered a job as a boy to take care POW Camp.

'I received the Honour Certificate from the white men in Ranau Government Office."

Pelula of Kampong Paka, near Ranau: "On another day, a Saturday, I gave the PW five cakes and one of them threw me this locket." (Locket, heart-shaped, gold with a photo of a woman inserted, was handed to 8 Aust. War Graves Unit). "The man who gave me the locket had only a few teeth in the top jaw and was aged about 30 years old. He was tall and very thin from lack of food, his eyes were grey ... his hair was dark brown inclined to curl."

Chapter Seven

KUCHING

Extracts from Peter Lee's Home Made 1945 Diary
25th March to 21st June 1945

Palm Sunday: March 25th 1945: In this little book, the second of my attempts at bookbinding, it is fitting that the opening pages should record the most momentous event in our collective lives during the past 3 years. On March 8th 1942 we lost contact with Freedom. Since that day we have been taught the meaning of freedom, through lack of it, in the hard school of experience. Today we had our first glimpse of Freedom again when Kuching was 'visited' by two American aircraft, fittingly enough two 4-engined 'Liberator' bombers, symbolical of that Liberty which we all hope will soon be ours again. At 10.30 a.m. I was thinking out the day's menus in the cookhouse when Cpl. Wilson came in with the news that two 4-engined aircraft were overhead. Without any thought, without even having seen them, I yelled out: "The Yanks are here!" and rushed out to see them. The day was a glorious one – the best we had had for over a week, and there in the azure blue of a sky dotted with patches of fleecy white cloud, were two silver aircraft flying at about 15000 ft. Suddenly from the second, slightly behind its mate, a puff of smoke comes out from its tail. Smoke? No – again mental response is

instantaneous and the word frames itself before the thought is conscious –
Pamphlets!!!

More and more stream out from the two machines, break up and stream earth-
wards in a widening stream. By now the whole Camp knows the glad tidings,
and all faces are upturned to the sky. The Japanese, too, have noticed them by
now and the gongs start beating all over the area. After seeing the Cookhouse
staff into their trench, I go across the garden to the No. 1 Hut trenches, cut
into the slight bank opposite. They are full by now, and in a bit of a mess. The
heavy rains we have been having have resulted in landfalls, and standing
water makes part of the dugouts useless. The Aussies over the wire are
already in their trenches, and everyone is in great spirits. Speculation,
hypotheses, forecasts fly round like sparks from a Roman candle. Were the
pamphlets intended for us, or for the native population? Who knows? They
are still coming down, and are drifting well away from the Camp area.
Disappointing, but the aircraft are still about, and everybody is keyed up.
Events follow in a surprisingly leisurely fashion. First, two reconnaissance
flights over the aerodrome at a high level during which one bomb appears to
have been dropped. Then, dropping down in a power dive from about 12000
– 1000 or less feet, more bombs or perhaps concentrated cannon fire, and a
third and last flight which seemed to concentrate on machine gunning. The
sight of one of these tremendous aircraft doing a left-hand bank just over the
trees between this Camp and the aerodrome causes loud expressions of
delight from everyone in our trench. The machines go away, and after a short
interval the "All Clear" is sounded. So ends our first, and we hope not our
last, visitation from our Allies. As I had always anticipated, the raid had a
very marked tonic effect on the Camp's morale, and provided a much needed
variant to conversation. Throughout the rest of the day, wherever one went,
the topic was always the same – excited speculation on where these planes
might be operating from, what the strategic purpose of the raid was, and what
the pamphlets might contain, tempered by anxiety about the position of our
Other Ranks' working party which is still being employed on the aerodrome.
To settle this latter point, the C.O. asked for an immediate interview with Col.
Suga, and asked for the withdrawal of all British troops at that place. Col.
Suga gave his assurance that he had already issued an order to that effect, but
that he would expedite it in view of the C.O's request [NB: The 'drome party
was stopped two days later and the 50 odd ORs quartered on the 'drome
returned to this Camp a day or so after that.] At this interview Col. Suga in
reply to a question on food, again reiterated the difficulty they were having in
getting food into Kuching. Ships were being torpedoed and bombed, and
communication by sea with Jesselton and Sandakan was now cut off. The
only possible way of getting ships through was by strong air escort all the
way, which was rather difficult as their aircraft were very busy transporting

Japanese officers. He gave the welcome news that Red Cross supplies had arrived in Japan some time previously via Russia, and that an allotment for POWs in this area had subsequently arrived in Singapore. The allocation for Borneo would be about the same as last time – 1 parcel per 6 persons, but that his problem was to get transport to bring it across, in view of the risk of sinkings. The C.O. suggested that medical supplies at any rate, might be brought across by aircraft. Suga promised to look into this. Of war news, Col. Suga would only say that the fighting in Europe was fierce and had reached a climax, and that out here there was fierce fighting in the Philippines.

Good Friday March 30th: After a week of expectancy and intense discussion, we had our second air raid today. Again the Air-Raid Precaution system seemed defective, as the warning was not given until the aircraft had appeared overhead. The day was sunny, with again patches or banks of white clouds. At about 1145 aircraft were heard approaching, high up, and shortly afterwards 9-12 appeared in a patch of blue sky at about 10,000 feet. They were evidently not Liberators – that much we could say, before things happened with startling suddenness. I turned towards the cookhouse, then looked again at the sky, and in what seemed like a split second two of the machines had peeled off and were doing a steep bank at tree-top height. As their undersides were towards us we could see that they had twin engines, twin fuselages and twin rudders – LIGHTNINGS – FIGHTERS !! These two words jumped into one's mind, and brought a whole flood of jumbled questions and speculations to the surface. Where were they operating from ? Let me think, what was their range, 1000-1500 miles ?? It was an exciting development. After machine gunning the aerodrome they made off, and again left a lot of "morale" uplift behind them. We later learnt that there were no casualties, British or Japanese from either this or the previous raid, but after this latest development all working parties on the aerodrome were discontinued. The remaining Allied troops on the 'drome, about 150 Dutch, were sent back to this area the following day.

April 4th Wednesday: To chronicle our 3rd raid, which up to date have been in 5 day cycles! This time ample warning was given, as we received the "possible" shortly after 10 a.m. At about 11, Dai Davies noticed a very distinct vapour trail being made due south of the Camp, which continued round to about due west in a dead straight line of white against the blue as though it had been ruled by a ruler. At 12 the imminent was given, and as we went to the trenches the first formation of six 4-engined aircraft in two "Vies" of three each, appeared from due west at about 12000 ft. These were quickly followed by three more formations of like number, making 24 in all, a magnificent sight with their undersides showing silver against the blue of a patchy sky, and the sun glinting on their turrets and fuselages. After making leisurely reconnaissance over the area, three machines dropped bombs, visible from this Camp, in the direction of either Pending or the river mouth. Shortly after their detonation a lightish concentration of black smoke was seen to rise from that place. More comment during the rest of the day as usual, the atmosphere being distinctly cheerful. During the past two days we have received 2500 lbs of tapioca and kladi root, scheduled for ten days, 12th-22nd April. On account of this we have decreased our rice consumption to 50 lbs. daily, and increased our root consumption to 325-350 lbs. representing our lowest and highest consumption respectively.

Retrospect: The past two to three months have been trying from both a camp and personal point of view. The food situation has been persistently uncertain and obscure, and has usually involved almost starvation rations for the first 5-10 days of the month, followed after a struggle by slightly better rations. This has resulted in a generally unsettled feeling in the Camp, which, combined with the very damp, wet weather we have been having (and which now seems to have broken – April 5th) has shown itself in an outbreak of petty quarrels, querulousness and general lack of amiability. I must confess that I have not been unaffected by all these things, and have inclined to be irritable myself – however I have made an effort to overcome it, which I think has now been successful! Another disturbing factor has been the absence of lighting since March 10th, when the power plant in the town broke down, we are told this involved the break up of bridge schools, poker parties and the small groups of reading enthusiasts who used to gather under our meagre 40W bulbs (6 in toto) every evening. Health has been gradually dropping lower, presumably less on account of lack of bulk foods, as of proteins and fats. Quite a number of people weigh themselves each month, and as their weight almost invariably shows a decline their worries increase pro rata. The last time I weighed myself, sometime about the beginning of March, my figure was 8 stone 6 lbs. As we are unable to do anything personally about this loss in weight, I have taken what seems to me to be the only logical step in the circumstances – I have given up "weighing and worrying"!!

There have been one or two concerts and sing-songs since I wrote my last notes, but generally speaking they are pitiful affairs. One hesitates to criticise without having any contribution to make oneself, but some of the "turns" are really ultra bad. The audiences too are generally apathetic and listless, although whether this is a case of cause and effect it is difficult to say. Everyone here lives secretly in a dream world of his own; his thoughts constantly straying to the things of the past and hopes for the future. I see brother officers attempting to read books, their gaze wandering after the first page or even line, to the scene outside or the distraction surrounding them. I do it myself, particularly if the book is complex or difficult to read and one's body is tired. There is a tendency for stray sentences or paragraphs to conjure up pictures of what has been or might be; descriptions that remind one of some well-loved person or place and transport the mind from the sordid present to that past which the mind very often gilds in colours perhaps unmerited by the particular experience. After being deprived of priceless liberty for over 3 years, and shut up in places to which the tremendous march of world history comes but indistinctly to the ear, it is all perhaps natural.

Wednesday April 11th: Completely "out" of ration root crop today, and now dependent on garden produce and our very small stock of rice. No further sign of Allied Air Forces, although observations posts seem to be manned every day.

Funerals are now a daily occurrence – often two and three per day. Area round Cemetery being cleared of rubber trees. Coffins are now used only to take corpses to the Cemetery and for the Service, and are then brought back to Camp for the next death. In spite of it all, the morale of the men seems high. During "possible", 3 boards, each 5' x 4', lettered P.O.W. are displayed around the area.

Very impressed with Howard Springs' "Fame is the Spur", modelled, I imagine on Ramsay MacDonald's career, with smatterings of those of I.H. Thomas, Phillip Snowden etc. His diagnosis of a politician's character is ruthless, but fair. All the characters are finely drawn, and he displays great insight into human nature of widely differing types.

Talk last night dwelt on post-war travel, on which I am very keen. Possibility world car tour, making living by articles, addressing meetings etc. – approach Morris for car etc.?? America, South America, Japan, China, F.I.C. Siam, Malaya, Burma, India, Africa, Turkey or Persia, Russia and home via Balkans or Scandinavia??

Tuesday April 16th: 1.13 p.m. Heard heavy drone of high-flying aircraft – left my lunch to investigate and eventually picked out tiny plane in sky about 30,000 ft. flying N.W.-S.E. Over the aerodrome it changed direction and doubled back on its tracks. We got the 'imminent' warning shortly afterwards, closed windows and doors, doused cookhouse fires, (a new order received 3 days ago) and went to the trenches. Nothing more happened. We were given the "All Clear" about 20 minutes later. General opinion was that the aircraft was on reconnaissance. The day was glorious, warm and sunny, with a slight breeze, a sky of almost Mediterranean blue with odd drifting patches of billowy white cloud.

Today we also received 2900-odd lbs. tapioca and kladi root from the largest consignment of root crop that has yet come into this area. There is also a very large pile of cooking bananas from which we have expectations!! The C.O. rather worried about the rice position, as we have no indication as yet as to if and when rice for … will be coming in. Tried to allay his anxiety to some extent – am putting on a completely riceless days … think 500 lbs. root which should satisfy the bulk food … It was also … a month ago that we had our inspection on the Square at 3 o'clock in the morning. This was done by a Japanese sentry and NCO by the light of candles and consisted of an examination of our bodies … scratches, blood, mud etc. We eventually found out that the ration store had been broken into by 2 Other Ranks who, when surprised by a sentry, bolted through the barbed wire. Rain had fallen very heavily, and as the search was carried out very promptly detection was easy – one man was identified by the state of his body and clothing and the other gave himself up.

Japanese Headquarters, Kuching

Women's Camp – Kuching

Julie Willmott (nee Tuxford): There were 30 children in the camp; I was the eldest, one little Australian girl, Rosemary, would always sing "Goodnight Daddy" and her father would hear her across the way in his camp.

I remember the men in the camp decided they would get eggs for the children in the Women's Camp; I would go through the fence at night to collect the eggs which one of the men would have buried in a marked spot under a tree. One night when Auntie Doreen was standing guard at the fence she saw that one guard was looking rather suspiciously at her and by the time I got back with the eggs there were two guards there. I was wearing a long dark coat and I squatted down on the ground hiding the eggs under the coat. I heard Auntie saying 'Oh she's not well not well' to the guards and they suggested that they lift me up and take me to the toilet but we said 'No no no' and eventually they went away and we got the eggs back safely. But Grandma was very very cross with me and hurt that I had not told her I was going for the eggs and she forbade me to do such a thing again.

I became a woman while in the camp and Grandma made me wear a bra because I was growing and she used to pull it tight around me and tell me I must wear it as tight as I can and I would say but I can't breathe and try and let it out a little bit but Grandma would say No you must wear it tight. We used to be made to get

Group: Far right front row: Julie Tuxford – Free!   Pic: AWM.116938.

238

out of bed in the middle of the night – sometimes three times during a night – and the Japanese would search our hut and push us around with the end of their rifles – some of the women would have their babies in their arms and they would scream in fright – we could never understand why they pushed us around and then later we would hear that they were looking for so-and-so. There was one soldier who was very kind, he was a Formosan, he spoke good English, and if he had any extra food he would tell us he would leave it at the bottom of the fence, we used to tell him that he would get hurt if he was caught and he would say No no – food for all – food for all.

I was Confirmed too while we were in Camp, Grandma wanted me Confirmed and Agnes Keith made me a beautiful dress to wear out of one of her evening gowns – lovely cream coloured material – the other ladies all helped her – and the Padre came in from the other Camp to conduct the Service – I remember that very clearly and at the ceremony I felt Jesus Christ very close to me. Dr. Stookes, Mrs. Keith, Auntie Doreen and Grandma – they were all there.

I used to pass the Camp quite often – their camp was the first one as you came down from Suga's house; the men were always busy and always looked nice – they were the only ones that shaved – they never lost their pride – the Captain never ever did not have a shirt on – always.

I learnt the word 'mate' and afterwards I learnt 'She's apples!' Captain Mosher would say 'If Julie can say She's apples we're right!' We would always say 'Good day mate' to each other and they would tell me to look after my teeth – I remember the Australians washing, shaving and always wore a hat –

I remember seeing some sort of drink, it looked like raspberry drink, in Dr. Yamamoto's office, and I was told not to touch it, he said to me 'Don't touch it – it's not for drinking' and when I told Grandma and she asked me if I was sure that was what he had said and I said yes then Grandma asked me if I had touched any and did I know what it was but I said no I hadn't touched it I didn't know what it was then Grandma said 'We must keep alive we must keep alive'. That was about three or four days before the Australians arrived to free us. Grandma knew what that drink was for she was a Doctor's wife.

I always found Major Suga very kind to me and the other children; he would talk to me as one of the older children and he would tell me things – some I didn't understand – but he would tell me not to tell anyone of the things he talked about. I never knew him to hurt, beat or kill any one but at times he would just disappear and then a reign of terror would begin until he came back again. The Japanese soldiers used to beat people up.

I was fifteen by now and we used to have a job of collecting vegetables from a common place just near the guard house and underneath Major Suga's house which was on a hill; you could see all the gardens; there was a guard house just opposite the Catholic section where the Padres were and then the Men's section where Dad could see me every day – I was pulling the cart for the vegetables by myself and going along the road I could see the head and shoulders of a man wearing a slouch hat and I thought that was a peculiar thing, then when I got near he said

'Good morning mate!' and I said 'Oh who are you? but wait a minute I've got to bow to this Japanese soldier' and he said "No you don't – you're free!" I said "Are we? are you an American?" and he said 'No – we're Aussie!' He asked me where I was going and I told him I was going for food and he said to forget about that and go back to the Women's Camp. I remember running back past the camp and calling out 'Dad, Dad, we're free!' Dad was there and he told me he knew and to go and tell Grandma, I was running and falling down skinning my knees but I kept running and got to Grandma and told her we were free and we were all there then Captain Glover came up and met Grandma and she told him 'My gosh you're a fine looking young man!' and all the adults sat down but I was running round calling out and telling everybody that we were free.

The day we were released Major Suga stood there in the Quadrangle, he was wearing his sword, and Dad said to me 'Come on Jule we'll go and say goodbye to Major Suga' I said to him 'Do you think we should Dad? we don't want to get into trouble' but Dad said that we wouldn't. Major General Wootten was there and I went across to him and asked him may I go across and speak to Major Suga and he said of course I could. So we went across to him and I told him I would never forget him and he said to me "Remember me and my sword, I value it very much, I have no family now they were all killed in Hiroshima – I have nothing left now – at least I never killed anybody."

George Tuxford was ten years old when he was interned with his father in the Men's Camp in Kuching. His father gave him the job of looking after the drinking water for the men when they were out on the working parties. This job gave George time to "scout about" as he called it and, in time, he could visit his friends in the Women's Camp. To do this he would creep up a drainage gutter between the two Camps away from the sight of the guards. "One day," he said, "I thought I would try my luck with the new guard and walk between the H.Q. on the hill and the Women's Camp, but to my horror, I ran into Major Suga as he was coming to his office. I smartly bowed, waited, still bowing. He came to me and said "Up! What is your name?" I replied, "George, Sir", and bowed. "Ar – George-ee" he said, "Come with me." The guard was now running towards me, he didn't see Major Suga until he came around the building. He stopped, gave his explanation to Major Suga I suppose – he was a very worried man I can remember! Major Suga said something, he smiled at me, bowed and left back to his guard-box.

"Come!" Major Suga said again. He made me go in front of him and now many other Japanese came out to see their boss, and a very frightened boy of 10 with a water-bottle not yet filled with water. All bowed. I didn't know what was going to happen. I stop to bow, Major Suga pushed me gently and said "Go!" and into his office. I went, was told to sit and given a rice biscuit which I put into my pocket. He asked again my name and I said, in Japanese, answering his English, that my name was George. I had learned this a long time ago and it had saved me many times. He burst out laughing, Nagai and the others came to see what was funny.

Major Suga said something, I guess about me. my understanding of Japanese was limited, Lt. Nagai said in English "Where is your father working today?" I pointed to a group of men we could see from the verandah. A guard was called in, he bowed, they gave him an order and he went out, I was worried because I thought Dad was going to be beaten for not looking after me. Soon the guard came back with Dad, they both bowed and Major Suga said to Dad, "Your son?" then I was told to go outside. I forgot to bow and Dad said "Bow son!" I turned and bowed and went out. I just sat on the step outside, worried and waiting, waiting for the worst. Dad came out by himself and he said nothing, just got my hand and gave me a hug as we walked back to his job. The other men came round to see what had happened but the guard said "Kora-Kora!" and we had to go back to work.

"Next morning at Tengko, as the rest marched out to work, Lt. Nagai at the gate stopped Dad and me and took us to the Major's office. Major Suga soon arrived in his Ford car, we all bowed, including Lt. Nagai. "You like playing with friends?" Major Suga said to me. I said, "Yes Sir". "Now you can play all you want with friends in Women's Camp" he said, "Must be back Tengko all time, I tell guards O.K. you can go in Women's Camp." Always, unbeknown to all, I was well established with friends long time, since the gardening started!

"From then on my moving around anywhere was easy and put to good use, visiting the Women's Camp was good until some Nuns got the idea I should join the School group – I soon made excuse about not being able to attend and got work to do !

"Major Suga was kind to all us children, he would give us fruit and rice cakes and take us rides in his car.

"But later the guards changed and new ones came that were not so friendly and I stopped going across the Parade Ground to the Women's Camp on my own for fear of a beating for Dad.

"I remember – not sure of the time – Major Suga took me in his car, with Dad, and told to get on a small ship, with some Japanese and we returned to Jesselton and Mum."

Flt. Lieut. Edward Grey-Jones' Diary

courtesy of Peter E.I. Lee.

No. 3 Camp (British Officers) of P.O.W. Camp at Lintang Barracks, Kuching, Sarawak

15.08.45: We were just about to start breakfast when Lt.Col. Whiting came into our hut and announced: "Gentlemen, I want no shouting or cheering nor any visible signs of elation at what I am now going to tell you. Remember we are prisoners of war and under Japanese observation.

"Gentlemen, the war is over (a gasp only) the Japanese Emperor has issued a rescript of unconditional surrender."

He then went on to tell us about the atomic bombs dropped on Hiroshima and Nagasaki, and their devastating effect.

22.08.45: This afternoon, Lt.Col. Suga called for representative parties from all camps except the Women & Children's at a meeting in front of his office. I went along. The only Japanese present were Suga, Lt. Ojima and an interpreter. (No guards).

Suga announced that "peace was coming soon, peace would be here very soon." He stressed the bombing of Japanese women and children by the atomic bomb, saying that the Japs waged war with soldiers and did not kill civilians and women and children to win wars. The Jap. Emperor, in order to save further loss of life had signed an order of unconditional surrender, but that this had to be ratified in ten days time.

He spoke with apparent emotion, and I'll give him marks that he didn't surround us with guards in case of an outbreak amongst us. Actually it passed off very quietly, due mainly to the fact that it was news a week old to us, although he did not know it.

He had the effrontery to tell us that he had given orders for our food to be increased in quantity and that he would do his utmost to obtain canteen for us, i.e. supplies of tobacco, bananas, sugar, blachang etc.

This, after repeatedly stating that there was no food left in the area, and we had been existing on 6 ozs. rice per head per day for the last several months.

Speech by Lt. Col. Suga
to Allied Prisoners of War and Internees
Kuching, 24th August, 1945.

"Good afternoon, everbody … Please sit down. At last I have some good news for you; peace is coming – it is at hand! You must keep calm and not excitement. Now I will tell you some news. The Americans have used Atomic Bomb, which causes much devastation, on Japan. On the 6th of this month they used it on Hiroshima City … (long pause) … nearly all the people, the citizens … were killed; nearly all the houses were burnt down. Japanese Government protested, but on the 9th the Americans again used Atomic Bomb, on Nagasaki City … Nagasaki City like Hiroshima City … (pause) … Japanese fight with soldiers, aeroplanes, ships, and guns – not with civilians, women and children … Japanese people, Asiatic peoples – do not bomb civilians   women and children … but nowadays war turn upside down … Our Emperor … our Japanese Emperor … very worried … he want to stop war. So Emperor sent message to Allies to say he will accept Potdam … Potdam … Potdam declaration. But perhaps you do not know about Potdam. Now I will tell you another news … (long pause) When German surrender … Allied Premier and President had grand conference at Potdam, where they made a declaration saying how they would treat the peoples after the War. Our Emperor accept Potdam Declaration … Now I will tell you another news … On the 9th of this month Mr. Stalin … Mr. Stalin of Soviet Roosia declare war on Japan … Mr. Stalin, with whom Japan had treaty for friendship and no fighting during the war, make attack on Japan … Our Emperor could not stand sight of bombing of Japanese women and children, and say must stop war … on the 15th he issue a Rescript and accept Potdam Declaration … (long pause) … But outside Japan many Japanese soldiers unbeaten – in Indo-China, Thailand, Singapore, Manchuria, Burma, Sumatra, Java, Borneo, Celebes, etc. Generals and soldiers not want to stop war; make much excitement … they say they will fight on to last man – to the last soldier. But Japanese respect Imperial House, and in Japan must obey Emperor's orders, so Generals and soldiers say will withdraw Japanese nationality and fight on … Japanese Emperor very worried – send Prince to highest Command – but Generals and soldiers still much excitement, still say must fight on, so they occupy the high-lands here and there, and make ready strong points … Situation very critical. (pause) … But my way is straight … I, as Commandant of Prisoners' and Internees' Camps must obey Japanese Emperor's orders and accept Rescript, and I will protect you all to my best possible … As you all know, I have always done my best for you, and I have told my subordinate officers to give you more food and clothing. You must tell your sick comrades – those who are sick in bed – that I will cure their sick-ness – that I will get them something for their sickness. You must tell them to be cheerful, to keep up their high spirits. You must all keep up your morale. Peace is coming, it is near at hand, but you must be patient. Do you understand? ... If there any questions that you wish to ask me you must tell your Camp Masters and I will see them".[1]

23.08.45: According to promise (for once) we were given extra supplies of rice, and we have bumped our daily consumption up to 12 ozs. I am told by ex-rubber planters that they used to issue 22 ozs. rice per day per Tamil labourer.

24-29.08.45: The Japs are fairly doling out rice and tapioca root to us, also have increased our daily issue of greens.

Jap. made gym. shoes, silly little singlets, khaki jackets (out sizes only) made in England, tooth powder in paper packets, bamboo tooth brushes and such-like articles have also been handed out. Some people have even been given leather boots. All these things we have repeatedly asked for, and have been told: "no stores or clothing at all in Kuching".

30.08.45: At 11.00 a.m. an R.A.A.F. transport plane arrived (a Douglas), escorted by three fighters (Mosquito), and dropped 24 parachutes on the men's camp. They contained medical supplies, including a complete set of surgical instruments, tinned food, fresh bread, cigarettes and tobacco and matches.

The containers are about 6' long and 2' in diameter. They also dropped about a dozen parcels of clothing without parachutes. Also some copies of "Table Tops", a newsheet issued by the Australian Military Forces Abroad, at Brunei (Nos.: 83,84 & 85 dated 25th, 26th and 27th August 1945.)

The barbed wire "knife rest" which was our gate, was removed and abolished from today. We were all thrilled to watch the supplies being dropped, but the Japanese made us stay inside our huts, with the windows and doors shut. This regulation caused the R.A.A.F. to think that there were only a few hundred prisoners at Kuching (this information later from Air Commodore Scherger, A.O.C. Labuan.)

A few days later we exhibited the actual numbers of PWs and Internees for the R.A.A.F. to see – which they did.

31.08.45: The day opened with a really wonderful breakfast, the best I have tasted since being taken prisoner.

Note by Peter Lee:

I can't recall who recorded this, but I can say it is a practically verbatim copy of what Suga said to us on the Square of the Batu Lintang POW Camp on 24/8/45, announcing Japan's Capitulation.

One pint of bubor (rice gruel) with a raw egg beaten up in it, ⅛th pint sugar, ½ pint coffee, one fried rice rissole with tomato sauce, one egg (baked in a rubber pot) and the piece de resistance, a chunk of bread and butter, the first bread and butter for 3¼ years! We in hut one were lucky and got a second cup of coffee – "lagi" ("more" in Malay).

11 a.m. According to schedule, the transport plane arrived with an escort of Mosquitoes from Labuan, and dropped 14 parachutes and a dozen or so smaller parcels. They also dropped a message in the pocket of a shirt (weighted with a tin of bully beef) saying:- "Please indicate by forming a human cross if you are receiving the supplies alright, or a human circle if you are not". The Australian Officers, to whom Lt. Ojima handed the message, immediately stood in the form of a cross. I later heard that this was duly observed.

No sentries are on guard inside the wire as from today; only perimeter guards maintained. At noon I went up, with others, to the Jap office to search for my diary, books, and one or two other small things they had taken from me from time to time. Was successful in rescuing the first part of my diary.

There seemed to be a "free for all" up there – women, internees, priests, officers, all mixing together and swopping news. There were, to my great surprise, two British M.Ps. POWs, (Red Caps) on duty guarding the parachute supplies.

"Lights Out" was at 11 p.m., an hour later than usual. Our lights consist of small pieces of rubber shoes burning on a rubber cup full of sand. One man has to be constantly on duty, tending the flame.

01.09.45: No visit by the R.A.A.F. today. Had some metasulphanilamide (dropped from air) put on an ulcer on the side of my foot. Am suffering from beri-beri in both feet and ankles. Am Orderly Officer today – for the last time – but there is practically nothing to do.

The Japanese (trying to make amends) put on a Japanese cinema show in town this evening and officers' camps were invited to send parties. 25 or 20 went from our camp, but I couldn't (and in any case wouldn't) go because of the march there and back.

02.09.45: Sunday. A C. of E. and an R. C. Service was held in our camp before breakfast. The "Grocer", in other words the R.A.A.F. transport plane arrived shortly before noon and dropped further supplies. Five of the loads broke away from their parachutes, and one or two 'chutes failed to open. Some medical supplies were broken and spoilt.

Permission was officially given today to visit the other camps in the area, from 4-7 p.m., but as I do not know anyone in the other camps, it is of little use to me.

The Australian officers' choir and sextette came over to our camp at 8.30 p.m. and gave us an excellent entertainment which finished with "God Save the King" at 10.15 p.m. This was the first occasion we have been able to sing the National Anthem for over three years, as it was strictly forbidden it was sung therefore with gusto and feeling. Quite a thrill – about 120 English officers and men, 20 or more Australian officers, 2 Americans (one of them being Laidlaw, the dentist from Shanghai, an internee) and a few Dutch officers.

03.09.45: Lt.Col. Whiting came into our hut while we were drinking our 7 a.m. cup of tea and informed us that the peace ratification was signed at 11 a.m. yesterday on board the USS MISSOURI. A nice surprise, as we had been told that the signing was to be postponed for two days.

No supplies dropped today, although the usual fighter patrol visited us.

A/C. Littlewood, R.A.F., died and was buried today. He was the only man I knew, outside our own camp. Unable to attend his funeral because of my swollen feet.

The Japs turned on the electric light this evening for the first time since March 11th. To balance this, the water was turned off at 4 p.m.

04.09.45: All roll-calls dispensed with now. A nasty shortage of rice was experienced at tiffin time, due to our last bag of rice proving absolutely inedible (and we can eat practically anything). The Japs changed it, and we got further supplies in the afternoon.

Two 'grocer' planes arrived in the morning, and another in the afternoon. That's the stuff – Send it down David. Much more bread than before – it works out at six men per large loaf. We also received an issue of a 2 oz. tin tobacco each. Mine to Jacko.

Very hot in the afternoon – 92° at my bed space. I am getting rather browned off with this waiting. The question everyone is asking is "When are they coming?" or "When do we go?"!!

No water all day, which means mighty little to drink and none to wash in. The evening meal (rice) was cooked in very thick well water. The well is just a hole we have dug in the garden – swarming in frogs and tadpoles.

In all, 66 parachutes were dropped today, and I understand that a message was with them expressing surprise at the number of PWs and Internees here

(2017), whereas the RAAF estimated it at 300 or so. Hence the increased quantity of supplies. We were all issued with two tins of matches today – the first match I have touched or ever seen for over three years.

05.09.45: Water turned on for a couple of hours during the night, which has filled up our kongs – but still none for washing. Two "grocer" planes arrived during the day and dropped 38 loads. Japs supplying us with peanuts, soya sauce, blachang, and a couple of small thin vests each – size 32 only.

Rollo and I were issued with a tin of condensed milk between us. We were frightened to start on it, as it was so good and precious. I don't think a soul in the camp would exchange his half tin for a bottle whiskey.

At noon, according to arrangement, a Catalina arrived and flew over the camp for a while, later landing in the estuary of the river. We all waved and some passengers, standing in the open doorway of the Cat. waved back. Col. A.G. Wilson, a staff officer of General Wootton's (9th Aust. Div.), was on board coming to arrange details of surrender with the local Jap commander, Maj. Gen. Yamamura.

Colonels Walsh (A.I.F.), Whimster (R.A.O.C.) and Maas (Dutch Forces) went into town with Col. Suga and had lunch with him.

The Cat. is reported still to be here at 6 p.m. and it is understood that Col. Walsh with Suga and the Japanese delegation leave for Labuan on her tomorrow morning.

Managed to swop 2 ozs. tin tobacco for two eggs and 3 packets of cigarette paper for one egg, and to top it all, Ronnie Green came along and gave me a further 2 eggs presento. I hadn't had any eggs for some while, so this was "big licks". Whipped one up with my rice at dinner and added some condensed milk – like a custard.

06.09.45: 7.45 a.m. Tea with milk and sugar!! 8 a.m. Breakfast: 1½ pints bubor with milk and sugar, hunk of bread and butter, one sausage and a boiled egg – a civilized meal (almost!).

No "Grocer" today, but a Cat. flew over very low about teatime bringing Suga and party back from Labuan. Col. Walsh is staying the night at Labuan.

I represented the R.A.F. at a tea party given in the Mess to the two senior doctors, Col. King (RAMC) and Col. Shepherd (Aust.) A nice dinner was served, practically entirely on Red Cross rations – no rice was used.

07.09.45: A 'biscuit bomber' arrived and dropped 'chutes at 11.15 a.m. A Cat. arrived at lunch time bringing Col. Walsh, two Australian medical officers and an up-to-date wireless set. Two more 'biscuit bombers' arrived at 3.15 p.m. and dropped a lot of stuff.

Unfortunately one case, still attached to its parachute, hit an internee named Hammond who was just coming out of his hut. He was killed outright – knocked his brains out – age 35, and single. Another case slipped from its parachute and crashed through the roof of the work-shop, narrowly missing some POWs. at work there. The two planes flew round and round, very low, after dropping their loads – waving to us and not knowing the damage they had done – 5 chutes fell in our garden.

We had a guest-night after dinner for which the Concert Party of the men's camp came over and gave a show. I helped Rollo to entertain an internee friend of his called Ward (a Sarawak Govt. servant). Tea and a jam doughnut was served – the latter much appreciated.

Bought 1½ lbs. of gula-apong (treacle sugar) over the fence from a Jap sentry for Jap. $40.

Lights out at 11.45 p.m. – the latest night for years.

08.09.45: The Union Jack was hoisted in the men's camp at 7 a.m. this morning with honours.

L/Bombardier Jones, a barber from the men's camp, is working here every morning now and I had a good hair cut. I have asked him to trade my yesterday's issue of Jap. cigarettes (4 pkts. of 20) for eight eggs – received later. "Biscuit bomber" arrived as usual.

At 11.30 we received a visit by the two M.Os from Labuan. The senior one, a Lt.Col., gave us a short talk, saying that from here we would be taken to Labuan, where we will receive a fine reception, but when – he couldn't say – so we must be patient. After Labuan, he didn't know where we would go, but he assured us that we would be returned to our homes at the earliest possible moment.

There seems to be some hitch in the arrangements for our release. The Japanese General in charge of all Borneo, named Baba, won't play ball apparently, and is hiding himself in a village near Jesselton.

The two Aussie doctors were accompanied on their tour of inspection by Colonels King and Shepherd, two other Aussie doctors (POWs) and trailing along in the rear, completely snubbed was the so-called Jap doctor – Yamamoto. He was kept well in his place.

The internees sent their Concert Party over at 8 p.m. and performed for our benefit, but unfortunately rain stopped play right in the middle of a conjuring trick by Dr. O'Connor.

The water was turned on again, permanently, thanks to the efforts of Teddy Edwards. Yesterday I had to have a bath down in the dirty stream-cum-drain that runs through our garden. Very unpleasant. We have all been given a course of "Atebrin" (14 tablets) to take, as a preventive against malaria.

Johnstone, my neighbour on the left, has taken to snoring, due, I imagine, to the heavy meals he eats. He must have woken me up 7 or 8 times last night.

09.09.45: No visit from RAAF today. After tea, Rollo and I called on Father Wheelan at the R.C. priest's camp – nice chap in spite of being a missionary – he comes from Wallasey. Was introduced to Father Parsons (of Hull) and Father Ruis (a Dutchman). Then on to the hospital to visit Jones and Whitworth – followed by a stroll round the men's camp. Back by 6.15 for a 'tomato juice cocktail' and dinner at 6.30. Early dinner because of the "Victory" concert in the men's camp. Didn't go to the latter and didn't miss much.

10.09.45: Due to a good pressure of water I was able to resume my daily toil, i.e. cleaning down the bathing point and surroundings. Won a tube of toothpaste in a draw for a limited quantity dropped by 'chute. The first toothpaste for three years!!

Was issued with a tin of boot-polish today, so all I need now is a pair of boots or shoes to use it on. Also a pot of shaving cream – a luxury after Japanese issue soap.

Some of the officers have moved into the men's camp to live and to assist in the running of it. As Lee is over there, Hardie and Jones in hospital, I am S.A.F.O.!!

11.09.45: The secret wireless set, which has been in operation on and off for the last three years in the men's camp, was on exhibition in this camp today. It is wonderful to think it was made, including the generator, in the camp, when sudden searches were in vogue and death the expected penalty. When the whole camp was cut off from the town supply of electricity in February this year, the operators of the set were undismayed, but set to and built a generator. They did not possess nor could obtain an old generator off a motor-car or anything like that. They started from scratch with odd bits of tin and iron and what have you. It took four months to build of which three were spent in making the tools (lathe etc.) with which to make it. Their security precautions consisted of 3 fuzes in circuit with the generator and the set. Two of these fuzes were in the two nearest huts to the two gates. When the set was in operation a man sat at each fuze, and watched the gate. Upon the entry of a Jap, he would pull the fuze out thereby causing the set to go dead and in 25 seconds the set was underneath the kitchen stove with red hot coals above it. The system worked – it was never discovered.

Now that I am putting on weight, I am starting to sweat again, after months and months without sweating even when the temperature was 92° in the shade. Also, at night, I am no longer kept awake by feeling cold in spite of wearing both my shirts and having a blanket over me inside a mosquito net.

This morning we were permitted to write a letter to our next-of-kin, on one side of the paper only, the envelope to be left open for possible censoring. The letters were to be flown to Labuan today. I, as usual, wrote to Dad. Wonder if and when he will get it.

At 4.45 p.m. a white car with a Red Cross on it arrived up at Suga's office, containing Brigadier Eastick of the 9th Aust. Div. and Captain Jennings, U.S.N. Also a lorry with a cinema man, war correspondent and a few others.

An immediate parade was called for on the main square "in the best dress possible." I have just returned from it, and am feeling frightfully bucked. The General was introduced to the crowds on the square by Lt.Col. Walsh, the senior British officer amongst us, amidst terrific cheering. There were present parties from all camps, Australian British and Dutch officers, interned men and interned women and children, British ORs, Padres, R.C. Fathers, Indian troops, and Dutch native troops.

He started off by telling us that he had been sent here by Lt. Gen. Wootton, to take the formal surrender of the Jap. commander, Maj. Gen. Yamamura, which thing he had just done this afternoon and that we were now all free people. Terrific cheers and hat waving – and some tears – of relief. He went on to say that some of us would be moved to Labuan tomorrow, some a few days later and some a few days later still. In the meanwhile we would have to stay in our present camps for a night or two while better quarters were being fixed up for us in town. He was full of good cheer.

The American Captain only said a few words, but how stirring they were: "Ladies and Gentlemen, this is my first experience of this sort. This is worth many a battle at sea, many a hard day and night at sea. This is what we have been fighting for, and we have succeeded." Enormous applause greeted this utterance and the officer making it (a fine looking man) was obviously moved himself. I had to swallow hard myself.

Col. Suga stood at the corner of the square, looking like the manager of a bee-farm, and was entirely ignored.

Officers at Kuching after Japanese Surrender   Pic: AWM.116932.

Group L. to R.: Brigadier Eastick, Colonel Walsh and Colonel Suga, after Japanese Surrender.
Pic: AWM.116924.

General Wootton is to make a flying visit here tomorrow, literally and metaphorically, at noon. We all parade again at that hour.

Among the party which arrived today and took over the town of Kuching were 3 Padres, C. of E., Congregationalist, and R. C., who are holding their respective Thanksgiving services at 10 a.m. tomorrow.

We had marched (or hobbled) back to our camp about a quarter to six, and were sitting talking about it, when Whiting, our acting C.O., commonly known as 'Blanco', came into our hut and announced "the following officers will stand-by from noon tomorrow for removal to Labuan: Lt. Farwell, F/O Pethybridge, F/Lt. Grey-Jones, F/Lt. Rollinson, and F/Lt. Jackson". You could have knocked me down with a bulldozer! We are classed as "walking sick". I am as excited as a June groom, and I am sure I shall never get to sleep tonight.

Tomorrow I am going to walk out of here a free man – after three and a half years of living below coolie level. Much below as regards food. This year we have been starving to death and have buried about 480 men including 4 officers and 2 batmen from this sector of the camp.

What a day it has been. The 11th of September – a day to remember –

12.09.45: The roll-call of the men's camp this morning, taken by our officers, revealed only two men absent (Australian). After breakfast I started packing up in the hope of the promised move, and lo and behold, at 11.45 the Adjutant cried out: "All officers and men who are standing by for the move – up at the top office in ten minutes." It is almost unbelievable that anything should take place on time, after 3½ years of the Jap idea of it, but it was so.

In due course we moved off in two lorries down to Kuching. We passed two small parties of Jap soldiers marching away from the town, still carrying rifles. They looked somewhat dejected, while we of course had fixed grins from ear to ear. On arrival in the town, our Aussie driver and officer escort pulled up at an erstwhile native cafe, now a 9th Div. Canteen and Restroom, where we de-lorried and were given sweet biscuits and tea. We sat in cane armchairs at round tables covered with magazines – the first touch of civilization. I rose to my feet (not without difficulty) to go and obtain a second cup of tea, but a huge Aussie quickly took my mug, that is my 'cup and saucer', off me remarking "Okay pal, sit down, it's your holiday today!" A foretaste of the welcome and kindness to come.

After resting for half an hour, we moved on board an American submarine chaser for conveyance down river and out to the roads. We sang:

"When we sail down the river to the sea,
And this Jail becomes another memory,
When we're free as we were in days of yore,
And we sing as we never sang before.
"Let the Chinese and the Dutchmen and the Dyaks fight about it
They can have their Borneo and we can do without it
When we sail down the river to the sea
There'll be hap-hap-happy days for you and me!"

as we drew away from the wharf, the theme song of the Kuching POWs, written and composed by one of them, and sung at the end of every Concert.

The sub-chaser's galley got cracking for us and produced piles of Vienna sausages (hot) and slices of cheese (iced). It all disappeared as fast as they could hand it up. Very much appreciated.

About 4 p.m. we arrived alongside the American destroyer escort ship, USS DOYLE C. BARNES, D.E. 353, and were duly installed below decks, in cots (3 deep) in spare crew's quarters – it was rather hot. Naturally the officer's quarters or the "Officers Country" as their signs read, could not accommodate so many of us, i.e. 23 British officers, 2 Dutch officers, an Internee doctor from Labuan and four of our batmen. The RAF were represented by myself (again SAFO), Jackson, Rollinson, Pethybridge and the batman, Stridgeon.

After a rather tiring and exciting day, I promptly threw a fit in four spasms. Uncontrollable champing of the teeth, rigours, shouting and sobbing and a copious flow of tears. The Chief Pharmacist's Mate (CPM) was called and hung on to my hands, bathed my brow, etc., until it was over. He informed me later that it was not epileptic, which I was glad to hear. He diagnosed "mental hysteria! due to over excitement and strain while in a low physical condition." I guess that is about right. I had a similar attack about 2 months ago.

So, at 6.30 p.m. when the others went to feed on the Mess-deck, I was helped up on to deck where it was much cooler as we were now under way, and was soon surrounded by a crowd of 'Gobs' (a harsh epithet for damn decent chaps) listening to my story. Shortly, my dinner arrived on a tray (a la American cafeteria style) and the steward who brought it cleared the decks by saying "You guys had better evacuate while this officer gets his supper" and they all very politely "evacuated" until I had finished.

After dinner, when it was dark, they staged a cinema show on the after deck. Tropical night, quite calm, quarter moon, music, friends and free – what more?!

The show started off with a newsreel which kept us PWs gaping like country cousins – the Queen reviewing the WRENS outside Buckingham palace – nearly upset me again. I find I can take great misery better than great happiness.

Between 11 pm and midnight I consumed four enormous beef sandwiches and two cups of coffee, while conversing with a huge Negro steward whose arms at the biceps were as thick as my thighs!

Went to bed about midnight but in spite of tiring day, I could not get to sleep for quite a while, from sheer happiness and relief.

13.09.45: And now to describe the breakfast, the meal we have all been planning and dreaming about for years. The cooks said that the 30 of us consumed as much as the rest of the ship's company, but I think and hope that that was a bit of hyperbole.

Personally I ate a plate of porridge, 4 fried eggs, 2 boiled eggs, 4 rounds of toast, a helping of fried ham, 2 helpings of bubble of squeak, rounded off with toast and jam. Loads of coffee of course (Maxwell House). Jacko and Ronnie managed 9 eggs each and Lt. Harris consumed no less than 18!

For tiffin we were given steak and onions, followed by strawberry ice cream and the American Navy's idea of ice-cream is about half-a-crown portion as

Group: Centre: Lieut. W.R.K. Henley. VX.33025. 2/6 Hvy. A.A. Bty., A.I.F. in Kuching on 2nd day of landing with Commanders of MT Boats, USN.   Pic: W.R.K. Henley

compared to our 3d or 6d. This tiffin defeated some but not me. Admittedly I had to stand up for an hour or so afterwards.

Arrived at Labuan Island about tea time and were taken ashore in two Dukws (amphibian cars) which came alongside the BARNES, then to the beach, (where the 9th Div. had made their landing in June) up on to the road and straight to the 2nd/4th Aust. Gen. Hospital where we alighted or is it 'disembarked'?

The officer's section is three long tents with double roofing and raisable side curtains, containing 28 beds in each. Real hospital beds, with spring mattresses and three pillows. The first time I have slept in a bed since hospital at Changi in September 1942. Pulse this evening 110.

The Aust. Red Cross girls came round and deluged us with comforts, including what they call a dilly-bag containing cigarettes, magazines, newspapers, toilet articles, sweets, chocolate etc. The one who visited us is called Lilian Entwistle. We had already had a free go at the canteen on board the BARNES – so we now have duplicate sets of toilet articles.

14.09.45: Threw nearly all my clothes out for burning this morning, as they were much tattered, scabie-infested, and probably housed a few bed bugs. What was not burnt, was taken away for sterilising.

Had my feet dressed with some new dope which looks like sulphur but ain't.

Had a thorough medical inspection by Lt. Col. Lamphee. He says I need to put on weight – blood count 73. He told me that I should eat plenty of meat and eggs, and yet we have nearly all been put on light diet – strange.

All I got at tiffin today was a spoonful of boiled tripe – stuff I've always disliked! So I filled up on seven slices of bread and jam.

To celebrate the occasion of our release, and to be a real devil, I smoked ten Capstan cigarettes, but didn't see anything in them, so have decided to quit before they become a habit. Also I was given a glass of Australian beer, which left me cold – in fact I rather disliked it!

15.09.45: Was inspected by the dentist after tiffin – he says there are eight extractions necessary, including five stumps. Many fillings required, and finally a plate (or plates) will be made. Store teeth at last!! This is what comes of not visiting the dentist for four years. I have the Japs to thank.

Weight today – 9 st. 1. (127) in pyjamas.

Another batch of our officers arrived this evening, while Rollo and Don

Westwood left by sea to Morotai and thence by Liberator to Australia. I now have Steve Day on my left and Joe Sinnett on my right.

Cabled to Dad this morning – a general cable (same wording for everyone).

16.09.45: What promised to be a dull day developed in the after noon when I was paid a visit by Air Commodore Scherger, the A.O.C. 1st Tactical Air Force, R.A.A.F. and Group Capt. Pierce, his number two. They stayed about half an hour, talking to Jacko and I. When we are allowed out we are invited down to the airfield there to be shown round all the latest crates, and the A.O.C. added "Call in on me and I'll have some beer on the ice for you". He was extremely pleasant and easy going. I said that it had been my intention of calling on him as soon as I could, and as soon as I got some clothes to go out in. He immediately said he would fix us up with an outfit of RAAF tropical campaign uniform, and that he would send up a storekeeper in the morning to get our orders.

Next I brought up the question of money as none of us have anything except worthless Japanese notes. He replied: "Certainly, how much do you want?" Jacko mumbled something about a few dollars just to buy one or two things we needed from the Canteen. The A.O.C. snapped back: "I'll send you $50 each tomorrow."

We yarned away about the relief of Kuching, latest aircraft etc. I showed him my last war pilot's log book, which I had just recently recovered from the Japs and which was lying with some other papers in front of me. He looked through the early pages and said: "Let's see how many hours you did before going solo – Ah! here it is – 4 hours 35 minutes, and I took over 14 hours!"

He informed me that he had been honoured with the command of the Royal Australian Air Force of Occupation in Japan. The arrival of Col. Lamphee terminated the chat with reiterations from the A.O.C. re our visit, clothing etc.

The doctor then had a look at me and decided to move me to a C.C.S. down on the sea coast, about 6 miles away. Jacko and some 18 others are going also. Another step towards home.

Then a pay-sergeant (A.I.F.) arrived and issued us each with an Australian Pay-book so that we can draw pocket money as required. All released PW officers are on the same rate, Two pounds Ten shillings per week, to be debited in due course to our respective accounts. However, the first credit entry in the book was a present from the Australian Government of five pounds Sterling (Six pounds five shillings Aust.)

Posted my third letter to Dad this evening. Free and airmail.

A more filling dinner than usual and I participated in a tin of bully beef at 9 p.m. washed down with a glass of beer – issued to us. It, the beer, tasted alright but did not afford 10% of the thrill of the first piece of bread and butter on August 31st.

Pethybridge returned from a picnic party and tour round, with news of the Sandakan parties which we left behind there in August '43. According to the Japanese admissions, not a soul is left alive of either camp, Australian or British. We left about 500 men with 5 R.A.F. and 5 Army Officers; the Australian party was much bigger.

Those who didn't die of starvation and disease, were killed on the "death march" to Ranau, or shot by the guards for attempting to escape.

Suga, the Jap. commandant of all the POW Camps in Borneo, committed suicide here in Labuan last night. He cut his throat with a table knife, and got his batman to finish him off by crowning him with a beer-bottle full of sand. He saved us the trouble of shooting him. How often have I had to salute and bow to him, and listen to his bombastic speeches. And so perish all aggressors.

17.09.45: The pay sergeant came round again this morning and I drew $30 at $ = 2/11d. Aust. or 2/4d. Sterling.

Eight of us RAF officers and Mockeridge, the batman, were called for and taken to the RAAF Store park to draw kit and clothes. So now we are alright – it it nice to have some new, clean clothes again after wearing rags for so long. Got back to 2/4th AGH for a hurried late lunch, and at 1.45 an ambulance called to take us to the C.C.S. There were about 10 or 12 ambulances in the convoy (one-way traffic on the road in places) and it was very slow and hot. Took us over an hour and a half to do the six miles. The C.C.S. is a canvas camp among the coconut trees along the west coast. One side of our long tent (30 beds) is parallel, and opens on to, the beach. The O/C. is Lt.Col. R.G. Worcester and the name is 2nd/1st Casualty Clearing Station. Not so comfortable as the A.G.H. but more pleasant surroundings. I am now the proud possessor of an electric torch – like a kid with a new toy – after stumbling around in the dark for three years.

Went for a short walk up the beach towards the Convalescent Camp. The beach is used as a highway and loads of lorries, Ducks, Jeeps, motor cycles, ambulances go up and down, to say nothing of bulldozers, carryalls and motor cranes at work there.

A warmish evening (82°) and we were all in bed and lights out by 10.30 p.m. There is a gramophone loud speaker installed up one of the trees, and we had a recital of records, but nearly all "popular" music, which was pretty bum.

18.09.45: General medical inspection again today. Weight 130 lbs. Blood pressure 110/70. Eyesight 6/6. R & L. Ear nose and throat OK. No sugar, no albumen and no worms.

Spent the morning in fitting up my new uniform. Lee and MacIntosh came to visit us in the afternoon – no news. Went for a 3/4 hour walk up and down the beach after high tea. Getting stronger every day. Had a look at my medical record in which I was described as a "thin grey haired man."

Split a bottle of beer with Hobbs in the evening, 20¢ the half. Our ration of beer is two bottles per week only.

19.09.45: Had an examination by another dentist (Capt. Sutton) this morning. He more or less confirmed the AGH man, and proceeded to pull out 3 molars from my right upper jaw, with an injection of procaine first. Mostly came out in bits.

Our Ward had a preliminary inspection by the ADMS (Assistant Director Medical Service) this morning, and at 2.30. Gen. Wootton came round – he asked me how I was, and was I getting enough to eat? Very, very fat and jovial. Visited a few of our men in the evening and afterwards the usual walk on the beach. Concert at night – did not attend.

I was having a swill down in the officers' bath house this morning when suddenly an iguana clattered across the concrete floor and out on the other side. Two or three natives armed with parangs, and many ORs were in full cry after it. It was slain in the dentist's tent – nearly four feet long from head to tip of tail. I leapt upon the seat, like a nervous woman with a mouse in the room!

20.09.45: Dentist again in the morning. Another extraction and drilling for three fillings. Gums rather sore and am on soft diet. The sores on my right ankle have broken out again, due I think to the purple coloured ointment they put on. We are now trying Eusol wet packs. An hour's walk this evening – dead low water.

Sweated very heavily on going to sleep, although it was not particularly hot. Had to change pyjamas – soaked through. Later in the night, it rained in on me and I had to have the sheet changed and dry towels put down. Woke up at "Lights on" (6.30 am) drenched with sweat again. In all, rather a wet night.

21.09.45: This morning, the Sisters invited six of us patients over to 'elevenses' at 10.30. We stayed there an hour and consumed tea and cream cake. Very nice of them.

Wrote my first, and a long letter to Lydia. Rain in the evening no walk.

22.09.45: Dentist at 9 a.m. Two more teeth extracted, making total to date – six. I have a total of 12 fillings to be done. Weight this morning 135 lbs. Had my sores dressed with Penicillin – sulphanilamide powder this afternoon.

Have received confirmation that of the 838 officers and men of the British Army and Air Force (including myself) who were taken to Jesselton in October 1942 only 33 now remain alive of which I am one – obviously.

Went for two walks today. Improving.

23.09.45: Wrote to Iris White this morning. During my walk this evening I saw some Jap prisoners behind the barbed wire. They look much better that way. Most of the Ward seem to have gone to the movies, but I am a bit tired and am turning in early.

24.09.45: Five years ago today I left Shanghai. Wrote to Robin. After lunch, Jacko, Brown, Pethybridge, self, Mockeridge and Folly went in to No. 25 A.S.P. and drew some further equipment, ribbons etc. The officers there (S/L. McGuinness, F/L. Barrow and F/O. Rule) asked us into their Mess for a drink, and on leaving the S/L. presented me with a bottle of gin. Such generosity and an open invitation to dinner. Gave the gin to Jacko. Rather tired after our bumpy trip, so turned in at 8 p.m.

25.09.45: Sewing all morning, fixing up rank stripes, hat pugaree and flash, wings etc. Dentist at 3 p.m. – more drilling, with injection. Then a swim with Jacko – first since Jesselton, found myself pretty fagged after 10 mins. or so. Sister Ling gave me a pair of white cotton underpants (Red Cross issue) to bathe in. I sewed up the front.

26.09.45: Had five fillings done after lunch as it is rumoured we are all off tomorrow, Jacko has arranged dinner at 25 A.S.P. for tomorrow but it looks doubtful now.

These amphibian boat-lorries are called ducks, spelt officially DUKW. Length 31' height 7½' width 8¼' Gross weight 9⅗ tons. Speed on land 50 mph, on water 6 to 7 knots. Engine 34 hp. G.M.C.

Major Dowling (the MO.) came round the Ward about 8 pm and told me that I was not fit to travel. So that's that. None going from this C.C.S., but all from the Convalescent Camp.

27.09.45: At 4.30, Jacko, Pethy and self went into 25 A.S.P. by jeep and had the evening meal with the Mess there. After the meal, we watched them practising cricket in a net cage (wire netting). Then to the movies – a good news-reel, bombing of Berlin and actual fighting in the streets. Labuan after the attack etc. The main picture was "To Have and To Have not". Fair. Went back to their Mess for a couple of whiskey and water, and so home by one of their jeeps. Back at 11.10 – rather tired.

28.09.45: Extract from today's edition of "Platypus" – the local news sheet:

"KUCHING MASS EXECUTION PLAN REVEALED"

"When he arrived in Sydney on Wednesday night (the 26th) with other repatriated ex POWs, Dr. Marcus Clarke of Double Bay, former Govt. medical officer in B.N.B. disclosed that the Jap. capitulation saved 1500 military and civilian prisoners from being butchered by their guards at Kuching last Saturday week.

"Dr. Clarke discovered plans for the massacre among the belongings of a Jap. Lieut. who was one of the camp officers. The papers found named Sept. 15th as the date of the execution" unquote.

We have heard from another Doctor (a German Jew) who has arrived here and is bedded in this Ward, that the above is quite true. The sick and older men were to be shot, and the remainder marched inland – there were to be no survivors. Being the 4th oldest member of our particular camp, I would doubtless have had the privelige of being shot, and probably forced to dig my own grave first.

Yamamoto, the so-called Jap doctor' had been ordered to poison the women and children. (He later admitted this on interrogation.)

Such are the Japanese.

Second inoculation against typhoid today (½cc) and I am feeling it more than I usually do.

Pethybridge and I dry the dishes in the Mess after lunch and tea today and breakfast tomorrow.

29.09.45: After lunch, we all received a hamper (a carton) from the Australian Comforts Fund containing:

1 tin Xmas pudding	1 tin jujubes
1 tin peaches	2 oz. tin tobacco
1 tin salted peanuts	Tube of toothpaste
Pot Shaving cream	Face cloth
Note pad	Booklet
Tin of talc	Housewife
Pkt. Gillette blades	Pkt. cig. papers
and a pkt. of envelopes.	

Had touch of toothache in evening so called on the dentist who was still working at 9 p.m. He fixed me up.

One hour's sharp walk this evening.

30.09.45: Official weight 144 lbs. (10 st. 4 lbs) which means that I have added 9 lbs. in the last 7 days.

At 7.30 p.m. Hay and I walked to the cinema at 9th Div. H.Q. and saw a most interesting Newsreel of the "Kamikaze" (suicide) air attacks on U.S. Aircraft Carrier SARATOGA, taken from on board that ship.

The main picture "Music for the Millions" was one of these 'child prodigy' films, so popular in the States, and which I can't stand. Margaret O'Brien. Sentimental tosh. Walked back again after the show 25 mins. Wrote to Dad 29/30th and posted it today. Still no reply to our cables.

01.10.45: Spent most of the morning drying things out after a very heavy rain storm during the night. Shared my Xmas pudding out at tiffin and found it very good.

About 4 p.m. Lady Louis Mountbatten arrived and inspected the camp. She came into this Ward, and shook hands with all of us in turn, and talked to each of us individually for a minute or so.

Japanese prisoners being marched through Kuching by local constabulary, September, 1945.

261

She was accompanied by various officers from Brigadier down to Captain. Group Capt. (Dr.) Hill, R.A.F., came and sat on my bed and talked for quite a while. He was in Singapore in 1939 and was relieved by W/Cr. Coffey.

In my talk with Lady Louis, I told her that in spite of all our troubles we never had any doubt as to the ultimate outcome of the war. She replied that even so, it must have seemed to be endless (our captivity) and that we must have wondered when the British were going to do something. She said that her husband found it very difficult fighting his way down Burma, with practically nothing.

I guess her age to be 50, although she still has a girlish figure. Her face is somewhat lined.

I pointed to Jacko on my right and Pethybridge and Brown on my left, and said that we were four R.A.F. officers who had been together all through the 3½ years. She made some remark about the good old R.A.F.; sticking together etc.

02.10.45: Packed up and was taken by ambulance, together with Green and Roche, to the Prisoners of War and Internees Reception Camp (commonly known as the 'Con' for Convalescent, Camp) about 1¼ miles along the beach. Another step in the right direction. Settled in, as best we may.

The camp is not very comfortable, nor is the food adequate for us who are all trying to build up the body. A writing room or shed rather is provided, and also a bar. There is an excellent open-air cinema and concert stage.

Walked back to the C.C.S. in the evening to retrieve my black rubber coat which I'd left behind, and to hear the news that W/Cr. Byrne brought. Main points are:

On arrival in England we go straight to Cosforth? (near Wolverhampton) where we are given full details of our financial position – 300 clothing coupons – 600 miles motoring coupons – Ten pounds – and then sent home on 42 days leave on full pay, with double civilian ration cards.

After Leave, report back to Cosforth for very thorough medical overhaul. The R.A.F. are not going to discharge us until we are as fit as when we joined.

Hospital or convalescent home if treatment is necessary. If not, another three weeks leave, still on full pay. Then demobilisation if required (preference given to POWs from the Far East). Granted a present? or gratuity? of:

One day's pay for each month as POW.

One day's pay for each month Service in the East.

If one wants to stay on in the Service – there is no age limit – one is sent on a month's refresher course, then 10 days leave, then posting in U.K. and the first posting is at one's choice as far as possible.

W/Cr. Byrne was a PW himself for four years in Germany. He is flying round the Far East, interviewing liberated RAF personnel. He arrived from Balikpapen this morning and is off to Singapore this afternoon. He holds out a good hope of us being flown home, or part of the way at any rate.

Had a couple of glasses of Australian Port with Ronnie Green – not bad for those who like port, and then on to the movies where we saw "I'll Be Seeing You" – Ginger Rogers and a grown-up Shirley Temple – bunk.

03.10.45: Very small breakfast which I had to help out with biscuits.

Inspected, very perfunctorily, by the doctor, then a walk up to the surf beach, about a mile and a half. Arrived there just in time to catch the duck back again. High tide while walking there, so occasionally I had to make slight detours into the jungle. Came across a notice reading "Danger! Beware Land Mines and Booby Traps". I retraced my steps to the beach, and took my shoes off and paddled.

Was interrogated in the afternoon by Lt. Robertson re experiences as a POW and filled in quite a long interrogation form.

After a very light evening meal I went for a walk on the beach and met one of the Dutch Fathers (ex Kuching) who struck me as a very decent fellow. He is a missionary in Borneo. We watched a Malay woman and boy doping small pools left in the rocks and collecting the stupified fish. They were only tiddlers, but this poisoning by tuba root is commonly used upcountry in the rivers, where big fish are taken.

Joined Roche for continuation of my walk to the surf beach and back. Had a few drinks and then six of us had a feed in our tent with a spare camp bed for a table. Bully, tongue, biscuits followed by peaches and Xmas pudding. All tinned stuff. We were all darned hungry. Turned in at 10 p.m. but was rudely awoken at 12.30 by a drunk OR. who fell over me and my bed, and could not get up again without my assistance. He was looking for hut No. 28 in 'A' lines, not in 'B' (the officers) lines. Helped him home. He has apparently swiped my comb. Didn't get to sleep again till 4.30 – must have been the Xmas pud, or maybe the Australian gin that upset my nerves.

04.10.45: Drew a jersey and a small waterproof kitbag from the Q.M. Stores.

After lunch, I got a lift in a lorry as far as the loading beaches down past the remains of the town of Victoria and from there I hopped a jeep out to the 2/6th A.G.H. Had a talk with Hardie and Jones. Then Hardie gave me a lift in a jeep out to 9th Div. H.Q. where he interviewed the D.A.A.G. We had tea in the H.Q. Mess. Then on with Hardie to 2/1st C.C.S. where we talked with the blokes. Thumbed a lift along to the Con camp, bath, evening meal, walk, change and cinema. "Rainbow Island" – Dorothy Lamour. Rotten.

05.10.45: Went and had a talk with S/Ldr. Birchall (RAAF) for half an hour, about RAF matters and personnel.

Then for a swim at the surf beach – very nice, but too calm. Travelled by the duck ferry service each way. The duck, while there, was towing a surf board around by wheels or propeller as necessary. Walked to C.C.S. and back after tea. No news there. Was introduced in the bar here to Brigadier Lumsden? of the British Marines. He is en-route by air from Melbourne to Singapore for a conference.

Attended a concert given in our camp by the 6th Aust. Div. Concert party. Good show. Supper in our tent and then to bed.

06.10.45: Went for a walk lasting an hour and 40 mins. this evening. Lt. Watts, an ex PW from Bangkok, arrived by plane from Singapore today. He has been sent by W/Cr. Byrne to collect and fly back with the R.A.F. personnel. He has cabled Byrne, and we await the reply.

Had a few drinks with him – gave him supper in our tent, and so to bed.

07.10.45: Spent most of the morning in sorting out my kit – putting the least valuable articles in the suitcase, to be abandoned or left for forwarding, if the weight of our baggage is limited.

Took Watts round the camp for a while in the afternoon, and after tea he and I walked to C.C.S. and back. Weighed myself while I was there 11 stone (154 lbs.) an increase of 10 lbs. in the last 7 days, and 3 stone since the middle of August. A wet and stormy night. Jacko came back with us to sample the Australian gin.

Our tent leaks in several places and the high wind blew the rain in to drench all our clothes and bedding.

08.10.45: Still no reply to Watts' cable and the RAF are still standing by. Met and had a talk with W/Cr. Kay, RAF. He is with B.B.C.A.U. He worked under Air Marshall Welsh for a time. Knows Ruth Welsh also. She is a big shot in the WAAFs apparently.

A quiet and uneventful day.

09.10.45: Third inoculation against typhoid (2cc). To C.C.S. after tea – taking news to them. Saw the dentist and arranged for fittings tomorrow. Walked back and changed, then to movies "Three Fiddlers" (Tommy Trinder). Pretty poor. Supper with Ronnie Green.

10.10.45: To C.C.S. immediately after breakfast and stayed there till tea-time, having impressions and fittings for my new store teeth. Back by 4.30 to hear that we are leaving by air tomorrow morning. Met and had a chat with Capt. MacLaren, one of the six Australian officers who escaped from Sandakan by native boat in the Spring of 1943. There was a party in the Mess to welcome four British Red Cross dames. Did not attend. Supper with Ronnie and to bed at midnight.

11.10.45: Arose at 6 a.m. Finished packing and then had breakfast, the best one we've had while in the Con camp.

Left camp at 7.15 – Hardie, Lee, self, Major Orbell (Paratroops), 6 RAF Other Ranks and 7 Army ORs. Arrived air-strip about 8. Waited till 8.45, then emplaned in a Dakota (31 Sqdn.) We were joined at 9, the take off hour, by Jacko, Pethy, Brown and Wag. Pryce. Altogether 21 passengers with baggage. Airborne 9.10 a.m. and arrived Singapore, (Kallang) at 2.40 (5½ hours). Put our watches back 1½ hrs. All crowded into a lorry and taken out to Seaview Hotel where all the officers except Hardie are to be quartered. Had lunch – unpacked a bit – drew sheets, towels, cigarettes etc. from the stores. Tea and cake supplied by a mobile NAAFI Canteen at 11 and 3 each day.

In the evening Lee and I went for a 2 hour run around in a rotten old taxi which cost us $12, but we considered it worth while. Called at 17 Scotts Rd., – now occupied by an Indian Army cinema Unit.

Absolutely no news or trace of any of my baggage. A Chinese couple were living in my old pavilion. The main house had been repaired after the bombing, but was entirely stripped of furniture. Indian soldiers occupied the servant's old quarters and the room my baggage was left in.

Then out to Tengah aerodrome – two Spitfire Squadrons were stationed there. Saw 2 to 300 Jap. prisoners, a working party, being marched out of the 'drome back to their camp, 3½ miles away. They looked fit, well nourished, but glum. We were told by the guard at the gate that the prisoners work very well.

Gave a lift into town to two RAF men dropping them at the Cathay cinema, and so back to dinner. A proper cold bath after dinner – luxury.

The ENSA put a concert on in the dining hall, but feeling tired I have written this up and now to a real bed.

12.10.45: Went in to Cables and Wireless in the morning and sent a cable off to Dad, reply paid. Looked for RJ's old office but nothing left there. Called Chartered Bank, which had opened this week, and found that my September 1941 pay had arrived on the 10.02.42 and my balance was $150.44. I drew the lot. Lunch at the Monico with Jacko and Lee. Bought a watch for $50 – seems a good bargain at the present high prices, but is probably only worth about $25 to $30. Back to Seaview for tea and dinner. Was introduced to W/Cdr. Byrne. After dinner, 5 of us went to the Great World. Beer there cost $3 per small bottle. Had a dish of Mee-hoon – rather poor. Finished the evening at a roadside stall near the Seaview hotel with a large bottle of beer @ $4.

13.10.45: Jacko, Bruno and I went into town. Coffee and ice cream at the G.H. cafe. Curry tiffin at the Islamic Restaurant in North Bridge Rd. Quite a good feed but the bill was $13.20 for three of us. Had a sleep in the afternoon, then a short walk up Amber Rd.

Talked for 20 mins. or so with a Mrs. Ferguson. Electric lights did not come on until 11 p.m. so had dinner by the light of a couple of torches. A mobile cinema unit put on a show at 8.15 – 16 mm.

The sound effects were hopeless. News reel was interesting, but I went to bed half way through the main picture, as I could not under stand a word being said.

14.10.45: Walked along to Katong village with Jacko and Bruno in the morning. Ice cream and coffee at a cafe there. Visited Beach House and mouched round. At 4 p.m. I walked to the Control Tower on Kallang airstrip, searching for my teeth which were to be forwarded to me by air. Unsuccessful. Saw the Duke of Gloucester's "York" on the tarmac. A huge machine. Also some Liberators, Halifaxes, amphibian Catalinas, and numerous Dakotas (31 Sqdn.) A telegram from Dad arrived in the afternoon, in reply to mine of 2 days ago. The first news from home since we were released – a poor show (everyone else the same). I was very pleased to get it and assume that all is well. After dinner, Jacko, Brown, Pethy, Wag and self went to the Roxy cinema where we were given the Chinese Manager's box – free. He is an old friend of Jacko's. Saw Deanna Durbin in "Nice Girl" an old picture, but good.

15.10.45: We were supposed to leave today, but it is now post poned until tomor-row. Called at the Vehicle Register Office re claiming for my car – told to claim in London. Called at Post Office and searched through the Borneo PW mail – unsuccessfully. After dinner six of us went to the Great World to see

Kuching cemetery, September 1945.

the All-In Wrestling. All lights in Singapore went out at 9.30 p.m. and the entertainment was completed by the light of a Jeep's headlamps. Did not think much of this wrestling, the first time I've seen it. So obviously faked. The taxi broke down on the way back. Started to walk into Singapore in the hopes of a lift. Then it started to rain. In the darkness, I fell into an open drain about two feet deep and skinned my knees. Painful and rather a shock. Got a lift in a Jeep to the Padang, walked in the torrential rain to Raffles Hotel, where we fortunately were lent a small car by W/Cdr. Byrne. The car had no roof or side curtains and by the time we had navigated it, through a solid wall of rain, to the Seaview Hotel we were somewhat wet.

16.10.45: Told to stand by to leave in the afternoon. So all of us packed up. When packing was finished we were told that our departure was postponed, but that we must stand by until further notice.

A dance was held in the Seaview Hotel at night – very crowded and quite a success I gather. Was feeling rotten and aching all over, probably due to my fall yesterday, so went to bed early.

17.10.45: Had a cup of coffee with Hardie and wife at the G.H. cafe with Lee. Called S.V.C. H.Q. and heard that R.J. was safe.

Lunched at Singapore Restaurant with Lee and Wag Price. A Dakota left for Penang and Rangoon this afternoon and took six passengers – no RAF though. Why? Went in to the Rex Hotel at 7.30 p.m. and joined the Hardies and 3 Naval officers for some cocktails (supplied by Navy). Then on to a good dinner at the Monico, specially ordered by Hardie, with beer (supplied by the Navy). After, we went to a dance at the old Dutch Club, now a cafe-restaurant. Finished at midnight. Did not dance as I am too unsteady on my feet. Was kindly brought home to Seaview in the Naval jeep.

18.10.45: Standing by as usual. Wrote to R.J. Slept in the afternoon. At 6 p.m. we were all suddenly shifted out of our room to make space for more women and children due to arrive by air. Moved over to Meyer's flats. At 7, Lee, Pethy, Brown and I went into the Rex Hotel and picked up Hardie. Then on to the Southern Hotel for a Chinese dinner – 10 courses, very good but very expensive. $17 each. Got back about 10 pm to find we are under orders to leave by air tomorrow.

19.10.45: Went over to the hotel after breakfast and found our room still vacant and unswept. More masterly staff work. 11 a.m. packed up and left by 3 ton truck for Kallang air port. Stopped off at the reception centre for lunch. Waited about, called at the Control Tower etc. and eventually boarded a Dakota at 1.45 pm. Door shut at 2 and we had a pretty hot ten minutes while they got the star board engine to start. Airborne, with 18 passengers at 2.12 p.m.

Arrived Butterworth 5.08, but as there was insufficient accommodation for us, we hopped over to Penang Island and landed there 10 mins. later. (Total 3 hrs. 6 mins.) Bussed from plane, in pouring rain, to a sort of Rest House where we spent the night. Most of the party went in to Georgetown after dinner, only 4 of us stayed behind. To bed at 9.30. rather tired.

20.10.45: Arose 6.30, breakfast 7.00, moved off by bus 7.30 and airborne at 8.15 a.m. Same Dakota and crew, but two more airmen passengers making a total of 20, viz. RAF 12 officers 4 ORs, Army 1 Officer and 3 IORs. Arrived Mingaladon airfield (Rangoon) at 2.00 pm after a pleasant uneventful trip (5 hrs. 45 mins.)

A very large airfield – no one to meet us – given lunch of sandwiches in an old brick building. F/L. Monk turned up 2 hrs. after we had landed. Taken to a hospital in a lorry – had to carry our own luggage upstairs, erect our own beds, mosquito nets etc., in a dysentery ward! No consideration shown to us as officers let alone ex POWs -

The reception, treatment and organisation was unbelievably bad or non-existent. I had to ask the patients (ORB) to let me have some dinner – fetch it myself – supply my own eating irons and mug – or I wouldn't have got any. As it was, all the sweet was scoffed before I got there. A very poor show – but who can we appeal to? Imagine putting us under-nourished POWs, who are trying to get our strength back, into a dysentery ward and leaving us to fend for ourselves entirely.

We have been given 2 pkts. of chocolate each – made for World War I I should think. Are we browned off? Everyone but Jacko and I have gone into Rangoon. I found the six hours flying a bit sleep making, so turned in early.

21.10.45: Left hospital at 1 p.m. (Thank God) and trucked to the air strip, where we emplaned on a French Dakota. Took off for Calcutta 1.50 p.m. with 23 passengers. Owing to slight trouble with the port engine, the destination was switched to Jessore where we landed at 5.56 (4 hrs. 6 mins.). Very low clouds, and pouring rain for the last hour. Put up for the night in an officers' Mess. Went to bed about 8 p.m., without dinner, too tired to wait for it.

22.10.45: Arose at 7.30, breakfasted and took off in another Dakota at 9.47. Landed Calcutta 10.17 (30 mins.) Met Wade of Shanghai, in fact he flew with us from Mingaladon to Jessore. He lives at Jessore temporarily, it being the HQs of Force 136 of which he is a member.

We landed at Calcutta because Alipore air strip was U/S owing to the heavy rains. Pouring rain when we landed. No one to meet us, as we expected. After a long wait we were driven in to the Grand Hotel. Another wait and we were then driven out to Belvedere, the Viceroy's palace, which has been taken over by RAPWI (Released Allied Prisoners of War and Internees).

Had a good lunch, and then spent the afternoon visiting all the various authorities who wished to see us. M.O., Pay, Intelligence, Red Cross, RTO etc. Got my Burma and Malayan money changed. Also drew Rs.230. I was vaccinated again, as it had not taken at Labuan.

Settled into our quarters in an Army hut. Quite comfortable and clean. Had a couple of whiskey and sodas with the Quartermaster, Lt. Graham of Wirral, before dinner. A quiet evening talking and so to bed.

23.10.45: Bought fountain pen and lighter, visited Red Cross store, visited "Quiz" room etc.

After lunch we went shopping with a volunteer lady driver, in her car. I was feeling sick and rotten, but managed to stay the course till we got back at 5 p.m., when I went straight to bed. Bought a pair of black shoes and an RAF cap – so feel better equipped. Met Mrs. Hodges at the Army & Navy Store. What an expensive shop. Did not take dinner – feeling rotten and a bit of a temperature.

24.10.45: Spent the entire morning packing and weighing, re-parking a re-weighing, and finally dispatching my suitcase, per parcel post, to Cardross. 21¾ lbs. on which the postage was only Rs.2.8.

Visited the doctor in the afternoon, who sounded my chest and gave me some cough mixture and ephedrine tablets. After dinner, a pleasant classical concert by ENSA in the main hall.

25.10.45: Walked into town, starting at 9.30 – shopping – back by bus at 12.30. We were informed at 1 p.m. that we were leaving by air tomorrow (BOAC Sunderland) and that we should have all luggage and belongings ready to go and be weighed in at 3 p.m.

Shortly after three, we trucked down to the other end of the Chowringhee, up to the 4th floor of a building where the BOAC offices area. Weighed in OK and tickets issued. Arrived back 5 p.m. feeling rotten. (Temp. 101.4°) Went to bed, worried indeed about whether to go or not. However, my problem was solved for me. The whole party is not going, whether it's a cancellation or only a postponement, we know not. No dinner.

26.10.45: A good night's rest and my temp down to normal, thank goodness. Saw Dr. and got further mixture and ephedrine.

Schofield arrived in camp. Under orders to move tomorrow by BOAC as arranged for today. All the other six ex-Kuching officers went to Mrs. Hodges' for dinner, but I stayed behind as I was not quite up to a party. Listened to an American Army Sgt. singing in the main hall after dinner – a nice baritone voice. To bed about ten, but didn't sleep much owing to asthma (slight).

27.10.45: Called 3 a.m., breakfast 3.30, moved off in two trucks 4.30 a.m. Waited at the Great Eastern Hotel for an hour, and then on to Barrakpore, arriving there at a quarter past six. A cup of tea then on board the Short Empire flying boat "Couee":

Airborne	6.50	alighted	Allahabad	9.55	3.05
	10.48		Gwalior	12.33	1.45
	12.45		Rajsamand	2.40	1.55
	3.17		Karachi	6.32	3.15
					10.00

Highest temp. 92° lowest 65° en route.

After filling in application for a further passage to U.K., had tea and cakes, then bussed in to the Army Transit Camp on the edge of the Race Course, via various ports of call en route.

Lee stayed behind in Calcutta with a touch of 'flu, which I think is what I have also. Pethybridge and Brown have decided to go to Bombay by train, so Jacko and I are the only two of our party left. Had dinner in quite a decent officers' Mess and so to bed – very tired.

28.10.45: Sunday. Immediately after breakfast we were told to pack up ready to move, whereto and when unknown.

11 a.m. Seventeen of us with baggage were taken out by lorry to the R.A.F. No.9 transit Camp at Mauripur (about 8 miles out). No one expected us, but they have shoved us into tents – Jacko, Harvey and I sharing a four bed tent. Feeling rotten, had lunch and went to bed. Got up for dinner and back again to bed. The large airfield which adjoins this camp was operating all night, like a busy air port.

We expect to be here about a week as they say a bottleneck has been formed due to the gales in Europe.

29.10.45: Spent the morning drawing RAF battle dress, one suit of winter under-clothes and a blue shirt and collars. Had an early lunch and went to bed for the rest of the day. No tea or dinner. Feeling lousy – cough, upset stomach (100.4°)

271

30.10.45: I took two Aspros last night, which produced a good sweat, and I feel much better this morning. Am dosing myself with Maclean's stomach powder also.

At 1.30, Jacko and Harvey got orders to weigh in preparatory to a take off, per Sunderland at 6 a.m. tomorrow. I tried to get on to the same plane, but without success. It is the first time Jacko and I have been parted since he arrived in Singapore May 1941. A pity, on the very last lap. They are due in England on Saturday. I have been told I'll probably go 24 hrs. later. I hope so.

Was having a drink in the lounge of the officers' Mess about 7 pm., with Jacko and Foley (of Johore) when who should come in and hail me but R.C. Stewart, now a Lt.Col. He is flying home on 61 days leave. Had quite a yarn with him and was very pleased to meet an old friend. He has been through the Burma Campaign with the 14th and 12th Divs. To bed after dinner. I see I shall have to take care of myself for a while. Not as fit as I thought I was. Weight today in KD slacks – 11 stone = 154 lbs.

31.10.45: Jacko and Harvey were called at 3 a.m. and left at 4. Did some washing before breakfast, which was all dry by 11 a.m. At noon I visited the Reception office and found I was due to leave in the afternoon – to be ready 1.45 p.m.

Packed up and moved over to the airfield at 2 p.m. Hung around there, weighing in, tea etc. and eventually boarded a "Liberator". 21 passengers including 7 ex POWs and a supernumary crew of 5.

Rather crowded and no leg room. We all got seats, but upright ones in which I found it impossible to sleep. Airborne at 4.25. The pilot told me he was going to break the journey at Habbaniyah, after 7 hours flying. However, due to bad weather in the Persian Gulf he did not do so and we flew on for eleven hours and a quarter, landing at Lydda 3.40 a.m. on 01.11.45 (Total 11 hrs. 15 mins.) Clocks put back about 3 hrs. after arrival. Messed about with canteen, exchange, finding quarters etc. and finally to bed about 3 a.m. local time, very very tired.

01.11.45: Early tea at 6.30 – did not get up for breakfast, but little sleep was possible owing to the flies. At 2 pm, I went in to Tel-Aviv by truck with a Lt. Walsh (Indian Artillery). A decent young man on his way back from leave. Walked around this entirely Jewish town – everything very expensive – I was unable to get a Thermos which I looked for. Had some excellent coffee and cakes. Caught the 6 pm truck back to camp. (No. 236 Transit Camp No. 3 Wing). Dinner and bed.

02.11.45: Still no news of our draft or I should say my draft (I have been put in charge of it). No. LIB.749s departure. Spent most of the morning trying to obtain a coat to go home in. It seems difficult. Bought a dark scarf from the Curio shop. Had arranged to hitch-hike my way to the Officers Shop at Sarafaud in the afternoon, there to buy myself a trench-coat. Fortunately a friend found out and informed me that they would not sell them to RAF officers. So I'll have to make do with the Singapore Policeman's raincoat. Went for a walk in the evening, then a bottle of stout, dinner and bed.

My draft, with a Col. Hill and Dr. O'Donnell added, is under orders to leave tomorrow evening at 6.40 pm. It looks like being a tiring trip in a Liberator.

03.11.45: Saturday. Packed up and took it easy during the day. At 7, draft LIB.749 assembled at No. 3 Wing office, and moved off to the airfield by truck. Stopped at the Exchange Control and changed our Palestine money for sterling. Hung around for quite a while. Loaded the luggage on board the Liberator and eventually took off at 8.45 pm. I was I/C draft and so got a seat right aft next to Col. Hill. Landed at an airfield, Castel Benito, near Tripoli at 4.30 a.m. after a quiet trip.

04.11.45: Took off again at 5.45 a.m. G.M.T. crossed over Tunis, Sardinia, struck the coast of France somewhere around Toulon and ran into some bad weather. Pilot climbed above it to 18 or 20 thousand feet. Oxygen masks were donned. Crossed the North coast at Cherbourg, over the Channel which looked very calm, and landed at the Transport Command aerodrome at Merryfield, Taunton, 2.00 pm. (Total 16 hours). That makes a total of 56 hours and 12 minutes actual flying time from Labuan to Taunton.

By train from Taunton at 5.15 and arrived London about 9.00 pm. Waited for transport and were then taken to the wrong place. Eventually arrived at the Endsleigh Hotel (an RAF transit camp) where I had a snack, 1/2 pint of draft beer, and stayed the night. Rang up Cardross and spoke to Dad, Rita and Hazel.

05.11.45; Up early and young Binsted, LAC Willgoss, AC.1 Hemmingway, and self, caught the 9.10 from Paddington, changed at Wolverhampton, and arrived Cosford about 1.30. Spent the afternoon and evening being interviewed by various people – medical exam – drew some more clothing etc. Had a long talk with the Accounting officer.

Went to bed after dinner to catch up on my sleep account a bit.

06.11.45: Left Cosford at 10.23 and arrived Paddington about 2.30. Saw the R.T.O. and transport, in the shape of a private car driven by a Red Cross lady, was laid on for me. She drove me right out to Cardross, a great relief as I was worried how to manage with three kit bags.

The journey's end, and thank God.

Lieut. Alan Dant was a member of the Federated Malay States Volunteer Forces and was a resident in Kuching prior to the commencement of hostilities. He remained in Kuching after the Japanese capitulation and was in a position to observe the progress of the War Trials. In 1946 he wrote a Bulletin which was circulated to his colleagues, and the following are extracts of interest:

Copy: News from Kuching

Japanese:

The last Japanese were removed about the end of March and were sent to Labuan en route for Formosa. The only real Japanese we knew were one and all war criminals and were sent earlier from Labuan to Morotai for trial. Amongst the last batch to go direct to Formosa were the half a dozen odd 'good boys', who had been marked down for special treatment. During their internment from September 1945 until March 1946 they had to be separated from the other ex-guards as more than once they had been attacked by their fellows. They included Yoshimura, Takechi (the Bull-Frog), Takko, Nichi and Mori. That they returned home safely to Taiwan and have now been demobbed and are happy is borne out by a letter I have recently had from Yoshimura, written in the most astounding English imaginable, asking whether I was interested in importing soya beans from Taiwan and exporting thence rice, rubber and manufactured goods. He is a little premature, but he has evidently the right ideas.

The Australian War Crimes team worked in Kuching until the end of January and did a very fine job. A full dossier was compiled listing the name of every guard together with every one of his nicknames, his description, his record – good or bad – and what had become of him. I really was pleasantly surprised to see for myself the thoroughness with which these files had been drawn up.

Of the total of about 120 guards, more than 70 had some crime or other ascribed to them, even if it was merely face slapping on one occasion only. There was one instance only of which I have personal knowledge, which was not recorded. One day in June 1945 I saw Takko lose his temper and mete out justice in the Japanese approved method. However I said nothing about it, for otherwise he had an excellent record, and the victim in question was one of the worse specimens of the Dutch O.R. Camp, who in all probability merited a lot more than he received.

The Criminals Themselves:

A few days before Christmas 1945 four officers, Nekata, Ojima, Takino and Yamamota, were all found guilty at Labuan and sentenced to death. Nekata and Yamamota met their due deserts and were hung in Morotai some weeks later. Their crimes were general brutality, torture and causing death, and in the case of the latter misappropriation and deliberate withholding of medical supplies. Ojima's crime was condoning ill-treatment and being responsible for the deaths of prisoners, and his sentence was commuted to five years' imprisonment. The last information I had of Takino, who was charged with failure to supply sufficient food and supplies, thereby causing death, was that he was awaiting confirmation of death sentence from Melbourne. I understand however that as a result of representations by POWs and Internees, a very strong recommendation to mercy had been put forward to the Authorities, and that it was probable that it would receive consideration. This was in April last, since when I have had no news. For myself, if Takino is executed, or given anything more than a purely nominal sentence, I shall not be satisfied that justice has been done.

I was most interested in Suga, and the light in which he was regarded by his own guards. The result of my questions revealed that they all liked him immensely, although they admitted that ex-officio he must be held responsible for all the ill-treatment and brutality. They all firmly believed that he was a 'good man', that he was undoubtedly on the side of the prisoners, and that he could have made things unbelievably worse for us than he did, especially if he had carried out orders. Independent investigation has substantiated beyond a doubt that when things were getting tough from May onwards, *on no less than three occasions he received direct orders to send us all on the much discussed 'death march'*, and that in each case he flatly refused to do so, saying that none would survive. There is no doubt that had he lived he would have been executed, if for nothing else, for his direct responsibility in the Sandakan affair, but I think he would have died honourably as did General Homma and not in the disgrace that was quite rightly handed out to Yamashita, the "Tiger of Malaya". When I left Labuan in September I was convinced Suga had had a "Jekyll and Hyde" personality and he could be, if he wished, the Devil Incarnate. Now, I am quite convinced that but for Suga, not one of us would now be alive. It has been proved, in contradiction to the rumours believed while we were in camp, that he had no official connection with the Kempe Tai.

My conclusions regarding Suga have been reached from three different sources: talking with our late Japanese guards, discussions with War Crimes Investigators who have attempted to get every story corroborated, and, most important of all, conversations with civilian Chinese and Malays to whom Suga constantly appealed for help in his endeavours to obtain better treatment for us. He undoubtedly had faults, but I think we owe him a great deal.

With regard to the NCO's, some have met their deserts, others I feel have been dealt with harshly. Life sentences were given to Shimitzu (Clark Gable), Yoshimota (Fred Archer) about whom I am sorry, and the 'Sailor', whilst fifteen years was handed out to Kogo (The Bear), Uwabe (The Sword Swallower), Osakasa (Henry), Beppo, Myamota (the Medical Sergeant- Major), Furnunisi, the 'ex-Ensign' assistant paymaster, and 'Conscientious'. Some of these are undoubtedly harsh, for I think we did receive some measure of protection from them. Still we shall never know exactly what did go on "up at the top" in the Japanese lines, and it is certainly better that they should be over-punished than that they should receive too lenient treatment.

The "plums" received varying sentences, in accordance with the enormity of their offences, ranging from life to a few months only.

Inagaki and Kubu, the Interpreters, were given Life. Sometimes I think they should both have died, at others I reflect that possibly life imprisonment will make them suffer more. Against this latter, there is always the fear that they will receive far better treatment as prisoners than we did – they will be kept short of nothing and the only thing they will lose is their freedom. Probably in the unhappy event of their ultimately being transferred to serve their sentences in civil prisons in Japan, they will receive preferential treatment and in any event I am convinced that, as sure as fate, before many months have elapsed, there will be a general amnesty and they will be completely free again. On the other hand, for those who like myself are afraid that British justice does not always deal out sufficiently harsh treatment where it is deserved, it gives me genuine satisfaction to report that both Inagaki and Kubu were last seen behind wire in Morotai as late as April being driven round the compound by a relay of suitably equipped Australian M.P.s and were, in fact, "going through it" daily, in no uncertain degree.

The only man who has apparently escaped his deserts is friend Hidato, of fond memory. He is listed in the official record as "having escaped from custody in Kuching early in October 1945". He has apparently wandered off into the interior and defied all attempts to locate him. The Officer-in-Charge of War Crimes was a bit worried because he could not get a suitable description and was afraid that he would not be able to identify Hidato. He was very pleased when I assured him that whatever disguise the gentleman adopted I should pretty soon be able to spot him. Ultimately he is bound to be caught for as there are now no Japanese left officially he will eventually be found.

About ten of the harmless Japanese successfully pleaded that they were Sarawak born and had never been away from Kuching all their lives and so were permitted to stay when the mass exodus took place. Among these were the Contractor, Fukumaru, now deprived of his profiteering and poor little Iwanaga who has now lost another 2 inches round his waist. The latter has been in to see me three times asking for a job, but whilst I have nothing particular against him, I have many objections to having a Japanese working in my office.

Nothing could have pleased me more than his comment about Colonel Suga which coincided with my own assessment of this man. He had finally had to accede to the demands of higher authority and planned for us to go on a "death march" on September 15th. Only the atom bomb had saved us and so we must be included in those thousands who owe it their lives which would owe it their lives which would have been lost had the war continued longer.

Sandakan
July 1942 – August 1945

Captain Moffitt stated at the trial of Captain Hoshijima Susumu:

"Hoshijima, at first a Lieutenant and later a Captain, was in charge of the Compound and PW labour at the 'drome from the time of their arrival in August 1942 until the middle of May 1945; he was, in fact, in charge of the actual construction of the 'drome.

"He is directly responsible for 1100 deaths which occurred while he was in charge but is indirectly responsible for 1290 other deaths for he handed all these men over to the command of Captain Takakuwa and within two months they had all perished except six. 470 went on the first march to Ranau at the end of January 1945; 536 on the second march on 29 May 1945. Many were slaughtered or died on the way and others died soon after arrival. 75 prisoners were sent on the third march and they too died. The men who were left behind at Sandakan were too sick to move and were all dead within six or eight weeks of Hoshijima leaving.

"Hoshijima had to construct an airfield, which he did, but his policy was to feed the healthy for they could work and to ignore the pleas for food from the sick and starving. When Major Flemming complained to him of his policy Hoshijima replied that the sick were of no use, they could not work, the Red Cross Convention was of no consequence, the men were all under the rule of the Japanese Army and must obey him.

"The construction work was finished on 10 January 1945, the Japanese policy was one of when the job was done the prisoners became an encumbrance and were not worth feeding. This story is one of amazing spirit, comradeship, sacrifice and ingenuity amid this barbarity.

"Food and medicines in 1945 were not plentiful at Sandakan but the PWs never need have died. The shortages are used as an excuse for this tragedy but the facts will show that there was no desire or attempt to keep the PWs alive; in fact Hoshijima admitted that while 1100 men perished, not one Japanese died.

"There are four charges against Hoshijima:

"The First Charge – refers to a special type of extreme torture in a small cage devised by Hoshijima in which a number of PW, possibly 15, died.

"The Second Charge – relates to the flogging and brutality meted out to the PWs over three years; men were maimed and the harsh treatment did vitally contribute to the final tragedy. It would have been bad enough for fit men but for sick and tired men it meant the final physical and mental breakdown.

"The Third Charge – refers to the systematic denial of medical supplies to hundreds of bed-ridden and dying PWs over the whole 2-1/2 years and to the starvation of the PW from June 1944 onwards.

"The Fourth Charge – refers to forcing sick men, cripples, people suffering ulcers, beri beri, malaria and dysentery with savage beatings to do heavy work thus ensuring their certain deaths.

"There were three Compounds: No.1 Compound held the original 1496 Australians; No.2 Compound 750 English and No.3 500 Australians who arrived later. All the Compounds were in the same area. When the 320 went to Kuching, No.3 Compound in September 1943 was shifted into No.1 and No.3 was used as a hospital for PWs. In October 1944, the hospital was moved back to No.1 Compound. There is no survivor from No.2 Compound so we cannot say what happened there up till 1945. The death rate was much higher in that Compound. Evidence is given by the 320 who marched out earlier for brutality was well under way in 1942 and 1943.

"Hoshijima admits the rice cuts with lack of medical supplies were responsible for many of the deaths. After June 1944 when there was a rice cut the men still worked on; deaths increased. From August 1942 to September 1944 about 120 Australians and 90 Englishmen died. Coffins were made for the men to about June 1944 when the death rate outstripped the PWs assigned to make coffins; PWs were then buried naked without coffins.

"When the military airfield work was finished the PWs were then put on to gardening, bomb disposal and wood carrying. No further rice was officially issued to the PW at the Compound after 10 January 1945. Japanese rations remained the same. The PWs had managed to save 170 200 lb. bags of rice to meet any emergency, these they held in their own store and the Japanese owed them a credit of 70 bags. The only rice issue they were given was these 70 bags; the PW used 20 till they went to Ranau in May, 30 were taken from them and issued as 10 days rations as they left on the march. The other 23 bags were left behind for the PWs too sick to move.

"In January-February 1945 the issue was just under 100 grams of rice per day per man (about 3 ounces). Later it dropped to 2 ounces a day compared with the 17 ounces a day they were getting when airfield construction was at its height. Hoshijima admits this change-over from rice to soft watery foods caused deaths.

"The officer in charge of the 'Q' Store at Sandakan, Arai, says from January to March 1945, rice issue was 300 grams for working PWs and 200 for sick, this was issued in bulk each month to the Compound and it was left to the Japanese to make the division; the PW never got their rice issue. It was Hoshijima's responsibility to see the rice issue was given to the PWs but his job was done, the airfield was completed and there was no need to feed the PWs.

"There can be no question of superior orders or general scarcity of food as an excuse; when the PWs were starving the Japanese at the Compound had more rice and other food than they wanted. They continually had rice or other food left over after a meal. Figures will show they were getting more than their ration – they were eating the PWs food.

"As soon as the rice issue was completely cut in January 1945 the death rate sky-rocketed and in March 1945, 317 PWs died (221 Australians and 96 English); deliberate massacre by starvation. Because of the so-called 'scarcity of rations' at the end of March Q.M. Arai discussed with Hoshijima officially cutting out the PW rice issue to the Compound; Hoshijima raised no objection and said: "If H.Q. approves that is alright with me". H.Q. did approve the recommendation but Hoshijima had already cut the rice issue of his own accord.

"There was a meat ration for PW in 1945 but they never received it. Beasts were killed but all went to the Japanese; the PWs got the entrails only and even then the heart and liver had been removed. In 1945 they only got six meals of maggotty fish; the men lived on watery food made of potato leaves, watercress, potatoes and tapioca. Arai issued many things for the PWs but they never got beyond the Japanese store. Hoshijima forbade trade with the local people who had fruit and fish and were willing to sell to the PWs. Men were flogged and caged for trying to buy food or who were caught trying to creep through the wire to get potatoes for their dying mates.

When the PWs were leaving Changi they were told there would be plenty of medicines at Sandakan for them however they did take unofficially 5 boxes of medicines which was very little for the number of PWs. Throughout their whole three years at Sandakan, despite complaints to Hoshijima, they received virtually no medical supplies from the Japanese. Men died with beri-beri, dysentery and malaria with little or no medical attention. Hoshijima's excuse was that there was no medicine available but he made no effort to acquire any. Doctor Taylor, a doctor from the Civilian Hospital which he ran until July 1943 said that when the PWs arrived in Sandakan he had enough drugs and medicines to do the whole of British North Borneo for two years. He requested permission to give medicines to the PWs but Hoshijima refused saying he was getting supplies in by air but none came. Dr. Taylor arranged for small amounts of medicine to be smuggled into the Compound, this was usually done by giving the small amounts to the Padre or Army Doctor at the burial services. Late in 1944 30 large boxes of medicine marked "U.S. RED CROSS" arrived at the Compound and were put in the Japanese Store. The Japanese refused to issue the stores to the PWs and the guards traded medicine and vital quinine to the desperate PWs for their watches and clothes. It was British quinine.

"The sick cannot work – let them die – was Hoshijima's policy. Malaria took terrific toll of these weekend men. Men in the cage out in the open all night were only allowed their loin-cloths. No blankets or mosquito nets were permitted although some of them owned them. The ground area was swampy and there were thousands of mosquitos.

"When Sandakan was taken from the Japanese there were about 160,000 quinine tablets there – sufficient to treat many thousand cases of malaria. One night, Captain Picone, the Army Doctor, was about to do an urgent operation on a burst duodenal ulcer. As there was no Japanese guard about he borrowed a globe from the guard room. He was beaten, then made to stand to attention for two hours outside the guard room while the patient waited. Hoshijima's attitude was obvious.

"Sick men were driven to work both on the airfield and in the garden. If there insufficient fit men a Japanese private would make a medical inspection and order men onto the job. Doctors who objected to this treatment of the sick were beaten; men with bandages on their ulcer or on any part of their body were kicked and beaten on the bandaged area to see how bad it was. Cripples were beaten with their own rough crutches to make them work harder. 'No Duty' men were given what the PW knew as 'sun-treatment' which meant they would be forced to stand and stare at the sun. One occasion the reason for this was that their officer endeavoured to have them removed from the 'heavy duty' to the 'light duty' section of the airfield. On another occasion all sick who could walk, doctors, orderlies and cooks, except two or three, were sent to the airfield to work leaving 300 bed patients without attention. Some of the sick had to be assisted there. Hoshijima saw them at the airfield. Food cuts for the whole Compound were used for punishment of one or two men for offences. All this harsh treatment on starving, sick overworked men hastened their deaths.

"Hoshijima approved the construction of a punishment cage in the Compound in 1942. It was 4'6" x 5'6" x 4'6" high; men could not stand up or lie down properly at night; the floor was bare boards, the walls were two inch sticks two inches apart. The PWs were exposed to all weather conditions and the mosquitoes. To get into the cage the prisoner had to crawl and the terms of imprisonment ranged from a few days to 30 days. A larger cage was built later and some PWs were sentenced for the duration, serving most of their time there. They had no blankets, no mosquito net and wore only their loin-cloth. For the first seven days they would receive no food and then only limited food; they were made to sit strictly to attention all day – being taken out and beaten if they relaxed. They were only allowed to go to the latrines twice a day and had to urinate through the bars. They were taken out twice a day for 'PT' which consisted of beating with sword sticks; often men had to be carried back to the cage. Sick men, men with hands bound behind their back, were put in the cage. On one occasion seven PWs were in this tiny cage for four days, one man actually died as a result of his treatment while there. His weight fell from 12 stone to 6 stone in 15 days, he did not die from disease. Two others were taken out to die and did die within a day or two of release; about 15 men died because of this treatment and they were all put in the cage on Hoshijima's express order.

"Tortures and beatings were a daily occurrence for three years. Hoshijima employed four men as bashers with sword sticks to flog the men and to drive them to work harder and harder at the airfield. For laziness or fancied laziness by one or two men, whole parties of 50 or 60 would be lined up, made to stand to attention then bashed on the back, face, or any part of their body, with sticks, hoes, rifle butts or canes. Some were deliberately kicked in the testicles; then they were made to stand looking directly at the sun, without hats or shirts, holding their hands sometimes with weights in them straight out in front. This procedure sometimes lasted for more than an hour. Officers were treated the same. Two men had their eyes knocked out, one having his eye gouged out by Hoshijima himself. Many had their teeth knocked our or jaws broken, Hoshijima saw many of these beatings but never tried to stop them, in fact, he admits he did a lot of the beating himself. His favourite trick was to make an officer stand to attention and 'king hit' him, after knocking him back to his feet with kicks he would repeat the performance two or three times.

Hoshijima stated that superior orders and shortages prevented the supply of food and medicine but he did absolutely nothing to remedy the position, in fact, he deliberately withheld food and medicines available to him for the PWs. His policy throughout that the sick were useless, an encumbrance, and should not be fed and when the airfield was completed the PWs would no longer be needed and there would be no point in feeding them as they could not serve the Japanese Army shows his true attitude towards the PWs.

"There have been many PW camps in this war with grim records, but the name of Sandakan PW Camp and the tragedy it represents will live as a blot on the barbaric Japanese Army. The man responsible stands before the Court; this sadist, although his method of slaughter was more subtle, ranks with the Beast of Belsen."

Captain Hoshijima Susumu was hanged at Rabaul on 6 April 1946.

Summary of Military Court Proceedings
Dealing with Japanese War Criminals

Members: L/Col. R.T. Cochrane, AASC 9 Aust. Div.
L/Col. J. Maxwell-Hall, BBCAU
Maj. A.J. Greville, HQ 9 Aust. Div.

Convened by: Brig. W.J.V. Windeyer

Place of Assembly: Labuan

Court Siting:

Prosecuting Officer: Lt. R. Balzer, HQ 9 Aust. Div.

Defending Officer: Maj. Matsumura, Susumu
Capt. Eto, Kunihiko
Col. Yamada, Setsuo
HQ 37 Japanese Army

Charges: (1) ILL TREATMENT OF PRISONERS in that they at Kuching between 15 May 1942 and 20 Aug. 45 being officers of the Borneo Prisoners of War and Internees Guard Unit having the custody and charge of prisoners of war and civilian internees ordered, authorised and permitted men under their command to make frequent cruel assaults inflicting grievous bodily harm on the said prisoners and internees.
(2) ILL TREATMENT … civilian internees denied to the said internees and prisoners sufficient food, medical supplies and medical attention whereby many of the said prisoners and internees died.
(3) ILL TREATMENT … civilian internees forced certain of the said prisoners of war and civilian internees when sick and starving to do heavy manual labour whereby many of the said prisoners and internees died.

AWC	Accused	Finding	Sentence	Remarks
792	Nakata, Takito	Guilty	Death by Shooting	Capt.
802	Ojima, Takao	Guilty	Death by Shooting	1/Lt.
836	Takino, Motoi	Guilty	Death by Shooting	Capt.
859	Yamamoto, Katsuji	Guilty	Death by Shooting	Lieut.

Trial No. 14.
SUMMARY OF PROCEEDINGS
OF AN AUSTRALIAN MILITARY COURT

Court Convened by: Brig. T.C. Eastick

Place of Assembly: Labuan

Date of Trial: 22nd January 1946 to 31st January 1946 (both dates inclusive).

Member: Maj. A.J. Greville, HQ 9 Aust. Div.

Maj. B.C. Blackburn, HQ 9 Aust. Div.

Capt. G.H. Dow, HQ 9 Aust. Div.

Prosecuting Officer: Lt. R. Balzer, HQ 9 Aust. Div.

Defending Officers: Maj. Matsamura Susumu

Capt. Eto, Kunihiko

HQ 37 Japanese Army

Notice of petition against finding and sentences lodged.

Petition against finding and sentences lodged.

Charge: VIOLATION OF THE LAWS AND USAGES OF WAR in that they at Kuching between 15 May 1942 and 12th September 1945 when members of the Borneo Prisoner of War and Internees Guard Unit engaged in guarding prisoners, namely, prisoners of war and internees did frequently assault and cruelly beat certain of the said prisoners in violation of the Laws and Usages of War.

AWC	Accused	Finding	Sentence	Remarks
817	Shoji Kuraji (S/M)	Guilty	Imprisonment for 1 year	
778	Matsutaka Katsushi (S/M) "Potato Jones"	Guilty	Imprisonment for 7 years	
759	Kogo Shigeru (Sgt.) "Bear Banjo Bill"	Guilty	Imprisonment for 20 years	
701	Asakusa Katsuji (Sgt.) "Ash Can Harry"	Guilty	Imprisonment for 15 years	
739	Inagaki Tetsuo (Lt.)	Guilty	Imprisonment for 10 years	Interpreter
764	Kubo Akihiko (Lt.)	Guilty	Imprisonment for Life	Interpreter
766	Kyogawa Tomio (Gd.) "Big Pig" "Benny Lynch" "Basher"	Guilty	Imprisonment for 15 years	
767	Kyose Norisuke (Gd.)	Guilty	Imprisonment for 10 years	
773	Matsuda Takeishi (Gd.) "Junior Ball Kicker"	Guilty	Imprisonment for 15 years	

AWC	Accused	Finding	Sentence	Remarks
805	Okamoto Keimei (Gd.) "Myrna Loy" "Weasel"	Guilty	Imprisonment for 15 years	
742	Ishimoto Yoshio (Gd.) "Stammering Steve"	Guilty	Imprisonment for 15 years	
845	Tsuda Seiji (Gd.)	Guilty	Imprisonment for 10 years	
705	Fujimoto Yoshio (Gd.) "Halitosis Harry"	Guilty	Imprisonment for 3 years	
825	Tagawa Nobuyuki (Gd.) "Intercourse" 'Little Col" "Little Gen"	Guilty	Imprisonment for 10 years	
823	Suzuki Nomobu (Gd.) "Makan Basher"	Guilty	Imprisonment for 15 years	
863	Yasumoto Yoshio (Gd.) "Ball Kicker" "Maggots" "Conjuror"	Guilty	Imprisonment for 20 years	
719	Hayama Takeo (Gd.) "Fish Face" "Joe Louis" "Gold Tooth" "Gold Pisa"	Guilty	Imprisonment for 10 years	
771	Matsuda Buichi (Gd.) "Smiler"	Guilty	Imprisonment for 7 years	
741	Ishii Hideo (Gd.)	Guilty	Imprisonment for 15 years	
829	Takamura Shoji (Gd.) "Lantern Jaw" "Moon Rat"	Guilty	Imprisonment for 10 years	
838	Tokuda Masatake (Gd.) "Knocky"	Guilty	Imprisonment for 15 years	
770	Matsubayashi Takeo (Gd.) "Roman Nose"	Guilty	Imprisonment for 10 years	
828	Takami Tsuneo (Gd.)	Guilty	Imprisonment for 5 years	
754	Kimura Seijiro (Gd.)	Guilty	Imprisonment for 15 years	
790	Nagayoshi Seiichi (Gd.) "Kick the Can"	Guilty	Imprisonment for 3 years	
753	Kawamura Katsuo (Gd.) "Black Horse" "Pig Man"	Guilty	Imprisonment for 10 years	

AWC	Accused	Finding	Sentence	Remarks
746	Kaneko Shigemori (Gd.) "Cemento" "Tinkle"	Guilty	Imprisonment for 15 years	
738	Imagawa Masamune (Gd.) "Big Marmite"	Guilty	Imprisonment for 12 years	
750	Kato Tadeo (Gd.) "No.1 Ball Kicker" "Hands Up"	Guilty	Imprisonment for 15 years	
706	Fujimura Shigeru (Gd.)	Guilty	Imprisonment for 10 years	
834	Takenaga Shigematsu (Gd.) "Colorado Kid"	Guilty	Imprisonment for 5 years	
758	Kobayashi Terue (Gd.) "Pimples" "Pock Face"	Guilty	Imprisonment for 12 years	
788	Nagamura Eiki (Gd.)	Guilty	Imprisonment for 7 years	
749	Kasama Eiji (Gd.)	Guilty	Imprisonment for 7 years	
807	Okabayashi Takemitsu (Gd.) "Grass Cutter" "Moon Face"	Guilty	Imprisonment for 15 years	
707	Fujita Yoshio (Gd.) "Woman Beater" "Little Marmite"	Guilty	Imprisonment for 3 years	
839	Tomibayashi Teruo (Gd.) "Tommy Bash"	Guilty	Imprisonment for 3 years	
867	Yoshida Koichi (Gd.)	Guilty	Imprisonment for 7 years	
831	Takeda Jiro (Gd.)	Not Guilty		
806	Okamura Yoshiaki (Gd.) "The Eyetie"	Not Guilty		
804	Okamoto Shozo (Gd.) "Steady"	Guilty	Imprisonment for 3 years	
818	Sugiyama Seiichi (Gd.)	Guilty	Imprisonment for 10 years	
713	Fukushima Kenji (Gd.)	Not Guilty		
760	Koike Yasushi (Cpl.) "Hospital Pig" "King Kong"	Guilty	Imprisonment for 10 years	
815	Shimizu Kanji (S/M.) "Bottle Legs" "Spann" "Papaya Legs"	Guilty	Imprisonment for 7 years	

Chapter Eight

SANDAKAN

After the Destruction of the Camp

After the departure of the second march and the burning of the Camp, the Japanese were also burning the last of the buildings in and around Sandakan town. By this time, what was once the capitol of Sabah was now a smoking ruin.

The prisoners left at the Camp site had no cover, no medical supplies, little food and no hope. They were left exposed to the elements. General Baba said at his Trial he ordered the prisoners to be cared for and when they recovered from their illness and ill-health, they were to rejoin those at Ranau.

It was General Baba's 37 Army Senior Staff Officer who ordered the destruction of the Camp including medical supplies, Camp records and that no medical officers were to remain with those men left behind.

Initially all prisoners were herded into No.1 Compound and, after the departure of the 75 in what is described as the third march and the massacre of 23 who were taken out to the old English camp site near the airfield and murdered, the remainder were moved into the No.2 Compound in open space opposite the Japanese guard house. It was in this locality where a large number of graves were found.

Lieut. Moritaki, who was second in command to Takakuwa, was absent when the second march departed he returned to the camp site on June 1st. Some reports stated he had been to Jesselton, however it was known he was at Kemansi to investigate the possibility of establishing a camp for the PWs. Takakuwa would have conveyed instructions to Moritaki to dispose of the prisoners

There is no record of what Moritaki was up to for the first ten days in June; S/M. Morozumi testified he received orders from Moritaki to send the 75 on the third march and to massacre the 23.

There is evidence Moritaki would have disposed of those senior PWs left at the camp – prisoners he had known for over two years, the keeper of hospital and camp records, the administrators.

It was known all forms of identification were removed from the prisoners, War Graves personnel are reported to have found a large number of identification tags in a hollow log; records were burnt. The scene was set to destroy all evidence, even the bass saxophone belonging to the English Compound was later found in a mass grave; Moritaki would have been ordered to oversee the disposal of the prisoners and their records.

Ikido Yoshio, one of the guards left behind in the camp with Morozumi, claimed to have accounted for the 292 POWs too ill to be included in the second march. He confirmed Lieut. Moritaki returned from Kemansi on 1 June. Ikido was not questioned on Moritaki's activities from the time of his return to 10 June, when 75 PWs were rounded up, without any belongings, and were last seen in diminishing groups – they would have commenced killing these 75 PWs once they reached the jungle track: it was in this general locality many remains were later found. (A member of the War Graves Unit recalled finding the bodies of an Australian and a Japanese by the side of the track and a heavy stick with a nail in the end nearby.)

Frequent inspection of the pitiful prisoners was carried out and, as they died, they were thrown into drains and covered over with earth. It was the camp site which was described by the War Graves Unit as the No.3 Cemetery, some were buried in a circle.

The various statements by Morozumi and his 16 Formosan guards make no mention of Moritaki's activities up to the time of his death on 18 July except that he was the responsible officer and that he was suffering from malaria.

Colonel Cummins' Sandakan Force of 1100, now under Major Gannon, arrived there on three R.A.N. Corvettes on 9 September 1945. His first concern was to establish whether there were any POWs located at the 8 Mile Camp. Colonel Otsuka informed him that the last PW died in early August and the Japanese responsible for guarding the POWs had left the area for Jesselton.

The 3 Australian Contact and Enquiry Unit, under Captain Cocks assisted by Lieut. E.K. Robinson and with him Captain Houghton of 23 War Graves Unit and other assistants, arrived at the camp site to carry out an investigation into the fate of the POWs left at the camp site after the 536 POWs were taken on the second march and the graves of those who died earlier in the established Cemetery in the camp.

Assisted by Japanese prisoners a thorough search was made of the area and a considerable quantity of pay-books and relics were found. Captain Houghton located No.2 Cemetery and opened a cross-section of the graves; he reported that many of these contained only one body however some contained as many as eight. Lt.Col. Johnstone, 9 Field Ambulance, was present when these graves were opened and he estimated the bodies had been there four or five months. (The graves containing 8 bodies may have contained those murdered after the departure of the second march.)

The War Trials of those Japanese responsible for the fate of the PWs in Borneo were now nearing an end; Captain Hoshijima and Captain Yamamoto were hanged at Rabaul on 6 April 1946. The 8 Military District, with its Headquarters at Rabaul, was now the responsible military authority for this area. All the Japanese convicted were now at Rabaul, some were appealing against their sentence. Amongst these were Sgt.Maj. Morozumi and twelve guards who had been convicted for the massacre of 23 of those left at the 8 Mile Camp. Morozumi received a life-sentence; he claimed that he was carrying out orders given to him by Lieut. Moritaki who was the officer in charge of the camp, at that time 1st/Lieut. Iwashita took 75 PWs who could walk on what is described as the third march; evidence is that there was only one Japanese survivor from this group who reached Ranau – it was Lt. Suzuki who was later shot by a disgruntled guard; the last of these 75 PWs allegedly were seen in the 42 Mile locality.

The British Borneo Civil Administration Unit moved into Sandakan in October 1945 after the Occupation troops moved out and Captain A.A. Rowland, who had been interned at Kuching, was placed in charge of the North Borneo Constabulary; now he too set about his own investigation into atrocities committed during the Japanese Occupation.

The Prosecutors returned to Australia in March 1946 – no further War Trials were conducted from Labuan, this responsibility now came under the 8 Military District, Rabaul; the War Crimes Section in Singapore were still interested in investigating crimes carried out in Borneo by the Japanese.

War Crimes investigators must have lost interest at this time in not providing a dental officer to accompany the War Graves Unit on the massive task of recovering those murdered by the guards who were now in detention at Rabaul.

After 50 years, War Graves personnel have been interviewed to try and ascertain other crimes which may have occurred after the departure of the second march. It is established that Moritaki was absent when the second march departed, however, it is documented he returned to Sandakan on June 1st. It is likely that Moritaki would have received orders to kill the remaining prisoners. It has been established through the evidence of Morozumi that he received orders from Moritaki to dispatch all those who could walk on the third march, after which they rounded up the remaining PWs who were taken to a rubber plantation near the airfield and massacred.

The sadistic Moritaki would have made up his mind to dispose of the senior PWs, those responsible for keeping records and who were witnesses to atrocities committed, the rescue of whom, in the event of an Allied invasion, would cause the Japanese great embarrassment.

When the 31 War Graves Unit first arrived at Sandakan at the end of March

1946, they were the only troops stationed in the area. The strength of the Unit was about 15, initially they were accommodated under canvas until Captain Johnstone received permission to construct huts using local materials. He wasted no time in surveying a site for the Cemetery and, with the assistance of about 100 Javanese who had originally been brought from Java as prisoners, cleared large areas of ground searching for graves.

Within a short time the area for No.1 Cemetery was cleared and the inexperienced Unit now began the ghastly task of recovery. The men were still sleeping under canvas; one night a scream woke the camp – the men raced down to the tent from where the scream had come to find a shocked digger who explained he had had a dream. His mates asked him what had happened and he told them that a cloudy misty figure had appeared by his bed and said to him: "Don't be frightened – the Japanese killed me – my name is so and so – and they buried me down the 8 Mile near a big tree not far from the side of the road." Before everyone settled down again for the night, Lieut. Brazier made a note of the man's dream; next day he took Ray Battram and two Javanese down the road where they cleared an area, found a depression and began digging – here they found the remains of an Australian together with his pay-book.

Work commenced in May 1946 in establishing a new Cemetery on what was the site of the aerodrome.

Sandakan Cemetery: "a little track … came to a cross with a plaque …"   PIC: AWM.

The evidence given by Ikida that there were 292 left behind in the camp when Takakuwa testified there were 288; it is likely Moritaki, having known the responsible POWs since 1942, would have decided to give the leaders an honourable execution and arranged for the Javanese labourers to prepare graves at the entrance to the No.1 Cemetery several hundred yards down the road, this locality would dispel any thoughts of murder.

From evidence given by Battram, who actually recovered over 600 remains in No.1 Cemetery, it is obvious they were not fully aware of the historical background of the last days at the camp; he stated: "There was a little track, just a little foot-pad, leading up to the ridge to the Cemetery where there was a cross on which there was a small plaque made from a mess-tin and it was engraved "To The Memory of British & Australian Fallen in Malaya". (sic).

This little plaque was actually at the entrance to the Cemetery. He continued: "Nearby I found a group of several separate graves containing remains which had been beheaded." Battram was certain of the execution because he remembered some of the skulls showed it had taken more than one stroke to kill them and the skull was separated from the body.

Arriving at the burial sites, as was the practice of the Japanese, each man would have been blindfolded and placed by his grave. The Japanese would have considered the ceremonial execution an honourable way to die – Moritaki would have felt more relaxed having removed the leaders of the camp; it is likely he would have committed many other atrocities during early June.

It is known there were only three or four Japanese in the area during this period with rank qualifying them to carry a sword: Lieut. Moritaki; 1st/Lieut. Iwashita (who left Sandakan on June 11 with the 75 PWs on the third march); Sgt.Maj. Morozumi and Hinato Genzo of the Kempe Tai.

It seems this ceremonial execution would have been known to others and may have been known to 37 Army Command; as Staff Officer Colonel Takayama stated during War Crimes proceedings: "They were out of communication with Sandakan until June 10 following the PT boats' attack on May 27" – a statement made to avoid any knowledge of what was happening at Sandakan.

There is a discrepancy of about 50 not accounted for on the camp site; it appears those 50 were disposed of by Moritaki in early June and this may account for the 8 to a grave in No.2 Cemetery and the discovery of those beheaded at the No.1 Cemetery.

The 23 and 8 War Graves Units first carried out a reconnaissance of the death march route and left markers identifying the remains where they found them, their men were instructed to locate only as a Searcher and the Recovery Party would follow later. Recovery was determined by weather conditions and at this time most of the work was carried out around the 8 Mile Camp site.

Beheadings were rare in relation to the great numbers of remains found – these perhaps could be attributed to the same Japanese officers. All evidence pointed to Lieut. Moritaki as the responsible Japanese officer who would have killed the Englishman and other leaders in the camp.

When the investigators were searching for Moritaki, the local people told them he died on 18 July; it was not until Wong Hiong eventually testified that he had helped dig the grave and bury Moritaki in his uniform, not far from the Japanese flagpole by the parade ground, that Cpl. Evans of 31 War Graves Unit took a party to locate and open the grave; the Javanese who had worked for Moritaki said when they saw the body: "That's him alright – you can tell by his four gold teeth." The Authorities were now satisfied Moritaki, the Japanese officer responsible for all atrocities at Sandakan, was dead.

Sgt. W.A.C. Russell of S.R.D. had been in the area three months before the Japanese Capitulation and was initially attached to the first POW Enquiry Group as a guide and interpreter. Russell knew the area well between Sandakan and Boto and was acquainted with the various village chiefs; it was Russell who recommended to the Authorities that local people, who had assisted prisoners of war, should be rewarded. This recommendation was adopted in 1946 and 31 War Graves were advised that an Australian/British Reward Mission under Major H.W.S. Jackson would be arriving by the end of the year to complete this task. Public notices were displayed in Sandakan, inviting people who had had contact with the prisoners to come forward and state their claim.

The party arrived in January 1947, led by Major Jackson (Australian), Major Dyce (British Army) and two Correspondents from the Australian Broadcasting

No. 3 Cemetery , Sandakan. Persons standing at location of last prisoner killed on site of No. 2 Compound. The original huts would have been located around the ridge , they were destroyed by fire on 29 May 1945.   Pic: Australian Archives.

Commission, Colin Simpson and William McFarlane. Word soon spread that the Reward Party was in the area and quite a few local people were contacted to be interviewed.

While at Sandakan, a Chinese, Wong Hiong, was interviewed regarding his story of an alleged crucifixion. Up to this time War Graves staff had not heard of the account in such a detailed manner as was produced by Colin Simpson. They had heard a prisoner had been nailed to a tree and finally executed but there were many rumours and stories; nothing surprised them. Wong Hiong made his first statement on this alleged crime to Colin Simpson (ABC), Major Jackson (AIF), S/Sgt. Bunter (War Graves) and Mr. Wong Yun Siew of the Agricultural Department, and he would have been aware of the potential for reward. Wong Hiong told his story and detailed a crucifixion of the leader of the English camp; he described him as a Naval Captain and the tallest man he had seen at 6'6"; he described his clothes – the type of cap he wore – how he had been detained in a wire cage overnight and next day taken out and nailed to a specially prepared cross which was about 7 ft. high. The man's hands were nailed to the cross and the Japanese officer carrying out this crime stood on a chair to hammer an 8 inch nail through the man's head – flesh from his body was removed. The body remained on the cross for some weeks and then the cross and the body were finally burnt and all the ashes were washed away by the rain.

Major Jackson was convinced of the story and the following day he cabled Army Headquarters in Melbourne for the attention of Director of Prisoners of War and Internees, stating that: "In my opinion this youth is a reliable witness, some of the information given by him checks with information that 31 War Graves have received."

War Crimes Section, Army H.Q. Melbourne, examined the report and ordered Major Jackson to interrogate Wong Hiong again, this took place on 16 January 1947 but this time cracks began to appear in Wong's account of the alleged atrocity. Major Jackson credited this to different Interpreter.

The Japanese never permitted Australians or British POWs at Sandakan to mix with each other, they were not allowed to talk to each other, any such contact was a serious offence and it is unlikely the Japanese would have found a Naval officer and placed him in any of the Compounds – or any other British or Dutch officer fitting the description as given by Wong. The only Naval officer at Sandakan, Lieut. Sligo, R.N.V.R. attached A.I.F., with 'B' Force, died on 31 August 1942.

Further investigation was made of the Japanese alleged witnesses who were serving 12 years' sentence at Rabaul; on 25 March the Military Board requested 31 War Graves to put Wong Hiong's evidence into Affidavit form, covering the two interviews, namely, the execution of the British camp leader (Wong's description of the Naval officer as the British camp leader), and the execution of the last surviving PWs, and also attached identification photographs of the three Japanese alleged to have been witnesses: Noshikawa Moriji, Noshikawa Yoshinori and S/M. Morozumi. Wong had to sign the Affidavit and the identified photographs.

The request for interrogation of Japanese in custody in Rabaul was dispatched

Peter Beaumont on track leading to Camp and pointing to boiler in centre of picture. ''Big Tree'' in background.   Pic: AWM.

Searcher party returning past 8 Mile Police Station.   Pic: AWM.

and again the crime experts there questioned Morozumi and his guards. They all testified if what was described by Wong Hiong had occurred they would have known about it.

Ali Asa worked as a Fireman at the Power Station there for the Japanese from August 1942 to August 1945 and he recalled: "When the first raid came 24 October 1944 the fires were not allowed to be lit at night and on 25 December 1944 I was transferred to the Japanese camp where I worked as a water boy. At the time of the raids the PWs were very thin and all were hungry; their main food was yam and they had no salt whatsoever.

"There were three PW camps, No.1 Australian, No.2. British and No.3 Australian. Before the air raids in 1944 the men in No.3 camp were taken to No.1 camp, leaving No.3 camp empty. I remember when the PW were taken on the marches, the first march occurred about February 1945, they came from No.1 and 2 camps. The men from No.2 camp left two days after the first party.

"I never saw a big wooden cross around the camps, I could see the camps but could not see inside them.

"Wong Hiong never told me that he had seen a PW executed."

War Crimes Section now requested Captain J. Burnett of War Graves to arrange for Wong to sign an Affidavit in connection with the statements he had made regarding: crucifixion 1) massacre of 23 PWs near the airfield and 3) the last PW who was beheaded.

Following this Affidavit, Wong Hiong was taken to the site of the alleged crucifixion which was in No.1 Camp and not in No.2 as claimed and within five yards of this spot a body was recovered. Wong Hiong also indicated the locality of the grave site where the last PW was beheaded and was believed to be an Australian.

Captain Burnett cabled Melbourne:
"War Crimes Section – Melbourne:
" … One (.) Body recovered five yards from spot indicated by Wong Hiong. (.) Skull found between thigh and shin bones (.) Body exhumed by Lieut. Sticpewich (.) Remains exhumed 8 Aug 47 (.)
" … Two (.) Body recovered centre Number 1 PW Camp on 12 Aug 47 (.) Right leg cut off 2 inches below knees (.) Twisted wire and 4 six inch nails 4 three inch nails recovered with body (.) Impossible to state if nails had been driven through feet and hands (.)"

Flt. Lieut. Peter Lee, who was in the camp up until August 1943, stated there was no one to fit this description of the victim described by Wong in the Camp.

Wong Hiong claimed the last PW to be killed was executed; Captain Burnett was requested to take Wong to the site of this execution which he did, and they found the body described in the cable. Part one of the cable confirmed that a PW had been beheaded, believed to have been the last one alive; Part two described the victim alleged to have been crucified which is completely in conflict with Wong's previous statement that he had been nailed to a cross and the cross and the victim's body had been burnt and the ashes washed away in the rain.

The discovery of the victim described as having been crucified and seen by Wong corresponds with a story the War Graves personnel heard when they first arrived – that a PW had been wired to a tree and murdered by a Japanese officer. Wong's first series of interrogations appears to have been distorted by an interpreter, as all Wong Hiong's future statements proved to be substantive.

The Australian Army Authority became aware Major Dyce had also sent a report to ALFSEA and they too were investigating the alleged atrocity. LANDFORCE Melbourne established the fact the victim was an Englishman (and probably the identity) and dis-

Saxophone recovered from mass grave, British Cemetery . Pic: G. Robinson

patched all material to the War Crimes Singapore. If the victim was an officer and his identity is known it is likely other officers, whose deaths are shown as late June early July, would have been disposed of about the same time.

It is likely too that this was one of many crimes committed by Moritaki soon after he returned from Kemansi early in June 1945.

Captain Burnett paid Wong Hiong a further $20 for this statement:

"During 1944 and 1945 I was employed by the Japs at the PW Camp Mile 8 Sandakan as cook and later as personal boy to Morozumi Hisao, which work I did up to the morning the Japs left the PW Camp, Sandakan.

"The morning before the Japs left this area I witnessed the following. All the Japs had started to pack up and on this morning they were all extra quiet and about 0700 hours after they had finished breakfast, Morozumi Hisao took a sword from its sheath which was hanging on the wall of the shelter. It was not the usual sword he wore generally.

"Then Morozumi ordered me not to leave the place. I got suspicious of something was about to happen, so after Morozumi had led the remaining Jap guards off in the direction of the PW Camp I came out and climbed a rubber tree. I was familiar with the layout of the PW Camp and had been inside it on several occasions and given the only PW alive on this day food. I was caught and punished for doing this about two weeks previous by Morozumi.

"From the rubber tree I saw Morozumi standing at a spot on the side of the hill alongside a slit trench in No.2 PW Compound.

"I saw four Japs, Nishikawa Yoshinori, Fukuda Nobuo, Nagata Shinichi, Goto Yoshitaro, dragging the last PW to be alive at this Camp from his shelter of blanket and groundsheet. These four Jap guards beat and kicked the PW and brutally moved him up to where Morozumi was waiting with the rest of the Jap guards.

"The PW's description is as follows: about 6 ft. tall, black hair, had a beard, had false teeth. I used to see him wash them when he washed his face at the water hole. I did on several occasions give this PW food.

"Hinata Genzo was the one who forced the PW to kneel down, and then Nagata Shinichi placed a piece of black cloth around the PW's face covering what appeared to be his eyes. The PW was facing north and Morozumi was standing on his left with the sword in his hand facing east. Morozumi then lifted the sword up over his head gripping it with both hands, and with one downward motion he brought the sword down with terrific force on to the neck of the PW. The PW's head disappeared from sight and the body slumped over. Then Morozumi kicked the body of the PW into the slit trench out of my sight. The Jap guards then started to shovel dirt in on top of the PW.

"At seeing what I had witnessed I became afraid and went back to my work and carried on. The Japs came back shortly after and continued to pack as they were leaving for Jesselton, which they did so at about 0700 hours the following day.

"I cannot remember the date of this happening, but I saw aeroplanes dropping pamphlets a few days later, and I was told that the war was finished."

Later in September 1947, the War Graves personnel returned to Australia. Proud of what they had achieved, they still suffered from the memories of the dreadful discoveries and ghastly sights they had uncovered in their work over the past two years.

Ray Battram recalled: "I had returned home to Glebe in Sydney and on Saturday afternoon I went down to the local Pub, "The Burton". I had grown up around Glebe and knew most people and they knew me. Drinking with a mate, relaxing and trying to get out of my mind the horror of the ghastly jobs we had just finished with, I was shattered back to reality when an old man I had known for years and who had lost his only son in Borneo in the War, called out to me across the Bar: "Did you find my boy up there?"

In 1945, relatives of those lost in the Borneo theatre of war received little or no information as to the circumstances of or the locality of the death of their menfolk, their searching has been on-going.

War Graves Recovery Unit group.
From left – standing: Fred (Doc) Bedford – R.A.M.C. Medical Orderly; Bill (Snow) Thornley – O/R.; Ossie Carr – Clerk; Tukidjam – Javanese; Len Evans – Driver; Allan Wilkie – Stores; Two Civil Administrators; Geoff Johnston (Captain) – O/C Departing; Don Hawkins – from elsewhere; Major Blow, D.S.O.; Captain J. Burnett, M.M. – O/C Taking Over.
From Left – squatting: Peter Beaumont – Signwriter, Ray (Darkie) Battram – O/R.

Pic: R. Battram.

Colonel Suga committed suicide with assistance from his batman. Shown still holding the knife.
From left to right: Harold MC Manus, C.P.O. Stone of USS HUSTON; Lt. Reg Dixon, A.I.F.

Pic: Reg Dixon

Christopher Elliott, in 1945, visited Sabah on a search for information about his brother, Donald Elliott, R.A.F. He again visited there in 1994 and his daughter, Anne, visited Sandakan and Ranau in January 1996. This is her tribute:

To the Spirit of Donald Elliott

You don't know me.
But I know you.
Through my father,
he has not forgotten you
and never will.
His life has been greatly affected
by your death.
He always looked up to you, you were his hero.
I will never forget.
Hope that you are at peace here.
And that you didn't suffer too much pain.
And that you can forgive your enemies
for what they did to you.
I thought of you at the VJ Day March
in Pall Mall, London.
I stood and watched the veterans walk
by – the lucky ones.
I was quite choked but proud.
You did it for me and the likes of me.
Thank you.
I think things would have been
different if you were still around.
But life isn't always fair, is it?

By Anne Elliott

British Memorial,
Kundasang, Sabah.

HONOUR ROLL

JESSELTON PARTY:

Comprised Royal Artillery and Royal Air Force personnel from Java and assembled at Jesselton (now Kota Kinabalu).

The names are taken from original Nominal Rolls believed to have been typed there and correspond with War Graves Registers.

This group was then transported to Sandakan where all but 10 Officers were removed in August 1943 to Kuching – none of those left at Sandakan survived.

The following codes indicate the place of death:

S	Reported died Sandakan.
S/L	About 100 men were sent to Labuan.
S/L/B	Some of the above were returned to Brunei area. There were no survivors.
L	Those sent from Kuching to Labuan.
L/B	Those reported to have reached Brunei.
DM	Died between Sandakan and Ranau.
R	Died at Ranau.
Space	Believed died Sandakan or on march to Ranau.

KUCHING:

Shown as 'K'. Died at Kuching, buried in the Camp Cemetery and later transferred to Labuan War Cemetery. A few graves identified and found at Labuan were transferred to this Cemetery.

BALLALE:

The Gunner 600 Party which left Changi 18 October 1942.

The Nominal Roll supplied by Allied Land Forces South East Asia Command (ALFSEAC) to Australian Military Force is incomplete: the first part records deaths recorded on Singapore Memorial; part two records names on Roll and do not appear on Singapore Memorial; part three lists those 18 who were recovered by Australian Forces.

SUEZ MARU:

Names of Royal Artillery and Royal Air Force personnel returning from Amboina to Java. Their ship, SUEZ MARU, was torpedoed and sunk; those who survived the sinking were massacred in the water. Date of death 29 November 1943.

CAPTAIN J.F.D. MILLS' PARTY
ROYAL ARTILLERY REGIMENTS

Number	Rank	Name	Regiment	Place of Origin	D.O.D.	Age	Place Died
806843	S/Sgt.	Ackland, G.J.	R.A. attd. HQ.16 HAA	Lwr. Edmonton, Middlesex	01.10.44	32	S/L/B
1753250	Gnr.	Adrian, William	48 Bty. 21 LAA	Darwen, Lancashire	31.12.44	36	S/L
11052160	Gnr.	Allen, John	242 Bty. 48 LAA	Mistley, Essex	17.06.45	24	S/L/B
1546011	Gnr.	Amoss, A.C.	242 Bty. 48 LAA	Wigan, Lancashire	19.05.45	39	S/L
1808928	Gnr.	Anderton, W.C.	242 Bty. 48 LAA	Oldham, Lancashire	16.05.45	23	S/L/B
1821279	Gnr.	Andrews, Harold	69 Bty. 21 LAA		22.03.45	34	
1734002	Gnr.	Aplin, E.C.	242 Bty. 48 LAA		29.03.45	31	DM
1826533	Gnr.	Archibald, T.M.	48 Bty. 21 LAA	Danderhall, Midlothian	22.02.45	37	
1818392	Gnr.	Ashmore, Harold	48 Bty. 21 LAA	Cinder Hall, Nottinghamshire	29.05.45	42	S
1768731	Gnr.	Avenell, J.B.	48 Bty. 21 LAA	Morpeth, Northumberland	14.03.45	24	S/L/B
1758991	Gnr.	Bagwell, A.A.C.	242 Bty. 48 LAA		27.02.45	36	S
1729649	Gnr.	Baker, T.C.	239 Bty. 77 HAA	Dorney, Buckinghamshire	21.03.45	35	S
1587669	Bdr.	Baker, W.G.	H.Q. 77 HAA		31.03.45		S
10630599	Pte.	Barber, A.T.	Catering attd. RAOC	Pershore, Worcestershire	01.11.44	28	S/L
1548153	Gnr.	Bareham, W.J.	95 Bty. 48 LAA	Witham, Essex	19.02.45	30	DM
1639343	Gnr.	Barker, M.E.	49 Bty. 48 LAA	Forest Gate, Essex	16.04.45	34	
1624395	Gnr.	Barnes, F.W.	48 Bty. 21 LAA		25.03.43	35	S
1563244	Gnr.	Bartlett, A.E.	48 Bty. 21 LAA	Hampstead, London	22.05.45	34	S/L
1773551	Gnr.	Batty, L.G.	242 Bty. 48 LAA	Liverpool	27.04.45	24	S
1753256	Gnr.	Baulcombe, H.J.	48 Bty. 21 LAA	Deptford, London	20.02.45	36	DM
1539977	L/Bdr.	Bayer, J.H.	89 Bty. 35 LAA		29.03.45	26	DM
2313139	L/Sgt.	Beck, J.T.	Royal Corps. Sigs.	Sheldon, Birmingham	21.03.45	47	DM
1808958	Gnr.	Bellamy, H.W.	242 Bty. 48 LAA		20.04.45		S
1549477	Gnr.	Benn, E.T.	48 Bty. 21 LAA		15.07.45	29	S
7641587	Cftsmn.	Bennett, R.J.	R.E.M.E.	Palmers Green, Middlesex	01.05.45	33	S
1623453	Gnr.	Bentley, William	241 Bty. 77 HAA	Dukinfield, Cheshire	17.02.45	34	S/L
6025672	Pte.	Bexfield, F.G.	RAOC attd. 21 LAA	West Hampstead, London	27.11.44	30	S/L

300

Number	Rank	Name	Regiment	Place of Origin	D.O.D.	Age	Place Died
2595407	Dvr.	Bird, C.G.	21 LAA Sig. Sec.	Rushden, Northamptonshire	26.12.44	33	S
1549846	Gnr.	Bird, F.L.	95 Bty. 48 LAA	Colchester, Essex	12.06.45	28	S
2365066	Sgmn.	Bird, M.C.	21 LAA Sig. Sec.	Colchester, Essex	22.05.43	34	S
1826537	Gnr.	Black, L.W.	21 LAA Regt.	Glasgow	13.02.45	38	DM
1827759	Gnr.	Blake, T.J.	48 Bty. 21 LAA	Hafod, Swansea	13.02.45		S
1743053	Gnr.	Bourne, Ralph	78 Bty. 35 LAA		12.02.45	36	
1554749	Gnr.	Boyd, John	242 Bty. 48 LAA	Sprotborough, Yorkshire	04.05.45	29	
1639234	Gnr.	Bramley, C.A.	49 Bty. 48 LAA	Tottenham, Middlesex	24.03.45	29	
17824213	Gnr.	Bratt, Frederick	49 Bty. 48 LAA		08.07.45	40	R
1563142	Gnr.	Bristow, A.J.	48 Bty. 21 LAA	Hammersmith, London	05.12.44	31	S/L
10630573	Pte.	Britten, E.D.G.	Catering attd. RAOC		20.01.45	28	S/L/B
1052486	L/Bdr.	Broadbent, Frank	242 Bty. 48 LAA		13.03.45	34	
1483222	BQMS	Broom, C.L.	78 Bty. 35 LAA	Shipley, Yorkshire	16.02.45	34	S
11052208	Bdr.	Brown, R.H.	242 Bty. 48 LAA	Urmston, Lancashire	14.04.45	23	S
1624402	Gnr.	Brown, William	48 Bty. 21 LAA	St. Pancras, London	08.02.45	34	S
1679320	Gnr.	Buckingham, H.F.	40 Bty. 48 LAA	Oxford	05.06.45	31	S
11052162	Gnr.	Buckle, Henry	242 Bty. 48 LAA	Patricroft, Lancashire	19.04.45	32	S
1543092	Gnr.	Bundock, G.E.	49 Bty. 48 LAA	Canterbury	21.04.45	41	S
1523544	Gnr.	Burdett, Noel	48 Bty. 21 LAA	New Costessey, Norfolk	10.03.45	36	S
11052489	Gnr.	Burgess, Richard	242 Bty. 48 LAA	Washington, Co. Durham	21.02.45	33	S
6550836	Bdr.	Burke, George	242 Bty. 48 LAA		19.03.45	28	DM
1522707	Sgt.	Butt, H.J.	242 Bty. 48 LAA	Fulborn, Cambridgeshire	24.03.45	26	DM
11052492	Gnr.	Campbell, T.McG.	242 Bty. 48 LAA	South Shields, Co. Durham	08.03.45	23	S
45230	L/Cpl.	Cann, W.G.	21 LAA Wkshps., RAOC		28.03.45	34	S
1543769	L/Bdr.	Carson, Charles	95 Bty. 48 LAA		06.06.45	28	S
1760033	Gnr.	Carver, Percy	48 Bty. 21 LAA	West Kingsdown, Kent	06.03.45	38	S
1808873	Gnr.	Challis, George	49 Bty. 48 LAA	West Glossop, Derbyshire	01.04.45	35	S
1472376	Gnr.	Charles, John	12 Bty. 6 HAA	Monkton, Co. Durham	25.07.45	23	R
1722457	Gnr.	Charlesworth, R.S.	48 Bty. 21 LAA	Hebden Bridge, Yorkshire	18.02.45	37	S
1481942	Gnr.	Cherry, F.A.	48 Bty. 21 LAA		02.04.45		S
210573	Lieut.	Chopping, G.N.	R.A.S.C.	Colchester, Essex	12.08.45	26	R
1485577	Bdr.	Clarke, C.B.	48 Bty. 21 LAA		07.10.44	32	S/L

301

Number	Rank	Name	Regiment	Place of Origin	D.O.D.	Age	Place Died
890423	Gnr.	Cliff, Sydney	95 Bty. 48 LAA		20.01.45		S
1758836	Gnr.	Clouter, F.J.	242 Bty. 48 LAA		22.11.44		S
2365045	Sgmn.	Coffin, Ernest	21 LAA Sig. Sec.		09.06.45	24	S
1801573	Gnr.	Cole, F.G.H.	242 Bty. 48 LAA	Bristol	10.04.45	29	S
1563036	Gnr.	Collins, D.G.	48 Bty. 21 LAA	Edmonton, Middlesex	14.07.45	32	R
1465809	Sgt.	Cook, P.V.	95 Bty. 48 LAA		21.12.44	35	S/L
7651327	Cftsmn.	Copley, Arthur	21 LAA Wkshps. REME	Blandford, Dorsetshire	01.10.44	35	S/L/B
1481518	Gnr.	Coppin, E.J.	49 Bty. 48 LAA	Bow, London	13.06.45	35	S
1609558	Gnr.	Costello, Michael	242 Bty. 48 LAA	Warrington, Lancashire	12.06.45	33	S
328892	Dvr.	Cox, Albert	21 LAA Sig. Sec.		01.04.45		S
1799368	Gnr.	Cox, A.J.	242 Bty. 48 LAA		09.11.44	23	S/L
1833690	Gnr.	Cox, J.W.	21 LAA Regt.		18.03.45	37	
1735774	L/Bdr.	Cretten, W.R.	242 Bty. 48 LAA	Harringay, Middlesex	18.12.44	34	S/L
1624414	Gnr.	Croft, E.W.G.	48 Bty. 21 LAA	Charlton, London	19.12.44	25	S/L
11052500	Gnr.	Crombie, Robert	242 Bty. 48 LAA	Sunderland, Co. Durham	15.02.45	23	
10630780	Pte.	Crow, W.S.	Catering attd. R.A.		11.03.45	28	S/L
1724978	Gnr.	Cryer, Ernest	48 Bty. 21 LAA	Todmorden, Lancashire	01.03.45	39	DM
4530985	Sgt.	Cunningham, Edward	Royal Corps. Sigs.	Leeds, Yorkshire	21.03.45	38	
111986	Capt.	Daniels, F.L.K. MID	R.A.M.C.	Copnor, Hampshire	06.08.45	39	R
10631347	Pte.	Daniels, Peter	Army Catering Corps.	Arlesey, Bedfordshire	28.10.44	28	S/L
1618676	Gnr.	Davies, C.A.C.	15 Bty. 6 HAA	Wigan, Lancashire	16.06.45	35	
1687169	Gnr.	Davis, Edward	242 Bty. 48 LAA	Brockley, London	25.07.45	33	R
1724923	Gnr.	Davison, G.M.	48 Bty. 21 LAA	Leeds, Yorkshire	09.02.45	38	S
1547776	Gnr.	Day, F.A.	95 Bty. 48 LAA		09.03.45	40	S/L/B
6214464	Sgmn.	Dennison, A.C.	21 LAA Sig. Sec.		02.06.45	23	DM
1682887	Cftsmn.	Dobson, E.A.	21 LAA Wkshps.,REME	Rycroft, Yorkshire	18.10.44	30	S/L
7641419	L/Cpl.	Dunnett, John	21 LAA Wkshps.,RAOC		07.06.45	31	S
1484235	Sgt.	Eaden, R.S.	48 Bty. 21 LAA		10.03.45	39	DM
1718393	Gnr.	East, E.J.	242 Bty. 48 LAA		02.05.45	34	
7592247	S/Sgt.	Edwards, Jack	REME attd. 21 LAA	Barnstable, Devon	05.08.45	27	R
2571825	L/Sgt.	Edwards, S.E.	21 LAA Sig. Sec.	Upton Park, Essex	24.03.45	28	DM
1801590	Gnr.	Efford, P.H.	242 Bty. 48 LAA		08.02.45		S

302

Number	Rank	Name	Regiment	Place of Origin	D.O.D.	Age	Place Died
11052571	Bdr.	Engstrom, R.C.B.	242 Bty. 48 LAA	Sunderland, Co. Durham	11.06.45	24	S
11052572	Gnr.	Epstine, Adrian	242 Bty. 48 LAA		27.02.45	23	
6009485	Gnr.	Evans, F.G.	15 Bty. 16 HAA		28.03.45	29	
1827284	Gnr.	Evans, T.F.	48 Bty. 21 LAA	Llanelly, Carmarthenshire	14.07.45	30	S
1624364	Gnr.	Everett, Harry	48 Bty. 21 LAA	Poplar, London	25.11.44	34	S/L
1801594	Gnr.	Faulks, C.H.	242 Bty. 48 LAA	Rettondon, Essex	16.02.45	27	S
1624366	Gnr.	Feast, A.H.	48 Bty. 21 LAA	Newbury, Berkshire	16.01.45	27	S/L
1481404	Bdr.	Fenner, R.A.	48 Bty. 21 LAA		17.02.45	30	
1736236	Gnr.	Fielding, T.O.	69 Bty. 21 LAA	Ilford, Essex	20.06.45	36	DM
1827434	Gnr.	Filbey, C.H.	48 Bty. 21 LAA		14.03.45	23	S/L
1824279	Gnr.	Fillingham, William	242 Bty. 48 LAA	Shaw, Lancashire	12.06.45	36	S
7910723	L/Bdr.	Finch, R.F.	49 Bty. 48 LAA	Clacton-on-Sea, Essex	14.01.45	24	S
11052575	Gnr.	Finnigan, William	242 Bty. 48 LAA		27.03.45	24	S
13062006	Pte.	Fishwick, William	175 Coy.Pioneer Corps.		01.03.45	30	
1445018	L/Sgt.	Fitzgerald, H.J.	240 Bty. 77 HAA	Newport, Monmouthshire	17.01.45	33	S
1653727	Sgt.	Forster, J.J.	95 Bty. 48 LAA	Watford, Hertfordshire	08.07.45	34	R
11052577	L/Bdr.	Forster, J.W.	242 Bty. 48 LAA	Gilesgate Moor, Durham	14.03.45	40	S/L/B
11051978	Gnr.	Foster, Leonard	242 Bty. 48 LAA		26.03.45	23	
1649394	Gnr.	Frampton, E.J.	95 Bty. 48 LAA		15.02.45		S
3448705	Gnr.	Frater, Arnold	69 Bty. 21 LAA		12.03.45	22	
1779965	L/Bdr.	Frost, D.A.	21 LAA Regt.	Prestbury, Cheshire	05.03.45	23	
1482073	Gnr.	Frost, Norman	21 LAA Regt.	Enfield, Middlesex	15.07.45	30	R
10532948	Cftsmn.	Gallagher, Joseph	R.E.M.E.	Mossend, Bellshill, Lanarks.	25.01.45	24	S
1478319	Bdr.	Gane, John	48 Bty. 21 LAA		22.02.45	31	S
1626799	Gnr.	Gardiner, A.L.	239 Bty. 77 HAA	East Ham, Sussex	02.12.44	24	S
1549335	Gnr.	Gardner, H.D.	48 Bty. 21 LAA		08.12.44	28	S
11052581	Gnr.	Garman, Henry	242 Bty. 48 LAA	Sunderland, Co. Durham	27.04.45	23	S
11052582	Gnr.	Geddes, William	242 Bty. 48 LAA	East Howdon, Northumberland	02.04.45	24	S
1563233	Gnr.	Gould, W.J.	48 Bty. 21 LAA		22.01.45		S
2326186	Sgt.	Graham, Andrew	Royal Corps. Sigs.		15.06.45	31	
1653681	Gnr.	Green, H.W.	95 Bty. 48 LAA	Norwich	17.06.45	34	S
1105288	Gnr.	Gregson, Alfred	242 Bty. 48 LAA	Deans Bank, Co. Durham	16.03.45	23	DM

Number	Rank	Name	Regiment	Place of Origin	D.O.D.	Age	Place Died
1560157	Bdr.	Grewcock, L.H.	242 Bty. 48 LAA	Reading, Berkshire	13.02.45	29	R
1449675	Bdr.	Griffiths, D.M.	239 Bty. 77 HAA		22.07.45	27	
1550169	Gnr.	Groves, Frederick	95 Bty. 48 LAA	Hayes, Middlesex	07.03.45	28	S
2365078	Sgmn.	Gwilliam, F.H.	21 LAA Sig. Sec.		19.01.45		S
4436237	Sgt.	Hall, J.E.W.	242 Bty. 48 LAA	Clacton-on-Sea, Essex	09.05.45	45	S
1801604	Gnr.	Hall, Robert	242 Bty. 48 LAA	Westcliff-on-Sea, Essex	09.04.45	29	S
1550136	Gnr.	Hallsey, G.T.	49 Bty. 48 LAA		14.03.45	29	S
1485582	L/Bdr.	Hammond, B.I.	48 Bty. 21 LAA	Cheshunt, Hertfordshire	11.05.43	29	S
1594882	Bdr.	Hanley, J.B.	242 Bty. 48 LAA		31.03.45		S
11052590	Gnr.	Hannant, N.J.	242 Bty. 48 LAA	Consett, Co. Durham	13.12.45	24	DM
1808998	Gnr.	Hardacre, George	242 Bty. 48 LAA		10.03.45	23	S
2359095	Sgmn.	Hardman, Joseph	21 LAA Sig. Sec.		22.04.45		S
1653779	Gnr.	Harold, R.R.	95 Bty. 48 LAA	Diss, Norfolk	31.03.45	29	S
1482076	L/Sgt.	Harrington, D.F.	48 Bty. 21 LAA	Enfield, Middlesex	31.03.45	29	S
2313178	Cpl.	Harrold, J.G.	Royal Corps. Sigs.	Frecheville, Sheffield	21.03.45	36	
1624327	L/Bdr.	Hart, Maurice	48 Bty. 21 LAA	Denmark Hill, London	16.04.45	32	S
788277	Gnr.	Hastie, John	95 Bty. 48 LAA	Cowgate, Newcastle-on-Tyne	13.02.45	36	S/L
1801607	Gnr.	Hawkins, E.R.	242 Bty. 48 LAA		31.03.45		S
1478315	Bdr.	Hayward, S.A.	48 Bty. 21 LAA	Tottenham, Middlesex	07.07.45	31	S
1793073	Gnr.	Hazeltine, John	242 Bty. 48 LAA	Royton, Lancashire	07.06.45	24	S
1817400	Gnr.	Hazzard, E.J.	21 LAA Regt.	Streatham, London	22.02.45	36	S
7630609	S/Sgt.	Henshall, N.H.	21 LAA Wkshps.,REME	Willaston, Cheshire	06.03.45	28	DM
11052510	Gnr.	Hessey, Samuel	242 Bty. 48 LAA	Gateshead, Co. Durham	15.02.45	23	S/L
1490211	Gnr.	Hewitt, H.W.	48 Bty. 21 LAA	North Earlham, Norwich	30.12.44	38	S/L
1738670	Gnr.	Heywood, C.J.	242 Bty. 48 LAA		06.05.45	38	S
2351736	Sgmn.	Hill, John	6 HAA Sig. Sec.	Radcliffe, Lancashire	27.05.45	33	S
1793075	Gnr.	Hill, W.R.	242 Bty. 48 LAA	St. Helens, Lancashire	17.02.45	24	
2085011	Gnr.	Hirstle, Lewis	48 Bty. 21 LAA	Dewsbury, Yorkshire	27.03.45	32	S
11052237	Gnr.	Hodgkinson, Derek	242 Bty. 48 LAA	Hull	21.03.45	24	S
2369914	Sgmn.	Hodgson, Roy	21 LAA Sig. Sec.	Kingsbury, Middlesex	02.08.45	24	R
7595624	L/Cpl.	Hoggett, W.V.	R.E.M.E.	Walthamstow, Essex	02.04.45	34	S
1817403	Gnr.	Holder, C.J.	48 Bty. 21 LAA	Dummer, Hampshire	14.06.45	27	S
1614385	L/Sgt.	Holder, H.J.	242 Bty. 48 LAA		06.03.45	32	S

Number	Rank	Name	Regiment	Place of Origin	D.O.D.	Age	Place Died
T/271319	Gnr.	Hood, George	RASC. attd 77 HAA	Hanley, Stoke-on-Trent	29.09.44	36	S/L
1791066	Gnr.	Hoof, Arthur	242 Bty. 48 LAA		08.01.45	24	S
1549831	Bdr.	Hopkins, A.H.	78 Bty. 35 LAA	Poole, Dorsetshire	27.11.44	28	S/L
11052169	Gnr.	Hopkinson, Henry	242 Bty. 48 LAA		11.03.45	29	
2358564	Sgmn.	Horrell, Frank	21 LAA Sig. Sec.	Lustleigh, Devon	30.03.45		S
7625164	Cftsmn.	Hughes, D.J.	21 LAA Wkshp.,REME	Cricklewood, Middlesex	17.06.45	28	
2357584	L/Cpl.	Humphreys, J.H.	21 LAA Sig. Sec.	East Finchley, Middlesex	20.06.45	38	S
11051947	Bdr.	Hutchinson, John	242 Bty. 48 LAA	Leeds, Yorkshire	04.02.45	23	S
749649	Gnr.	Iles, R.J.	243 Bty. 77 HAA	Cardiff	30.06.45	41	
1481402	Bdr.	Ireland, H.S.	48 Bty. 21 LAA	Enfield, Middlesex	13.02.45	31	S
1478314	WO.II	Jacobi, H.C.	48 Bty. 21 LAA	Potters Bar, Middlesex	26.03.45	38	DM
1818777	Gnr.	James, Brinley	48 Bty. 21 LAA	Trebanos, Glamorgan	31.12.44	39	S/L
1801620	Gnr.	James, S.E.	242 Bty. 48 LAA	Winchmore Hill, Buckinghamshire	21.12.44	29	S/L
11051585	Gnr.	Jardine, Albert	242 Bty. 48 LAA	Salford, Lancashire	15.02.45	23	DM
1801622	Gnr.	Jenkins, A.W.E.	242 Bty. 48 LAA	Stepney Green, London	20.01.45	29	S/L
1824284	Gnr.	Johnson, J.E.	69 Bty. 21 LAA	Blackburn, Lancashire	30.03.45	36	S
2359829	Cpl.	Johnson, K.A.	21 LAA Sig. Sec.		30.06.45	28	S
764188	Gnr.	Johnston, Joseph	48 Bty. 21 LAA	Walworth, London	28.11.44	37	S/L
11052206	Bdr.	Jones, Cyril	242 Bty. 48 LAA		20.04.45	24	S
1482052	Gnr.	Jones, E.B.	48 Bty. 21 LAA		08.03.45	30	S
T/3660151	Dvr.	Jones, J.H.	R.A.S.C.	Salford, Lancashire	06.03.45	28	DM
11051560	Gnr.	Jones, Thomas	242 Bty. 48 LAA	Crosby, Liverpool	07.02.45	23	S
11052172	Gnr.	Kaeo, C.R.V.	242 Bty. 48 LAA	Poulton, Cheshire	31.12.44	25	S/L
1735580	Gnr.	Keable, L.A.	242 Bty. 48 LAA	Charsfield, Suffolk	14.06.45	24	S
11052201	Gnr.	Keaveney, P.E.	242 Bty. 48 LAA	St. Helens, Lancashire	12.05.45	23	S
1792626	Gnr.	Keeble, Norman	95 Bty. 48 LAA		05.06.45	33	S
S/97325	Pte.	Kibble, Edward	R.A.S.C.		15.12.44	26	
1486999	Sgt.	Kidby, H.G.	242 Bty. 48 LAA		21.03.45	38	
2596745	Cpl.	Knowles, J.H.	21 LAA Sig. Sec.	Barrow-in-Furness, Lancs.	01.02.45	24	
11051562	Gnr.	Knutton, Herbert	242 Bty. 48 LAA	Blackpool, Lancashire	21.04.43	33	S

305

Number	Rank	Name	Regiment	Place of Origin	D.O.D.	Age	Place Died
6343400	WO.II	Laing, Ronald	95 Bty. 48 LAA		20.03.45	28	DM
850234	Gnr.	Lanham, Harry	12 Bty. 6 HAA		26.04.45	27	S
6607693	Bdr.	Law, D.R.	48 Bty. 21 LAA	West Sleekburn, Northumberland	07.06.45	38	DM
2576710	Sgt.	LeClercq, R.R.	Royal Corps. Sigs.	Broxbourne, Hertfordshire	03.06.45	35	S
5485976	Gnr.	Lee, J.A.	242 Bty. 48 LAA	Hornchurch, Essex	24.12.44	44	S/L
10530427	Cftsmn.	Lester, C.F.	R.E.M.E.	Hornchurch, Essex	01.07.44	37	S
1821409	Gnr.	Levins, Patrick	242 Bty. 48 LAA	Catford, London	04.04.45		S
5336958	Dvr.	Lewis, V.A.	21 LAA Sig. Sec.	Bootle, Lancashire	22.05.45	23	S
1483259	S/Sgt.	Litten, A.J.E.	89 Bty. 35 LAA	Watford, Hertfordshire	13.03.45	40	S
1826674	Gnr.	Lockhart, John	21 LAA Regt.	Oxford	04.05.45	41	R
T/3659933	Dvr.	Lomas, G.T.	142 Tpt.Coy.,RASC	Salford, Lancashire	01.07.45	31	S
1801632	Gnr.	Long, George	242 Bty. 48 LAA		21.02.45	29	S
875205	Gnr.	Longhurst, L.E.	48 Bty. 21 LAA	Kings Heath, Birmingham	22.06.45	24	S
1591194	Gnr.	Longworth, Thomas	239 Bty. 77 HAA		17.03.45	24	S
11051563	Gnr.	Luscott, Thomas	242 Bty. 48 LAA	Stockport, Cheshire	02.03.45	23	S
1795847	Gnr.	McArthur, Peter	242 Bty. 48 LAA	Comrie, Perthshire	08.04.45	24	S
1430013	Sgt.	McComisky, Henry	242 Bty. 48 LAA		20.12.44	27	S
1779808	Gnr.	McCulloch, W.H.	79 Bty. 21 LAA		16.02.45	22	
1543177	Gnr.	McDonald, J.A.	69 Bty. 21 LAA	Port Dinorwic, Caernarvonshire	03.07.45	33	S
11052541	Gnr.	McGough, Matthew	242 Bty. 48 LAA	Southwick, Co. Durham	30.03.45	25	S
1481925	Gnr.	McMeechan, Charles	242 Bty. 48 LAA	Fallin, Stirlingshire	18.05.45	35	S
1828416	L/Bdr.	McMenemy, Daniel	48 Bty. 21 LAA	Glasgow	16.02.45	37	S
1771927	Gnr.	McNab, C.P.	48 Bty. 21 LAA	Gravesend, Kent	15.03.45	35	S
1719997	Gnr.	Mace, A.F.	12 Bty. 6 HAA	Gloucester	17.03.45	35	S
1826599	Gnr.	Madeley, J.W.	21 LAA Regt.	Ardwick, Manchester	12.04.45	31	S
1543181	Gnr.	Maguire, Christopher	69 Bty. 21 LAA	Liverpool	28.04.45	43	S
1543128	Gnr.	Maguire, Joseph	69 Bty. 21 LAA	Heywood, Lancashire	03.04.45	35	S
11052533	Gnr.	Mannix, James	242 Bty. 48 LAA		10.05.45	23	S
1563176	Gnr.	Mansi, L.L.	42 Bty. 21 LAA	Cranfield, Bedfordshire	01.01.45	33	S/L
11052209	Gnr.	Marsden, James	242 Bty. 48 LAA		07.06.45	23	
1482079	Gnr.	Martin, J.R.	48 Bty. 21 LAA	Muswell Hill, Middlesex	14.02.45	31	
7621809	Cftsmn.	Mason, E.J.	21 LAA Wkshp.,REME		17.03,45	27	S/L/B

306

Number	Rank	Name	Regiment	Place of Origin	D.O.D.	Age	Place Died
1809130	Gnr.	Mason, William	H.Q., 48 LAA Regt.	Standish, Lancashire	05.03.45	34	
11052535	Bdr.	Matthews, Thomas	242 Bty. 48 LAA	Sunderland, Co. Durham	27.11.44	23	S
1771509	L/Bdr.	Mayhew, H.J.	242 Bty. 48 LAA		14.12.44	39	S/L
1550385	Gnr.	Mears, R.M.	95 Bty. 48 LAA	Finsbury Park, Middlesex	09.11.43	22	S
11052238	Gnr.	Mellor, Edward	242 Bty. 48 LAA	Swinton, Lancashire	16.02.45	36	S
11263050	Gnr.	Mellor, Sydney	21 LAA Regt.	Ashton-under-Lyne, Lancs.	15.06.45	35	S
2989071	Pte.	Metcalfe, Alfred	Argyll&Suth.Hghldrs.		11.12.44	30	S/L
1563286	L/Bdr.	Mileman, A.E.	49 Bty. 21 LAA		16.02.45		S
10530484	Cftsmn.	Miles, C.F.	REME attd. 21 LAA	Tunbridge Wells, Kent	05.12.44	38	S/L
1801526	Gnr.	Miles, G.A.	242 Bty. 48 LAA	Harlow, Essex	07.06.45	29	S
1482805	Sgt.	Miller, H.L.	242 Bty. 48 LAA	Clacton-on-Sea, Essex	18.02.45	35	
73787	Capt.	Mills, J.F.D.	77 HAA Regt.		03.07.45	30	S
13056355	Cpl.	Mitchell, Frank	Pioneer Corps.	Bury, Lancashire	13.06.45	28	S/L
1560196	Sgt.	Moore, J.E.	242 Bty. 48 LAA		08.04.45	33	S
1801645	Gnr.	Morris, R.S.	242 Bty. 48 LAA	Reigate, Surrey	05.03.45	29	S
11052176	Bdr.	Morris, Ronald	242 Bty. 48 LAA	Moston, Manchester	06.03.45	31	S
T/273326	L/Cpl.	Morrison, H.M.A.	RASC attd. R.A.	Mortlake, Surrey	10.03.45	36	S
1774747	Gnr.	Morton, Fred	48 Bty. 21 LAA	Ashton, Cheshire	13.05.43	27	S
1801649	Gnr.	Myers, Steve	48 LAA Regt.	Rayleigh, Essex	01.03.45	27	
1733113	Gnr.	Newall, J.E.	48 Bty. 21 LAA		25.03.45	35	S
2361041	Sgmn.	Newton, A.H.	Royal Corps. Sigs.	Portsmouth	14.04.45	27	S
S/166240	Pte.	Nicholas, J.L.	Fld. Bakery, RASC	Llanelly, Carmarthenshire	16.07.45	28	
2367016	Dvr.	Nickson, S.D.	RCS.21LAA.RA. Sig Sec	Liverpool	15.02.45	32	S
1556628	Gnr.	Noble, John	242 Bty. 48 LAA	Carlisle	14.04.45	28	S
11051912	Gnr.	Northfield, Alan	242 Bty. 48 LAA		14.04.45	23	
1791497	Gnr.	Norton, Bernard	48 Bty. 21 LAA		15.06.45	23	S
1599632	Gnr.	Oakham, G.J.	48 Bty. 21 LAA	Canterbury	13.03.45	31	S/L
1599633	Gnr.	Olding, A.E.	48 Bty. 21 LAA		29.01.45	27	S
1801656	Gnr.	Oliver, H.S.	242 Bty. 48 LAA	Westminster, London	12.03.45	34	
2371592	Sgmn.	O'Shea, D.M.P.	21 LAA Sig. Sec.		19.06.45	24	S

307

Number	Rank	Name	Regiment	Place of Origin	D.O.D.	Age	Place Died
1434295	L/Sgt.	Palmer, H.J.	240 Bty. 77 HAA	Ely, Cardiff	17.03.45	24	R
1548600	Gnr.	Parker, L.N.J.	48 Bty. 21 LAA	Walthamstow, Essex	22.03.45	28	
1455182	Gnr.	Parks, Kenneth	48 Bty. 21 LAA	Hall Green, Birmingham	07.03.45	23	S/L/B
1458305	Gnr.	Parsons, F.J.H.	239 Bty. 77 HAA		14.03.45	33	
11052548	Gnr.	Paterson, Robert	242 Bty. 48 LAA	Sunderland, Co. Durham	18.05.43	34	S
11052549	Gnr.	Patrick, F.W.	242 Bty. 48 LAA		28.03.45	23	
1550073	Gnr.	Payne, Benjamin	48 Bty. 21 LAA	Islington, London	06.03.45	29	S
1828363	Gnr.	Peat, J.H.	48 Bty. 21 LAA	Mansfield, Nottinghamshire	15.04.45	32	S
1794569	Gnr.	Peel, Joseph	242 Bty. 48 LAA	Craven, Yorkshire	09.05.45	23	
1681252	Gnr.	Penn, E.W.	48 Bty. 21 LAA	Harold Hill, Essex	01.10.44	27	S/L
1611674	Bdr.	Penrose, S.H.	242 Bty. 48 LAA		21.04.45	33	S/L/B
1485584	Bdr.	Perry, G.H.	48 Bty. 21 LAA		24.03.45	38	
1801663	Gnr.	Petherwick, N.G.	95 Bty. 48 LAA		14.04.45		S
1684046	Gnr.	Picot, E.J.	95 Bty. 48 LAA	St. Helier, Channel Islands	30.07.45	32	S/L
11052180	L/Bdr.	Platt, J.S.	242 Bty. 48 LAA	Stockport, Cheshire	12.03.45	24	
1563098	L/Bdr.	Pope, C.E.	48 Bty. 21 LAA	Oldham, Lancashire	30.12.44	31	S/L
1801666	Gnr.	Portsmouth, R.A.	242 Bty. 48 LAA	Hayes, Middlesex	09.07.45	25	S
1467253	Gnr.	Potter, A.H.	48 Bty. 21 LAA		26.05.43		S
1801667	Gnr.	Potter, E.R.	242 Bty. 48 LAA		01.01.45	28	S/L
2320640	Sgmn.	Powell, S.G.T.	21 LAA Sig. Sec.	Hauxwell, Yorkshire	23.09.44	32	S/L
11052555	Gnr.	Pratt, J.C.	242 Bty. 48 LAA	Ashington, Northumberland	06.02.45	24	S
1481396	L/Bdr.	Prentice, D.E.	48 Bty. 21 LAA	Palmers Green, Middlesex	06.05.45	29	S
1828364	Gnr.	Presland, R.A.	48 Bty. 21 LAA	Irthlingborough, Northamps.	12.06.43	40	S
1549478	Gnr.	Pretlove, John	48 Bty. 21 LAA	South Tottenham, Middlesex	17.02.45	35	S/L
7607960	Cftsmn.	Privett, D.E.	R.E.M.E.	Cosham, Hampshire	30.03.45	24	S
7586000	Sgt.	Prouten, George	78 Bty. 35 LAA	Old Basing, Hampshire	14.06.45	54	
11053325	Gnr.	Rafferty, James	242 Bty. 48 LAA	Willington Quay, Northumb.	19.02.45	24	S/L
1801690	Gnr.	Rawlings, Daniel	242 Bty. 48 LAA	Chingford, Essex	20.01.45	29	S/L/B
1809011	Gnr.	Read, James	242 Bty. 48 LAA	Wigan, Lancashire	02.07.45	24	S
1828365	Gnr.	Redman, Cyril	21 LAA Regt.		04.01.45	34	S
11051564	Gnr.	Reid, K.W.	242 Bty. 48 LAA		28.01.45	23	
1550563	Gnr.	Relf, A.T.R.	49 Bty. 48 LAA		07.12.44	30	S/L

308

Number	Rank	Name	Regiment	Place of Origin	D.O.D.	Age	Place Died
1717708	Sgt.	Richards, T.H.I.	242 Bty. 48 LAA	Wearne, Somerset	22.03.45	35	S
842317	Gnr.	Roberts, Bois	48 Bty. 21 LAA		18.02.45	28	S
2317202	Sgt.	Roberts, R.J.	77 HAA Sig. Sec.		06.03.45	38	DM
923333	L/Bdr.	Roberts, W.L.	48 Bty. 21 LAA		18.07.45	23	DM
1826671	L/Bdr.	Robinson, A.W.	21 LAA Regt.	Bangor, Caernarvonshire	11.03.45	31	S
1771878	Gnr.	Rocker, S.S.	48 Bty. 21 LAA	Earby, Yorkshire	14.03.45	24	
1828420	Gnr.	Rodden, M.J.	48 Bty. 21 LAA	Wickford, Essex	28.02.45	36	
1772638	L/Bdr.	Rogers, E.R.	69 Bty. 21 LAA	Greenock, Renfrewshire	30.06.45	30	S
851182	Sgt.	Rogers, J.W.	49 Bty. 48 LAA	Widnes, Lancashire	13.03.45	28	DM
359128	Lieut.	Rolfe, I.D.	21 LAA Regt.	Bradfield, Essex	27.01.45	25	S
818029	Sgt.	Rooker, J.H.	12 Bty. 6 HAA	Portsmouth	04.08.45	31	R
1481395	Bdr.	Rookwood, L.J.	48 Bty. 21 LAA	Enfield, Middlesex	27.02.45	29	S
1621236	Gnr.	Ross, J.G.	95 Bty. 48 LAA		20.02.45	32	
1488316	Gnr.	Rudling, J.W.P.	242 Bty. 48 LAA	Hadleigh, Essex	24.10.44	32	S/L
1592423	Gnr.	Russell, H.G.	48 Bty. 21 LAA	Lake Alfred, Florida, USA	08.03.45	30	
13051168	Pte.	Russell, John	Pioneer Corps.	Paisley, Renfrewshire	22.04.45	38	S
2358051	Sgmn.	Sadler, F.E.	21 LAA Sig. Sec.	Shelford, Cambridgeshire	22.07.45	36	R
2329580	Sgmn.	Said, Alfred	77 HAA Sig. Sec.		06.03.45	23	S
874036	BQMS	Salter, A.H.	15 Bty. 6 HAA		19.03.45	38	
11051931	Gnr.	Saville, Walter	242 Bty. 48 LAA	Claygate, Surrey	01.03.45	24	S
1827438	Gnr.	Scott, J.G.	242 Bty. 48 LAA	Sheffield	03.01.45	39	S
1531000	Gnr.	Scott, R.G.	48 Bty. 21 LAA	Walthamstow, Essex	13.04.45	27	S
11052595	Gnr.	Scott, Thomas	242 Bty. 48 LAA	Newcastle-on-Tyne	01.09.44	23	S/L
1828366	Gnr.	Seamarks, W.H.	48 Bty. 21 LAA	Rushden, Northamptonshire	06.02.45	21	
1498952	Sgt.	Sharp, Harry	21 LAA Regt.	Scotforth, Lancaster	28.03.45	26	S
1801674	Gnr.	Shaw, A.W.	242 Bty. 48 LAA	Canning Town, Essex	05.02.45	32	S
11051876	L/Bdr.	Shearsmith, Douglas	242 Bty. 48 LAA	Hull	14.06.45	23	S
1483130	Sgt.	Shipley, George	48 Bty. 21 LAA		17.03.45	31	S
1632166	Gnr.	Shippen, J.W.	242 Bty. 48 LAA	Altrincham, Cheshire	15.03.45	34	
1465066	Gnr.	Shrubshall, W.F.	48 Bty. 21 LAA	Sheerness, Kent	18.03.45	35	
11051567	Gnr.	Shuffleton, J.A.	242 Bty. 48 LAA		24.03.45		
1592521	Bdr.	Sime, J.R.	48 Bty. 21 LAA		28.05.45		S

Number	Rank	Name	Regiment	Place of Origin	D.O.D.	Age	Place Died
774380	Gnr.	Simmonds, Frederick	15 Bty. 6 HAA	King's Heath, Birmingham	30.11.44	35	S/L
1574392	Pte.	Simmonds, T.J.N.	21 LAA Wkshp.		23.07.45	27	S
1592522	Gnr.	Simpson, Benjamin	48 Bty. 21 LAA	Stepney, London	25.03.45	32	S/L
1490053	Gnr.	Skilbeck, Ernest	48 Bty. 21 LAA		08.11.44	40	DM
1684076	Gnr.	Slade, A.E.	95 Bty. 48 LAA		17.02.45	35	S
S/116351	Sgt.	Small, J.N.	R.A.S.C.		04.03.45	29	S
1592523	Gnr.	Smith, A.C.	48 Bty. 21 LAA		04.02.45	32	S
1548866	Gnr.	Smith, A.E.W.	21 LAA Regt.	Kentish Town, London	21.02.45	28	S
1543768	Bdr.	Smith, George	242 Bty. 48 LAA		12.01.45		S
1687386	Gnr.	Sneddon, Thomas	242 Bty. 48 LAA	Putney, London	11.06.45	33	R
912788	Gnr.	Snell, Charles	48 Bty. 21 LAA	Roehampton, London	14.09.44	23	R
1736581	Sgt.	Sperring, A.J.	242 Bty. 48 LAA	Bristol	18.03.45	38	S/L
1828369	Gnr.	Starmer, W.C.	48 Bty. 21 LAA		09.05.43		S
1808986	Gnr.	Stephens, Joseph	242 Bty. 48 LAA	Liverpool	05.04.45	24	S
1826610	Gnr.	Stephenson, Allen	21 LAA Regt.	Burnley, Lancashire	14.06.45	31	S
2562597	Sgt.	Stevenson, A.B.	77 HAA Sig. Sec.	Falkirk, Stirlingshire	07.06.45	36	R
1592526	Gnr.	Stockwell, W.J.	48 Bty. 21 LAA	Clydach Vale, Glamorgan	29.07.45	34	R
6472087	Gnr.	Sweeney, Edward	95 Bty. 48 LAA		12.04.45	31	S
1687396	Gnr.	Sweeney, Michael	95 Bty. 48 LAA	Goodmayes, Essex	07.05.45	33	
10541432	Pte.	Sweeting, A.J.	RAOC attd. 21 LAA	Chelmsford, Essex	29.03.45	41	DM
1569412	Bdr.	Tabberer, J.H.	242 Bty. 48 LAA	New Malden, Surrey	27.03.45	31	
1056974	Gnr.	Tampin, G.W.	48 Bty. 21 LAA	Custom House, Essex	11.02.45	39	S
1549050	Gnr.	Tant, F.C.	48 Bty. 21 LAA		23.04.45	29	
1478296	Bdr.	Tasker, E.L.	48 Bty. 21 LAA		18.02.45	41	DM
1801686	Gnr.	Taylor, A.L.	242 Bty. 48 LAA		09.12.44	29	S/L
1554935	Gnr.	Taylor, Cyril	95 Bty. 48 LAA	Sheffield	28.02.45	28	S
2365065	Sgmn.	Taylor, J.C.	21 LAA Sig. Sec.	Hengrove, Bristol	29.09.43		S
1610093	Gnr.	Taylor, Wallace	242 Bty. 48 LAA		16.02.45		S
2314668	Cpl.	Teasdale, W.J.	21 LAA Sig. Sec.	Mitcham, Surrey	21.02.45	41	S
1563443	Gnr.	Tester, E.J.R.	49 Bty. 48 LAA	Sevenoaks, Kent	11.06.45	32	S
871106	Sgt.	Thomas, H.J.	242 Bty. 77 HAA	Pentre, Glamorgan	12.07.45	36	R
11052607	L/Bdr.	Thompson, Arthur	242 Bty. 48 LAA	Sunderland, Co. Durham	18.02.45	23	S/L/B

Number	Rank	Name	Regiment	Place of Origin	D.O.D.	Age	Place Died
1065901	Gnr.	Thornett, A.W.J.	15 Bty. 6 HAA	Wolvercote, Oxford	14.06.45	34	R
910445	Sgt.	Thoroughgood, C.R.	48 Bty. 21 LAA		14.03.45	24	R
1547322	Gnr.	Thorpe, A.G.	95 Bty. 48 LAA		14.02.45	28	
1801699	Gnr.	Thurston, R.G.	242 Bty. 48 LAA	Bridlington, Yorkshire	28.03.45	28	
5045809	L/Cpl.	Titley, Joseph	21 LAA Wkshp.,REME	Wolverhampton	04.02.45	37	S
1820579	Gnr.	Tominey, Thomas	48 Bty. 21 LAA	Glasgow	17.02.45	39	S/L
2346404	Sgmn.	Tomkinson, David	Royal Corps. Sigs.	Llandilo, Carmarthenshire	02.03.45	25	S
11052188	Gnr.	Tonkin, Jack	242 Bty. 48 LAA	Salford, Lancashire	17.04.45	23	
1710408	Gnr.	Tonkinson, J.S.	95 Bty. 48 LAA	Coventry	23.05.45	27	
5252779	L/Cpl.	Tovey, G.H.	Worcestershire Regt.	Kidderminster, Worcestershire	27.03.45	25	S/L
6199585	Gnr.	Trevorrow, H.D.	48 Bty. 21 LAA	Matelli, West Bengal, India	04.01.45	31	R
1563215	L/Bdr.	Tritton, V.J.	48 Bty. 21 LAA	Palmers Green, Middlesex	28.06.45	33	S
11052203	L/Bdr.	Tutty, J.G.	242 Bty. 48 LAA		09.06.45		
1801702	Gnr.	Varney, H.L.	242 Bty. 48 LAA	Lwr. Edmonton, Middlesex	22.04.45	29	S
1717709	Gnr.	Venton, C.L.	242 Bty. 48 LAA	Truro, Cornwall	06.02.45		S
2351753	L/Sgt.	Waidson, Fred	77 HAA Sig. Sec.	Wolsingham, Co. Durham	24.07.45	32	R
1801703	L/Bdr.	Waite, S.A.	242 Bty. 48 LAA	Beckenham, Kent	01.06.43	32	S
11052245	Gnr.	Wakefield, A.L.B.	242 Bty. 48 LAA	Eccles, Lancashire	30.12.44	38	S
1595423	Sgt.	Walker, N.G.	48 Bty. 21 LAA		29.03.45	35	R
1549851	L/Bdr.	Warwick, A.W.	48 Bty. 21 LAA		14.11.44		S/L
1826753	Gnr.	Watson, Peter	95 Bty. 48 LAA	Glasgow	07.06.45	29	S/L/B
5880971	L/Bdr.	Watts, J.T.	95 Bty. 48 LAA		15.01.45		S
1818166	Gnr.	Webb, D.T.	H.Q., 6 HAA Regt.		02.04.45	24	S
1827650	Gnr.	Webb, H.L.	242 Bty. 48 LAA	East Dulwich, London	13.02.45	36	S
1549144	Gnr.	Webster, W.B.	48 Bty. 21 LAA		12.12.44		S
1801707	Gnr.	Weller, E.H.	242 Bty. 48 LAA		18.02.45	41	
1796289	Gnr.	Wessendorff, J.G.	242 Bty. 48 LAA	Treherbert, Glamorgan	18.01.45	23	S/L/B
797493	Gnr.	Weston, Stanley	12 Bty. 6 HAA	Slough, Buckinghamshire	07.05.45	37	
1563267	L/Bdr.	White, C.E.	48 Bty. 21 LAA	Paddington, London	23.06.43	35	S
1801709	Gnr.	White, S.J.	242 Bty. 48 LAA	Bermondsey, London	08.12.44	28	S
1826645	Gnr.	Whittle, T.C.H.	21 LAA Regt.	Nelson, Lancashire	28.02.45	31	S/L

Number	Rank	Name	Regiment	Place of Origin	D.O.D.	Age	Place Died
546730	Gnr.	Whittle, William	48 LAA Regt.	Walton-on-the-Naze, Essex	08.03.45	37	S
11052615	Gnr.	Wilkinson, Joseph	242 Bty. 48 LAA		21.12.44		S
11051568	Gnr.	Wilkinson, W.A.	242 Bty. 48 LAA	Miles Platting, Manchester	09.01.45	24	S
1796292	Gnr.	Williams, C.E.	242 Bty. 48 LAA		06.01.45		S
1549135	Gnr.	Williams, G.W.	48 Bty. 21 LAA	Coolham, Sussex	29.11.44	33	
1827755	Gnr.	Williamson, John	49 Bty. 48 LAA	Newcastle-on-Tyne	04.03.45	36	
1563284	Sgt.	Willis, E.R.	48 Bty. 21 LAA	Abbots Langley	30.03.45	34	
744583	WO.II	Willis, F.A.J.	21 LAA Wkshps.,REME	Reading, Yorkshire	15.02.45	32	S
1801710	Gnr.	Wilson, C.J.	242 Bty. 48 LAA	Stoke Newington, London	28.03.45	30	S
1490050	Sgt.	Wilson, G.E.	48 Bty. 21 LAA	Tottenham, Middlesex	21.03.45	28	S
1765808	Bdr.	Wilson, John	242 Bty. 48 LAA	Carlisle	17.03.45	38	R
1602019	Gnr.	Wilson, William	48 Bty. 21 LAA	Kensington, London	13.11.44	31	S/L
1549189	L/Bdr.	Wix, D.J.	48 Bty. 21 LAA		24.04.45	29	S/L/B
1793202	L/Bdr.	Woods, A.A.	H.Q., 16 HAA Regt.	Bishop's Stortford, Herts.	12.03.45	28	
1478001	Bdr.	Woods, E.A.	48 Bty. 21 LAA	Ipswich, Suffolk	18.06.45	32	S
1478303	Bdr.	Woolbar, R.C.	48 Bty. 21 LAA	Ealing, Middlesex	28.02.45	33	
808768	Gnr.	Woolf, W.H.	15 Bty. 6 HAA		10.03.45	32	
1592537	Gnr.	Wright, A.E.	48 Bty. 21 LAA		17.03.45	33	S/L
1811565	Gnr.	Wright, George	21 LAA Regt.		05.04.45	23	S/L/B
2369767	Sgmn.	Wright, S.W.	21 LAA Sig. Sec.	Nechells, Birmingham	16.07.45	24	
1592538	Gnr.	York, R.W.J.	48 Bty. 21 LAA	Debden, Essex	16.06.45	30	S
109991	Lieut.	Young, P.H.	12 Bty. 6 HAA		26.07.45	27	S
1592540	Gnr.	Young, William	48 Bty. 21 LAA	Bow, London	01.11.43	33	

NOTE: 636112 Cpl. J.V. Holdsworth, R.A.F. War Graves Register gives date of death 07.01.43 – should read 07.01.45. Reported to have gone to Labuan in June 1944 – reached Brunei January 1945.

1367192 AC.2 R.C. McLellan, R.A.F. Register records date of death 03.01.43. Not recorded as having died at Jesselton. Other reports indicate date of death 03.01.45.

1222372 AC.1 Chadburn, E.F. R.A.F. Register records date of death 23.04.45. Should read 23.04.43. Died at Jesselton Civil Hospital.

ROYAL AIR FORCE
Taken from Squadron Leader Hardie's Nominal Roll

Number	Rank	Name	Regiment	Place of Origin	D.O.D.	Age	Place Died
1255028	LAC	Allison, K.G.	R.A.F. (VR)	St.Leonards-on-Sea, Sussex	07.01.45	30	S
751161	W.O.	Allsop, K.H.	R.A.F. (VR)		24.07.45		R
537890	Cpl.	Ashlin, Benjamin	R.A.F.		04.02.45		S
1278350	AC.2	Austin, T.H.	RAF(VR) 84 Sqdn.		17.02.45		DM
1000884	Cpl.	Aynsley, F.A.	R.A.F. (VR)	Benwell, Newcastle-on-Tyne	16.04.45	26	S
1121082	AC.1	Baguley, Leonard	R.A.F. (VR)	Sherwood, Nottingham	12.06.45	35	R
537877	Cpl.	Balls, A.J.	R.A.F.		19.04.45	27	S/L
996234	Cpl.	Barclay, George	R.A.F. (VR)	Glasgow	10.06.45	29	S/L/B
1251664	AC.1	Barnes, L.S.	R.A.F. (VR)	Hounslow, Middlesex	12.06.45	24	R
1285064	LAC	Bassett, Elgar	R.A.F. (VR)		23.03.45		S
618731	AC.1	Bates, E.C.S.	R.A.F. 211 Sqdn.		07.06.45	27	S
910546	LAC	Beale, E.P.	R.A.F. (VR)		04.04.45	26	S
643141	LAC	Beardshaw, Herbert	R.A.F. 84 Sqdn.	Kingstanding, Birmingham	20.02.45	39	DM
1530389	AC.1	Beardsley, John	R.A.F. (VR)	New Basford, Nottingham	29.03.45	24	S
640149	Cpl.	Beavis, V.F.	R.A.F. (VR)	Tottenham, Middlesex	05.02.45	25	L/B
1054179	AC.2	Beever, Eric	R.A.F. (VR)		10.02.45	25	S
644334	LAC	Bell, Albert	R.A.F.	Co. Armagh, Nthn. Ireland	29.03.45	27	DM
1371918	AC.2	Bell, G.A.	R.A.F.	Bridge of Marnoch, Banffs.	19.12.44	23	S/L
355412	W.O.	Bessant, J.W.	R.A.F.	Liverpool	04.04.45	45	S
952860	Cpl.	Bishop, E.G.	R.A.F. (VR)	Warrington, Lancashire	14.04.45	26	S
84844	Flt/Lt.	Blackledge, R.G. MID	RAF(VR) 232 Sqdn.	Newcastle-on-Tyne	10.06.45	33	S/L/B
1330503	AC.1	Blazley, T.W.	RAF(VR) 211 Sqdn.		04.06.45	22	
1201580	LAC	Bluck, H.G.	R.A.F. (VR)	Cambridge	14.03.43		
1366139	AC.1	Blyth, J.W.	RAF(VR) 211 Sqdn.	Largs, Ayrshire	16.06.45	24	S
1069332	AC.1	Booth, Frank	R.A.F. (VR)		04.03.45	30	S
565512	Sgt.	Boutcher, D.G.	R.A.F. 211 Sqdn.	Merlins Bridge, Pembrokeshire	15.04.45		S
362816	F/Sgt.	Bowden, J.A.	R.A.F. 205 Sqdn.		04.07.45		S
912488	LAC	Brackenbury, K.S.	R.A.F. (VR)		26.03.45		S

Number	Rank	Name	Regiment	Place of Origin	D.O.D.	Age	Place Died
636346	Cpl.	Bremner, Ian	R.A.F.	Charlton, London	21.03.45	25	S/L/B
565691	Sgt.	Brett, P.J.	R.A.F. 205 Sqdn.	Stansted, Essex	19.03.45	31	S
1207379	LAC	Brown, A.E.	R.A.F. (VR)	Bray, Berkshire	16.03.45	39	S
918625	AC.1	Brown, L.D.	R.A.F. (VR)	Prenton, Cheshire	04.12.44	28	S
1185141	LAC	Bull, W.G.	R.A.F. (VR)	Southall, Middlesex	26.09.44	33	R
63906	F/Offr.	Burgess, H.G.	R.A.F. (VR)	Stamford, Lincolnshire	03.08.45	41	R
994570	AC.1	Burgess, R.R.	R.A.F. (VR)	Blairgowrie, Perthshire	07.01.45	36	S
746177	Cpl.	Burroughs, J.G.	R.A.F. (VR)	Holland-on-Sea, Essex	07.06.45	25	S
990101	AC.2	Camberg, David	R.A.F. (VR)	Glasgow	18.04.45	25	S
927033	LAC	Campling, F.S.	RAF(VR) 258 Sqdn.		22.03.45		DM
561497	Sgt.	Cartwright, Edwin	R.A.F.	Wellingore, Lincolnshire	15.02.45	33	
117799	F/Offr.	Caruth, R.A.Y.	R.A.F.	Durban, South Africa	22.06.45		K
1162044	Cpl.	Castle, S.H.L.	R.A.F. (VR)	Isleworth, Middlesex	25.02.45	24	S
756298	AC.2	Cawsey, A.R.	R.A.F. (VR)	Gillingham, Kent	05.12.44	24	S/L
623055	Cpl.	Chapples, Ivor	R.A.F.		05.04.45	26	S
521265	Cpl.	Chinchen, H.J.	R.A.F.	Swanage, Dorsetshire	14.04.45	29	S
923452	Cpl.	Clark, A.C.	RAF(VR) 211 Sqdn.	Bermondsey, London	22.02.45	26	DM
551353	Sgt.	Clark, H.E.	R.A.F.		23.04.45	24	S
1158207	LAC	Clark, R.W.J.	R.A.F. (VR)	Exeter	21.12.44	40	S
1330266	AC.1	Clarke, H.B.	R.A.F. (VR)		28.02.45		DM
1478164	AC.2	Clavery, R.B.	R.A.F. (VR)		05.02.45		S/L/B
970707	Cpl.	Clayton, James	R.A.F. (VR)	Co. Down, Nthn. Ireland	02.03.45	28	S
1113486	AC.1	Cliff, Ronald	R.A.F. (VR)	Bolton, Lancashire	09.06.45	25	S
1216180	AC.1	Coggon, Harold	R.A.F. (VR)	Doncaster, Yorkshire	24.06.45	22	
536816	Cpl.	Coghlan, Nicholas	R.A.F.		19.03.45		
1175158	AC.1	Cole, E.F.	R.A.F. (VR)		19.01.44		
940191	LAC	Cole, P.W.	RAF(VR) 211 Sqdn.	Stuntney, Cambridgeshire	09.06.45	23	S
1220595	AC.1	Collins, A.E.	R.A.F. (VR)	Brighton, Sussex	26.03.45	37	S
913650	LAC	Coombs, John	R.A.F. (VR)	Lightwater, Surrey	07.07.45	31	S
1293357	AC.2	Cosham, K.F.	RAF(VR) 211 Sqdn.		08.03.45		R
1018560	AC.1	Cossens, R.E.	R.A.F. (VR)		05.07.45		S
1184669	LAC	Cossey, C.E.	R.A.F. (VR)		24.02.45		S

314

Number	Rank	Name	Regiment	Place of Origin	D.O.D.	Age	Place Died
120083	F/Offr.	Cressey, S.W.	R.A.F.	Ferntree Gully, Vic.,Australia	11.07.45	47	S
1036472	AC.1	Crone, J.K.	R.A.F. (VR)	Kendal, Westmorland	05.04.45	23	S
1158503	LAC	Crook, A.L.	R.A.F. (VR)		12.06.45		
1135172	AC.1	Curtis, R.S.	R.A.F. (VR)	Walthamstow, Essex	16.01.45	35	S
1296774	AC.1	Darby, P.E.	R.A.F. (VR)	Corfe Mullen, Dorsetshire	16.11.44	22	S
920886	AC.1	Davey, R.T.	RAF(VR) 211 Sqdn.	Exmouth, Devon	21.04.45	24	S/L/B
630718	Cpl.	Davey, William	R.A.F. 211 Sqdn.		16.09.44		S
1498158	AC.2	Davies, J.I.	R.A.F. (VR)		08.03.45		DM
633049	LAC	Davies, Lawrence	R.A.F.	Rainhill, Lancashire	30.04.45	26	S
1232082	AC.2	Davies, T.B.	RAF(VR) 211 Sqdn.	Sheffield	19.05.45	24	
1317077	AC.1	Davis, Christopher	RAF(VR) 211 Sqdn.		05.01.45	22	S/L/B
548711	AC.1	Deacon, W.J.	R.A.F.	Saltash, Cornwall	15.02.45	22	DM
1296952	AC.2	Doe, J.H.	RAF(VR) 242 Sqdn.		27.03.45	25	
940560	AC.2	Drew, J.S.	R.A.F. (VR)	Nth. Malvern, Worcestershire	21.03.45	22	
1282873	AC.2	Drew, R.E.	R.A.F. (VR)	Wembley Park, Middlesex	25.04.45	23	
949483	LAC	Duncan, J.B.	R.A.F. (VR)	Stockton-on-Tees, Co.Durham	24.02.45	27	S/L
959838	Cpl.	Durham, J.A.	R.A.F. (VR)	Tredegar, Monmouthshire	22.03.45	31	DM
962177	Cpl.	Durrant, R.J.	R.A.F. (VR)	Norwich	28.02.45	28	
643028	LAC	Dyer, W.V.	R.A.F.	Luxulyan, Cornwall	05.06.45	26	S
1208841	LAC	Edden, S.V.	R.A.F. (VR)	Tamworth, Staffordshire	19.03.45	31	S
1367265	AC.1	Elder, A.H.	R.A.F. (VR)	Kirkcaldy, Fife	22.04.45	38	S
574596	Cpl.	Elliott, D.V.	R.A.F.	Beccles, Suffolk	17.03.45	23	DM
946929	LAC	Endersby, R.W.	R.A.F. (VR)	Stoke, Coventry	16.01.45	24	S
1026512	LAC	Eyles, W.A.R.	R.A.F. (VR)	Northampton	12.03.45	31	
1286452	LAC	Failes, C.E.	R.A.F. (VR)	Acton, Middlesex	05.04.45	32	S
633556	Cpl.	Fairgray, Nelson	R.A.F. 84 Sqdn.		28.02.45		
1211363	AC.1	Feltham, M.R.	R.A.F. 211 Sqdn.	Bournemouth, Hampshire	02.07.45	24	R
627990	Cpl.	Fenn, Norman	R.A.F.		14.06.45		S
611918	LAC	Fisher, Eric	R.A.F. 84 Sqdn.		09.02.45		S
993389	Cpl.	Fisher, T.W.S.	R.A.F. (VR)		23.03.45	23	S

315

Number	Rank	Name	Regiment	Place of Origin	D.O.D.	Age	Place Died
1035626	AC.1	Fletcher, Jack	R.A.F. (VR)		29.03.45		DM
1136363	AC.2	Fletcher, S.N.	R.A.F. (VR)		03.03.45	25	S
1053276	AC.1	Flinn, M.M.	R.A.F. (VR)	Smethwick, Staffordshire	04.10.44		S
1108527	LAC	Foley, Michael	R.A.F. (VR)		21.07.45		R
1354824	LAC	Ford, E.A.	R.A.F. (VR)	Newcastle-on-Tyne	24.02.45	35	24
991523	LAC	Foster, Edwin	R.A.F. (VR)	Hull	07.06.45	27	
565537	Sgt.	Freeman, P.R.C.	R.A.F.	Higherford, Lancashire	03.04.45	29	S
				Felixstowe, Suffolk			
995893	AC.1	Garner, J.H.	R.A.F. (VR)	Stockport, Cheshire	15.12.44	30	S/L
927421	LAC	Garrad, E.F.	R.A.F. (VR)	Little Wakering, Essex	08.04.45	23	DM
1099099	AC.1	Gates, A.I.	RAF(VR) 211 Sqdn.	Plasmarl, Swansea	11.03.45	34	
774090	LAC	Gavigan, E.P.	RAF(VR) 211 Sqdn.	Kingston-on-Thames, Surrey	14.01.45	35	S
958618	AC.1	Gibbs, C.F.	R.A.F. (VR)	Alton, Hampshire	23.02.45	21	
1025146	AC.2	Giffen, William	R.A.F. (VR)		27.03.45		
1289933	LAC	Gilder, A.J.	R.A.F.		13.03.45		
643685	LAC	Glover, J.B.	R.A.F.	Broughton, Lincolnshire	03.04.45	28	S
126007	AC.1	Godlonton, A.G.	R.A.F. (VR)		06.04.45		S
1317118	AC.1	Gollop, W.D.	RAF(VR) 211 Sqdn.	Parkstone, Dorsetshire	30.06.45	24	
624736	LAC	Goodwin, F.R.	R.A.F. (VR)		06.03.45		
1242148	LAC	Gordon, H.C.	R.A.F. (VR)	Ashton-under-Lyne, Lancs.	12.05.45	32	DM
960165	AC.1	Granger, H.P.	R.A.F. (VR)		22.06.45		S
988973	LAC	Gray, J.D.	R.A.F. (VR)		31.12.44		
1105550	LAC	Green, Henry	R.A.F. (VR)	Wigan, Lancashire	16.03.45	24	
1134110	AC.2	Greenfield, Arthur	R.A.F. (VR)	Hull	03.01.45	28	S/L
994444	AC.2	Grice, R.W.	R.A.F. (VR)	Wigan, Lancashire	30.03.45	24	R
937097	LAC	Griffiths, E.S.	R.A.F. (VR)	Ellesmere, Shropshire	03.03.45	25	
1133340	AC.1	Griffiths, Idwai	R.A.F. (VR)	Tynywerglodd, Caernarvonshire	29.12.44	25	S
953230	AC.1	Groundon, F.G.	R.A.F. (VR)	Sunderland, Co. Durham	22.03.45	24	
635988	Cpl.	Guerin, Daniel	R.A.F.	Boherbue, Co.Cork, Irish Rep.	25.04.45	37	S
952345	AC.2	Guy, Graham	R.A.F. (VR)	Wakefield, Yorkshire	27.02.45	27	
1134150	LAC	Hall, Leslie	R.A.F. (VR)	Slaithwaite, Yorkshire	01.03.45	39	
648252	LAC	Hall, R.J.	R.A.F.	Ilford, Essex	20.06.45	26	S
972747	LAC	Harris, Bertie	R.A.F. 84 Sqdn.	Inverglen, Argyllshire	22.03.45	28	

316

Number	Rank	Name	Regiment	Place of Origin	D.O.D.	Age	Place Died
1127239	AC.2	Harris, C.W.	RAF(VR) 211 Sqdn.	West Benwell, Newcastle-on-Tyne	30.04.45	22	S
1145369	AC.2	Harris, John	R.A.F. (VR)	Birmingham	15.06.45		S
519284	Cpl.	Harrison, Harold	R.A.F.	Hucknall, Nottinghamshire	03.04.45	31	S
975322	Cpl.	Haslam, S.J.	R.A.F. (VR)	Dolton Rectory, Devon	21.06.45	27	S
1212107	AC.1	Hawkins, Clifford	R.A.F. (VR)		15.06.45		S
624395	LAC	Hayward, G.L.	R.A.F.	Hull	19.03.45	24	S/L/B
1189230	LAC	Hester, W.V.	R.A.F. (VR)	Aldershot, Hampshire	14.03.45		
1495268	AC.2	Hickson, Frank	RAF(VR) 211 Sqdn.	Rochdale, Lancashire	01.12.44	39	S
1151463	AC.1	Hill, L.W.	R.A.F. (VR)	Eton, Buckinghamshire	04.12.44	27	S/L
1180962	Cpl.	Hobbs, F.W.	R.A.F. (VR)	Luton, Bedfordshire	23.05.45	25	S
1087945	AC.1	Hodges, Thomas	RAF(VR) 211 Sqdn.		05.02.45		S
1039619	AC.2	Hodgkinson, Frank	RAF(VR) 211 Sqdn.	Blackburn, Lancashire	16.10.44	23	S
1104224	AC.1	Hodkinson, J.E.	R.A.F. (VR)	Middlewich, Cheshire	21.04.45	30	
1135446	AC.1	Holben, R.J.	R.A.F. (VR)	Hammersmith, London	05.04.45	35	
636112	Cpl.	Holdsworth, J.V.	R.A.F. 84 Sqdn.	Bradford, Yorkshire	07.01.4S	26	S/L/B
908080	LAC	Holman, R.F.	RAF(VR) 211 Sqdn.	Hadleigh, Suffolk	13.05.45	31	
1009942	LAC	Hornsby, A.E.	R.A.F. (VR)	Barmby Marsh, Yorkshire	07.02.45	30	S/L/B
1185599	LAC	Hudgell, H.E.	R.A.F. (VR)	Sawbridgeworth, Herts.	14.07.45	33	S
1218482	AC.2	Hughes, A.J.	RAF(VR) 242 Sqdn.		28.03.45		
1260445	AC.1	Hughes, B.F.	R.A.F. (VR)		11.07.45		R
1059747	AC.1	Humphries, W.G.	RAF(VR) 211 Sqdn.	Leeds, Yorkshire	24.05.45	23	S
563799	W.O.	Hynes, C.A.	R.A.F. 242 Sqdn.	Resolven, Glamorgan	06.03.45	31	S/L
1004986	LAC	Ingham, Harry	R.A.F. (VR)	Accrington, Lancashire	23.03.45	29	
1237236	AC.2	Jacobs, Alec	RAF(VR) 211 Sqdn.	Stepney, London	01.06.45	23	S
995708	AC.1	James, H.O.	R.A.F. (VR)	Southport, Lancashire	25.01.45	40	S
1349505	AC.2	Jamieson, John	R.A.F. (VR)	King's Park, Glasgow	23.03.45	40	
1367070	AC.1	Jazewcis, Wincas	R.A.F. (VR)		23.02.45	30	
1055869	AC.2	Jefferies, J.P.	RAF(VR) 211 Sqdn.		21.02.45		S
520582	Cpl.	Jefferson, H.T.A.	R.A.F.		05.04.45		S
1253333	AC.1	Jewell, W.J.	R.A.F. (VR)	Cardiff	03.04.45-	33	S
1273387	AC.1	Johnson, Ernest	R.A.F. (VR)	Swindon, Wiltshire	14.02.45		S/L

317

Number	Rank	Name	Regiment	Place of Origin	D.O.D.	Age	Place Died
653301	Cpl.	Jones, B.P.	R.A.F.	Llanelly, Carmarthenshire	15.04.45	24	S
1010911	LAC	Jones, M.P.	R.A.F. (VR)		13.07.45		S
970172	AC.1	Jones, Thomas	R.A.F. (VR)	Longsight, Manchester	27.03.45	27	S
1123171	AC.1	Jones, Tivy	R.A.F. (VR)		21.07.45	23	S
750336	AC.1	Jones, W.F.	R.A.F. (VR)	Osney, Oxfordshire	01.04.45		R
1106684	AC.2	Jordan, F.J.	R.A.F. (VR)	Liverpool	12.06.45	31	S
785110	AC.2	Joshua, J.M.	R.A.F. (VR)		10.06.45		S/L/B
538301	Cpl.	Joy, R.L.T.	R.A.F.	St. Andrews, Fife	02.12.44	26	S/L
1073264	AC.1	Kay, Raymond	RAF(VR) 211 Sqdn.	Sheffield	15.12.44		S/L/B
1195700	LAC	Kearney, F.W.	R.A.F. (VR)		21.02.45	32	DM
574679	Cpl.	Kemmler, J.M.	R.A.F.		02.04.45		S/L/B
941986	Cpl.	Kennerley, Kenneth	R.A.F. (VR)		25.04.45		S
1104252	LAC	Kent, G.H.	R.A.F. (VR)	Nuneaton, Warwickshire	19.06.45		S
642298	Cpl.	Kitchingham, Tom	R.A.F.	Margate	26.03.45	23	S
911965	Cpl.	Kleiser, E.L.	R.A.F. (VR)		28.03.45		S
1072004	AC.1	Knapper, G.W.	R.A.F. (VR)	Easington Coll., Co.Durham	15.06.45	24	S
1021437	AC.1	Lane, Alan	R.A.F. (VR)		14.02.45		S
1129837	AC.1	Larter, G.R.	R.A.F. (VR)	Rattlesden, Suffolk	21.02.45	39	DM
541973	Cpl.	Latham, Ralph	R.A.F.	Moulton, Cheshire	26.12.44	26	S
1276938	AC.1	Lawrence, E.G.	R.A.F. (VR)	Llanishen, Cardiff	06.02.45	38	S
641243	LAC	Lealand, Joseph	R.A.F.		23.04.45		S
613250	AC.1	Lee, Robert	R.A.F.	Shaw, Lancashire	30.03.45	24	S
1365472	AC.2	Leslie, George	R.A.F. (VR)		31.12.44	33	S
1007659	AC.1	Lewis, Albert	R.A.F. (VR)	Pontymister, Monmouthshire	05.01.45	39	S/L
142610	F/Offr.	Linge, A.J.	R.A.F. (VR)		26.06.45	53	DM
935211	W.O.	Littlewood, E.L.	RAF(VR) 205 Sqdn.	Hope, Derbyshire	17.03.45	28	DM
912998	AC.1	Lucas, C.R.G.	R.A.F. (VR)	Rainham, Essex	31.03.45	25	S
539798	AC.2	McCandless, J.R.	R.A.F.	Co.Down, Nthn.Ireland	11.08.45	28	R
1107403	AC.1	McConnell, W.S.	R.A.F. (VR)	Falkirk, Stirlingshire	13.03.45	25	
358213	Sgt.	McDermott, T.H.	R.A.F.	Braintree, Essex	27.07.45	40	R

318

Number	Rank	Name	Regiment	Place of Origin	D.O.D.	Age	Place Died
951784	LAC	McGregor, N.E.	R.A.F. (VR)	Leeds, Yorkshire	25.11.44	32	S
646134	Cpl.	McKeon, Leonard	R.A.F.	Stalybridge, Cheshire	27.03.45	26	
1367192	AC.2	McLellan, R.C.	R.A.F. (VR)	Glasgow	03.01.45	39	S
950231	LAC	McNee, S.R.	R.A.F. (VR)	Glasgow	23.01.45	26	R
935920	Cpl.	Mahon, E.O.	R.A.F. (VR)	Bradford, Yorkshire	30.06.45	37	S
1051577	LAC	Maitland, Thomas	R.A.F. (VR)	Castleside, Co. Durham	03.02.45	31	S/L
978638	AC.1	Marks, R.G.	R.A.F. (VR)	Blackrock,Co.Dublin,Ire.Rep.	08.11.44		DM
544332	Cpl.	Marriott, P.C.	R.A.F.	Barnwell, Northamptonshire	18.02.45	26	S
641845	Cpl.	Marsh, E.A.	R.A.F. (VR)	Barry, Glamorgan	05.06.45	23	S
933429	LAC	Matthews, T.R.	R.A.F. 211 Sqdn.	Ramsgate, Kent	14.07.45	23	S
1257180	AC.2	Maylam, H.E.	RAF(VR) 211 Sqdn.	Whitstable, Kent	10.05.45	32	R
505712	W.O.	Merchant, A.H.	R.A.F.	Plymouth	18.07.45	38	S
1326199	AC.1	Middleton, Norman	RAF(VR) 211 Sqdn.	Ashbourne, Derbyshire	30.03.45	33	
539095	LAC	Millar, P.R.	R.A.F. 211 Sqdn.	Bonnyrigg, Midlothian	21.07.45	31	S
1475234	AC.2	Millard, W.E.	R.A.F. (VR)	Gosforth, Newcastle-on-Tyne	28.01.45	40	S
637570	LAC	Miller, D.C.	R.A.F.	Parkstone, Dorsetshire	07.06.45	23	S
1151812	Cpl.	Milton, H.E.	R.A.F. (VR)	Folkestone	30.04.45	29	S
937975	Cpl.	Mitchell, A.W.	R.A.F. (VR)	Sheffield	03.06.45	31	S
645710	AC.1	Moore, Douglas	R.A.F.		27.02.45		DM
749641	Cpl.	Moore, F.W.A.	R.A.F. (VR)	Gillingham, Kent	15.02.45	25	
1028262	AC.1	Morris, Leonard	R.A.F. (VR)	Hyson Green, Notts	28.03.45	24	R
1286629	AC.1	Morton, G.S.	R.A.F. (VR)	Southall, Middlesex	27.12.44	27	S/L
1105761	LAC	Mullaney, James	RAF(VR) 211 Sqdn.	Liverpool	11.03.45	24	S/L/B
969870	Cpl.	Munro, John	R.A.F. (VR)		28.05.45	29	S/L/B
940019	AC.1	Nathan, G.M.	R.A.F. (VR)	Nottingham	14.02.45	28	DM
1294019	AC.1	Newman, F.K.	RAF(VR) 211 Sqdn.	Wandsworth, London	07.03.45	23	DM
1376881	AC.1	Newman, F.R.	R.A.F. (VR)		21.03.45		
913831	LAC	O'Keeffe, A.J.H.	RAF(VR) 205 Sqdn.	Walthamstow, Essex	26.01.45	26	S/L
956432	LAC	Oldroyd, H.G.	R.A.F. (VR)	Hull	16.04.45	27	
622104	AC.1	Orange, Thomas	R.A.F.		05.03.45		S/L
1300537	AC.1	Ormond, W.J.	R.A.F. (VR)	Hasguard, Pembrokeshire	04.09.44	34	S

319

Number	Rank	Name	Regiment	Place of Origin	D.O.D.	Age	Place Died
1103634	LAC	Orr, Hugh	R.A.F. (VR)	Hamilton, Lanarkshire	09.01.45	24	S
1390430	AC.1	Palmer, E.A.	R.A.F. (VR)	Hornsey, Middlesex	13.12.44	29	S/L/B
651872	LAC	Parfitt, A.W.C.	R.A.F.	Compton, Berkshire	07.03.45	25	R
523222	Cpl.	Parker, F.H.	R.A.F.		12.03.45		
1198371	AC.2	Parker, R.C.	RAF(VR) 211 Sqdn.	Iver Heath, Buckinghamshire	14.03.45	30	
575669	AC.1	Pask, J.K.	R.A.F.	Terrington, St.Clement, Norfolk	15.06.45	21	S
942946	LAC	Passey, F.M.	R.A.F. (VR)	Church Gresley, Derbyshire	13.05.45	25	
1169691	AC.1	Patchesa, H.A.	R.A.F. (VR)	Northampton	02.06.45	24	
1253054	AC.1	Paterson, Leslie	R.A.F. (VR)	Broxbourne, Hertfordshire	14.06.45		R
995058	LAC	Payne, W.E.	R.A.F.	Blackhall Rocks, Co. Durham	07.06.45	30	
1498100	AC.2	Pearce, Charles	R.A.F. (VR)	Kingstanding, Birmingham	05.03.45	23	DM
971437	Cpl.	Pearson, C.B.	R.A.F. (VR)	West Hartlepool, Co. Durham	02.06.45	30	R
648059	Cpl.	Pelan, H.G.	R.A.F.	Lisburn,Co.Antrim,Nth.Ireland	15.02.45	33	S
949022	LAC	Pennell, R.W.	R.A.F. (VR)	Rooksbridge, Somerset	23.01.45	30	S
1496245	AC.2	Pepper, W.J.	R.A.F. (VR)	Stanley, Lancashire	17.02.45	22	S/L
616800	LAC	Perkins, J.W.F.	R.A.F.		06.04.45		S
509897	Cpl.	Perry, H.S.	R.A.F.	Totley Rise, Yorkshire	15.05.45	40	
971938	LAC	Petheram, K.D.G.	R.A.F. (VR)	Mumbles, Glamorgan	20.03.45	24	
1255877	AC.1	Phillips, D.G.	R.A.F. (VR)	Neath, Glamorgan	13.03.45	36	
510644	Cpl.	Phillips, J.W.	R.A.F.	Llandilo, Carmarthenshire	04.10.44	37	S
572595	Cpl.	Pimblett, Eric	R.A.F.	Waterfoot, Lancashire	01.07.45	24	
536640	LAC	Pittendreigh, William	R.A.F.	Crudie, Aberdeenshire	12.03.45	26	
1103844	AC.1	Plummer, H.W.	R.A.F. (VR)	South Shields, Co. Durham	15.07.44	30	S
934876	AC.1	Polden, L.W.	R.A.F. (VR)	Sutton, Surrey	07.03.45	30	
533811	F/Sgt.	Potter, A.A.	R.A.F. (VR)	Stoke Gabriel, Devon	21.02.45	27	S
1441975	AC.2	Potts, L.G.	R.A.F. (VR)	Bow, London	19.05.45	21	
654215	AC.1	Powell, J.F.	R.A.F.	Milford Haven, Pembrokeshire	26.11.44	22	S
964703	LAC	Preston, A.A.	R.A.F. (VR)	Kirk Hallam, Derbyshire	07.03.45	32	S/L
1274285	AC.1	Price, D.J.	R.A.F. (VR)	Farnborough, Hampshire	21.02.45	32	DM
1087942	AC.2	Price, G.R.	R.A.F. (VR)		08.04.45	38	S
998580	LAC	Priddle, G.F.	R.A.F. (VR)	Torquay, Devon	12.06.45	32	R

Number	Rank	Name	Regiment	Place of Origin	D.O.D.	Age	Place Died
1250381	AC.1	Quy, E.C.	R.A.F. (VR)	Great Totham, Essex	01.03.45	32	S/L
1269585	AC.1	Ramsay, H.J.	R.A.F. (VR)	Kingsbury, Middlesex	30.06.45	25	S
1050595	LAC	Ramsay, J.O.	R.A.F. (VR)	Eyemouth, Berwickshire	29.01.45	35	S
623622	Sgt.	Ransome, Harry	R.A.F.	Altofts, Yorkshire	23.03.45	25	
1058262	AC.2	Ratcliffe, W.W.	RAF(VR) 211 Sqdn.		23.03.45		S/L
1296836	AC.1	Read, L.W.	RAF(VR) 211 Sqdn.	Charlton Marshall, Dorsetshire	30.11.44	23	
1177473	AC.1	Reeves, G.F.	R.A.F.	Angmering, Sussex	02.03.45	24	
993394	AC.1	Rennie, George	R.A.F.		15.07.45		S
1333041	AC.2	Richards, L.L.	R.A.F. (VR)	Brightlingsea, Essex	30.03.45	23	S
1271734	AC.1	Rickard, Thomas	R.A.F. (VR)	Staines, Middlesex	08.06.45	27	S
991984	AC.1	Rigby, William	R.A.F. (VR)	Wakefield, Yorkshire	12.03.45	26	S/L
1158722	AC.1	Robb, H.S.	R.A.F. (VR)		20.02.45		
1242271	AC.1	Roberts, O.G.	R.A.F. (VR)	Bedwas, Monmouthshire	12.12.44	30	S
1106425	AC.1	Robson, J.R.	RAF(VR) 211 Sqdn.		13.07.45	27	S
939135	LAC	Root, J.E.	R.A.F. (VR)	Hendon, Middlesex	24.04.45	27	S/L/B
1231820	AC.2	Rouchy, J.F.	R.A.F. (VR)		26.03.45		
1326197	AC.1	Rowarth, J.G.	R.A.F. (VR)	Sth.Normanton, Derbyshire	27.03.45	26	S/L/B
1283802	AC.1	Rowland, J.D.	R.A.F. (VR)		08.06.44		S
1164836	AC.1	Rowley, Albert	R.A.F. (VR)	Hanley, Stoke-on-Trent	02.12.44	33	S/L
620977	LAC	Sampson, F.S.	R.A.F.	Callington, Cornwall	05.02.45	24	
335329	W.O.	Sanders, T.W.	R.A.F.		27.12.44		S
1374118	AC.2	Sands, A.McG.	RAF(VR) 271 Sqdn.		02.08.45		R
543013	LAC	Sarginson, J.E.	R.A.F.	Gateshead, Co. Durham	09.02.45	26	S
750305	AC.1	Saunders, R.W.	R.A.F. (VR)	Abingdon, Berkshire	23.04.45	26	S
1270226	AC.2	Scotcher, F.R.	R.A.F. (VR)	Ipswich, Suffolk	21.04.45	24	S/L/B
1120396	AC.1	Seal, C.A.	RAF(VR) 211 Sqdn.		02.03.45	39	DM
642378	Cpl.	Seckington, Eric	R.A.F.	Birmingham	18.04.45	23	
938152	AC.2	Shackleton, Norman	R.A.F. (VR)	Carlisle	25.02.45	26	
1142345	AC.2	Shatwell, Charles	R.A.F. (VR)		30.11.44		S
947650	LAC	Shaw, G.P.	R.A.F. (VR)	Birkby, Huddersfield	08.12.44	23	S
1030209	LAC	Shaw, Reginald	R.A.F. (VR)	Coalville, Leicestershire	21.06.45	29	S

321

Number	Rank	Name	Regiment	Place of Origin	D.O.D.	Age	Place Died
752181	LAC	Sherriff, F.C.	RAF(VR) 205 Sqdn.	Hutton, Essex	05.06.45	40	S
944334	AC.1	Simpson, G.A.	RAF(VR) 211 Sqdn.		27.03.45	25	S
1232047	AC.1	Simpson, G.W.	R.A.F. (VR)		11.06.45	25	
1195232	AC.2	Sims, Eric	RAF(VR) 211 Sqdn.	Aylestone, Leicester	25.05.45	24	S
1269900	AC.1	Slater, J.E.	R.A.F. (VR)		02.06.45		
1069715	AC.1	Smith, G.B.	R.A.F. (VR)		15.03.45		
1030298	LAC	Smith, J.H.	R.A.F. (VR)	South Yardley, Birmingham	09.03.45	33	
956498	LAC	Smith, J.T.	R.A.F. (VR)	Coseley, Staffordshire	08.07.45	29	R
1025329	AC.1	Smith, S.J.	R.A.F. (VR)	Lwr.Openshaw, Manchester	01.08.45	38	R
1349504	AC.2	Smith, T.D.	R.A.F. (VR)	Cheadle, Cheshire	30.04.43	39	S
786355	AC.2	Soorier, M.K.	R.A.F. (VR)	Seramban, Malaya	03.06.45		
525345	Cpl	Soutar, D.C.	R.A.F.		01.11.44	33	S/L
1292960	AC.i	Southwell, J.R.	R.A.F. (VR)		03.05.45		
619442	LAC	Spencer, F.I.	R.A.F. 211 Sqdn.	Manchester	14.02.45	40	S
634384	LAC	Spuffard, E.N.	R.A.F.	Harringay, Middlesex	17.12.44	24	S/L
529174	F/Sgt.	Stammers, A.G.	R.A.F. 205 Sqdn.	Badingham, Suffolk	05.06.45	28	S
1387375	AC.1	Stapeley, O.W.	R.A.F. (VR)	Walthamstow, Essex	16.07.45	22	R
569396	Cpl.	Stephens, J.C.	R.A.F. 205 Sqdn.	Hampstead, London	14.04.45	25	S
933479	LAC	Sticklee, H.S.	R.A.F. (VR)	Romford, Essex	01.12.44	44	S
972854	Cpl.	Street, Alec	R.A.F. (VR)		16.02.45		S
644381	Cpl.	Summerfield, Victor	R.A.F.	Hampstead, London	03.03.45	27	
1103688	LAC	Swindell, George	R.A.F. (VR)	Sheffield	13.03.45	32	
1017354	AC.1	Symonds, A.G.	R.A.F. (VR)	Lockleaze, Bristol	15.03.45	32	
940694	LAC	Taylor, A.L.	RAF(VR) 211 Sqdn.	Rushden, Northamptonshire	28.03.45	28	
1206929	AC.1	Taylor, E.W.	R.A.F. (VR)		20.03.45		
508150	Sgt.	Tennent, B.G.R.	R.A.F.	Hendon, Middlesex	21.07.45	35	S
613325	Cpl.	Thomas, Benjamin	R.A.F.		02.04.45		
1050417	Cpl.	Thompson, E.H.	R.A.F. (VR)		23.04.45		
969695	LAC	Thompson, Robert	R.A.F. (VR)	Belfast, Nthn. Ireland	15.06.45	21	
816056	LAC	Thompson, S.T.	R.A.F.	Belfast, Nthn. Ireland	26.03.45		DM
647676	LAC	Tout, R.E.G.	R.A.F. 211 Sqdn.	Malvern Link, Worcs.	11.12.44	26	S/L
912890	LAC	Toye, J.W.	R.A.F. (VR)	Holborn, London	28.02.45	29	DM

Number	Rank	Name	Regiment	Place of Origin	D.O.D.	Age	Place Died
1055582	AC.1	Trickett, E.S.	R.A.F. (VR)		01.06.45		S
621324	W.O.	Tugwell, W.P.	R.A.F.		19.03.45	26	DM
574644	LAC	Turland, P.C.	R.A.F.		02.05.45	23	S
943084	LAC	Turnbull, E.D.	R.A.F. (VR)	Heston, Middlesex	03.04.45		S
646177	LAC	Umpleby, Edgar	R.A.F.	Escrick, Yorkshire	20.03.45	27	
942171	LAC	Urry, Fred	R.A.F. (VR)		18.03.45	27	
516884	Sgt.	Vickerman, Herbert	R.A.F.	Granchester, Cambridgeshire	07.06.45	31	S
937399	LAC	Walker, J.S.	R.A.F. (VR)	Northampton	24.02.45	24	
1352874	Cpl.	Wallace, R.A.	R.A.F. (VR)	East Newport, Fife	06.04.45		
304115	Cpl.	Walmsley, M.W.	R.A.F.		12.07.45		R
77336	Chpln.	Wanless, The Rev. J.T.	attd. R.A.F.		30.06.45		
940527	AC.1	Ware, John	R.A.F. (VR)	Dagenham, Essex	03.04.45	24	S
365809	F/Sgt.	Warner, S.L.	R.A.F.	Bognor Regis, Sussex	21.04.45	36	S
1073941	AC.1	Waterhouse, Charles	RAF(VR) 84 Sqdn.	Swinton, Lancashire	08.02.45	36	S
951267	AC.1	Watkins, K.O.	R.A.F. (VR)	Cardiff	24.01.45	28	S
625094	Cpl.	Watson, A.J.	R.A.F.	Cathays, Glamorgan	09.07.45	24	R
1450291	AC.2	Watson, W.T.T.	R.A.F. (VR)	Croydon, Surrey	05.05.45	22	
1251128	LAC	Watts, Ronald	R.A.F. (VR)	Hitchin, Hertfordshire	29.07.45	29	S
950703	Cpl.	Waud, K.J.	R.A.F. (VR)	Grimsby, Lincolnshire	08.03.45	26	
358244	Cpl.	Webster, William	R.A.F. 242 Sqdn.	Ramsgate, Kent	11.06.45	40	
940195	LAC	Weller, A.L.	RAF(VR) 211 Sqdn.	Brixton, London	15.02.45	24	S/L
1259096	LAC	Wells, E.W.	RAF(VR) 242 Sqdn.	Mill Hill, Middlesex	19.01.45	35	S
1292985	AC.1	Wells, F.G.	R.A.F. (VR)	Penge, Kent	29.05.45	23	
1354117	AC.1	Whitehead, R.M.	R.A.F. (VR)	Godstone, Surrey	14.02.45	23	DM
516891	W.O.	Whiteside, R.MacD.	R.A.F. (VR)	Ansdell, Lancashire	14.06.45	29	
1005976	AC.1	Wigglesworth, L.H.	RAF(VR) 27 Sqdn.	Rotherham, Yorkshire	10.06.45	24	S/L/B
1341518	AC.1	Wilkie, J.McE.	R.A.F. (VR)	Bankfoot, Perthshire	22.02.45	19	
1196742	AC.2	Williams, A.E.	R.A.F. (VR)	Thornbury, Gloucestershire	05.01.45	40	S
910168	LAC	Williams, C.R.	RAF(VR) 153 Sqdn.	Ipswich, Suffolk	10.01.45	33	
1077842	AC.2	Williams, J.L.	R.A.F. (VR)	Ammanford, Carmarthenshire	17.03.45	26	R

Number	Rank	Name	Regiment	Place of Origin	D.O.D.	Age	Place Died
1089246	AC.1	Williams, R.H.	R.A.F. (VR)	Horsington, Somerset	19.02.45	25	
613679	LAC	Williams, Stanley	R.A.F.	Sunderland, Co. Durham	28.04.45	32	
1128182	AC.1	Williams, T.H.	R.A.F. (VR)	King's Norton, Birmingham	18.06.45	35	S
957899	LAC	Willmoth, A.W.	R.A.F. (VR)	Acton, Middlesex	27.06.45	29	S
567026	Cpl.	Wilson, George	R.A.F.	New Mill, Banffshire	14.06.45	26	S
1076488	AC.2	Wilson, Leslie	R.A.F. (VR)	Harrogate, Yorkshire	22.06.45	24	
1175164	LAC	Winder, C.G.	R.A.F. (VR)	Newhaven, Sussex	16.04.45	25	S
956138	LAC	Wiper, Thomas	R.A.F. (VR)	Barnsley, Yorkshire	28.04.45	27	S
1499501	AC.1	Wragg, Ernest	R.A.F. (VR)	Ibstock, Leicestershire	18.03.45	24	S
624725	LAC	Wright, Kenneth	R.A.F. 84 Sqdn.	Derby	14.06.45	24	
702234	AC.1	York, Reginald	R.A.F.	Wimbledon, Surrey	05.04.45	26	S

Singapore Memorial
Labuan Party from Kuching

Number	Rank	Name	Regiment	Place of Origin	D.O.D.	Age	Place Died
13928	Cpl.	Allan, G.P.	F.M.S.V.F.	Helensburgh, Dumbartonshire	15.03.45	28	L
13740	Pte.	Allen, Walter	S.S.V.F.	Levenshulme, Manchester	25.04.45	28	L
2324132	Sgmn.	Allen, W.J.	RCS.,S'pore Ftrs. Sigs.	Magilligan, Co.Londonderry, Ire.	30.10.44	28	L
2879194	Pte.	Anderson, Francis	Gordon Highlanders		20.01.45	21	L
55914	Gnr.	Barber, J.H.	3 Bty. 6 HAA		27.08.44		L
3130487	Bdsmn.	Bartley, Raymond	Argyll&Suth.Hghldrs.	Dudley, Northumberland	20.01.45	25	L
1748708	Gnr.	Barton, G.F.T.	15 Bty. 6 HAA	Hurst, Berkshire	13.01.45	34	L
4862811	Pte.	Bell, A.H.	Leicestershire Regt.	Osbournby, Lincolnshire	30.10.44	30	L
T/873041	Dvr.	Bell, J.J.	RASC attd. 21 LAA	Co. Antrim, Nthn. Ireland	22.09.44	32	L
809160	Gnr.	Bennett, John	15 Bty. 6 HAA	Falkirk, Stirlingshire	23.09.44	32	L
113	Pte.	Bird, G.L.	S.S.V.F.	Westerham, Kent	17.01.45		L
2580987	Sgmn.	Blackburn, W.S.	Royal Corps. Sigs.	Motherwell, Lanarkshire	21.11.44	23	L
13014	Pte.	Blair, D.D.	S.S.V.F.		28.01.45		L
13336	Pte.	Blakeley, R.F.	S.S.V.F.	Forest Hill, London	29.10.44	27	L
206513	Sgt.	Bretherton, George	R.E.M.E.(WO.I IAOC)	Stokesley, Yorkshire	10.06.45	28	L
6147322	Pte.	Bridgewater, A.E,	East Surrey Regt.		30.09.44	24	L
1080700	Gnr.	Bridgman, J.H.	137 Fld.Regt., R.A.	Upper Holloway, London	25.10.44	32	L
6141393	Cpl.	Brown, C.H.	East Surrey Regt.	Fulham, London	28.03.45	29	L/B
T/141788	Dvr,	Brown, John	RASC attd. 21 LAA	Bordesley Green, Birmingham	23.11.44	25	L
7636612	Pte.	Brown, John	R.A.O.C.		04.12.44	28	L
12773	Sgt.	Brown, R.B.	S.S.V.F.		10.12.44		L
T/193795	Dvr.	Burridge, E.T.	RASC att, 6 HAA	Ogmore Vale, Glamorgan	18.11.44	29	L
863877	Gnr.	Caddick, Raymond	9 Coast Regt.	Lanesfield, Staffordshire	20.01.45	23	L/B
122826	Capt.	Campbell, C.F.	R.A.M.C.		10.06.45		L/B
1786768	Gnr.	Cartwright, S.A.	9 Coast Regt.	Cwmaman, Glamorgan	08.03.45	34	L
13433	L/Bdr.	Chambers, W,H.	S.S.V.F.	Westbury-on-Trym, Bristol	26.03.45	31	L/B
1057009	L/Bdr.	Champ, James	9 Coast Regt.	Blythe Bridge, Staffordshire	11.11.44	40	L

Number	Rank	Name	Regiment	Place of Origin	D.O.D.	Age	Place Died
2889844	Pte.	Codd, James	Gordon Highlanders	Watford, Hertfordshire	17.10.44	27	L
7647131	Sgt.	Collins, R,G,	RAOC attd. IAOC		03.01.45	28	L
11055388	Gnr.	Daisley, Herbert	9 Coast Regt.		26.12.44	30	L
7848	Sgt.	Davis, W.R.	F.M.S.V.F.	Wellington, New Zealand	01.04.45	33	L
2875907	Pte.	Dawson, James	Gordon Highlanders		29.01.45	28	L
1786948	Gnr.	Deacon, H.J.	11 Coast Regt.	Callington, Cornwall	20.01.45	24	L/B
13244	Pte.	Deans, A.G.	S.S.V.F.	Inshes, Inverness-shire	17.01.45	37	L
	Pte.	DeSouza, J.F.	S.S.V.F.		31.05.45		L
6141079	L/Cpl.	Donaldson, C.A.	East Surrey Regt.	Epsom, Surrey	24.02.45	27	L
5528	Sgt.	Eckford, E.F.	S.S.V.F.	Blackheath, London	13.11.44	28	L/B
3850247	WO.I(RSM)	Edge, Francis	Loyal Rgt.(Nth.Lancs)	Aldershot, Hampshire	20.01.45	41	L/B
4857745	Pte.	Edridge, S.R.	Leicestershire Regt.		28.09.44	27	L
2584203	CQMS	Edwards, T.K.	Royal Corps. Sigs.	Wallasey, Cheshire	05.12.44	38	L
2875364	Pte.	Elliott, K.I.	Gordon Highlanders	Broad Clyst, Devon	01.02.45	29	L/B
831692	Sgt.	Ellwood, W.J.	16 Def.Rgt., R.A.	Whitehaven, Cumberland	01.12.44	26	L
12532	Sgt.	Elsworth, Arthur	S.S.V.F.	Walton-on-Thames, Surrey	12.02.45	42	L
13300	L/Cpl.	Fennell, R.R.	S.S.V.F.		13.02.45		L
2191594	Pte.	Ferguson, J.G.R.	Argyll&Suth.Hghldrs.		20.01.45	27	L/B
813988	Pte.	Finley, William	Loyal Regt.(Nth.Lancs)		27.04.45	31	L/B
13105	Pte.	Fraser, Henry	F.M.S.V.F.	Rhynie, Aberdeenshire	17.11.44	34	L
2565876	Sgt.	Ghey, G.O.	Royal Corps. Sigs.		05.12.44	33	L
2875351	Pte.	Gibb, Alexander	Gordon Highlanders		29.09.44	31	L
2351310	L/Sgt.	Glover, V.T.	77 HAA Sig. Sec.	Meir, Stoke-on-Trent	06.02.45	31	L
5413	Pte.	Godber, J.G.	S.S.V.F.	Wallasey, Cheshire	27.04.45	30	L/B
2988091	L/Cpl.	Haddock, Arthur	Argyll&Suth.Hghldrs.		04.01.45	29	L
7540	S/Sgt.	Hall, F.W.	F.M.S.V.F.	Harlesden, Middlesex	18.04.45	35	L/B
2326825	Sgmn.	Hampson, Harold	Royal Corps. Sigs.		16.02.45	26	L
1577729	Gnr.	Hastings, W.W.	11 Coast Regt.	Camberwell, London	09.01.45	30	L

Number	Rank	Name	Regiment	Place of Origin	D.O.D.	Age	Place Died
1552184	Sgt.	Hawkins, J.J.	144 Bty. 35 LAA	Leicester	24.12.44	30	L
2876237	Pte.	Hay, James	Gordon Highlanders	Inverichnie, Banffshire	17.12.44	32	L
S/3384307	Cpl.	Hayes, Walter	RASC attd. 48 LAA	Preston, Lancashire	14.11.44	36	L
S/137704	Cpl.	Hedgington, A.V.	R.A.S.C.	Reading, Yorkshire	26.01.45	26	L
868388	Gnr.	Hirst, G.W.	7 Coast Regt.	Stannington, Yorkshire	17.11.44	27	L
934135	Gnr.	Hitchen, Thomas	137 Fld. Regt.		23.11.44	26	L
80431	L/Cpl.	Hogan, G.L.	S.S.V.F.		06.08.44	25	L
1765150	Gnr.	Holmes, Alfred	7 Coast Regt.	Bilston, Staffordshire	10.04.45	29	L/B
5615	Cpl.	Hooper, R.A.	S.S.V.F.		06.08.44	31	L/B
13007	Cpl.	Hubble, P.W.	F.M.S.V.F.	Guildford, Surrey	30.11.44		L
13862	Gnr.	Hutchings, B.L.	S.S,V,F,	Westbrook, Margate	25.04.45	23	L/B
13857	Pte.	Hutchings, N.W,	S.S.V.F.	Westbrook, Margate	06.08.44	21	L/B
2876622	L/Cpl.	Imray, James	Gordon Highlanders	Fife Keith, Banffshire	23.10.44	30	L
2986059	Pte.	Innes, Alexander	Argyll&Suth.Hghldrs,		17.04.45	25	L
1709753	Gnr.	Jackson, Arthur	5 Searchlight	Huyton, Lancashire	23.03.45	34	L
13778	Pte.	Janacek, Rudolf	S.S.V.F.		13.02.45		L
1452858	Bdr.	Jenkins, Haydn	239 Bty. 77 HAA	Church Village, Glamorgan	08.10.44	32	L
950928	Gnr.	Kendall, S.D.	137 Fld. Regt.	Lancaster	01.10.44	25	L
903380	Gnr.	Kendrey, D.W.	122 Fld. Regt.	Bradford, Yorkshire	28.11.44	25	L
13227	L/Bdr,	Kennedy, L.H.	S.S.V.F.	Parkstone, Dorsetshire	27.04.45	33	L/B
29135	Sgmn.	Kenneison, A,R,	S.S.V.F.		11.10.44		L
2885228	Pte.	Laing, Douglas	Gordon Highlanders	Banchory, Kincardineshire	18.12.44	28	L
2042048	Gnr.	Lambert, Harry	7 Bty. 9 Coast Rgt.	Parson Cross, Sheffield	04.12.44	26	L
13790	Pte.	Laurie, W.I.	S.S.V.F.	Wishaw, Lanarkshire	04.03.45	40	L/B
153993	Dvr.	Lawcock, C.E.	Royal Corps. Sigs.		23.02.45	28	L
13329	L/Cpl.	Leijssius, Irving	Bde.HQ., S.S.V.F.	Singapore	26.03.45	28	L/B
12927	Cpl.	Lennane, W.Q.	S.S.V.F.	North Finchley, Middlesex	15.09.44	34	L/B
2876246	Sgt.	Leslie, James	Intelligence Corps.		08.02.45	32	L
T/274821	Dvr.	London, H.W.	RASC attd. 77 HAA	Rochdale, Lancashire	12.10.44	23	L
12886	Sgt.	Lord, A.O.	S.S.V.F.		...03.45	26	L/B

Number	Rank	Name	Regiment	Place of Origin	D.O.D.	Age	Place Died
13889	Pte.	Loveday, J.A.	S.S.V.F.	Singapore	06.08.44	28	L
2876734	Pte.	McAllan, James	Gordon Highlanders	Aberdeen	20.01.45	29	L
1786904	Gnr.	McCarthy, F.W.	7 Coast Regt., R.A.	Watford, Hertfordshire	28.02.45	33	L
13471	Pte.	McConigley, John	S.S.V.F.	Las Vegas, Nevada, U.S.A.	13.11.44	38	L
13404	Cpl.	McCutcheon, A.Q.	S.S.V.F.	Malvern, Vic., Australia	02.04.45		L/B
407734	Pte.	MacDonald, Donald	Gordon Highlanders	Arnisort, Isle of Skye	25.02.45	29	L
6031	Pte.	McDougall, G.H.	F.M.S.V.F.		16.03.45	34	L/B
T/7047342	Dvr.	McGurk, B.D.	R.A.S.C.	Newry, Co.Down, Nthn.Ireland	23.02.45	22	L
2981666	L/Cpl.	McLardie, Robert	Argyll&Suth.Hghldrs.		20.01.45	24	L
13460	Pte.	McLean, C.G.	S.S.V.F.		26.11.44	27	L
241080	Pte.	McMeekin, W.G.	Catering attd. R.A.O.C.	Kilwinning, Ayrshire	30.11.44	25	L
2982101	Pte.	Macleod, Alexander	Argyll&Suth.Hghldrs.	Leverburgh, Isle of Harris	18.11.44	26	L
13536	Gnr.	Major, J.S.	S.S.V.F.	Wallington, Surrey	25.01.45		L
2878815	Pte.	Malcolm, J.A.	Gordon Highlanders	Stonehaven, Kincardineshire	25.11.44	25	L
T/66644	Dvr.	Mapplebeck, Joseph	RASC attd. R.A.	Rotherham, Yorkshire	11.12.44	24	L
851512	Gnr.	Mason, J.H.	9 Coast Regt.	Liverpool	21.11.44	30	L/B
1518125	Pte.	Matthews, S.A.	R.A.O.C.		04.01.45	24	L
835003	Gnr.	Maxwell, Reginald	7 Coast Regt.	Derby	25.02.45	29	L
2875778	Pte.	Mennie, James	Gordon Highlanders	Rothiemay, Banffshire	19.12.44	31	L
2324118	Sgmn.	Millar, R.D.	Royal Corps. Sigs.	Co. Tyrone, Nthn. Ireland	05.01.45	27	L
813507	Bdr.	Millard, Ronald	78 Bty. 35 LAA	Reading, Berkshire	11.11.44	29	L
2878400	Pte.	Milne, Harold	Gordon Highlanders		20.11.44	27	L
13826	Pte.	Mitchell, A.J.M.	S.S.V.F.	Rayner's Lane, Middlesex	29.11.44	21	L
5071	Cpl.	Montigney, L.M.	F.M.S.V.F.		05.04.45	40	L
836561	L/Bdr.	Moran, Frank	5 Fld. Regt., R.A.		07.02.45	35	L
2979965	Pte.	Moreton, George	Argyll&Suth.Highldrs.	Blackpool, Lancashire	30.01.45	23	L
2981025	C/Sgt.	Moyes, A.D.	Argyll&Suth.Hghldrs.		13.01.45	25	L
12931	L/Bdr.	Mulvey, W.T.	S.S.V.F.		12.04.45	31	L/B
5826901	Pte.	Murray, H.J.	Suffolk Regiment		19.11.44	26	L
6142221	L/Cpl.	Musgrave, Albert	East Surrey Regt.		20.01.45	27	L/B
2369069	L/Cpl.	Newton, H.O.	Royal Corps. Sigs.	Codnor, Derbyshire	18.04.45	26	L/B
860089	Gnr.	O'Brien, F.W.	11 Coast Regt.	St. Phillips, Bristol	03.04.45	31	L/B
13753	Pte.	Oppenheim, L.A.	S.S.V.F.	Sydney, N.S.W., Australia	15.02.45		L

328

Number	Rank	Name	Regiment	Place of Origin	D.O.D.	Age	Place Died
6025	Pte.	Osborne, William	F.M.S.V.F.	New Cumnock, Ayrshire	06.08.44	33	L
1726135	Gnr.	Padfield, R.F.	3 Bty. 6 HAA	Bournemouth, Hampshire	21.11.44	33	L
1069558	S/Sgt.	Parker, J.J.	155(Lanarks)Fld.Regt.	Urmston, Lancashire	28.12.44	33	L
2878968	Pte.	Penman, Thomas	Gordon Highlanders		31.03.45	26	L
2878058	Pte.	Petrie, W.McG.	Gordon Highlanders		23.11.44	26	L
1629590	L/Bdr.	Phillips, W.A.	5 Searchlight Regt.	Wallasey, Cheshire	15.04.45	34	L/B
T/6291	L/Cpl.	Philpots, J.H,	R.A.S.C. (WO.I IAOC)		10.02.45		L
2974400	WO.II	Porter, A.S.	Argyll&Suth.Hghldrs,		09.12.44	36	L
943675	Gnr.	Pothan, R.F.	Royal Artillery	Bloxwich, Staffordshire	10.06.45	26	L/B
1577762	Gnr.	Purdey, T.H.	11 Coast Regt.	Sunbury-on-Thames, Middlesex	16.04.45	29	L/B
13439	Cpl,	Read, F.E.	S.S.V.F.	Brockley, London	10.04.45	23	L/B
4859359	Gnr.	Redfern, F.A.	9 Coast Regt.		04.12.44	26	L/B
2876868	Pte.	Reid, George	Gordon Highlanders		06.08.44	34	L
13965	Pte.	Richardson, E.M.	F.M.S.V.F.		19.02.45	36	L
12646	Sgt.	Ritchie, G.O.	S.S.V.F.	Leeds, Yorkshire	17.11.44	31	L
2026157	Sgmn.	Ritchie, Robert	RCS S'pore Ftrs Sigs.		21.12.44	39	L
5520	L/Cpl.	Rowland, F.E.	S.S.V.F.	Kuala Lumpur, Malaya	01.10.44		L
12661	Pte.	Russell, J.W.	S.S.V.F.	Springburn, Glasgow	04.10.44		L
1061074	Bdr.	Russell, W.H.	Royal Artillery	Dragon's Green, Sussex	01.04.45	39	L
T/276655	Dvr,	Ryan, R.W.	R.A.S.C.	Feltham, Middlesex		23	L/B
2979863	Pte.	Shanks, W.P.	Argyll&Suth.Hghldrs.	Falkirk, Stirlingshire	11.12.44	27	L
4863445	Pte.	Shepherd, J.F.	Leicestershire Regt.		09.02.45	29	L
	Gnr.	Sherriff, A.G.	S.S.V.F.	Auckland, New Zealand	31.10.44		L
963487	Gnr.	Shun, C.W.A.	155(Lanarks) Fld.Regt.	Clapham, London	05.11.44	25	L
3854734	Cpl.	Simms, Arthur	S'pore Ftrs.Coy.MP		06.10.44		L
T/133780	Cpl.	Smith, C.F.	RASC attd. 35 LAA	Newbiggin-by-the-Sea, Northumb.	28.10.44	36	L
1525417	Gnr.	Smith, Douglas	5 Fld.Regt., R.A.	Stoke Newington, London	07.11.44	27	L
12846	Sgt.	Smith, F.N.J.	S.S.V.F.	Singapore	20.12.44	32	L
950883	L/Bdr.	Smith, James	137 Fld.Regt., R.A.	Acton Bridge, Cheshire	26.09.44	27	L
13798	L/Sgt.	Sowden, G.C.	F.M.S.V.F.	Singapore	31.10.44	30	L
6070	Pte.	Spare, G.H.	S.S.V.F.	Worthing, Sussex	07.02.45		L

Number	Rank	Name	Regiment	Place of Origin	D.O.D.	Age	Place Died
5496402	L/Cpl.	Staplehurst, Arthur	East Surrey Regt.		19.11.44	29	L
842018	Gnr.	Stewart, James	9 Coast Regt.		21.12.44	28	L
6102	L/Cpl.	Stokes, Wilfred	F.M.S.V.F.	Bournemouth, Hampshire	06.08.44	34	L
13411	Pte.	Storch, A.G.	F.M.S.V.F.	Malaga, Spain	22.01.45	27	L
13853	Pte.	Sullivan, L.K.	B.H.Q., S.S.V.F.	Singapore	19.11.44		L
963490	L/Bdr.	Tadman, T.W.	155(Lanarks)Fld.Regt.	West Norwood, London	03.04.45	25	L/B
2876366	Pte.	Tennant, Charles	Gordon Highlanders	Edinville, Banffshire	10.09.44	33	L
3322299	Pte.	Thomson, John	Gordon Highlanders	Arbroath, Angus	19.04.45	29	L/B
1877435	Spr.	Thornton, A.K.	Bomb Disp.Coy., R.E.	Castleford, Yorkshire	20.01.45	24	L
3322905	Pte.	Trench, J.P.	Argyll&Suth.Hghldrs.	Widdrington Station, Northumb.	13.02.45	30	L
13828	Gnr.	Turcan, J.P.	S' pore R.A., SSVF	Edinburgh	44	30	L
13800	Pte.	Usher, G.J.D.	S.S.V.F.		16.01.45	21	L
13882	Pte.	Van Cuylenburg, R.H.M.	B.H.Q., S.S.V.F.	Singapore	29.11.44	19	L/B
T/259972	Dvr.	Vasey, Douglas	R.A.S.C.	Derby	04.12.44	32	L
13777	Pte.	Vitek, K.	S.S.V.F.		18.03.45		L
953823	Gnr.	Wain, Frederick	155(Lanarks)Fld.Regt.		20.02.45	25	L
4810	Pte.	Wales, H.P.	S.S.V.F.	Stockport, Cheshire	06.08.44	29	L/B
5731183	Sgt.	Walker, S.E.	Dorsetshire Regt. (WO.I. IAOC)		05.03.45		L
860279	Sgt.	Ward, C.V.	R.A.., (WO.I IAOC)		10.06.45		L
5346	Cpl.	Wark, David	S.S.V.F.		24.11.44		L
1436429	LAC	Weir, V.E.D.	R.A.F. (V.R.)	Hendon, Middlesex	30.05.45	28	L
2335364	Cpl.	Wharf, T.A.	Royal Corps. Sigs.	Middlesbrough, Yorkshire	31.03.45	27	L
13929	Pte.	Wicksteed, P.H.	F.M.S.V.F.	Perth, Western Australia	06.08.44	32	L/B
4858034	Pte.	Wilkinson, T.W.	Leicestershire Regt.		29.04.45	27	L/B
2883814	Pte.	Will, R.C.	Gordon Highlanders		05.12.44	26	L
1438673	Gnr.	Wilson, C.G.	9 Coast Regt.	Cogan, Glamorgan	27.04.45	24	L/B
2876580	Pte.	Wiseman, Robert	Gordon Highlanders		19.06.44	32	L

A.I.F. Died on Labuan

Number	Rank	Name	Regiment	Place of Origin	D.O.D.	Age
NX.39989	Pte.	Adams, A.M. (S/A. White, A.M.)	G.B.D., A.I.F,	Homebush, N.S.W.	26.01.45	22
NX.37694	Pte.	Crome, E.J.	2/20 Bn.	Woollahra, N.S.W.	28.02.45	20
VX.61084	Pte.	Ford, W.D.	2/29 Bn.	West Melbourne, Victoria	03.12.44	23
NX.67801	Pte.	Geelan, William	2/19 Bn.	Wentworthville, N.S.W.	04.01.45	24
VX.20450	Pte.	Radcliffe, K.E.	2/2 Pnr. Bn.	Prahran, Victoria	28.09.44	25
WX.11900	Cpl.	Tyrrell, Albert	2/2 Pnr. Bn.	Nedlands, Western Australia	24.06.45	40
NX.19562	Spr.	Zinn, A.C.	2/6 Fd.Coy., RAE	Cape Town, South Africa	20.11.44	37

(annotations in Regiment column:) Ex,) Kuching,] Party ex,] Sandakan.)

Royal Navy – Died Labuan

Number	Rank	Name	Regiment	Place of Origin	D.O.D.	Age
DK.134337		Burnett, E.	R.N.V.R.			
D/137704		Credfer	HMS SULTAN			
6962		Elwood	R.A.N.			
831692		Kelly, H.A.	R.N.			
19225		Simpson, W.	R.N.			
CKX.104981		Summers				
P1/6100191						

Graves Recovered Labaun/Brunei

Number	Rank	Name	Regiment	Place of Origin	D.O.D.	Age
572157	Cpl.	Griffiths, George	R.A.F.	Liverpool, England	22.09.44	
6045	Pte.	Innes, J.C.	Kedah Vol. attd. SSVF	Sydney, N.S.W.	10.05.45	
T/121530	Dvr.	Jowitt, R.H.	RASC. attd. R.A.	Ripley, Derbyshire	16.05.45	26
905624	L/Sgt.	Lumb, T.G.	137 Fld.Rgt., R.A.	Cleveleys, Lancashire	08.09.44	
912788	Gnr.	Snell, Charles	48 Bty. 21 LAA	Roehampton, London	14.09.44	23
1540237	Gnr.	Stokes, A.H.	89 Bty. 35 LAA		12.07.45	27

331

Number	Rank	Name	Regiment	Place of Origin	D.O.D.	Age	Place Died
1539955	Gnr.	Abbs, J.S.	89 Bty. 35 LAA		07.04.45	25	K
1700392	Gnr.	Adams, h.C.	78 Bty. 35 LAA	Nottingham	05.07.45	35	K
1714841	Bdr.	Adams, R.C.	49 Bty. 48 LAA		20.07.45	30	K
10555271	Pte.	Adamson, R.P.A.	77 HAA Wkshps.,RAOC	Kew, Surrey	23.09.43	22	K
1548943	Gnr.	Aldis, E.A.A.	49 Bty. 48 LAA	Ipswich, Suffolk	30.03.45	29	K
1793058	Gnr.	Alldritt, Henry	89 Bty. 35 LAA	Kirkdale, Liverpool	12.09.45	24	K
211620	Capt.	Anderson, T.V.N.		Winchester	03.10.45	38	K
S/1983921	Sgt.	Andrew, G.S.	R.A.S.C.	Newmilns, Ayrshire	01.07.45	27	K
13021999	Pte.	Andrews, F.J.	R.A.O.C.	Port Glasgow, Renfrewshire	24.08.45	28	K
5670376	Sgt.	Annett, W.L.	The Loyals(Nth.Lancs)	Bruton, Somerset	17.07.45	30	K
T/274791	Dvr.	Archer, John	RASC. attd. R.A.	Wakefield, Yorkshire	20.08.45	31	K
T/276035	L/Cpl.	Arnold, John	RASC. attd. R.A.		13.08.45		K
2329451	Sgmn.	Arthington-Davey, W.H.	Royal Corps. Sigs.		17.06.45	25	K
54366	Spr.	Arthur, Andrew	Royal Engineers		19.G7.45	39	K
2352967	L/Cpl.	Ashworth, Tom	Royal Corps. Sigs.	Blackpool, Lancashire	13.11.44	33	K
7610473	Cftsmn.	Atkinson, A.G.C.	R.E.M.E.	Middlesbrough, Yorkshire	05.08.45	25	K
1555642	Sgt.	Attwell, A.W.	78 Bty. 35 LAA		18.04.44	29	K
5572520	L/Cpl.	Bacon, Albert	RASC attd. R.A.	Wallington, Surrey	05.06.45	27	K
13202	Pte.	Ball, D.H.	F.M.S.V.F.	Wimbledon, Surrey	26.08.45	31	K
872536	Gnr.	Banbury, G.L.	9 Coast Regt., R.A.	Weymouth, Dorsetshire	12.04.44	24	K
5387158	Sgt.	Bannister, F.H.J.	Oxfds. & Bucks. L/Inf.	Oxford	11.08.45	27	K
T/252189	L/Cpl.	Barnes, F.S.	R.A.S.C.		27.03.44	39	K
7637773	Pte.	Barratt, Leonard	R.A.O.C.	Bulwell, Nottingham	30.08.45	32	K
5385426	Pte.	Barson, W.J.	R.A.O.C.	North Hinksey, Berkshire	12.11.42	27	K
169Q767	L/Sgt.	Bartlett, Charles	166 Bty. 48 LAA	Dorchester, Dorsetshire	25.05.45	37	K
1732185	Gnr.	Beadsley, Amos	H.Q. 35 LAA Regt.	Chelsea, London	22.02.45	41	K

Number	Rank	Name	Regiment	Place of Origin	D.O.D.	Age	Place Died
1783500	Gnr.	Beale, A.E.T.	89 Bty. 35 LAA		05.07.45	34	K
13736	Pte.	Beattie, D.P.	S.S.V.F.	Sanderstead, Surrey	21.06.45	33	K
6004638	Gnr.	Beckwith, Charles	15 Bty. 6 HAA	Halstead, Essex	17.03.45	42	K
791677	Gnr.	Bedford, Lawrence	156 HAA Regt.	Barnsley, Yorkshire	05.06.45	36	K
4680391	L/Cpl.	Bell, Joseph	Military Police	New Rossington, Yorkshire	14.06.45	28	K
1700420	Gnr.	Belshaw, Frank	78 Bty. 35 LAA		02.07.45	35	K
59795	Sgt.	Bentley, Herbert	Royal Corps. Sigs.		17.08.45		K
T/65011	Sgt.	Berry, J.S.	RASC attd. R.A.	Westminster, London	13.04.45	32	K
851343	Sgt.	Bills, C.L.	16 Def.Regt., R.A.		03.10.45	29	K
3854887	Pte.	Birch, W.A.	The Loyals(Nth.Lancs)	Bolton, Lancashire	12.08.44	30	K
4390355	Sgmn.	Bland, Kenneth	48 LAA Sig. Sec.		27.08.45	37	K
1549166	Gnr.	Blundell, Harold	48 Bty. 21 LAA	Liverpool	06.03.45	33	K
781252	L/Bdr.	Boddy, H.G.	12 Bty. 6 HAA	South Wraxall, Yorkshire	30.07.45	37	K
983313	Gnr.	Boldry, Ernest	9 Coast Regt. R.A.	Doncaster, Yorkshire	09.08.45	25	K
1831429	Gnr.	Bond, J.W.	78 Bty. 35 LAA	King's Lynn, Norfolk	25.07.45	38	K
842006	Bdr.	Bonham, J.H.	9 Coast Regt. R.A.	Leicester	01.05.45	30	K
7636869	Pte.	Bowden, F.L.	77 HAA Wkshp.,RAOC	Catford, London	09.06.45	31	K
1078821	Gnr.	Bower, Albert	5 Fld.Regt., R.A.		02.07.45	38	K
T/7045724	Dvr.	Bowes, R.T.	R.A.S.C.		02.07.45		K
5381297	Gnr.	Bowles, P.H.	89 Bty. 35 LAA	Headington, Oxford	08.04.45	29	K
T/88461	Dvr.	Bowman, Harry	RASC attd. R.A.	Forfar, Angus	11.07.45	27	K
6042	Pte.	Boyde, R.A.	S.S.V.F.		06.06.45		K
1812897	Gnr.	Boyle, J.L.	21 LAA Regt.	Sowerby Bridge, Yorkshire	03.07.45	30	K
13056059	Pte.	Brabin, M.J.	Pioneer Corps.	Bootle, Lancashire	12.08.45	25	K
1700381	Gnr.	Brain, G.W.	89 Bty. 35 LAA	Mablethorpe, Lincolnshire	01.09.45	35	K
1556489	Sgt.	Braybrook, W.C.	78 Bty. 35 LAA	Hanwell, Middlesex	07.08.45	43	K
13087114	Pte.	Broomhead, Ernest	Pioneer Corps.		21.03.45	35	K
T/3662562	L/Cpl.	Brough, Arthur	R.A.S.C.	Carlton, Nottinghamshire	10.06.45	38	K
987421	L/Bdr.	Brough, J.T.	5 Fld.Regt. R.A.	Barrowford, Lancashire	25.04.45	32	K
10558856	Pte.	Broughton, Arthur	R.A.O.C.	Doncaster, Yorkshire	24.07.45	29	K
2359490	Sgmn.	Broughton, S.D.	48 LAA Sig. Sec.	Manchester	04.08.44	39	K
1597152	L/Bdr.	Brown, A.J.	79 Bty. 21 LAA	Black Rock, Lancashire	13.08.45	31	K
4614304	Pte.	Brown, Herbert	R.A.O.C.		29.06.45	28	K

333

Number	Rank	Name	Regiment	Place of Origin	D.O.D.	Age	Place Died
1605321	Gnr.	Brown, J.J.	29 Bty. 3 HAA	Chesterfield, Derbyshire	05.07.45	36	K
T/267504	Dvr.	Brown, Leslie	RASC attd. R.A.	Sanderstead, Surrey	16.08.45	24	K
13396	Pte.	Brown, N.C.	S.S.V.F.		19.06.45	31	K
1729673	Gnr.	Bryant, S.G.	78 Bty. 35 LAA	Christchurch, Hampshire	14.04.45	34	K
1086737	Gnr.	Buckley, S.H.	1 HAA Regt. R.A.		07.08.45	26	K
1827210	Gnr.	Bullock, W.A.	78 Bty. 35 LAA		13.06.45	36	K
1827211	Gnr.	Bundick, F.J.	78 Bty. 35 LAA	Westcliff-on-Sea, Essex	27.04.45	39	K
13707	Pte.	Burley, E.J.P.	S.S.V.F.	East Sheen, Surrey	26.08.45	31	K
1169950	Cpl.	Burnham, Arthur	R.A.F. (VR)	Long Eaton, Derbyshire	14.09.45	25	K
T/3662393	Dvr.	Bush, T.H.	R.A.S.C.	Liverpool	26.03.45	32	K
T/113022	Sgt.	Butlin, M.C.	R.A.S.C.		28.11.44	25	K
1809081	Gnr.	Cahill, James	78 Bty. 35 LAA		28.06.45	24	K
T/5339471	Dvr.	Calder, Frederick	RASC attd. R.A.	Bethnal Green, London	16.02.45	27	K
977220	Gnr.	Campbell, Rodger	155 F/Rgt.,(Lanarks)	Kilwinning, Ayrshire	15.02.45	24	K
1833316	Gnr.	Carey, J.E.	49 Bty. 48 LAA	Clifton, Bristol	12.06.45	39	K
2876334	Pte.	Carle, James	Gordon Highlanders	St. Fergus, Aberdeenshire	13.05.45	35	K
847812	Bdr.	Carney, William	3 HAA Regt., R.A.		09.08.45	34	K
1073330	L/Sgt.	Carr, J.F.	80 A/Tank Regt.		08.06.45	36	K
1831434	Gnr.	Carroll, Harry	78 Bty. 35 LAA		16.06.45	37	K
10553622	Pte.	Carter, G.H.	48 LAA Wkshps.,RAOC	Watford, Hertfordshire	13.06.45	24	K
13274	L/Cpl.	Cassells, Alastair	S.S.V.F.	Edinburgh	04.07.45		K
1057876	Gnr.	Castle, Ernest	7 Coast Regt., R.A.	Halling, Kent	01.03.44	39	K
1817292	L/Bdr.	Castle, G.H.	12 Bty. 6 HAA	Norbiton, Surrey	04.08.45	25	K
1700347	Gnr.	Cave, J.V.	78 Bty. 35 LAA	Long Eaton, Derbyshire	19.01.45	37	K
T/166252	L/Sgt.	Chadwick, Walter	RASC attd. R.A.	Radcliffe, Lancashire	02.06.45	27	K
T/169695	Cpl.	Chandler, E.W.F.	RASC attd. R.A.	Reading, Berkshire	31.05.45	28	K
1426290	Gnr.	Chandler, L.W.	15 Bty. 6 HAA	Minchinhampton, Gloucestshre.	29.05.43	42	K
899044	Gnr.	Chant, W.G.	48 Bty. 21 HAA	St. Marylebone, London	15.08.45	25	K
1700351	Gnr.	Chaplin, William	78 Bty. 35 LAA		08.09.45	36	K
T/253095	Dvr.	Chapman, A.E.	RASC attd. R.A.	Coalville, Leicestershire	05.08.45	24	K
T/231141	Dvr.	Chapman, F.W.	RASC attd. R.A.	Liverpool	01.07.45	29	K
1831437	Gnr.	Chapman, Walter	78 Bty. 35 LAA		28.11.44	40	K

334

Number	Rank	Name	Regiment	Place of Origin	D.O.D.	Age	Place Died
805194	Gnr.	Charles, S.E.G.	12 Bty. 6 HAA	Hampton, Middlesex	18.07.45	33	K
1550218	Sgt.	Cheeseman, Louis	144 Bty. 35 LAA		19.05.45	32	K
T/273743	Dvr.	Cheesman, Alfred	RASC attd. R.A.	Ilford, Essex	31.03.45	38	K
1624407	Gnr.	Childs, A.V.	48 Bty. 21 LAA	Stoneleigh, Surrey	07.05.45	39	K
5491811	L/Cpl.	Chiverton, Frederick	Military Police		04.07.45	40	K
1555831	Sgt.	Clarke, R.D.	79 Bty. 21 LAA	Wimbledon, Surrey	02.09.45	32	K
1807817	Gnr.	Clarkson, Irvin	78 Bty. 35 LAA	Birkenhead	18.06.45	36	K
640532	LAC	Clement, E.L.	R.A.F. 84 Sqdn.	Abington, Northampton	05.09.45	23	K
1551607	Bdr.	Coak, W.H.	78 Bty. 35 LAA	Shirley, Southampton	24.06.45	29	K
1549336	Gnr.	Coble, Thomas	48 Bty. 21 LAA	Dagenham, Essex	28.05.45	34	K
84877	L/Cpl.	Collins, G.H.	Catering attd. R.A.	Linton, Kent	22.11.44	44	K
5158	L/Cpl.	Comper, G.F.	S.S.V.F.	Wembley, Middlesex	14.06.45	37	K
1572965	Gnr.	Cook, E.J.	78 Bty. 35 LAA	Woking, Surrey	01.05.45	33	K
1058449	Gnr.	Cook, Isaac	9 Coast Regt., R.A.	Sacriston, Co. Durham	27.06.45	41	K
1766329	Gnr.	Cook, R.W.	48 Bty. 21 LAA		25.06.45	24	K
1679443	Gnr.	Cook, W.H.	49 Bty. 48 LAA		13.07.45	38	K
1472346	Bdr.	Cooke, T.H.	240 Bty. 77 HAA	Ely, Cardiff	11.09.45	34	K
1609769	Gnr.	Cooksey, Joseph	49 Bty. 48 LAA	Notton, Yorkshire	18.07.45	24	K
1729695	Gnr.	Coomber, G.H.	78 Bty. 35 LAA	Cosham, Portsmouth	06.09.45	35	K
10558668	Pte.	Cope, J.A.	R.A.O.C.		13.05.45	28	K
7664672	Cpl.	Copper, C.W.	R.A.O.C.	Twickenham, Middlesex	29.07.45	27	K
1614718	Gnr.	Corderoy, A.A.H.	79 Bty. 21 LAA		18.04.44	31	K
2367654	Sgmn.	Corke, G.J.	48 LAA Sig. Sec.	Norwich	14.09.45	39	K
2979670	Pte.	Cornish, Thomas	Argyll&Suth.Hldrs.		25.07.45	31	K
1782176	Gnr.	Couldwell, L.G.	78 Bty. 35 LAA	Worrall, Yorkshire	19.08.45	25	K
2357202	Cpl.	Coventry, D.K.	48 LAA Sig. Sec.	Edinburgh	08.07.45	31	K
S/227609	Sgt.	Crabb, A.E.	R.A.S.C.	Orpington, Kent	03.08.45	36	K
13342	L/Cpl.	Crawley, Arthur	S.S.V.F.		22.08.45		K
T/238828	Dvr.	Crawley, R.A.	RASC attd. R.A.	Watford, Hertfordshire	12.09.45	39	K
T/271962	Dvr.	Crawshaw, Harold	RASC attd. R.A.		12.08.45		K
7620310	Pte.	Creber, E.R.	R.A.O.C.	Ideford, Devon	17.08.45	30	K
1270410	AC.1	Crittenden, H.H.	RAF(VR) 62 Sqdn.		03.07.45		K
7611773	Pte.	Cross, C.E.	R.A.O.C.	Muswell Hill, Middlesex	28.05.45	26	K

335

Number	Rank	Name	Regiment	Place of Origin	D.O.D.	Age	Place Died
T/3194308	Dvr.	Cruikshank, J.B.	RASC attd. R.A.	Edinburgh	12.05.45	30	K
T/272655	Dvr.	Cubbin, Harry	RASC attd. R.A.		04.06.45		K
1577709	Gnr.	Curran, F.M.	7 Coast Regt., R.A.	Portobello, Midlothian	16.02.44	31	K
13278	Sgt.	Curties, G.A.	S.S.V.F.		27.05.45		K
805094	Cpl.	Cuttell, H.R.	R.A.F. (Aux.A.F.)	Selly Oak, Birmingham	21.05.45	43	K
1700316	Gnr.	Danby, Leonard	78 Bty. 35 LAA	Nuthall, Nottinghamshire	17.08.45	33	K
1502885	Gnr.	Daniels, Albert	12 Bty. 6 HAA	Goldenhill, Stoke-on-Trent	30.07.45	29	K
2216672	Cpl.	Davey, H.H.	41 Ftrss.Coy., R.E.	Worthing, Sussex	26.08.45	36	K
117	Gnr.	Davey, W.H.	S.S.V.F.	Etmelo, Transvaal, Sth.Africa	02.07.45		K
1523822	Gnr.	Davidson, Robert	35 LAA Regt.	Sauchie, Clackmannanshire	08.08.45	43	K
840530	L/Sgt.	Davies, Jack	7 Coast Regt., R.A.		16.04.44	30	K
1796066	Gnr.	Davies, Thomas	49 Bty. 48 LAA		30.05.45	39	K
1026444	Gnr.	Davis, Joseph	7 Coast Regt., R.A.		13.08.45	44	K
1639157	Sgt.	Dawe, G.H.	78 Bty. 35 LAA	Sydenham, London	29.07.45	35	K
7597684	Pte.	Dawkins, Stanley	R.A.O.C.	Middlesbrough, Yorkshire	23.08.45	25	K
T/254306	Dvr.	Dawney, A.J.	RASC attd. R.A.	Dalston, London	02.06.45	39	K
S/266353	Pte.	Day, D.A.	RASC attd. R.A.	Canterbury	05.08.45	24	K
1080766	Gnr.	Dellow, R.V.	137 Fld.Regt., R.A.		29.05.45	32	K
S/68648	Pte.	Dennis, A.G.	R.A.S.C.	Acton, Middlesex	16.08.45	38	K
S/4922511	Pte.	Dingley, E.R.	RASC attd. 48 LAA	Handsworth, Birmingham	06.07.45	31	K
1833260	Gnr.	Dixon, J.W.	242 Bty. 48 LAA	Clevedon, Somerset	27.04.45	38	K
3246	Sgt.	Dodd, J.H.	S.S.V.F.	Jesmond, Newcastle-on-Tyne	06.07.45		K
1771667	Gnr.	Donovan, T.J.	78 Bty. 35 LAA		03.08.45	24	K
1691941	Gnr.	Dormor, G.E.	78 Bty. 35 LAA		15.06.45	37	K
5125531	Sgt.	Dorton, L.E.	Royal Warwcks. Regt.		18.07.45	40	K
T/275979	Dvr.	Downs, Robert	RASC attd. R.A.	Lichfield, Staffordshire	03.08.45	34	K
1550214	Gnr.	Dudley, K.W.	78 Bty. 35 LAA		22.07.45	28	K
1826504	Gnr.	Duncan, James	48 Bty. 21 LAA	Montrose, Angus	21.04.45	39	K
1075653	Gnr.	Dunstan, R.E.	78 Bty. 35 LAA	Wood Green, Middlesex	03.05.45	29	K
T/6711094	Dvr.	Durbridge, J.A.	RASC attd. R.A.	Battersea, London	20.08.45	39	K
1818021	Gnr.	Dyke, J.H.	15 Bty. 6 HAA	Barry Island, Glamorgan	06.01.45	37	K

Number	Rank	Name	Regiment	Place of Origin	D.O.D.	Age	Place Died
847359	Gnr.	Eaton, Ralph	12 Bty. 6 HAA		30.10.43	26	K
1807848	Gnr.	Edge, Herbert	49 Bty. 48 LAA	Glossop, Derbyshire	13.06.45	36	K
T/276789	Dvr.	Edwards, Alun	RASC attd. R.A.	Rhyl, Flintshire	07.09.45	35	K
1833723	Gnr.	Elmes, A.R.D.	21 LAA Regt.	Tooting, Surrey	10.09.45	33	K
785109	AC.2	Every, G.A.	R.A.F. (VR)		20.05.45		K
1782195	Gnr.	Exley, Tom	78 Bty. 35 LAA	Yeadon, Yorkshire	16.04.45	41	K
1700275	Gnr.	Fairbrother, H.S.	78 Bty. 35 LAA	Stapleford, Nottinghamshire	18.05.45	36	K
T/254315	Dvr.	Fairweather, Robert	RASC attd. R.A.	Longsight, Manchester	28.10.44	39	K
4618266	Pte.	Farr, Jack	R.A.O.C.		25.02.44	26	K
1735656	Gnr.	Farrer, P.C.	78 Bty. 35 LAA	Bedford	29.04.45	39	K
1563143	Gnr.	Farrow, A.R.	48 Bty. 21 LAA		30.06.45	33	K
7251740	Sgt.	Feely, Joseph	Intelligence Corps.		28.07.45	48	K
1784469	Gnr.	Fergus, William	78 Bty. 35 LAA	Portobello, Midlothian	28.10.42	38	K
1624367	Gnr.	Field, C.G.	48 Bty. 21 LAA	Tufnell Park, London	29.12.44	34	K
T/775809	L/Cpl.	Firth, Ernest	RASC attd. R.A.		14.02.45		K
1653624	Gnr.	Fisk, E.G.	49 Bty. 48 LAA	Clacton-on-Sea, Essex	17.05.45	34	K
1653625	Gnr.	Fitch, K.G.	49 Bty. 48 LAA		02.08.45	34	K
10532579	Pte.	Fletcher, W.F.	R.A.O.C.	Prestwood, Worcestershire	25.04.44	33	K
1873513	L/Cpl.	Forbes, E.R.	41 Ftrss.Coy., R.E.	Clare, Co.Tyrone, Nthn.Ire.	15.08.45	28	K
860657	Gnr.	Ford, F.G.	9 Coast Regt., R.A.	Daybrook, Nottinghamshire	02.07.45	28	K
5989008	Spr.	Fossey, J.I.	35 Ftrss.Coy., R.E.	Hemel Hempstead, Herts.	23.08.45	29	K
1578956	Sgt.	Foster, Jack	REME attd. IAOC	Halifax, Yorkshire	07.05.45	29	K
S/259620	Pte.	Fowler, Eric	R.A.S.C.	Forest Gate, Essex	09.08.45	23	K
2080869	Bdr.	Fox, Arthur	78 Bty. 35 LAA	Watford, Hertfordshire	17.07.45	31	K
7655183	Pte.	Fox, Harold	77 HAA Wkshp., RAOC		06.08.45	37	K
998500	AC.1	Fozzard, Harold	R.A.F. (VR)	Batley, Yorkshire	23.01.45	25	K
1729740	Gnr.	Frampton, T.G.	78 Bty. 35 LAA	Totton, Hampshire	25.12.44	33	K
1826510	Gnr.	Fraser, Alexander	78 Bty. 35 LAA		27.05.45	37	K
922876	Bdr.	Freedman, M.F.	5 Fld.Regt., R.A.		31.07.45	43	K
1794139	Gnr.	Furey, Thomas	78 Bty. 35 LAA		12.09.45	24	K
T/210034	Pte.	Garrett, L.E.	RASC attd. R.A.	Kineton, Warwickshire	23.07.45	34	K

337

Number	Rank	Name	Regiment	Place of Origin	D.O.D.	Age	Place Died
T/240437	L/Cpl.	Gaw, Hugh	RASC attd. R.A.	Prestwick, Ayrshire	01.07.45	39	K
1653654	Sgt.	Gent, J.A.	49 Bty. 48 LAA	Grays, Essex	19.05.45	34	K
1788144	Gnr.	Gibbon, W.H.	5 S/Light Regt. R.A.		14.05.45	39	K
1776471	Gnr.	Gibbs, F.H.	89 Bty. 35 LAA	Homerton, London	10.08.45	41	K
3054623	Bdr.	Glen, C.J.	78 Bty. 35 LAA	Uphall, West Lothian	22.01.45	37	K
1782202	Gnr.	Glew, G.T.	78 Bty. 35 LAA	Hull	19.08.45	41	K
1653708	Sgt.	Goddard, Jack	49 Bty. 48 LAA	Ware, Hertfordshire	13.06.45	34	K
1458291	Sgt.	Goff, A.J.	21 LAA Regt.	Hove, Sussex	26.07.45	25	K
1594942	Bdr.	Gofton, Harold	78 Bty. 35 LAA	Grimethorpe, Yorkshire	09.09.45	31	K
1874304	Spr.	Golden, Henry	41 Ftrss.Coy., R.E.	Ince, Wigan, Lancashire	21.07.45	26	K
11052583	Gnr.	Goldsbrough, G.H.	242 Bty. 48 LAA		05.03.45	25	K
1547428	Gnr.	Gough, F.H.	78 Bty. 35 LAA	Newton Purcell, Oxfordshire	24.07.45	41	K
815600	Sgt.	Gough, T.H.	78 Bty. 35 LAA	Sheldon, Birmingham	05.12.42	35	K
7639324	Pte.	Gould, C.A.	R.A.O.C.	Blackburn, Lancashire	13.08.45	33	K
T/3061176	Dvr.	Gowrie, C.M.	RASC attd. R.A.	Newtongrange, Midlothian	07.06.45	25	K
11052585	Gnr.	Graham, Joseph	242 Bty. 48 LAA		31.01.45	23	K
80117	Sgt.	Gray, R.W.	S.S.V.F.		29.05.45	46	K
853282	Sgt.	Greenwood, Ernest	7 Coast Regt., R.A.	Rossendale, Lancashire	11.06.45	29	K
T/328731	Dvr.	Greenwood, H.G.	RASC attd. 42 LAA	Brockley, London	05.08.45	25	K
1609536	Gnr.	Gregory, Harold	78 Bty. 35 LAA	Oldham, Lancashire	07.07.45	32	K
1726216	Gnr.	Griffin, W.J.	3 Bty. 6 HAA		07.06.45	39	K
4178171	Gnr.	Griffiths, R.J.	R.A. attd. RAOC		09.07.44	42	K
S/237422	Pte.	Gudgeon, M.W.	R.A.S.C.	South Shields, Co. Durham	11.06.45	27	K
1554817	Gnr.	Hacking, J.D.	49 Bty. 48 LAA		13.05.45	29	K
845419	Gnr.	Hall, J.B.	9 Coast Regt., R.A.	Middle Stobswood, Northumb.	10.05.45	31	K
T/3194395	Dvr.	Hall, W.D.	RASC attd. R.A.	Kirkton, Dumfriesshire	28.03.45	30	K
1700254	Gnr.	Hallam, Arthur	78 Bty. 35 LAA	Burton-Joyce, Nottinghamshire	26.03.45	35	K
1725594	Gnr.	Hallam, Joseph	12 Bty. 6 HAA	Blurton, Stoke-on-Trent	03.07.45	30	K
T/66719	Dvr.	Hamilton, David	RASC attd. R.A.	Cleator Moor, Cumberland	11.09.45	27	K
1831444	Gnr.	Hammersley, E.A.	78 Bty. 35 LAA	Southwold, Suffolk	03.05.45	24	K
1679410	Gnr.	Hammond, A.A.	49 Bty. 48 LAA	Harpley, Norfolk	21.04.45	42	K

338

Number	Rank	Name	Regiment	Place of Origin	D.O.D.	Age	Place Died
1817101	Gnr.	Hammond, C.G.	12 Bty. 6 HAA	Walkden, Lancashire	31.10.43	40	K
7639277	Pte.	Hampson. Arthur	R.A.O.C.		01.12.42	31	K
12835	L/Cpl.	Hansen, C.B.	S.S.V.F.	Copenhagen, Denmark	23.08.45	29	K
1580892	Gnr.	Harding, A.R.	12 Bty. 6 HAA		03.07.45	31	K
2050195	Gnr.	Harding, C.F.	12 Bty. 6 HAA	St. Mary Cray, Kent	14.05.45	25	K
1700258	Gnr.	Hardy, Albert	78 Bty. 35 LAA	Sutton-in-Ashfield, Notts.	03.04.43	37	K
T/191579	Cpl.	Hardy, A.J.	RASC attd. R.A.	Ross-on-Wye, Herefordshire	02.02.45	31	K
1626510	Gnr.	Harris, G.H.	49 Bty. 48 LAA	Bushey, Hertfordshire	03.09.45	34	K
6199768	L/Cpl.	Harris, Herbert	Military Police		04.08.45	34	K
1732109	Gnr.	Harris, Samuel	15 Bty. 6 HAA		15.06.45	33	K
1071502	Gnr.	Harrison, Albert	15 Bty. 6 HAA	Carlisle	22.07.45	39	K
1569468	Gnr.	Harrison, John	12 Bty. 6 HAA	Barnsley, Yorkshire	11.05.45	25	K
1626521	Gnr.	Harvey, G.M.	49 Bty. 48 LAA	Norwich	25.07.45	29	K
1569031	Gnr.	Harwood, C.T.	12 Bty. 6 HAA	Burton-on-Trent	22.05.45	30	K
T/109516	Dvr.	Hay, Alfred	R.A.S.C.	Paisley, Renfrewshire	09.12.44	27	K
3056490	L/Cpl.	Hay, William	R.A.S.C.	Edinburgh	22.08.45	38	K
1038868	AC.1	Hazel, Walter	R.A.F. (VR)	Chelmsford, Essex	17.08.45	33	K
7591940	Cftsmn.	Herbert, G.R.	R.E.M.E.		04.01.45	43	K
917559	Sgt.	Higgin, L.D.	5 Fld.Regt., R.A.		26.07.45	32	K
1787190	Gnr.	Higgs, D.J.	7 Coast Regt., R.A.		15.04.45	24	K
1556524	Bdr.	Hill, K.W.	144 Bty. 35 LAA		18.07.45	35	K
856137	Gnr.	Hindmoor, J.C.	9 Coast Regt., R.A.	Horrington, Cumberland	30.07.45	27	K
1794591	Gnr.	Hirst, M.S.	49 Bty. 48 LAA	Purston, Yorkshire	30.07.45	22	K
10555491	Pte.	Hobson, Cyril	R.A.O.C.	Ilkeston, Derbyshire	23.05.44	32	K
1678778	Gnr.	Hockham, H.A.	49 Bty. 48 LAA	Kingston-on-Thames, Surrey	29.05.45	32	K
10536165	Gnr.	Hodge, A.A.	R.A.O.C.		10.08.45	29	K
1470587	Gnr.	Hodge, William	9 Coast Regt., R.A.	Renfrewshire	19.07.45	42	K
T/270409	Pte.	Hodges, C.H.	R.A.S.C.	Highbury, London	10.11.44	33	K
T/4970081	L/Cpl.	Hole, W.L.	RASC attd. R.A.	New Lenton, Nottingham	20.07.45	34	K
T/209290	Dvr.	Holgate, Joseph	RASC attd. R.A.	Sheffield	01.02.43	31	K
224889	L/Cpl.	Hookham, A.E.	Military Police	Brixton, London	14.05.45	28	K
1758778	Gnr.	Horton, Arthur	48 LAA Regt.		29.05.45		K
1775970	L/Bdr.	Hounsham, R.W.	49 Bty. 48 LAA	Upper Norwood, Surrey	22.09.44	37	K

Number	Rank	Name	Regiment	Place of Origin	D.O.D.	Age	Place Died
7603708	Cpl.	Howard, B.G.H.	R.A.O.C.	Bournemouth, Hampshire	12.08.45	27	K
1801507	Gnr.	Howard, D.T.	49 Bty. 48 LAA	Southfields, London	29.03.43	27	K
13028061	Sgt.	Howard, George	Pioneer Corps.		29.05.45	45	K
T/3774381	Dvr.	Howard, W.S.	R.A.S.C.	Bootle, Lancashire	20.02.45	26	K
2336787	Sgmn.	Howes, W.F.	Royal Corps. Sigs.	Belevedere, Kent	28.05.45	28	K
T/272664	Dvr.	Hulme, Jack	RASC attd. R.A.	Leigh, Lancashire	15.07.45	31	K
1492790	Gnr.	Humphries, J.T.	7 Coast Regt., R.A.	Llandyssul, Cardiganshire	15.07.45	26	K
T/272693	Dvr.	Hyde, Joseph	RASC attd. R.A.		23.07.45		K
1714942	Gnr.	Iles, Bert	H.Q., 6 HAA	Kingswood, Gloucestershire	20.11.44	34	K
1572802	Gnr.	Impett, H.C.	49 Bty. 48 LAA	Margate	21.07.45	33	K
3854855	L/Sgt.	Isherwood, John	The Loyals(Nth.Lancs)	Bolton, Lancashire	29.05.45	32	K
1794597	Gnr.	Jackson, A.E.	242 Bty. 48 LAA		03.04.45	24	K
S/191065	Pte.	James, C.D.R.	R.A.S.C.	St. Marylebone, London	08.05.45	25	K
T/3911936	Dvr.	James, F.P.	RASC attd. R.A.	Brynmawr, Brecknockshire	11.05.45	25	K
363409	2/Lt.	James, Norman	R.A.O.C.	Leeds, Yorkshire	13.11.42	26	K
1809089	Gnr.	Jamieson, Robert	49 Bty. 48 LAA		02.07.45	24	K
7588534	L/Cpl.	Jacques, Charles	48 LAA Wkshps.,REME	East Peckham, Kent	15.07.45	21	K
7626785	Cpl.	Jeffrey, George	R.A.O.C.		18.03.44	28	K
1486760	L/Bdr.	Jeffrey, W.S.R.	242 Bty. 48 LAA		24.08.45	35	K
1489169	Bdr.	Jenkins, E.D.	48 LAA Regt.	Clacton-on-Sea, Essex	06.12.42	36	K
T/276799	Dvr.	Jenkins, Rhydian	RASC attd. R.A.	Llanelly, Carmarthenshire	06.06.45	27	K
T/2765655	Dvr.	Johnson, Thomas	RASC attd. R.A.	Thurnscoe, Yorkshire	06.01.45	40	K
1700235	Gnr.	Johnson, T.A.	78 Bty. 35 LAA	Nottingham	12.06.45	35	K
5530	L/Cpl.	Jones, A.R.	S.S.V.F.	Surbiton, Surrey	07.05.45	39	K
1796410	Gnr.	Jones, Charles	49 Bty. 48 LAA	Flint	02.07.45	24	K
1796118	Gnr.	Jones, Gwilym	242 Bty. 48 LAA	Llandudno Jn.,Caernarvonshire	16.07.45	24	K
3971411	Cftsmn.	Jones, M.G.	48 LAA Wkshps., REME	Lampeter, Cardiganshire	19.07.45	29	K
1765670	Gnr.	Jones, Thomas	49 Bty. 48 LAA	Liverpool	21.07.45	41	K
T/275988	Dvr.	Jones, W.E.	RASC attd. R.A.	Oakengates, Shropshire	16.07.45	28	K
2368733	Sgmn.	Judson, C.N.	48 LAA Sig. Sec.	Boston, Lincolnshire	13.06.45	25	K
13056467	Pte.	Kaighan, A.N.	Pioneer Corps.	Whitehaven, Cumberland	28.07.45	25	K

340

Number	Rank	Name	Regiment	Place of Origin	Age	D.O.D.	Place Died
T/7020561	Dvr.	Kearsey, H.J.	RASC attd. R.A.	Plaistow	36	21.06.45	K
1617411	Gnr.	Keartland, J.L.	5 S/Light Regt., R.A.	Erdington, Birmingham	34	06.07.45	K
T/59605	Dvr.	Keegan, J.R.	R.A.S.C.	West Kensington, London	29	24.08.45	K
2371464	Sgmn.	Keith, Edwin	48 LAA Sig. Sec.		31	19.11.42	K
10533117	Pte.	Kelleway, John	R.A.O.C.			18.08.45	K
10555497	Pte.	Kent, Alfred	77 HAA Wkshp.,RAOC	Derby	31	15.06.45	K
1482078	L/Bdr.	Kilbey, H.H.	48 Bty. 21 LAA	Winchmore Hill, Middlesex	36	30.06.45	K
1562985	Gnr.	Kimber, M.L.	78 Bty. 35 LAA	Reading, Yorkshire	33	17.08.45	K
S/188124	Cpl.	Kimberley, Ernest	RASC attd. R.A.		29	18.06.45	K
1446108	Pte.	Kingham, Harry	77 HAA Wkshps., RAOC	Mitcham, Surrey	40	24.05.45	K
T/3132928	Dvr.	Knaggs, Reginald	RASC attd. R.A.	Burnholme, Yorkshire	26	04.08.45	K
1105122	Gnr.	Laing, D.A.K.L.	155(Lanarks), Regt.		36	03.08.45	K
800055	L/Cpl.	Lambert, W.L.	Intelligence Corps.	Bootham, York	34	19.08.45	K
7608285	Cpl.	Land, E.F.	R.A.O.C.	Dagenham, Essex	35	17.05.45	K
T/71005	L/Cpl.	Launder, R.G.	RASC attd. R.A.	Halnaker, Sussex	24	03.08.45	K
763289	Gnr.	Laurie, A.J.	12 Bty. 6 HAA			18.06.45	K
1788238	Gnr.	Lawrence, H.J.	49 Bty. 48 LAA	Plumstead, London	39	25.07.45	K
T/242430	Dvr.	Lawson, Frederick	R.A.S.C.	Sunderland, Co. Durham	35	10.11.44	K
1700190	Gnr.	Lawson, George	78 Bty. 35 LAA		35	25.08.45	K
T/272698	Dvr.	Lawson, Thomas	RASC attd. R.A.	Nelson, Lancashire	24	16.07.45	K
13822	L/Cpl.	Leach, A.L.	S.S.V.F.	Singapore	23	24.07.45	K
5110808	Dvr.	Lewis, Wilfred	Royal Corps. Sigs.	Whittington, Shropshire	22	07.08.45	K
1028484	AC.2	Lilly, Wilson	R.A.F. (VR)	Larne,Co.Antrim,Nthn.Ireland	22	11.08.45	K
1543452	Gnr.	Lindsay, Jack	78 Bty. 35 LAA	Abingdon, Berkshire	45	09.09.45	K
1719024	Gnr.	Line, William	15 Bty. 6 HAA		36	14.08.45	K
10553002	Pte.	Lippard, H.F.	77 HAA Wkshps.,RAOC	Welling, Kent	42	09.08.45	K
1549236	Gnr.	Lipscombe, A.F.	78 Bty. 35 LAA		29	11.08.45	K
11263023	Gnr.	Little, Stanley	21 LAA Regt.	Carlisle	32	25.07.45	K
544907	Cpl.	Littlewood, Harry	R.A.F.	Marsh, Huddersfield	30	03.09.45	K
1710463	Gnr.	Logan, John	49 Bty. 48 LAA	Glasgow	33	15.06.45	K
T/5057241	Dvr.	McAuslane, Peter	RASC attd. R.A.			05.08.45	K
4528500	Bdr.	McCarthy, Charles	R.A.attd. 1 HAA Rgt.		40	24.05.45	K

Number	Rank	Name	Regiment	Place of Origin	D.O.D.	Age	Place Died
2357334	Sgmn.	McGlone, E.M.	48 LAA Sig. Sec.	Killorglin, Co. Kerry, Ire.Rep.	09.08.45	35	K
1179324	AC.1	McGowan, R.J.	R.A.F. (VR)	Crediton, Devon	11.05.45	30	K
80027	Cpl.	Mackenzie, A.S.	S.S.V.F.		23.03.45	39	K
764864	Gnr.	Mackett, G.W.	78 Bty. 35 LAA		31.07.45	38	K
13719	Pte.	McLaren, Moray	S.S.V.F.	Davenham, Cheshire	03.09.45	37	K
T/236831	Dvr.	McLaughlin, John	RASC attd. R.A.	Uddingston, Lanarkshire	05.04.45	30	K
863940	Gnr.	McLean, Robert	5 Fld.Regt., R.A.	Clydebank, Dunbartonshire	31.08.45	28	K
6011	Pte.	McLeod, Alexander	S.S.V.F.		19.03.45	40	K
S/244635	Pte.	McMahon, Francis	R.A.S.C.	Corby, Northamptonshire	24.06.45	29	K
3662438	Dvr.	Maddox, Frank	R.A.S.C.	Hulme, Manchester	17.06.45	37	K
2327754	L/Cpl.	Major, H.A.	Royal Corps. Sigs.	Fulham, London	08.07.45	26	K
1700210	Gnr.	Manners, Claude	79 Bty. 35 LAA	Nottingham	10.12.44	37	K
123478	Lieut.	Marchmont, A.G.	R.A.O.C.	Australia	21.05.45		K
2821202	L/Cpl.	Marjeram, D.F.	Military Police	Brixton Hill, London	21.09.45	29	K
1700153	Gnr.	Marriott, E.J.	78 Bty. 35 LAA	Old Lenton, Nottingham	04.07.45	29	K
7633046	Cpl.	Marshall, Donald	R.E.M.E.	Leeds, Yorkshire	25.03.43	27	K
10557862	Pte.	Marshall, Geoffrey	R.A.O.C.	Lancaster	02.07.45	24	K
963862	Gnr.	Martin, George	122 Fld.Regt., R.A.	New Farnley, Yorkshire	11.09.45	28	K
1595230	Bdr.	Masters, E.E.	78 Bty. 35 LAA	Haverah Park, Yorkshire	03.08.45	34	K
2876443	L/Cpl.	Matthew, George	Intelligence Corps.		05.02.43	31	K
T/156992	Dvr.	Matthews, G.W.	RASC attd. R.A.	St. Albans, Hertfordshire	14.09.44	27	K
1643440	Gnr.	Mayes, G.H.	3 Bty. 6 HAA		09.08.44	32	K
7639038	Pte.	Maynard, A.W.	77 HAA Wkshps., RAOC	Fawley Green,Buckinghamshire	10.09.45	27	K
1736031	Gnr.	Merry, E.C.	49 Bty. 48 LAA	Middleton Cheney, Oxfordshire	13.08.45	35	K
13069	Pte.	Miller, R.D.	S.S.V.F.	Barnton, Midlothian	18.06.45	31	K
6202201	Gnr.	Miller, W.A.	78 Bty. 35 LAA	Yiewsley, Middlesex	09.09.45	27	K
1743070	Gnr.	Mills, John	78 Bty. 35 LAA	Westhoughton, Lancashire	07.09.45	37	K
S/222311	Pte.	Miskell, Michael	R.A.S.C.	New Ollerton, Nottinghamshire	15.02.45	30	K
1597166	L/Bdr.	Molloy, John	69 Bty. 21 LAA	Miles Platting, Manchester	06.07.45	32	K
1054168	Bdr.	Montgomery, William	5 Fld.Regt., R.A.		14.06.45	43	K
1515998	Gnr.	Mooney, W.T.	78 Bty. 35 LAA		09.06.45	26	K
T/3911978	Dvr.	Morgan, Evan	RASC attd. R.A.	Bonymaen, Swansea	10.02.45	25	K
10555110	Pte.	Morris, C.A.	R.A.O.C.	Mansfield, Nottinghamshire	06.08.45	24	K

Number	Rank	Name	Regiment	Place of Origin	D.O.D.	Age	Place Died
812242	Gnr.	Morris, G.E.	H.Q., 6 HAA	Wheatley, Oxfordshire	22.10.42	31	K
T/3064226	Dvr.	Morrison, Robert	RASC attd. R.A.		08.08.45	34	K
1807859	Gnr.	Morton, Edward	49 Bty. 48 LAA	Ashton-under-Lyne, Lancs.	05.04.45	35	K
868929	Gnr.	Mountain, G.A.	9 Coast Regt., R.A.	Spilsby, Lincolnshire	26.07.45	28	K
10559996	Pte.	Muirhead, George	77 HAA Wkshps.,RAOC		10.06.45	24	K
T/3137085	Dvr.	Munn, R.W.	RASC attd. R.A.	Springburn, Glasgow	24.02.45	36	K
1577753	L/Bdr.	Nash, W.F.J.	11 Coast Regt.R.A.		09.08.45	33	K
T/3779194	Dvr.	Naughton, A.C.	R.A.S.C.	Walton, Liverpool	23.07.45	24	K
3958889	Gnr.	Nightingale, C.G.	15 Bty. 6 HAA	Landore, Swansea	07.12.44	30	K
815147	Gnr.	Nisbet, Charles	12 Bty. 6 HAA		16.07.45	34	K
T/156225	Dvr.	Nixon, Charles	RASC attd. R.A.		23.10.44	26	K
1542864	Sgt.	Nixon, J.H.S.	49 Bty. 48 LAA	Brighton, Sussex	30.04.45	29	K
4742741	Gnr.	Nixon, J.T.	9 Coast Regt., R.A.	Rochdale, Lancashire	05.02.44	37	K
7642691	Cftsmn.	Noble, William	77 HAA Wkshps., REME	Gateshead, Co. Durham	09.08.45	31	K
T/66651	Dvr.	Nolan, J.E.	RASC attd. R.A.	Hanley, Stoke-on-Trent	14.07.45	25	K
1749568	Gnr.	Norcott, S.G.	15 Bty. 6 HAA	Leeds, Yorkshire	16.06.45	39	K
T/193233	Dvr.	Norfolk, W.T.	RASC attd. R.A.		17.06.45		K
T/273841	Dvr.	Norris, Frank	RASC attd. R.A.		16.03.45		K
T/266390	Dvr.	Norris, G.W.	RASC attd. R.A.		19.09.45		K
7630850	Pte.	Norwood, A.H.	R.A.O.C.		03.07.45	30	K
1829524	Gnr.	Nott, G.F.	12 Bty. 6 HAA		08.01.45	23	K
3052322	Sgt.	O'Donnell, William	73 Bty. 35 LAA	Greenock, Renfrewshire	13.08.45	42	K
12358	Pte.	O'Dwyer, P.J.	S.S.V.F.	East Croydon, Surrey	26.08.45	38	K
1594937	Gnr.	Oliver, Michael	49 Bty. 48 LAA		31.08.45	24	K
4129535	Pte.	Oliver, W.G.H.	RAOC attd. R.A.	Tavistock, Devon	26.07.45	29	K
7653808	Cftsmn.	Orchard, R.J.	48 LAA Wkshps., REME	Peverell, Plymouth	21.02.45	24	K
13347	Pte.	O'Reilly, F.H.	S.S.V.F.		04.08.45		K
1701600	Gnr.	Osborne, Albert	78 Bty. 35 LAA	Birmingham	22.10.42	29	K
T/155210	Dvr.	Osborne, John	RASC attd. R.A.	Liverpool	18.08.45	27	K
2359273	Cpl.	Owen, M.D.	48 LAA Sig. Sec.	Newtown, Montgomeryshire	23.08.45	37	K
868630	Gnr.	Oxley, D.E.	9 Coast Regt., R.A.		26.05.45	26	K

343

Number	Rank	Name	Regiment	Place of Origin	D.O.D.	Age	Place Died
1189749	AC.1	Pafford, Frederick	R.A.F. (VR)	Millbrook, Southampton	07.07.45	29	K
1735053	Gnr.	Partner, George	95 Bty. 48 LAA	Kirkwall, Orkney	27.06.45	35	K
T/272009	Dvr.	Peat, R.W.	RASC attd. R.A.	Leeds, Yorkshire	05.05.45	31	K
1681654	Gnr.	Pegram, Thomas	49 Bty. 48 LAA	South Chingford, Essex	13.12.44	35	K
5123137	Cftsmn.	Perella, L.D.	48 LAA Wkshps.,REME	Ontario, Canada	16.07.45	23	K
872397	Gnr.	Peters, Herbert	7 Coast Regt., R.A.	West Hartlepool, Co.Durham	29.04.44	24	K
122650	Capt.	Phillips, H.M.B.	R.E.M.E.		26.11.43		K
2819229	L/Cpl.	Phimister, J.A.	Military Police		06.08.45	30	K
10554591	Pte.	Pickering, Arthur	77 HAA Wkshps.,RAOC	Leeds, Yorkshire	06.07.45	32	K
1736043	Gnr.	Pilcher, C.W.	95 Bty. 48 LAA	Southampton	09.01.43	34	K
2327421	CQMS	Plowman, Verdun	Royal Corps. Sigs.		09.08.45	29	K
T/162865	Dvr.	Plume, L.G.	RASC attd. R.A.		27.08.45		K
1821236	Gnr.	Plunkett, Peter	78 Bty. 35 LAA	Preston, Lancashire	10.04.45	25	K
6012	Lieut.	Pomeroy-Giles, Jack	Malacca Def. Corps.	West Bridgeford, Nottingham	20.06.45		K
	Lieut.	Pool, Albert	S.S.V.F.	Ripon, Yorkshire	17.07.45	49	K
6619382	Bdr.	Poole, A.A.	15 Bty. 6 HAA	Bricket Wood, Hertfordshire	19.07.45	36	K
1749852	L/Bdr.	Potsey, Joseph	49 Bty. 48 LAA		16.06.45	37	K
T/276804	L/Cpl.	Powell, A.E.	RASC attd. R.A.	Connah's Quay, Flintshire	24.07.45	33	K
1549569	Gnr.	Poynter, G.H.W.	78 Bty. 35 LAA		10.05.45	30	K
7794	Bdr.	Price, Eric	F.M.S.V.F.	Blackley, Manchester	05.09.44	31	K
3963390	L/Cpl.	Price, Evan	The Welch Regt.		20.05.44	24	K
T/252310	Dvr.	Price, J.A.	R.A.S.C.	Walthamstow, Essex	03.02.45	24	K
879897	Gnr.	Price, J.J.	12 Bty. 6 HAA	Manchester	13.05.44	25	K
1809068	Gnr.	Pritchard, Joseph	40 Bty. 48 LAA	New Mills, Derbyshire	14.07.45	24	K
13783	L/Cpl.	Proctor, Harold	S.S.V.F.	St.Annes-on-Sea, Lancashire	20.08.45	41	K
T/233091	Dvr.	Proctor, Alfred	RASC attd. R.A.	Yardley Wood, Birmingham	19.07.45	34	K
1759906	Gnr.	Pryke, E.A.	144 Bty. 35 LAA	Croydon, Surrey	15.04.44	37	K
1817339	Gnr.	Quy, W.E.	12 Bty. 6 HAA	Barking, Essex	21.08.45	37	K
2979776	Pte.	Rankin, George	Argyll&Suth.Hghldrs.	Salford, Lancashire	01.05.45	29	K
1809188	Gnr.	Rawson, George	49 Bty. 48 LAA		05.07.45	38	K
1734315	Gnr.	Read, Charles	95 Bty. 48 LAA	Greenford, Middlesex	21.08.45	34	K

Number	Rank	Name	Regiment	Place of Origin	D.O.D.	Age	Place Died
1801691	Gnr.	Read, R.H.	49 Bty. 48 LAA		25.09.44	28	K
7644503	Cftsmn.	Reader, William	R.E.M.E.	Sandiacre, Nottinghamshire	15.04.45	24	K
7683631	L/Cpl.	Reading, F.A.	Military Police	Llandudno, Caernarvonshire	12.06.45	34	K
T/2765378	Dvr.	Redmayne, Harold	RASC attd. R.A.		18.07.45		K
10555574	Pte.	Reilly, John	77 HAA Wkshps.,RAOC		20.08.45	30	K
T/276131	Dvr.	Reynolds, Arthur	R.A.S.C.	Morden, Surrey	10.06.44	21	K
885245	S/Sgt.	Rice, T.W.	137 Fld.Regt.R.A.	St.Annes-on-Sea, Lancashire	23.03.44	37	K
T/235403	Dvr.	Richardson, A.C.	RASC attd. R.A.		16.06.45		K
3526145	Pte.	Ricketts, A.W.	The Manchester Regt.		04.08.45	30	K
1652023	Gnr.	Ricketts, Henry	78 Bty. 35 LAA		04.06.45	33	K
784188	Gnr.	Ridley, Ralph	15 Bty. 6 HAA		25.07.45	38	K
1777656	Gnr.	Ridley, Spencer	78 Bty. 35 LAA	Nutley, Sussex	20.01.44	40	K
1563479	L/Bdr.	Rigby, S.C.	78 Bty. 35 LAA	Ryde	10.07.45	34	K
S/5957414	Pte.	Rilstone, Richard	R.A.S.C.	Bowes Park, Middlesex	27.08.45	27	K
T/275999	Dvr.	Rimmington, H.	RASC attd. R.A.		16.07.45		K
T/258525	L/Cpl.	Roberts, Edward	RASC attd. R.A.	Wrexham, Denbighshire	20.08.45	29	K
11051926	Gnr.	Robertshaw, Willcock	242 Bty. 48 LAA	Batley, Yorkshire	01.07.45	23	K
2879166	L/Cpl.	Robertson, Charles	Military Police	Fife Keith, Banffshire	26.08.45	24	K
2879183	Pte.	Robertson, R.B.	Gordon Highlanders		17.07.45		K
851206	L/Sgt.	Robson, William	9 Coast Regt., R.A.	Stirchley, Birmingham	01.08.45	32	K
901951	L/Bdr.	Rogers, Merfyn	48 Bty. 21 LAA	Pen-y-Craig, Glamorgan	22.08.45	24	K
1827101	Gnr.	Rosen, Solomon	78 Bty. 35 LAA	Dagenham, Essex	12.07.45	31	K
7616563	Pte.	Ross, Donald	R.A.O.C.	Barking, Essex	28.07.45	26	K
T/866808	Dvr.	Ross, W.C.	RASC attd. R.A.	Leeds, Yorkshire	02.04.44	23	K
T/2865468	Dvr.	Rough, Albert	RASC attd. R.A.	Brentford, Middlesex	31.03.45	29	K
1635236	Gnr.	Rough, W.H.	78 Bty. 35 LAA	Isleworth, Middlesex	31.08.45	39	K
1592422	Gnr.	Rowe, Henry	49 Bty. 48 LAA	Westminster, London	29.05.45	32	K
1791068	Gnr.	Royle, E.M.	78 Bty. 35 LAA	Lytham-St.-Annes, Lancashire	13.01.45	24	K
1551858	Gnr.	Rumble, A.E.	78 Bty. 35 LAA	Reading, Yorkshire	30.08.45	30	K
1736429	Gnr.	Rush, A.G.	49 Bty. 48 LAA	Mottingham, Kent	23.04.45	37	K
1779361	Gnr.	Russell, G.L.	78 Bty. 35 LAA	Letterkenny, Co.Donegal, Ire.	26.06.43	22	K
47637	Lt.Col.	Russell, M.C.	The East Surrey Regt.	Horsell, Surrey	05.06.43	32	K

Number	Rank	Name	Regiment	Place of Origin	D.O.D.	Age	Place Died
T/254172	Dvr.	Sadler, T.F.	RASC attd. R.A.	Redhill, Surrey	22.05.45	39	K
10540990	Cftsmn.	Salmon, N.F.	R.E.M.E.	Hastings, Sussex	24.08.45	41	K
T/235215	Pte.	Salmons, George	RASC attd. R.A.	Warminster, Wiltshire	04.06.45	39	K
7605279	Sgt.	Sansom, Walter	RAOC attd. R.A.	West Hartlepool, Co. Durham	17.05.44	29	K
784108	Sgt.	Sargison, A.L.	15 Bty. 6 HAA	Dalston, Cumberland	27.12.44	32	K
7600538	S/Sgt.	Savage, S.P.	R.E.M.E.	Stroud, Gloucestershire	25.07.45	37	K
1759156	Gnr.	Saville, W.F.	49 Bty. 48 LAA	Beckenham, Kent	03.08.45	40	K
T/3050103	Dvr.	Scott, J.H.	RASC attd. R.A.	Springburn, Glasgow	11.08.45	39	K
1758925	Gnr.	Scott, W.A.	78 Bty. 35 LAA	Kingston-on-Thames, Surrey	06.09.45	34	K
T/3196543	Dvr.	Servant, David	RASC attd. R.A.	Dumbarton	05.01.45	32	K
1555915	Gnr.	Seward, K.F.	78 Bty. 35 LAA	Hermitage, Berkshire	11.05.45	32	K
5883104	Cpl.	Sharman, Harry	Northamptonshire Rgt.		02.05.45	30	K
1643331	Gnr.	Sharp, M.S.	15 Bty. 6 HAA		28.07.45	34	K
13315	Pte.	Sharpe-Smith, I.M.	F.M.S.V.F.		23.08.45		K
6461032	Gnr.	Sharpley, R.R.	48 Bty. 21 LAA	Sudbury, Middlesex	30.07.45	26	K
1777933	Gnr.	Sheldon, Harry	78 Bty. 35 LAA	Matlock, Derbyshire	22.05.45	35	K
7586992	Cpl.	Shelley, E.A.H.	R.A.O.C.	Didcot, Berkshire	12.07.45	29	K
1438675	Gnr.	Sheward, R.A.	16 Def.Fld.Rgt.,RA	Northfield, Birmingham	02.06.45	23	K
6472825	Gnr.	Shore, Theodore	48 Bty. 21 LAA	Southgate, Middlesex	07.07.45	27	K
1827679	Gnr.	Sidebotham, Frederick	48 LAA Regt.		20.04.45	28	K
T/271382	Dvr.	Sidebotham, Samuel	RASC attd. R.A.	West Bromwich, Staffordshire	21.07.45	38	K
1692990	Gnr.	Sider, W.J.	49 Bty. 48 LAA	Camberwell, London	05.06.45	36	K
T/230445	Dvr.	Siggins, S.E.	RASC attd. R.A.	Bow, London	10.02.45	24	K
T/3662446	L/Cpl.	Sighe, George	R.A.S.C.		01.09.45		K
1826605	Gnr.	Simm, John	21 LAA Regt.	Leigh, Lancashire	22.04.44	30	K
6142757	Pte.	Simmons, R.T.	East Surrey Regt.		16.08.45	26	K
1065084	Gnr.	Simpson, J.W.	12 Bty. 6 HAA		13.03.45	39	K
1458636	Gnr.	Simpson, Walter	80 A/Tk. Regt.	Glasgow	14.07.45	26	K
1828621	Gnr.	Slater, E.H.	48 LAA Regt.		21.08.45		K
8343115	Gnr.	Smale, V.J.	16 Def.Fld.Regt.		15.06.45	29	K
1701637	Gnr.	Smith, A.H.	110 Bty. 35 LAA	Hockley, Birmingham	02.07.45	30	K
T/2765590	Dvr.	Smith, Charles	RASC attd. R.A.		30.08.45	24	K
1543480	Gnr.	Smith, Frederick	49 Bty. 48 LAA	Colchester, Essex	25.07.45	33	K

Number	Rank	Name	Regiment	Place of Origin	D.O.D.	Age	Place Died
3914774	Pte.	Smith, H.R.	R.A.O.C.	Glamorgan	27.10.42	35	K
T/88715	Dvr.	Smith, L.S.	RASC attd. R.A.		13.06.45	25	K
1716347	Gnr.	Smith, T.L.	95 Bty. 48 LAA	Bingham, Nottinghamshire	18.08.45	39	K
117114	F/Offr.	Smith, V.H.	R.A.F. (VR)	Victoria Park, Western Aust.	21.07.45	44	K
810792	Sgmn.	Smith, W.C.	Royal Corps. Sigs.	Norwich	09.09.45	32	K
10556467	Pte.	Smith, W.C.	48 LAA Wkshps.RAOC	Wincobank, Yorkshire	31.03.44	39	K
1786965	Gnr.	Snell, R.G.	16 Def.Fld. Regt.	St.Stephen, Cornwall	23.06.45	24	K
S/5730820	Sgt.	Snook, H.S.	R.A.S.C.	Uplands, Bristol	14.03.45	30	K
13128	Pte.	Sovereign-Smith, G.A.	S.S.V.F.	Romford, Essex	22.07.45	39	K
926567	Bdr.	Spafford, Maurice	122 Fld.Regt.	Huddersfield	15.03.45	40	K
5828700	Sgt.	Spooner, E.J.	The Suffolk Regt.		16.11.42	25	K
931345	LAC	Stafford, J.L.	R.A.F. (VR)	Gabalfa, Glamorgan	19.07.45	35	K
7646270	Sgt.	Statham, C.W.	R.E.M.E.	St.Albans, Hertfordshire	28.07.45	35	K
1713506	Gnr.	Steingart, Sidney	78 Bty. 35 LAA	Stepney, London	24.08.45	37	K
4916668	Gnr.	Stephens, G.A.	12 Bty. 6 HAA	Walsall, Staffordshire	17.05.45	23	K
1072717	Gnr.	Stephenson, George	12 Bty. 6 HAA	Sutton-in-Ashfield, Notts.	21.06.45	37	K
1788700	Gnr.	Stephenson, Thomas	78 Bty. 35 LAA	Epsom, Surrey	14.03.44	39	K
13056239	Pte.	Stevenson, Albert	Pioneer Corps.	Accrington, Lancashire	11.05.45	26	K
2874959	L/Cpl.	Stewart, Gordon	Gordon Highlanders		24.06.45	31	K
1264280	AC.1	Stiven, J.G.	R.A.F. (VR)	Fulham, London	24.03.45	33	K
6344	Cpl.	Strahan, A.C.	F.M.S.V.F.	Southsea, Hampshire	10.08.45		K
1830244	Gnr.	Stratton, James	78 Bty. 35 LAA		17.08.45	33	K
T/3196979	Dvr.	Stuart, Duncan	RASC attd. R.A.	Glasgow	10.10.44	33	K
T/266413	Dvr.	Stump, Leonard	RASC attd. R.A.	Homerton, London	23.06.45	24	K
1057481	Gnr.	Summons, J.M.	7 Coast Regt.		22.07.45	42	K
944578	Gnr.	Sutcliffe, S.A.	137 Fld. Regt.	Rochdale, Lancashire	02.01.43	24	K
13063683	Pte.	Sutcliffe, Willie	77 HAA Wkshp.,RAOC	Barrowford, Lancashire	09.02.45	33	K
2330585	Sgt.	Suttie, D.H. MID	80 A/Tk.Rgt.Sig. Sec.	Dundee	21.08.45	27	K
819824	Bdr.	Tate, John	15 Bty. 6 HAA		07.08.45	28	K
13693	Sgmn.	Tayler, P.B.	S.S.V.F.		11.08.45		K
13056329	Pte.	Taylor, H.E.	Pioneer Corps.	Liverpool	10.05.45	28	K
T/254418	Dvr.	Taylor, S.J.	RASC attd. R.A.	Burslem, Stoke-on-Trent	07.07.45	41	K

Number	Rank	Name	Regiment	Place of Origin	D.O.D.	Age	Place Died
1690759	Gnr.	Taylor, W.H.	49 Bty. 48 LAA	Maisemore, Gloucestershire	31.03.44	23	K
1556398	Gnr.	Tester, L.G.	49 Bty. 48 LAA	Chipstead, Kent	29.05.45	35	K
2568691	Pte.	Thom, D.I.	Gordon Highlanders		24.08.45	30	K
T/215964	Dvr.	Thomson, J.C.	RASC attd. R.A.	Prestonpans, East Lothian	01.07.45	31	K
1788715	Gnr.	Tibbit, B.A.	78 Bty. 35 LAA	Lee, London	19.04.44	34	K
401276	Gnr.	Tiley, Joseph	12 Bty. 6 HAA	Calne, Wiltshire	02.06.45	35	K
2336483	Dvr.	Till, E.E.	48 LAA Regt. Sig. Sec.	Grimsby, Lincolnshire	01.03.45	25	K
T/1102835	Dvr.	Timperley, Arthur	RASC attd. R.A.	Clayton, Manchester	27.07.45	39	K
13056297	Pte.	Tipping, W.D.	Pioneer Corps.		03.02.43	24	K
T/3656936	Dvr.	Tipton, Robert	R.A.S.C.	Bradford, Manchester	07.06.45	27	K
986617	Gnr.	Titman, H.A.	12 Bty. 6 HAA	Stamford, Lincolnshire	29.04.45	30	K
T/272029	Dvr.	Tomlinson, John	RASC attd. R.A.	Leeds, Yorkshire	08.05.43	26	K
2030965	Gnr.	Toner, A.J.	12 Bty. 6 HAA	Newcastle-on-Tyne	30.07.45	30	K
1550569	L/Bdr.	Tozer, A.E.	78 Bty. 35 LAA	Bournemouth, Hampshire	23.08.45	29	K
13024745	Pte.	Traynor, Patrick	Pioneer Corps.	Co.Antrim, Nthn.Ireland	05.11.42	44	K
6142250	Pte.	Treasure, P.C.	East Surrey Regt.		24.06.45	25	K
1550521	Gnr.	Trinder, H.W.	78 Bty. 35 LAA	Maidenhead, Berkshire	29.07.45	30	K
1700044	Gnr.	Turgoose, G.H.	89 Bty. 35 LAA	Carlton, Nottinghamshire	29.04.45	39	K
T/4038049	Dvr.	Turner, J.H.	RASC attd. R.A.		17.06.45	25	K
1787168	Gnr.	Turner, William	7 Coast Regt.	Whitchurch Hall, Oxfordshire	03.12.43	22	K
T/266498	L/Cpl.	Umney, A.C.	RASC attd. R.A.	Newport Pagnell	18.06.45	38	K
867307	Gnr.	Unitt, Herbert	15 Bty. 6 HAA		02.11.42	24	K
T/2765609	Dvr.	Vanner, J.E.	RASC attd. R.A.	Gateshead, Co. Durham	05.08.45	35	K
T/272032	Dvr.	Verity, Ralph	RASC attd. R.A.	Bradford, Yorkshire	02.04.45		K
1873511	L/Cpl.	Verner, R.G.	36 Ftrss.Coy., R.E.	Co. Tyrone, Nthn. Ireland	30.07.45	33	K
T/199740	Cpl.	Wadd, J.E.	RASC attd. R.A.	Leicester	14.05.45	34	K
T/235542	Pte.	Wainwright, Arthur	RASC attd. R.A.	Ripley, Derbyshire	12.08.45	29	K
T/222011	Dvr.	Waite, G.E.	R.A.S.C.	Kingwood Common, Oxfordshire	09.06.45	35	K
10556356	Pte.	Walker, Frederick	48 LAA Wkshps.,RAOC	Spondon, Derbyshire	01.05.45	37	K
817872	Sgmn.	Walker, G.A.	Royal Corps. Sigs.	Liverpool	10.07.45	30	K

348

Number	Rank	Name	Regiment	Place of Origin	D.O.D.	Age	Place Died
851531	Gnr.	Walker, J.A.	9 Coast Regt.	Glasgow	07.05.45	33	K
856129	Gnr.	Walker, J.B.	9 Coast Regt.		14.04.44	30	K
6282550	Gnr.	Wallis, P.H.	49 Bty. 48 LAA	East Farleigh, Kent	17.08.45	44	K
7634808	Sgt.	Walter, J.F.S.	R.E.M.E.	Menston, Yorkshire	06.08.45	23	K
1532925	Gnr.	Walters, O.C.	78 Bty. 35 LAA	Wellington, Somerset	17.05.45	24	K
T/3660143	Dvr.	Walton, John	R.A.S.C.		31.07.45		K
1470054	Gnr.	Ward, C.D.	7 Coast Regt.	Portsmouth	21.06.45	25	K
T/276005	Dvr.	Ward, F.C.	RASC attd. R.A.		25.06.45		K
1489170	L/Bdr.	Warren, John	49 Bty. 48 LAA	Stepney, London	09.04.45	40	K
7046761	Dvr.	Watson, Jack	R.A.S.C.	Birmingham	05.08.45	27	K
T/272033	Dvr.	Watson, W.A.	RASC attd. R.A.	Pitsmoor, Sheffield	12.09.45	31	K
1735694	Bdr.	Watt, S.M.	49 Bty. 48 LAA	Hatfield, Hertfordshire	19.07.45	38	K
T/2765485	L/Cpl.	Webb, J.H.	RASC attd. R.A.		24.08.45		K
1827651	Gnr.	Weeden, E.A.	49 Bty. 48 LAA	Stratford, Essex	16.07.45	35	K
1818167	Gnr.	Weeks, H.A.	3 Bty. 6 HAA	Gorseinon, Glamorgan	12.08.45	25	K
1058984	L/Bdr.	Wells, George	15 Bty. 6 HAA		27.03.45	43	K
1478030	Sgt.	Wells, Stephen	78 Bty. 35 LAA	Bourne, Surrey	22.07.45	25	K
T/206777	Dvr.	West, Jack	RASC attd. R.A.	Harmenden, Hertfordshire	28.07.45	31	K
S/274430	Pte.	White, E.G.	RASC attd. R.A.	Abercynon, Glamorgan	23.07.45	39	K
1520131	Gnr.	White, R.J.	78 Bty. 35 LAA	Bournemouth, Hampshire	24.03.45	36	K
1550212	Sgt.	Whittington, B.A.	78 Bty. 35 LAA	Newport, Isle of Wight	07.07.45	29	K
7625070	Pte.	Whyte, D.W.	R.A.O.C.		10.06.45	28	K
13692	Pte.	Wickett, D.J.	F.M.S.V.F.	West Brompton, London	16.08.43	30	K
1556564	Gnr.	Wicks, R.J.	78 Bty. 35 LAA	Reading, Berkshire	21.05.45	32	K
1810723	Gnr.	Wilkinson, William	15 Bty. 6 HAA	Longton, Stoke-on-Trent	09.06.45	41	K
10540791	Pte.	Williams, H.E.	R.A.O.C.		09.08.45	30	K
926521	AC.1	Williams, N.H.	RAF(VR) 242 Sqdn.	Stithians, Cornwall	15.01.45	26	K
1759203	Gnr.	Wilmshurst, E.A.	78 Bty. 35 LAA	Bethnal Green, London	08.04.45	34	K
T/2752433	Drv.	Wilson, Archibald	RASC attd. R.A.		30.07.45		K
5344	Cpl.	Wilson, D.E.	S.S.V.F.	Fulham, London	13.03.45	32	K
T/272037	Dvr.	Wilson, Geoffrey	RASC attd. R.A.	Bradford, Yorkshire	30.07.45	25	K
1750908	Gnr.	Wilson, John	78 Bty. 35 LAA	Port Dundas, Glasgow	22.06.45	37	K
856897	Gnr.	Wilson, J.M.	15 Bty. 6 HAA	South Stanley, Co. Durham	05.04.45-	27	K

Number	Rank	Name	Regiment	Place of Origin	D.O.D.	Age	Place Died
853738	Gnr.	Wilson, J.B.	9 Coast Regt.		17.11.43	29	K
646298	AC.1	Wilson, T.W.	R.A.F.	Burghead, Morayshire	14.08.45	25	K
868713	Gnr.	Wiltshire, A.L.	3 Bty. 6 HAA		09.04.45	27	K
1826381	Gnr.	Winskill, Thomas	49 Bty. 48 LAA	Chopwell, Co. Durham	11.08.45	42	K
T/258393	Dvr.	Winter, Tom	R.A.S.C.	Carnforth, Lancashire	07.05.45	24	K
T/50255	Sgt.	Wisdom, A.J.E.	RASC attd. R.A.	Ryde, Isle of Wight	08.06.45	44	K
1533070	Gnr.	Wolstenholme, Samuel	78 Bty. 35 LAA	Kendal, Westmorland	16.03.45	25	K
4218	Pte.	Wood, J.H.	S.S.V.F.	Woodford Green, Essex	16.09.43	37	K
T/203821	Dvr.	Wood, W.W.	RASC attd. R.A.	Paddington, London	12.06.45	34	K
13063195	Cftsmn.	Woodman, A.H.	R.E.M.E.	Bristol	13.08.45	29	K
1522934	Gnr.	Worby, Harry	49 Bty. 48 LAA	Ipswich, Suffolk	16.07.45	35	K
1766414	Gnr.	Worner, H.H.	49 Bty. 48 LAA		27.12.44	31	K
258467	Pte.	Worswick, Thomas	Catering attd. RASC	Darwen, Lancashire	13.11.44	34	K
1556562	Gnr.	Wright, J.A.	78 Bty. 35 LAA	Reading, Berkshire	05.07.45	33	K
1610942	Gnr.	Yaxley, W.E.	49 Bty. 48 LAA	Belvedere, Kent	25.05.45	34	K
2366594	Sgmn.	Youens, W.J.F.	48 LAA Sig. Sec.		01.12.44	39	K
805122	Gnr.	Young, James	H.Q., 6 HAA Regt.	High Spen, Co. Durham	20.07.45	34	K

Royal Artillery Regiment Personnel
Lost at Sea "Suez Maru"
29 November 1943

Number	Rank	Name	Regiment	Place of Origin	D.O.D.	Age	Place Died
975543	Gnr.	Agar, J.R.	232 Bty. 77 HAA	Etruria, Stoke-on-Trent	29.11.43	27	
554863	Tpr.	Alton, George	3rd Hussars, R.A.C.	Brampton, Derbyshire	29.11.43	27	
858461	L/Sgt.	Argust, T.J.	241 Bty. 77 HAA		29.11.43	27	
2323853	Dvr.	Arnold, William	RCS. 77 MAA. Sig. Sec.	Middleton Tyas, Yorkshire	29.11.43	28	
1776004	Gnr.	Ashby, T.J.	89 Bty. 55 LAA	Mill Hill, Middlesex	29.11.43	23	
1646062	Gnr.	Bartlett, R.W.	240 Bty. 77 HAA		29.11.43	36	
552028	Tpr.	Barson, W.J.	3rd Kings Own Hsrs.RAC.	Botley, Berkshire	29.11.43	30	
1646452	Gnr.	Baxter, N.F.R.J.	239 Bty. 77 HAA	Hampstead, London	29.11.43	29	
1646453	Gnr.	Baylis, P.H.	241 Bty. 77 HAA	Fulham, London	29.11.43	31	
883260	Bdr.	Beard, Kenneth	240 Bty. 77 HAA		29.11.43	23	
T/3197011	Dvr.	Beesley, Thomas	RASC.attd. 21 LAA		29.11.43	32	
1555676	Gnr.	Bennell, W.J.	21 LAA Regt.	Byfleet, Surrey	29.11.43	30	
7931567	Tpr.	Bennett, Ellis	3rd Kings Own Hsrs.RAC	Hollingworth, Manchester	29.11.43	33	
781554	Gnr.	Bessant, T.E.	15 Bty. 6 HAA		29.11.43	33	
1771730	L/Bdr.	Blake, H.G.	241 Bty. 77 HAA		29.11.43	38	
2056513	Gnr.	Bogie, J.W.	239 Bty. 77 HAA	Gosport, Hampshire	29.11.43	22	
1734919	Gnr.	Boswell, Arthur	12 Bty. 6 HAA	Stockport, Cheshire	29.11.43	35	
1545633	Bdr.	Bowins, Edwin	89 Bty. 35 LAA	Tackley, Oxfordshire	29.11.43	30	
1808638	Gnr.	Boyton, S.W.	241 Bty. 77 HAA	Hook End, Essex	29.11.43	22	
2359179	Sgmn.	Brooks, Ronald	RCS.77 MAA.Sig. Sec.		29.11.43	23	
392206	Cpl.	Buck, E.N.	3rd Kigs Own Hsrs.RAC	Hanging Houghton, Northamptons	29.11.43	43	
T/204369	Dvr.	Bumpus, Richard	RASC.attd. 77 HAA	Sileby, Leicestershire	29.11.43	27	
554363	Tpr.	Butler, R.D.	3rd Kings Own Hsrs.RAC	Bognor Regis, Sussex	29.11.43	27	
1706299	L/Bdr.	Butler, W.H.	239 Bty. 77 HAA	Burslem, Stoke-on-Trent	29.11.43	30	
1491669	Gnr.	Buzzacott, S.J.	241 Bty. 77 HAA	Kentish Town, London	29.11.43	25	

351

Number	Rank	Name	Regiment	Place of Origin	D.O.D.	Age	Place Died
7905199	Tpr.	Callaghan, Charles	3rd Kings Own Hsrs.RAC		29.11.43	26	
553865	Tpr.	Carter, Sidney	3rd Kings Own Hsrs.RAC		29.11.43	28	
839063	Gnr.	Clarke, A.S.	241 Bty. 77 HAA	Rhondda, Glamorgan	29.11.43	27	
2578462	Cpl.	Clarke, W.A.	RCS.77 HAA. Sig. Sec.		29.11.43	22	
1444944	L/Bdr.	Coleman, D.C.	241 Bty. 77 HAA	Ystrad, Glamorgan	29.11.43	36	
1491692	Gnr.	Coleman, G.J.	239 Bty. 77 HAA	Kentish Town, London	29.11.43	24	
7607793	Pte.	Cooper, R.H.	RAOC.attd. 48 LAA	Perry Barr, Birmingham	29.11.43	26	
857848	L/Bdr.	Coughlin, Michael	240 Bty. 77 HAA	Canton, Cardiff	29.11.43	30	
1706343	Gnr.	Couley, Thomas	239 Bty. 77 HAA		29.11.43	35	
1444948	Gnr.	Cowell, R.W.F.	240 Bty. 77 HAA	Leckwith, Glamorgan	29.11.43	23	
T/279213	Dvr.	Crowther, Allan	142 Tpt.Coy.RASC	Idle, Yorlcshire	29.11.43	31	
1719728	Gnr.	Davenport, R.J.	21 LAA Regt.,R.A.		29.11.43	34	
223662	Capt.	Davey, H.G.A.	General List		29.11.43	36	
1474423	Bdr.	Davies, J.S.	239 Bty. 77 HAA	Ystradmynach, Glamorgan	29.11.43	33	
1779354	Gnr.	Davies, W.E.	241 Bty. 77 HAA	Cardiff	29.11.43	22	
1635984	Gnr.	Davis, F.G.W.	240 Bty. 77 HAA	Caddlngton, Bedfordshire	29.11.43	32	
1762524	Gnr.	Davis, Jack	126 Bty. 44 LAA	Parkstone, Dorsetshire	29.11.43	38	
1794622	Gnr.	Dawson, George	240 Bty. 77 HAA	Brinsworth, Yorkshire	29.11.43	32	
6918688	Tpr.	Denyer, W.C.	Loyals(Nth.Lancs.)Rgt.	Danbury, Essex	29.11.43	27	
552316	Cpl.	Dickson, Robert	3rd Kings Own Hsrs.RAC		29.11.43	33	
2357678	Sgmn.	Digsby, J.J.	RCS.77 HAA. Sig. Sec.		29.11.43	33	
1654019	Gnr.	Dring, Edwin	21 LAA.Regt. R.A.	Penge, Kent	29.11.43	31	
7933280	Tpr.	Dunning, Norman	3rd Kings Own Hsrs.RAC	Rhyl, Flintshire	29.11.43	31	
T/3456500	Dvr.	Edmondson, Frank	142 Gen.Tpt.Coy.RASC	Higher Walton, Lancashire	29.11.43	28	
2351273	Sgmn.	Edmondson, Robert	RCS.77 HAA. Sig. Sec.	Chadsmoor, Staffordshire	29.11.43	27	
4913355	Tpr.	Edwards, F.E.	3rd Kings Own Hsrs.RAC	Widnes, Lancashire	29.11.43	28	
1743083	L/Bdr.	Ellwood, Bernard	241 Bty. 77 HAA	Crawley, Sussex	23.11.43	35	
553240	Sgt.	Emery, A.W.J.	3rd Kings Own Hsrs.RAC	Tottenham, Middlesex	29.11.43	28	
1614637	Bdr.	Emms, D.C.	79 Bty. 21 LAA		29.11.43	30	
7608356	Pte.	Entwistle, William	RAOC. attd. 48 LAA		29.11.43	29	

Number	Rank	Name	Regiment	Place of Origin	D.O.D.	Age	Place Died
1074199	Gnr.	Falconer, H.K.	79 Bty. 35 LAA	York	29.11.43	32	
550681	Sgt.	Farmer, Albert	3rd Kings Own Hsrs.RAC		29.11.43	27	
1434031	Gnr.	Fawcett, John	241 Bty. 77 HAA		29.11.43	38	
1623465	Gnr.	Ferguson, R.A.	240 Bty. 77 HAA	Appley Bridge, Lancashire	29.11.43	33	
1807016	Gnr.	Fitch, L.E.	79 Bty. 21 LAA	Waltham Abbey, Essex	29.11.43	22	
1614639	Gnr.	Foster, C.H.	79 Bty. 21 LAA	East Sheen, Surrey	29.11.43	30	
1794521	Gnr.	Frith, Jack	239 Bty. 77 HAA	Hyde, Cheshire	29.11.43	23	
2366953	Sgmn.	Fullarton, A.F.	RCS.77 HAA. Sig. Sec.	Wood Green, Middlesex	29.11.43	35	
1609535	Gnr.	Garner, Walter	239 Bty. 77 HAA	Stockport, Cheshire	29.11.43	31	
1807736	Gnr.	Gell, W.P.	240 Bty. 77 HAA		29.11.43	22	
1491801	Gnr.	George, H.C.	239 Bty. 77 HAA	Marylebone, London	29.11.43	24	
T/182497	Dvr.	Glennon, A.E.	RASC.attd. 77 HAA	Wythenshawe, Manchester	29.11.43		
1733525	Gnr.	Goodier, Clifford	241 Bty. 77 HAA		29.11.43	36	
1646355	Gnr.	Gosling, W.E.	241 Bty. 77 HAA		29.11.43	29	
1491824	L/Sgt.	Grady, M.E.	239 Bty. 77 HAA	Ramsgate, Kent	29.11.43	25	
1822265	Gnr.	Grant, G.L.	21 LAA Regt.	Dumfries	29.11.43	35	
1491825	L/Bdr.	Greaves, J.T.	240 Bty. 77 HAA	Streatham, London	29.11.43	25	
2042674	Gnr.	Griffin, J.Y.	21 LAA Regt.	Brixton, London	29.11.43	28	
1591190	L/Bdr.	Guest, Harold	239 Bty. 77 HAA	Miles Platting, Manchester	29.11.43	23	
918269	Gnr.	Guilar, Peter	241 Bty. 77 HAA		29.11.43	21	
1706476	Gnr.	Hadley, Arthur	240 Bty. 77 HAA		29.11.43	25	
7625227	Sgt.	Hall, T.F.	R.E.M.E.		29.11.43	29	
2063179	Gnr.	Harding, C.H.	241 Bty. 77 HAA	Loughborough, Leicestershire	29.11.43	23	
7894655	Tpr.	Harrison, Victor	3rd Kings Own Hsrs.RAC	Selsey, Gloucestershire	29.11.43	23	
1807575	Gnr.	Haywood, C.T.	240 Bty. 77 HAA	Breaston, Derbyshire	29.11.43	31	
1604973	Gnr.	Healey, S.E.	241 Bty. 77 HAA	Nottingham	29.11.43	34	
1746331	Gnr.	Herley, J.M.	12 Bty. 6 HAA		29.11.43	33	
1646112	Bdr.	Hillier, H.G.	240 Bty. 77 HAA	Street, Somerset	29.11.43	30	
1517804	Bdr.	Hurrell, Leonard	241 Bty. 77 HAA		29.11.43	24	
1870889	Spr.	Hutchins, D.W. MID	35 Ftrss.Coy.R.E.	Harlesden, Middlesex	29.11.43	26	

Number	Rank	Name	Regiment	Place of Origin	D.O.D.	Age	Place Died
2351640	Sgmn.	Hyde, George	RCS. 6 HAA. Sig. Sec.	Chester	29.11.43	27	
1587861	L/Bdr.	James, R.W.	241 Bty. 77 HAA		29.11.43	30	
554343	Cpl.	Jarvis, F.W.	3rd Kings Own Hsrs.RAC	Buckingham	29.11.43	27	
1443870	Gnr.	John, L.W.	240 Bty. 77 HAA	Cardiff	29.11.43	35	
1512208	L/Bdr.	Johnson, T.J.	241 Bty. 77 HAA	Wolverhampton	29.11.43	24	
883016	Gnr.	Jones, B.W.	239 Bty. 77 HAA	Penyrheol, Glamorgan	29.11.43	25	
2367018	Sgmn.	Jones, Ernest	RCS. 77 HAA Sig. Sec.		29.11.43	30	
1459948	Gnr.	Jones, J.W.	239 Bty. 77 HAA		29.11.43	42	
1580632	Gnr.	Jones, Lewis	15 Bty. 6 HAA	King's Cross, London	29.11.43	29	
4191764	Gnr.	Jones, William	85 Anti Tank Rgt. RA	Flint	29.11.43	25	
3439328	Sgt.	Jones, W.J.	241 Bty. 77 HAA	Tonypandy, Glamorgan	29.11.43	40	
1442911	Gnr.	Jones, Winser	239 Bty. 77 HAA	Abertridwr, Glamorgan	29.11.43	25	
1548354	Gnr.	Joseph, J.H.	21 LAA Regt.		29.11.43	27	
7925299	Tpr.	King, H.P.	3rd Kings Own Hsrs.RAC	Bitterne, Southampton	29.11.43	37	
1808704	Gnr.	Knowles, W.R.	239 Bty. 77 HAA	Great Yarmouth, Norfolk	29.11.43	23	
1645999	Gnr.	Lewis, O.T.	240 Bty. 77 HAA	Camborne, Cornwall	29.11.43	23	
1563570	Bdr.	Lintott, S.J.	89 Bty. 35 LAA	St. John's, Woking, Surrey	29.11.43	36	
1582380	Gnr.	Lloyd, J.H.	239 Bty. 77 HAA		29.11.43	29	
1587717	L/Sgt.	Locke, C.A.	241 Bty. 77 HAA	Prestwood, Buckinghamshire	29.11.43	29	
2370030	Sgmn.	Lund, Cyril	RCS. 77 HAA. Sig. Sec.		29.11.43	30	
1746273	Gnr.	Luxford, S.H.	241 Bty. 77 HAA	East Grinstead, Sussex	29.11.43	36	
T/3064085	Dvr.	McCallum, Robert	RASC.attd. 21 LAA		29.11.43	30	
2346442	L/Cpl.	McHugh, P.J.	RCS. 77 HAA Sig. Sec.	Oldham, Lancashire	29.11.43	29	
2877464	Cpl.	McIvor, W.J.	R.A.O.C.	Keith, Banffshire	29.11.43	27	
2326759	Sgmn.	McManus, James	RCS. 77 HAA Sig. Sec.		29.11.43	25	
3385975	Tpr.	Marriott, E.H.	3rd Kings Own Hsrs.RAC	King's Heath, Northampton	29.11.43	24	
1591196	Gnr.	Marsh, J.H.	239 Bty. 77 HAA		29.11.43	23	
1605582	Gnr.	Marshall, J.W.	241 Bty. 77 HAA	South Shields, Co. Durham	29.11.43	33	
554672	Tpr.	Martin, H.S.	3rd Kings Own Hsrs.RAC	St. Helen's, Lancashire	29.11.43	29	

354

Number	Rank	Name	Regiment	Place of Origin	D.O.D.	Age	Place Died
1794617	Gnr.	Maskill, Raymond	241 Bty. 77 HAA		29.11.43	22	
3856946	Gnr.	Meadows, James	15 Bty. 6 HAA		29.11.43	23	
1645950	Gnr.	Medway, R.P.	239 Bty. 77 HAA	Exeter	29.11.43	30	
1807626	Gnr.	Mee, James	239 Bty. 77 HAA	Sandiacre, Derbyshire	29.11.43	24	
1835097	Gnr.	Megins, D.T.	239 Bty. 77 HAA	Maesteg, Glamorgan	29.11.43	21	
1807628	Gnr.	Milner, Henry	239 Bty. 77 HAA	Mansfield, Nottinghamshire	29.11.43	22	
5886739	Sgmn.	Mold, Jack	RCS. 77 HAA Sig. Sec.	Whitnash, Warwickshire	29.11.43	24	
552648	Cpl.	Morris, G.F.	3rd Kings Own Hsrs.RAC	Shrewsbury, Shropshire	29.11.43	29	
1657365	Gnr.	Morrow, Alex	239 Bty. 77 HAA	Donegal, Northern Ireland	29.11.43	34	
1706536	Gnr.	Mosley, Henry	239 Bty. 77 HAA		29.11.43	34	
1587875	L/Bdr.	Moulton, Ernest	241 Bty. 77 HAA		29.11.43	37	
S/2226241	Pte.	Murphy, Alexander	R.A.S.C.		29.11.43	23	
1793083	Gnr.	Murray, James	239 Bty. 77 HAA	Maryport, Cumberland	29.11.43	23	
1636090	Gnr.	Naylor, Cooper	241 Bty. 77 HAA	Pudsey, Yorkshire	29.11.43	32	
1475012	Gnr.	Nevill, J.L.	15 Bty. 6 HAA	Hillingdon, Middlesex	29.11.43	31	
2354843	Dvr.	Oldfield, Horace	RCS. 77 HAA Sig. Sec.	Hampstead, London	29.11.43	37	
1646529	Gnr.	Osborn, R.V.	241 Bty. 77 HAA	Bournemouth, Hampshire	29.11.43	29	
3184681	Gnr.	Osborne, F.C.	12 Bty. 6 HAA	Dowlais, Glamorgan	29.11.43	35	
1627446	Gnr.	Owens, Edward	241 Bty. 77 HAA		29.11.43	35	
7932239	Tpr.	Page, E.J.	3rd Kings Own Hsrs. RAC	Norwich	29.11.43	33	
1643469	Gnr.	Palmer, A.F.	15 Bty. 6 HAA	St. Pancras, London	29.11.43	32	
5248434	Tpr.	Perry, William	3rd Kings Own Hsrs. RAC	Woodsetton, Staffordshire	29.11.43	34	
6016330	Cftsmn.	Phillips, R.J.	REME. attd. 21 LAA	Goodmayes, Essex	29.11.43	23	
405502	Cpl.	Powell, George	3rd Kings Own Hsrs. RAC	Leeds, Yorkshire	29.11.43	30	
402661	Cpl.	Preece, G.J.	3rd Kings Own Hsrs. RAC		29.11.43	34	
1732105	Gnr.	Pritchard, F.J.	241 Bty. 77 HAA		29.11.43	23	
1808708	Gnr.	Ransome, J.A.	240 Bty. 77 HAA	Docking, Norfolk	29.11.43	22	
2366447	Sgmn.	Reynolds, H.M.	RCS. 77 HAA Sig. Sec.	Weobley, Herefordshire	29.11.43	22	
1826603	Gnr.	Rigby, Peter	21 LAA Regt.	Over Hulton, Lancashire	29.11.43	29	

Number	Rank	Name	Regiment	Place of Origin	D.O.D.	Age	Place Died
S/238808	Pte.	Roberts, Jack	Fld.Bakery, RASC	Cambridge	29.11.43	23	
1582438	Gnr.	Robertson, R.C.	239 Bty. 77 HAA		29.11.43		
1605469	Gnr.	Robinson, Thomas	241 Bty. 77 HAA		29.11.43	35	
748122	BQMS	Rowe, R.H.	241 Bty. 77 HAA	Gelli Pentre, Glamorgan	29.11.43	38	
1807346	Gnr.	Saban, C.V.	79 Bty. 21 LAA		29.11.43	22	
1626641	L/Bdr.	Sage, Norman	239 Bty. 77 HAA	Upper Norwood, Surrey	29.11.43	29	
1751252	Bdr.	Saunders, N.E.	239 Bty. 77 HAA	Redland, Gloucestershire	29.11.43	35	
1064369	L/Bdr.	Scarbrough, H.T.	239 Bty. 77 HAA		29.11.43	37	
2579558	Sgmn.	Sharpe, J.I.G.	RCS. 77 HAA Sig. Sec.	St.John's Wood, London	29.11.43	22	
1826738	Gnr.	Smith, Kenneth	79 Bty. 21 LAA	Rutherglen, Lanarkshire	29.11.43	37	
1482054	Sgt.	Spence, L.F.	48 Bty. 21 LAA	Banstead, Surrey	29.11.43	28	
3535743	Pte.	Spurling, William	Manchester Regt.	Burtonwood, Lancashire	29.11.43	29	
553192	Cpl.	Stanford, W.L.J.	3rd Kings Own Hsrs.RAC	Darlington, Co. Durham	29.11.43	30	
1770727	Gnr.	Stanley, S.E.	15 Bty. 6 HAA	Oadby, Leicestershire	29.11.43	23	
1736274	Gnr.	Steam, Sidney	79 Bty. 21 LAA		29.11.43	36	
1502670	Gnr.	Steed, William	15 Bty. 6 HAA	Walsall, Staffordshire	29.11.43	25	
1439392	Gnr.	Steedman, E.	12 Bty. 6 HAA	Edinburgh	29.11.43	36	
1549377	Gnr.	Steventon, G.V.H.	21 LAA Regt.	Stockwell, London	29.11.43	29	
543906	Cpl.	Stigant, E.W.C.	3rd Kings Own Hsrs.RAC	Gosport, Hampshire	29.11.43	37	
1646008	Gnr.	Stone, E.J.	239 Bty. 77 HAA	Wiveliscombe, Somerset	29.11.43	29	
1807387	Gnr.	Stoneham, S.W.	21 LAA Regt.		29.11.43	22	
3855662	L/Cpl.	Stringfellow, William	Intelligence Corps.	Hindley, Lancashire	29.11.43	30	
747928	BSM	Sumption, Edward	241 Bty. 77 HAA	Pentre, Glamorgan	29.11.43	52	
822321	Gnr.	Sunley, L.H.	21 LAA Regt.	Alverstoke, Hampshire	29.11.43	29	
T/89779	Sgt.	Sweeny, R.R.	R.A.S.C.	Harrogate, Yorkshire	29.11.43	37	
T/254047	Dvr.	Taylor, Ronald	RASC.attd. 48 LAA	Belper, Derbyshire	29.11.43	23	
1447543	Gnr.	Thomas, W.C.	239 Bty. 77 HAA		29.11.43	29	
T/157214	Dvr.	Thorpe, Albert	RASC. attd. 48 LAA	Atherton, Lancashire	29.11.43	25	
818155	L/Bdr.	Tinsley, C.W.	239 Bty. 77 HAA	Crayford, Kent	29.11.43	32	
1427519	Sgt.	Toole, G.M.	15 Bty. 6 HAA	Basingstoke, Hampshire	29.11.43	23	
1807700	Gnr.	Toon, A.A.	240 Bty. 77 HAA	Leicester	29.11.43	22	

Number	Rank	Name	Regiment	Place of Origin	D.O.D.	Age	Place Died
T/68799	Dvr.	Tregaskis, W.J.	RASC. attd. 21 LAA	Plymouth	29.11.43	22	
1646054	Gnr.	Tucker, Harold	239 Bty. 77 HAA	Chulmleigh, Devon	29.11.43	28	
3527946	Tpr.	Turner, W.D.	3rd Kings Own Hsrs.RAC	Dukinfield, Cheshire	29.11.43	26	
1502708	Gnr.	Varney, T.E.	15 Bty. 6 HAA		29.11.43	25	
845146	Gnr.	Walker, A.N.	9 Coast Rgt.,R.A.	Leeds, Yorkshire	29.11.43	27	
984512	Bdr.	Walker, Jack	241 Bty. 77 HAA		29.11.43	28	
1706719	Gnr.	Wardell, M.W.	239 Bty. 77 HAA	Kingstanding, Birmingham	29.11.43	33	
2352277	L/Cpl.	Waring, E.G.	RCS. 77 HAA. Sig .Sec.	Morley, Yorkshire	29.11.43	33	
1458782	L/Bdr.	Watts, F.J.	240 Bty. 77 HAA		29.11.43	35	
1065009	Gnr.	Wayman, C.T.	12 Bty. 6 HAA	Chaxhill, Gloucestershire	29.11.43	36	
1507596	Gnr.	Webb, A.F.	241 Bty. 77 HAA	Laindon, Essex	29.11.43	25	
833203	Sgt.	Webb, C.O.	239 Bty. 77 HAA	Tenby, Pembrokeshire	29.11.43	30	
1808716	L/Bdr.	Whitman, W.J.	239 Bty. 77 HAA	Leighton Buzzard, Bedfordshire	29.11.43	29	
1545761	Gnr.	Wilkinson, C.F.St.G.	21 LAA Reg.	Neasden, Middlesex	29.11.43	29	
7899863	Tpr.	Williams, Arnold	3rd Kings Own Hsrs.RAC	Chester	29.11.43	25	
405133	Cpl.	Williams, E.C.	3rd Kings Own Hsrs.RAC	Folkestone	29.11.43	29	
553616	Tpr.	Williamson, Kenneth	3rd Kings Own Hsrs.RAC		29.11.43	30	
7629277	Pte.	Wood, P.D.	RAOC.attd. R.A.	Taunton, Somerset	29.11.43	32	
1555770	L/Bdr.	Woodman, L.H.	21 LAA Regt.	Malmesbury, Wiltshire	29.11.43	29	
1819219	Gnr.	Yudkin, Abraham	48 Bty. 21 LAA	Hackney, London	29.11.43	29	

Royal Air Force Personnel
Lost at Sea "Suez Maru"
29 November 1943

Number	Rank	Name	Regiment	Place of Origin	D.O.D.	Age	Place Died
1308868	Cpl.	Abbott, W.J.	RAF (VR) 242 Sqdn.	Hayes, Bromley, Kent	29.11.43	33	
539725	LAC	Alderson, J.B.	R.A.F. 220 Sqdn.	Darlington, Co. Durham	29.11.43	24	
918239	LAC	Andrews, E.W.	R.A.F. (VR)		29.11.43	23	
935929	Cpl.	Ashworth, S.G.	R.A.F. (VR)	Coulsdon, Surrey	29.11.43		
926840	LAC	Badcock, I.K.F.	RAF (VR) 242 Sqdn.	New Milton, Hampshire	29.11.43	31	
1132321	LAC	Barber, G.J.W.	R.A.F. (VR)	Ilford, Essex	29.11.43		
626496	Cpl.	Beatty, M.A.A.	R.A.F. 84 Sqdn.	Tunbridge Wells, Kent	29.11.43	23	
1040478	AC.2	Bell, William	R.A.F. (VR)	Whitehaven, Cumberland	29.11.43	33	
847141	LAC	Bennett, A.H.	RAF (Aux. A.F.)	Leyton, Essex	29.11.43	29	
515790	W.O.	Bere, C.H.	R.A.F. 62 Sqdn.	Tiverton, Devon	29.11.43	32	
1023130	AC.2	Blackwood, David	R.A.F. (VR)	Addiewell, Midlothian	29.11.43	26	
634798	LAC	Blakely, A.G.	R.A.F.	Kington, Herefordshire	29.11.43	22	
654650	LAC	Bonner, I.F.	R.A.F.	Birmingham	29.11.43	24	
1152607	Cpl.	Boulton, Ben	R.A.F. (VR)	Burslem, Stoke-on-Trent	29.11.43	30	
1265463	AC.1	Bracegirdle, Phil	R.A.F. (VR)		29.11.43	31	
1156249	AC.1	Brant, J.E.	R.A.F. (VR)		29.11.43		
47467	F/Offr.	Brentnall, A.S.	R.A.F. 84 Sqdn.	Gonerby Hill Foot, Lincolnshire	29.11.43	37	
522691	Sgt.	Broadhurst, James	R.A.F.	Peterborough, Northhamptonshire	29.11.43	29	
1440802	AC.2	Brockman, G.R.H.	R.A.F. (VR)	Gillingham, Kent	29.11.43	20	
993595	AC.2	Brodie, W.F.P.	R.A.F. (VR)	Rattray, Perthshire	29.11.43	29	
1368857	AC.1	Bromley, Thomas	R.A.F. (VR)	Barrhead, Glasgow	29.11.43	22	
1231177	AC.1	Brooker, D.A.	R.A.F. (VR)	West Malling, Kent	29.11.43	20	
634480	LAC	Brookes, Alec	R.A.F. 232 Sqdn.	Walsall, Staffordshire	29.11.43	22	
524715	Cpl.	Brown, Leslie	R.A.F.		29.11.43	37	
950438	AC.1	Brown, R.A.	R.A.F. (VR)	Glasgow	29.11.43	25	
1407313	AC.2	Brown, V.L.C.	RAF (VR) 605 Sqdn.	Buckland Brewer, Devon	29.11.43	23	

358

Number	Rank	Name	Regiment	Place of Origin	D.O.D.	Age	Place Died
958014	Cpl.	Burt, Walter	R.A.F. (VR)	Doncaster, Yorkshire	29.11.43	26	
814176	AC.2	Burton, G.H.	RAF(Aux.AF) 211 Sqdn.	Bircotes, Nottinghamshire	29.11.43	21	
991671	Cpl.	Carlin, J.E.	R.A.F. (VR)		29.11.43	41	
1098479	AC.2	Carroll, Robert	RAF (VR) 211 Sqdn.		29.11.43		
1229958	AC.2	Chambers, S.J.A.	R.A.F. (VR)		29.11.43		
645028	Cpl.	Chandler, H.G.E.	R.A.F. 84 Sqdn.		29.11.43	27	
1059606	LAC	Chapman, W.L.	R.A.F. (VR)	Aberdeen	29.11.43	23	
1211362	AC.1	Checketts, E.E.	RAF (VR) 605 Sqdn.	Worcester	29.11.43	21	
1011674	AC.1	Clegg, H.C.	R.A.F. (VR)	Worsborough Dale, Yorkshire	29.11.43		
1335299	F/Sgt.	Clement, G.W.	RAF (VR) 99 Sqdn.		29.11.43		
1016297	AC.1	Coates, Bernard	RAF (VR) 84 Sqdn.	Farsley, Yorkshire	29.11.43	31	
651422	Cpl.	Cole, R.A.	R.A.F.	Lostwithiel, Cornwall	29.11.43	22	
537707	Cpl.	Collingwood, R.A.	R.A.F. 84 Sqdn.	Gateshead, Co. Durham	29.11.43	25	
1012371	LAC	Connett, J.H.	R.A.F. (VR)	Plymouth	29.11.43	31	
1531976	AC.2	Cousins, A.W.C.	R.A.F. 242 Sqdn.	Stockport, Cheshire	29.11.43	44	
530013	LAC	Croston, Thomas	R.A.F. 211 Sqdn.	Westhoughton, Lancashire	29.11.43	27	
979836	Cpl.	Currie, D.R.	R.A.F. (VR)	Stirling	29.11.43	23	
1136563	AC.2	Daft, William	R.A.F. (VR)	Stapleford, Nottinghamshire	29.11.43	29	
539874	Sgt.	Darwen, G.G.	R.A.F. 84 Sqdn.	Bridlington, Yorkshire	29.11.43	26	
1226089	AC.1	Dicks, S.W.	R.A.F. (VR)	Isham, Northamptonshire	29.11.43		
1031192	AC.1	Dixon, William	R.A.F. (VR)	Preston, Lancashire	29.11.43	23	
985788	W.O.	Dodds, R.A.	R.A.F.		29.11.43	24	
954800	LAC	Donaldson, John	RAF (VR) 211 Sqdn.		29.11.43		
1204528	Cpl.	Dron, C.P.	R.A.F. (VR)	Whitley Bay, Northumberland	29.11.43		
548567	Cpl.	Dunlop, R.A.	R.A.F.		29.11.43		
1265129	AC.2	Dunphy, C.T.	R.A.F. (VR)		29.11.43	32	
1143310	AC.1	Earl, C.S.	RAF (VR) 605 Sqdn.	Cheltenham, Gloucestershire	29.11.43	43	
903009	LAC	Edis, Jim	RAF (VR) 84 Sqdn.		29.11.43		
1286282	AC.1	Elias, T.I.	R.A.F. (VR)	Swansea	29.11.43	27	
1484330	AC.2	Ellison, Edward	R.A.F. (VR)	Birkenhead	29.11.43	21	

Number	Rank	Name	Regiment	Place of Origin	D.O.D.	Age	Place Died
1004122	AC.2	Entwistle, Stanley	R.A.F. (VR)	Blackburn, Lancashire	29.11.43		
929550	LAC	Evans, T.J.	R.A.F. (VR)	Burry Port, Carmarthenshire	29.11.43	30	
1082200	AC.2	Fairhurst, Albert	R.A.F. (VR)		29.11.43		
1165931	LAC	Farnell, A.S.	R.A.F. (VR)		29.11.43	23	
632931	Cpl.	Fawcett, Henry	R.A.F.	Bearpark, Co. Durham	29.11.43	23	
1360261	AC.1	Files, Frank	RAF (VR) 100 Sqdn.		29.11.43		
1184503	AC.2	Filmer, Brian	R.A.F. (VR)	Willington Quay, Northumberland	29.11.43	31	
1090680	AC.2	Flavell, J.W.	R.A.F. (VR)	West Dulwich, London	29.11.43	24	
937854	Cpl.	Foster, J.R.	R.A.F. (VR)	Sunderland, Co. Durham	29.11.43	29	
905642	AC.1	Frost, L.A.	R.A.F. (VR)		29.11.43		
1102563	Cpl.	Fulton, Alan	R.A.F. (VR)	Wallsend, Northumberland	29.11.43	28	
1006617	Cpl.	Gelder, William	R.A.F. (VR)	Accrington, Lancashire	29.11.43	34	
1141703	LAC	Gelling, Arthur	R.A.F. (VR)	Widnes, Lancashire	29.11.43	22	
546442	Cpl.	Gleeson, Terence	R.A.F.		29.11.43		
117803	F/Offr.	Godfree, J.H.W.	R.A.F.	Natal, South Africa	29.11.43	48	
1061437	AC.2	Goldberg, Charles	R.A.F. (VR)	Leeds, Yorkshire	29.11.43		
1056822	AC.2	Gorst, Fred	RAF (VR) 84 Sqdn.	Preston, Lancashire	29.11.43	23	
611159	LAC	Graveson, James	R.A.F. 62 Sqdn.	Maryport, Cumberland	29.11.43	23	
535963	Cpl.	Gray, T.Y.	R.A.F.	Maryhill, Glasgow	29.11.43	33	
116815	F/Offr.	Gregg, J.F.F.	R.A.F.	Armagh, Northern Ireland	29.11.43	40	
936592	LAC	Griffin, William	R.A.F. (VR)		29.11.43		
955915	LAC	Griffith, John	R.A.F. (VR)	Llanllyfni, Caernarvonshire	29.11.43	24	
913137	LAC	Groombridge, J.G.	RAF (VR) 211 Sqdn.	Crowborough, Sussex	29.11.43	37	
1254212	AC.1	Grunis, Abe	R.A.F. (VR)		29.11.43		
1480589	AC.2	Halliday, J.H.	R.A.F. (VR)	South Shields, Co. Durham	29.11.43	22	
901652	LAC	Hambridge, A.R.V.	RAF (VR) 84 Sqdn.		29.11.43		
626473	LAC	Hanley, J.C.	R.A.F.		29.11.43		
930495	LAC	Hardy, Robert	R.A.F. (VR)		29.11.43		
1210798	AC.1	Harnden, John	R.A.F. (VR)		29.11.43		
1213243	AC.1	Harris, A.F.	RAF (VR) 605 Sqdn.		29.11.43		

Number	Rank	Name	Regiment	Place of Origin	D.O.D.	Age	Place Died
616344	Cpl.	Harrison, Herbert	R.A.F.	Brackley, Northamptonshire	29.11.43	24	
1529018	F/Sgt.	Hawkins, Kenneth	RAF (VR) 99 Sqdn.	Leeds, Yorkshire	29.11.43	23	
1235829	AC.1	Hayes, W.J.	R.A.F. (VR)	Bramford, Suffolk	29.11.43		
1205956	AC.2	Heath, R.A.	R.A.F. (VR)	Fromefield, Frome, Somerset	29.11.43	33	
156510	LAC	Hedgecox, William	R.A.F.	Barnsley, Yorkshire	29.11.43	43	
1304949	AC.1	Hicks, Walter	R.A.F. (VR)	Hornchurch, Essex	29.11.43	23	
1157359	AC.1	Holman, A.L.	RAF (VR) 36 Sqdn.	Callington, Cornwall	29.11.43	27	
1252122	W.O.	Hough, H.H.	RAF (VR) 84 Sqdn.		29.11.43		
991586	AC.1	Hoyles, Frank	RAF (VR) 84 Sqdn.		29.11.43		
1280482	AC.1	Hulley, P.O'D.	R.A.F. (VR)	Lewisham, London	29.11.43	26	
1173380	AC.1	Hunt, J.H.	R.A.F. (VR)	Barnet, Hertfordshire	29.11.43	29	
903136	LAC	Hutchinson, R.S.	R.A.F. (VR)	Plympton, Devon	29.11.43	24	
978595	AC.1	Jones, C.E.W.	RAF (VR) 84 Sqdn.	Fenham, Newcastle-on-Tyne	29.11.43	26	
532739	Cpl.	Jones, E.A.	R.A.F.	Stonehouse, Gloucestershire	29.11.43	29	
575062	AC.1	Jones, G.L.M.	R.A.F.	Bath, Somerset	29.11.43	21	
1379347	Sgt.	Joynson, A.L.	RAF (VR) 99 Sqdn.	Monton Green, Lancashire	29.11.43	23	
1152011	W.O.	Juby, D.A.	R.A.F. (VR)	Norwich	29.11.43	27	
1214661	AC.1	Kaines, A.L.	R.A.F. (VR)	Milton, Berkshire	29.11.43	35	
531925	F/Sgt.	Kemp, Stanley	R.A.F. 605 Sqdn.	Blackpool, Lancashire	29.11.43	25	
1387333	AC.1	Kidd, J.T.	R.A.F. (VR)	Bethnal Green, London	29.11.43	22	
1430241	AC.1	King, J.T.	R.A.F. (VR)	Great Brickhill, Buckinghamshire	29.11.43	22	
1309078	AC.1	King, M.G.	R.A.F. (VR)	Lower Kingswood, Surrey	29.11.43	34	
1194884	AC.2	Knight, H.G.T.	R.A.F. (VR)	Partridge Green, Sussex	29.11.43	21	
950227	Cpl.	Knightley, G.B.	R.A.F. (VR)	Cheadle, Staffordshire	29.11.43	29	
1134274	AC.1	Knock, W.F.	R.A.F. (VR)	Ingatestone, Essex	29.11.43	37	
762154	LAC	Lawe, N.E.	R.A.F. (VR)	Stafford	29.11.43	34	
1250653	LAC	Lawes, N.J.A.	R.A.F. (VR)		29.11.43		
614399	Cpl.	Lawson, Harold	R.A.F.	Wallasey, Cheshire	29.11.43	32	
1166195	AC.1	Lawson, L.C.	R.A.F. (VR)	New Southgate, Middlesex	29.11.43	26	
979864	AC.1	Leach, R.C.	R.A.F. (VR)	Mannamead, Plymouth	29.11.43	27	

Number	Rank	Name	Regiment	Place of Origin	D.O.D.	Age	Place Died
622386	AC.1	Lee, W.A.	R.A.F. 211 Sqdn.	St. Ninians, Stirling	29.11.43		
1286884	AC.1	Leeper, D.J.	R.A.F.	Reigate, Surrey	29.11.43	32	
570612	Cpl.	Lees, F.N.	R.A.F.	Wallasey, Cheshire	29.11.43	23	
1164591	LAC	Leeves, William	R.A.F. (VR)	Jarvis Brook, Sussex	29.11.43	34	
621301	Cpl.	Lewis, B.F.	R.A.F.		29.11.43		
1022389	AC.2	Lindsay, Samuel	R.A.F. (VR)	Dalmarnock, Glasgow	29.11.43	32	
538172	AC.1	Litherland, John	R.A.F.	Bewsey, Lancashire	29.11.43		
1046901	AC.1	Love, C.F.	RAF (VR) 605 Sqdn.	Ashingdon, Essex	29.11.43	38	
1286202	LAC	Lowle, H.D.	R.A.F. (VR)	West Brompton, London	29.11.43	30	
1335703	Sgt.	McColley, J.E.	RAF (VR) 99 Sqdn.	New Cross, London	29.11.43	20	
550582	F/Sgt.	McCormack, J.W.	R.A.F.		29.11.43		
634665	AC.1	Macey, H.V.	R.A.F.	Dursley, Gloucestershire	29.11.43	21	
978073	AC.1	McGuinness, Robert	R.A.F. (VR)	Belfast, Northern Ireland	29.11.43	20	
1056500	LAC	McIntyre, R.A.S.	R.A.F. (VR)	Port Glasgow, Renfrewshire	29.11.43	29	
1180421	W.O.	Mackillop, D.J.	RAF (VR) 84 Sqdn.	Woolland, Dorsetshire	29.11.43		
1062210	Cpl.	McLean, Angus	RAF (VR) 84 Sqdn.	Ibrox, Glasgow	29.11.43	30	
621000	AC.1	McPhillips, Thomas	R.A.F.	Dunfermline, Fife	29.11.43		
1366673	AC.2	Mair, George	R.A.F. (VR)		29.11.43	29	
958215	AC.2	Martin, J.R.	R.A.F. (VR)	Yiewsley, Middlesex	29.11.43		
1205241	AC.2	Martin, R.J.	R.A.F. (VR)	Abbey Wood, London	29.11.43	35	
632671	LAC	Mason, E.H.	R.A.F.	St. Pancras, London	29.11.43	32	
1234797	LAC	Mason, W.D.	RAF (VR) 242 Sqdn.	Vennington, Shropshire	29.11.43	22	
979553	LAC	Maxwell, David	RAF (VR) 36 Sqdn.	Tillicoultry, Clackmannanshire	29.11.43	28	
570306	LAC	Maynard, V.F.	R.A.F.	Pembroke Dock	29.11.43	22	
1174733	AC.1	Metcalfe, Matthew	R.A.F. (VR)		29.11.43	23	
1112966	LAC	Minton, F.A.	RAF (VR) 23 Sqdn.	Liverpool	29.11.43	28	
980427	LAC	Morgan, F.A.J.	R.A.F. (VR)	Dublin, Irish Republic	29.11.43	22	
912211	AC.2	Morgan, R.G.	RAF (VR) 34 Sqdn.	Streatham, London	29.11.43	23	
1292710	AC.1	Morris, E.W.	RAF (VR) 242 Sqdn.		29.11.43	23	
527412	Cpl.	Morris, R.V.	R.A.F.		29.11.43		
1190136	AC.2	Mundin, H.K.	R.A.F. (VR)	South Wigston, Leicestershire	29.11.43	22	

Number	Rank	Name	Regiment	Place of Origin	D.O.D.	Age	Place Died
1204043	F/Sgt.	Nash, R.C.	RAF (VR) 99 Sqdn.	Somerford, Staffordshire	29.11.43	23	
1000551	LAC	Nicholson, R.W.	R.A.F. (VR)	Darlington, Co. Durham	29.11.43	23	
1234542	AC.2	Niehorster, G.E.	R.A.F. (VR)	Enfield, Middlesex	29.11.43	21	
615574	Cpl.	North, D.E.	R.A.F.	North Finchley, Middlesex	29.11.43	25	
1441079	AC.2	Owen, W.E.	R.A.F. (VR)		29.11.43		
903290	Cpl.	Palmer, J.E.	RAF (VR) 605 Sqdn.		29.11.43		
1447475	AC.1	Parsons, W.G.	R.A.F. (VR)	Gorleston-on-Sea, Norfolk	29.11.43	36	
701363	Cpl.	Permain, James	R.A.F. (VR)	Freemantle, Southampton	29.11.43		
1575597	F/Sgt.	Perry, V.D.	RAF (VR) 99 Sqdn.	Sherwood Rise, Nottingham	29.11.43		
929224	LAC	Philpott, Sidney	R.A.F. (VR)	Canvey Island, Essex	29.11.43	23	
1012421	LAC	Pont, A.L.F.	RAF (VR) 605 Sqdn.	Northfield, Birmingham	29.11.43	30	
631904	AC.1	Pope, P.F.	R.A.F. 84 Sqdn.	Hucknall, Nottinghamshire	29.11.43	20	
1284061	AC.1	Powell, E.J.	R.A.F. (VR)	Southall, Middlesex	29.11.43	26	
1017978	AC.2	Pownall, J.S.	R.A.F. (VR)	St. Helens, Lancashire	29.11.43	33	
1158337	LAC	Prime, A.J.	R.A.F. (VR)	Lower Cam, Gloucestershire	29.11.43	23	
1309574	AC.1	Prime, C.H.	R.A.F. (VR)		29.11.43		
640281	LAC	Pusey, J.W.	R.A.F.	Windsor, Berkshire	29.11.43	23	
1177682	AC.2	Radford, Norman	R.A.F. (VR)	Leicester	29.11.43	22	
1006943	AC.1	Ratcliffe, Leonard	RAF (VR) 84 Sqdn.	New Mills, Derbyshire	29.11.43	29	
649039	LAC	Reay, R.F.G.	R.A.F.	Walthamstow, Essex	29.11.43	23	
1063513	LAC	Reid, E.M.	R.A.F. (VR)		29.11.43		
1108806	AC.2	Renshaw, William	R.A.F. (VR)	Wing, Buckinghamshire	29.11.43	25	
1124266	AC.1	Reynolds, Arthur	R.A.F. (VR)		29.11.43		
1137513	AC.1	Richardson, Alfred	RAF (VR) 84 Sqdn.	Chadderton, Lancashire	29.11.43	34	
925034	LAC	Ringrow, F.C.	R.A.F. (VR)	Rainham, Essex	29.11.43	23	
1340008	AC.1	Robertson, Albert	RAF (VR) 84 Sqdn.		29.11.43	22	
1019835	AC.1	Robson, J.E.	RAF (VR) 84 Sqdn.	Ambleside, Westmorland	29.11.43	31	
1256012	LAC	Romain, Louis	R.A.F. (VR)	Kentish Town, London	29.11.43	28	
654537	Cpl.	Sant, R.T.	R.A.F.	Middlewich, Cheshire	29.11.43	21	

363

Number	Rank	Name	Regiment	Place of Origin	D.O.D.	Age	Place Died
1019586	AC.2	Shaw, V.T.	RAF (VR) 62 Sqdn.	Southport, Lancashire	29.11.43	31	
518753	F/Sgt.	Shimells, Leonard	R.A.F.		29.11.43		
906113	AC.1	Shouler, D.W.	RAF (VR) 605 Sqdn.	Torquay, Devon	29.11.43	23	
1074216	AC.2	Shuttleworth, D.A.	R.A.F. (VR)	Burnley, Lancashire	29.11.43	32	
803509	Cpl.	Sim, J.H.	R.A.F. (Aux. A.F.)		29.11.43		
1156987	LAC	Small, S.R.	RAF (VR) 84 Sqdn.	Wandsworth, London	29.11.43	28	
956483	LAC	Smart, Jack	R.A.F. (VR)	Penyfai, Glamorgan	29.11.43	25	
1261758	Cpl.	Smith, A.B.J.	RAF (VR) 84 Sqdn.	Exeter	29.11.43	21	
1055923	LAC	Smith, A.H.	R.A.F. (VR)	Colne, Lancashire	29.11.43	23	
972275	LAC	Smith, Donald	RAF (VR) 62 Sqdn.		29.11.43		
975668	AC.2	Smith, E.M.	R.A.F. (VR)	New Costessey, Norfolk	29.11.43	23	
1103013	LAC	Smith, H.L.	R.A.F. (VR)	Liverpool	29.11.43		
1377011	LAC	Smith, H.J.	R.A.F. (VR)		29.11.43		
1319147	AC.2	Sprake, R.J.L.	R.A.F. (VR)	Bridport, Dorsetshire	29.11.43	22	
573094	Cpl.	Standley, P.J.	R.A.F.	Kingsteignton, Devon	29.11.43	21	
925188	LAC	Staniland, E.J.	R.A.F. (VR)	Hanwell, Middlesex	29.11.43		
625564	Cpl.	Stedman, J.W.	R.A.F. 62 Sqdn.	Romford, Essex	29.11.43	24	
1378172	AC.1	Streater, V.S.	R.A.F. (VR)	Chingford, Essex	29.11.43	32	
627036	LAC	Stuart, B.W.J.	R.A.F.	Walmer, Kent	29.11.43	23	
610989	Sgt.	Swaffield, N.G.	R.A.F.	Southsea, Hampshire	29.11.43		
1167039	AC.1	Tanguy, R.L.	RAF (VR) 242 Sqdn.		29.11.43		
577270	AC.1	Taylor, Frank	R.A.F.		29.11.43		
1259891	AC.1	Taylor, L.G.	R.A.F. (VR)	East Ham, Essex	29.11.43	23	
941699	LAC	Teasdale, G.N.	R.A.F. (VR)	Grimsby, Lincolnshire	29.11.43	25	
805530	LAC	Tooth, C.G.	RAF(Aux.A.F.)605 Sqdn.	King's Norton, Birmingham	29.11.43	28	
591817	LAC	Tozer, L.R.	R.A.F. 100 Sqdn.	Tonteg, Glamorgan	29.11.43	21	
550100	Sgt.	Tully, W.E.	R.A.F. 84 Sqdn.	Sheffield	29.11.43	25	
1208373	AC.2	Utting, Harold	RAF (VR) 62 Sqdn.	Romford, Essex	29.11.43	27	
944211	AC.1	Vincent, D.R.	RAF (VR) 84 Sqdn.	Handsworth, Birmingham	29.11.43	27	

Number	Rank	Name	Regiment	Place of Origin	D.O.D.	Age	Place Died
1190515	AC.1	Walker, A.C.C.	R.A.F. (VR)		29.11.43		
1023094	AC.2	Walton, A.N.C.	RAF (VR) 62 Sqdn.	Newton-le-Willows, Lancashire	29.11.43		
1287882	LAC	Watson, C.P.	R.A.F. (VR)	Ipswich, Suffolk	29.11.43	22	
611113	LAC	Webb, H.J.	R.A.F.		29.11.43		
411484	F/Lieut.	White, G.P.	R.N.Z.A.F.	Wellington, New Zealand	29.11.43	24	
1235505	AC.2	Wigley, G.V.	RAF (VR) 242 Sqdn.		29.11.43	22	
1010120	LAC	Wilcock, H.R.	R.A.F. (VR)	Salford, Lancashire	29.11.43	30	
1121640	LAC	Williams, E.S.	R.A.F. (VR)	Wolstanton, Staffordshire	29.11.43	27	
629130	LAC	Williams, H.E.J.	R.A.F.	Saltash, Cornwall	29.11.43	22	
626147	AC.1	Williams, J.D.	R.A.F.		29.11.43		
953620	LAC	Williams, R.J.	RAF (VR) 200 Sqdn.	Leicester	29.11.43	23	
1316108	AC.2	Wing, F.J.	RAF (VR) 242 Sqdn.	Islip, Oxfordshire	29.11.43	21	
511113	W.O.	Wright, G.C.	R.A.F. 84 Sqdn.		29.11.43		
1259752	LAC	Yallop, W.E.F.	R.A.F. (VR)	Beccles, Suffolk	29.11.43	23	

The Nominal Roll provided by Allied Land Forces South East Asia Command seems incomplete.

Number	Rank	Name	Regiment	Place of Origin	D.O.D.	Age	Place Died
133194	Capt.	Aldridge,B.H.M.	R.A.M.C.		05.03.43		
1427501	Gnr.	Allison, John	3 HAA Regt.		05.03.43	27	
1426791	Gnr.	Anderson, Sidney	9 Coast Regt.		05.03.43	30	
151926	Lieut.	Andrew, L.D.	3 HAA Regt.	Crouch End, Middlesex	05.03.43	29	
1700403	L.Bdr.	Ansell, H.W.H.	144 Bty. 35 LAA	Blackpool, Lancashire	05.03.43	32	
1773841	Gnr.	Ardy, W.A.	144 Bty. 35 LAA	Tooting, Surrey	05.03.43	38	
984218	Gnr.	Armitage, W.S.	R.A.attd. 1 HAA. RIA	Salford, Lancashire	05.03.43	27	
1793059	Gnr.	Ashton, Ernest	89 Bty. 35 LAA		05.03.43	22	
1799306	Gnr.	Atcheler, W.V.	47 Coast Obs. R.A.	Bermondsey, London	05.03.43	37	
1700407	Gnr.	Ayre, Albert	144 Bty. 35 LAA	Derby	08.07.43	35	
2044898	Gnr.	Bacon, D.W.	89 Bty. 35 LAA		15.11.42	21	
2597280	Sgmn.	Bailey, L.J.	35 LAA Regt.Sig. Sec.		05.03.43	21	
1799969	Gnr.	Baker, W.R.	144 Bty. 35 LAA		05.03.43	26	
1799970	Gnr.	Balch, P.F.	144 Bty. 35 LAA		05.03.43	21	
1817008	Gnr.	Ball, K.S.	3 Bty. 6 HAA	Newport, Monmouthshire	05.03.43	21	
853226	Gnr.	Banks, G.E.	9 Coast Regt.		05.03.43	27	
1078333	Gnr.	Bannerman, J.C.	5 Sch.Light Regt.	Hounslow, Middlesex	05.03.43	32	
1466975	Gnr.	Barker, Douglas	7 Coast Regt.		05.03.43	21	
872336	L/Sgt.	Barker, James	5 Sch.Light Regt.		05.03.43	27	
3857636	Gnr.	Barlow, Henry	3 Bty. 6 HAA	Bolton, Lancashire	05.03.43	21	
5103648	Gnr.	Barnett, J.W.	21 Bty. 3 HAA	Ladywood, Birmingham	05.03.43	36	
7009882	Gnr.	Barr, Samuel	7 Coast Regt.		27.03.43	36	
1739282	Gnr.	Barrett, A.C.	7 Coast Regt.	Rudgwick, Sussex	05.03.43	32	
850961	L/Bdr.	Barrett, Joseph	9 Coast Regt.	Dublin, Irish Republic	05.03.43	25	

Number	Rank	Name	Regiment	Place of Origin	D.O.D.	Age	Place Died
1573055	Gnr.	Bartlett, Bert	H.Q., 35 LAA Rgt.	Guildford, Surrey	05.03.43	31	
11053926	Gnr.	Bartley, M.S.T.	9 Coast Regt.	Surbiton, Surrey	05.03.43	32	
166810	Lieut.	Bass, E.W.	35 LAA Regt.	Cambridge	05.03.43	31	
15258	Lt.Col.	Bassett, John	35 LAA Regt.		05.03.43	45	
148084	Lieut.	Bedford, J.W.	2 AA.Rgt.HK&S.R.A.		05.03.43		
6967898	Gnr.	Bennett, Dennis	5 Sch.Light Regt.	Feltham, Middlesex	05.03.43	23	
6895053	Sgt.	Bennett, R.H.	2 HAA Regt.	Earl's Court, London	05.03.43	26	
194408	Lieut.	Bennett, W.F.	RA. sec.2AA.HK&S.RA		05.03.43		
872634	Bdr.	Bennett, W.J.	7 Coast Regt.	Amersham, Buckinghamshire	05.03.43	24	
1709676	Gnr.	Beresford, George	5 Sch.Light Regt.	Longsight, Manchester	05.03.43	31	
1786922	Gnr.	Bergin, Jeremiah	7 Coast Regt.	Sunderland, Co. Durham	23.04.43	22	
860801	Bdr.	Bevan, W.R.	9 Coast Regt.	Singapore	05.03.43	26	
843557	Gnr.	Bickerton, Robert	9 Coast Regt.		05.03.43	26	
877075	Gnr.	Billingham, S.C.	144 Bty. 35 LAA	Sparkbrook, Birmingham	05.03.43	22	
5989180	Gnr.	Bladon, F.C.	9 Coast Regt.		05.03.43	25	
1818199	Gnr.	Blake, F.H.	9 Coast Regt.	Newport, Monmouthshire	05.03.43	21	
542937	Sgt.	Blinko, A.M.	144 Bty. 35 LAA	High Wycombe, Buckinghamshire	05.03.43	39	
1556546	Gnr.	Bond, R.J.	144 Bty. 35 LAA	Sheffield	05.03.43	29	
843518	Sgt.	Bosanquet, D.G.A.	5 Sch.Light Regt.	Dawlish, Devon	05.03.43	28	
1523727	Gnr.	Boswell, E.G.	144 Bty. 35 LAA		05.03.43	29	
1487094	Gnr.	Bowell, N.H.	H.Q., 35 LAA Regt.		05.03.43	39	
850079	Bdr.	Bowers, G.H.	9 Coast Regt.		05.03.43	26	
1523402	Gnr.	Boxall, H.G.F.	H.Q.,35 LAA Regt.		05.03.43	28	
1577687	Gnr.	Boyd, L.H.	11 Coast Regt.	Macclesfield, Cheshire	05.03.43	27	
1777964	Gnr.	Bradley, Tom	89 Bty. 35 LAA		05.03.43	22	
1718501	Gnr.	Bragg, J.H.	5 Sch.Light Regt.	Kenton, Middlesex	05.03.43	35	
73731	Lieut.	Brancker, P.L.	2 HAA. Rgt.HK&S.RA	Heswall, Cheshire	05.03.43	28	
2053950	Gnr.	Brandwood, William	11 Bty. 3 HAA	Failsworth, Lancashire	05.03.43	26	
768162	Gnr.	Braybrook, G.E.	16 Def.Rgt., R.A.	Kempston, Bedfordshire	05.03.43	33	
984474	Gnr.	Brazier, A.L.	3 HAA Regt.	Hockley, Birmingham	05.03.43	27	
2568474	Gnr.	Breddy, A.W.	16 Def.Rgt., R.A.	Manchester	05.03.43	26	
1629460	Gnr.	Brierley, Fred	5 Sch.Light Regt.	Royton, Lancashire	05.03.43	31	
1065905	WO.I.	Broadfoot, Robert	H.Q., 35 LAA Regt.		05.03.43	32	

Number	Rank	Name	Regiment	Place of Origin	D.O.D.	Age	Place Died
1543426	Bdr.	Brockbank, J.W.	144 Bty. 35 LAA	Reading, Berkshire	05.03.43	30	
1524208	Gnr.	Brooker, A.E.	144 Bty. 35 LAA		05.03.43	35	
1781666	Gnr.	Brotton, J.G.	RA. attd. 1 HAA. RIA	Stokesley, Yorkshire	05.03.43	22	
825673	Gnr.	Brown, A.J.	7 Coast Regt.	Nottingham	05.03.43	26	
1777966	Gnr.	Brown, A.J.	144 Bty. 35 LAA	Leicester	05.03.43	22	
1572560	Gnr.	Brown, A.W.	16 Def.Rgt., R.A.	Wavertree, Liverpool	05.03.43	26	
1787125	Gnr.	Brownhood, Alex	7 Coast Regt.		05.03.43	38	
828276	Bdr.	Bryant, J.C.F.	9 Coast Regt.	Greenford, Middlesex	05.03.43	24	
853712	Gnr.	Budd, H.A.	7 Coast Regt.		05.03.43	25	
97594	Maj.	Bullock, Edward	144 Bty. 35 LAA	Bexhill-on-Sea, Sussex	05.03.43		
854118	Sgt.	Burdell, Stanley	16 Def.Regt., R.A.		05.03.43	26	
1831431	Gnr.	Burgess, A.W.	144 Bty. 35 LAA	Gorleston-on-Sea, Norfolk	05.03.43	37	
1427590	Gnr.	Burnell, Harry	9 Coast Regt.	Leeds, Yorkshire	05.03.43	24	
1773966	Gnr.	Callaghan, William	144 Bty. 35 LAA	Battersea, London	23.02.43	32	
872279	L/Bdr.	Capers, V.F.	5 Sch.Light Regt.	Leamington Spa, Warwickshire	05.03.43		
1779885	Gnr.	Capper, Harry	2 HAA Regt.		05.03.43	35	
1646045	Gnr.	Card, W.F.	3 Bty. 6 HAA		05.03.43	35	
1782171	Gnr.	Cariss, Laurence	144 Bty. 35 LAA	Bradford, Yorkshire	05.03.43	38	
10631243	Pte.	Carter, Harry	Catering.attd. 144 LAA	Wigston, Leicestershire	05.03.43	27	
876942	Gnr.	Chadwick, J.J.	9 Coast Regt.		05.03.43	27	
1069163	BQMS	Chapman, Ernest	7 Coast Regt.	Broomhill, Yorkshire	26.02.43	39	
1437803	Sgt.	Chellingsworth, J.K.	RA. attd. 1 HAA. RIA	Ross-on-Wye, Herefordshire	05.03.43	33	
825715	Bdr.	Cheyne, George	1 HAA Regt.	Dunlugas, Banffshire	05.03.43	27	
1470484	Bdr.	Chisholm, D.H.	16 Def.Regt.,RA	Malvern, South Australia	05.03.43	24	
847651	Gnr.	Chivers, Ernest	9 Coast Regt.	Calstone, Wiltshire	05.03.43	25	
11055178	Gnr.	Clargo, E.T.E.	9 Coast Regt.	Reading, Berkshire	05.03.43	22	
1818221	Gnr.	Clarke, Alfred	3 Bty. 6 HAA	Newport, Monmouthshire	05.03.43	22	
1831473	Gnr.	Clayton, Eric	144 Bty. 35 LAA	South Kirkby, Yorkshire	05.03.43	37	
1811400	Gnr.	Clements, T.H.	3 HAA Regt.	Kettering, Northamptonshire	05.03.43	31	
S/12781	WO.II	Close, H.C.	RASC.attd. HQ.MalayaCd.	South Kensington, London	05.03.43	42	
1709707	Gnr.	Clowes, Alexander	14 Bty. 5 Sch.Light	Farnworth, Lancashire	05.03.43	31	
973236	Gnr.	Coggings, Clifford	7 Coast Regt.	Leeds, Yorkshire	05.03.43	28	

368

Number	Rank	Name	Regiment	Place of Origin	D.O.D.	Age	Place Died
191983	Lt.(QM)	Coleby, A.E.	2 HAA. Rgt.HK&S.RA	Shoeburyness, Essex	05.03.43	39	
87490	Lieut.	Coleman, R.B.B.	9 A.A. Regt., RA	Co. Antrim, Nthn. Ireland	05.03.43	33	
1786770	Gnr.	Colin, Reginald	9 Coast Regt.		17.12.42	34	
1493197	Bdr.	Collings, Cecil	RA. attd. 1 HAA. RIA		05.03.43	24	
1556046	Gnr.	Collins, H.K.	144 Bty. 35 LAA		05.03.43	28	
1030737	WO.II	Collins, H.S.	7 Coast Regt.		27.04.43	45	
1412007	WO.II	Congdon, W.H.	7 Coast Regt.		26.02.43	47	
1781633	Gnr.	Conroy, Charles	RA. attd. 1 HAA. , RIA	Bradford, Yorkshire	05.03.43	38	
1629575	Gnr.	Conway, W.T.	14 Bty. 5 Sch.Light.	Miles Platting, Manchester	05.03.43	32	
1709678	Gnr.	Cook, Clement	5 Sch.Light Regt.	Congleton, Cheshire	21.02.43	32	
187476	Lieut.	Cook, D.C.	2 AA.Rgt., HK&S.RA	Leeds, Yorkshire	05.03.43	22	
1470588	Gnr.	Cooke, E.A.	9 Coast Regt.		05.03.43	39	
1709708	Gnr.	Cookson, Wilfred	5 Sch.Light Regt.	Colne, Lancashire	05.03.43	31	
1061053	Gnr.	Coomber, A.J.	7 Coast Regt.	Upper Billingford, Norfolk	05.03.43	36	
1709679	Gnr.	Cooper, George	14 Bty. 5 Sch.Light	Davyhulme, Lancashire	05.03.43	32	
1777876	Gnr.	Cooper, J.H.	144 Bty. 35 LAA		05.03.43	22	
986085	Gnr.	Cornwell, J.L.J.	3 LAA Regt.	Troon, Ayreshire	05.03.43	22	
90419	Lieut.	Couzens, J.P.	3 LAA Regt.	Hindhead, Surrey	05.03.43	22	
1686349	Gnr.	Cox, F.R.	5 Sch.Light Regt.	Ironville, Nottinghamshire	05.03.43	22	
1790089	Gnr.	Craig, James	144 Bty. 35 LAA	Thornliebank, Glasgow	05.03.43	22	
1603346	Gnr.	Creedon, D.K.	3 HAA Regt.		05.03.43	25	
1474744	Bdr.	Cregeen, Winston	1 HAA. Rgt. HK&S. RA		05.03.43	23	
1786772	Gnr.	Crick, Philip	7 Coast Regt.	Kidderminster, Worcestershire	05.03.43	33	
4029649	Gnr.	Crowhurst, H.W.	21 Bty. 3 HAA	Stepney, London	05.03.43	36	
863742	Gnr.	Cullen, A.G.	7 Coast Regt.	Mansfield, Nottinghamshire	05.03.43	26	
1049546	BQMS	Currie, J.H.	7 Coast Regt.		11.03.43	44	
190959	Lieut.	Curtis, R.H.	2 HAA Rgt. HK&S.RA	Risely, Berkshire	05.03.43	30	
106005	Capt.	Dance, E.G.	35 LAA Regt.		30.04.43		
1787344	Gnr.	Dargie, John	9 Coast Regt.	Ardler by Meigle, Perthshire	05.03.43	22	
1781644	Gnr.	Darley, Frank	RA. attd. 1 HAA. RIA	Bradford, Yorkshire	05.03.43	37	
76552	Lieut.	Davidson, J.D.	1 HAA Regt.	Fyfield, Berkshire	05.03.43		
170158	Lieut.	Davie, P.H.W.	5 Sch. Light Regt.	Bournemouth, Hampshire	06.04.43	33	

369

Number	Rank	Name	Regiment	Place of Origin	D.O.D.	Age	Place Died
1831442	Gnr.	Davies, H.G.	144 Bty. 35 LAA	Luton, Bedfordshire	05.03.43	26	
1481592	BQMS	Davies, J.R.	144 Bty. 35 LAA		05.03.43	30	
863923	Gnr.	Davison, J.E.	9 Coast Regt.	Sunderland, Co. Durham	05.03.43	26	
798990	WO.II	Davison, T.B.	9 Coast Regt.	Blyth, Northumberland	05.03.43	31	
1800374	Gnr.	Dawson, C.W.	144 Bty. 35 LAA		05.03.43	22	
1470532	Gnr.	De Jong, Eric	3 LAA Regt.		05.03.43	31	
145938	Lieut.	Dixon, J.N.	1 HAA Rgt. HK&S. R.A.	Reading, Berkshire	05.03.43	26	
1425311	L/Sgt.	Dodson, T.S.	9 Coast Regt.	Edinburgh	05.03.43	41	
1641410	Gnr.	Donkin, R.W.	5 Sch.Light Regt.	Golders Green, Middlesex	05.03.43	34	
1493217	Gnr.	Donovan, Lawrence	7 Coast Regt.		05.03.43	34	
1783857	Gnr.	Doyle, W.J.	RA. attd. 1 HAA. RIA	Penwyllt, Swansea	05.03.43	37	
1777887	Gnr.	Driver, E.A.	144 Bty. 35 LAA	Northampton	27.04.43	22	
S/7662263	Pte.	Drummond, Victor	RASC.attd. HQ.SporeFtrs.		05.03.43	23	
1710669	Gnr.	Drury, J.L.	7 Coast Regt.	Plumstead, London	05.03.43	36	
1577712	Gnr.	Dry, A.G.	11 Coast Regt.	Hemel Hempstead, Hertfordshire	05.03.43	26	
1770390	Gnr.	Duplock, J.A.	144 Bty. 35 LAA	Brighton, Sussex	05.03.43	22	
850331	Gnr.	Dye, R.J.	7 Coast Regt.	Darlington, Co. Durham	05.03.43	25	
840429	Gnr.	Dyer, A.G.	7 Coast Regt.	Wicken, Essex	05.03.43	29	
845425	L/Bdr.	Dyson, Alfred	7 Coast Regt.	Radford, Coventry	07.05.43	28	
1700329	L/Bdr.	Eastgate, A.L.	H.Q. 35 LAA Regt.	Newark, Nottinghamshire	05.03.43	33	
1470491	Gnr.	Edema, G.P.	7 Coast Regt.	Changi, Singapore	05.03.43	23	
69278	Lieut.	Elliott, O.G.	7 Coast Regt.		05.03.43	31	
1807010	Gnr.	Evans, W.B.	144 Bty. 35 LAA	Beddau, Glamorgan	05.03.43	21	
1629579	Gnr.	Fairbrother, George	5 Sch.Light Regt.		05.03.43	31	
1782191	Gnr.	Fawden, Herbert	89 Bty. 35 LAA	Pontefract, Yorkshire	05.03.43	39	
T/85438	Dvr.	Ferrol, D.M.	R.A.S.C.	Bridgeton, Glasgow	05.03.43	28	
1031920	Gnr.	Fidler, Thomas	7 Coast Regt.		05.03.43	42	
1426864	Gnr.	Finch, A.H.	9 Coast Regt.		05.03.43	26	
1486474	Gnr.	Finch, Ernest	89 Bty. 35 LAA		05.03.43	40	
76355	Lieut.	Finch, P.T.T.	1 HAA Regt.		05.03.43		
1700281	Gnr.	Fletcher, Harold	35 LAA Regt.		05.03.43	32	

370

Number	Rank	Name	Regiment	Place of Origin	D.O.D.	Age	Place Died
3307674	Gnr.	Fletcher, Stephen	9 Coast Regt.	Reydon, Suffolk	05.03.43	34	
853304	Gnr.	Flinders, Thomas	9 Coast Regt.	Hexthorpe, Yorkshire	05.03.43	25	
325278	Gnr.	Flory, Basil	Royal Artillery		05.03.43	21	
1789900	Gnr.	Ford, Samuel	144 Bty. 35 LAA	Burslem, Stoke-on-Trent	05.03.43	22	
6395526	Gnr.	Forder, V.S.	7 Coast Regt.		05.03.43	35	
863880	Gnr.	Fox, N.A.	16 Def.Rgt.,R.A.	Brigg, Lincolnshire	05.03.43	25	
5038611	Gnr.	Fragle, Ether	2 HAA Regt.	Oakengates, Shropshire	16.03.43	40	
1700287	L/Sgt.	Francis, Frank	144 Bty. 35 LAA	Sutton-in-Ashfield, Notts.	05.03.43	23	
1605293	Gnr.	Francis, R.L.	3 HAA Regt.	Treorchy, Glamorgan	05.03.43	30	
4977454	Gnr.	French, Kenneth	7 Coast Regt.		05.03.43	20	
1788821	Gnr.	Fridd, T.W.	144 Bty. 35 LAA	Surbiton, Surrey	05.03.43		
853539	Gnr.	Galbraith, W.J.	7 Coast Regt.		05.03.43	28	
1061618	Gnr.	Gale, F.T.	7 Coast Regt.	Tooting, Surrey	05.03.43	38	
64137	Maj.	Galloway, J.B.	6(S)HAA. Bty.,HK&S.R.A.		05.03.43		
1785885	Gnr.	Gamon, E.W.	144 Bty. 35 LAA	Plaistow, Essex	05.03.43	32	
1470503	Gnr.	Gardiner, A.E.J.	1 HAA Regt.		05.03.43	35	
109362	Lieut.	Game, D.A.	9 Coast Regt.		02.03.43	29	
113035	Capt.	Gee, R.L.	11 Bty., 7 HAA		05.03.43	40	
109917	Lieut.	Gemmell, R.F.	RA. attd. 1 HAA. RIA.	Broxbourne, Hertfordshire	05.03.43	26	
126298	Lieut.	Gerrard, G.H.	R.A. attd. RIA		05.03.43	28	
62284	L/Bdr.	Gibson, Joseph	Royal Artillery	Hull	05.03.43	24	
186637	Lieut.	Gibson, M.C.	2 AA Regt., HK&S.RA	Epsom, Surrey	05.03.43	22	
800411	Gnr.	Gibson, Peter	9 Coast Regt.		05.03.43	33	
838738	Gnr.	Gildon, A.L.	9 Coast Regt.	Auckland, New Zealand	05.03.43	28	
1414579	Gnr.	Ginn, H.R.	3 Bty. 6 HAA		05.03.43	42	
872440	Gnr.	Gleason, G.H.	11 Bty. 3 HAA		05.03.43		
880575	Gnr.	Goldsmith, F.A.	9 Coast Regt.		05.03.43	24	
3763444	Gnr.	Gorman, M.G.	9 Coast Regt.		05.03.43	38	
973684	Gnr.	Gouge, J.W.G.	7 Coast Regt.	Isle of Grain, Kent	05.03.43	32	
872407	Gnr.	Grant, G.A.	9 Coast Regt.		05.03.43	27	
1552488	Bdr.	Gray, E.G.	HQ. 35 LAA Regt.	Oxford	18.02.43-	28	
1806163	Gnr.	Gray, Victor	144 Bty. 35 LAA	Douglas, Isle of Man	05.03.43	31	

Number	Rank	Name	Regiment	Place of Origin	Age	Place Died
856742	Gnr.	Grayson, Kenneth	11 Bty. 3 HAA		24	
1478927	Gnr.	Greenfield, D.H.	144 Bty. 35 LAA		23	
1788837	Gnr.	Greenhill, J.J.	144 Bty. 35 LAA	South Ealing, Middlesex	37	
63693	Maj.	Greenwood, Frank	RA. sec.2 HAA. HK&S.RA			
180950	Lieut.	Gribble, H.W.	RA. sec.1 HAA. RIA	Norwich	23	
165304	Lieut.	Griffith, H.S.L.	RA. attd. 1 HAA. HK&S.RA	Porthleven, Cornwall		
1817097	Gnr.	Griffiths, Farnham	3 Bty. 6 HAA	Llandilo, Carmarthenshire	22	
1709714	Gnr.	Griffiths, George	5 Sch.Light.Regt.	Leyland, Lancashire	32	
1547696	L/Bdr.	Grills, George	144 Bty. 35 LAA	Torquay, Devon	40	
812061	BQMS.	Gutteridge, W.J.	3 LAA Regt. RA	Copnor, Hampshire	26	
1544538	Gnr.	Hall, Frank	HQ. 35 LAA Regt.	Ascot, Berkshire	37	
851582	Gnr.	Hallas, A.E.	9 Coast Regt.		29	
113037	Capt.	Halsted, H.N.P.R.	7 Coast Regt.	Co.Waterford, Irish Republic	30	
1493006	Gnr.	Hamerton, R.S.	9 Coast Regt.	Moss Side, Manchester	25	
1416695	BQMS.	Hamilton, R.W.	9 Coast Regt.	Earlsfield, London	41	
1547025	Sgt.	Hansen, John	144 Bty. 35 LAA		26	
1822094	Gnr.	Hardie, W.R.	9 Coast Regt.	Birkenhead	28	
51851	Maj.	Hargreaves, Frank	3 HAA Regt.			
1629523	Gnr.	Hartley, A.M.	5 Sch.Light Regt.	Blackburn, Lancashire	26	
842151	Gnr.	Haslam, Charles	3 HAA Regt.	Oldham, Lancashire	26	
6630613	Gnr.	Hatton, M.F.	78 Bty. 35 LAA		40	
1782214	Gnr.	Havercroft, Wilfred	H.Q. 35 LAA Regt.	Hull	22	
1427350	Gnr.	Hawkins, N.H.	9 Coast Regt.		23	
1562901	Gnr.	Hayers, G.W.	144 Bty. 35 LAA	Beaconsfield, Buckinghamshire	29	
1808516	Gnr.	Hayward, W.D.	H.Q. 35 LAA Regt.		22	
1609683	Gnr.	Heanan, John	3 Bty. 6 HAA	Jarrow, Co. Durham	22	
11054357	Gnr.	Hellen, A.H.	9 Coast Regt.		33	
186652	Lieut.	Hewitt, D.E.	RA. attd. 1 HAA RIA			
1413555	S/Sgt.	Hick, C.W.	9 Coast Regt.	Isle of Walney, Lancashire	39	
1018043	Bdr.	Higginbottom, W.A.	9 Coast Regt.	Wandsworth, London	37	
172635	Lieut.	Hill, B.O'N.	2 HA Rgt., HK&S.RA			
1483245	Sgt.	Hill, Frederick	144 Bty. 35 LAA		37	

Number	Rank	Name	Regiment	Place of Origin	D.O.D.	Age	Place Died
835266	Bdr.	Hill, G.V.	7 Coast Regt.	Paddington, London	05.03.43	27	
872024	Gnr.	Hill, Raymond	7 Coast Regt.	Shirley, Southampton	05.03.43	25	
1426716	Gnr.	Hill, Thomas	9 Coast Regt.	Hindley, Lancashire	05.03.43	29	
975802	Gnr.	Hindmarsh, James	9 Coast Regt.		05.03.43	24	
1440018	Bdr.	Hinton, Donald	RA. attd. 1 HAA. HK&S.RA	Taplow, Buckinghamshire	05.03.43	26	
1483246	S/Sgt.	Hoddinott, H.F.	144 Bty. 35 LAA		05.03.43	29	
1427552	Gnr.	Hogan, Charles	9 Coast Regt.	Birmingham	05.03.43	22	
1787102	Gnr.	Holland, Harry	7 Coast Regt.	Parson Cross, Sheffield	16.04.43	38	
1700222	Gnr.	Hollimould, Leslie	144 Bty. 35 LAA	Bobbers Mill, Nottingham	05.03.43	23	
1720230	Gnr.	Holmes, C.T.	3 Bty. 6 HAA		02.05.43	33	
1427505	Gnr.	Hooman, J.L.	9 Coast Regt.		05.03.43	22	
2051781	Gnr.	Hooper, Eric	3 Bty. 6 HAA	Liverpool	05.03.43	21	
1438729	Gnr.	Hooper, G.E.	16 Def.Regt., RA	Lee, London	05.03.43	22	
1629582	Gnr.	Hooper, G.H.	5 Sch.Light Regt.	Salford, Lancashire	05.03.43	31	
1571047	Gnr.	Horn, Leslie	9 Coast Regt.	Swineshead, Lincolnshire	05.03.43	29	
4199389	Bdr.	Home, J.P.	1 HAA Regt.	Cardiff	05.03.43	26	
194457	Lieut.	Houlton, J.C.F.	1 HAA Rgt.,HK&S.RA	Sherborne, Gloucestershire	05.03.43		
850288	Bdr.	Howard, T.R.	7 Coast Regt.		05.03.43	28	
1438636	Gnr.	Howell, S.G.	9 Coast Regt.		05.03.43	23	
872387	Bdr.	Hubbard, Charles	5 Sch.Light Regt.		05.03.43	26	
1700228	L/Bdr.	Huggins, F.E.	146 Bty. 35 LAA		05.03.43	23	
5109079	L/Sgt.	Hunt, E.T.	5 Sch.Light Regt.		05.03.43	26	
845394	Gnr.	Hunt, G.G.	7 Coast Regt.	Lowbands, Worcestershire	05.03.43	26	
835260	Sgt.	Hunter, James	3 Bty.6 HAA	Wigan, Lancashire	05.03.43	28	
180966	Lieut.	Huntington, N.J.S.	3 HAA. HK&S.RA	Thorpe Bay, Essex	05.03.43	22	
1799493	Gnr.	Hurricks, R.C.	144 Bty. 35 LAA	Ipswich, Suffolk	05.03.43	21	
1561730	Bdr.	Husband, C.H.	2 HAA Regt.		05.03.43	25	
179236	Lieut.	Hutchins, R.J.	RA. sec.3 HAA., RIA	Shepherd's Bush, London	05.03.43	25	
1700230	Gnr.	Hutchinson, H.W.	144 Bty. 35 LAA	Daybrook, Nottinghamshire	05.03.43	29	
1709690	Gnr.	Hutchinson, Leslie	5 Sch.Light Regt.		05.03.43	31	
872644	Bdr.	Hutchinson, William	1 HAA Regt.	Ribbleton, Lancashire	05.03.43	26	
2085023	L/Bdr.	Hutton-Taylor, E.S.	5 Sch.Light Regt.		01.03.43	29	
5615198	Gnr.	Hyne, C.G.	3 LAA Regt.	Dartmouth, Devon	05.03.43	33	

Number	Rank	Name	Regiment	Place of Origin	D.O.D.	Age	Place Died
1426678	Gnr.	Ingarfield, Harry	9 Coast Regt.		05.03.43	27	
2047759	Gnr.	Irish, T.H.	5 Sch. Light Regt.		05.03.43	23	
180967	Lieut.	Jackson, F.W.	89 Bty. 35 LAA	Whyteleafe, Surrey	08.03.43	43	
1493032	L/Bdr.	James, D.F.	7 Coast Regt.	Llandilo, Carmarthenshire	05.03.43	24	
1724622	Gnr.	James, G.H.	7 Coast Regt.		05.03.43	28	
1556296	Bdr.	James, Leslie	89 Bty. 35 LAA	Weymouth, Dorsetshire	05.03.43	28	
1629554	L/Bdr.	Jardine, Stanley	5 Sch.Light Regt.	Bootle, Lancashire	05.03.43	31	
155418	Lieut.	Jenkins, S.M.	1 HAA Regt.	Saltney, Chester	05.03.43	30	
1543986	Gnr.	Jennings, Harry	3 LAA Regt.	Bridgwater, Somerset	10.03.43	42	
73050	Lieut.	Jermyn, Peter	1 HAA Regt.,HK&S.RA	Exmouth, Devon	05.03.43	25	
1737869	Gnr.	Jervis, Harry	144 Bty. 35 LAA	Middlesbrough, Yorkshire	05.03.43	34	
866439	Bdr.	Johnson, C.G.	9 Bty. 1 HAA		05.03.43	24	
1629470	Gnr.	Johnson, C.T.	5 Sch.Light Regt.	Widnes, Lancashire	05.03.43	31	
1573751	Gnr.	Johnson, Frederick	5 Sch.Light Regt.	Kilburn, Middlesex	05.03.43	28	
172664	Lieut.	Johnson, G.H.	RA. att.1 HAA. RIA		05.03.43	36	
1552580	Gnr.	Johnson, Thomas	144 Bty. 35 LAA		05.03.43		
4130609	Gnr.	Johnson, W.W.	3 LAA Regt.		05.03.43	25	
1805904	Gnr.	Johnson, W.W.	3 HAA Regt.	Kettering, Northamptonshire	05.03.43	20	
1808054	Gnr.	Johnston, A.McC.	Coast Regt.,R.A.		05.03.43	21	
1629587	Gnr.	Johnston, George	5 Sch.Light Regt.	Fleetwood, Lancashire	05.03.43	31	
1483253	Gnr.	Jones, C.A.	H.Q. 35 LAA Regt.	Havant, Hampshire	05.03.43	33	
868617	L/Sgt.	Jones, Edward	5 Sch.Light Regt.		09.04.43	27	
1532755	Gnr.	Jones, Frank	144 Bty. 35 LAA	Calder Grove, Yorkshire	05.03.43	25	
164302	Lieut.	Jones, J.C.	1 HAA Regt. R.A.		05.03.43	27	
822522	L/Bdr.	Jones, J.E.	2 HAA Regt.		05.03.43	25	
1457641	Gnr.	Jones, Joseph	9 Coast Regt.	Mold, Flintshire	05.03.43	24	
1605162	Gnr.	Jones, W.J.	3 HAA Regt.		05.03.43	27	
1479512	L/Bdr.	Joy, K.C.	89 Bty. 35 LAA	Oxford	05.03.43	32	
6460102	Gnr.	Kay, E.A.	9 Coast Regt.	Balham, London	05.03.43	25	
398459	Bdr.	Kay, Leo	3 HAA Regt.	Over Haddon, Derbyshire	20.08.43	34	
1438698	Gnr.	Keyes, Peter	9 Coast Regt.	Co. Leix, Irish Republic	05.03.43	23	

Number	Rank	Name	Regiment	Place of Origin	D.O.D.	Age	Place Died
1625734	Gnr.	Killien, G.P.	5 Sch.Light Regt.	Plymouth	05.03.43	33	
856831	Bdr.	Kitson, J.R.	9 Coast Regt.		05.03.43	26	
752389	Gnr.	Knowles, T.A.	9 Coast Regt.	Edinburgh	05.03.43	37	
4683662	Sgt.	Knox, Leslie	R.A.M.C.		05.03.43	36	
1427507	Gnr.	Kreike, W.H.	9 Coast Regt.	Stoke Newington, London	05.03.43	25	
815566	L/Bdr.	Lamb, Donald	3 Bty. 6 HAA		05.03.43	28	
1058477	WO.II	Lambourne, T.E.J.	7 Coast Regt.		21.10.42	33	
1569486	Gnr.	Lance, Eric	H.Q., 6 HAA Regt.		23.03.43	30	
1639049	Gnr.	Landells, W.K.	144 Bty. 35 LAA	Wood Green, Middlesex	05.03.43	33	
875987	Gnr.	Lascelles, Frank	9 Coast Regt.	Kirkcaldy, Fife	05.03.43	23	
1763388	Gnr.	Law, R.G.	49 Coast Obs., R.A.	Marylebone, London	24.02.43	36	
182793	Lieut.	Lawson, J.L.	RA. sec. 2 HAA,HK&S.RA	Swindon, Wiltshire	05.03.43	32	
6407501	Gnr.	Lehman, Henry	RA. attd. 1 HAA. RIA		05.03.43	29	
1577853	Gnr.	Leitch, John	11 Coast Regt.	Cardenden, Fife	20.06.43	23	
2986305	Gnr.	Leslie, J.A.	RA. attd. 1 HAA. ,RIA	Glasgow	05.03.43	25	
1669410	Sgt.	Lewis, Robert	5 Sch.Light Regt.	Corsham, Wiltshire	05.03.43	42	
1472953	Gnr.	Lewis, W.D.	144 Bty. 35 LAA		05.03.43	42	
1709571	Gnr.	Ley, J.C.	5 Sch.Light Regt.		05.03.43	31	
MZ/17462	Capt.	Lillico, J.W.	Indian Med. Serv.	Hemel Hempstead, Hertfordshire	18.10.42		
5726631	Gnr.	Lillington, S.W.	5 Sch.Light Regt.	Lewell, Dorsetshire	05.03.43	20	
1700199	Gnr.	Lockwood, William	5 Bn. Suffolk Regt.	Bulwell, Nottingham	05.03.43	32	
881569	Bdr.	Longfield, E.T.	2 HAA Regt.	Braunton, Devon	05.03.43	31	
1629472	Gnr.	Lord, Francis	5 Sch.Light Regt.		05.03.43	31	
69042	Capt.	Loring, G.N.	10 Bty. 1 AA.HK&S.RA.	Twyford, Hampshire	05.03.43	27	
872289	Gnr.	Lowery, John	9 Coast Regt.	St. Helens, Lancashire	05.03.43	25	
1753139	Bdr.	Lucas, A.H.	144 Bty. 35 LAA	East Ham, Essex	05.03.43	34	
98862	Lieut.	Lucas, H.A.	RA. sec.1 HAA. RIA	Grinstead, Sussex	05.03.43	25	
838982	Gnr.	McAughtrie, Thomas	3 Bty. 6 HAA		05.03.43	28	
182803	Lieut.	MacBean, Alexander	RA. attd. 1 HAA. RIA		05.03.43	24	
2053379	Gnr.	Macbeth, J.E.	3 HAA Regt.	Aberdeen	05.03.43	22	
780536	Sgt.	McCarten, Daniel	7 Coast Regt.		05.03.43	33	

375

Number	Rank	Name	Regiment	Place of Origin	D.O.D.	Age	Place Died
164294	Capt.	McCoubrey, R.T.	7 Coast Regt.	Belfast, Northern Ireland	15.06.43	37	
1787304	Gnr.	McCulloch, Robert	7 Coast Regt.		05.03.43	22	
835569	Bdr.	McElveen, Thomas	3 HAA Regt.	Belfast, Northern Ireland	05.03.43	27	
165311	Lieut.	McEwen, Edgar	28 LAA Regt.	Caterham, Surrey	05.03.43	49	
1610200	Gnr.	McGough, J.H.	3 Bty. 6 HAA	Burnley, Lancashire	01.03.43	21	
856404	Gnr.	McGull, James	16 Def. Regt.		05.03.43	25	
1709542	Gnr.	Mackenzie, Leslie	5 Sch.Light Regt.		05.03.43	31	
1474227	Gnr.	McNab, Joseph	RA. attd. 1 HAA., RIA		05.03.43	31	
2580832	Dvr.	Macpherson, Ian	35 LAA.Regt.Sig. Sec.	Maryhill, Glasgow	05.03.43	22	
1766458	Gnr.	Macrae, Alexander	144 Bty. 35 LAA	Lochcarron, Ross and Cromarty	05.03.43	34	
1547502	Gnr.	MacWilliam, C.A.	9 Coast Regt.	Inverkeithing, Fife	05.03.43	26	
863511	Gnr.	Mahoney, James	7 Coast Regt.		05.03.43	27	
1427482	Gnr.	Mann, H.G.	9 Coast Regt.		05.03.43	28	
5182509	Gnr.	Manning, E.A.	9 Coast Regt.		05.03.43		
2057105	Gnr.	Marshall, M.S.	5 Sch. Light Regt.	East Molesey, Surrey	05.03.43	40	
886405	Gnr.	Marskell, H.A.	9 Coast Regt.		05.03.43	23	
6975341	Gnr.	Martin, Walter	2 HAA Regt.		05.03.43	39	
1788805	Gnr.	Maryon, W.H.	144 Bty. 35 LAA	Walthamstow, Essex	05.03.43		
138385	Lieut.	Maslen, J.N.M.	RA. attd. 1 HAA. RIA	Bournemouth, Hampshire	19.02.43	32	
1750774	Gnr.	Matheson, Kenneth	RA. attd. 1 HAA., RIA		05.03.43	29	
845309	Gnr.	Matthews, W.T.	7 Coast Regt.	Ramsgate, Kent	05.03.43	26	
1427146	Gnr.	Maxwell, R.W.	16 Def. Regt., RA		05.03.43	29	
1438702	Gnr.	Maylin, G.A.	9 Coast Regt.	Henlow, Bedfordshire	05.03.43	22	
860616	Gnr.	Menzies, Stewart	9 Coast Regt.		05.03.43	25	
2059512	L/Bdr.	Meredith, L.A.G.	5 Sch.Light Regt.	Hounslow, Middlesex	05.03.43	22	
1552493	Gnr.	Merriman, G.R.M.	144 Bty. 35 LAA		05.03.43	29	
1709755	Gnr.	Millar, W.S.	5 Sch.Light Regt.		05.03.43	31	
880746	Gnr.	Miller, D.N.	16 Def.Regt., RA	Horwich, Lancashire	05.03.43	23	
1460158	Bdr.	Miller, D.F.	RA. attd. 1 HAA., RIA	Ryde, Isle of Wight	05.03.43	28	
1641427	Gnr.	Miller, J.W.F.	5 Sch.Light Regt.	Cockburnspath, Berwickshire	05.03.43	32	
1470513	Gnr.	Millington, William	3 HAA Regt.	Singapore	05.03.43	24	
1550516	Gnr.	Mitchell, R.W.	144 Bty. 35 LAA		05.03.43	27	
821579	Gnr.	Moderate, J.R.	3 Bty. 6 HAA	Glasgow	05.03.43	30	

376

Number	Rank	Name	Regiment	Place of Origin	D.O.D.	Age	Place Died
1756775	Gnr.	Moon, V.H.	RA. attd. 1 HAA., RIA	Brighton, Sussex	05.03.43	35	
1642614	L/Sgt.	Moore, R.W.	144 Bty. 35 LAA	Hinckley, Leicestershire	05.03.43	23	
1786748	Gnr.	Moran, John	16 Def.Regt., RA	Co. Mayo, Irish Republic	05.03.43	35	
1649516	Gnr.	Morton, A.J.	5 Sch.Light Regt.	Reading, Berkshire	05.03.43	27	
1753154	Gnr.	Moss, A.A.	144 Bty. 35 LAA		05.03.43	34	
6083529	L/Bdr.	Moth, Horace	144 Bty. 35 LAA	Lichfield, Staffordshire	12.12.42	35	
1541719	Gnr.	Moule, F.J.	11 Coast Regt.	Cookley, Worcestershire	05.03.43	24	
1470084	Gnr.	Muir, A.M.	9 Coast Regt.	Rosewell, Midlothian	05.03.43	26	
1456810	Gnr.	Mundy, G.T.	144 Bty. 35 LAA		05.03.43	25	
1735867	Gnr.	Munton, Harry	89 Bty. 35 LAA	Stockport, Cheshire	05.03.43	34	
826416	Gnr.	Murphy, James	3 Bty. 6 HAA	Willenhall, Staffordshire	06.11.42	30	
1537327	Gnr.	Murphy, J.E.	3 Bty. 6 HAA	Lancaster	05.03.43	23	
1427603	Gnr.	Murphy, J.P.	9 Coast Regt.	Shildon, Co. Durham	05.03.43	26	
73398	Capt.	Nairn, P.T.	54 AA Regt. RA	Kensington, London	05.03.43	25	
1783586	Gnr.	Napaul, Leonard	144 Bty. 35 LAA		05.03.43	27	
6203841	Gnr.	Nappin, F.C.	5 Sch.Light Regt.	Kilburn, Middlesex	19.05.43	24	
1520482	Sgt.	Napthine, E.S.	144 Bty. 35 LAA	Sonning, Berkshire	05.03.43	25	
1493082	Gnr.	Neate, R.R.	7 Coast Regt.	Caerphilly, Glamorgan	05.03.43	24	
7372907	Pte.	Neaves, P.J.	198 Fld.Amb., RAMC	Little Shelford, Cambridgeshire	05.03.43	26	
201704	Lieut.	Neill, Eric	RA. attd. 1 HAA., RIA	Benton, Northumberland	05.03.43		
1065669	L/Sgt.	Neville, J.E.	7 Coast Regt.	Woodbridge, Suffolk	05.03.43	31	
872557	L/Bdr.	Nixon, W.R.	3 HAA. Regt.		05.03.43	25	
850096	Gnr.	Nolan, C.P.	7 Coast Regt.	Kenton, Middlesex	05.03.43	26	
86082	Lieut.	Noon, John	RA. sec.1 HAA.,HK&S.RA	Newbury, Berkshire	02.02.43	27	
89591	Lieut.	Norris, B.R.H.	1 HAA Regt.	Hill Head, Hampshire	05.03.43	22	
1627882	Gnr.	Norris, S.J.	5 Sch.Light Regt.	West Ewell, Surry	05.03.43	31	
860668	Gnr.	North, Willie	16 Def.Regt., RA	Huddersfield	05.03.43	25	
1075780	Gnr.	Oates, E.A.	9 Coast Regt.		05.03.43	32	
1412689	WO.I	O'Brien, James	16 Def.Regt., RA	Edinburgh	05.03.43	40	
S/143595	Pte.	O'Brien, J.D.P.	R.A.S.C.		05.03.43	23	
1470142	Gnr.	Odhams, M.A.	3 LAA Rgt., HK&S.RA		26.04.43	22	

Number	Rank	Name	Regiment	Place of Origin	D.O.D.	Age	Place Died
1629498	Gnr.	Oldham, L.V.	5 Sch.Light Regt.	Whaley Bridge, Cheshire	05.03.43	31	
1607481	Gnr.	Ormesher, R.E.	5 Sch.Light Regt.	Widnes, Lancashire	05.03.43	31	
850606	Gnr.	O'Shea, Michael	7 Coast Regt.		05.03.43	25	
858930	Gnr.	Otter, R.H.	9 Coast Regt.	Easton, Dorsetshire	05.03.43	25	
2049	Capt.	Oxley, M.H.	7 Heavy Bt., R.A.		25.02.43		
194502	Lieut.	Palk, P.B.U.	2 AA Rgt., HK&S.RA.		05.03.43		
1754082	L/Bdr.	Palmer, G.M.	48 Coast Obs., RA	Chingford, Essex	05.03.43	34	
1523717	Gnr.	Passenger, R.A.C.	144/35 LAA Regt.	Flackwell Heath, Buckinghamshire	02.03.43	25	
868970	Gnr.	Paternoster, Herbert	9 Coast Regt.		05.03.43	25	
11000463	Gnr.	Patin, L.G.H.	7 Coast Regt.	Pakefield, Suffolk	05.03.43	27	
851467	Gnr.	Payne, A.W.	7 Coast Regt.	Hoole, Cheshire	05.03.43	26	
929806	Gnr.	Payne, F.W.	89 Bty. 35 LAA	Ruislip Manor, Middlesex	05.03.43	30	
1431029	Gnr.	Pearce, C.W.	7 Coast Regt.		05.03.43	23	
197700	Lieut.	Perls, O.I.R.	3 LAA Regt., HK&S.RA		05.03.43	27	
835997	Bdr.	Perrott, W.G.L.	5 Sch.Light Regt.	Hampstead, London	12.05.43	27	
1688866	Gnr.	Perry, W.H.	144 Bty. 35 LAA	Co. Wicklow, Irish Republic	05.03.43	28	
1592836	Gnr.	Pettit, A.A.	5 Sch.Light Regt.		05.03.43		
1577757	Gnr.	Pickering, C.J.	11 Coast Regt.	Tolworth, Surrey	05.03.43	26	
1486661	Gnr.	Pike, E.R.	H.Q., 35 LAA Regt.	North Finchley, Middlesex	05.03.43	27	
862963	Gnr.	Plumstead, J.R.L.	7 Coast Regt	Ealing, Middlesex	21.01.43,	41	
4684717	Gnr.	Porteous, W.G.	2 HAA Regt.	Westcliff-on-sea, Essex	05.03.43	25	
179326	Lieut.	Potts, G.M,	Royal Artillery	Leeds, Yorkshire	05.03.43	38	
1605186	Gnr.	Powell, I.T.	3 HAA Regt.	Pontygwaith, Glamorgan	01.05.43	38	
863176	Gnr.	Price, J.H.	9 Coast Regt.		05.03.43	21	
1700142	Gnr.	Quinney, J.O.	144 Bty. 35 LAA	Hucknall, Nottinghamshire	21.01.43	26	
151237	Lieut.	Rackham, A.W.	3 LAA Regt., HK&S.RA		05.03.43		
872579	Bdr.	Radford, Harold	5 Sch.Light Regt.	Toll Bar, Yorkshire	05.03.43	23	
1426958	L/Bdr.	Rae, Colin	9 Coast Regt.	Carronshore, Stirlingshire	05.03.43	22	
1522719	Sgt.	Rainey, E.W.	144 Bty. 35 LAA	Perivale, Middlesex	05.03.43	32	
851142	Gnr.	Ralphs, Reginald	9 Coast Regt.	Ironbridge, Shropshire	05.03.43	26	

Number	Rank	Name	Regiment	Place of Origin	D.O.D.	Age	Place Died
1549644	Gnr.	Ranscombe, A.F.W.	144 Bty. 35 LAA	Great Marlow, Buckinghamshire	06.03.43	26	
1540199	Gnr.	Rawles, L.A.	H.Q. 35 LAA Regt.	Wembley, Middlesex	05.03.43	24	
1779217	Gnr.	Raynsford, A.J.	144 Bty. 35 LAA		05.03.43		
869131	Bdr.	Reah, T.A.	1 HAA Regt.		05.03.43	24	
1545919	Gnr.	Redgrave, H.L.	H.Q. 35 LAA Regt.	Amersham, Buckinghamshire	05.03.43	46	
1605252	Gnr.	Rees, B.D.	2 HAA Regt. R.A.	Bridgend, Glamorgan	05.03.43	30	
1485821	Bdr.	Rees, J.H.	2 HAA Regt. R.A.	Dowlais, Glamorgan	05.03.43	32	
1713949	Gnr.	Rehm, D.P.	5 Sch.Light Regt.	Paddington, London	05.03.43	26	
1426910	Gnr.	Reynolds, Joseph	7 Coast Regt.	Ossett, Yorkshire	05.03.43		
1489517	L/Bdr.	Richards, B.A.	H.Q. 35 LAA Regt.	Oxford	09.02.43	40	
169546	Lieut.	Richards, C.C.	1 HAA Regt., HK&S.RA.	Stoke Bishop, Bristol	05.03.43	35	
T/137840	Cpl.	Richardson, Douglas	RASC.attd. 122Fld.Rgt.		05.03.43	23	
1424286	BQMS	Rigby, A.T.	2 HAA Regt.		25.02.43	38	
850953	Bdr.	Roberts, Harry	1 HAA Regt.		05.03.43	27	
11054811	Gnr.	Roberts, J.R.	Royal Artillery	Beddington, Surrey	05.03.43	32	
158708	Lieut.	Robertson, D.R.	2 AA.Rgt.,HK&S.RA	Perth	05.03.43		
1601713	Gnr.	Robins, E.F.	144 Bty. 35 LAA		05.03.43	22	
7365033	Pte.	Robinson, Charles	198 Fld.Amb.,RAMC	Poplar, London	05.03.43	21	
835652	Gnr.	Robinson, Harry	7 Coast Regt.		05.03.43	29	
828431	Gnr.	Robinson, Joseph	9 Coast Regt.		05.03.43	31	
1427118	Gnr.	Robinson, W.L.	11 Bty. 3 HAA	Holloway, London	05.03.43	25	
1779033	Gnr.	Rogers, C.S.F.	3 HAA Regt.	Robin Hood's Bay, Yorkshire	05.03.43	22	
872662	Gnr.	Ross, A.L.	3 HAA Regt.	Coventry	05.03.43	25	
1782368	Gnr.	Rowland, Jack	144 Bty. 35 LAA	Winsford, Cheshire	05.03.43	22	
1573039	Gnr.	Rowland, J.W.	144 Bty. 35 LAA	Leatherhead, Surrey	05.03.43	30	
3716111	Gnr.	Rowlands, A.O.	2 HAA Regt.	Birkenhead	05.03.43	29	
1770686	Gnr.	Rudkin, Wilfred	11 Coast Regt.		05.03.43	30	
776315	Sgt.	Rushmer, George	RA. attd. 1 HAA. ,RIA		05.03.43	32	
1543466	L/Bdr.	Rutter, J.H.	144 Bty. 35 LAA	Bassaleg, Monmouthshire	05.03.43	29	
1549403	Bdr.	Ryan, R.M.O.	35 LAA Regt.	Maidenhead, Berkshire	03.12.42	31	
214688	Lieut.	Salmon, P.J.	RA. sec.1 HAA. , RIA		05.03.43		
934927	Gnr.	Sampson, J.A.	1 HAA Regt.	Feltham, Middlesex	05.03.43	23	

379

Number	Rank	Name	Regiment	Place of Origin	D.O.D.	Age	Place Died
158715	Lieut.	Sanders, H.A.	16 Bty. 3 LAA	Wimbledon, Surrey	05.03.43	26	
3446184	Bdr.	Sandiford, Joseph	RA. attd. 1 HAA. , RIA	Bury, Lancashire	05.03.43	28	
1427569	Gnr.	Saucier, K.R.J.	9 Coast Regt.		05.03.43	23	
4380965	BQMS	Saunders, Cyril	9 Coast Regt.	Portobello, Midlothian	26.07.43 -	42	
1810694	Gnr.	Scarth, John	3 HAA Regt.	Stirchley, Birmingham	25.02.43	33	
1787075	Gnr.	Schofield, Wilfred	7 Coast Regt.	Rawtenstall, Lancashire	05.03.43	22	
1556147	Sgt.	Scott, A.D.C.	144 Bty. 35 LAA		05.03.43		
1427444	Gnr.	Shanklin, Henry	3 HAA Regt.	Fletchertown, Cumberland	05.03.43	22	
7372727	Pte.	Sharman, K.L.	198 Fld.Amb., RAMC	Foxton, Hertfordshire	05.03.43	26	
863096	Gnr.	Sharp, C.J.	9 Coast Regt.		05.03.43		
818750	Gnr.	Shatwell, James	3 Bty. 6 HAA	West Bollington, Cheshire	13.06.43	30	
853213	Gnr.	Shaw, J.W.	9 Coast Regt.	Aldershot, Hampshire	05.03.43	25	
1426846	Gnr.	Shaw, Thomas	9 Coast Regt.		05.03.43		
1700115	Gnr.	Sheldon, Arthur	144 Bty. 35 LAA	Stapleford, Nottinghamshire	05.03.43	27	
1782243	Gnr.	Sheldon, J.E.	144 Bty. 35 LAA	Woodlands, Yorkshire	05.03.43	26	
1801865	Gnr.	Short, E.E.	144 Bty. 35 LAA	Leyton, Essex	05.03.43	31	
863518	Gnr.	Shuter, James	7 Coast Regt.		05.03.43		
1801866	Gnr.	Silver, Samuel	144 Bty. 35 LAA	Leytonstone, Essex	24.04.43	32	
1757520	Gnr.	Simes, Reginald	89 Bty. 35 LAA		05.03.43		
1790071	Gnr.	Simmonds, P.A.	144 Bty. 35 LAA	Godalming, Surrey	05.03.43	37	
1508000	Gnr.	Siney, A.T.	3 HAA Regt.		05.03.43		
1427241	Gnr.	Slater, Samuel	9 Coast Regt.		05.03.43		
1700064	L/Bdr.	Small, C.T.	144 Bty. 35 LAA	Lenton, Nottinghamshire	05.03.43	22	
1602965	Gnr.	Smart, R.H.	1 HAA Regt.	Ringwood, Hampshire	07.03.43	29	
1700066	Gnr.	Smelt, James	H.Q. 35 LAA Regt.		05.03.43	22	
1799435	Gnr.	Smith, A.G.P.	144 Bty. 35 LAA	Boxworth, Cambridgeshire	05.03.43	21	
1603305	Gnr.	Smith, D.R.	3 HAA Regt.	Drayton Beauchamp, Bucks.	05.03.43	22	
158730	Lieut.	Smith, G.E.M.	2 AA.Rgt., HK&S.RA	Ware, Hertfordshire	05.03.43		
2821116	Gnr.	Smith, G.W.	9 Coast Regt.	Oldham, Lancashire	05.03.43	25	
1739275	Gnr.	Smith, S.L.	7 Coast Regt.		05.03.43	32	
833834	Gnr.	Smith, Thomas	9 Coast Regt.		05.03.43	27	
1786966	Gnr.	Sollars, J.T.	7 Coast Regt.	Barnwood, Gloucestershire	05.03.43	21	
836697	L/Bdr.	Soutter, W.A.	3 Bty. 6 HAA	Liverpool	20.01.43	26	

380

Number	Rank	Name	Regiment	Place of Origin	D.O.D.	Age	Place Died
4855807	Bdr.	Spencer, F.G.	16 Def.Regt., RA	Coalville, Leicestershire	05.03.43	32	
863855	Gnr.	Spencer, Freeman	9 Coast Regt.	Ilkeston, Derbyshire	05.03.43	28	
1415761	Sgt.	Spranklen, S.R.	3 LAA Regt.	Fleet, Hampshire	05.03.43	41	
1828138	Gnr.	Stacy, Henry	144 Bty. 35 LAA	Norwich	05.03.43	34	
1716837	Gnr.	Stadden, William	3 Bty. 6 HAA	St. George, Bristol	07.04.43	34	
1573220	L/Bdr.	Stagg, A.F.	89 Bty. 35 LAA	Reading, Berkshire	05.03.43	32	
1811768	Gnr.	Stainton, William	9 Coast Regt.	Mumbles, Glamorgan	05.03.43	26	
40639	Maj.	Steele, A.P.	Royal Artillery	Dumfries	05.03.43	38	
836130	L/Bdr.	Steer, F.T.	7 Coast Regt.	Sheffield	05.03.43	26	
872458	Gnr.	Stephens, Howard	3 HAA Regt.		05.03.43	27	
1712301	Gnr.	Stevens, A.H.	9 Coast Regt.	North Kensington, London	05.03.43	33	
1415430	BQMS	Stokes, John	7 Coast Regt.	Blackhill, Co. Durham	28.11.42	41	
1550525	Gnr.	Strange, R.E.	144 Bty. 35 LAA	High Wycombe, Buckinghamshire	05.03.43	27	
156870	Lieut.	Sturt, J.E.	Royal Artillery	Epsom, Surrey	05.03.43	33	
856041	Gnr.	Stych, S.J.	9 Coast Regt.	Edgbaston, Birmingham	05.03.43	26	
1426946	Gnr.	Sunshine, Edward	9 Coast Regt.	Old Swan, Liverpool	05.03.43	23	
5378004	Gnr.	Sutton, W.H.	3 HAA Regt.	North Kensington, London	05.03.43	37	
842437	Gnr.	Swinburn, Leslie	9 Coast Regt.	Doncaster, Yorkshire	05.03.43	26	
1641568	Gnr.	Tabor, H.R.	38 Coast Obs.,R.A.	Chingford, Essex	05.03.43	31	
1700031	Gnr.	Taylor, E.G.	144 Bty. 35 LAA	Nottingham	05.03.43	33	
1707573	Gnr.	Taylor, H.J.	RA. attd. 1 HAA. , RIA	Great Wyrley, Staffordshire	05.03.43	33	
2050213	Gnr.	Taylor-Kane, Frank	3 HAA Regt.	Mayfield, Leicester	05.03.43	22	
1700036	Gnr.	Theaker, T.G.	144 Bty. 35 LAA		05.03.43	33	
1703236	Gnr.	Thomas, David	2 HAA Regt.	Bootle, Lancashire	05.03.43	29	
850807	L/Sgt.	Thomas, G.R.	5 Sch.Light Regt.		05.03.43	26	
1549714	Gnr.	Thompson, J.E.	35 LAA Regt.	Boarstall, Buckinghamshire	05.03.43	26	
1433290	Gnr.	Thomson, James	9 Coast Regt.	East Wemyss, Fife	05.03.43	22	
154216	Lt.(QM)	Thorpe, R.H.	9 Coast Regt.	Birkenhead	05.03.43	23	
1067343	Gnr.	Thurston, C.J.	3 HAA Regt.	Taunton, Somerset	05.03.43	35	
1547026	L/Bdr.	Tilling, T.H.	144 Bty. 35 LAA		05.03.43		
846687	Gnr.	Todd, E.D.	9 Coast Regt.	Cosham, Portsmouth	05.03.43	25	
727930	Gnr.	Tomlin, G.J.	11 Coast Regt.		05.03.43	42	

Number	Rank	Name	Regiment	Place of Origin	D.O.D.	Age	Place Died
6200068	Bdr.	Tumilty, C.E.	7 Coast Regt.	Edmonton, Middlesex	05.03.43		
1806028	Gnr.	Tunnicliff, C.R.	3 HAA Regt.	Hyson Green, Nottingham	05.03.43	21	
775353	Gnr.	Turner, A.J.	144 Bty. 35 LAA		05.03.43		
1709732	Gnr.	Turner, B.A.	14 Bty. 5 Sch.Lt.Rgt.	Warrington, Lancashire	23.03.43	31	
4076834	Gnr.	Turner, E.I.	9 Coast Regt.		05.03.43		
1776966	Gnr.	Vanstone, J.E.	144 Bty. 35 LAA	Islington, London	05.03.43	22	
871455	L/Bdr.	Venables, R.S.	7 Coast Regt.	Gosport, Hampshire	05.03.43	23	
831491	Gnr.	Viggers, T.J.	9 Coast Regt.		05.03.43		
850890	L/Bdr.	Wainwright, J.W.	9 Coast Regt.		05.03.43	28	
1479525	Sgt.	Walker, E.B.	89 Bty. 35 LAA		05.03.43	30	
1769585	Gnr.	Walsh, Michael	9 Coast Regt.	Co.Wexford, Irish Republic	05.03.43	27	
1061364	Sgt.	Ward, C.W.	3 Bty. 6 HAA		06.11.42	33	
853631	Gnr.	Ward, George	3 HAA Regt.	Rochdale, Lancashire	05.03.43	27	
1547780	Gnr.	Ward, George	H.Q., 35 LAA Regt.	High Wycombe, Buckinghamshire	26.10.42	26	
59606	Gnr.	Ward, G.H.	3 LAA Regt.	Singapore	05.03.43		
1484136	Gnr.	Ward, L.H.	3 LAA Regt.	Farnham, Surrey	05.03.43	39	
802087	L/Sgt.	Warman, William	5 Sch.Light Regt.		05.03.43	32	
155024	L/Bdr.	Warren, Albert	89 Bty. 35 LAA		05.03.43	23	
786171	Gnr.	Watson, R.L.	H.Q., 35 LAA Regt.		05.03.43	32	
871205	Gnr.	Webber, P.A.	9 Coast Regt.	Scaynes Hill, Sussex	05.03.43	26	
824223	Gnr.	Webster, W.J. (S/A. Jackson, W.J.)	5 Fld.Regt., R.A.	Aberdeen	05.03.43	29	
1798902	Bdr.	Weir, James	144 Bty. 35 LAA	Hucknall, Nottinghamshire	05.03.43	21	
1073551	L/Sgt.	Welbelove, Sidney	5 Sch.Light Regt.	Westcliff-on-Sea, Essex	05.03.43	34	
150046	Lt.(QM)	Welford, K.W.D.	35 LAA Regt.	Chelsea, London	23.01.43	27	
1577805	Gnr.	Wells, F.J.	11 Coast Regt.		05.03.43	29	
1722940	Gnr.	West, Clifford	31 Coast Bty., R.A.		23.02.43	28	
1524210	Bdr.	West, E.D.	144 Bty. 35 LAA	Leicester	05.03.43	25	
845906	Gnr.	Whatley, G.F.	9 Coast Regt.	Mannamead, Plymouth	05.03.43	29	
1793534	L/Bdr.	Whyatt, C.C.	3 Bty. 6 HAA	Shoeburyness, Essex	05.03.43	22	
190126	Lieut.	Wiebkin, P.M.J.	2 HAA. Rgt.HK&S.RA.	Wimbledon, Surrey	05.03.43		

382

Number	Rank	Name	Regiment	Place of Origin	D.O.D.	Age	Place Died
838126	Gnr.	Wilkes, G.D.	9 Coast Regt.	Plymouth	05.03.43	28	
4534555	Gnr.	Wilkinson, Bobbie	3 HAA Regt.		05.03.43	31	
827841	Gnr.	Williams, F.H.	9 Coast Regt.	Liverpool	05.03.43	27	
1546111	Sgt.	Williams, W.J.C.	78 Bty. 35 LAA		05.03.43	29	
847572	Gnr.	Wills, H.J.	9 Coast Regt.	South Molten, Devon	05.03.43	25	
1561724	Gnr.	Willson, W.J.	3 Bty. 6 HAA	Surbiton, Surrey	05.03.43	24	
1777919	Gnr.	Wilson, J.W.	144 Bty. 35 LAA	Codnor, Derbyshire	05.03.43	22	
86912	Lieut.	Wilson, Norman	29 Heavy Bty. R.A.		05.03.43		
1721238	Gnr.	Wilson, W.R.	RA. attd. 1 HAA. RIA.	Falkirk, Stirlingshire	05.03.43	34	
164300	Capt.	Wilton, A.C.	11 Coast Regt.		05.03.43		
4394979	Gnr.	Wimpenny, V.H.	RA. attd. 1 HAA. RIA		05.03.43		
172845	Lieut.	Windows, H.B.	3 Bty. 6 HAA	Birlingham, Worcestershire	05.03.43	26	
4000412	Gnr.	Wood, H.L.	7 Coast Regt.		05.03.43		
851954	Gnr.	Wood, J.H.	16 Def.Regt.,RA	High Lane, Co. Durham	05.03.43	27	
1470573	Gnr.	Woodford, L.E.	Royal Artillery		05.03.43		
186368	Lieut.	Woodhead, R.G.	2 AA. Rgt., HK&S.RA		05.03.43		
78898	Capt.	Woods, W.T.	8 Hvy. Bty., HK&S.Arty.	Dartford, Kent	05.03.43	47	
1787274	Gnr.	Yarrow, B.C.	7 Coast Regt.	Peterborough, Northamptonshire	05.03.43	36	
859180	L/Bdr.	York, H.A.	3 HAA Regt. R.A.	Luton, Bedfordshire	05.03.43	24	
1483240	L/Sgt.	Young, W.E.	89 Bty. 35 LAA	Rose Hill, Oxford	05.03.43	34	

NOTE: Where the date of death is shown other than 5 March 1943, the deaths occurred at Rabaul with the exception of W.O.II Lambourne, T.E.J., who was buried at sea.

The Ballale Party were killed between December 1942 and 30th June 1943.

The Officer who was executed the day after the transport arrived has not been identified.

This Incomplete List is Taken from Roll Supplied by Allied Landforce South East Asia Command To Australian Military Force Melbourne.

Not listed on Singapore Memorial Register.

Number	Rank	Name	Regiment	
2053776	Gnr.	Bennett, J.G.	9 Coast. R.A.	
	Gnr.	Bryant, C.		Not identified. Could be Bryant, J.E.C.
		Clarke, M.		No I.D.
1421477	Sgt.	Dolsky, P.	11 Coast Regt.	
4386990	Gnr.	Doyle, J.	3 LAA. H.K.S.R.A.	
1489085	Gnr.	Evans, E.H.	3 H.A.A.	
1467981	L/Sgt.	Gould,	2 HAA. H.K.S.R.A.	
1426716		Hills,		No I.D.
1438692	Gnr.	Hodson,	9 Coast. R.A.	
863857	L/Bdr.	Johnson, A.	9 Coast. R.A.	
1605160	Gnr.	Jones, T.A.	3 H.A.A.	
221426	Gnr.	Kirk, A.V.	7 Coast.	
132914	Capt.	Mallett, R.E.	16 Def. Regt.	
3308320	Gnr.	McGuire, James	3 HAA Regt.	
872219	L/Bdr.	Murphy, W.	3 HAA. ?	
	Gnr.	Neahan, J.		No I.D.
850801		O'Connor, J.J.	7 Coast R.A.	
	L/Bdr.	Parker,	R.A.	
4914924	Sgt. (AC)	Pass, S.C.		H.Q. Air Defence.
2366341	Sig.	Pike, A.C.C.	R.C.O.S. 35 LAA.	
1438739		Richards, A.	7 Coast. Regt. R.A.	?
		Stanley, C.		No
1749560	Gnr.	Weaver, R.	3 H.A.A.	
1477522	Gnr.	Winter, A.P.	35 LAA.	
1627812	Bdr.	Waller, F.	35 LAA	

Survivors Rescued by Australian Forces

Number	Rank	Name	Regiment
851969	L/Bdr.	Ahern, T.	R.A.
1899596	Gnr.	Baker, A.T.	3 A.A. Regt.
843976	Bdr.	Burglass, H.M.	H.K.S.R.A.
1700369	L/Bdr.	Blythe, J.	35 LAA Regt.
2048251	L/Bdr.	Docherty, F.J.	316 Bat. 5 Regt.
	L/Sgt.	Dunne,	
850014	Gnr.	Fowler, J.	7 Coast Regt.
163296	Gnr.	Gabber, B.	6 Hy. A.A. Regt.
1604796	Gnr.	Jones, W.	3 A.A. Regt.
1063742	L/Sgt.	Matts, N.	R.A.
1492839	Gnr.	Moore, G.N.	7 Coast Regt.
957291	L/Bdr.	Murphy, W.	3 Hy. A.A. Regt.
1058699	L/Bdr.	Newell, C.D.	7 Coast Regt.
845373	L/Sgt.	Nolan, T.	R.A.
168209	Gnr.	Slater, F.W.	5 SL Regt.
1805994	Gnr.	Smelt, L.	35 LAA Regt.
1492562	Gnr.	Walker, T.K.	7 Coast Regt.
868015	Gnr.	Whyte, G.	11/3 H.A.A. Regt.

Captain R.A. Bird — Royal Artillery
Captain Alan Bazel1 — Royal Artillery
Captain Donald Yates Corps. — Royal Army Ordinance
Lieut. Dai Davies — Royal Corps Signals
Captain W.L. Wallis — 48 Bty. Royal Artillery
Captain Ian Foulkes — Royal Artillery

Notes

Sandakan: the origin of the name "Sandakan" – oral tradition from the word "Sandak" meaning a Lease from the Sultan of Sulu.

William Prior was the first Lessee. This was about 1870.

All care has been taken to transcribe the diaries as written and remain as written to retain the spontaneous recording of the time.

The Labuan Honour Roll may not be complete as a number of names were found in a mutilated state. Some items found, including identity discs belonging to personnel who were never in Borneo and returned home, probably came from other prisoner of war camps. An item belonging to Driver Foot, NX.49400, was found. Foot was lost following the sinking of the RAKUYU MARU on 12 September 1944. The Japanese at Kuching had no knowledge of names found in the Brunei area.

The Japanese have overstated the number of men sent from Sandakan to Labuan.

Some place names differ, according to the source. I have adopted those most commonly used.

Names are indexed as in the text and in places refer to the 'nickname' used in Camp.

Names of places of origin are taken from War Graves Registers and some of these have been found to be incorrect.

References

The principal source for Japanese War Criminals tried by the 9 Australian Division War Crimes Court can be found in the trial of General Baba, the Commander of the 37 Army in Borneo. Australian Archives A.C.T. CRS.A471 Item 81631.

The trial of Captain Hoshijima Susumu, Commander of the Sandakan Prisoner of War Compound. Item 80777 of the same Reference.

The trial of Captain Takakuwa Takuo and Captain Watanabe Genzo. A471 Item 80771.

Further text I relied on my extensive library of taped interviews with survivors; 'Z' Special personnel and many people who were closely connected with the Sangakan tragedy. I also used numerous records in Australian Archives relating to British prisoners of war in Borneo.

SUEZ MARU references Australian Archives MP742/1/0 Item 336/1/2026.

The Gunners' 600 Party – Australian Archives B3856/0 Item 144/14/75.

David Bergamini "Imperial Conspiracy".

The four Editions of "Sandakan – The Last March" Don Wall. (4th Edition – ISBN 0646231707).

"Abandoned?" Don Wall – ISBN 0731691695.

Diary of an Unknown British Soldier – AWM.54/253/1/11.

Index – Kill the Prisoners!

Last picture taken as Hereward entered the British army in July, 1940.

Gnr. Hereward Russell. 48 Bty. 21 LAA.
Pic and caption: Elizabeth Kessler, "Lilies at the Gate", Chicago Spectrum Press, Evanston, Illinois, 60201 USA
ISBN 1-886094-1